New Scholarship that Makes *Real Communication* the Authoritative Source

Substantial revisions in listening and group communication chapters reflect dramatic changes in the field. Updated coverage of mediated communication incorporates exciting new research and practical advice on communicating via technology, including discussions of social networking, privacy, cyberbullying, and trolling.

"Understanding Mass and Mediated Communication" Appendix in Every Book

Due to our increasingly virtual and plugged-in world, this formerly optional chapter is now included in each new copy of the book.

A Spotlight on Thinking Critically About Ethics, Culture, and Technology

Feature boxes throughout the text offer compelling stories of ethical dilemmas, communication across cultures, and the impact of technology. Questions after each feature help students consider various communication strategies that could be applied to the situation.

Innovative Tools in Each Chapter Help Students Learn and Apply Communication Concepts

► **A self-assessment quiz** (which can be answered in LaunchPad) invites students to examine their own communication in light of scholarly concepts discussed.

► **And You? questions** in the margins challenge students to think critically about how they might respond to a situation discussed in the text.

► **Real Reference guides** help students grasp important ideas quickly, make connections among the topics, and study for the test.

Real Communication

An Introduction

THIRD EDITION

DAN O'HAIR
University of Kentucky

MARY WIEMANN
Emeritus, Santa Barbara City College

DOROTHY IMRICH MULLIN
University of California, Santa Barbara

JASON TEVEN
California State University, Fullerton

Bedford/St. Martin's
Boston • New York

For Bedford/St. Martin's

Vice President, Editorial, Macmillan Higher Education Humanities: Edwin Hill
Publisher for Communication: Erika Gutierrez
Senior Developmental Editor: Julia Bartz
Production Editor: Annette Pagliaro Sweeney
Senior Production Supervisor: Steven Cestaro
Marketing Manager: Thomas Digiano
Project Coordination, Design, Composition: Cenveo® Publisher Services
Photo Researcher: Magellan Visual, Inc.
Director of Rights and Permissions: Hilary Newman
Senior Art Director: Anna Palchik
Cover Design: Cenveo® Publisher Services
Cover Art: Copyright © Getty Images
Printing and Binding: RR Donnelley and Sons

Manufactured in the United States of America.

9   8   7   6   5   4
f   e   d   c   b   a

For information, write: Bedford/St. Martin's, 75 Arlington Street, Boston, MA 02116
    (617-399-4000)

ISBN 978-1-4576-6292-8 (Paperback)
ISBN 978-1-4576-8540-8 (Loose-leaf Edition)

Acknowledgments

Text acknowledgments and copyrights appear at the back of the book on page R-36, which
constitutes an extension of the copyright page. Art acknowledgments and copyrights appear on
the same page as the art selections they cover. It is a violation of the law to reproduce these
selections by any means whatsoever without the written permission of the copyright holder.

preface

Now is a fascinating time to teach human communication. The field of interpersonal communication is evolving as new channels for communication develop; mediated communication is redefining the term *group*, making organizations flatter and generating new challenges for leadership and conflict management; public speaking is becoming a more crucial communication tool in too many professions to list; and the discipline as a whole is evolving at what seems like light speed, especially as scholars work to keep up with the profound changes wrought by technology. Our goal for *Real Communication* is to capture the dynamic and evolving nature of our discipline in a way that truly engages students while encouraging them to assess their own communication experiences and to consider the communication concepts at work in the world around them.

As scholars, we see communication concepts at work every day—in our interactions with others, in the screenplays of the films and TV shows we watch, in the carefully choreographed language of political campaigns, and in the subtle and blatant messages of advertising and marketing. But as instructors, we know that making these connections clear to students can be a challenge, especially in a course that requires us to cover diverse areas of the field (some of which may be outside of our area of expertise or research interest) all in approximately fourteen weeks. Perhaps the most disheartening comment we hear from students and from colleagues—who find themselves pressed for time and depending on their textbook to cover the basics—is that the course materials don't reflect real life or the real world. As one student told us some years ago, "I just don't see myself or anyone like me in the book we used. It's filled with examples about fake people. It's not real."

We developed *Real Communication* in response to those challenges. With this text, we wanted to reimagine the human communication course and what an effective textbook for it might look like. The answer came in addressing the course challenges: we have to make it real, make it relevant, and help students make sense of the course. This was the birth of *Real Communication: An Introduction*, inspired by our colleagues and students who reminded us that a truly effective book would give a cohesive view of human communication—and the discipline that studies it—and that it would feel, well, *real*. Books about hypothetical people will never drive home the point that effective, appropriate, and ethical communication can truly change our personal and professional lives.

The content of the book itself is the result of years of interactions, of communicating with students and colleagues, all in the service of creating the best possible introductory text. We include the strongest and most relevant scholarship—both classic and cutting edge. To create a truly innovative and effective learning tool for the introductory course, we applied the content and scholarship to real and compelling people. We talked to students, instructors, and professionals from around the country, seeking personal stories about how they used what they learned in the classroom. We searched countless media sources and real-world locations for inventive and intriguing ways to illustrate communication concepts at work. We found our examples in the communication playing out in the world around us, whether in scenarios from reality television programs or examples taken from mainstream movies, the national political scene, sporting and cultural events, or even visits to the grocery store. We involved instructors from all over the United States in reviews and discussion groups to get a true sense of what they want and need from a communication textbook. And as we followed up with students, both in our own classrooms and in focus groups around the country, we found them excited to engage with communication scholarship and practice key communication skills in their own lives, making the discipline *relevant* in a whole new way. In response, we designed in-text pedagogical features and other learning tools to match. Finally, throughout the process, we looked for opportunities to draw more clear-cut connections between the various parts of our exceptionally broad discipline. On the one hand, we created unique pedagogical callouts that draw students' attention to important connections between different areas of communication; on the other hand, we carefully tailored coverage in the text itself to highlight the ways that fundamental principles help us understand widely divergent aspects of communication. Perception, for example, merits its own chapter, but we also show how it informs conflict management, public speaking, and interpersonal and organizational communication. By taking this approach, we encourage students to see that the value of these concepts goes well beyond their "assigned" chapter and applies to a variety of contexts that students experience every day.

The overwhelming response to our first edition told us that we were on to something—and the success of the second edition confirmed it. Over and over, we've heard from instructors and students that our approach—friendly, familiar, scholarly, and *real*—provides a solid foundation for understanding and appreciating the nuances of modern communication in a way that is thought provoking, fun, and engaging. We are delighted to have heard from students who not only read our book but also keep thinking about what they've read long after they put it back on the shelf, applying the concepts they've learned to their own communication every day.

This positive response makes us even more excited about the new and improved third edition that you hold in your hands. This edition matches cutting-edge content with powerful digital tools. All chapters have been revised to include new scholarship, updated and realistic examples, and a focus on emerging technologies. We're also excited to offer a powerful (and easy-to-use) learning platform called LaunchPad, which combines the full e-book with curated videos, quizzes, activities, instructor's resources, and LearningCurve—an adaptive quizzing program. Finally, each copy of the book will include the formerly optional chapter, Understanding Mass and Mediated Communication, given the topic's relevance in our modern, connected age.

Features

The very *best* coverage of human communication. All of the coverage you expect from a human communication textbook is presented here in compelling fashion: essential concepts and models of communication, self, perception, culture, language, nonverbal communication, listening, interpersonal relationships, interpersonal conflict, small group communication, organizational communication, public speaking, interviewing, and mass and mediated communication. But we've also included topics and research relevant in today's fast-changing world, topics often underrepresented in competing texts: cyberbullying, organizational ethics, physical ability and public speaking, learning disabilities and listening, culture and language, nonverbal cues, mediated communication, and much more. And we consistently emphasize the concept of *competence* throughout, encouraging students to think about their verbal and nonverbal messages and the feedback they receive from their communication partners in the larger relational, situational, and cultural contexts.

Real Communication **is, well, real.** It incorporates stories, tales, and interviews with former communication students plus insights and examples derived from communication scholars into each of the book's boxes, examples, and features. These rich materials ring true because they *are* true. And the book invites readers in with numerous self-examination features that allow them to consider their own experiences, evaluate their own communication skills, and integrate their knowledge into improved, more effective behaviors.

Engaging examples—from pop culture and beyond—bring concepts to life and connect with students' lived experience. Today's students are interconnected as no generation has ever been. *Real Communication* harnesses this reality by illuminating communication concepts through students' shared experience of culture through novels, film, and TV; the viral language of the Internet; the borderless interactions of online social networking; and the influence of current events in an age of round-the-clock news. This perspective informs the examples, features, and overall voice with which we introduce the discipline.

Highlights *connections* among the different aspects of the course. On every page, *Real Communication* highlights ways that the different areas of our discipline support and inform one another. Along with relevant coverage in the main text and running examples that in some cases span several chapters, marginal CONNECT notes throughout the book help students truly make sense of the human communication course—and the discipline. These unique callouts draw *concrete links* between coverage areas in different parts of the text—for example, explaining that understanding interpersonal conflict can lead to improved leadership in a small group or that the steps students take to organize a speech can help them organize a group meeting.

Learning tools and apparatus that help students understand, internalize, and practice communication concepts and skills.

▶ **Attention-grabbing opening and closing vignettes.** Each chapter of *Real Communication* is bookended with a topic that we think will resonate with students, from teams at Pixar working to represent their characters' nonverbal behavior, to Captain Ray Holt leading an unruly police squad in *Brooklyn*

Nine-Nine. At the end of each chapter, we revisit the opening story to show students how the principles and theories they've learned apply to the opening example.

▶ **Critical thinking boxes on ethics, culture, and technology.** From the ethics of résumé "padding" to insight into how work–life balance differs across the globe to the etiquette of Facebook friending, the boxes in *Real Communication* offer students the opportunity to think critically about the ways in which communication concepts play out in a variety of situations.

▶ **Unique features that provide personal takes on communication.** In each chapter, Real Communicator boxes highlight how real people improved their lives by applying communication concepts. These interviews with real people explore the countless ways in which the application of communication concepts can help our careers, from choreographer Aaron Tolson teaching dancers of all ages and backgrounds to admissions director Vanessa Gonzales traveling to recruit international students. And throughout the text, What About You? self-assessments and marginal And You? questions prompt students to build self-awareness and assess their own communication in light of research.

▶ **Powerful study tools for student success.** The Real Reference study tool at the end of each chapter contains a focused overview of the chapter's key concepts and terms, linked to specific pages in the chapter. Before each Real Reference, Things to Try activities encourage students to further explore the concepts and principles presented in the chapter. This edition also contains LearningCurve, which offers adaptive quizzes for each chapter, as well as nearly three hundred videos (new full-length speeches, key term videos, and more) that visually explain key concepts.

What's New in the Third Edition?

Our goal for this edition was twofold: to keep *Real Communication* at the forefront of the discipline with its engaging coverage and practical theory, and to provide powerful digital tools to make student learning more individualized and immersive. We were pleased to invite Dorothy Imrich Mullin and Jason Tevin to become full-fledged members of the author team. These noted scholars and course coordinators brought their formidable expertise, writing talents, and enthusiasm to the table. Through numerous brainstorming sessions, we discussed instructor and student feedback and explored our own ideas for making *Real Communication* even more current, authoritative, and dynamic. These sessions paid off. Flip through any chapter to see recent scholarship, updated and realistic examples, and an even stronger focus on ethics, culture, and technology. Some specific changes include the following:

▶ **Substantial revisions in the listening and group communication chapters to reflect changes in the field.** New listening research includes interaction management and the effects of physical appearance. The group chapters (Chapters 9 and 10) explore Gersick's punctuated equilibrium model, social ostracism, group status, and leadership qualities.

▶ **Cutting-edge coverage of mediated communication that examines how we communicate now.** *Real Communication* incorporates exciting research and practical advice on communicating via technology, along with student-oriented topics like social networking, privacy, and trolling.

▶ **New and updated sample speeches accompanied by new full-length videos.** These speeches, entitled "Social Media, Social Identity, and Social Causes" and "Preventing Cyberbullying," explore relevant topics in written and visual formats to help students improve their own public speaking skills. To learn more about the videos, see the LaunchPad section that follows.

▶ **Focus on real people in real careers.** Our revamped Real Communicator boxes, which can be found in every chapter, include a fascinating look at how communication study has launched many diverse careers, from doctor, to media research professional, to actress (just see the box on Octavia Spencer!). Our "Real Communicators" both share career advice and show students that communication study can lead to a wide variety of professions.

▶ **Inclusion of the "Understanding Mass and Mediated Communication" Appendix in every book.** Due to our increasingly virtual and plugged-in world, this formerly optional chapter is now included in each new copy of the book. The chapter includes updated information and scholarship on niche programming, narrowcasting, framing, Internet Gaming Disorder, agenda setting, and digital disparities.

▶ **Updated examples that keep students reading and learning essential course concepts.** These include modern-day issues (from celebrity activism to perceptions of the Tea Party) and familiar faces (from Sheryl Sandberg to *The Bachelorette*) that illuminate theories for students.

As for our digital content, we're thrilled to introduce LaunchPad, a dynamic and easy-to-use platform. LaunchPad makes instructors' lives easier by putting everything in one place, combining the full e-book with carefully chosen videos, quizzes, activities, instructor's resources, and LearningCurve. LaunchPad—which can be packaged for free with *Real Communication* or purchased separately—allows instructors to create reading, video, or quiz assignments in seconds, as well as embed their own videos or custom content. Instructors can also keep an eye on their class's progress throughout the semester for individual students and for individual assignments.

LaunchPad comes fully loaded with powerful learning tools, including the following:

▶ **LearningCurve, an adaptive and personalized quizzing program that puts the concept of "testing to learn" into action.** Chapter callouts prompt students to tackle the gamelike LearningCurve quizzes to test their knowledge and reinforce learning. Based on cognitive research on how students learn, this adaptive quizzing program motivates students to engage with course materials. The reporting tools let you see what students understand so you can adapt your teaching to their needs.

▶ **New full-length student speech videos that illustrate speech techniques and serve as speech models.** In addition to the two full-length speeches from the text, LaunchPad includes two more polished, professionally shot, full-length speeches (on freeganism and becoming a socially conscious consumer), plus key Needs Improvement clips that help students recognize how to avoid common pitfalls. Each speech and clip comes with multiple-choice questions so that students can analyze the speaker's techniques and apply them to their own assignments. These four full-length student speech videos bring the grand total of full-length student speech videos to twenty-eight.

▶ **Almost 300 videos** that visually explain important concepts and show public speaking in action.

Digital and Print Formats

For more information on these formats and packaging information, please visit the online catalog at **macmillanhighered.com/realcomm/catalog.**

LaunchPad is a dynamic new platform that dramatically enhances teaching and learning. LaunchPad combines the full e-book with carefully chosen videos, quizzes, activities, instructor's resources, and LearningCurve. Offering a student-friendly approach and an organization designed for easy assignability in a simple user interface, LaunchPad also allows instructors to create assignments, embed video or custom content, and track students' progress with Gradebook. LaunchPad can be ordered on its own or packaged for *free* with *Real Communication*. Learn more at **launchpadworks.com.**

Real Communication **is available as a print text.** To get the most out of the book, package LaunchPad for free with the text.

The loose-leaf edition of *Real Communication* **features the same print text in a convenient, budget-priced format,** designed to fit into any three-ring binder. Package LaunchPad with the looseleaf edition for free.

The Bedford e-Book to Go for *Real Communication* **includes the same content as the print book.** It also provides an affordable, tech-savvy PDF e-book option for students. Instructors can customize the e-book by adding their own content and deleting or rearranging chapters. Learn more about custom Bedford e-Books to Go at **macmillanhighered.com/ebooks**—where you can also learn more about other e-book versions of *Real Communication* in a variety of formats including Kindle, CourseSmart, Barnes & Noble Nook-Study, Know, Cafe-Scribe, and Chegg.

Resources for Students

For more information on these resources or to learn about package options, please visit the online catalog at **macmillanhighered.com/realcomm/catalog.**

The Essential Guide to Intercultural Communication **by Jennifer Willis-Rivera (University of Wisconsin, River Falls).** This useful guide offers an overview of key communication areas, including perception, verbal and nonverbal communication, interpersonal relationships, and organizations, from a uniquely intercultural perspective. Enhancing the discussion are contemporary and fun examples drawn from real life as well as an entire chapter devoted to intercultural communication in popular culture.

The Essential Guide to Rhetoric **by William M. Keith (University of Wisconsin, Milwaukee) and Christian O. Lundberg (University of North Carolina, Chapel Hill).** This handy guide is a powerful addition to the public speaking portion of the human communication course, providing an accessible and balanced overview of key historical and contemporary rhetorical theories. Written by two leaders in the field, this brief introduction uses concrete, relevant examples and jargon-free language to bring concepts to life.

The Essential Guide to Presentation Software **by Allison Joy Bailey (University of North Georgia) and Rob Patterson (University of Virginia).** This guide shows students how presentation software can be used to support but not overtake their speeches. Sample screens and practical advice make this an indispensable resource for students preparing electronic visual aids.

Outlining and Organizing Your Speech **by Merry Buchanan (University of Central Oklahoma).** This student workbook provides step-by-step guidance for preparing informative, persuasive, and professional presentations and gives students the opportunity to practice the critical skills of conducting audience analysis, dealing with communication apprehension, selecting a speech topic and purpose, researching support materials, organizing and outlining, developing introductions and conclusions, enhancing language and delivery, and preparing and using presentation aids.

Media Career Guide: Preparing for Jobs in the 21st Century **by Sherri Hope Culver (Temple University) and James Seguin (Robert Morris University).** Practical and student friendly, this guide includes a comprehensive directory of media jobs, practical tips, and career guidance for students considering a major in communication studies and mass media.

Research and Documentation in the Digital Age, **Sixth Edition, by Diana Hacker and Barbara Fister (Gustavus Adolphus College).** This handy booklet covers everything students need for college research assignments at the library and on the Internet, including advice for finding and evaluating Internet sources.

Resources for Instructors

For more information or to order or download these resources, please visit the online catalog at **macmillanhighered.com/realcomm/catalog.**

Instructor's Resource Manual. This downloadable manual contains helpful tips and teaching assistance for new and seasoned instructors alike. Content includes learning objectives, lecture outlines, general classroom activities, and review questions as well as suggestions for setting up a syllabus, tips on managing your classroom, and general notes on teaching the course. Also available in LaunchPad.

Computerized Test Bank for *Real Communication* by Al Golden (Joliet Junior College). The Computerized Test Bank includes multiple-choice, true/false, short answer, and essay questions keyed to various levels of difficulty. The questions appear in easy-to-use software that allows instructors to add, edit, re-sequence, and print questions and answers. Instructors can also export questions into a variety of formats, including Blackboard, Desire2Learn, and Moodle. The Computerized Test Bank can be downloaded from the Instructor Resources tab of the book's catalog page, and the content is also loaded in the LaunchPad question bank administrator.

PowerPoint Slides for *Real Communication* provide support for important concepts addressed in each chapter, including graphics of key figures and questions for class discussion. The slides are available for download from the Instructor Resources tab of the book's catalog page and they are also available in LaunchPad.

***ESL Students in the Public Speaking Classroom: A Guide for Instructors* by Robbin Crabtree (Loyola Marymount University) and David Alan Sapp (Fairfield University).** This professional resource provides support for new and experienced instructors of public speaking courses whose classrooms include ESL and other linguistically diverse students. Based on landmark research and years of their own teaching experience, the authors provide insights about the variety of non-native English-speaking students (including speakers of global English varieties), practical techniques that can be used to help these students succeed in their assignments, and ideas for leveraging this cultural asset for the education of *all* students in the public speaking classroom.

***Coordinating the Communication Course: A Guidebook,* by Deanna Fassett and John Warren.** This professional resource offers the most practical advice on every topic that is central to the coordinator/director role. Starting with setting a strong foundation, this professional resource continues on with thoughtful guidance, tips, and best practices on crucial topics such as creating community across multiple sections, orchestrating meaningful assessment, hiring and training instructors, and more. Model course materials, recommended readings, and insights from successful coordinators make this resource a must-have for anyone directing a course in communication.

Professional and student speeches. Available on DVD, volume 19 of the esteemed Great Speeches series offers dynamic professional speeches for today's classroom, featuring such compelling speakers as Bill Clinton, Christopher Reeve, and the Dalai Lama. Additional professional videos are available from the Bedford/St. Martin's Video Library. In addition, three recordings of student speeches (featuring students of varying abilities from Texas Tech and the University of Oklahoma) provide models for study and analysis. These professional and student speech resources are free to qualified adopters. Please contact your sales representative for more information.

Customize *Real Communication*. Add your own content or more of ours. Qualified adopters will have the ability to create a version of *Real Communication* that exactly matches their specific needs. Learn more about custom options at **macmillanhighered.com/catalog/other/custom_solutions.**

Acknowledgments

First and foremost, we owe a great deal of gratitude to our families and friends who supported us and listened to us as we worked through ideas for the book, who made us laugh during bouts of writer's block, and who were understanding when we had to cancel plans to meet deadlines. Dan thanks his wife, Mary John; his son, Jonathan; and his daughter and son-in-law, Erica and Anders, and their daughter Fiona. Mary thanks her husband, John; her daughter and son-in-law, Molly and Chad, and their children William and Jackson; and her son and daughter-in-law, John and Andrea. Dolly thanks her husband, Charles, and their Aussie Shepherd, Britney. Jason thanks his daughters, Magdalena and Julia, for their constant love and support. You will always remain our litmus tests for just how real our communication is across its many applications. In addition, we wish to credit and thank Gus Friedrich and John Wiemann, whose contributions to this book and our discipline are far too many to list. And, of course, we must thank our students and graduate student teaching assistants—including Daniel Bernard, Cory Cunningham, Kim Potts, Vanessa Gonzales, Cynthia Inda, and Michel Haigh, among countless others—who continue to inspire us as teachers. We're grateful for the frank discussions that have opened our eyes to many of the challenges of this course from your point of view, and we are grateful for your helpful and thoughtful suggestions on examples.

We are likewise grateful to several colleagues who contributed to the first edition of *Real Communication*: Marion Boyer of Kalamazoo Valley Community College; Charee Mooney of Arizona State University; Celeste Simons of the University of Texas at Austin; Michele Wendell-Senter of the Art Institute of Washington; and Bobette Wolesensky of Palm Beach Community College.

We would also like to thank everyone at Macmillan Education who helped make this book possible, including former Vice President of Editorial Denise Wydra and Director of Production Sue Brown. We owe a particular debt of gratitude to our editorial colleagues: Publisher Erika Gutierrez for her leadership and passion for education; Senior Developmental Editors Karen Schultz Moore and Julia Bartz for their creativity, tenacity, constructive advice, calmness, and vision to create a book that truly reaches students; Contributing Editor Ann Kirby-Payne for her talent, dedication, and sense of humor that can be felt on each page of the book; Editorial Assistant Caitlin Crandell for her artistic eye in organizing and executing our stunning art program; Media Editor Tom Kane for managing all of the video material with professionalism and grace; and Associate Editor Alexis Smith for leading the exciting and complex development of the text's LearningCurve. Without the production staff at Macmillan Education, this manuscript would be nothing more than black words on white paper fresh from our printers (with quite a few typos to boot!). So we thank Managing Editor Shuli Traub for her leadership; Project Editor Annette Pagliaro Sweeney for her calm dedication and superior organizational skills; and Assistant Director of Editing/Design and Production Elise S. Kaiser. Also, we credit Art Director Lucy Krikorian; our permissions specialists, Linda Winters and Eve Lehmann; and our capable photo researcher, Sue McDermott Barlow. Finally, we wish to thank Macmillan Education's extraordinary marketing staff for their incredible commitment and excitement about our book—and their willingness to share that excitement with others: Marketing Manager Tom Digiano and Senior Market Development Manager Sally Constable.

Finally, books simply do not happen without the feedback and suggestions of respected colleagues who read drafts of every chapter and tell us what works and what doesn't. Thank you for being part of this process: Ashley Alfaro, Tarrant County College Southeast Campus; Jonathan Bowman, University of San Diego; Braze Brickwedel, Tallahassee Community College; Aaron Burton, Bowling Green State University; Anna Carmon, Indiana University-Purdue University Columbus; Tim Chandler, Hardin-Simmons University; Katie Fischer Clune, Rockhurst University; Jennifer Fairchild, East Kentucky University; LaKresha Graham, Rockhurst University; Deborah Hefferin, Broward College; Laura Janusik, Rockhurst University; Mignon Kucia, Mississippi College; Melanie Laliker, Bridgewater College; Amy Lenoce, Naugatuck Valley City College; Kate Magsamen-Conrad, Bowling Green State University; Marc Martin, Holy Names University; Amanda Melniczek, Guilford Tech Community College; John Modaff, Moorehead State University; Pamela Morris, University of Wisconsin–La Crosse; Courtney Neujahr, California State University–Fullerton; Dan Rogers, Cedar Valley College; Charlie Pavitt, University of Delaware; Johnny Rowing, College of Western Idaho; Joe Sheller, Mount Mercy University; Yasmin Shenoy, University of Hartford; Maggie Sullivan, Loras College; Elizabeth Tolman, South Dakota State University; Rikki Tremblay, California State University–Fullerton; Gwen Wittenbaum, Michigan State University.

about the authors

Dan O'Hair is dean of the University of Kentucky College of Communication and Information. He is past presidential professor in the Department of Communication at the University of Oklahoma and past president of the National Communication Association. He is coauthor or coeditor of eighteen communication texts and scholarly volumes and has published more than ninety research articles and chapters in dozens of communication, psychology, and health journals and books. He is a frequent presenter at national and international communication conferences, is on the editorial boards of various journals, and has served on numerous committees and task forces for regional and national communication associations.

Mary Wiemann is professor emeritus in the Department of Communication at Santa Barbara City College in California. Her books, book chapters, journal articles, student and instructor manuals, and online instructional materials all reflect her commitment to making effective communication real and accessible for students. A recipient of awards for outstanding teaching, she is also a communication laboratory innovator and has directed classroom research projects in the community college setting. She serves on the editorial board of the *Journal of Literacy and Technology,* is a frequent presenter at the National Communication Association convention, and has held a number of offices in the Human Communication and Technology Division of that organization.

Dorothy "Dolly" Imrich Mullin is a continuing lecturer in the Department of Communication at the University of California, Santa Barbara. Her published research is in the area of media policy and effects. Her current focus is on teaching communication to undergraduates. She specializes in large introductory communication courses, including research methods and theory, and has been recognized for her efforts with a Distinguished Teaching Award. She also trains and supervises the graduate student teaching assistants, working to develop and promote excellent teaching skills among the professors of the future.

Jason Teven, an award-winning scholar and teacher, is professor of Human Communication Studies at California State University, Fullerton. He has published widely in academic journals and is devoted to programmatic research and the social scientific approach to human communication, with research relating to credibility, caring, and social influence within instructional, interpersonal, and organizational communication contexts. His most recent scholarly activities include the examination of superior–subordinate relationships within organizations; communication competence; and the impact of personality traits on communication within the workplace and interpersonal relationships. One of his instructional innovations includes the development of an undergraduate Teaching Associate (lab director) program for the basic course in Human Communication.

brief contents

contents

Check out *Real Communication*'s **LaunchPad** at **bedfordstmartins.com/realcomm** for videos, quizzes, **LearningCurve**, and more.

For videos and LearningCurve quizzing within LaunchPad, go to **bedfordstmartins.com/realcomm**

▶ ✓ For videos and LearningCurve quizzing within LaunchPad, go to **bedfordstmartins.com/realcomm**

▶ ✓ For videos and LearningCurve quizzing within LaunchPad, go to **bedfordstmartins.com/realcomm**

 For videos and LearningCurve quizzing within LaunchPad, go to **bedfordstmartins.com/realcomm**

---

chapter 6

 For videos and LearningCurve quizzing within LaunchPad, go to **bedfordstmartins.com/realcomm**

For videos and LearningCurve quizzing within LaunchPad, go to **bedfordstmartins.com/realcomm**

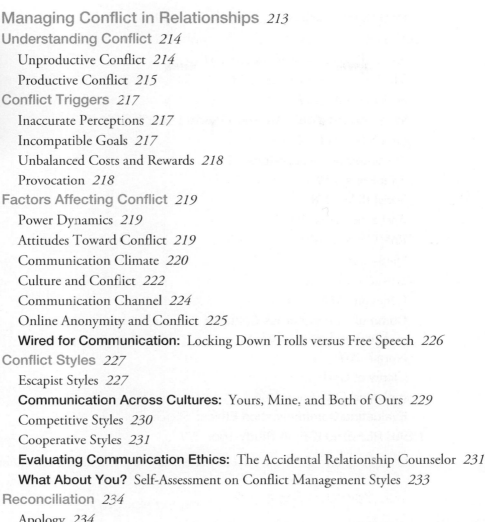

For videos and LearningCurve quizzing within LaunchPad, go to **bedfordstmartins.com/realcomm**

PART THREE

Group and Organizational Communication *241*

For videos and LearningCurve quizzing within LaunchPad, go to **bedfordstmartins.com/realcomm**

For videos and LearningCurve quizzing within LaunchPad, go to **bedfordstmartins.com/realcomm**

For videos and LearningCurve quizzing within LaunchPad, go to **bedfordstmartins.com/realcomm**

PART FOUR

Public Speaking *333*

 For videos and LearningCurve quizzing within LaunchPad, go to **bedfordstmartins.com/realcomm**

For videos and LearningCurve quizzing within LaunchPad, go to **bedfordstmartins.com/realcomm**

For videos and LearningCurve quizzing within LaunchPad, go to **bedfordstmartins.com/realcomm**

▶✓ For videos and LearningCurve quizzing within LaunchPac, go to **bedfordstmartins.com/realcomm**

For videos and LearningCurve quizzing within LaunchPad, go to **bedfordstmartins.com/realcomm**

PART ONE

Basic Communication Processes

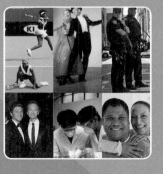

The power of social media brought everyone from surfers to marathon runners together in recovery efforts after Hurricane Sandy. © Nancy Siesel/Demotix/Corbis

COAL FREE FUTURE

✓ **LearningCurve** can help you master the material in this chapter. Go to **bedfordstmartins.com/realcomm**.

Communication: Essential Human Behavior

The water had receded within hours, but the isolation was just beginning. When Hurricane Sandy sent a fourteen-foot storm surge barreling across New York City's tiny Rockaway peninsula, homes and cars were destroyed and the community of 130,000 was left without power, phones, or transportation. Those lucky enough to charge their phones with a generator found signals were fleeting for the first week or so; one might manage to get one text or tweet out before the connection was gone. Radio became the only news outlet, although the mayor's daily briefings proved difficult to catch for people with a lot of cleanup work to do. Nonetheless, news that the New York Marathon, scheduled for the following weekend, would go on as planned sent locals reeling, wondering if anyone on the mainland even knew how bad things were (Boyle, 2012).

But elsewhere, social networks were buzzing. Surfers from the mainland converged on the Facebook page of the local surf club, figured out what was needed, and began gathering supplies and arranging car pools to get volunteers to the scene (Tockett, 2012). The very networks that organized protests of the financial sector the year before became vital information hubs as well: occupy Wall Street had become Occupy Sandy (Feuer, 2012). Churches, civic groups, schools, and everyday citizens showed up en masse to help their fellow New Yorkers. And when the city finally did cancel the marathon, runners who had trained all year for the event joined the volunteer efforts (Macur & Eder, 2012).

With cold weather bearing down, weary neighbors found themselves gathering—around small bonfires on the street, in homes with working generators, and around the trucks that delivered warm meals. Eventually, comfort tents popped up, providing residents with information, food, water, in-person support—and a place to charge those cell phones.

After you have finished reading this chapter, you will be able to

- Define the communication process

- Describe the functions of communication

- Assess the quality or value of communication by examining its six characteristics

- Define what communication scholars consider to be competent communication

- Describe the visual representations, or models, of communication

- Describe why communication is vital to everyone

Communication is the process by which we use symbols, signs, and behaviors to exchange information. That process is so crucial that communication is described as "the process through which the social fabric of relationships, groups, organizations, societies, and world order—and disorder—is created and maintained" (Ruben, 2005, pp. 294–295). Successful communication allows us to satisfy our most basic needs, from finding food and shelter to functioning in our communities and developing meaningful relationships—like many Sandy victims did after the storm. But because communication is such a natural part of our daily lives, we often take it for granted, which can make communication breakdowns all the more difficult. Failures in communication—from the loss of electronic communication to the decision to hold a marathon in the aftermath of a disaster—can lead to feelings of isolation, frustration, and anger.

Communication challenges exist in every profession and every personal relationship. For example, communication professor (and reserve police officer) Howard Giles claims that 97 percent of law enforcement practices involve communication skills (Giles et al., 2006). But police academies usually spend little time teaching those skills. Most citizens lack these crucial skills as well. One professor who teaches college-level communication classes to prisoners notes "the vast majority of my imprisoned students have been caged, in large part, because of their communicative illiteracy" (Hartnett, 2010, p. 68).

Effective communicators understand how their communication choices affect *others* and why *others'* communication choices affect *them* as they do. So in this chapter, we introduce you to this exciting discipline by looking at why we communicate, how we communicate, and what it means to communicate well. Then we examine ways of visualizing the communication process and consider the history of this rich field.

We Must Communicate: The Functional Perspective

We communicate from the moment we're born. A baby's cry lets everyone within earshot know that something isn't right: he's hungry, cold, or has a painful ear infection. Throughout our lives, we spend a huge amount of time communicating with others to ensure that our needs are met—though in more sophisticated ways than we did as infants. We talk, listen, smile, and nod; we write up résumés and go on dates. In these ways, we learn, express ourselves, form relationships, and gain employment. This **functional perspective** of communication examines how our communication helps (or doesn't help) us accomplish our goals in personal, group, organizational, public, or technologically mediated situations.

There are usually multiple goals at play in any given situation. For example, you may want to host Thanksgiving this year to illustrate your adult status in the family, but your older sister may insist on keeping the holiday at her home out of tradition. You and she must try to make Thanksgiving happen (one goal) without alienating each other (another goal). These goals may be accomplished in different ways. You might ask your sister to alternate years hosting the holidays; you might drag your mother into it and ask her to advocate for you with your

Everyone has ideas about what constitutes good communication. But just how correct are those ideas? Do your personal theories of communication match what social science tells us about the way we communicate? Consider the following questions:

BOX 1.1

COMMUNICATION IS *NOT* JUST COMMON SENSE

▶ **Does talking equal effective communication?** Have you ever sat through a conversation in which a relative kept repeating the same boring stories and you couldn't get a word in edgewise? Simply talking isn't always effective on its own. To communicate effectively, you also need to be thoughtful about what you are saying, remain silent at times, and use listening skills and appropriate nonverbal behaviors.

▶ **Do body movements (often called "body language") constitute a language?** As you will learn in Chapter 4, nonverbal communication is important and useful, but there is no direct translation for what body movements mean. Because nonverbal communication can be interpreted in many different ways, it is not a true language.

▶ **Is more control necessarily better in communication?** Although we admire people who can articulate their point of view, if we think they are trying to trick us or force us, we resist what they are saying. A candidate's speech may be beautifully crafted with clever slogans, for example, but he still can't make you vote for him.

▶ **Are most communication behaviors inborn and entirely natural?** No. Although we are certainly born with some ability to communicate, most of the skills we need to be effective communicators must be learned— otherwise, we'd go through life crying whenever we needed something. The best communicators never stop learning.

▶ **Is speaking well more important than listening?** If you talk and nobody listens, has communication taken place? No—because communication is a two-way street (even when you are just talking to yourself!), and listening is a crucial part of the process.

Many of us believe that we can rely on our *own* common sense to guide us, even though we think that other people's common sense fails them miserably (Watts, 2011). Don't fall for the commonsense "trap." Realize that communication takes work, adaptation, and careful attention to the situation.

sister. You might even try to bully your sister into letting you host. (Of course, some of these strategies may be more effective than others!) Lastly, goals may change over time. For instance, you might initially have thought you wanted to host Thanksgiving but then realized your small apartment can't comfortably fit your large family.

A long line of research conducted in a variety of contexts—including work groups, families, and friendships—has found that this goal-oriented communication serves one or more primary functions, such as expressing affiliation, managing relationships, or influencing others (Wiemann & Krueger, 1980). Let's consider each of these functions, keeping in mind that they are often intertwined.

AND YOU?

Consider a communication situation in which you played a part today. What was your communication goal? Were you up front and honest about your goal or did you keep your goal largely to yourself? For example, if you wanted to get your roommate to clean the mess in the kitchen, did you state this directly or did you complain about the mess without making a request?

Expressing Affiliation

Affiliation is the feeling of connectedness you have with others. You show how you want to be associated with someone by expressing liking, love, or respect— or, alternatively, dislike, hatred, or disrespect (Wiemann, 2009).

Obviously, it feels good to be loved and admired. But affiliation may also meet practical needs, as when you show respect for your boss, who can offer you stability and security in your job. Other times affiliation may fulfill the need for companionship, intellectual stimulation, or a sense of belonging with a valued group of people.

Affiliation can be expressed in many different ways—verbally ("I love you") and nonverbally (a big hug), and through face-to-face or mediated channels (like sending text messages or using social networking sites). In fact, we are increasingly using media technologies to develop and maintain a positive sense of connection with each other (Walther & Ramirez, 2009), especially with people who are far away physically. A supportive text message from a friend can help you face a difficult personal situation with confidence. A simple click of the "Like" thumbs-up icon on Facebook can show that you are a fan of your brother's new band.

Managing Relationships

All communication "works" (or not) within the context of **relationships**—the interconnections between two or more people. As mentioned earlier, communication allows us to express affiliation, and that can certainly be important in relationships. But relationships involve more than just affiliation—such as how intimately we get to know one another or how we handle conflict (as we'll see in Chapters 7 and 8). We need effective communication to be able to manage these aspects of our relationships.

AND YOU?

Have you ever been in a relationship in which you liked someone but at times felt a bit disconnected from the person? What messages did the person send (or not send) that gave you this feeling? What did you do to try to reestablish the connection?

Relationships also involve **interdependence**, meaning that what we do affects others and what others do affects us. For example, Jamie flips burgers to get a paycheck to help pay for college—that's her goal. Her boss depends on Jamie to do her job well and keep the business profitable. And the customers, who just want an inexpensive and quick lunch, depend on both of them. Jamie, the boss, and the lunch customers are interdependent. Jamie and her boss must communicate to get along well and yet keep their relationship professional. Similarly, Jamie and her boss use communication to establish a trusting and loyal relationship with their customers without getting to know each of them on a personal level.

Communication is also important for managing relationships over time. Perhaps you made a best friend in kindergarten and you and he have remained close despite physical distance and the introduction of new friends and romantic partners into the mix. Verbal and nonverbal behaviors (see Chapters 3 and 4) likely had a big role in maintaining this relationship: You video chat with your friend once a month, keep up with each other on Facebook, and text him on his birthday, reinforcing the relationship with laughs and words of encouragement. You've also likely lost friendships as time has passed. Perhaps you broke up with your high school sweetheart when the two of you went to separate colleges. Your phone calls and visits became less frequent and—when you did speak—you found your communication uncomfortable and strained. The kinds of verbal and nonverbal relational "work" you do in managing relationships may signal their health or demise, revealing how communication functions to establish and maintain your relationships happily or unhappily.

● CONTESTANTS IN DEMANDING COMPETITIONS such as *The Amazing Race* know that it would be impossible to achieve goals without cooperation and clear communication. Heather Wines/CBS via Getty Images

Influencing Others

Most communication is influential in one way or another. Some influence is intentional: a politician uses gestures strategically during a press conference to shape how voters perceive her. Other influence is unintentional: Michaela's lack of eye contact during an after-class meeting gives her professor the sense that she lacks confidence, but she's really just having trouble with her contact lenses.

The ability of one person, group, or organization to influence others and the way in which their interactions are conducted is called **control**. Unlike affection, which you can give and receive infinitely, control is finite: the more control one person has in a relationship or situation, the less the others tend to have. Distribution of control is worked out through communication—by how people talk with each other, what they say, and when they interact. This negotiation of control may seem like a power struggle at times. But it is a necessary aspect of every type of relationship: family, friends, romantic partners, colleagues, doctors and patients, teachers and students, advertisers and consumers.

The amount of control you have over others or that they have over you varies depending on the situation and each person's status. Sometimes control shifts from one party to another. For example, as a new bank employee, Manny

CONNECT

As you learn in Chapter 16, persuasive speaking is an attempt to influence others' attitudes, beliefs, or behaviors. It may seem as though the speaker has all of the control in the speaking situation, but this isn't the case. The audience members can exert influence on the speaker through a variety of nonverbal cues (like eye contact and facial expressions) that may cause the speaker to alter his or her behavior.

real communicator

NAME: Vicky Turk
OCCUPATION: Human Resources

I love my job—and I think I'm pretty good at it, thanks in part to the skills I gained as an undergraduate Communication major. I'm currently a human resources professional at a global financial data and media company, and I handle everything in an employee's "life cycle." From hiring to relations with coworkers, relocation, flexible work arrangements, immigration, and even separation from the company, I am the employee's go-to person.

You might think that people in this high-intensity environment arrive with the communication skills they need to succeed. Sadly, this isn't true; just because you're a manager doesn't mean that you effectively negotiate conflict with a subordinate. Or just because you're an incredibly successful accountant doesn't mean that you're a natural at leading a group toward a particular goal. The fact is that communication isn't common sense; I spend a good deal of time helping people navigate stressful work/life situations that could be alleviated or improved with better listening, nonverbal, intercultural, conflict management, and group work skills. Much of the time, I find myself reaching for these very tools!

For example, when I'm mediating a manager–employee conflict or one between colleagues, I remind myself that people—regardless of professional status—like to feel that someone is truly, actively listening to them when they're sharing their perspective, particularly in a heated situation. I've found that I can defuse all sorts of problems by hearing the parties out, not showing what I feel or think internally (monitoring my nonverbal behaviors), and modeling how to navigate a way through differing perceptions without threatening any of the individuals involved. Once people feel that I'm on their side, they listen less defensively and we usually find a resolution.

I remember my college professors stressing that competent communicators need to be agile and adjust their behaviors rapidly to meet the needs of intense and quickly changing situations. Being able to do this confidently is essential when working in Human Resources. (This is also true of other people-oriented professions, such as teaching, counseling, and consulting.) After all, verbal and nonverbal behavior that might be effective and appropriate with one individual in one situation at one particular moment in time might not be effective and appropriate elsewhere—and you don't always have a lot of time to sit and think about it.

I consider myself extremely fortunate to have a wonderful and interesting job that constantly challenges me to refine my skills and learn new ones. Some people may have questioned my decision to major in Communication because it "doesn't produce direct job skills." Clearly I've proved the naysayers wrong. I can always take a course or a workshop to learn a programming language, improve my Web design skills, or learn other equally important skills in today's economy. But I rest assured and reflect gratefully that I spent four years studying the ins and outs of human communication. I would not be where I am today had my studies taken me in a different direction.

looks to his manager, Alexis, for direction and advice about how to do his job well. The unequal control distribution is appropriate and meets Manny's and Alexis's expectations of their job responsibilities. But as Manny becomes more comfortable in the job, he will likely take more control, and Alexis will let him work more independently. This redistribution of control is a natural process.

How We Communicate

It's 8:45 A.M. in New York City. A woman walks up to a street vendor's cart, smiles and nods quickly at the vendor, and says, "Regular." The man promptly prepares her a small coffee with milk and two sugars. He hands her the coffee; she hands him some money, says "thanks," and continues on her way.

With only two words spoken, an entire business transaction has been carried out to the satisfaction of both parties. But what exactly occurred? The characteristics of communication can explain.

● **FOR MOST LEARNING** environments to be successful, teachers should have more control than students in the classroom. © David Grossman/The Image Works

Characteristics of Communication

Communication has six defining characteristics: the extent to which the message is *symbolic*, the extent to which the *code is shared*, the degree to which the message is *culturally bound*, the sender's perceived *intentionality*, the presence of a *channel*, and the degree to which the encoding and decoding of messages are *transactional*. That's quite a mouthful, so let's look at each characteristic more closely.

Communication Is Symbolic

Communication relies on the use of **symbols**—arbitrary constructions (usually language or behaviors) that refer to objects: people, things, and ideas. The stronger the connection is between symbol and object, the clearer the intended meaning, and vice versa. For example, our customer greeted the street vendor with a smile and a nod—behaviors clearly indicating the idea of "greeting."

A symbol can take on a new meaning if at least two people agree that it will have that meaning for them. A romantic couple might share a specific "look" that communicates their mutual affection; three friends might have a gesture that signifies an inside joke. Social groups, such as fraternities and sororities or sports teams, might use a handshake, password, or article of clothing to set themselves apart from others. We cover the use of such verbal and nonverbal symbols more deeply in Chapters 3, 4, and 5.

As we discuss in Chapter 3, the most arbitrary symbolic behavior is language. There is no particular reason why the letters *t-r-e-e* should represent a very large plant form, but they do. And in Chapter 4, you learn that gestures serve a similar purpose. Holding up your thumb while clenching your other fingers stands for "good job" in U.S. culture, though you likely don't need to have this fact explained.

CONNECT

As you learn in Chapter 5, culture can dictate communication norms, such as defining personal space. In Mediterranean cultures, for instance, men stand close together and frequently touch during conversation. But in North American cultures, the appropriate conversational distance is generally about three feet, and men seldom touch each other during social interaction, except when they shake hands in greeting.

Communication Requires a Shared Code

A **code** is a set of symbols that are joined to create a meaningful message. For communication to take place, the participants must share the code to encode and decode messages. **Encoding** is the process of mentally constructing a message—putting it into a symbol that can be sent to someone. **Decoding** is the process of interpreting and assigning meaning to a message that gets received. If the relational partners are using the same code, they are more likely to encode and decode messages accurately and arrive at the shared meaning they want to communicate.

Speaking a common language is the most obvious example of sharing a communication code, though it is certainly not the only one. Baseball teams, for example, develop elaborate codes for various pitches and plays, which players communicate through hand gestures and body movements (removing a baseball cap, holding up three fingers and shaking them twice). Similarly, consider the emoticons, texting, and chat room shorthand we all use when communicating through mediated channels—especially when we're in a hurry.

Communication Is Linked to Culture

If you've ever traveled abroad, or even through the different neighborhoods of a large city, you know that communication is linked to culture. *Culture* refers to the shared beliefs, values, and practices of a group of people. A group's culture includes the language (or languages) and other symbols used by group members as well as the norms and rules about appropriate behavior.

Most people are members of several co-cultures simultaneously. *Co-cultures* are smaller groups of people within a larger culture that are distinguished by features such as race, religion, age, generation, political affiliation, gender, sexual orientation, economic status, educational level, occupation, and a host of other factors.

Consider Angela, who identifies with a number of co-cultures: she is an American, an African American, a woman, a Midwesterner, a married lawyer with two children, a person with an income over $100,000 a year, a Democrat, and a Baptist. Each of these co-cultures carries different meanings for Angela and affects her communication—including the language she speaks, how she presents herself to others, how she evaluates her effectiveness, and how she interprets others' behavior (Chen & Starosta, 1996; Zarrinabadi, 2012).

Cultural identities can even form around interests and hobbies. For example, a music critic at Pitchfork.com might distinguish among rock, soul, and hip-hop and might even break those styles down further, using terms like *old-school, freestyle, classic, punk, techno,* and *R&B.* For someone less involved or less interested in the music scene, such distinctions might seem unimportant—it's all just popular music. We uncover the cultural complexities of communication in Chapter 5.

Communication Can Be Unintentional

Some communication is *intentional*, such as messaging a friend to let her know you'll be away from your computer and using a mutually understood code (BRB!). Other communication is *spontaneous* and therefore unintentional (Buck, 1988; Motley, 1990). For example, you communicate a message when you blush, even though blushing is an involuntary action. The distinction between the two types of communication can be described as the difference between *giving* information and *giving off* information (Goffman, 1967).

These distinctions are important: we tend to see involuntary messages as more honest and reliable because the person giving off the information doesn't have the opportunity to censor it. However, most spontaneous messages are ambiguous: Is your face red because you're embarrassed? Because you're angry? Because you've had a hot cup of tea? Because you just ran up six flights of stairs? Other surrounding cues may give us more clues to the meaning, but in the end our final assessment can still be questionable. The most successful communicators are sensitive to the fact that both intended and unintended messages exert an impact on the people around them.

Communication Occurs Through Various Channels

Once, the only means of communication—the only channel—was face-to-face contact. But as society became more sophisticated, other channels emerged. Smoke signals, handwritten correspondence, telegraph, telephone, e-mail, and text messaging are all examples. A **channel** is simply the method through which communication occurs. We must have a channel to communicate.

Most people in technologically advanced societies use many channels to communicate, though they are not always proficient at adapting communication for the channel being used. Do you have a friend who leaves five-minute voice mail messages on your cell phone as though speaking directly with you? Or do you have a cousin who shares deeply private information with all of her six hundred Facebook "friends"? We all need to identify the channel that will work best for certain messages, at certain points in our relationships with certain people, and then adapt our messages to that medium.

Communication Is Transactional

You may recall when CBS and Warner Brothers halted production of the hit comedy *Two and a Half Men* after actor Charlie Sheen made many derogatory, insulting remarks about the sitcom's creator, Chuck Lorre (Carter, 2011). Lorre's refusal to continue the show in the aftermath of Sheen's hostility carried a huge financial loss for all parties, but nothing seemed possible to reverse the turn of events and the show was only resumed after Sheen was replaced by Ashton Kutcher. That's because communication is a **transactional** process: it involves people exchanging messages in both *sender* and *receiver* roles, and their messages are interdependent—influenced by those of their partner—and irreversible. Once a message has been sent (intentionally or not) and received, it *cannot* be taken back, nor can it be repeated in precisely the same way. It is an ongoing process that can be immediate (as in a real-time conversation) or delayed (as in the case of a text message exchange).

AND YOU?

Have you ever given off an unintentional message that was improperly decoded? (For example, you yawn during an argument because you're tired from work, but your romantic partner assumes you are bored and uninterested.) What did you do to clarify that message? Was it effective?

Choosing the appropriate channel for a specific message is important, particularly when conflict is involved. As you learn in Chapter 8, breaking up with someone via Facebook rather than through a more personal channel (like face to face) can worsen an already difficult situation. Such channels don't allow for nonverbal communication (tone of voice, eye contact, etc.), which helps you present difficult news clearly and sensitively.

● **CHARLIE SHEEN'S OFFENSIVE** behavior not only damaged his own career but also impacted everyone else involved in *Two and a Half Men*. CBS/Photofest

As we illustrate throughout this book, whenever you communicate with others, you influence them in some way. Equally important, you are influenced *by* others. What you say to a person is influenced by what he or she says to you, and vice versa. In the end, every conversation or interaction you have changes you (and the other person), even if only in some small way, as it adds to your life experiences.

Assessing Communicative Value

To understand communication more fully, you assess the quality, or communicative value, of your communication. You do this by examining how well the communication demonstrates the six characteristics discussed earlier. If the symbols are well chosen, the code shared, and the messages sent as intended, the interaction has high communicative value, and misunderstandings are less likely.

For example, recall the coffee purchase described at the beginning of this section. The woman and the street vendor share a clear, if unwritten, code: in New York City, "regular" coffee means coffee with milk and two sugars. The code has a cultural meaning unique to New York. Even within the city, it is somewhat specialized, limited to street vendors and delicatessens. Had she said the same word to the counterperson at a Seattle's Best coffee shop on the West Coast—or even at the Starbucks just down the street—she might have received a perplexed stare in reply. See Table 1.1 for a more detailed breakdown of this transaction.

TABLE 1.1

COMMUNICATION CHARACTERISTICS: ANATOMY OF A COFFEE SALE
Approaching the study of communication through its characteristics will help you evaluate behaviors you encounter in terms of their communicative value. As you can see, the simple coffee sale described in the text is clearly communicative, meeting all six criteria.

Characteristic	Behavior
Communication is symbolic.	Both parties speak English.
Communication requires a shared code.	Both parties understand the meaning of "regular." Both parties understand the smile and nod greeting.
Communication is linked to culture.	Both parties are New Yorkers.
Communication need not be intentional.	The woman knows the meanings of her words and gestures; they are not ambiguous to the street vendor.
Communication occurs through various channels.	This example uses the spoken word, gestures, and eye contact.
Communication is transactional.	The woman understands the message she is giving, and the man understands the message he is receiving.

Communicating Competently

Communicating is inherently complex because people and situations vary. For example, in the classic film *Walk the Line*, singer-songwriter Johnny Cash is thoroughly at ease in front of an audience but falls apart when communicating at home. Cash's relationship with his wife, Vivian, seems marked by a lack of understanding, dishonesty, and an inability to connect on a personal level. The Academy Award–winning film reveals that Johnny Cash has a set of useful and unique talents but that he must adapt them to suit the needs of different people and situations. He does this in his second, successful marriage to June Carter Cash.

● **ALTHOUGH JOHNNY CASH** (played by Joaquin Phoenix in the film *Walk the Line*) had a great connection and rapport with his fans, his first marriage was far less successful.

In studying communication, our goal is to become competent communicators. We do not mean merely adequate or "good enough." Indeed, communication scholars use the term **competent communication** to describe communication that is effective and appropriate for a given situation, in which the communicators evaluate and reassess their own communication process (Wiemann & Backlund, 1980). We examine each of these aspects of competent communication in the following sections.

Competent Communication Is Process-Oriented

An old sports adage says, "It's not whether you win or lose; it's how you play the game." This means that the *process* (how you play) is more important than the *outcome* (who wins and who loses). In communication, an **outcome** has to do with the product of an interchange. In a negotiation, for example, the outcome may be that you get a good deal on a product or get a contract signed. Competent communication is also concerned with **process**—the means by which participants arrived at an outcome. Although outcomes obviously still play a role in a process analysis, *what* is said and *how* it is said have great significance.

● **IN OCTOBER 2013,** protesters called for effective communication when Congress failed to negotiate an agreement about the 2014 fiscal budget, shutting down the American government for over two weeks.

When it comes to process, communicators who strive to create mutually satisfying outcomes are the most competent (Wiemann, 1977). A study of fathers and daughters, for example, found that the most satisfactory relationships involved a matching of needs and a balancing of control (Punyanunt-Carter, 2005). Asif, for example, hoped his daughter Laila would attend his alma mater. In the summer before Laila's senior year of high school, the two visited the university as well as several others. They worked together on her college applications and debated the merits of each school. Both Asif and Laila describe their relationship as satisfying and note that the process of searching for the right

school made them even closer, even though Laila ultimately did not choose her father's alma mater.

Ethical considerations are a crucial part of the communication process. **Ethics** is the study of morals, specifically the moral choices individuals make in their relationships with others. Your personal values, along with your culture's values, provide guidance on how to construct your messages appropriately and how to analyze messages directed toward you (Casmir, 1997; Christians & Traber, 1997). Ethical concerns arise whenever standards of right and wrong significantly affect our communication behavior (Johansson & Stohl, 2012). For example, the communication of a political spokesperson who lies or twists the truth to garner a jump in the polls for a candidate is not competent but instead is unethical, manipulative, and exploitative.

Questions of right and wrong arise whenever people communicate. Ethical communication is fundamental to responsible thinking, decision-making, and the development of relationships and communities within and across contexts, cultures, channels, and media. Moreover, ethical communication enhances human worth and dignity by fostering truthfulness, fairness, responsibility, personal integrity, and respect for self and others. We believe that unethical communication threatens the quality of all communication and consequently the well-being of individuals and the society in which we live. Therefore we, the members of the National Communication Association, endorse and are committed to practicing the following principles of ethical communication:

▶ We advocate truthfulness, accuracy, honesty, and reason as essential to the integrity of communication.

▶ We endorse freedom of expression, diversity of perspective, and tolerance of dissent to achieve the informed and responsible decision-making fundamental to a civil society.

▶ We strive to understand and respect other communicators before evaluating and responding to their messages.

▶ We promote access to communication resources and opportunities as necessary to fulfill human potential and contribute to the well-being of families, communities, and society.

▶ We promote communication climates of caring and mutual understanding that respect the unique needs and characteristics of individual communicators.

▶ We condemn communication that degrades individuals and humanity through distortion, intimidation, coercion, and violence, and through the expression of intolerance and hatred.

▶ We are committed to the courageous expression of personal convictions in pursuit of fairness and justice.

▶ We advocate sharing information, opinions, and feelings when facing significant choices while also respecting privacy and confidentiality.

▶ We accept responsibility for the short- and long-term consequences for our own communication and expect the same of others.

Competent Communication Is Appropriate and Effective

Lena Dunham stars in the HBO series *Girls* as Hannah, a twenty-something in Brooklyn with writerly ambitions. Due to her self-involvement, Hannah is not a particularly skilled communicator, and one incident in the third season makes this abundantly clear. Hannah attends the funeral of the editor who was helping her publish a memoir—and ends up asking his widow to help connect her to another publisher. Shocked at her timing, the widow asks her to leave.

If you've ever laughed or cringed at someone else's inappropriate question or comment, you already understand that for communication to be competent it needs to be both effective and appropriate. You would not speak to your grandmother in the same way you talk to your friends; nor would a lawyer ask her husband to complete a task the same way she would ask her office assistant. Competent, successful communicators adjust their behavior to suit particular individuals and situations; the characters in *Girls* do neither.

● **WHILE STARTING OUT** in the world of publishing, Hannah from *Girls* doesn't always make the best communication choices. Ali Paige Goldstein/© HBO/Courtesy Everett Collection

Appropriate Behavior

During his spring 2013 European tour, popular music star Justin Bieber visited Amsterdam's Anne Frank House, a popular museum dedicated to the legacy of the World War II teenage diarist, Anne Frank. Frank's family, and four other Jewish friends, hid from the Nazis in secret rooms in the house until they were discovered and arrested in 1944. Frank's widely read *Diary of Anne Frank* provides a first-person account of daily life under such strenuous conditions in the midst of one of history's most horrifying genocides. Sadly, Justin Bieber missed the solemn and reflective nature of his visit when he signed the museum's guestbook, "Truly inspiring to be able to come here. Anne was a great girl. Hopefully she would have been a belieber" (Duke, 2013). When the message was later posted to the museum's Facebook page, fans were outraged that the singer hoped that Anne Frank, a teenager whose memories give a face to the tens of thousands of lives uprooted and extinguished by the Nazi regime, would have been a "belieber"—a girl head-over-heels in love with Justin Bieber (Duke, 2013).

Communication is appropriate when it meets the demands of the situation as well as the expectations of others present (whether physically or virtually). In almost all situations, cultural norms and rules set the standards for expectations. Although Justin Bieber may have thought his comment would show appreciation for Frank as a regular teenager who liked celebrities, he violated norms about modesty and respect in a reflective historical place. He made his admiration of a woman whose story inspires millions appear to be more about himself.

Sometimes even those whose profession it is to communicate, such as journalists, can also be inappropriate. After the disastrous 2013 Santa Maria, Brazil, nightclub fire that killed almost 250 people, reporters jockeyed for the "most

One skill that can help you communicate appropriately is *self-monitoring*. As you learn in Chapter 2, the ability to monitor yourself and your environment for clues on how to behave is quite powerful. At a party, you can assess how formal or informal a situation is, what types of messages are considered acceptable or off-limits, and so on. Such knowledge allows you to tailor your communication to be competent in your environment.

● JUSTIN BIEBER'S
ENTRY in the guestbook
at the Anne Frank House
showed a disregard for
cultural norms and rules.
Bradley Kanaris/Getty Images

The relational context
usually determines how
much information you are
willing to share (or *self-
disclose*) with another
individual. In Chapter 7,
you'll learn more about
why it's competent to avoid
telling your manager about
the fight you had with your
significant other but why
it might enhance intimacy
to share such information
with your close friend or
sibling.

dramatic-grieving-parent interview"; cartoons depicted young people going in one door of the club and coming out another escorted by death with a scythe (Xersenesky, 2013). Appropriate care and tact for the victims and their families were inappropriately ignored in the rush to share sensationalist stories.

Successful communicators know what is and isn't appropriate in a variety of situations. Moreover, they have **behavioral flexibility**: the ability to use a number of different behaviors depending on the situation. So while you might love to talk about politics or your grades when you're with your friends, you might decide that these topics aren't appropriate during Passover dinner at your aunt's house.

Effective Behavior

Behaving appropriately is not enough in itself. Competent communication must also be effective—it must help you meet your goals. This can be challenging, because it's not always easy to know what messages will work best—and you may have more than one goal (Canary, Cody, & Smith, 1994). For example, Travis and his fiancée, Leah, are arguing over whose family they will visit over the July 4th long weekend. Travis has conflicting goals: he wants to see his family for the holiday, but he also wants Leah to be happy.

If you have some knowledge of your communication partner's expectations, you can more easily determine which messages will be more effective than others. If Travis knows that Leah would like to spend the holiday with her family because she wants to see her elderly grandmother, he might suggest that they spend the four-day weekend with his family but their weeklong August vacation with her family. In addition, prioritizing your goals can help you construct effective messages. If Leah knows that her grandmother is ailing, she may decide that going home for July 4th is a more important goal than pleasing Travis. She can then tell him that she's sorry to let him down but that she absolutely must return home.

Communication behavior that is effective in one setting might not be suitable in others. For example, many students feel that their best teachers are those who are organized and logical (Kramer & Pier, 1999). But if your roommate handed you a detailed schedule of what you should do every day in your apartment during the upcoming semester, you might find this behavior strange and annoying.

Competent Communication Involves Communication Skills

Having exemplary skills in one area does not make someone competent overall: your mechanic may work wonders on your car, but that doesn't mean he can give you a great haircut. The same idea is true for great communicators: a politician who delivers a great speech may falter during a debate or interview; a social worker who conveys instructions clearly to her staff may have trouble clarifying her points during a meeting with the hospital board.

WIREDFORCOMMUNICATION

E-Mail Etiquette: How *Not* to Communicate with Your Professor

> From: student@college.edu
> Sent: Tuesday, September 9, 2014 11:42 A.M.
> To: professor@college.edu
> Subject: hey
> hey, sorry i missed class today . . . i had a little too much fun last nite had a rough time waking up ;)
> can you E-mail me your teaching notes ASAP? Tnx.

E-mails, when used effectively, are a valuable educational tool. They allow college students to ask questions outside of class and let professors provide instant feedback, making instructors more accessible than ever before. And while that's a great thing, many professors are complaining that some student e-mails are inappropriate.

Informal

Overly casual messages bother instructors and affect their perceptions of students' credibility (Stevens, Houser, & Cowan, 2009). Your message should be formal. It should open with a salutation ("Dear Professor Smith"), continue with a person/class identifier ("I'm Vera Yun in your 9:30 T/R conflict class"), and close with a proper signature ("Thanks in advance, Vera"). The rules of grammar, spelling, and capitalization all apply. There should be a clear subject line that should be appropriate to the content of the e-mail (otherwise, your professor may reject your e-mail as spam).

Inappropriate

The e-mail shown here is wholly inappropriate for student-professor correspondence. There's a halfhearted attempt at an apology and a thinly veiled reference to being hung over on the day of class. Here, as with any communication, it's important to analyze your audience. There are some things you can say to your friends that you shouldn't say to your professor. Review your draft before you send it; if you think you've written something that you think *might* offend or be inappropriate, take it out!

Demanding

Many professors complain that student e-mails are becoming increasingly pushy in tone. Recipients of poor grades send nasty notes, absent students demand teaching notes, and many students send more than ten e-mails a day, expecting their professors to be available around the clock.

Some guidelines: don't clutter inboxes with a barrage of requests, and give recipients plenty of time to respond. Use the tools that your professor has provided, such as the course syllabus, assignment sheets, or notes posted on a Web site before you e-mail; you may find that you already have what you need. And if you skipped class, don't ask your professor what you missed; that's what classmates are for.

THINK ABOUT THIS

❶ What is the value of an effective and appropriate subject line in an e-mail message? In what ways might the subject line influence your instructor's impression of the message and its sender?

❷ Why might students tend to use e-mail when a phone call or an office visit would be more appropriate? In what ways does the choice of communication channel influence the content and style of the message?

❸ What are the advantages of e-mail over other channels of communication when contacting a professor? How might a student capitalize on those advantages?

Communication skills are behavioral abilities based on social under-standings that are used to achieve particular goals (such as asking for a raise, maintaining a relationship, or working on a team). Some of us may instinc-tively be better at communication than others, but all of us can benefit from experience and practice at developing our skills to find the best choice of words or the most appropriate tone of voice to use with our relational partners or work teams.

People who are judged as incompetent in some situations often don't know that they are unskilled; their inflated image of themselves seems to block their awareness (Dunning & Kruger, 1999). For example, suppose you see yourself as a great team player. During the evaluation at the end of a class project, you're surprised to learn that your teammates see you as "bossy." This feedback suggests that while you may be good at leading a team, you're less adept at working along-side others as an equal. The lesson? You may need to master some new com-munication skills to be a competent group member. In fact, having a number of skills increases your behavioral options, thereby boosting your odds of success in communicating with others.

Competent Communication Involves Using Technology

Communicating competently in face-to-face situations is complex. Adding tech-nology to the mix can present even more challenges (Cupach & Spitzberg, 2011; Wright et al., 2013). So, can you measure the effectiveness and appropriateness of communication when you are on the phone or using a social networking site in the same way as when you are face to face? Research indicates that the answer is yes . . . and no.

As we've seen, competent communication must meet the goals of the com-municators and be effective and appropriate for the situation. But our goals can sometimes be enhanced by the simultaneous use of more than one technology. For example, while chatting online or on the phone, many people locate info on the Web to share with a communication partner or to back up their own argu-ments (Walther, Van Der Heide, Tong, Carr, & Atkin, 2010; Lipinski-Harten & Tafarodi, 2012). If they were talking face to face with someone, using the Web at the same time might be considered rude.

The technology channels you use can also change others' perceptions of your communication competence. Texting a "thank you" might be an appropriate way to thank a friend for a compliment, but it probably won't impress your great-uncle Fred after he gives you a generous graduation gift. He'll likely be expecting a low-tech, handwritten thank-you note.

Finally, research shows that if you are comfortable with a particular technol-ogy, you will see yourself as more competent with that technology and use it to accomplish your goals more often (Keaten & Kelly, 2008). For example, you may feel comfortable applying for jobs online; you are familiar with the technol-ogies involved and are willing to wait for an electronic response. You would likely describe yourself as competent with these technologies (Bakke, 2010), whereas your parents or grandparents may question your use of them for job hunting if they are less familiar with them.

what about you?

Assessing your own competence is a useful step in understanding and improving your personal communication behaviors.

Complete the following questionnaire, evaluating your behavior with a long-standing partner in mind (for example, close friend, family member, romantic partner). Rate each on the following scale: 5 = strongly agree; 4 = agree; 3 = undecided or neutral; 2 = disagree; and 1 = strongly disagree. Then add your responses and check the key for feedback on your competence.

_____ 1. I find it easy to get along with others.
_____ 2. I am "rewarding" to talk to.
_____ 3. I can deal with others effectively.
_____ 4. I am a good listener.
_____ 5. I won't argue with someone just to prove I'm right.
_____ 6. I generally know how others feel.
_____ 7. I let others know I understand them.
_____ 8. I am relaxed and comfortable when speaking.
_____ 9. I listen to what people say to me.
_____ 10. I generally know what type of behavior is appropriate in any given situation.
_____ 11. I typically do not make unusual demands on my friends.
_____ 12. I am an effective conversationalist.
_____ 13. I am supportive of others.
_____ 14. I am sensitive to others' needs of the moment.
_____ 15. I pay attention to the conversation.
_____ 16. I am generally relaxed when conversing with a new acquaintance.
_____ 17. I am interested in what my partner(s) have to say.
_____ 18. I am a likeable person.
_____ 19. I am flexible.
_____ 20. I generally say the right thing at the right time.

74–100: You perceive yourself as highly competent; you are comfortable with your communication behavior and are usually both appropriate and effective in your communication.

47–73: You are competent at times but are sometimes unsure of what to say or do when you communicate with others. Sometimes you care more about being effective than appropriate, and at other times you worry more about being appropriate than being effective.

20–46: You frequently find yourself tense in communication situations, worried about how to adapt to your partner and the situation. You may be unconcerned or not tuned into the communication situation.

Note: your scores may change across situations (and with different people).

Source: Adapted from J. M. Wiemann (1977). Used with permission.

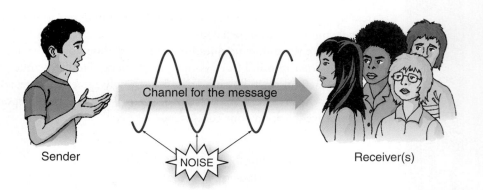

Channel for the message

Sender

NOISE

Receiver(s)

FIGURE 1.1
LINEAR MODEL

Modeling Communication

As we've stated, the communication process is infinitely complex. For this reason, scholars have generated different models, or visual representations, of the process to help deepen our understanding of communication. Let's look at three such models: linear, interaction, and competent communication.

The Linear Model

In the **linear model** of communication (see Figure 1.1), scholars proposed that a **sender** originates communication with words or actions constituting the **message**. The message is then carried through a *channel* (air and sound waves, written or visual, over telephone lines, cables, or electronic transmissions). Along the way, some interference, called **noise**, occurs. Because of the noise, the message arrives at the **receiver** changed in some way from the original (Shannon & Weaver, 1949).

The linear model depicts communication as occurring in only one direction: from sender to receiver. So, although this model may be useful for showing how electronic signals (such as television and radio) are transmitted to the public, it does not show the receiver's role in interpreting meaning or in sending simultaneous feedback to the sender in a conversation. For this reason, scholars have dismissed the linear model as not particularly useful for understanding most kinds of communication, particularly interactive forms.

The Interaction Model

The **interaction model** shows communication as a two-directional process that incorporates feedback into communication between sender and receiver (see Figure 1.2). **Feedback** is a message from the receiver to the sender that illustrates how the receiver is responding. As with the linear model, noise may occur along the way.

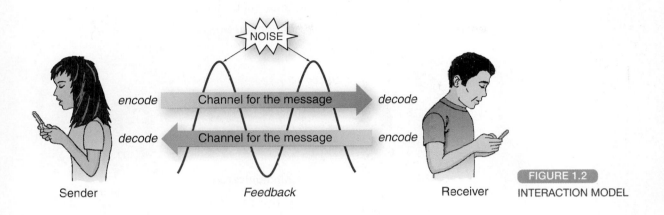

NOISE

encode   Channel for the message   decode

decode   Channel for the message   encode

Sender   *Feedback*   Receiver

FIGURE 1.2

INTERACTION MODEL

Feedback can be a verbal message (your friend invites you to a party on Friday night, and you reply, "About nine?"), a nonverbal message (your roommate is telling you about a movie, and you look up, smile, and nod while you are listening), or both (you frown while saying, "I don't think I understand"). Through feedback, communicators in the interaction model are both senders and receivers of messages.

Instant messaging is a good example of how the interaction model can be applied in mediated situations; you get feedback, but it's not in "real time." For example, while G-chatting, Melissa takes some time in composing her response to Howard's last comment; during the delay, Howard may log off, thinking that Melissa has lost interest.

The Competent Communication Model

Though the linear and interaction models describe some communication processes, neither captures the complexity of competent communication that we talked about in the preceding section (Wiemann & Backlund, 1980).

To illustrate this complex process, we developed a model of communication that shows effective and appropriate communication (see Figure 1.3). This **competent communication model** not only includes feedback, but also it shows communication as an ongoing, *transactional* process: the individuals (or groups or organizations) are *interdependent*—their actions affect one another—and they exchange irreversible messages.

In this model, arrows show the links between communication behaviors by representing messages being sent and received. In face-to-face communication, the behaviors of both communicators influence each individual at the same time. For example, Cliff smiles and nods at Jalissa without saying anything as Jalissa talks about the meeting she hosted for her book club. Through these behaviors, Cliff is sending messages of encouragement while receiving her verbal messages. Jalissa sends messages about the book she chose for that week's discussion, as well as the foods she selected and prepared for the get-together. But she is also receiving messages from Cliff that she interprets as positive interest. Both Cliff

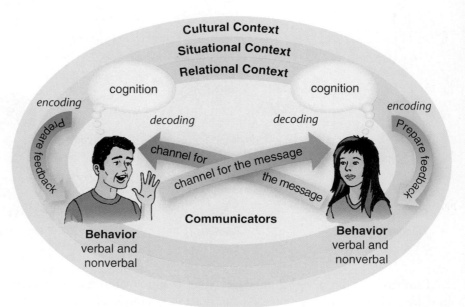

FIGURE 1.3

COMPETENT
COMMUNICATION MODEL

and Jalissa are simultaneously encoding (sending) and decoding (receiving) communication behavior.

This transaction changes slightly with different types of communication. For example, in a mediated form of communication—a Facebook posting or texting, for example—the sending and receiving of messages may not be simultaneous. In such cases, the communicators are more likely to take turns, or a delay in time may elapse between messages. In mass media such as TV or radio, feedback may be even more limited and delayed—audience reactions to a TV show are typically gauged only by the Nielsen ratings (how many people watched) or by comments posted by fans on their blogs.

The competent communication model takes into account not only the transactional nature of communication but also the role of communicators themselves—their internal thoughts and influences as well as the various contexts in which they operate. There are four main spheres of influence at play in the competent communication model:

▶ The *communicators*. Two individuals are shown here, but many variations are possible: one speaking to an audience of two hundred, six individuals in a group meeting, and so on.

▶ The *relationships* among the communicators.

▶ The *situation* in which the communication occurs.

▶ The *cultural setting* that frames the interaction.

Let's take a closer look at each of these influences.

The Communicators

The most obvious elements in any communication are the communicators themselves. When sending and receiving messages, each communicator is influenced by **cognitions**, the thoughts they have about themselves and others, including their understanding and awareness of who they are (smart, funny, compassionate), how well they like themselves, and how successful they think they are. We discuss this in depth in Chapter 2. For now, just understand that your cognitions influence your behavior when you communicate. **Behavior** is observable communication, including verbal messages (words) and nonverbal messages (facial expressions, body movements, clothing, gestures). Your cognitions are encoded into the messages you send, which are then decoded by your communication partner into his or her own cognitions that influence the interpretation of your message and the preparation of feedback to you.

This constant cycle can be seen in the following example. Devon knows that he's a good student, but he struggles with math and science courses. This embarrasses him because his mother is a doctor and his brother is an engineer. He rarely feels like he will succeed in these areas. He tells his friend Kayla that he can't figure out why he failed his recent physics exam because he studied for days beforehand. When he says this, his eyes are downcast and he looks angry. Kayla receives and decodes Devon's message, and because she prides herself on being a good listener and not reacting overly emotionally, she encodes and sends a feedback message of her own: she calmly asks whether Devon contacted his physics professor or an academic tutor for extra help. Devon receives and decodes Kayla's message in light of his own cognitions about being a poor science student. He notices that Kayla made very direct eye contact, didn't smile, and didn't express sympathy. He concludes that she is accusing him of not working hard enough. He sends feedback of his own—his eyes are large and his arms are crossed and he loudly and sarcastically states, "Right, yeah, I guess I was just too dumb to think about that."

Because communication situations have so many "moving parts," they can vary greatly. More successful communicators often have a high degree of **cognitive complexity**. That is, they can consider multiple scenarios, formulate multiple theories, and make multiple interpretations when encoding and decoding messages. In this case, both Kayla and Devon could have considered other possible interpretations and responses to be more competent communicators.

AND YOU?

Recall a communication situation in which you felt uncomfortable. Perhaps you were thinking that your partner disapproved of you or of what you were saying or doing. What were your thoughts (cognitions) about yourself? About your partner? What could you say or do to clarify the situation? What kind of feedback would be most effective?

The Relational Context

As we discussed earlier, from mundane business transactions to intimate discussions, all communication occurs within the context of a relationship. In the competent communication model, this relational context is represented by the inner sphere in Figure 1.3. A kiss, for example, has a different meaning when bestowed on your mother than it does when shared with your romantic partner. When you make a new acquaintance, saying "Let's be friends" can be an exciting invitation to get to know someone new, but the same message shared with someone you've been dating for a year shuts down intimacy. The relationship itself is influenced by its past history as well as both parties' expectations for the current situation and for the future.

● **THE MEANING** of a kiss changes depending on the context. A kiss between mother and child doesn't have the same meaning as a kiss between romantic partners. (left) © Mango Productions/Corbis; (right) © Robert Fried/Alamy

A relational history is the sum of the shared experiences of the individuals involved in the relationship. References to this common history (such as inside jokes) can be important in defining a relationship, because such references indicate to you, your partner, and others that there is something special about this bond. Your relational history may also affect what is appropriate in a particular circumstance. For example, you may give advice to a sibling or close friend without worrying about politeness, but you might be careful with someone you haven't known for very long. Relational history can complicate matters when

EVALUATING**COMMUNICATION**ETHICS

THINK ABOUT THIS

Friends with Money

You know that students at your large state school come from all kinds of backgrounds and circumstances. You also know that you have it easier than some and you try not to resent those who seem to have it easier than you. But your new roommate, Cameron, is beginning to frustrate you. Although you both think of yourselves as "ordinary middle-class guys," it's becoming clear that he comes from a more privileged background than do you. While you are taking out loans, along with help from your parents, to pay your tuition, Cameron's tuition is paid in full up front. And he is the only one of your friends who doesn't have a part-time job during the school year; his parents supply him with spending money on a regular basis.

He's a really nice guy, and you share a lot of the same interests, but he continues to suggest excursions—such as eating out or going to concerts—that you just can't afford. When he notes that your favorite band is playing the local arena next weekend and that tickets are "only $75," you feel jealous and angry that he could be so clueless. What do you do?

❶ What relational, situational, and cultural factors are involved in this ethical communication dilemma?

❷ Is Cameron fully responsible for properly decoding these contextual cues? Do you have a responsibility here as well? Explain your answers.

❸ How might you construct a competent and ethical response to Cameron to help make him aware of your frustrations without insulting or alienating him?

you're communicating on social networking sites like Facebook. Your "friends" probably include those who are currently very close to you as well as those who are distant (for example, former elementary school classmates). Even if you direct your post to one friend in particular, all your friends can see it, so you might be letting those distant relationships in on a private joke (or making them feel left out).

Our communication is also shaped by our expectations and goals for the relationship. Expectations and goals can be quite different. For example, high school sweethearts may want their relationship to continue (a goal) but at the same time anticipate that going to college in different states could lead to a breakup (an expectation). Clearly, our expectations and goals differ according to each relationship. They change during the course of both short conversations and over the life span of a relationship.

The Situational Context

The situational context is represented by the middle sphere in the competent communication model and includes the social environment (a loud, boisterous party versus an intimate dinner for two), the physical place (at home in the kitchen versus at Chicago's O'Hare International Airport), specific events and situations (a wedding versus a funeral), and even a specific mediated place (a private message versus a tweet). The situational context also includes where you live and work, your home or office decorations, the time of day or night, and the current events in the particular environment at the time (Mease & Terry, 2012).

For example, Kevin gets home from work and asks Rhiannon what's for dinner. If she shrieks, Kevin might conclude that she is mad at him, but if he considers the situational context, he might reinterpret her response. He might notice that his wife is still in her suit, meaning she just got home from a long day at work. He might notice that the kitchen sink is clogged, the dog has gotten sick on the living room rug, and the clean laundry is still sitting, unfolded, on the couch. By considering the situation, Kevin may calmly ask Rhiannon about these situational factors rather than get defensive and start an argument.

AND YOU?

What relational, situational, and cultural contexts are influencing you as you read this book? Consider your gender, ethnicity, academic or socioeconomic background, and other factors. Have you studied communication or speech before? Have you taken a course with this professor before? What expectations and goals do you have for this book and this course?

● **WHEN IT COMES** to interacting with parents and older relatives, different cultures teach different values. (left) Purestock/Getty Images; (right) © Bonnie Kami/PhotoEdit

Organizations also develop their own cultures, which have a huge impact on communication. You might work for a company that encourages casual dress, informal meetings, and the ability to openly share thoughts with management. Or you might work for an organization that is more formal and hierarchical. Your communication needs to be adjusted to be competent in a particular *organizational culture*, a point we address in Chapter 11.

The Cultural Context

Finally, we must discuss the fact that all communication takes place within the powerful context of the surrounding culture, represented by the outermost sphere of the competent communication model. Culture is the backdrop for the situation, the relationship, and the communicators themselves. As you will learn in Chapter 5, the communication aspects of culture encompass more than nationality; culture also includes race, gender, religion, sexual orientation, group identities, and so on. This cultural "mix" can create tensions and challenges, but also incredible opportunities (Sprain & Boromisza-Habashi, 2013).

Culture influences which of our messages are considered to be appropriate and effective and strongly affects our cognitions. For example, Hannah comes from a culture that shows respect for elders by not questioning their authority and by cherishing possessions that have been passed down in the family for generations. Cole, by contrast, was raised in a culture that encourages him to talk back to and question elders and that values new possessions over old ones. Both Hannah and Cole view their own behaviors as natural and may view the other's behavior as odd or abnormal. If they are to become friends, colleagues, or romantic partners, each would benefit from becoming sensitive to the other's cultural background.

Cultural identity—how individuals view themselves as members of a specific culture—influences the communication choices people make and how they interpret the messages they receive from others (Lindsley, 1999). Cultural identity is reinforced by the messages people receive from those in similar cultures. In our example, both Hannah's and Cole's cognitions have been reinforced by their respective friends and family, who share their cultural identity.

The Study of Communication

If you've never studied communication before, right now you might feel like you know more about messages and relationships and communication contexts than you ever thought you'd need to know! But there is still so much more to study that can profoundly affect your friendships, romantic relationships, group memberships, career, and overall success in life. You've seen that communicating well—effectively, appropriately, and ethically—is not an innate ability; it is a process we can all improve on throughout our lives.

So what's behind this discipline? What do communication scholars (like the authors of this book) do? Well, in democracies from ancient Greece to the United States, scholars realized early on that communication was the key to participation in government and civic life. Rhetoric (the art of speaking) has been considered a crucial aspect of a well-rounded education from Aristotle to this day (Simonson, Peck, Craig, & Jackson, 2013). Public speaking was taught in America's first universities, partly to reinforce the powerful effect that speaking out can have on society (Dues & Brown, 2004). A similar concern for the public's welfare lay behind the addition of professional journalism courses to university curricula early in the twentieth century. At that time, the sensationalistic excesses of the "penny press" highlighted the need for news writers who were trained in both the technical aspects of reporting and the ethical responsibilities of journalists in a free society.

COMMUNICATIONACROSSCULTURES

THINK ABOUT THIS

Judging Sex and Gender

Upon learning that she would be replaced on the U.S. Supreme Court by John Roberts, retiring Justice Sandra Day O'Connor was pleased, but not completely. "He's good in every way," she responded, "except he's not a woman" (Balz & Fears, 2005). Appointed in 1981 by Ronald Reagan, O'Connor was the first woman ever to serve on the nation's highest court. Her disappointment that the court would once again include only one woman (O'Connor's colleague Ruth Bader Ginsberg, appointed in 1993 by Bill Clinton) would prove short lived: within six years, the court would be a full third female.[1]

If women make up roughly half of the U.S. population, it should logically follow that they will comprise a large portion of the courts as well. On the other hand, if justice is indeed blind, the sex (or race, ethnicity, religion, and so on) of individual justices should not matter. There is some argument over whether female justices rule differently than male justices—some research suggests that having three or more women on a panel can change the way the panel reaches decisions, even when the panel is predominantly male. Does gender affect the way justices come to decisions? There is some evidence that it does.

Consider the case of Savana Redding, a middle school student who, having been accused of supplying classmates with prescription strength ibuprofen, was stripped down to her underwear by two female school administrators, who searched through her underwear for the pills. None were found. Feeling that her Fourth Amendment protection from unreasonable search and seizure had been violated, Redding and her family sued the school district, and the case eventually found its way to the Supreme Court. Judging from the comments made by justices during arguments, Savana's case looked bleak, as justices didn't seem to understand why the situation was a big deal. "In my experience when I was 8 or 10 or 12 years old, you know, we did take our clothes off once a day, we changed for gym," noted Justice Stephen Breyer (Lithwick, 2009). But Justice Ginsberg, as a female, took a very different view and spoke out both in the press and to her colleagues about how humiliating such an experience could be for a teenage girl. "They have never been a 13-year-old girl," she told one reporter. "It's a very sensitive age for a girl. I didn't think that my colleagues, some of them, quite understood" (quoted in Biskupic, 2009). The Court eventually ruled that Redding's rights had indeed been violated, in an 8–1 decision. Today, the Court's three female Justices are often in agreement, but it remains unclear whether that is due to ideology (all three are fairly liberal) or to gender (Liptak, 2013).

① A Does it strike you as surprising that Ginsberg saw the case of Savana Redding differently than did her male colleagues? How might each justice's personal experiences— their specific relational and cultural context—influence their decisions?

② Why is it that sex and gender have become such issues in the past thirty years, particularly on the Supreme Court? Do you think gender might have influenced the decisions of the 101 men (all but one of them white) who preceded Sandra Day O'Connor to the bench during the court's first 190 years?

③ Consider also the unique situational context of the Savana Redding case. Would justices have thought about it differently if she were a teenage boy? If she were older? Younger? If the drugs she was suspected of hiding were stronger than ibuprofen?

[1]Justice Sonia Sotomayor was appointed in 2009; Justice Elena Kagan was appointed in 2010.

Today, communication continues to be a dynamic and multifaceted discipline focused on improving interactions and relationships, including those between two individuals, between individuals of different cultures, between speakers or media producers and audiences, within small groups, in large organizations, and among nations and international organizations. (Table 1.2 illustrates some of the major areas of specialization and the focus of each.) The research in our field draws clear connections between these assorted types of relationships (Berger, Roloff, & Roskos-Ewoldsen, 2010). Furthermore, the principles of communication laid out in this chapter can be successfully applied to many different communication situations and contexts. For example, as technology advances, communication becomes more complicated, expansive, and sometimes unclear. For most of human existence, an interpersonal relationship was limited to face-to-face interactions, later enhanced by mediated communication via the written word and the telephone. But today, individuals strike up personal and business relationships through e-mail, social networking groups, and phone contact across the globe, often without ever facing each other in person.

Throughout this book, we explore how communication skills, concepts, and theories apply to various communication situations and offer scholarship from five distinct areas of the discipline:

▶ *Basic Communication Processes.* All communication involves the basic processes of perception, verbal communication, nonverbal communication, intercultural communication, and listening. Skills that we develop in these areas inform the way we handle communication in a variety of contexts, from talking with friends to making presentations in front of a class or a large public audience. In the remainder of Part 1 of the book, you will learn how these basic processes affect every communication situation.

▶ *Interpersonal Communication.* As social animals, we human beings cannot avoid forming interpersonal relationships and interacting with other individuals. Interpersonal communication is the study of communication between **dyads**, or pairs of individuals. Most students find this study particularly relevant to their lives as they negotiate their friendships, romantic relationships, and family relationships. We investigate the exciting, nerve-racking, fun, confusing, tumultuous, and rewarding world of relationships and conflict in Part 2 of this book. An in-depth analysis of interviewing—one of the most daunting and important types of interpersonal communication—is offered in Appendix A at the back of the book.

▶ *Group and Organizational Communication.* If you've ever tried to run a professional meeting, manage a class or work group, or plan a day trip for a bunch of friends, you know that as the number of people involved in a conversation, activity, or project increases, communication becomes more complicated. By studying interactions in groups and organizations, communication scholars help create strategies for managing the flow of information and interactions among individuals in groups. We'll explore this in Part 3 of the book.

TABLE 1.2

THE BROAD FIELD OF COMMUNICATION RESEARCH TODAY

Area of Study	Focus of Study
Argumentation and debate	Persuasion, reasoning, logic, and presentation
Communication technology and telecommunication studies	Development and application of technologies across communication contexts
Conflict management	Reducing adversarial messages in personal, organizational, and community contexts
Family communication	Communication between parents and children and between generations
Health communication	Communication messages of health care providers and patients
Instructional and developmental communication	Teaching effectiveness and life span communication
Intercultural communication	Communication rules and values across cultures and co-cultures
Interpersonal communication	Basic two-person (dyadic) processes
Intergroup communication	Effects of communication within and between groups on social relationships
Journalism	Producing and analyzing written, visual, and auditory messages for public dissemination
Language and social interaction	Word acquisition and use in communication messages
Marketing	Communicating the value of products or services to customers
Mass communication and media studies	Designing and producing media messages and identifying and evaluating media effects
New media	Digital interactivity involving user feedback and on-demand access to content
Nonverbal communication	Nonlanguage codes that communicate
Organizational communication	Communication efficiency and effectiveness in business and other organizations
Political communication	Study of politicians, voters, and audiences and their impact on one another
Public relations	Message production designed to improve the image of individuals and organizations
Relational communication	Communication in close relationships such as romances, families, and friendships
Rhetorical theory and criticism	Analyzing speeches and other public messages
Visual communication	Effectiveness of advertising and other visual media

Informed by: Bryant, J., & Pribanic-Smith, E. J. (2010). A historical overview of research in communication science (pp. 21–36). In C. R. Berger, M. E. Roloff, M. E., & D. R. Roskos-Ewoldsen (Eds.) (2010). *The handbook of communication science* (2nd ed.). Thousand Oaks, CA: Sage Publications, Inc.

► *Public Speaking.* Don't panic! We're going to provide a lot of help and guidance to assist you as you become a competent public speaker. Even if you've never had to speak in front of a group before, in Part 4 you'll learn not only how to research and develop a presentation but also how to connect with your audience on a personal level. We also offer tips on becoming a more critical audience member whether you are engaged with a speaker in a lecture hall, a protest rally, or a professional conference.

► *Mass Communication.* Has your little brother tried to karate-kick the dog (or you) after watching a martial arts cartoon? Did you feel depressed after *Glee* aired its last episode? TV, radio, film, and much of the Internet are important parts of American culture and can be significant parts of our individual lives as well. Professional communicators in the mass media industries work hard to get and keep our attention. But audiences have the power to reject media messages too. In Appendix B, we explore the study of mass communication and new technology, including the forces that shape media messages and the effects media messages can have on the attitudes and behaviors of audiences.

We are confident that this book will provide you with an enjoyable reading experience as well as help you improve your communication. As a result, your life, your work, your relationships, and your ability to speak out will all be enhanced.

AND YOU?

Did you choose to take this course, or is it required? Regardless of why you're here, what do you hope to learn? What kind of communication most interests or intrigues you? What part of this book or course do you think will be most applicable to your life, future study, or professional career?

BACK TO ▶ After Hurricane Sandy

 At the beginning of the chapter, we talked about how Hurricane Sandy left one area of New York City not only physically devastated but also isolated in terms of communication and services. Let's consider the importance of different channels of communication in an emergency.

► Different channels of communication are crucial in the aftermath of a hurricane. The loss of landline phones, which normally work in the event of a blackout, left the elderly and housebound particularly vulnerable. Here, face-to-face communication became vital: checking in on neighbors and door-to-door canvassing saved lives. Meanwhile, established organizations like FEMA and the Red Cross were largely overshadowed by the efforts of small, informal groups that formed and reacted quickly to provide help for those affected. Without social networking, it's unlikely that those seeking to help would have been able to connect as effectively with one another and with those in need (Nessen, 2012).

► Those outside the affected area might have seen the logic in Mayor Michael Bloomberg's initial decision to hold the marathon as planned: After all, it would bring much needed revenue to the city, which was facing a costly rebuilding effort. But the mayor failed to consider the situational context for hundreds of thousands of New Yorkers still reeling from the storm. To residents of the low-lying parts of the city, it seemed not only insensitive but also impractical and dangerous to divert police and emergency services to cover the marathon when large portions of the city were still lacking power and basic necessities.

▶ Spotty cellular service meant that people in the affected areas were more likely to see texts or Facebook posts than to have access to reliable on-line news coverage. Former locals who lived elsewhere began posting updates for their peninsula-bound friends and family, forming micro-communication networks that traditional media could not replicate. At the same time, residents left without electricity for months on end were forced to confront their own reliance on electronic telecommunications and gained a new appreciation for old-school news outlets like radio and newspapers.

▶ The storm had an unexpected effect on relationships. Neighbors checked on neighbors, shared what they had, and gathered to complain, commiserate, and comfort one another. Residents noted that in the aftermath of the storm, they became friends with neighbors they'd never spoken with before (Hardt, 2012). Real-world social networks were reinforced as local clubs, charitable organizations, and fraternal organizations were formed or strengthened by residents moved to help one another and their community recover.

THINGS TO TRY ▶ Activities

1. LaunchPad for *Real Communication* offers key term videos and encourages self-assessment through adaptive quizzing. Go to **bedfordstmartins.com/realcomm** to get access to:

✔ **LearningCurve** Adaptive Quizzes.   ⊙ Video clips that illustrate key concepts, highlighted in teal in the Real Reference section that follows.

2. Think of someone (a family member, a celebrity, a politician, a friend, a professor) who exhibits competent communication in a particular context. What behaviors does this person exhibit that make him or her particularly effective? Would you want to model some of your own communication behavior after this person? Why or why not?

3. Keep a log of all the different channels (face to face, written, computer mediated, telephonic, others) you use to communicate during the course of one morning or afternoon. Do you regularly communicate with a particular person via a specific channel? (For example, do you talk with your mother mostly over the phone, your romantic partner through text messages, and your childhood best friend via Facebook postings?) What channels do you prefer to use when

sending different types of messages (long and short messages, positive and negative messages, business and personal messages, and so on)?

4. Describe two communication situations, one in which the communication was appropriate but not effective, and one in which the communication was effective but not very appropriate. Analyze these situations, considering the situation and relationship.

5. Consider a scene from a favorite film or novel. Imagine how it would change if you had not seen the rest of the film or read the entire novel. Would you come away from it with the same meaning if you did not understand the relational context between the characters or the situational context within the larger story?

Now that you have finished reading this chapter, you can:

Define the communication process:

- **Communication** is the process by which we use symbols, signs, and behaviors to exchange information (p. 4).
- Communication is much more complex than "common sense" (pp. 4–5).

Describe the functions of communication:

- The **functional perspective** examines how communication behaviors work (or don't work) to accomplish goals (p. 4).
- **Relationships** are the interconnections, or interdependence, between two or more people that function to achieve some goal (p. 6).
- Relationship **interdependence** means that what we do affects others, and vice versa (p. 7).
- There are three primary functions in communication:
  - Expressing **affiliation**, or feelings for others (p. 6).
  - relationships (pp. 6–7).
  - Negotiating **control**, over others (pp. 7–9).

Assess the quality or value of communication by examining its six characteristics:

- Communication relies on **symbols**, arbitrary constructions related to the people, things, or concepts to which they refer (p. 9).
- Communication requires a shared **code**, or a set of symbols, that creates a meaningful message; **encoding** is the process of producing and sending a message, whereas **decoding** is the process of receiving a message and making sense of it (p. 10).
- Communication is linked to *culture*, the shared beliefs, values, and practices of a group of people, and *co-cultures*, smaller groups within a culture (p. 10).
- Communication may be intentional or spontaneous (p. 11).
- Communication requires a **channel**, the method through which it occurs (p. 11).
- Communication is a **transactional** process: you influence others while they influence you (pp. 11–12).

Define what communication scholars consider to be competent communication:

- **Competent communication** is more **process** than **outcome** focused (pp. 13–14).

- **Ethics** is the study of morals (p. 14).
- Communication is appropriate when it meets the demands of the situation (p. 15).
- **Behavioral flexibility** involves knowing and using a number of different behaviors to achieve appropriate communication (p. 16).
- Communication is effective when it achieves desired goals (p. 16).
- **Communication skills** are behaviors that help communicators achieve their goals (p. 18).

Describe the visual representations, or models, of communication:

- In the **linear model**, a **sender** originates the **message**, carried through a channel—perhaps interfered with by **noise**—to the **receiver** (p. 20).
- The **interaction model** expands on the linear model by including **feedback** between the receiver and the sender (pp. 20–21).
- The **competent communication model** is a transactional model incorporating three contextual spheres in which individuals communicate (pp. 21–22).
  - *Communicators:* **Cognitions**, thoughts communicators have about themselves, influence **behavior**, observable communication, and how the message is interpreted before preparing feedback. **Cognitive complexity** enables communicators to think about multiple and subtle nuances in the messages of their partners (p. 23).
  - *Relational context:* Communication occurs within the context of a relationship and is influenced by the relational history (pp. 23–25).
  - *Situational context:* The circumstances surrounding communication, influence communication (p. 25).
  - *Cultural context:* Cultural identity, how individuals view themselves as a member of a specific culture, influences communication choices (p. 26).

Describe why communication is vital to everyone:

- The informed citizens become aware of the power of speaking out (p. 26).
- Interactions and relationships occur between **dyads**, groups, organizations, speakers and audiences, and mass and mediated contexts (pp. 28–30).

○──── **Whether he's playing** a beat poet on film or singing and dancing on Broadway, Daniel Radcliffe will always remind audiences of *Harry Potter*. Clay Enos/©Sony Classics/Courtesy Everett Collection

✓ **LearningCurve** can help you master the material in this chapter.
Go to **bedfordstmartins.com/realcomm**.

chapter 2

Perceiving the Self and Others

To you, growing up might seem like a long and arduous journey, but for many people watching you, it seems like you've gone from an adorable child to the person you are today in the blink of an eye. Now consider what it might be like to grow up in front of the entire world, to have millions of people appear shocked at the fact that you are "suddenly" an adult. Oh, and imagine that in addition to constantly reminding them that you don't need a babysitter, you also have to gently inform them that you are not, in fact, a wizard.

That's pretty much the life of actor Daniel Radcliffe, better known to a generation of movie fans as Harry Potter. Stepping away from *Potter* proved difficult, but as the franchise came to a close, Radcliffe tried his best to seek out roles that would put some distance between himself and Harry. He sought out difficult roles on stage, taking on nude scenes as a tormented teen in the stage productions of *Equus* and learning to sing and dance for a Broadway revival of *How to Succeed in Business Without Even Trying*. He tackled characters that were nothing like Harry in a string of small, independent films: a Victorian widower in *The Woman in Black* and an American, openly gay, aspiring poet in *Kill Your Darlings*. Nonetheless, he knows that he can never truly leave Harry behind: "I have to accept the fact that my face is going to remind people of Harry because I played that character" (Dominus, 2013).

Yet as much as the specter of Harry Potter loomed over Radcliffe, so did another stereotype: that of the "Child Star." Many young actors who captured audiences' attention before him saw their careers fizzle once they hit puberty. Others, having gotten too rich and too famous too soon, attracted more attention for offscreen exploits and mishaps than for onscreen work. For Radcliffe, and other young actors who grew up on screen, being taken seriously may require a set of perceptive skills that they just don't teach at Hogwarts.

After you have finished reading this chapter, you will be able to

○ Describe how our personal perspective on the world influences our communication

○ Explain how we use and misuse schemas when communicating with others

○ Define the attributions we use to explain behavior

○ Describe cultural differences that influence perception

○ Identify how our self-concept—who we think we are—influences communication

○ Describe how our cognitions about ourselves and our behavior affect our communication with others

The challenge of acting is to create a believable character, to make audiences think the fictional person on stage or on screen is a real person, in a real situation. Of course, an actor must also be able to shed that character—and all the associations that go with it—if he or she wants to go on to a successful career with rich and varied roles. To do that, actors must constantly alter the way that we consider, interpret, and understand who they are. In communication terms, that means changing our perceptions.

We all have unique ways of perceiving ourselves, others, and the world around us, and we communicate based on those perceptions. **Perception** is a cognitive process through which we interpret our experiences and form our own unique understandings. Those thoughts, or cognitions, influence how and what we communicate to others. They also affect how we interpret others' behaviors and messages. Thus, understanding the role that perception plays in communication is crucial to our success as communicators. In this chapter, we explore how our personal perspective on the world influences our communication, how we make sense of our experiences, how culture influences our perceptions, how we think about ourselves and others, and how these factors affect our communication behavior.

Perception: Making Sense of Your World

It's eight o'clock on a Wednesday night, and a roomful of singles are gathered at an Atlanta hot spot for an interesting event: over the next hour and a half, each woman will be introduced to no fewer than twenty eligible men. The problem: she'll have only three minutes with each. Every pair will divulge their first names, perhaps their occupations, where they're from, and why they're there.

Speed dating is popular in many metropolitan areas in the United States, England, and India. Organized by upstart companies that promise to screen applicants and put together large groups of potentially compatible singles, the event is arranged so that each person meets anywhere from ten to twenty potential mates. They spend usually less than ten minutes with each to see if there is any "chemistry." But how much can one person learn about another in just a few minutes?

Actually, first impressions can generate quite a bit of information. Irina might tell Adam that she's twenty-nine, is a public relations executive, was born in Milwaukee but has lived in Atlanta for seven years, and has a passion for *film noir*. Adam might hear all this but also notice that Irina is tall and attractive, that she makes steady eye contact, and that she has assertive mannerisms. This information might lead him to draw conclusions; for example, "She's probably more successful than I am." Adam might also notice that Irina is what he considers a "funky" dresser—she wears lots of brightly colored bead jewelry along with her conservative business suit. This, and her mention of *film noir*, puts him off a bit—he wonders if she's an "artsy" type. His last girlfriend was into art and was always dragging him off to gallery openings that he found painfully boring and pretentious. He feels a little intimidated by Irina and decides that they probably aren't compatible.

Even during brief encounters—like Adam's meeting with Irina—we are bombarded with information: the other person's words, tone of voice, facial expressions, degree of eye contact. Through **communication processing**, we gather, organize, and evaluate all this information. Although we receive information through our senses, this is just the beginning of the process. How we interpret that information is unique to each of us, influenced by how we organize perceptions into our existing memory bases, called *schemas*.

Schemas: Organizing Perceptions

As you receive information, you strive to make sense of it. To do so, you consider not only the new information but also how it fits with information you already have. For example, in evaluating Irina, speed dater Adam makes associations with his own relationship experience and his assumptions about assertive women. He compares Irina to his old girlfriend ("artsy") and to himself, guessing about her professional success. Adam is making sense of the interaction's many inputs through **schemas**, mental structures that put together related bits of information (Fiske & Taylor, 1991) (see Figure 2.1). Once put together, these chunks of information form patterns that we use to create meaning. Schemas present various opportunities and challenges as we discuss later.

The Function of Schemas

Your schemas help you understand how things (like a job interview or a first date) work or should work. Communicators retrieve schemas from memory and interpret new information, people, and situations in accordance with those schemas. For example, imagine that during your walk across campus, a classmate approaches and says, "Hey, what's up?" An existing schema (based on memories of past encounters) tells you that you will exchange hellos and then, after some small talk, go your separate ways. When you recognize one component of a schema, the entire schema is activated and helps you to know what to say or how to behave in a particular situation.

Schemas are fairly stable once they are established, but they can also change somewhat as you go through life perceiving new or conflicting bits of information about different people and situations. For example, the **interaction appearance theory** helps explain how people change their perceptions of someone, particularly their physical attractiveness, the more they interact (Albada, Knapp, & Theune, 2002). You probably have noticed that people become more or less attractive to you as you get to know them better. For example, you might find a colleague more attractive after you discover her quirky sense of humor or less attractive when you experience his short temper.

● **WHEN OTHERS** approach you at a speed-dating event, you immediately start forming opinions about them. How they're dressed, the sound of their voice, and their smile all play into whether or not you feel a connection with these potential partners. Chris Hondros/ Getty Images

AND YOU?

Think back to your first impressions of two different people, one whom you immediately liked and one who made a negative impression. What role might your schemas have played in these first impressions? Did these individuals remind you of other people you like or dislike? Did they exhibit traits that you have found attractive or unattractive in others?

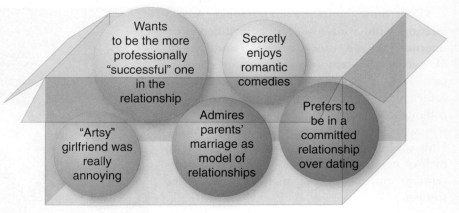

FIGURE 2.1

ADAM'S SCHEMA ABOUT DATING AND RELATIONSHIPS Our schemas affect our communication and our relationships. Here is Adam's schema for dating and relationships, represented as a box containing pieces of information from various sources in his life.

Challenges with Schemas and Perception

To send and receive messages that are effective and appropriate, you must be able to process information in a way that not only makes sense to you but that also is accurately perceived by others. Schemas can help you do all of this. However, sometimes schemas can make you a less perceptive communicator; they may cloud your judgment or cause you to rely on stereotypes (discussed later in this chapter) or misinformation. Communication researchers note that schemas present several challenges to competent communication.

If you've ever found yourself saying "Uh-huh" at the wrong time because you weren't paying attention during a conversation, you know that listening and mindlessness are a bad combination. In Chapter 6, you learn that competent listening involves being an *active*, rather than *passive*, participant in your communication situations and requires you to make conscious choices to decode messages.

▶ *Mindlessness.* Schemas may make you a less critical processor of information by producing a state of **mindlessness**, during which you process information passively. Mindlessness helps you handle some transactions automatically; for example, you don't have to consciously think about how to place an order every time you go to a restaurant. But mindlessness can create problems, too—including reduced cognitive activity (you have fewer thoughts), inaccurate recall (you can't remember simple things), and uncritical evaluation (you don't question wrong or incomplete information) (Roloff, 1980). The remedy for mindlessness is to pay attention to your schemas, a process called **mindfulness**. Mindfulness involves being aware of yourself and tuning out distractions to focus; it has a variety of benefits from higher test scores to reduced public speaking anxiety (Huston, 2010; Jacobs, 2013).

▶ *Selective perception.* Whereas mindlessness is passive, **selective perception**— that is, biased perception—constitutes active thought. If you listen to testimony at a trial, you may notice that one witness will remember the exact time of the accident while another will describe the color and make of the cars involved. They both saw the same accident but remembered different parts. Additionally, we often selectively pay attention to the information that is consistent with our schemas. In our speed-dating example, Adam hears what Irina says, how she says it, and what she looks like. But other information, such as Irina's warm smile and easy laugh, might escape his notice if it challenges his notion of what an "artsy" person is like.

▶ *Distorted perception.* If five people watch a televised debate between two political candidates, they will likely have five different interpretations of what took place and what was important. The strong supporter of one candidate may overestimate the greatness of his candidate's performance and undervalue the other candidate's arguments. In addition, we have a tendency to judge events based on vivid information. If you pay attention to sensational news stories, you may believe that you are at great risk of dying in a terrorist attack in the United States, whereas you actually have a much greater chance of being in a fatal car crash (Pomeroy, 2013).

▶ *Undue influence.* When you give greater credibility or importance to something shown or said than should be the case, you are falling victim to **undue influence**. For example, corporations know that using celebrities to endorse their products can increase sales; even though we know actress Kaley Cuoco isn't a mechanic or a travel agent, her fans might trust that her endorsement of Toyota and Priceline.com signals quality. Similarly, consumers can be influenced by buyer reviews of products, not realizing that a reviewer may have been given free products or other inducements to produce a positive review.

● **IN THE HUNGER GAMES,** players have to make sense of evolving schemas in order to survive, adapting to strange creatures, changing landscapes, and sudden rule violations that threaten their lives in the arena. Alessandra Montalto/The New York Times/Redux

Attributions: Interpreting Your Perceptions

Our schemas help us organize the information we perceive about people, but we also have a need to explain *why* people say what they do or act in certain ways. The judgments that we make to explain behavior are known as **attributions** (Jones, 1990). Consider the following exchange:

EMMA　I'm heading over to Mark's place to help him study for our midterm. He has really been struggling this semester.

CALEB　Well, he was never exactly a rocket scientist.

Emma might attribute Caleb's comment to his personality ("Caleb is obnoxious!") or to the situation ("Wow, something has put Caleb in a bad mood"). When we attribute behavior to someone's personality (or something within the person's control), we call that an *internal* attribution. When we attribute it to the situation (or something outside the person's control), that's an *external* attribution. How do we decide? If Emma considers her experience with Caleb and remembers that he is not usually so blunt or harsh about other people, she will likely attribute his behavior to the situation, not his personality.

AND YOU?

Think of an individual whom you hold in very high regard, such as a parent, a favorite professor, a mentor, or a media pundit. How do this person's opinions influence your perceptions about specific matters? Is this an undue influence? Why or why not?

Unfortunately, we are not completely rational in how we make attributions. The **fundamental attribution error** is a bias we have that causes us to overemphasize internal causes and underestimate external causes of behaviors we observe in others (McLeod, Detenber, & Eveland, 2001; Ross & Nisbett, 1991). (For example, we might assume that "Mark failed the midterm because he was too lazy to study.") The error works in the opposite way when we make attributions about ourselves. Owing to the **self-serving bias**, we usually attribute our own successes to internal factors ("I got an 'A' because I'm smart") and attribute our failures to external effects ("I failed the midterm because my professor stinks").

Improving Your Perceptions

Improving your perceptions is helpful in many communication situations. In Chapter 12, you learn how considering different aspects of an audience's demographic background can help you to target your message specifically to them (or know what to talk about in the first place).

Making accurate perceptions can be challenging. For example, in the classic basketball film *Hoosiers*, Gene Hackman plays Hickory High basketball coach Norman Dale. Dale's small-town players are intimidated by the cavernous arena where they'll be playing for the Indiana state championship. Though they know the court is regulation size, it looks enormous to them. Dale uses a tape measure to confirm the height of the basket and the distance from the foul line. Only then do they believe that the court is the same size as the one they play on in their gym. This restores their confidence.

The following suggestions can help you improve your perception abilities and thus become a better communicator.

▶ *Be thoughtful when you seek explanations.* Look beyond the most obvious explanation for what you observe. For example, your roommate, usually tidy, may have left your place a mess this morning. Rather than declaring that he is a slob, consider whether he felt ill last night or whether he needed to rush off to an exam. Being thoughtful sometimes means just pausing to give yourself time to evaluate. If someone's Facebook status update offends you, don't comment right away. Be mindful by taking a deep breath and thinking through your reaction so you can reduce negative perceptions and their effects (Partnoy, 2012).

▶ *Look beyond first impressions.* Don't rely completely on your first impressions; these often lead to inaccurate conclusions. Consider Meghan, who frequently comes off as loud when people first meet her, but her manner springs from a love for meeting new people, so she enthusiastically asks questions while getting to know them. Hold off forming a judgment until you can gather further perceptions.

▶ *Question your assumptions.* Don't assume that you know what others think, feel, or believe based on their group affiliations or a host of other cultural factors. For example, many traditional-aged, residential college students assume that most other college students are busy getting drunk and having casual sex. Research shows, however, that many students are far less comfortable with these behaviors than they assume *other* students are (Reiber & Garcia, 2010). Thinking that everyone else in your demographic believes the opposite of you is a common perceptual error (Beiser, 2013).

Perception in a Diverse World

A few generations ago, people may have gone months without coming into contact with someone from a different village or neighborhood. A wheelchair-bound child may have been unable to attend public schools. In parts of this country, white and black Americans were not permitted to sit at the same lunch counter. Today, people from all walks of life learn, work, and play together. And through technology, we can communicate with others across vast distances. A student in Louisville, Kentucky, can chat online with a student from Bangladesh. A salesperson in Omaha, Nebraska, may work full-time with clients in Tokyo. In order to communicate effectively, we must stretch our perceptions to "see through the eyes, hearts, and minds of people from cultures" other than our own (Chen & Starosta, 2008, p. 215). In this section, we do precisely that by examining the cultural context and perceptual barriers.

The Cultural Context

Many students are fans of A&E Television's hit series, *Duck Dynasty*, which chronicles the lives of the Robertson family from rural Louisiana who struck it rich with their family business making products for duck hunters. Students

● **DO YOU SHARE** a cultural identity with any of these groups? Factors such as age, gender, race, religious beliefs, sexual orientation—even where you grew up—affect your own perceptions and the perceptions of others. (top left) Digital Vision/Getty Images; (top right) Michael Williamson/The Washington Post/Getty Images; (bottom left) PATRICK ANDRADE/Landov; (bottom right) Tom Shaw/Getty Images

can get pretty riled up talking about it! Some find the show offensive, perpetuating stereotypes about individuals from the rural southern United States (especially after cast member Phil Robertson was taken off the show temporarily after making anti-gay remarks); others find the show empowering with positive portrayals of family interactions and the possibility of socioeconomic mobility.

COMMUNICATIONACROSSCULTURES

Perceptions of Hair Color: A Gray Area

Anne Kreamer took at close look at a photograph of herself standing alongside her teenaged daughter and suddenly came to a realization. She didn't look, as she imagined, as her daughter's "faintly hip older friend," but rather as a "schlubby, middle-aged woman with her hair dyed too dark." Inspired to authenticity, and with a bit of curiosity about what she really looked like, Kreamer decided, once and for all, to ditch the dye. She documented the long, arduous process of growing out her natural gray hair for *More Magazine*. "I had never thought closely or critically about what the color of my hair was communicating to the world. It was simply what I had done for 25 years, and what I assumed looked good and right" (Kreamer, 2006).

Kreamer estimated that 75 percent of American women dye their hair—and in our youth-obsessed culture, it's likely that a good portion of those in their thirties and older do it to cover gray hair. Gray hair is fraught with cultural meaning: for a woman, it might imply that she's past her prime. Many women worry that going gray will harm their careers (and there is some evidence that they're correct) (Sixel, 2011). And although gray hair on men has long been considered "distinguished," the number of men choosing to cover their gray is rising (Daswani, 2012).

Women typically begin dying their hair because they feel they're too young to be gray; but at some point, like Kreamer, they might feel that they're ready to embrace their authentic color—and with it, their authentic age. And that, too, can imply meaning. After Kreamer grew out her hair, she tried a little experiment. She went to an online dating site and created a profile that included a photo of herself with her new silver locks. In three weeks, the silver-haired profile garnered three hundred looks and seven winks. After a three-week hiatus, Kreamer posted again, using a different name but an identical profile—except this time, her hair color in her photo was digitally altered to look darker. The brown-haired version received a mere seventy looks and two winks in a three-week period. She tried the same experiment in different cities, and although total numbers differed, the gray-haired image always drew more attention than the brown-haired one. Kreamer theorizes that her natural look sent a specific message: "I was beginning to think that gray hair might actually be an advantage in a dating situation, a signal that says *I'm not hiding anything* from the get-go" (Kreamer, 2007).

THINK ABOUT THIS

❶ What do you think is the "appropriate" age for a woman (or a man) to go gray? What message does it send if a younger person opts not to cover his or her gray?

❷ Do our perceptions of gray hair change with age? Does gray hair carry the same meaning at age 30 that it does at age 40? At age 50? At age 60?

❸ Why might more men be opting to cover their gray? Have perceptions of age and masculinity changed, or are men simply more comfortable at a salon than they used to be?

As you likely know from experience, culture is an incredibly powerful context of communication: it has a profound effect on the way we perceive events, as well as ourselves and others. Think back to the competent communication model in Chapter 1. The ring that comprises the cultural context is made up of variables that make our perceptions unique: race, ethnicity, religion, politics, gender, sexual orientation, age, education, role, occupation, abilities/disabilities, geography, and so on. These differences are known as *diversity* (Loden & Rosener, 1991). (Also see our discussion of co-cultural variation in Chapter 5.) Even your positive or negative perceptions of a show like *Duck Dynasty* are linked to your perceptions about age, education, occupation, geography, religion, and a host of other factors. To communicate effectively and appropriately in today's world, you must possess an understanding of and appreciation for people who perceive others differently than you do. It's also important to understand the way your unique background affects your perceptions.

Perceptual Barriers

Karl Krayer is a communication consultant who does diversity training for corporations, schools, and other organizations. Based on his experience, Krayer notes that successful intercultural communication requires mindfulness, respect for others, and accurate perceptions of situations. "Resistance to cultural diversity usually boils down to ignorance," he says. "Once people understand other cultural groups better, it doesn't take long to see . . . people working cooperatively together for a common cause" (personal communication, May 19, 2004). In our diverse world, perceptual challenges can present barriers to competent communication, including narrow perspectives, stereotyping, and prejudice.

A Narrow Perspective

When Hurricane Katrina devastated the city of New Orleans, leaving countless residents trapped on rooftops or huddled in the Superdome for shelter, many Americans wondered why New Orleans residents didn't just get into their cars and leave the city when the flood warnings were announced. For many upper- and middle-class Americans, the idea that a family might not own a car, might not have enough money to stay in an out-of-town hotel, or might fear that their abandoned home would be looted never crossed their minds. Their own experiences clouded their perception of other people's reality. Individuals who fail to consider other cultural perspectives in this manner have **cultural myopia**, a form of nearsightedness grounded in the belief that one's own culture is appropriate and relevant in all situations and to all people (Loden & Rosener, 1991).

To ensure that *diversity* is respected in professional situations, organizations (as well as the U.S. government) enact policies and codes of behavior to protect employees from hurtful, antagonistic communication regarding their race, religion, national origin, sexual orientation, age, and abilities. This type of derogatory communication, known as *harassment*, is discussed in Chapter 11.

● **MANY NEW ORLEANS RESIDENTS** who did not evacuate for Hurricane Katrina found themselves without food, water, or shelter. They perceived their government as abandoning them, while outsiders perceived the residents as crazy for not leaving. AP Photo/Eric Gay

Cultural myopia is especially dangerous when members of the dominant group in a society are unaware of, or are insensitive toward, the needs and values of other members in the same society.

Stereotyping

CONNECT

As you learn in Chapter 5, stereotypes can lead to *discrimination* in which your thoughts about an individual or group lead to specific behaviors. So if you believe that all sorority members are poor students (and you dislike them for this belief), you may discriminate against a Zeta Tau Alpha member in your study group, believing her incapable of handling the workload.

Schemas can be dangerous in a diverse society if we rely too much on them to make generalizations about groups of people. For example, **stereotyping** is the act of assuming that individuals, because they belong to certain groups, have a set of attitudes, behaviors, skills, morals, or habits. It is applying a type of group schema to people that is fixed or set, so that when you meet an individual from this group, you apply your set of perceptions of the entire group to that individual.

Stereotypes may be positive, negative, or neutral; they may be about a group to which you belong or one that is different from your own. If you have a negative stereotype about corporate executives, for example, you may think that they are all greedy and unethical, even though many (if not most) are hardworking, honest men and women who have climbed the corporate ladder. On the other hand, a positive stereotype might blind you to bad behaviors that don't conform to your ideas.

Such stereotyping plays a role in the way we perceive individual behaviors. In a study of the effects of friends' posts on Facebook (Walther, Van Der Heide, Kim, Westerman, & Tong, 2008), researchers found that for men, negative posts about their "misbehavior" (such as excessive drunkenness and sexual exploits) resulted in perceptions of greater attractiveness. But the same kinds of posts produced very negative judgments when posted about women. These negative impressions can reinforce double standards about the acceptability of certain behaviors among men versus women (Baile, Steeves, Brukell, & Regan, 2013). Gender stereotypes, indeed, run deep across contexts. Participants in one research study viewed only the heads of two social robots, one with longer hair and curved lips (feminine) and one with shorter hair and straight lips (masculine). Participants perceived the long-haired robot as more suited for household chores and caring for children and the elderly and the short-haired one as ready to repair technical devices or guard a house (Eyssel & Kuchenbrandt, 2012).

● **STEREOTYPES OF DUCK DYNASTY'S** cast members might lead some to think they'd feel out of place in a New York City hotel—but they actually feel right at home. Gurney Productions / © A&E / Courtesy Everett Collection

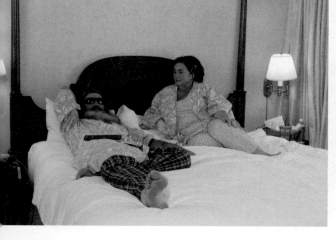

Prejudice

Negative stereotypes may lead to **prejudice**, a deep-seated feeling of unkindness and ill will toward particular groups, often accompanied by feelings of superiority over those groups. In its most extreme form, prejudice can lead to a belief that the lives of some people are worth less than those of others. Indeed, the institution of slavery in the United States flourished based on this belief. Even today, the cultural landscape of almost every nation is dotted with groups that advocate the notion of racial superiority.

Prejudice involves prejudging a person or persons negatively, usually without efforts to discover the relevant facts. Although we often associate prejudice with race and ethnicity, such snap judgments about people may also be based on any type of group membership (for example, gender, social class, age, religion, disability). It can take even very limited visual or communication cues to trigger these prejudices. For example, one of the stars of the aforementioned TV show *Duck Dynasty* was escorted out of a New York City hotel when he asked to find the restroom. The hotel staff assumed that his long, scruffy beard meant that he was a "homeless" person rather than a paying guest! The staff no doubt also committed the fundamental attribution error, discussed earlier in this chapter, by assuming a set of negative personal traits that goes along with being homeless (or bearded). We'll discuss these perceptual errors further—and ways to remove them—in Chapter 5.

Cognitions About Ourselves

Imagine spending the first nineteen years of your life without an official first name. That's what "Baby Boy" Pauson did. His father disappeared and his mother never got around to picking a name for his birth certificate. People referred to him as Max (after his mother, Maxine), yet his official records still noted his legal name as "Baby Boy." Tormented, teased, and bounced around for years, Pauson perceived himself as an outcast and escaped through comic books, animation, and fantasy. It wasn't until he entered San Francisco's School of the Arts that he discovered that others valued his creativity and nonconformity. He finally found a lawyer who helped him create an official identity with the weighty name he had imagined for himself as a child—Maximus Julius Pauson (Eckholm, 2010).

For most of us, our name (or nickname) is an important element in our *cognitions*, or thoughts about ourselves. For example, many women who marry debate whether to change their last names: some worry that losing the last name they were born with might signify the loss of a personal identity; others see changing their name as a way to communicate their relationship status or signify a new family identity. We introduce ourselves using the names we prefer (our full name, a nickname, or a moniker like "coach" or "doc"), based on the way we perceive ourselves and want others to perceive us. Though you may not have struggled with your name, you—like all people—have certainly struggled with the challenge of understanding and projecting your identity in order to become a more competent communicator. Three important influences on our thoughts about ourselves are self-concept, self-esteem, and self-efficacy (see Figure 2.2). We discuss each of these in turn.

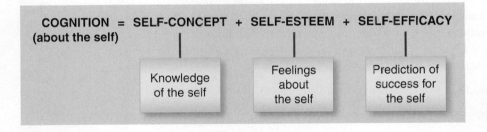

COGNITION = SELF-CONCEPT + SELF-ESTEEM + SELF-EFFICACY
(about the self)

| Knowledge of the self | Feelings about the self | Prediction of success for the self |

FIGURE 2.2

UNDERSTANDING COGNITION

what about you?

Need for Cognition Scale

Individuals have different perceptions about the thinking process. Some really enjoy grappling with complex ideas and innovating new ways of thinking, whereas others prefer to rely on familiar ways of handling people and situations. Consider the questions that follow and note how well they fit your experiences according to the following scale: 5 = extremely characteristic of you; 4 = somewhat characteristic; 3 = neither characteristic nor uncharacteristic; 2 = somewhat uncharacteristic; and 1 = extremely uncharacteristic. Then add up your score and refer to the following analysis.

_____ 1. I prefer complex problems to simple problems.

_____ 2. I like to have the responsibility of handling a situation that requires a lot of thinking.

_____ 3. Thinking is my idea of fun.

_____ 4. I would rather do something challenging than something that requires little thought.

_____ 5. I look forward to situations in which I will have to think in depth about something.

_____ 6. I find satisfaction in deliberating hard and for long hours.

_____ 7. I prefer to think about long-term projects rather than small, daily ones.

_____ 8. I dislike tasks that require little thought once I've learned them.

_____ 9. The idea of relying on thought to make my way to the top appeals to me.

_____ 10. I really enjoy a task that involves coming up with new solutions to a problem.

_____ 11. Learning new ways of thinking excites me.

_____ 12. I prefer my life to be filled with puzzles that I must solve.

_____ 13. The notion of thinking abstractly is appealing to me.

_____ 14. I would prefer a task that is intellectual, difficult, and important to one that is somewhat important but does not require much thought.

_____ 15. I feel satisfaction after completing a task that required a lot of mental effort.

_____ 16. I usually end up deliberating about issues even when they do not affect me personally.

51–80: **High need for cognition.** You enjoy the thinking process and are self-motivated to apply your thinking skills to a variety of situations. You select important information and tend to be conscientious and open to new experiences.

33–50: **Medium need for cognition.** You find some satisfaction in expending mental effort but also find comfort in tasks that are established and predictable.

16–32: **Low need for cognition.** You enjoy completing less taxing, daily tasks that don't require a lot of reflection. You generally find thinking about difficult tasks unsatisfying. You prefer relying on your tried-and-true ways of thinking and you don't like to be presented with puzzles to solve.

Source: Adapted from J. T. Cacioppo & R. E. Petty (1984).

Self-Concept: Who You Think You Are

Six-year old Coy Mathis has long hair, loves to wear pink dresses, and tears up when anyone refers to her as a boy. She was born biologically male but identifies as female. Her parents and doctors agree that her gender identity is simply part of who Coy is as a human being (Frosch, 2013). So, who are *you*? You may describe yourself to others as a male, a female, a college student, a Latino, a Buddhist, a heterosexual, a biology major, an uncle, a mother, or a friend. But who you are involves much more.

As we discussed in Chapter 1, your awareness and understanding of who you are—as interpreted and influenced by your thoughts, actions, abilities, values, goals, and ideals—is your **self-concept**. You develop a self-concept by thinking about your strengths and weaknesses, observing your behavior in a wide variety of situations, witnessing your own reactions to situations, and watching others' reactions to you (Snyder, 1979). You form beliefs about yourself as active and scattered, as conservative and funny, as plain and popular—and so on. You even form beliefs about how you tend to behave and how you expect to be treated in a variety of social situations. These are your cognitions. Remember from the model in Chapter 1 that both cognition and behavior make a communicator.

Your self-concept powerfully shapes your communication with others. It can affect what you think of other people, because your perception of others is related to how you think of yourself (Edwards, 1990). If attributes like honesty and wit are important to you, you will consider them important traits in other people. If you think that swearing makes you appear vulgar, you will likely think the same of others when they use foul language. When you interact with others, your self-concept comes into play as well. As we shall see when we discuss self-esteem and self-efficacy, it can affect how apprehensive you get in certain communication situations (McCroskey, 1997), whether you're even willing to interact with others (Cegala, 1981), and how you approach someone with a request (timidly or with confidence).

So while your self-concept strongly influences how and when you communicate with others, the reverse is also true: when you interact with other people, you get impressions from them that reveal what they think about you as a person and as a communicator. This information gets reincorporated into your self-concept. *Direct evidence* comes in the form of compliments, insults, support, or negative remarks. *Indirect evidence* that influences your self-concept might be revealed through innuendo, gossip, subtle nonverbal cues, or a lack of communication. For instance, if you ask a friend to evaluate your promise as a contestant on *America's Got Talent* and he changes the subject, you might get the impression that you're not such a great singer after all.

Our interactions with others, and their responses to us, often cause us to compare ourselves to others as we develop our ideas about ourselves. **Social comparison theory** (Bishop, 2000; Festinger, 1954) explains that we are driven to gain an accurate sense of self by examining our qualities and abilities in comparison to others. For example, if you are the least financially well-off among your friends, you may consider yourself as poor; given the same income and resources but a circle of less fortunate friends, you might think of yourself as well-off. Images in the media can have a similar effect. For example, if you compare your body shape with models in fashion magazines, you might come to believe that you have

● **ISIS KING,** former America's Next Top Model contestant, was the first transgender woman to compete on the show and became a public advocate for transgender youth. Anthony Behar/Sipa USA/Newscom

flat hair, thin eyelashes, or short legs! The beliefs we develop about ourselves—our bodies, our personalities, our abilities—exert a powerful influence on our lives, our relationships, and our communication. Struggles with self-concept—the way we perceive ourselves—are closely related to the way we feel about ourselves, of course, so we next examine how these feelings relate to communication.

Self-Esteem: How You Feel About Yourself

Self-esteem refers to how you feel about yourself, including your worth—your value as a person. Self-esteem consists of attitudes, the positive and negative feelings we have in a given situation about our abilities, traits, thoughts, emotions, behavior, and appearance. Self-concept and self-esteem are closely related: people need to know themselves before they can have attitudes about themselves. Consequently, many researchers believe that the self-concept forms first, and self-esteem emerges later (Greenwalk, Bellezza, & Banaji, 1988).

You have probably noticed that people with high self-esteem have confidence in what they do, how they think, and how they perform. That's partly because these individuals are better able to incorporate their successes into their self-concept. This projection of confidence led the high-end Italian clothing company Canali to make former Yankee baseball pitcher Mariano Rivera the first sports-figure star in its advertising campaign history (Araton, 2010). Rivera's self-assurance and self-control add to the perception of Canali's elegant clothing.

Research shows that people with high self-esteem are more confident in their interpersonal relationships, too—perhaps because they tend to believe that being friendly is a positive trait that will cause others to be friendly in return (Baldwin & Keelan, 1999). For example, Facebook posts and pictures of your family and friends not only communicate your self-worth to others but also encourage "likes" and "comments" back from them (Jacobs, 2013). Research also shows that perceived commitment from a romantic partner enhances self-esteem (Rill, Balocchi, Hopper, Denker, & Olson, 2009). Thus, individuals with high self-esteem may not feel a strong need for public displays of affection. By contrast, someone with low self-esteem might press their romantic partner to show affection in public, so others can see that "someone loves me!"

● **YANKEES PITCHER**
Mariano Rivera brings an essence of elegant self-assurance and self-control to an ad for Canali's high-end clothing. Neilson Barnard/WireImage for New York Magazine/Getty Images

Research suggests that some people have low self-esteem, or a poor view of themselves, because they lack accurate information about themselves or they mistrust the knowledge they do possess. For example, you may feel that you are a poor student because you have to study constantly to keep up your grades in German class. Your German professor, however, might find that your efforts and the improvement you've made over the semester reveal that you are a good, hardworking student. Low self-esteem may also result from unreasonable comparisons to other people or to cultural stereotypes. If your self-concept about your body shape is based on comparisons with media personalities, that perception can affect your self-esteem. Indeed, exposure to images of body "perfection" in the media has been linked to negative body image and even eating disorders (Bishop, 2000; Hendriks, 2002; Jacobs, 2013). In fact, a recent study shows that men exposed to idealized male bodies in even brief music video clips reported decreased body and muscle tone satisfaction (Mulgrew & Volcevski-Kostas, 2012).

EVALUATINGCOMMUNICATIONETHICS

Ethics and the Self-Concept

You and your romantic partner, Peyton, have been together for three years and have supported each other through many ups and downs, particularly in your professional lives. Both of you have successful careers and have made sacrifices to help each other achieve personal and professional goals. Most recently, the two of you moved to Washington, D.C., from Saint Louis so that Peyton could accept a promotion with a large financial investment firm. Since you were thrilled for Peyton's career opportunity and since you are able to work from a home office, you consented to the move. But it has been difficult because Peyton works long hours and your entire family and most of your close friends are still in Saint Louis.

Peyton comes home early one afternoon to announce that the investment firm has offered another promotion to a position that would require travel from Monday to Friday two weeks out of the month. Peyton talks excitedly about the increase in status and in pay and the new opportunities that the position would afford you both. Your immediate reaction is one of anger. How could Peyton consider taking a position that required so much travel, especially since this would leave you alone in a city where you know few people and where you work alone out of your home? Hadn't you sacrificed enough by moving halfway across the country for Peyton's career?

You confront Peyton, who is first surprised and then angry. "I thought we were working for the same thing—a better opportunity for our future," Peyton says. "I am good to you, and I give you everything you want. I thought I could count on you to support me in this. It is not like it will be much different from the way it is now since I work so late. After all, I'll be home every weekend."

You are hurt. You value harmony in your home and your relationships, and you value time spent with your partner. You believe that you are a flexible, reasonable person who appreciates joint decision-making. You feel that you have been supportive and that you have made Peyton's career a priority in your home. Peyton's reaction, however, sends a much different message that makes you uneasy. You are upset by the different ways that you and Peyton perceive the situation and the ensuing communication difficulties.

1 Consider the different elements that make up both your self-concept and your partner's. What do you each value? What are your goals and ideals? What are your thoughts and beliefs about work, relationships, and other important matters?

2 How might your self-concept have affected the way that you perceived Peyton's message about the promotion? How might the message have affected your self-esteem?

3 Now take Peyton's perspective. How might your partner's self-concept have affected the way that the news of the promotion was shared with you? How might your reaction have affected Peyton's self-esteem?

Similarly, comparing your life to the (supposedly) exciting lives presented by others on Facebook can have negative effects on your self-esteem (Chou & Edge, 2012). In contrast, becoming more "self-aware" by updating and giving thought to a positive presentation of your own Facebook profile appears to enhance self-esteem rather than diminish it (Gonzalez & Hancock, 2011; Toma, 2013).

Self-Efficacy: Assessing Your Own Abilities

Actor Peter Dinklage won a Golden Globe award for his portrayal of the complex Tyrion Lannister in HBO's popular original series, *Game of Thrones* (Kois, 2012); he received an Emmy nomination for the same role. But there

● **WHAT CAN WE** learn about the power of self-concept and self-esteem in our own lives from Peter Dinklage's success? Helen Sloan /© HBO/Courtesy Everett Collection

Self-fulfilling prophecies are deeply tied to verbal and nonverbal communication. If you believe you will ace a job interview because you are well prepared, you will likely stand tall and make confident eye contact with your interviewer (Chapter 3) and use appropriate and effective language (Chapter 4) to describe your skill set. Your confidence just may land you the position you want!

was a time when such recognition seemed far off as Dinklage attempted to jump-start an acting career while living in a rat-infested Brooklyn apartment without heat. It's not that he didn't have offers for decent-paying parts; it's that he turned them down. Dinklage is a little person (diagnosed with achondroplasia—a common cause of dwarfism) who refused to play elves or leprechauns, roles that would forever tie his talents to his stature. When he played Tom Thumb in a vaudevillian play, he so impressed director Tom McCarthy that McCarthy rewrote a script for "The Station Agent" to make Dinklage the leading man. A series of roles later, Dinklage earned the success he desired without playing parts that he felt would demean him—all because he believed he could "play the romantic lead and get the girl" (quoted in Kois, 2012).

Dinklage's experiences reveal the power of self-efficacy, which is the third factor influencing our cognitions about ourselves. Like Dinklage, you have an overall view of all aspects of yourself (self-concept), as well as an evaluation of how you feel about yourself in a particular area at any given moment in time (self-esteem). Based on this information, you approach a communication situation with an eye toward the *likelihood* of presenting yourself effectively. This ability to predict actual success from self-concept and self-esteem is **self-efficacy** (Bandura, 1982). Your perceptions of self-efficacy guide your ultimate choice of communication situations, making you much more likely to engage in communication when you believe you will probably be successful and avoid situations where you believe your self-efficacy to be low.

Even though a person's lack of effort is most often caused by perceptions of low self-efficacy, people with very high levels of self-efficacy sometimes become overconfident (Bandura, 1982; Harris & Hahn, 2011). For example, some students believe that if they understood their professors' lectures well while sitting in class, then they wouldn't really need to study their notes very much after that to prepare for exams. Those students often end up shocked later at how much information they did not remember.

Self-efficacy affects your ability to cope with failure and stress. Feelings of low self-efficacy may cause you to dwell on your shortcomings. If you already feel inadequate and then fail at something, a snowball effect occurs as the failure takes a toll on your self-esteem; stress and negative feelings result, lowering your feelings of self-efficacy even more. For example, Jessie is job hunting but worries that she does not do well in interviews. Every time she goes to an interview and then doesn't get a job offer, her self-efficacy drops. She lowers her expectations for herself, and her interview performance worsens as well. By contrast, people with high self-efficacy are less emotionally battered by failures because they usually chalk up disappointments to a "bad day" or some other external factor.

Perceptions of your self-efficacy may lead to a **self-fulfilling prophecy**—a prediction that causes you to change your behavior in a way that makes the prediction more likely to occur. If you go to a party believing that others don't enjoy your company, for example, you'll probably stand apart, not talking to anyone

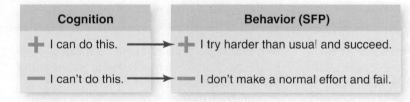

Self-Fulfilling Prophecy (SFP)

Cognition	Behavior (SFP)
➕ I can do this. ⟶	➕ I try harder than usual and succeed.
➖ I can't do this. ⟶	➖ I don't make a normal effort and fail.

Self-fulfilling prophecy imposed on others:

My behavior	Their cognition	Their behavior (SFP)
➕ You can do it. ⟶	➕ I can do this. ⟶	➕ Try harder than usual and succeed.
➖ You can't do this. ⟶	➖ I can't do this. ⟶	➖ Don't try as hard and fail.

FIGURE 2.3

THE SELF-FULFILLING PROPHECY

and making no effort to be friendly. Others won't like you, so your prophecy gets fulfilled. Self-efficacy and self-fulfilling prophecy are thus related. Low self-efficacy often causes you to exert less effort to prepare or participate than you would in situations in which you are comfortable and have high self-efficacy. When you do not prepare for or participate in a situation (such as at the party), your behavior causes the prediction to come true, creating a self-fulfilling prophecy (see Figure 2.3). One study of international soccer tournaments found teams that had a history of losing (even if the current players were not a part of the losing effort) were significantly less likely to win the penalty shoot-outs that decide a tied game (Jordet, Hartman, & Jelle Vuijk, 2012). Why? It's possible that the players choked under a high degree of performance pressure, unable to predict their own success from past performances. It is also possible that they hurried their preparation and thus created their own demise.

Self-fulfilling prophecies don't always produce negative results. If you announce plans to improve your grades after a lackluster semester and then work harder than usual to accomplish your goal, your prediction may result in an improved GPA. But even the simple act of announcing your goals to others—for example, tweeting your intention to quit smoking or to run a marathon—can create a commitment to making a positive self-fulfilling prophecy come true (Willard & Gramzow, 2008).

Assessing Our Perceptions of Self

Whenever you communicate, you receive feedback from people that allows you to assess your strengths and weaknesses. These assessments of self are important before, during, and after you have communicated. You evaluate your expectations, execution, and outcomes in three ways: self-actualization, self-adequacy, and self-denigration.

real communicator

NAME: Lisa M. Turay, CSJ
OCCUPATION: Woman Religious, Women's Wellness Counselor

Call me "Lisa." That's how I introduce myself to all the mothers I counsel at our women's wellness clinic. I don't hide the fact that I am a Catholic nun—Sister Lisa is clearly on my name badge—but I like to give clients the choice to call me by either name. After all, focusing strongly on my status in religious life invokes a set of perceptions on the part of clients that they may or may not find comfortable. Given the highly personal and deeply emotional situations we discuss, my client's comfort is my top priority.

I've always enjoyed working with children and teens and was excited to expand my counseling skills by working with mothers and babies. As I learned from my undergraduate communication courses and my graduate counseling courses, a good counselor doesn't need to be "the same" as his or her clients or have experienced what they've experienced; rather, he or she needs to practice the communication skills of perspective-taking and empathic listening. By doing so, I am able to help my clients get through some of the most stressful times in their lives: having babies, losing babies, and dealing with personal and family stresses surrounding babies.

Pregnant and postpartum (after-birth) women experience a wide range of physical and emotional changes. Imbalanced hormones coupled with physical challenges (like lack of sleep or impaired mobility) can reduce a woman to tears. Postpartum women often need to be reminded to eat well, attend to personal hygiene, and sleep when the baby sleeps. They are often exhausted and overwhelmed; week 3 or 4 after the birth of a child is like hitting the wall when you run—but by week 6, most can see the "finish line." I help these women adjust their sometimes negative thinking about their current situations. There are so many schemas surrounding babies and parenthood. Negative ones like "I'm a bad mother because the baby keeps crying" or "I'll never sleep again" need to be challenged. Seeing moms come to terms

with realistic perceptions about parenthood—and begin to adjust to this new phase of life—is one of the most rewarding parts of my job.

Unfortunately, grief counseling is a necessary and very difficult part of my job. The loss of a pregnancy (particularly past the first trimester) and the death of a newborn are among the most difficult things an individual can face in adult life. Well-meaning friends and family members sometimes rely on mindless scripts of what to say in such situations (for example, "Oh, it was probably for the best" or "These things happen for a reason"). Too many times women hear, "Oh, you're young; you can have another child" when they are thinking, "Did I do something wrong? Am I fit to be a mother?" My job is not to sugarcoat the pain or offer false assurances, but rather to give these women a safe space to grieve, to be silent, and to ask questions. They need support and an understanding about the process of grief.

I also work closely with moms and expectant moms—and sometimes their entire family units—on issues related to self-concept, self-esteem, and self-efficacy. For example, some women and men fear that they won't be "good" parents or they have trouble seeing themselves in the parental role. Sometimes they're overwhelmed by the idea of change; sometimes they're paralyzed by unrealistic expectations of perfection or a fear of failure. I help them walk through these thoughts and encourage them to seek out reassurance and realistic expectations. For example, some expectant fathers fear that the baby will replace them in the eyes of the mother; sometimes just expressing this concern to the expectant mom in a productive way can diminish this worry.

The most enjoyable and satisfying part of my job is when women come to me early on in pregnancy, and I get to make the journey with them. Many women bring their babies in when they have their three-week and six-week postpartum checkups so that we can share in their joy. My counseling allows me to participate in the transformation to new life: a privilege that words cannot describe.

Self-Actualization

The most positive evaluation you can make about your competence level is referred to as **self-actualization**—the feelings and thoughts you get when you know that you have negotiated a communication situation as well as you possibly could. At times like these, you have a sense of fulfillment and satisfaction. For example, Shari, a school psychologist, was having problems with the third-grade teacher of one of the students she counsels. The teacher seemed uninterested in the student's performance, would not return Shari's phone calls or e-mails, and seemed curt and aloof when they did speak. Shari finally decided to confront the teacher. Although she was nervous at first about saying the right thing, she later felt very good about the experience. The teacher had seemed shocked at the criticism but offered an apology. At the end of the meeting, Shari was quite content that she had been honest and assertive, as well as fair and understanding. This positive assessment of her behavior led to a higher level of self-esteem. When Shari needs to confront someone in the future, she will likely feel more confident about doing so.

Self-Adequacy

At times you may think that your communication performance was not stellar, but it was good enough. When you assess your communication competence as sufficient or acceptable, you feel a sense of **self-adequacy**, which is less intensely positive than self-actualization. Feelings of self-adequacy can lead you in two directions: toward contentment or toward a desire for self-improvement.

Suppose that Phil has been working hard to improve his public speaking abilities and does a satisfactory job when he speaks to his fraternity about its goals for charitable work in the coming year. He might feel very satisfied about his speech, but he realizes that with a little more effort and practice, he could have been even more persuasive. In this case, Phil's reaction is one of *self-improvement*. He tells himself that he wants to be more competent in his communication, regardless of his current level.

Although self-improvement is a good motivation, in some circumstances being satisfied or content with your self-adequacy is sufficient. For example, Lilia has a long history of communication difficulties with her mother. Their relationship is characterized by sarcastic and unkind comments and interactions. But during her last visit home, Lilia and her mother managed to not get into an argument. So Lilia felt good about her communication with her mom. The two didn't become best friends or resolve all their old problems, but Lilia thought she communicated well under the circumstances. She was content with her self-adequacy.

Self-Denigration

The most negative assessment you can make about a communication experience is **self-denigration**: criticizing or attacking yourself. This occurs most often when communicators overemphasize their weaknesses

AND YOU?

Think about a communication situation in your own life in which you believe that you achieved self-adequacy. Were you content with the outcome of the situation, or did you still desire more self-improvement? Why? Is it possible to feel both contentment as well as a desire for self-improvement in your communication situation?

● **SELF-DENIGRATING BEHAVIORS** can only hurt your performance, so the next time you feel like saying to yourself "I'll never be able to understand calculus" instead try thinking "Let's see if I can figure this out!" Irina Zolina/Shutterstock

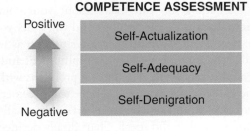

FIGURE 2.4

**ASSESSING OUR
PERCEPTIONS OF SELF**

To avoid self-denigration,
consider the situational
and relational contexts discussed in Chapter 1. You
may judge yourself harshly
for not communicating as
easily with your aunt Irma as
you do with your friend Joe,
but different environments—
as well as unique relational
histories with different individuals—make that goal.
Rather, assess your com-
munication with your aunt
in light of the constraints of
that particular relationship
and situation.

or shortcomings ("I knew I'd end up fumbling over my words and repeating myself—I am such a klutz!"). Most self-denigration is unnecessary and unwarranted. Even more important, it prevents real improvement. Hunter, for example, thinks that his sister is stubborn and judgmental and that he cannot talk to her. He says, "I always lose it with her, and I yell at her because there is nothing I can say that she will listen to!" Rather than just accepting the idea that nothing he says will ever "work," Hunter needs to assess his communication behaviors more reasonably: what specific words and nonverbal behaviors (like eye rolling) might he have used with his sister when she "didn't listen"? What were some different communication behaviors he used during times when he actually had positive interactions with his sister? Hunter can also plan for communication improvement ("Next time, I will not raise my voice, and I will look at and listen to my sister until she is finished talking, before I say anything back to her"). Thus, our assessments of our competence run from self-actualization on the positive end of the spectrum to self-denigration on the negative end (see Figure 2.4).

Behavior: Managing Our Identities

As you've learned, you define yourself through your self-concept and your ideas about self-esteem and self-efficacy. But you also make decisions about how to share these internal viewpoints with others. This is manifested in your verbal and nonverbal behaviors.

We all have aspects of ourselves that we want to share and aspects that we would rather keep private. Many of the choices we make in our communication behavior, from the clothes we wear to the way we speak, are determined by how we want others to perceive us. In this section, we consider how we let the world know just who we think we are and how our communication with others can shape their perceptions of us.

Let's examine the process illustrated in Figure 2.5 for a moment. At the core of this process is the self. The self has cognitions that consist of self-concept (knowing and understanding the self), self-esteem (evaluating the self), and self-efficacy (predicting the self's success)—all of which we've discussed. These cognitions influence our verbal and nonverbal behaviors, which

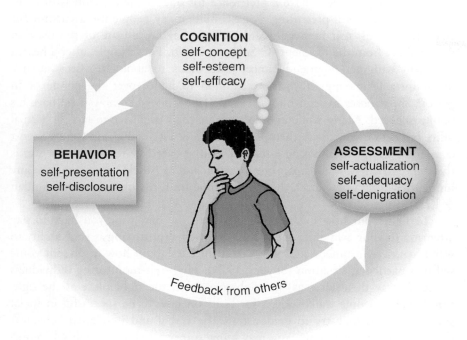

COGNITION
self-concept
self-esteem
self-efficacy

BEHAVIOR
self-presentation
self-disclosure

ASSESSMENT
self-actualization
self-adequacy
self-denigration

Feedback from others

FIGURE 2.5

THE SELF The self is composed of our cognitions, our behavior, and our self-assessments. These factors work together to affect our communication.

consist of self-presentation and self-disclosure, two terms we will explain soon. Our behavior generates feedback from others, which leads to our assessments of self-actualization, self-adequacy, and self-denigration. These judgments of our performance then affect our cognitions. As you read about self-presentation, self-disclosure, and feedback in the coming pages, refer to this illustration to remind yourself of the roles these play in your interactions with others.

Self-Presentation

You let others know about yourself through **self-presentation**—intentional communication designed to show elements of the self for strategic purposes. For example, if you want to create the impression among your coworkers that you are competent at your job as a teacher, you might mention during conversations how you've successfully handled disciplinary situations or how you've designed innovative lessons to make long division fun.

We all tend to focus on self-presentation when we are being evaluated, formally or informally, by others (Canary & Cody, 1993). For example, you probably behave very differently when you are meeting your significant other's parents for the first time than when you're hanging out with your friends or your own family.

Self-presentation can take many forms. You can present yourself through face-to-face conversation, through e-mail or text messaging, and Twitter and

AND YOU?

Like Julie, you have probably encountered situations in which you chose to engage in either face-to-face communication or mediated communication (for example, text messaging, posting on Facebook, e-mailing). Why did you choose a particular channel? If you chose a mediated channel, did you feel safer from an unknown reaction as the research suggests? Why or why not?

Facebook. You may even have a preference for one of these channels of communication when self-presenting. For example, many people use asynchronous channels (e-mail, text messages, cards) when they are unsure of the reaction they will get from the recipient (O'Sullivan, 2000). For example, after a heated argument with her boyfriend Lance, Julie wants to apologize. Because she's uncomfortable making this self-presentation to Lance over the phone or in person, she chooses to send him a text message when she knows he'll have his phone silenced. Many students also prefer e-mail over face-to-face or virtual office hours to interact with their professors (Li & Pitts, 2009). In fact, the most common reasons for choosing e-mail or texting over face-to-face interaction is the ability to carefully construct our messages and to "shield" ourselves from any immediate negative feedback that might come from the other person (Riordan & Kreuz, 2010).

To figure out how to present yourself in the best way, you have to pay attention to your own and others' behavior. **Self-monitoring** is your ability to watch your environment and others in it for cues about how to present yourself in a particular situation (Snyder, 1974). High-self-monitoring individuals try to portray themselves as "the right person in the right place at the right time." These people watch others for hints on how to be successful in social situations. And they try to demonstrate the verbal and nonverbal behaviors that seem most appropriate. You may know someone who is a high-self-monitoring communicator. During class, this person always sits in a certain strategic position, gets involved in discussions when others do so, gestures in a similar manner to others, and when it is time to let others talk, is very strategic with silence. These "sufficiently skilled actors" can display situation-appropriate communication behaviors. Low-self-monitoring individuals are not nearly so sensitive to situational cues that prescribe communication behavior. They communicate according to their deep-seated values or their feelings of the moment. They do not see the need to adapt to situations or people; rather, they feel that controlling their style of communication would be "false." If low self-monitors anticipate a communication situation that is different from their own self-presentation style, they will either avoid the situation or accept the fact that their communication may not please all the parties involved.

Communicating successfully involves finding the appropriate level of self-monitoring for the situation and the people involved. It might seem like high self-monitors are the winners in social interaction, but this isn't always the case. High self-monitors can drive themselves crazy by focusing on every little thing that they say and do (Wright, Holloway, & Roloff, 2007). They might also become manipulative in their carefully crafted efforts

● **PLACES OF WORSHIP** often have dress codes, whether they are explicitly stated or not. People may feel that you are being disrespectful and inappropriate if you ignore these rules and do things your own way. Wathiq Khuzaie /Getty Images

to impress people. Perhaps you have experienced social media users who brag about being at a great party for the "benefit" of the people who aren't there (Harmon, 2011). And consider those who ineffectually disguise bragging over social media by self-denigrating ("Can't seem to fit into those size two jeans, despite my daily workouts")—on Twitter they've earned their own hashtag: #humblebrag.

By contrast, competent communicators will monitor their self-presentation just enough to present themselves effectively but without forgetting that communication involves others. They also know that you can't control what *others* do around you that may affect your efforts to present yourself effectively—including what your friends post on your Facebook timeline!

Self-Disclosure

Angelica is a stylish dresser; has a lovely apartment in Austin, Texas; eats out at nice restaurants regularly; and drives a new car. But she has a secret: she is drowning in debt, barely keeping up with her minimum credit card payments. She looks around at her friends, all the same age as she and living similar lifestyles. She wonders if they make more money than she does or if they, too, are over their heads in debt. One night while she's having coffee with her best friend, Tonya, Angelica comes clean about her situation: she can't go on their upcoming trip to Cozumel, she tells Tonya, because her credit cards are maxed out.

When you reveal yourself to others by sharing information about yourself—as Angelica has done with Tonya—you engage in **self-disclosure**. Voluntary self-disclosure functions to develop ordinary social relationships (Antaki, Barnes, & Leudar, 2005) but has more impact or creates more intimacy if it goes below surface information (Tamir & Mitchell, 2012). For example, telling someone that you like snacking on raw vegetables is surface information, but explaining to them why you became a vegetarian is deeper self-disclosure.

Self-disclosure can help you confirm your self-concept or improve your self-esteem; it can also enable you to obtain reassurance or comfort from a trusted friend (Miller, Cooke, Tsang, & Morgan, 1992). For example, Angelica might suspect that Tonya is also living on credit; if Tonya discloses that she is, her confession might reassure Angelica that it's OK to buy things she can't afford on credit because everyone else is doing it. However, if Tonya reveals that she makes more money than Angelica, or that she manages her money more wisely, Angelica's self-concept may incur some damage. As you may remember from Chapter 1, information you receive about your self is termed *feedback*. The feedback Angelica receives from Tonya will be in response to her self-disclosure. That same feedback—and how she interprets it—will also influence Angelica's perception of herself.

How you incorporate feedback into the self depends on several factors. One of the most important factors is your *sensitivity level* to feedback. Research demonstrates that some individuals are highly sensitive, whereas others are largely unaffected by the feedback they receive (Edwards, 1990). Presumably, people who are more sensitive to feedback are susceptible

CONNECT

The process we use to choose the information we are willing to share with others has long fascinated researchers. In Chapter 7, we examine the *social penetration theory*, which uses an onion as a metaphor to show how we move from superficial confessions to more intimate ones. Your outer "layer" might consist of disclosure about where you are from, but as you peel away the layers, your disclosures become more personal.

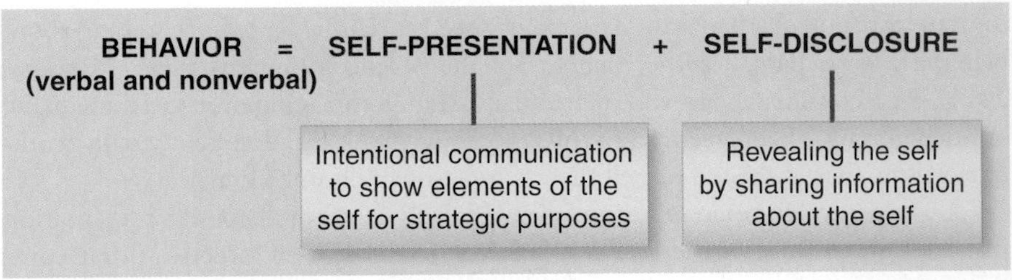

BEHAVIOR   =   SELF-PRESENTATION   +   SELF-DISCLOSURE
(verbal and nonverbal)

| Intentional communication to show elements of the self for strategic purposes | Revealing the self by sharing information about the self |

FIGURE 2.6

UNDERSTANDING
BEHAVIOR

and receptive to information about their abilities, knowledge, and talents. Low-sensitive people would be less responsive to such information. For example, when Olympic short track skater Apolo Ohno bombed at the Olympic trials in 1998, he wasn't interested in hearing that his efforts weren't sufficient. He was demonstrating a low sensitivity level to the advice and feedback from his coach, friends, and family. Ohno's father sent him to a secluded cabin for eight days to contemplate his career. After that, Ohno decided that he was ready to receive the feedback that he needed to improve his game. He developed a higher sensitivity to feedback, went on to win eight Olympic medals (Bishop, 2010), and finished the World Championships in the gold, silver, or bronze medal position eighteen times. Figure 2.6 illustrates how self-presentation and self-disclosure constitute the behavior segment of "The Self," seen in Figure 2.5.

Technology: Managing the Self and Perceptions

If you're wondering how your friend Ned is doing, all you need to do is check out his Facebook profile—right? There you see photographs of his recent visit with his longtime girlfriend's family in Texas. You read funny status updates about his apartment hunt. And you see that others wrote on his wall to congratulate him on his recent promotion. Life is going well for Ned, so you send him a private message to let him know that you're glad for him. Would you be surprised if Ned responded to share that he is considering a breakup with his girlfriend, that he hates his job, and that he can't afford a decent apartment because his student loans are crushing him? How is this possible (you wonder) when Ned's profile seems to indicate that his life is fulfilling and happy?

This is possible because blogs, tweets, chat rooms, and dating and social networking sites allow you to control the presentation of self far more carefully than in face-to-face encounters. When you manage the self online, you can much more easily choose what to reveal and what to conceal. You can decide whether you will reveal your gender, ethnicity, and race, as well as your religious or political preferences. What's more, you can edit, revise, and organize the information you disclose before the message goes out. In this way, you can present an image that is smart, charming, and eloquent, even if you tend to be nervous or timid in face-to-face communication. You are ultimately the one who controls this

WIREDFORCOMMUNICATION

Avatars: Virtual Personas and Perception

Thirteen-year-old Desmond, better known in cyberspace as Captain Obvious, is modifying his avatar in the online role-playing game *Borderlands II*. He calls the character Butch. Butch will be making his way through a series of quests on the far-off planet Pandora while wearing an eye patch and a dockworker's skull cap. Desmond describes Butch as "psychotic." But when other players look at Butch, are they drawing conclusions about Desmond? Research suggests that they might be.

Avatars can be chosen for any number of reasons, including as a way to draw attention to yourself, to give others a glimpse of your interests, or to capture some aspect of your personality (Suler, 2007). The characteristics of selected avatars are important to both behavior and perception. Researchers who looked at players in the massive online role-playing game *Second Life* suggest that avatars are "highly controlled information transmitters, well-suited to strategic self-presentation that can be used to communicate any of the selves" (Bélisle & Bodur, 2010). Put simply, specific cues in avatars communicate certain aspects of the self. For example, male avatars with long hair or stylish hairstyles were widely perceived as more extroverted, whereas those with jeans, gray shirts, long-sleeved shirts, or black hair were perceived as introverted. So when players choose specific attributes for avatars—from the way they look to what they wear—it's likely that they are making their choices in order to convey specific personal attributes.

But what if you didn't design the character yourself? Could your online behavior be affected by the cues of a randomly assigned avatar? Maybe. Nick Yee and Jeremy Bailenson (2007) found that people's behavior was affected by the physical characteristics of the avatar assigned to them. For example, people who were assigned to more attractive avatars self-disclosed more and talked more intimately with others than those assigned less attractive avatars.

For Desmond and Butch, of course, things may be more complicated. *Second Life* is a virtual world that is supposed to mirror ours, complete with its own economy, culture, religions, and relationships. *Borderlands*, however, is a scripted fantasy story that occurs on a faraway planet. Long-sleeved shirts may suggest introversion on *Second Life*'s virtual Earth, but it's unclear what they might indicate on the planet Pandora.

THINK ABOUT THIS

❶ Does it surprise you that avatars can influence perceptions in such a way?

❷ When you create an avatar—be it an elaborate skin on *Second Life* or a rudimentary Mii on your Wii console—how do you choose its attributes?

❸ Does context matter? Do you think avatars function differently in different games or virtual environments?

information; the media you choose are not responsible for what you share or how you share it (Keller, 2013).

In Ned's case, he chose to present a self that is carefree and happy—even though his current situation is quite the opposite. Of course, it is important to remember as a user of social media that if you can choose what to present about yourself, so too can everyone else. Recall that recent studies (for example, Kross

AND YOU?

Randomly select five of your Facebook friends and visit their profiles. Consider their status updates, their friends' posts about them, the pages they like, and so on. What type of impression does their profile make on you? What words would you use to describe these individuals? Do you believe they present themselves accurately?

et al., 2013) have found that more time spent on Facebook seeing everyone else's seemingly "fabulous" lives can make you feel worse about yourself and your own life!

In addition, how *you* present yourself online may not be the only factor in how you come across to others. Statements made by your friends on Facebook, for example, can significantly affect people's impressions of you. One study found that when people post on their friend's wall positive statements about their friend's behavior, their friend's credibility and "social attractiveness" increased, compared to negative statements (for example, about excessive drunkenness or sexual behavior); in addition, the perceived attractiveness of friends affected perceptions of self-attractiveness (Walther, Van Der Heide, Kim, Westerman, & Tong, 2008). Even the number and type of friends you have on Facebook can have an influence—if you have "too few" or "too many" friends, your reputation could suffer (Tong, Van Der Heide, Langwell, & Walther, 2008).

BACK TO ▸ Boy Wizard No More.

At the beginning of this chapter, we talked about how child actors (like Daniel Radcliffe) struggle with audiences' perceptions of them. Let's reflect on what communication and perception scholarship might have to say about this phenomenon.

▸ When an audience's perception of a performer becomes deeply embedded in the popular psyche, it's easy for actors to get pigeonholed into particular roles, a type of stereotyping known as *typecasting* in the business. Some simply stick to the characters they're known for (Samuel L. Jackson usually plays a tough guy, Dame Maggie Smith is the go-to actress for British matriarchs, and Sandra Bullock rarely plays a villain). But others work hard to resist typecasting: Bill Murray, Robin Williams, Denzel Washington, Anne Hathaway, and the late Heath Ledger all garnered critical praise (and in some cases Oscars) for playing against type. For Radcliffe, the key to gaining respect as an actor has been to take on projects quite different from the *Harry Potter* blockbuster franchise—challenging roles on stage and in small independent films.

▸ Note that "former child star" also calls to mind schemas unrelated to particular roles. The brief careers of Gary Coleman and Macaulay Culkin are testaments to audiences' tendency to lose interest in precocious children once they outgrow childish roles, and the erratic personal lives of Lindsay Lohan, Amanda Bynes, and Miley Cyrus often overshadow the long, steady careers of former child stars like Keenan Thompson, Jodie Foster, Jason Bateman, Joseph Gordon-Levitt, and Anne Hathaway. We also ignore the countless child stars who have gone on to successful careers behind the camera (like Ron Howard and Peter Billingsley) or to happy, successful, and somewhat anonymous lives outside Hollywood. In other words, the fundamental attribution error makes us remember the messes while we forget all about the quieter successes.

▸ Radcliffe also struggles with perceptions about child stars and worries that everyone he meets—especially colleagues on the set—will expect him to be spoiled and demanding. He works to replace such stereotypes with his own cognitions: his self-concept of being a hardworking professional. The actor says he tries to counter those perceptions by introducing himself humbly when he meets someone new ("Hi, I'm Dan"), even though he knows that they already know who he is. He also relies on a uniquely British brand of self-deprecating humor that he calls the "comedy of embarrassment" to break the ice, apologizing for not being a wizard or for growing up and making fans feel old, and frequently mocking his own fame, his luck, or his diminutive stature (Dominus, 2013). Finally, he makes it a point to be the consummate professional on set, bearing in mind his father's advice: "On a film set there's always somebody who's going to be causing a delay. . . . Make sure it's never you" (Dominus, 2013, p. 28).

THINGS TO TRY ▸ Activities

1. LaunchPad for *Real Communication* offers key term videos and encourages self-assessment through adaptive quizzing. Go to **bedfordstmartins.com/realcomm** to get access to:

✓ **LearningCurve** Adaptive Quizzes.

▸ Video clips that illustrate key concepts, highlighted in teal in the Real Reference section that follows.

2. Describe how you managed an impression of yourself in a face-to-face interaction and a mediated one. Describe your conscious preparations for this impression management, and then describe the outcome. What contributed to your successful or unsuccessful management of self? Were the impression-management strategies you employed in the face-to-face interaction different from the mediated situation?

3. Take a look at the text of a presidential speech online at www.whitehouse.gov. After reading the complete speech, consider how the speech is characterized in various sources (blogs, liberal and conservative news sources, late-night comedy and satires). How do perceptions of the speech change from one source to another? Does your perception of the speech change as you consider the points of view of these various sources?

4. Think about a co-culture (age, sexual orientation, socioeconomic status, race, religion, and so on) with which you identify. Then make a list of stereotypes that are associated with that group. In what ways do you conform to such stereotypes? In what ways do you not conform? Do you identify with more than one culture? If so, are there any stereotypes on your list that contradict each other? How might intersection of these cultures (for example, being a white, Christian, thirty-year-old stay-at-home dad or being a fifty-year-old

Hispanic lesbian scientist) affect your perception of yourself as well as others' perceptions of you?

5. Watch some television programming or flip through a magazine that is typically geared toward a particular group. Pay close attention to the advertisements you see. Are they geared toward the groups that are expected to be watching the programming? If so, do you see instances in which the commercials allow for flexibility and mindfulness (for example, any advertising geared toward women during football games)? If you are a member of the group being targeted during such programming, do you find yourself more or less persuaded by the message based on stereotypes about your group?

Now that you have finished reading this chapter, you can:

Describe how our personal perspective on the world influences our communication:

▶ **Perception** is the cognitive process that helps us make sense of the world (p. 36).
▶ **Communication processing** is how we gather, organize, and evaluate the information we receive (p. 37).
▶ Because we are constantly bombarded with information we must sift through it to determine what is important and what to remember (p. 37).

Explain how we use and misuse schemas when communicating with others:

▶ **Schemas** are mental structures we use to connect bits of information together (p. 37).
▶ Schemas function to help us understand how things work and decide how to act.
▶ Schemas evolve as we select new information and situations (p. 37).
▶ **Interaction appearance theory** explains how people change their perception of someone else as they spend more time together (p. 37).
▶ Schemas present four challenges that derail good communication. **Mindlessness** is a passive response to information. This can be corrected by **mindfulness**, which helps us focus on the task at hand. The challenge **selective perception** presents is that it allows bias to influence our thoughts. **Undue influence** allows other sources too much say (pp. 38–39).

Define the attributions we use to explain behavior:

▶ When we need to explain why someone says or does something in a manner that does not fit our schemas, we look to attributions (pp. 39–40).
▶ The **fundamental attribution error** explains our tendency to assume that another person's wrong behavior stems from an internal flaw, whereas the **self-serving bias** attributes our own failures to external causes (p. 40).
▶ Improve your perceptions by verifying them, being thoughtful looking beyond first impressions, and questioning your assumptions (pp. 40–41).

Describe cultural differences that influence perception:

▶ Effective communication depends on understanding how diversity, the variables that make us unique, affects perception (p. 41).

▶ The failure to see beyond our own beliefs and circumstances, or **cultural myopia**, blinds us to alternative points of view (pp. 43–44).
▶ **Stereotyping**, or generalizing about people, limits our ability to see the individual and can lead to **prejudice**, ill will toward a particular group and a sense of one's own superiority (pp. 44–45).

Identify how our **self-concept**—who we think we are—influences communication:

▶ We receive both direct and indirect evidence about the self.
▶ We are more willing to interact in situations where we feel we have strengths and where our self-concept is confirmed by others (p. 47).
▶ We compare ourselves to others, even idealized images in the media, according to social comparison theory—often to our own disadvantage (pp. 47–48).
▶ **Self-esteem** is how we feel about ourselves in a particular situation (pp. 48–49).
▶ **Self-efficacy** is the ability to predict our effectiveness in a communication situation. Inaccurate self-efficacy may lead to a self-fulfilling prophecy, whereby we change our behavior in ways that make our prediction more likely to come true (pp. 49–51).
▶ We assess our communication effectiveness through the lenses of **self-actualization** (high performance), **self-adequacy** (adequate performance), and **self-denigration** (poor performance) (pp. 53–54).

Describe how our cognitions about ourselves and our behavior affect our communication with others:

▶ **Self-presentation** is intentional communication designed to let others know about ourselves (pp. 55–57).
▶ The tendency to watch our environment and others in it for cues as to how to present ourselves is called self-monitoring (pp. 56–57).
▶ Sharing important information about ourselves is self-disclosure (pp. 57–58).
▶ We can more easily control presentation of self online than in face-to-face encounters but that doesn't mean that everyone does it effectively (pp. 58–60).

Which of these pairs are partners? (top left) Getty Images; (top center) Metro-Goldwyn-Mayer/Getty Images; (top right) Getty Images; (bottom left) Bennett Raglin/WireImage for Tony Awards Productions/Getty Images; (bottom center) © Photofusion Picture Library/Alamy; (bottom right) Stockbyte/Getty Images.

3

Verbal
Communication

Anne Kerry was walking to the bank in her San Francisco neighborhood when she suddenly ran into Scott, an old college friend, accompanied by another young man. "Anne," he said warmly, "I want you to meet my partner, Bryan." Anne was surprised—she hadn't realized that Scott was gay. She asked, "How long have you two been together?" Both men looked at her quizzically before they realized what she was thinking. "No," said Scott, "I became a police officer. Bryan and I work patrol together." "I was embarrassed," said Anne. "I didn't mean to misunderstand their relationship. I just figured that 'partner' meant love interest."

Like many words in the English language, *partner* has a variety of definitions: it can mean anything from "an associate" to "a dancing companion" to "a group of two or more symbiotically associated organisms." But like Anne, many of us immediately jump to another definition: "half of a couple who live together or who are habitual companions." Indeed, the term is widely used by gays and lesbians seeking a label for their loved one. Some heterosexual couples have also embraced the term to reveal their committed state, particularly when they feel that they've outgrown the term *boyfriend* or *girlfriend* or are unwilling to use the terms *husband* and *wife*.

The fact is the labels we choose for our relationships have a huge impact on our communication. The term *partner* can give rise to ambiguity—is the person you introduce with this term a business colleague, someone you play tennis with, or your "significant other"? That ambiguity makes it difficult for others to grasp your intended meaning. Perhaps that's why some Massachusetts gays and lesbians who wed after the state was the first to ratify same-sex marriages avoid the term *partner*. Bob Buckley felt the power of such labels when his partner, Marty Scott, needed medical treatment. When hospital administrators asked his relationship to the patient, Buckley was able to say, simply, "husband" and was immediately allowed to stay with Scott, since spouses are afforded this privilege but partners are not (Jones, 2005).

After you have finished reading this chapter, you will be able to

- Describe the power of language—the system of symbols we use to think about and communicate our experiences and feelings

- Identify the ways language works to help people communicate— the five functional communication competencies

- Describe the ways that communicators create meaning with language

- Label problematic uses of language and their remedies

- Describe how language reflects, builds on, and determines context

As our opening vignette shows, the names used to describe our connections with others have power. This is true for all kinds of relationships. For example, calling your father "Dad" reveals less formality in your relationship than calling him "Father." In a stepfamily situation, calling your father's wife "Mom" indicates more closeness than using her first name. Choosing words can get complicated. That's why we dedicate this chapter to studying verbal communication, the way we communicate with language. **Language** is the system of symbols (words) that we use to think about and communicate experiences and feelings. Language is also governed by grammatical rules and is influenced by contexts.

Of course, nonverbal behaviors—pauses, tone of voice, and body movements—accompany the words we speak. Thus they are an integral part of our communication and we examine them in Chapter 4. But we now focus on the nature of language, its functions, how it creates meaning, problems with language, and contexts that influence our use of language.

The Nature of Language

In 1970, a "wild child" was discovered in California. Thirteen-year-old "Genie" had been chained in a small room with no toys and little food for nearly her entire life. Her abusive father gave her no hugs, no loving words, and no conversation. As a result, Genie never developed language. Medical doctors, linguists, and psychologists worked intensely with Genie for over seven years, hoping to give the girl a chance at life in a community with others. But despite their efforts, Genie never learned more than a few hundred words and was never able to form sentences of more than two or three words (Pines, 1997; "Secret," 1997). Genie's sad story highlights the complex nature of language: someone with Genie's background will never fully grasp that language is symbolic, has multiple meanings, is informed by our thoughts, and is shaped by grammar and context. We explore these four points in this chapter.

Language Is Symbolic

What comes to mind when you see the word *cat*? A furry childhood best friend? Fits of sneezing from allergies? Either way, the word evokes a response because it is a *symbol,* a sign representing a person, idea, or thing. Words evoke particular responses because speakers of that language agree that they do. Thus you can use words to communicate ideas and thoughts about particular subjects when you have a common language. Moreover, using words as symbols is a uniquely human ability (Wade, 2010).

Thought Informs Language

Jamal Henderson is preparing to apply to colleges. He keeps his father, Michael, involved in the process because he values his opinion. They both agree that Jamal should attend a "good college." But Michael feels hurt when Jamal starts talking seriously about urban universities in another state. He thinks his son has ruled out his own alma mater, the local campus of the state university system. Jamal and Michael have different thoughts about what a "good college" is. Their language and thoughts are related in their own minds, and each thinks he is using the term appropriately.

Your **cognitive language** is the system of symbols you use to describe people, things, and situations in your mind. It influences your language (Giles & Wiemann, 1987) and is related to your thoughts, attitudes, and the society in which you live (Bradac & Giles, 2005). Michael may think a "good college" is close to home, is involved in the local community, and offers small class sizes. Meanwhile, Jamal may think a "good college" presents the opportunity to live in a new city and to study with people from other countries.

Our thinking affects the language we use. But language also influences our thoughts. If you tell yourself that a coworker is an "idiot," the word may influence your future impressions of him. To illustrate, if he's quiet during a meeting, you might conclude that he knows nothing about the subject under discussion. On a much larger scale, we can have visceral reactions to the words or names assigned to people and places. For example, children assigned linguistically low-status names (like Alekzandra instead of Alexandra) tend to be treated differently by teachers, are more likely to be referred for special education, and are less likely to be perceived as gifted (Rochman, 2011). Indeed, the city of Stalingrad in Russia was renamed Volgograd because of the strong, negative reaction to a name associated with the violent dictator, Joseph Stalin (Roth, 2013).

Language Is Ruled by Grammar

If you are a fantasy or science-fiction fan, you know that the language in today's video games and television must be more than the alien gibberish of old. It must have complete structures that consistently make sense. So Hollywood hires "conlangers"—people who construct new languages with complete grammatical structures like those you see in the HBO series *Game of Thrones*' Dothraki or *Avatar*'s Na'vi (Chozick, 2011).

As your third-grade teacher likely told you, **grammar**—the system of rules for creating words, phrases, and sentences in a particular language—is important. Although good grammar doesn't always equal good communication, using correct grammar helps you communicate clearly. And pronunciation matters, too. For example, if you pronounce the word *tomato* "tommy-toe," others probably won't understand that you are referring to the red fruit that tastes really good on a hamburger. That's because grammar has *phonological rules* governing how words should be pronounced.

Similarly, grammar has *syntactic rules* guiding the placement of words in a sentence. If you shuffle the words in the sentence "I ran to the store to buy some milk" to "Store I to milk to ran the buy some," your meaning becomes unclear. Grammatical rules differ among languages. Native speakers of English, for example, must remember that the grammar of Romance languages (such as French and Spanish) requires a different syntax. For example, in English, adjectives typically precede a noun ("I have an intelligent dog"), whereas in Spanish, adjectives follow the noun (*"Tengo un perro intelegente,"* literally translated as

CONNECT

As you learn in Chapter 13, it's important for speakers to choose clear and appropriate language when planning a speech. If your terms are confusing or inappropriate for the speaking occasion, your audience will quickly lose interest in what you're saying. This is true whether you are attempting to inform or persuade your listeners or even speaking in honor of a special occasion.

"I have a dog intelligent"). To communicate clearly in Spanish, an English speaker must adjust.

Excellent grammar on its own will not automatically make you an outstanding communicator. Telling your professor in perfect English that her style of dress is a sorry flashback to the 1980s is still offensive and inappropriate. That's because competent communicators also consider the situational, relational, and cultural contexts whenever they use language.

Language Is Bound by Context

● **IT'S PROBABLY** a good idea to avoid regaling your grandmother with tales of your crazy spring-break shenanigans. Rubberball/Jupiter Images

Imagine a scenario in which your cousin prattles on and on about her wild spring break in Miami. Now imagine that she's talking to your eighty-year-old grandmother . . . at your niece's fifth birthday party . . . in front of a group of devoutly religious family members. These contrasting scenarios illustrate how language is bound by contexts such as our relationship with the people present, the situation we're in, and the cultural factors at play. Does Grandma really want to hear about your cousin's behavior? Is it really OK to talk about this at a little kid's party? What about respecting the beliefs and sensibilities of your family members?

Communication accommodation theory (CAT) explains how language and identity shape communication in various contexts. CAT argues that competent communicators adjust their language and nonverbal behaviors (see Chapter 4) to the person, group, and context (Giles, Coupland, & Coupland, 1991; Shepherd, Giles, & LePoire, 2001; Soliz & Giles, 2010). We examine the relational, situational, and cultural contexts later in this chapter. But for now, keep in mind that communicating competently involves accommodating to context.

The Functions of Language

One of the first phrases that eighteen-month-old Josie learned to use was "thank you." Had this toddler already mastered the rules of etiquette? Was she just picking up a habit from her parents? Or was she learning that certain phrases would help her get things she wants: a compliment, a smile, a cookie?

We all learn isolated words and grammar as we acquire language. Josie, for example, probably picked up the expression "thank you" from her parents, her older brother, or her babysitter. But to become a competent communicator, she must learn to use this and other symbols appropriately. If Josie uses "thank you" as a name for her stuffed bear, she's not using it appropriately, so she's not communicating effectively. **Communication acquisition** is the process of learning individual words in a language as well as how to use that language *appropriately* and *effectively* in various contexts. Just as Josie gets a smile from her parents for saying "thank you," using language competently helps us to achieve our goals.

Researchers have identified five competencies (Wood, 1982) for how language behaviors function: controlling, informing, feeling, imagining, and ritualizing. We all develop these competencies when we're young by interacting with family and peers and observing television and other media. These competencies remain important throughout our lives. For that reason, we now look at them more closely.

Using Language as a Means of Control

Language is used as an instrument of *control*, to exert influence over others and our environment. Josie's use of the phrase "thank you" impresses her mother, who reassures her that using the term makes her a "good girl." Such appropriate use of language can make children seem cute, smart, or polite, giving them the ability to present themselves in a positive light. Recall from Chapter 1 that *control* is actually a neutral term; it is a crucial social skill whether used in a positive or negative way. As an adult, Josie will be able to use language to control her environment by negotiating a pay raise or bargaining with a car dealer. However, she will also need to avoid negative control strategies, such as whining, ridiculing, insulting, threatening, or belittling, as these do not contribute to productive, successful communication.

For anyone who has been the victim of hurtful language and actions, speaking out—harnessing the power of language—can actually restore a sense of control. Tens of thousands of women have been brutally raped in the Congo, and their shame has kept them silent. Cultural taboos about gender and sexual behavior have also prevented them from sharing their stories. However, local and international aid groups have organized open forums to help victims talk about the atrocities, connect with others, and regain control of their lives. Words about such experiences are certainly hard to speak, but once these narratives are spoken, they can empower the speaker (Bartels et al., 2013; Gettleman, 2008).

Using language as an instrument of control is part of our *self-presentation*, discussed in Chapter 2. When you're on a job interview (see the Interviewing Appendix), you'll want to use clear, professional language that highlights your skills. Similarly, when delivering a speech (see Chapter 14), your language should let your audience know that you're engaged with and informed about your topic.

Using Language to Share Information

Have you ever asked a sick child to tell you "where it hurts," only to receive a vague and unhelpful answer? This is because young children are still developing the next functional competency, **informing**—using language to give and receive information. As an adult, if you've ever been asked for directions, you know that providing people with information that they can understand and understanding the information they're conveying to you are equally important skills.

There are four important aspects of informing: questioning, describing, reinforcing, and withholding.

▶ *Questioning* is something we learn at a young age and use throughout our lives. Young children hungry for information about their world quickly learn the power of the simple, one-word question "Why?"

▶ *Describing* helps us communicate our world to others. Parents and teachers may ask children to repeat directions to their school or their home or to detail the specifics of a story they've heard.

As indicated, sometimes competent language use means knowing when to withhold information or avoid topics. This is particularly important when developing and maintaining interpersonal relationships (Chapter 7). For example, strategic topic avoidance allows you to steer the conversation away from discussing your friend's recent painful breakup until she is ready to discuss it.

> ▶ *Reinforcing* information can help us become competent listeners. We might take notes or simply repeat the information to confirm our comprehension.

> ▶ *Withholding* information or opinions may be appropriate in some situations. For example, you may withhold your opposition to your manager's plan because you want to keep your job. Or you may elect not to reveal a piece of information that might embarrass a friend.

Together, these four skills form the basis of the informational competency that we use to communicate throughout our lives.

Using Language to Express Feelings

Poets, writers, and lyricists are celebrated for using language to capture and express emotions. But most expressions of feelings are less elaborately composed than a Shakespearean sonnet or an angry protest song. In everyday conversation and correspondence, we use language to send messages to others expressing how we feel about ourselves, them, or the situation. Young children can say, "I'm sad," and cry or laugh to communicate feelings. As you mature, you learn how to express a more complex set of emotions—liking, love, respect, empathy, hostility, and pride—and you may even intensify emotion by using words like *obsessed* rather than *love/like* (Goodman, 2013). The functional competency of expressing **feeling** is primarily relational: you let people know how much you value (or don't value) them by the emotions you express.

We all use language to express our feelings, but to be competent, we must do so appropriately and effectively. Many people don't communicate their emotions well. For example, Elliot expresses frustration with his staff by yelling at them; his staff responds by mocking Elliot at a local pub after work. Instead, Elliot could have said, "I'm *worried* that we're not going to make the deadline on this project"; someone on his staff could have said, "I'm feeling *tense* about making the deadline, too, but I'm also *confused* about why you yelled at me." Sometimes, appropriate and effective communication means avoiding expressing feelings that we consider inappropriate or risky in a given situation (Burleson, Holmstrom, & Gilstrap, 2005). For example,

Using language to express feelings competently can be a powerful addition to your communication skills in a variety of settings. In a small group (Chapter 9), you might need to express your frustration with the fact that you're doing most of the work. In an organization (Chapter 11), you might save your company time and money by effectively sharing your concerns about a project.

when Abby's boyfriend suggests sharing an apartment next semester, Abby changes the subject to avoid admitting that she's uncomfortable taking that step.

Using Language to Express Creativity

What do Katniss Everdeen, George Michael Bluth, Wonder Woman, and Sherlock Holmes have in common? Each is the product of the imagination of a writer or storyteller. And regardless of whether they were conceptualized as part of a novel, comic book, screenplay, or television series, each character and his or her story are primarily expressed through language.

Imagining is probably the most complex functional competency. It is the ability to think, play, and be creative in communication. Children imagine by pretending to be a superhero. Adults imagine, too. The way a song is worded, the way a play is scripted, and the way special effects coordinate with the message delivered in a film— these all stem from imagination. On the job, imagining is the ability to use language to convey a vision for a project to your coworkers (such as architects explaining blueprints and models). In a debate, imagining enables you to think ahead of your opponent, to put words to each side of an argument, and to use language in logical and convincing ways.

● **WHILE A TOAST** might be the perfect way to wish a couple happiness at their wedding shower, in the film *Bridesmaids* Annie and Helen inappropriately use it as an opportunity to compete for the role of best friend to the bride. Suzanne Hanover/© Universal Pictures/Courtesy Everett Collection

Using Language as Ritual

When little Josie says "thank you" for her cookie, it's a sign that she is learning the fifth functional competency: ritualizing. **Ritualizing** involves the rules for managing conversations and relationships. We begin learning these rules as children: peekaboo games require us to learn turn-taking in conversations. When we learn to say "hi" or "bye-bye" or "please," we internalize politeness rituals.

In adulthood, ritualizing effectively means saying and doing the "right" thing at weddings, funerals, dinners, athletic events, and other social gatherings. Simple exchanges, like telling a bride and groom "congratulations" or offering condolences to a grieving friend, are some ways we ritualize language. However, our ritualizing is not always that formal, nor is it limited to big events. In our everyday lives we use ritual comments to support one another in relationships, such as "Have a great day, Honey!" "You're going to nail that speech" or even just "I'll text you later. . . ."

Language and Meaning

Imagine three-year-old Damon sitting in a house of worship with his parents. He's having a great time banging his stuffed toys around until his mother grabs them away during a silent part of the service. Clearly upset, Damon calls her a nasty name. Mom's face turns bright red, and she escorts Damon out to the car. Damon associated his language with the concept of being unhappy; he was upset about Mom taking his toys, so he uttered the same word he had probably heard a family member use when unhappy with someone.

● **THE WORD** *SCHOOL* has multiple denotative meanings: it is not only the place where students learn but also a group of fish. (left) MaxyM/Shutterstock; (right) Comstock/Jupiter Images

Semantics involves the relationships among symbols, objects, people, and concepts; it refers to the *meaning* that words have for people, either because of their definitions or because of their placement in a sentence. Damon had probably observed reactions to the use of the nasty name, so he thought it meant "Give me my toys back." What Damon had not learned was **pragmatics**, the ability to use his culture's symbol systems appropriately. He may have gotten a few laughs by using the language in front of his family at home, but he didn't realize that it's inappropriate to use the word in other contexts. When you acquire language, you learn semantics, but when you learn *how* to use the verbal symbols of a culture appropriately, you learn pragmatics.

Key to understanding semantic and pragmatic meaning are three ideas that we now examine: the multiple meanings of words, their varying levels of abstraction, and their usage in particular groups.

Words Have Multiple Meanings

As you saw in the opening "partner" vignette, a single word can have many meanings. A dictionary can help you find the **denotative meaning** of a word— its basic, consistently accepted definition. But to be a competent communicator, you'll also need to consider a word's **connotative meaning**, people's emotional or attitudinal response to it. Consider the word *school*. It has several denotative meanings, including a building where education takes place and a large group of fish. But the word can also carry strong connotative meanings, based on your attitudes toward and experiences with school: it might bring back happy memories of class birthday parties in second grade, or it might make you feel anxious about final exams.

Obviously, choosing words carefully is important. Not only must you make sure the denotative meaning is clear (using the word *ostentatious* with a bunch of six-year-olds isn't going to help you explain anything), but you also have to be aware of the possible connotative meanings of the words you use (Hample, 1987). Consider the words people might choose at a party to introduce the person to whom they are married. They could say, "I'd like you to meet my *wife*," or ". . . my *spouse*" (or *bride, old lady, ball-and-chain, better half*). These terms denotatively mean the same thing—their marital partner. But connotatively, they might generate very different reactions (including possibly offending people). *Spouse* may have a positive connotation in some situations, such as in legal paperwork or a gender-neutral invitation ("spouses welcome"). But in a personal introduction, it may come across negatively, as too formal and lacking affection. Connotative reactions also depend on the people you're speaking to and your relationship to them—the same word may make your friends laugh but anger your family members.

Subtle differences in word meaning can even change your entire interpretation of an event. For example, your grandfather offers to give you $10,000 at your college graduation if you graduate with honors. Is his offer a bribe, a reward, or an incentive? How you and others perceive and process his offer depends on the meaning associated with the language used. You may resent your grandfather if you consider the money a *bribe*, feel proud if you earn your *reward*, or feel motivated by the *incentive*.

Abstraction

Language operates at many levels of abstraction, ranging from very vague to very specific. You might talk in such broad, vague terms that no one knows what you are staying ("Stuff is cool!"), or you can speak so specifically that people may think you are keeping notes for a court case against them: "I saw you at 10:32 P.M. on Friday, January 29, at the right-hand corner table of Harry's Bar with a six-foot-tall, brown-haired man wearing black jeans, boots, and a powder blue T-shirt."

The **abstraction ladder** (Hayakawa, 1964) illustrates the specific versus general levels of abstraction (see Figure 3.1). The top rungs of the ladder are high-level

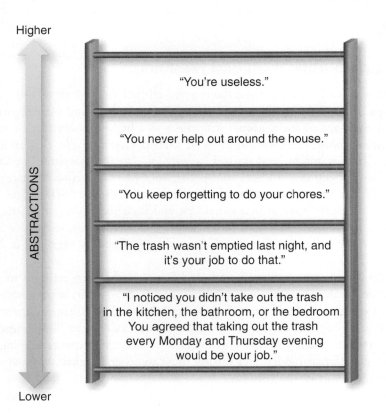

Higher

ABSTRACTIONS

"You're useless."

"You never help out around the house."

"You keep forgetting to do your chores."

"The trash wasn't emptied last night, and it's your job to do that."

"I noticed you didn't take out the trash in the kitchen, the bathroom, or the bedroom. You agreed that taking out the trash every Monday and Thursday evening would be your job."

Lower

FIGURE 3.1

THE ABSTRACTION LADDER

abstractions: these are the most general and vague. Lower-level abstractions are more specific and can help you understand more precisely what people mean. "Let's watch something interesting on Netflix" is a high abstraction that allows a wide range of choices (and the possibility of some really bad movies). Saying "I'd like to watch a historical drama tonight" (lower abstraction) is more likely to get you something you'll enjoy, whereas naming the exact movie ("Let's watch *Lincoln*") ensures satisfaction.

But even though lower abstractions ensure clarity, high abstractions can accomplish certain communication goals. Here are a few examples:

► *Evasion.* Avoiding specific details is evasion. A teenager might tell her parents that she is "going *out* with *some friends*" rather than "going to a party at Nell's house with Fernanda, Justin, and Derek."

► *Equivocation.* **Equivocation** involves using words that have imprecise meanings that can be interpreted multiple ways. Equivocation can help us get out of an uncomfortable situation, as when a friend asks what you think of her new sweater—which you think is hideous—and you reply, "It's . . . *colorful.*"

► *Euphemisms.* **Euphemisms** are words or phrases with neutral or positive connotations that we use to substitute for terms that might be perceived as upsetting. For example, you might say that your uncle "passed on" rather than "died" or that your mother had a "procedure" rather than an "operation."

● **SKATEBOARDERS HAVE** their own jargon for their fancy flips and tricks. If you're not a skateboarder, an "ollie" might be a foreign concept. Michael Sharkey/Getty Images

Group Identification and Meaning

Language also informs others about your affiliations and memberships. For example, **slang** is language that is informal, nonstandard, and usually particular to a specific age or social group; it operates as a high-level abstraction because meanings of slang are known only by its users during a specific time in history. A rock concert might be described as "groovy," "totally awesome," or "off the hook"—each expression places the speaker in a particular time or place in the world. Teenagers might alert each other online that they've "GTG" (got to go) because of "POS" (parent over shoulder), and their parents are none the wiser. Slang is often intensified by adjectives that increase emphasis, such as *absolutely, completely, extremely, totally, wickedly,* or *massively* (Palacios Martínez & Núñez Pertejo, 2012).

Related to slang is **jargon**, technical language that is specific to members of a given profession or activity or hobby group. Jargon may seem abstract and vague to those outside the group but conveys clear and precise meanings to those within the group. For example, when a fan of the model game Warhammer 40K speaks of "kit bashing," other fans understand that the speaker is taking parts from two different models and mixing them together. The rest of us, however, would probably just stare blankly.

AND YOU?

What kinds of slang or jargon do you regularly use? How did you become familiar with these terms? And how would you go about explaining these terms to someone who is unfamiliar with them?

WIREDFORCOMMUNICATION

Speaking in Code

There's a large contingent of educators and parents who think the key to securing a good-paying job after college lies with learning a foreign language. Envisioning a future in which China leads the world's economy, they push school boards to teach Mandarin or enroll their children in extracurricular immersion courses (McDonald, 2012). But what if there were another language just as likely to lead to fruitful employment, one that applied to just about every existing and emerging industry that not only could be taught in schools but also learned at home for little cost? And what if that language, already in use around the world, were based primarily on English?

That language—well, technically, *those languages*, since there are many—is computer code. Code essentially refers to the directions given to a computer to make it do what you want it to do. The apps you use to play games on your phone, the programs that spit out your credit card bill each month, the tools that small businesses use to manage supply chains and payroll, even the sensor that dings in your car when you forget to buckle up, all run on code. In every industry, from information tech to communications, manufacturing to agriculture, and food service to shipping, computers and code play a role. The most popular computer languages (like Ruby, Python, and C++) are "spoken" in just about every technologically advanced country, even though these languages are, by and large, based on English language keywords. But most Americans—even the digital natives who were raised on technology—simply don't know how to code, and so employers find themselves duking it out to hire the ones who do. "Our policy is literally to hire as many talented engineers as we can find," notes Facebook founder Mark Zuckerberg. "There just aren't enough people who are trained and have these skills today" (Zuckerberg, 2013). Others are careful to point out that coding is not just for engineers or engineering majors. It's a skill that will benefit anyone in just about any job. Huffington Post CTO John Pavley points out that even for nontech types, coding can open doors to satisfying work. "[N]on-technical people can learn to code, which will open doors to better jobs and a richer understanding of the rapidly changing world around us, where computer chips and software are finding their way into every aspect of our lives" (Pavley, 2013).

Pavley likens the divide between those who can and cannot code to the low levels of literacy during the Dark Ages, when the written word, along with the power it conferred, was the provenance of only a small elite. But there is a movement to bring the power of code to the masses. Organizations like CodeAcademy and Code.org advocate making more computer science courses available to students from kindergarten through high school and offer free coding lessons online for anyone interested in learning a programming language at home (Wingfield, 2013). Some even suggest making learning code an educational requirement along the lines of, or even in place of, a foreign language (Koerner, 2013). Other nations have already taken that step. Multilingual education may take on a whole new meaning.

THINK ABOUT THIS

1 In communication terms, what kind of code is *code*? Is it a language like English or Mandarin? Is it verbal communication or something else entirely?

2 Should schools require students to learn code the same way most schools require them to learn a foreign language? If computer languages can be learned fairly easily with a book via a Web-based class, why might it be important to offer them in schools?

3 Is the dominance of English in the programming world significant? What meaning might it carry in non-English-speaking contexts?

4 Consider your envisioned field of study and the career you hope to pursue after college. Do you think having some knowledge of computer code would be helpful for you?

Problematic Uses of Language

"I think we're still in a muddle with our language, because once you get words and a spoken language it gets harder to communicate" (Ewalt, 2005, para. 1). The famous primatologist Jane Goodall made this point when explaining why chimpanzees get over their disputes much faster than humans. They strike out at each other and then offer each other reassuring pats or embraces, and voilà, argument over. Not so with people: words can be really hard to forget.

As you've probably experienced, words can lead to confusion, hurt feelings, misunderstandings, and anger when we blurt things out before considering them (and their effects) carefully (Miller & Roloff, 2007). We sometimes engage in hurtful or hateful language, use labels in ways that others don't appreciate, reveal bias through our words, and use offensive or coarse language. And when we put thoughtless or hastily chosen words in e-mails or post them on Twitter or Facebook, they become "permanent," and we may have great difficulty taking them back (Riordan & Kreuz, 2010).

Hateful and Hurtful Language

After twenty-five minutes of hearing ethnic slurs from the crowd whenever he tried to score a goal, soccer star Kevin Prince Boateng kicked the ball into the crowd and walked off the field, accompanied by his teammates (Herman, 2013). Sadly, Boateng's story is not an isolated event: anti-Semitic chants plagued another soccer club, and fans have thrown food and screamed insults at black players in others. Such language that offends, threatens, or insults a person or group based on race, religion, gender, or other identifiable characteristics is **hatespeech** (Waltman & Haas, 2011). Hatespeech employs offensive words to deride the person or group; thus hatespeech often creates vividly negative images of groups in the minds of listeners while downplaying the unique qualities of individuals in those groups (Haas, 2012, p. 132).

Other language choices may not be intended to offend individuals based on cultural factors but are nonetheless hurtful. For example, do sports fans have the right to jeer at the opposing team? Should they be allowed to bellow at referees throughout the game? What about the instance of an opposing team fan reading loudly from the grand jury report of the Jerry Sandusky sexual abuse case at a Penn State game (Pennington, 2012)? Although none of these behaviors are technically against the law, they have communication effects and are often considered **hurtful language**—inappropriate, damaging, mean, sarcastic, or offensive statements that affect others in negative ways.

Labeling

Feminist. The literal definition of the term is "a person who advocates equal social, political, and all other rights for women and men." But who are these people who label themselves feminists? In our years of teaching undergraduates, we've heard plenty of students note that feminists are women who hate men and care only about professional success. But "there is no way to tell what a feminist

AND YOU?

Are you a feminist? What does the term *feminist* mean to you? If you hear someone called a feminist, what ideas or images does this bring to mind?

'looks' like. Feminists are young, old, women, men, feminine or masculine, and of varying ethnicities" (McClanahan, 2006, para. 5).

Feminists also hail from different religious backgrounds, causing some interesting discussions about the labels believers choose regarding their feminist viewpoints. When a group of Spanish Muslims approached city officials in Barcelona, Spain, about sponsoring a conference on Islamic feminism, one official responded with shock, noting that "Islamic feminism" must surely be a contradiction or an oxymoron (Nomani, 2005). Others have eschewed the feminist label entirely because of its connection to liberal politics. More recently, prominent conservative female politicians have donned the label "mama grizzly" to express the fierceness of pro-life, limited-government women (Torregrosa, 2010).

What these examples reveal is that the labels we choose for our beliefs affect how we communicate them to others (and how others respond). As these examples show, when we place gender, ethnic, class, occupation, or role labels on others, we ignore their individual differences (Sarich & Miele, 2004) and thus limit or constrict our communication. So if you think all feminists are liberal, secular, career-oriented women, you may miss out on the opportunity to understand the feminist views of your aunt who is a stay-at-home mom or your male neighbor who is a conservative Jew.

Biased Language

Some language is infused with subtle meanings that imply that a person or subject should be perceived in a particular way. This is known as **biased language**. For example, addressing an older person as "sweetie" or "dear" can be belittling (even if kindly intended) (Leland, 2008). In particular, older individuals struggling with dementia are sensitive to language that implies that they are childlike ("Did you eat your dinner like a good boy?") because they are struggling to maintain their dignity (Williams, Herman, Gajewski, & Wilson, 2009). In addition, there are many derogatory terms for women who engage in casual sex,

CONNECT

The federal government and organizations take derogatory labels that hurt and demean others quite seriously. Professional organizations typically provide employees with information regarding their *harassment* and *sexual harassment* policies, which are intended to protect employees from feeling threatened or attacked because of their race, religion, abilities, or other personal traits. We discuss this important issue in Chapter 11.

EVALUATINGCOMMUNICATIONETHICS

Résumé Language

You've just graduated with a B.A. in communication and are on the hunt for an entry-level position in marketing. You know that your résumé is strong in terms of your degree, relevant coursework, and good grades, but you're a bit worried that you may not have enough real-world experience. Since you had to work full time to pay college expenses, you couldn't afford to take the kinds of unpaid internships that look so impressive on a résumé; you waited tables all through college instead and graduated in five years instead of four.

You discuss these concerns with a friend who suggests making some changes in the language of your résumé. First, she suggests changing your entry date for college to make it look like you finished the degree in four years. Second, she suggests you cast your restaurant experience as a type of marketing internship in which you developed "people skills" and "sales skills" that helped you "analyze and synthesize" consumers and products. Finally, she tells you to use your cover letter to describe yourself as "a team player" who is "attentive to detail" and has "proven creativity."

You're worried that some aspects of your résumé might not be impressive enough, but you're not entirely sure that padding your résumé with vague language and empty jargon is the way to go. What will you do?

THINK ABOUT THIS

❶ Is it crucial that an employer know how long it took you to earn your B.A.? Is it unethical to simply note the date you finished it?

❷ Will you follow your friend's suggestion to use vague expressions like "team player"? In what ways might you use more precise terms to describe yourself?

❸ Rather than dressing it up as "marketing experience," might there be an honest way to use your restaurant experience to your advantage here?

though men who engage in similar behaviors in similar situations are afforded less derogatory labels (she is "easy"; he is a "player"). Such biased language perpetuates perceptions of women as less intelligent, less mentally healthy, and less competent than men in similar relationships or situations (Conley, 2011; Jacobs, 2012).

Biased language can also affect others' perceptions of you. For example, if you employ the vague "those guys" to describe coworkers in another department or a group of teens hanging out at the mall, others will likely see you as more biased than people who use concrete terms (for example, "the attorneys in the legal department" or "the high school students at FroYo") (Assilaméhou & Testé, 2013).

AND YOU?

Has anyone ever labeled you in a way that truly irritated or offended you? What terms did they use? Are you aware of any biased language that frequently seeps into conversations among your friends, family, or coworkers? How might you consider addressing such biases?

When language openly excludes certain groups or implies something negative about them, we often attempt to replace the biased language with more neutral terms, employing what is known as **politically correct language**. For example, the terms *firefighter*, *police officer*, and *chairperson* replace the sexist terms *fireman*, *policeman*, and *chairman*, reflecting and perhaps influencing the fact that these once male-dominated positions are now open to women as well. Critics of political correctness argue that such attempts at sensitivity and neutrality can undermine communication as they substitute euphemisms for clarity when dealing with difficult subjects and place certain words off-limits (O'Neill, 2011). But others note that there is value in always trying to be sensitive—and accurate—when we make choices regarding language.

Profanity and Civility

Comedians curse and audiences laugh; perhaps you have a relative who adds colorful words to his or her stories, which amuses your family members ("That's Uncle Mike for you!"). This was not the case for A.J. Clemente who cursed on air on his first day as a broadcaster for the North Dakota NBC affiliate KFYR. Clemente later explained that he was practicing his lines and nervously uttered the offensive words without realizing that his microphone was on; he also offered an apology for his behavior on Twitter. But in the end, he could not undo the impression he left with his new employer and was ultimately fired (ABC News, 2013; Grossman, 2013). Recent years have seen an increase in swearing over mediated channels (Butler & Fitzgerald, 2011), and some critics believe that public outrage over sex, violence, and profanity seems to have waned in recent decades (Steinberg, 2010). In fact, in the wake of Clemente's outburst, more than fifteen hundred fans wrote supportive notes on the station's Facebook page asking managers to reconsider their decision to let Clemente go. Twitter supporters also showed their support with #FreeAJ and #KeepAJ.

Profanity includes cursing and other expressions considered, rude, vulgar, or disrespectful. Such words get their social and emotional impact from the culture and can be perceived positively, neutrally, or negatively (Johnson, 2012) based on factors like the social setting (for example, friends at home watching televised sports) or the relationship. If A.J. Clemente had uttered the exact same words at a bar surrounded by friends, it would not have made national news. Rather, he cursed in a formal, professional environment.

Regardless of whether language is viewed as rude or appropriate based on the relational, cultural, or situational context, it should meet some standards of **civility**, the social norm for appropriate behavior. Crude, offensive, vulgar, and profane language can create uncomfortable and unproductive relationships and work environments (Johnson & Lewis, 2010). Following are five guidelines for the production of more civil language in the workplace (Troester & Mester, 2007), but most of them are applicable outside of the business context as well:

▶ Use no words rather than offensive ones.

▶ Use words appropriate to your specific listener.

▶ Choose temperate and accurate words over inflammatory ones when commenting on ideas, issues, or persons.

▶ Use objective, respectful, nondiscriminatory language.

▶ Use clean language at all times when at work.

Language in Context

You learned about the importance of context in Chapter 1 as part of our model of communication competence. Context is particularly important to our study of language in three ways: language reflects, builds on, and determines context.

▶ *Language reflects context.* The language we use reflects who we're around, where we are, and what sort of cultural factors are at play—that is, the context we're in. In different contexts, we use different **speech repertoires**—sets of complex language styles, behaviors, and skills that we have learned. Recall from the beginning of this chapter that we need to "accommodate" our communication (that is, adjust our way of speaking with other people). Having several speech repertoires at our disposal allows us to choose the most effective and appropriate way of speaking for a given relationship, situation, or cultural environment.

▶ *Language builds on context.* At the beginning of this chapter, we wondered about the difference between calling your stepmother "Mom" versus calling her by her first name. It's an example of language building on context. If your stepmother raised you and is your primary maternal figure, you might well call her "Mom." But if your relationship with her is strained, you are close to your own biological or adopted mother, or your stepmother entered your life once you were an adult, you may prefer to call her by her name. As you develop relationships, you learn how people prefer to be addressed (and how you are comfortable addressing them), and you adjust your language accordingly.

▶ *Language determines context.* We can also *create* context by the language we use. If your professor says, "Call me Veronica," one context is created (informal, first-name basis, more equal). If she says, "I'm Dr. Esquivel," you will likely have expectations for a more formal context (less personal, less equal). This context will then influence your choice of speech repertoires—you're more likely to tell "Veronica" about your weekend plans than "Dr. Esquivel."

With these points in mind, let's consider how language works in different situations, in our relationships, and in our cultures, as well as in mediated settings.

Situational Context

Different situations (being at a job interview, in a court of law, or at your Uncle Fred's sixtieth birthday party) call for different speech repertoires. **Code switching** is a type of accommodation in which communicators change from one repertoire or "code" to another as the situation warrants. The language you speak is one type of code. If you speak both English and Spanish, for example, you might speak English in the classroom or on the job but switch to Spanish with your family at home because it creates a special bond between family members (Gudykunst, 2004).

Another type of code that you may switch is the linguistic style—the use of slang, jargon, and grammar—that allows you to fit in with a particular group. These language accommodations may be ways to survive, to manage defensiveness, to manage identity, or to signal power or status in different situations (Dragojevic, Giles, & Watson, 2013). For instance, police officers use this type of accommodation when they adopt the street slang or foreign phrases used by citizens in the

AND YOU?

Consider the various situations you find yourself in over the course of a given day—at home, in the classroom, at a student activity, on the job, and so on. Do you have different speech repertoires for each situation? Does your language change further depending on who is present—your mother, your best friend, your professor?

COMMUNICATIONACROSSCULTURES

Teaching Twain

It is considered a classic of American literature, a truly groundbreaking novel that thumbed its nose at convention when it was published in 1885 and continues to challenge ideas about race, relationships, and language more than a century later.

At a time when respectable books were written in upper-middle-class English—and when slavery was still fresh in American memory—Mark Twain's *Adventures of Huckleberry Finn* told the story of the unlikely relationship between a free-spirited white boy and a fugitive slave, Jim, in everyday language. Twain carefully constructed Jim and Huck's conversations with words, inflections, and phonetic spellings that can shock modern readers. Most notably, Twain uses the "N-word" over two hundred times.

The book itself remains controversial as scholars and critics continue to argue about Twain's characters. It is consistently at or near the top of the American Library Association's annual list of books banned or challenged by parents or school boards. John Wallace, a former public school administrator, calls it "racist trash" and says that its use of the N-word is offensive, no matter what the context or how teachers try to explain it (D. L. Howard, 2004). Yet others come to the book's defense, noting that it was written as satire and that Twain's intention was "to subvert, not reinforce, racism" (Kennedy, 2003, p. 108). Temple University professor David Bradley notes that the word must be taken in the context of the times and situation: "What was Twain supposed to do, call them African-Americans?" (Rabinowitz, 1995, para. 16).

Teachers of American literature often find themselves struggling with self-censorship as they grapple with whether or not to speak the word aloud in class, since it may cause students to feel hurt and offended. This was certainly the case for Professor Alan Gribben of Auburn University at Montgomery, who created a revised edition of the work that replaces the N-word with the word *slave*. Professor Gribben explains: "I'm by no means sanitizing Mark Twain. The sharp social critiques are in there. The humor is intact. I just had the idea to get us away from obsessing about this one word, and just let the stories stand alone" (quoted in Bosman, 2011, para. 2). But critics passionately disagree, accusing Professor Gribben's publisher of censorship and sanitizing history. Author Jill Nelson notes that changing Twain's carefully chosen words to suit contemporary mores and eliminate hurt feelings "is an abdication of a teacher's responsibility to illuminate and guide students through an unfamiliar and perhaps difficult text" (Nelson, 2011, para. 3).

THINK ABOUT THIS

1 What meaning does the N-word carry for you? Does it seem appropriate to use it in a scholarly discussion? How do you feel about it being printed (or not printed) in this textbook? Does avoiding printing or saying the word give it more or less power?

2 If an instructor chose to use the word in class, how might he or she do so in a way that would be sensitive to students? Can students investigate the word's meaning and history without using it?

3 What is your opinion on Gribben's new edition? Are his editorial changes sensitive and helpful, or is he sanitizing history?

neighborhoods they patrol and when they use more formal, bureaucratic language when interacting with superiors, filling out reports, or testifying in court.

Similarly, you might decide to use **high language**—a more formal, polite, or "mainstream" language—in business contexts, in the classroom, and in formal social gatherings (as when trying to impress the parents of your new romantic interest). However, you would probably switch to more informal, easygoing **low language** (often involving slang) when you're in more casual or comfortable environments, such as watching a football game at a sports bar with your friends.

● **THE FORMAL,** high language that this young woman employs while at work with her colleagues differs from the more casual, low language that she probably uses when relaxing at home or socializing with friends. Ronnie Kaufman/Larry Hirshowitz/Blend Images/Getty Images

Our sex and gender can interact with the situation to affect our language use. For example, women and men adapt their language use to same-sex versus mixed-sex situations. When women speak with other women, they tend to discuss relationships and use words that are more affection-oriented (concerned with feelings, values, and attitudes). Men chatting with other men use more instrumentally oriented language (concerned with doing things and accomplishing tasks) (Reis, 1998). Gender also comes into play in workplace situations. Occupations that have been traditionally defined as "masculine" or "feminine" often develop a job culture and language that follow suit. Male nursery school teachers (a traditionally "feminine job") and fathers doing primary childcare may use feminine language at work; female police officers (a traditionally "masculine" job) may adopt more masculine language on patrol (Winter & Pauwels, 2006).

But as we've learned, competent communicators use the most effective and appropriate ways of interacting in a given situation. That may mean putting aside gendered speech "appropriate" for our sex. For instance, a successful male manager uses language that reflects liking and respect when building relationships in the workplace, and a successful female manager uses direct language to clarify instructions for completing an important task (Bates, 1988).

Relational Context

● **IN** *THE HELP,* Aibleen, played by Octavia Spencer, uses language to show the relationship between herself and her employer in 1960's Mississippi. Dale Robinette/© Walt Disney Studios Motion Pictures/Courtesy Everett Collection

Kathryn Stockett's bestseller *The Help* (2009), along with the 2011 film adaptation, is a fascinating representation of the relationships between black domestic servants and their white employers in Mississippi in the early 1960s. The dialogues (told in different voices) ring true because they reflect the relationships between and among women of different races, social classes, and experiences.

We all choose different language to communicate in different relationships: you don't speak to your grandmother the way you speak to your best friend, and we (college professors) don't speak to our students the way we speak to our colleagues. That's because language both reflects and creates the relational context. Let's consider some examples.

Michelle and Chris have been dating for a few weeks. After a movie one night, they run into one of Chris's colleagues. When Chris introduces Michelle as his *girlfriend*, Michelle is surprised. She hadn't thought of their relationship as being that serious yet. The English language allows us to communicate the status of many of our relationships quite clearly: mother, brother, aunt, grandfather, daughter, and so on. But as with the word *partner*, the language we use when communicating about other types of relationships can be confusing. Chris and Michelle are in the somewhat undefined state of "dating." When Chris uses the term *girlfriend* as a label for Michelle, this implies a more defined level of intimacy that Michelle isn't yet sure she feels. Chris certainly had other options, but each has its own issues. For example, if Chris had said that Michelle is a *friend*, it might have implied a lack of romantic interest (and might have hurt Michelle's feelings). The fact is the English language has very few terms to describe different levels of intimacy we have with friends and romantic partners (Bradac, 1983; Stollen & White, 2004).

Labels can also confer status and create understandings between and among individuals. If you say, "I'd like you to meet my boss, Edward Sanchez," you are describing both Mr. Sanchez's status and the professional relationship that you have with him; it tells others what language is appropriate in front of him. To indicate a more casual relationship, you might introduce him as, "Ed—we work together at Kohl's."

Cultural Context

Throughout this book, we remind you about the relationship between culture and communication (particularly in Chapter 5). Next we examine particular aspects of how the cultural context shapes our language, including the relationship among culture, words, and thoughts; the relationship between gender and language; and the impact of our region (where we grew up or where we live now) on our verbal choices.

Culture, Words, and Thought

As we have seen, our language use can affect our thoughts. Consider a study of the Pirahã tribe of Brazil (Gordon, 2004). The study shows that the Pirahã language does not have words for numbers above two—anything above two is simply called "many." When researchers laid a random number of familiar objects (like sticks and nuts) in a row, and asked the Pirahã to lay out the same number of objects in their own pile, tribe members were able to match the pile if there were three or fewer objects. But for numbers above three, they would only approximately match the pile, becoming less and less accurate as the number of objects increased. In addition, when researchers asked them to copy taps on the floor, the Pirahã did not copy the behavior beyond three taps. Researchers concluded that the limitation of words for numbers above two prevented the Pirahã from perceiving larger numbers (Biever, 2004).

The study's findings support the **Sapir-Whorf hypothesis** (also known as linguistic relativity theory), which holds that the words a culture uses (or doesn't use) influence the thinking of people from that culture (Sapir & Whorf, 1956). In other words, if a culture lacks a word for something (as the Pirahã lack words for higher numbers), members of that culture will have few thoughts about that thing or concept. Thus language influences or determines how we see the world around us, and speakers of different languages develop different views of the world relative to their language. For example, some languages (like Spanish, French, and German) assign a gender to objects. This is a bit of a foreign concept to many native speakers of English because English is gender-neutral—English speakers

AND YOU?

How do you label your romantic partner? Do you use different terms around different people in different situations? How do the terms you choose for each other affect your understanding of the status of the relationship?

CONNECT

The different language we use in different relationships is often affected by unique *communication climates* or atmospheres that encompass relationships. This is certainly true when experiencing interpersonal conflict (Chapter 8). For example, if you and your brother experience a *supportive climate*, your conflicts will likely be characterized by careful, considerate words and an openness to hearing each other's thoughts.

real communicator

NAME: Matt Burgess
OCCUPATION: Author and Creative Writing Instructor

The use of language has always been fascinating to me. When my first novel (*Dogfight: A Love Story*) was published, reviewers said I had an incredible ear for dialogue and the "poetry" of the street. I was flattered to have succeeded at putting the vivid language of my New York City neighborhood onto the printed page.

When I began writing stories in college, I used the more sophisticated terminology of my professors and student peers. But back home in Queens, I felt uncomfortable—almost guilty—using the high language of that urbane, professional context. Then I realized there was no reason to be anxious; the language of different economic, social, and cultural groups is rich with meaning. I really believe that this conscious decision helped my fiction become more realistic and reflective of the worlds around me. For example, when I try to capture the conversations in bodegas, bowling alleys, and barbershops, I use the casual, low language so familiar to me; it's filled with the slang, neighborhood references, and good-humored insults that I grew up around. Nonverbal communication is important to capture, too. Some people deliver an insult with a wink, smile, or vocal tone that expresses love and changes the literal meaning of the words spoken.

Precise language is important to my writing as well. For example, I avoid clichés and highly abstract language. If you say something happened "out of the blue," you don't really mean something came out of a color; this is a lazy language choice. Rather, I use precise words for clarity and interest: "She showed signs of satisfaction as she took possession of her reward" transforms into "Gilda grinned as she snatched the coin." (On a personal note, precise language is important in my marriage, too. When my wife says, "I particularly enjoyed the curry dish you spent an hour making tonight," I appreciate it even more than when she just says, "Thanks for fixing dinner.")

In addition to working on my second novel, I teach creative writing courses to both traditional students and older adults. One of my goals is to help them find their own unique voice as writers to say what they mean accurately and precisely while utilizing the unique words and speaking styles comfortable and familiar to them. This journey with language has been deeply rewarding to me and enriches my life. My hope as an author and teacher is that my readers and students will be able to say the same.

simply say *the shoe* whereas a Spanish speaker marks the word as masculine (*el zapato, el* being the masculine article); a French speaker marks the word as feminine (*la chaussure, la* being the feminine article). Marking an object as masculine or feminine changes a speaker's mental picture of the object. For example, German speakers describe a key (a masculine word in German) in traditionally masculine terms (*hard, heavy, jagged, metal, serrated,* and *useful*) whereas Spanish speakers describe a key (a feminine word in Spanish) in traditionally feminine terms (*golden, intricate, little, lovely, shiny,* and *tiny*) (Wasserman & Weseley, 2009).

Gender and Language

Cultural factors deeply affect our thinking and perception of gender roles, which are often inscribed with "different languages" for the masculine and the feminine (Gudykunst & Ting-Toomey, 1988). The idea that men and women speak entirely different languages is popular fodder for comedy, talk shows, and pop psychologists, so let's identify what actual differences have contributed to that view.

Women primarily see conversations as negotiations for closeness and connection with others, whereas men experience talk more as a struggle for control, independence, and hierarchy (Tannen, 1992). But either may use powerful, controlling language to define limits, authority, and relationships and less controlling language to express affection. Let's look at a few examples.

▶ *Interruptions.* Male speakers are thought to interrupt others in conversation more than female speakers, but the situation and the status of the speakers are better predictors than biological sex (Pearson, Turner, & Todd-Mancillas, 1991). For example, female professors can be expected to interrupt male students more often than those male students interrupt female professors, owing to the difference in power and status. But when status and situation are neutral, men tend to interrupt women considerably more often than women interrupt men (Ivy & Backlund, 2004).

▶ *Intensifiers.* Women's speech patterns, compared with men's, contain more words that heighten or intensify topics: ("so excited," "*very* happy") (Yaguchi, Iyeiri, & Baba, 2010). Consider the intensity level of "I'm upset" versus "I'm *really* upset."

▶ *Qualifiers, hedges, and disclaimers.* Language that sounds hesitant is perceived as being less powerful (often associated with women's speech). *Qualifiers* include terms like *kind of, sort of, maybe*, and *possibly.* *Hedges* are expressions such as "I think," "I feel," or "I guess." *Disclaimers* discount what you are about to say and can head off confrontation or avoid embarrassment: "I'm likely imagining things, but I thought I saw . . ." (Palomares, 2009).

▶ *Tag questions.* Another sign of hesitancy or uncertainty associated with feminine speech is the *tag question*, as in "That waitress was obnoxious, wasn't she?" Tag questions attempt to get your conversational partner to agree with you, establishing a connection based on similar opinions. They can also come across as threats (Ivy & Backlund, 2004); for example, "You're not going to smoke another cigarette, *are you*?"

▶ *Resistance messages.* Differences in the way men and women express resistance can have serious consequences. Specifically, date rape awareness programs advise women to use the word *no* when a male partner or friend makes an unwanted sexual advance. But a woman might instead say, "I don't have protection," choosing vague or evasive language over the direct *no* to avoid a scene. Men, however, sometimes perceive an indirect denial as a yes. Women's use of clear messages, coupled with men's increased understanding of women's preference for more indirect resistance messages, can lead to more competent communication in this crucial area (Lim & Roloff, 1999; Motley & Reeder, 1995).

CONNECT

Gendered language often affects mixed-sex small group settings. Women are typically encouraged to build rapport, using affectionate language to keep the peace and share power (Chapters 3 and 9). Men are rewarded for taking charge of a group and using direct, action-oriented language. Competent communicators must be aware of these differences in style and must promote group communication that encourages all members to share and challenge ideas in order to achieve group goals.

AND YOU?

What are your personal thoughts on sex, gender, and language? Do you think men and women speak different languages, or do you feel that we all speak more similarly than differently? How do your thoughts and opinions match up with the research we've cited in this chapter?

In summary, research has corroborated some differences in communication style due to sex (Kiesling, 1998), but many of those differences pale when we consider *gender* (the cultural meaning of sex), context, role, and task (Ewald, 2010; Mulac, Wiemann, Widenmann, & Gibson, 1988; Newman, Groom, Handelman, & Pennebaker, 2008). Relatedly, studying language from a sex-difference approach can be misleading, because it treats women (and men) as a homogenous "global category," paying little attention to differences in ethnicity, religion, sexuality, and economic status (Crawford, 1995). In fact, recent studies focus on how we present our different "faces" in interaction (Tannen, 2009, 2010) and how language choices are more about negotiating influence (power, hierarchy), solidarity (connection, intimacy), value formation, and identity rather than about sex (Tannen, Kendall, & Gorgon, 2007). Decades of research find that we are less bound by our sex than we are by the language choices we make. Thus, regardless of whether we are male or female, we can choose to use language that gives us more influence or creates more connection—or both.

Geography

Our editor from New Jersey assures us that even in such a small state, it makes a big difference if you are from North Jersey or South Jersey. (The status of people from the middle part of the state remains unclear, at least to us.) People in North Jersey eat subs (sandwiches that you buy at 7-Eleven or QuickChek) and Italian ice (a frozen dessert). The night before Halloween, when shaving cream and toilet paper abound, is Goosey Night or Cabbage Night. And "the city" is, of course, New York City. People from South Jersey eat hoagies (typically from a convenience store called Wawa) and water ice. The night before Halloween is Mischief Night. And going to "the city" means taking a trip to Philadelphia.

As this example illustrates, even for speakers of the same language who grow up just fifty miles apart, culture affects their language and their understanding of the world. Other examples are more extreme. Consider our friend Ada, who kindly shared an embarrassing moment with us (and is allowing us to tell you). When she came to the United States from Hong Kong, she knew she had to give up some of her Britishisms to communicate more effectively with her American-born classmates at Wesleyan University. This was never more apparent than when she asked a classmate for a rubber (to correct some mistakes in her notebook). She wanted an eraser; he thought she was asking for a condom. Needless to say, she was a bit perplexed by his response: "Maybe after class?"

AND YOU?

Think back to where you grew up—whether in the United States or abroad. Are there any terms that you use that would cause confusion to others who speak your native tongue? Have you ever been in a situation where you've used a regional term that caused an embarrassing miscommunication?

● **IS THIS A SUB** or a hoagie? Perhaps a hero or just a plain old sandwich?
© Foodcollection.com/Alamy

Mediated Contexts

Have you ever sent an e-mail or a text message that was misunderstood by the recipient? It has happened to all of us—and that's often because our e-mails, text messages, tweets, and wall postings lack the nonverbal cues and hints we provide in face-to-face conversation. So if you text your spouse to say that you both have to spend Friday night with your slightly quirky Aunt Ethel, and he texts you back "Great," is he really excited? Is he being sarcastic? "Great" could mean either thing, but you can't see his nonverbal reaction to know if he's smiling or grimacing and rolling his eyes. That's why communication in mediated contexts must be extra clear to be effective (DeAndrea & Walther, 2011).

Other characteristics of our online language can also influence communication. For example, people in computer-mediated groups who use powerful language, such as direct statements of their personal goals, are seen as more credible, attractive, and persuasive than those who use tentative language (hedges, disclaimers, and tag questions) (Adkins & Brashers, 1995). However, group-oriented language can be more persuasive and effective than language pushing personal goals. For example, one study of an international adolescent online forum found that students who were elected as "leaders" (Cassell, Huffaker, Tversky, & Ferriman, 2006) made references to group goals and synthesized other students' posts.

Interestingly, sex and gender can influence the language you use with technology. In online games, for example, people who were assigned avatars of their own gender were more likely to use gender-typical language (more emotional expressions and tentative language if assigned a feminine avatar) than those assigned mismatched avatars (Palomares & Lee, 2010). Another study found that people infer a person's sex from language cues online (for example, amount of self-disclosure, expression of emotion) and conform more to computer-mediated partners when they believe them to be male (Lee, 2007).

But technology affects language use in broader ways as well, including the proliferation of English as the language of the Internet. Individuals in Salt Lake City, São Paulo, and Stockholm can all communicate digitally, often in English. Critics often claim that because English dominates the mass media industries, English speakers' values and thinking are being imposed on the non-English-speaking world. Nevertheless, many non-Western countries have benefited from this proliferation, with countless jobs being relocated to places like India and Hong Kong (Friedman, 2007). Every day brings increasing language diversity to the Internet, and Internet-based translators make it much easier to translate material into innumerable languages (Danet & Herring, 2007).

● **TEXTING YOUR FRIEND** "Coffee?" is a perfect way to schedule a quick get-together, but if you're asking your professor to meet over a cup for career advice, it'd be smart to send a more formal email. Blend Images/Veer

Beliefs About "Talk"

As you've seen in this chapter, individuals value language as a way to gain control in conversations, to share information, express feelings, be creative, and so on. Others, however, are more comfortable with fewer words, even silence.

Complete the following questionnaire about your own beliefs about talking and language use, and rate the frequency that you engage in each behavior. Use the following scale: 5 = almost always; 4 = frequently; 3 = sometimes; 2 = not very often; and 1 = rarely. Then add your scores and consider where you fall on the following continuum.

_____ 1. I enjoy meeting and talking with people.

_____ 2. In general, I consider myself quite a talker.

_____ 3. I don't mind initiating conversations with strangers.

_____ 4. I like to voice my opinion.

_____ 5. In general, I enjoy talking.

_____ 6. I enjoy small talk.

_____ 7. I like people who talk a lot.

_____ 8. When talking, I find myself trying to influence others' opinions and feelings.

_____ 9. I believe talk is one way to increase intimacy.

_____ 10. Small talk is an enjoyable use of time.

_____ 11. I don't mind taking responsibility for breaking the ice when meeting someone for the first time.

_____ 12. I talk more when I feel I'm in control of a situation.

_____ 13. I feel uncomfortable with silences in a conversation.

_____ 14. In general, I like to be the first one to speak in a discussion.

_____ 15. I feel comfortable asking a stranger for information.

_____ 16. When in a discussion, I talk even if I'm unfamiliar with the topic.

_____ 17. I enjoy going out to meet and talk with people.

_____ 18. I find myself turning on the radio or TV just to hear the sound of someone's voice.

67–90: You enjoy and value talk and are not apprehensive about talking; you see talking as a social experience and, as a rule, you are uncomfortable with silence.

43–66: You have a more measured approach to talk, using it to accomplish goals and meet the norms of the situation. You are comfortable with silence and more likely to adjust your rate of talking to that of your partner(s).

18–42: You do not enjoy a lot of talk and prefer to use it with a purpose in mind. Silence is comfortable for you and you do not rush to fill it with words.

Note: Different cultures value talk in different ways (see Chapter 5), so it might be important for you to adapt your use of language or silence according to the situation. In addition, competent communicators remember that being appropriate and effective means talking up at times, being sociable with talk, but also knowing when to be quiet and let others talk.

Source: Adapted from Honeycutt & Wiemann (1999) and Wiemann, Chen, & Giles (1986).

Despite the controversies surrounding English, the Internet, and mass media, technology has, in some sense, created a language of its own. The language of text messaging and chat rooms frequently relies on acronyms (for example, IMO for "in my opinion"), some of which people use in other contexts and some of which has even made it into the *Oxford English Dictionary* (Editorial, 2011). Acronyms are useful in texting because they enable rapid keystroking, resulting in speed that makes this "fingered speech" more like spoken language (McWhorter, 2013). However, it's important to keep text language in its appropriate context. If your professor writes you an e-mail asking about your recent absences from class, it's probably not a good idea to respond with "NOYB, IMHO" ("none of your business, in my humble opinion"). That would show not only a lack of respect for your instructor (obviously) but also a lack of understanding regarding context. E-mail etiquette calls for more complete sentences.

BACK TO ▶ Our Partners

Our discussion of the word *partner* and its various meanings showed that the labels we choose are powerful—and can complicate our communication.

▶ The word *partner* has several denotative meanings, as we discussed earlier. But it can also have powerful connotative meanings. Let's look at romantic couples who choose the term *partner*. When some people hear an individual refer to his or her "partner," they may assume the individual is gay or lesbian. And they may have positive, negative, or neutral reactions based on their cultural background. Others may wonder if the individual is trying to hide his or her marital or legal status. Still others may see *partner* as a term that marks equality in romantic relationships.

▶ Abstraction plays an important role in the use of the term *partner*. Saying "This is my boyfriend" or "This is my business partner" is a low-level abstraction, offering others a clear definition of your status. But the term *partner* is a high-level abstraction, keeping your status and relationship considerably more vague.

▶ Considering the relational, situational, and cultural context is one way to make the term *partner* less abstract and vague. If you let your chemistry professor know that your "partner" needs some help with an experiment, the instructor understands that you mean your lab partner rather than your romantic partner or the person you play tennis with. Similarly, when introducing the love of your life to your elderly great-aunt, you might want to use a less ambiguous term. Your great-aunt may be of a generation that did not use the term *partner* to apply to a love interest.

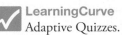 **Activities**

1. LaunchPad for *Real Communication* offers key term videos and encourages self-assessment through adaptive quizzing. Go to **bedfordstmartins.com/realcomm** to get access to:

✓ **LearningCurve**
Adaptive Quizzes.

▶ Video clips that illustrate key concepts, highlighted in teal in the Real Reference section that follows.

2. Take a look at a piece of writing you've produced (an essay, your résumé, or a private Facebook message to a friend). Do you use high or low levels of abstraction? Is your choice of language appropriate for the communication contexts involved? (For example, is your essay written in a way that is mindful of your relationship with your professor and the academic setting?)

3. Describe the similarities and differences you find in the language you use and the language a close friend or family member of the opposite sex uses over the course of a single conversation. What did you notice? Were there any misunderstandings or power struggles in this conversation? How do your findings match up with what the research we presented tells us?

4. Examine the language you use in mediated communication. Are there subtle ways in which you and your communication partners negotiate influence and create connectedness? Are any language choices related to sex or gender? What differences do you find in the language you use in mediated contexts from the language you use in face-to-face contexts?

5. Make a study of your Facebook (or other social networking) pages. Compile a list of the types of language used, including acronyms. Do you ever misunderstand the language in posts from your friends? Have you ever used language that was misinterpreted? Are you ever offended by the posts or "shares" of your friends? Describe how you could post in the future to avoid problems due to language.

Now that you have finished reading this chapter, you can:

Describe the power of **language**—the system of symbols we use to think about and communicate experiences and feelings:

▶ Words are symbols that have meanings agreed to by speakers of a language (p. 66).

▶ **Cognitive language** is what you use to describe people, things, and situations in your mind (p. 67).

▶ Correct **grammar**, the rules of a language, helps ensure clarity (p. 67).

▶ **Communication accommodation theory** illustrates how people should adapt their language and nonverbal behaviors to the person, group, or context (p. 68).

▶ Learning words and how to use them effectively is the process of **communication acquisition** (p. 68).

Identify how language helps people communicate—the five functional communication competencies:

▶ As an instrument of control (p. 69).

▶ For **informing**, including four aspects: questioning, describing, reinforcing, and withholding (p. 69).

▶ For expressing **feelings** to let people know how we value them (p. 70).

▶ For **imagining**, communicating a creative idea (p. 71).

▶ For **ritualizing**, managing conversations and relationships (p. 71).

Describe the ways that communicators create meaning with language:

▶ **Semantics** refers to the meaning that words have; **pragmatics** refers to the ability to use them appropriately (p. 72).

▶ A **denotative meaning** is the accepted definition of a word; its **connotative meaning** is the emotional or attitudinal response to it (p. 72).

▶ The **abstraction ladder** ranks communication from specific, which ensures clarity, to general and vague (p. 73).

▶ Some communication situations may call for abstractions: **evasion**, avoiding specifics; **equivocation**, using unclear terms; or **euphemisms**, using substitutions for possibly upsetting terms (p. 74).

▶ **Slang** is a group's informal language; **jargon** is a group's technical language (p. 74).

Label problematic uses of language and their remedies:

▶ **Hatespeech** is language that offends, threatens, or insults a person or group based on race, color, gender, or other identifiable characteristics (p. 76) whereas **hurtful language** includes words or expressions that are considered inappropriate, pretentious, damaging, mean, sarcastic, or offensive to others (p. 76).

▶ We ignore individual differences when we place gender, ethnic, or other role labels on people (pp. 76–77).

▶ **Biased language** has subtle meanings that influence perception negatively (pp. 77–78); using **politically correct language** attempts to meet culturally appropriate norms (p. 78).

▶ **Profanity** involves expressions that are considered insulting, rude, vulgar, or disrespectful (p. 79).

▶ **Civility** involves language that meets socially appropriate norms (p. 79).

Describe how language reflects, builds on, and determines context:

▶ We use different **speech repertoires** to find the most effective language for a given situation (p. 80).

▶ **Code switching** is a type of accommodation in which communicators change from one repertoire or "code" to another as the situation warrants (p. 80).

▶ **High language** is a more formal, polite, or "mainstream" language (p. 81).

▶ **Low language** is more informal and often involves slang (p. 81).

▶ We use language to create or reflect the context of a relationship (pp. 82–83).

▶ The **Sapir-Whorf hypothesis** (or linguistic relativity theory) suggests that our words influence our thinking (p. 83) by shaping or determining how we see the world; thus, speakers of different languages have different views of the world (p. 83).

▶ Although assuming that there are gender differences in communication can be misleading, some differences in masculine and feminine language exist. The use of interruptions, intensifiers, qualifiers, hedges, disclaimers, tag questions and resistance messages is linked with feminine versus masculine speech patterns (p. 85).

▶ The culture of the geographical area affects language (p. 86).

▶ Although communication technology has made English the dominant world language and has created a global society, the Internet also continues to create a language of its own (p. 87).

No dialogue is needed to convey Carl and Ellie's love for each other. MCD©Walt Disney Co./courtesy Everett Collection

LearningCurve can help you master the material in this chapter.
Go to bedfordstmartins.com/realcomm.

Nonverbal Communication

Can you tell a compelling, believable, and heartwarming love story in just four minutes—without using any words? The Academy Award–nominated *Up* does just that (Docter & Peterson, 2009). After opening with a simple meet-cute between young, quiet Carl and adventurous, talkative Ellie, the sequence that follows offers a montage of life moments, explained simply and graphically: they express affection by holding hands and devotion by the cross-my-heart gesture of their childhood. Their dreams of children are symbolized in visions of baby-shaped clouds, and as those dreams are crushed, their grief is conveyed by Ellie's silent sobs and Carl's quiet gestures of comfort. As the years go by, their plans to travel are shown with paintings and brochures; the financial struggles that thwart them are explained in tiny vignettes that detail home repairs, car troubles, and medical bills. Relying entirely on nonverbal behaviors—beautifully crafted and rendered by the artists at Pixar Studios—and set to a mesmerizing musical score, the sequence manages to clearly convey the events and emotions that shaped these two characters' decades-long romance, as well as Carl's loneliness and isolation after Ellie's death, without a word of dialogue.

The filmmakers at Pixar were no strangers to near "silent" films—their previous offering, the equally stunning and compelling *WALL-E*, included virtually no dialogue for the first forty minutes, in what the British newspaper *The Independent* called "a masterclass in non-verbal communication" (Quinn, 2008, para. 7). During those scenes, the film not only managed to create compelling characters out of a pair of robots and a lone, unspeaking cockroach, but also to explain a fairly complicated story line of environmental devastation in a simple, accessible way.

Telling a story on screen is complicated because filmmaking encompasses nonverbal performances (be it from actors or from animators). These performances include the visual choices made by the artists and directors, from colors used in a scene's background to the characters' clothing. For animators like the team at Pixar, the challenge is even more daunting. They must make inhuman objects—whether computer-generated "people" like Carl and Ellie, monsters like Mike Wazowski from *Monster's University*, or robots (or fish, toys, or insects)—into believable, humanlike characters who can effectively communicate complex information and emotions.

Likewise, in real life, we communicate with many tools other than language. In this chapter, we examine **nonverbal communication**—the process of intentionally or unintentionally signaling meaning through behavior other than words (Knapp & Hall, 2010). This definition encompasses a variety of actions, such as gestures, tone of voice, and eye behavior, as well as all aspects of physical appearance. We begin by examining the nature and functions of nonverbal communication. Then we move to the nonverbal codes that convey messages without words and conclude with an examination of important influences on nonverbal communication.

The Nature of Nonverbal Communication

A deaf woman signs a message to a companion. A colleague writes a note to you on a pad of paper during a boring meeting. A man taps his watch to signal to a friend that it's almost time for lunch. In all three instances, communication occurs without a word being spoken. But not all of all these examples are actually nonverbal communication. Studying the essential nature of nonverbal communication reveals why.

Nonverbal Behavior Is Communicative

You communicate nonverbally when you convey a message without using any words. But you also communicate nonverbally when you use nonverbal behaviors *in addition* to words: when you smile, frown, or gesture as you speak or when you use a particular tone or volume while talking (Giles & LePoire, 2006). For example, as a kid, maybe you knew when your parents were angry with you because they called you by your full name while using "that tone."

Consider the examples we gave above. American Sign Language (ASL), a visual language with its own grammatical structure used by hearing-impaired individuals in the United States and English-speaking Canada, is still verbal communication. It may be *nonvocal*, because the communicators don't use their voices. However, it is still a language, because it uses hand signals (rather than spoken words) as symbols and it has grammatical rules. The note that your colleague writes to you uses words, so it too is a form of verbal communication (written rather than spoken). Only the third example is nonverbal communication—tapping a watch signals meaning without use of linguistic symbols. Yet this example reminds us that nonverbal behavior and verbal communication are connected. Had the friends not made a verbal agreement to meet for lunch, the act of tapping the watch might be confusing.

Nonverbal Communication Is Often Spontaneous and Unintentional

The best poker players think a great deal about nonverbal communication. They know how to bluff, or convince their opponents that they are holding a better (or worse) hand than is actually the case. A player who figures out an opponent's "tell"—a nonverbal signal indicating a good or bad hand—can profit from this knowledge if he, quite literally, plays his cards right. Mike Caro, a poker professional and author of *The Body Language of Poker*, warns players not to look at the cards as they are laid out on the table. Players who look away from "the flop" have a strong hand, he explains. Those who stare at it—or at their cards—have a weak one. He also advises players to memorize their hand so opponents won't see them looking at their cards and glean cues from this action (Zimbushka, 2008).

Like poker players, we often send nonverbal messages unintentionally—we roll our eyes, laugh, slouch, or blush without meaning to. And our nonverbal behaviors can send powerful, unintended messages without us having much time to think through them (Capella & Greene, 1982). Great poker players know that they can't completely eliminate such behaviors. That's why many of them wear sunglasses while playing: they want to mask their eyes so their opponents can't pick up subtle and unintentional cues from their eye movements.

Nonverbal Communication Is Ambiguous

Professional players like Caro might have a system for reading nonverbal behaviors, but even they know that it's more of an art than a science. That's because nonverbal communication is inherently ambiguous. Blinking, stammering, or hesitations in speech can indicate deception. But they can also indicate anxiety or uncertainty. In many cases, you can pick up clues about the meaning of behavior from the situational context. If your friend is sighing deeply and blinking rapidly as she heads off to her biochemistry final exam, she's probably anxious. But you can't know for sure. Perhaps her boyfriend broke up with her

You make sense of your world and decode nonverbal behavior through *schemas*, your accumulated experience of people, roles, and situations (Chapter 2). So if you catch your friend in a lie, you might suspect, on the basis of your relational history, that whenever he avoids eye contact with you, he's lying. But competent communicators must think beyond schemas when determining the meaning of nonverbal communication.

● **DOES THIS CARD PLAYER** have a good or bad hand? Who knows? His poker face reveals nothing. Pablo Blazquez Dominguez/Getty Images

twenty minutes ago and she just doesn't feel like talking about it. For this reason, it's best to regard nonverbal behavior (and poker "tells") as cues to be checked out rather than as facts.

Nonverbal Communication Is More Believable Than Verbal Communication

Imagine you're grabbing lunch with your brother, talking a mile a minute about your exciting plans for after graduation. He's staring off into space. You wonder if you're boring him. But when you look closer, you notice that his face is ashen, he isn't making eye contact with you, and he hasn't shaved in a few days. You pause and ask, "Hey, is everything OK with you? You seem . . . not yourself." Your brother looks up somewhat startled, tries to smile, and says, "What? Oh! Yes, everything's great."

You've just experienced **channel discrepancy**, a situation in which one set of behaviors says one thing and another set says something different. In this case, your brother's verbal communication says he is fine, but his nonverbal communication says he is not fine at all. So which message do you believe? In most cases, you'll believe the nonverbal message. Like most of us, you assume your brother has less control over his nonverbal behaviors, so they are more "reliable" indicators of how he is feeling. Research supports your assumption. Studies show that we tend to give more weight to nonverbal behavior than to verbal behavior when we

▶ express spontaneous feelings (such as crying) (Burgoon & Hoobler, 2002)

▶ assess others' motives (as in deception) (Burgoon, Blair, & Strom, 2008)

▶ express rapport with others (for example, show liking) (Hullman, Goodnight, & Mougeotte, 2012)

▶ figure out others' meanings when there are few other behaviors to observe (Grahe & Bernieri, 1999; Knapp & Hall, 2010)

However, just because we tend to place more stock in nonverbal communication doesn't mean that we always interpret that communication accurately. Your brother might be fine, just as he says he is. Perhaps he is growing a "playoff beard" along with the rest of his hockey team and is thinking about the next day's game rather than listening to you talk about your plans. Even when we know others very well, we often fail to detect deception or read their nonverbal behaviors accurately (Knapp & Hall, 2010; Van Swol, Malhotr, & Braun, 2012; Vrij, 2006).

Functions of Nonverbal Communication

Now that we've established the essential nature of nonverbal communication, we can discuss how it helps us interact effectively in relationships. It's impossible to discuss every purpose that nonverbal behaviors serve, but next we highlight the most important ways that nonverbal behaviors work on their own—and in combination with verbal behaviors—to affect communication (Burgoon, Floyd, & Guerrero, 2010).

Reinforcing Verbal Messages

Nonverbal behavior clarifies meaning by reinforcing verbal messages in three ways: repeating, complementing, and accenting. **Repeating** mirrors the verbal message through a clear nonverbal cue that represents the exact same idea. For example, you hold up three fingers while saying "three" or shake your head at a toddler while saying "no." You can also reinforce verbal messages with **complementing**, nonverbal behavior that is consistent with the verbal message and often enhances it. For example, when you pat a friend on the back while saying, "You did a great job," you reinforce the message that your friend has done well.

Nonverbal behaviors are also used for **accenting**, or clarifying and emphasizing specific information in a verbal message. For example, suppose you want your friend to meet you at a local pub at 6 P.M. You can make eye contact as you talk (indicating that you are monitoring your friend's attention level) and touch the friend lightly on the forearm as you mention the pub on State Street ("Do you know the one I mean?").

Substituting Verbal Messages

Nonverbal cues can substitute for words. For example, a traffic officer's outstretched palm substitutes for the word *stop*. **Substituting** is common in situations where words are unavailable (communicating with someone who speaks a different language) or when speaking aloud would be inappropriate (at the symphony or during a religious service). Substitution cues signal information you'd rather not say aloud (raising your eyebrows at your partner to signal you want to leave a party) or help you communicate when you don't know the words to use (pointing to the location of pain to your doctor) (Rowbotham, Holler, Lloyd, & Wearden, 2012).

Sometimes you may nonverbally substitute silence for words. If your roommate is driving you nuts with her constant talking (while you're trying to write a paper), you may become silent and look away from her when she asks for your input on last night's episode of *Dancing with the Stars* (Giles, Coupland, & Wiemann, 1992). Silence may also be a sign of deference (as when you don't express your opinion because the other has higher status); it may also signal defiance (as when you refuse to answer someone who angers you) (Ng & Ng, 2012).

Contradicting Verbal Messages

Nonverbal communication functions to **contradict** the verbal when the behavioral cues convey the opposite of the verbal message. Sometimes this is unintentional, as when you clearly look upset but say that nothing's wrong, and you don't

● **WHEN A TRAFFIC COP** holds out one hand, you know to stop; she doesn't have to scream "STOP!" to get the intended effect. © Sandy Felsenthal/Corbis

AND YOU?

Have you ever experienced (or been responsible for) a failed attempt at sarcasm or teasing via a text message or social network posting? What, in your opinion, caused this communication breakdown? How might it have been avoided?

● **A SMELLY,** ugly little monster? Certainly not.

realize your nonverbal behavior is giving you away. Other times, contradicting behavior is intentional. For instance, Caroline sighs deeply to get Andy to ask, "What's wrong?" She can keep the attention coming by refusing to answer or by tersely stating, "Nothing." Although such tactics can get another person's attention, they're deceptive because they take advantage of the person's concern in order to serve selfish purposes.

Contradicting behavior is also part of what makes joking around, teasing, and the use of sarcasm (cutting remarks) so powerful. When you roll your eyes and say, "Wow, that was a captivating lecture," you let your classmate know that, despite your words, you found listening to your professor about as interesting as vacuuming. Contradicting behavior can work positively as well. For instance, your friend calls to your beloved dog, "Come here, you smelly, ugly little monster!" Your friend's smile, high pitch, and open arms reveal that your friend really thinks your dog is adorable.

Managing Impressions and Regulating Interactions

Nonverbal cues are used to manage the impressions and regulate interactions of communicators in a variety of relationships and situations (Cappella & Schreiber, 2006). This **interaction management** function occurs from the first time you meet someone and continues throughout the life span of your relationship. For example, you dress professionally for a job interview; your smile, firm handshake, and friendly tone convey your sincerity as you say, "This sounds like a wonderful organization to work for." The hiring manager's smiles and nods—or frowns and silence—in turn influence your behaviors back to her (Keating, 2006). Should you get the job, your nonverbal behaviors help you manage a tense situation with your boss by keeping a respectful distance and lowering your tone of voice. Additionally, nonverbal behavior (like smiles, eye contact, and so on) helps you manage your ongoing, everyday interactions with coworkers.

Nonverbal cues are also used in coordinating verbal interaction at the level of conversation—they help us **regulate** the back-and-forth flow of communication. For example, if you pause after saying "Hello" when answering your phone, you are offering the person on the other end a chance to self-identify and explain the purpose of the call. Face to face, you may hold your hand up while speaking to signal that you don't want to be interrupted or gesture broadly to indicate continued excitement about your topic (Cutica & Bucciarelli, 2011). Additionally, raising your hand in a face-to-face classroom setting lets your professor know that you have a question or information to share.

If conversational regulation doesn't go smoothly, there can be negative consequences. For example, if you successfully interrupt others when they are speaking, you may gain influence, but they may like you less. On the other hand, if you allow interruptions, others may perceive you as less influential (Farley, 2008). Naturally, the situational context plays a role. It's more serious to interrupt (or be interrupted) during a debate or a business meeting, whereas some interruption is acceptable during casual conversations with friends. Matching your regulation behaviors to those of your partner makes interactions go smoothly (Schmidt, Morr, Fitzpatrick, & Richardson, 2012).

AND YOU?

Imagine that you are listening to a friend tell a long story in a face-to-face setting. How might you regulate the interaction to show that you're listening or that you'd like to interject a comment? Would these actions change if the conversation were taking place via instant messaging or in a chat room? How so?

Creating Immediacy

Nonverbal communication can also create **immediacy**, a feeling of closeness, involvement, and warmth between people (Andersen, Guerrero, & Jones, 2006; Prager, 2000). Such behaviors include sitting or standing close to another person, turning and leaning toward the individual, smiling, making eye contact, and touching appropriately (Andersen, 1998; Andersen, Guerrero, Buller, & Jorgensen, 1998). Even adding "smiley face" emoticons to your e-mail messages has been found to increase perceptions of immediacy and liking (Yoo, 2007).

Immediacy behaviors help you form and manage impressions, particularly if you want to have more social influence. The implications for interpersonal relationships are clear: physical contact, eye contact, smiling, and other gestures tell your romantic partner, your family members, and close friends that you love and care for them and that you want to be near them. In the professional world, multiple studies find that physicians, nurses, and staff who engage in immediacy behaviors have patients who are less fearful of them and more satisfied with their medical care (Richmond, Smith, Heisel, & McCroskey, 2001; Wanzer, Booth-Butterfield, & Gruber, 2004). And if you are a supervisor at work, combine positive messages with immediacy behaviors to enhance your likeability and credibility (Teven, 2007).

Deceiving Others

In the historical drama *Argo*, Central Intelligence Agency officer Tony Mendez rescues six American agents stranded in Tehran, Iran, during the 1979 Iranian hostage crisis. Mendez executes his rescue without a single weapon. Rather, he deceives Iranian officials by having the agents pose as a Canadian movie crew scouting locations in Iran (Dargis, 2012). Mendez and the hostages (both in the film and in real life) pulled off their deception by carefully learning their "roles" in the fabricated story and by consciously monitoring their nonverbal communication to reveal confidence and poise.

Although most of us will never engage in such a dramatic example of **deception**—the attempt to convince others of something that is false (O'Hair & Cody, 1994)—we will admit to occasionally engaging in it (if we're being honest). Sometimes we deceive to protect others, as when you tell your friend that no one noticed her torn slacks. Other times, we deceive out of fear, as when victims of abuse blame their injuries on falls or accidents. However, deception can have

● **MENDEZ AND THE OTHER** agents had to develop detailed backstories in order to pull off their plan: to convincingly pose as a Canadian film crew in Iran. © Warner Bros. Pictures/ Courtesy Everett Collection

what about you?

Nonverbal Immediacy Scale

The following statements describe the level of involvement, warmth, and closeness (immediacy) that some people attempt to achieve when communicating with others.

Please indicate in the space at the left of each item the degree to which you believe the statement applies to you in a given conversation with a stranger. Please use the following five-point scale: 1 = never; 2 = rarely; 3 = occasionally; 4 = often; and 5 = very often.

_____ 1. I use my hands and arms to gesture while talking to people.

_____ 2. I touch others on the shoulder or arm while talking to them.

_____ 3. I use an excited voice while talking to people.

_____ 4. I look at or toward others while talking to them.

_____ 5. I don't move away from others when they touch me while we are talking.

_____ 6. I have a relaxed body position when I talk to people.

_____ 7. I smile while talking to people.

_____ 8. I make eye contact while talking to people.

_____ 9. My facial expressions show others I care about the conversation.

_____ 10. I sit close to people while talking with them.

_____ 11. My voice is warm when I talk to people.

_____ 12. I use a variety of vocal expressions when I talk to people.

_____ 13. I lean slightly toward people when I talk with them.

_____ 14. I am animated when I talk to people.

_____ 15. I express myself through facial expressions when I talk with people.

_____ 16. I move closer to people when I talk to them.

_____ 17. I turn my body toward others during conversations.

_____ 18. I nod in response to others' assertions.

Add your scores for 1–18 here:_____

67–90: You communicate a high level of immediacy in your nonverbal behavior. Be careful not to exceed others', particularly strangers', comfort levels, however (that is, watch out for people who shrink back, look away, or have negative facial expressions, as you may be getting too close or touching too much).

43–66: You communicate immediacy in many situations. Your nonverbal expressions of interest and warmth are likely to make new people in your life more comfortable, too.

18–42: You don't communicate immediacy behaviors very often. Consider increasing your nonverbal immediacy behaviors to help you manage impressions and initiate more satisfying relationships.

Source: Adapted from V. P. Richmond, J. C. McCroskey, and A. D. Johnson, A. D. (2003).

malicious and self-serving motives, as in the solicitor who tries to get your social security number and other personal data in order to commit identity theft.

You may be drawn in by a solicitor who sounds warm and friendly, but it is more likely that you will look for the opposite type of behavior to sniff out a liar (Canary, Cody, & Manusov, 2008). People who appear anxious, who avoid making eye contact, who blink frequently, or who have frequent and awkward body movements seem deceptive (Leal & Vrij, 2008). However, research shows that although these cues make us more suspicious, they do not actually make us more accurate at detecting deception (Van Swol, Braun, & Kolb, 2013). This is partly because people's "honest" or "dishonest" demeanor is often inconsistent with whether they are actually telling the truth or lying (Levine et al., 2011). Liars often appear anxious only if concerned about the lie or about getting caught (Canary, Cody, & Manusov, 2008). On one hand, if the lie is unimportant, liars may instead be relaxed and controlled. On the other hand, someone accused of lying may show nonverbal or physiological signs of anxiety even if not guilty. This is one reason why so-called lie detectors (and the newer brain scans) are not reliable measures of deception (Kirchner, 2013).

Nonverbal Communication Codes

Ask any fans of *The Big Bang Theory* about the brilliant Dr. Sheldon Cooper's greatest struggle and they'll quickly respond with "understanding other people." More specifically, Sheldon confesses to having an immensely difficult time interpreting others' emotions (like sadness or disappointment) and responding empathically. And—played out to great comic effect on the show—he seems completely unable to decode others' sarcasm. (At one point, his friend and roommate, Leonard, has to hold up a sign that says "SARCASM" to help Sheldon navigate a particularly intense conversation with their neighbor, Penny!)

Truth be told, Sheldon struggles to interpret and understand **nonverbal codes**, the symbols we use to send messages without, or in addition to, words. Although we divide these codes into categories for simplicity and clarity, nonverbal behaviors seldom communicate meaning in isolation; as you saw in the last section, clusters of nonverbal behaviors (hugs, smiles, eye contact) function together to regulate behavior or convey immediacy. The codes we examine here are gestures and body movements, facial expressions, eye behavior, voice, physical appearance, space and environment, touch, and time.

Gestures and Body Movements

Did you succumb to the dance craze and Internet meme the "Harlem Shake"? If so, you've joined millions in the silly, shimmying body movements that communicate sexuality one moment and hilarity the next—all without words (Cvitanic, 2013). You have probably heard others call such body movements "body language," but the way you move your body is not a language at all— "Harlem Shaking" has no specific, consistently understood definition. Such behavior is called **kinesics**—gestures and body movements that send nonverbal messages. When Eva motions her arm to include Jane in a conversation, or Rodney walks into an interview standing tall to project confidence, you are witnessing

CONNECT

Kinesics is important when delivering a speech, as your body movements should support your words. For example, illustrators help clarify a point for your audience; confident posture reassures your listeners that you're prepared and organized. Certain adaptors (like yawning), however, can leave the audience with the impression that you are bored with your own speech. We discuss these issues in Chapter 14.

real communicator

NAME: Octavia Spencer
OCCUPATION: Academy Award Winning Actress

I've always wanted to work in the film industry, though I never dreamed it would be in front of the camera. But in 1995, I got a small part opposite Sandra Bullock in the hit film *A Time to Kill*, and I was on my way. Since that time, I've had a number of roles on stage, screen, and television.

What I do want everyone reading this interview to realize is that my success is tied to a number of the topics you're studying right now—particularly nonverbal communication. For example, pretty much anyone can read a script out loud, but *how* you read it is what counts in this industry. The tone of voice, the timing, the pause that is just long enough to get people to look up and pay attention—these are the keys to getting (and staying) employed!

Vocal cues alone are incredibly important in acting. When I was the voice of "Minny" on the audio version of the book *The Help* (Kathryn Stockett's *New York Times* bestseller), I had to study the appropriate accents, timing, and inflections to make my performance truly authentic. Later, when I played the same role for the film, I realized just how much more meaning and feeling I was able to communicate when I could use facial expressions and body movements to express my character.

Most of my roles are comedic and, let me tell you, acting in comedies isn't a barrel of laughs. It's incredibly challenging work. Facial expressions in particular have to be appropriate and come at just the right moment (otherwise, they aren't at all funny). Often there are ten different facial expressions I have to produce in less than one minute to show surprise, hurt, outrage, confusion, acceptance, determination, confidence, liking, disgust, and pleasure. Oh, and it has to appear natural, too.

In addition, the way I tilt my head or hold my body changes the information I'm trying to convey. For example, I played Dr. Evilini, a witch with dual personalities, on *Wizards of Waverly Place*. As one personality, my head was bent, and my voice low pitched with a diabolical, screeching laugh. The other personality had a normal voice, and I kept my body erect, though my eyes were always wide with expression. Because the show's target audience was primarily comprised of children, every movement was exaggerated to ensure its comedic value.

At the end of the day, I am truly grateful to be doing something that I absolutely enjoy—and none of it would be possible without a close study of nonverbal communication.

kinesic behaviors. And although there is not a specific message conveyed, research shows that we're fairly good at deciphering others' emotions from their gestures and movements (Montepare, Koff, Zaitchik, & Alberet, 1999).

There are five main categories of gestures and movements that convey meaning nonverbally (Ekman & Friesen, 1969):

▶ **Emblems** are often used to substitute for words, because they have a more definition-like meaning for the people who use them. The "thumbs up" and "okay" signs are both emblems that most Americans would recognize and understand. During his inauguration parade, Barack Obama greeted the marching band from his old high school with an emblem fellow Hawaiians would understand: a shaka sign—a pinkie and thumb salute that is widely regarded as a representation of the "aloha spirit."

▶ **Illustrators** reinforce verbal messages and help visually explain what is being said. Holding your hands two feet apart while saying, "The fish was *this* big!" is an illustrator. Illustrators can also be used to increase influence in relationships, as when we emphasize our words with pointing or sketching a thought in the air (Dunbar & Burgoon, 2005).

▶ **Regulators** help us manage our interactions. Raising your hand and lifting your head, for example, indicate that you want to speak. Raising your eyebrows usually indicates you want information from others (Flecha-García, 2010). Both regulators and illustrators often pair with vocal signals to enhance communication, as when you say, "I, I, I …" while holding up your index finger to break into conversation (regulators) or emphasize the word "*this*" in the preceding fish example (illustrator).

▶ **Adaptors** satisfy some physical or psychological need, such as rubbing your eyes when you're tired or twisting your hair when you're nervous or bored. Usually not conscious behaviors, adaptors are used to reduce bodily tension. Because they may be more frequent when someone is stressed, impatient, or bored, they are often interpreted as indicators of negative feelings (Goss & O'Hair, 1988).

▶ **Affect displays** are nonverbal gestures that convey feelings, moods, and reactions. Slumping in a chair may indicate fatigue or boredom; a fist thrust high in the air indicates joy when your team scores a touchdown. Setting your jaw and hitting your fist on the table may indicate your anger or frustration. Affect is also displayed through facial expressions, as discussed next.

Facial Expressions

Consider the character Spock, the half-Vulcan, half-human science officer from *Star Trek* who suppresses his emotions at all costs in the pursuit of pure logic. Both of the actors who have played Spock (Leonard Nimoy in the original television series and Zachary Quinto in the 2013 film) had their human eyebrows replaced with artificial "Vulcan" ones: because Spock's eyebrows—and eye expressions in general—appear less human, his emotions seem less human too.

● **WITH THOSE** Vulcan eyebrows, Spock portrays little emotion. © Paramount. Courtesy Everett Collection

As humans, we are wired to use our faces to indicate emotions (Fridlund & Russell, 2006). Although the reasons behind our facial expressions might be difficult to ascertain, several specific expressions are common across all cultures (Ekman & Friesen, 1971). A smile, for example, usually indicates happiness; a frown, sadness; raised eyebrows tend to indicate surprise, and wrinkled eyebrows, concern (see Figure 4.1).

Blind children, who cannot learn to mimic facial movements through sight, exhibit sadness, anger, disgust, fear, interest, surprise, and happiness in the same way that sighted people exhibit these feelings (Eibl-Eibesfeldt, 1973). These seven primary facial expressions are thus considered inborn, whereas most other expressions are learned from our culture (Gagnon, Gosselin, Hudon-ven der Buhs, Larocque, & Milliard, 2010). There is some evidence that pride also may be a universally recognized emotion (Tracy & Robins, 2008).

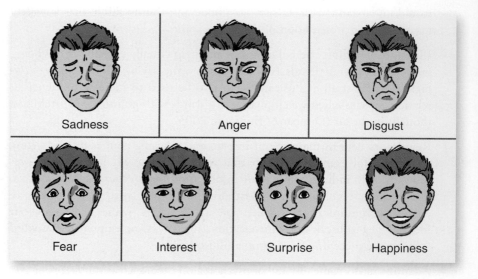

FIGURE 4.1

CROSS-CULTURAL PRIMARY FACIAL EXPRESSIONS Research shows that these seven expressions of emotion exist in all cultures and are inborn.

Although we're fairly adept at deciphering these common expressions of emotion, we're not necessarily experts at decoding all facial expressions (Bavelas & Chovil, 2006). That's because the human face can produce more than a thousand different expressions (and as many as twenty thousand if you take into account all of the combinations of the different facial areas) (Ekman, Friesen, & Ellsworth, 1972; Harrigan & Taing, 1997). Moreover, our emotions can be concealed by facial management techniques, conscious manipulation of our faces to convey a particular expression.

One common facial management technique is **masking**, replacing an expression that shows true feeling with an expression that shows appropriate feeling for a given interaction. Actors use masking all the time. But you also use it when you smile at customers at the restaurant where you work even though you're in a horrible mood and wish they'd leave (Richmond, McCroskey, & Payne, 1991).

Eye Behavior

When Rooney Mara portrayed Lisbeth Salander in the film adaptation of *The Girl with the Dragon Tattoo* (2011), she learned to move and gesture in ways to convey the hurt and fury her avenging character experiences. But Mara said that her character's eye behavior was particularly hard to master. Contrary to the norms of interaction, Salander never looks into the face of others, keeping her gaze downcast or sideways (Ryzik, 2012). **Oculesics** is the study of the use of the eyes to communicate—which includes Salander's gaze aversion.

Newborn infants (two to five days old) stare significantly longer at faces offering a direct gaze rather than an averted one. The babies orient themselves more often toward the face that makes eye contact with them. Babies as young as three months old smile less when adults avert their gaze and begin smiling more when adults resume eye contact (Farroni, Csibra, Simion, & Johnson, 2002).

There are some cultural variations in gazing with children. For example, European American parents gaze more at their children, especially between mothers and sons. Mexican American parents, on the other hand, spend less time making

CONNECT

Despite differing cultural norms regarding direct eye contact, it remains an important part of giving speeches and succeeding in job interviews in the United States. In both situations, eye contact signals respect for your audience and confidence in your abilities and preparedness. You learn more about the challenges of eye contact, and how to move past them, in Chapter 14 and the Interviewing Appendix.

eye contact with children. Accordingly, children gaze more directly at fathers in European American homes than in Mexican American homes (Schofield, Parke, Castañeda, & Coltrane, 2008). Perhaps children in Mexican American homes gaze less directly at fathers as a sign of respect for the cultural hierarchy in the family.

The human gaze remains important beyond childhood. You use direct eye contact with a hiring manager in a job interview in the United States to make a stronger impression. In more personal relationships, you look at a friend differently than you look at your significant other and very differently from someone you dislike intensely. Each glance can send a message of liking, loving, attraction, or contempt (see Table 4.1).

Voice

When the University of Arizona opened the National Institute for Civil Discourse, they wanted to promote compromise and understanding among groups famously at odds with one another (Dooling, 2011). They quickly found out that it was not only the words used that stood in the way of civility, but it was also the vocal tone. Imagine yourself saying, "I respect your right to believe that" with a calm, balanced tone; now imagine saying the same words with a sarcastic tone while emphasizing the word *right*. You could communicate genuine respect in the first instance or disgust and intolerance in the second.

The vocalized sounds that accompany our words are nonverbal behaviors called **paralanguage**. **Pitch** in language involves variations in the voice (higher or lower) that give prominence to certain words or syllables. Vocal **tone** is a modulation of the voice, usually expressing a particular feeling or mood; you may notice your friend sounds "down" or hear the excitement in your teammate's revelry about your win. Vocal **volume** is how loud or soft the voice is—think of the softness of a whisper or the thunder of an angry shout.

In addition to pitch, tone, and volume, paralanguage also involves behaviors like pauses, hesitations, vocal quality, accents, and the rate and rhythm of speech. It exhibits qualities like hoarseness, nasality, smoothness, or deepness, and it may sound precise, clipped, slurred, or shrill. Teenage girls are sometimes mocked for using uptalk (making statements into questions? "Right?") or for guttural flutter of the vocal cords called "vocal fry," as in comedienne Maya Rudolph's mimicry of poet Maya Angelou on *Saturday Night Live* (Quenqua, 2012).

We all have preferences about which voices are most attractive—angry, demanding voices are usually perceived as annoying—and whiny voices *really* annoying (Sokol, Webster, Thompson, & Stevens, 2005). Look no further than your favorite radio DJs or newscasters to examine the vocal qualities people enjoy the most. These individuals tend to have smooth voices and find a middle ground between precise and fluid speech. Pronunciation matters too—and can identify individuals as coming from another country or region. Thus, our Missouri readers may know that residents disagree on whether to pronounce their home state as "Missouruh" (which tags a speaker as being from a rural part of the state) or "Misoureeee," indicating a more urban environment. Interestingly, politicians often pronounce it both ways to cover their bases (Wheaton, 2012).

● **NPR MUSIC HOST** Bob Boilen uses a precise, accentless voice on the air. Max Hirshfeld/Redux

TABLE 4.1

THE POWER OF EYE CONTACT

Function of Eye Contact	Image	Example
Influences attitude change	 © ACE STOCK LIMITED/Alamy	Looking at someone to get the person to trust you or comply with your wishes
Indicates a degree of arousal	 John Henley/Getty Images	Glancing across a crowded room to signal attraction or interest; looking at a customer attentively in the interest of receiving positive evaluations—and sales (Ford, 1999)
Expresses emotion	 Vladimir Godnik/Getty Images	Soft eyes of loving looks; frightened eyes of a startled person; hard eyes of an angry person
Regulates interaction	 © Image Source/Alamy	Looking more at a conversational partner when listening; regulating eye contact to assume or give up the speaking role (Wiemann & Knapp, 1999)
Indicates power	 ColorBlind Images/Getty Images	Direct, prolonged gaze to convey dominance; avoidance of eye contact to signal submissiveness (Burgoon & Dunbar, 2006)
Forms impressions	 Frank Herholdt /Getty Images	Making eye contact with an audience to communicate confidence and sincerity

Source: Leathers (1986). Adapted with permission.

Meanwhile, **vocalizations** are paralinguistic utterances that give information about our emotional or physical state, such as laughing, crying, sighing, yawning, or moaning. Other vocalizations simply replace words or create non-word fillers in conversations. You might clear your throat to get someone's attention or use "Shhhh" to quiet a crowd, and most of us tend to insert "umm's" and "ah's" into conversation when we're taking a moment to think. Sometimes such **back-channel cues** signal when we want to talk versus when we're encouraging others to continue talking ("oh," "uh-huh").

Physical Appearance

If you've ever seen a reality television makeover show (from *The Biggest Loser* to *What Not to Wear*), you know that many people wish to alter their appearance to elicit positive changes in their personal and professional lives. Although what you wear—or the way you fix your hair or makeup—may not speak directly to your abilities or define you as a person, it communicates messages about you nonetheless. In fact, the initial impression your appearance makes may affect your future interactions with others (DeKay, 2009).

Most people in Western society are well aware of the significance of appearance. Research shows that society affords attractive people certain advantages. For instance, attractive students receive more interaction from their teachers (Richmond et al., 1991), and "good-looking" job candidates have a greater chance of being hired (Molloy, 1983; Shannon & Stark, 2003). Jurors find attractive defendants innocent more often (Efran, 1974), although discussion and deliberation can mitigate this bias (Patry, 2008). Appearance affects not only perceptions of attractiveness but also judgments about a person's background, character, personality, status, and future behavior (Guerrero & Floyd, 2006).

Perceptions about appearance and attractiveness are inferred not only from physical characteristics like body shape and size, facial features, skin color, height, and hair color but also from the clothing you wear, which can reveal quite a bit about your status, economic level, social background, goals, and satisfaction (Crane, 2000). In fact, your clothing choice can also speak to your communication intentions. When Queen Elizabeth II became the first British monarch to visit the Irish Republic after decades of discord, she wore a suit in emerald green, the proud color of the Emerald Isle. Clearly her choice signaled a hoped-for reconciliation (Dowd, 2012).

We also infer a great deal of meaning from **artifacts**—accessories carried or used on the body for decoration or identification. For example, the expensive Rolex watch that your uncle wears sends a very different message about wealth and status than a ten-dollar watch would. Other artifacts, such as briefcases, tattoos, earrings, nose rings, nail polish, and engagement and wedding rings, also convey messages about your relational status, your gender, and even how willing you are to defy conventions. Tattoos, for example, send a variety of messages. Some descendants of Holocaust survivors inscribe the concentration camp identification numbers of their ancestors onto their forearms to communicate their desire to remember their relatives and never forget the atrocities perpetuated by the Nazi regime (Rudoren, 2012). On a lighter note, research finds that men view a butterfly tattoo on the back of a sunbathing woman as a sign that she may be receptive to his romantic overtures (Guéguen, 2012).

CONNECT

Using vocalizations like "uh-huh" can help others perceive you as an effective listener (Chapter 6). When a loved one discusses a difficult situation, you want to allow the person to speak and not constantly interrupt with your own words. Vocalizations tell your partner that you're listening and that you're actively engaged in the conversation.

CONNECT

Chapter 11 explains that the artifacts you exhibit in a professional setting both reflect and shape the organization's culture—its beliefs, values, and ways of doing things. Competent communicators must be mindful of the messages their artifacts send in light of the larger organizational picture.

● **REALITY SHOWS** like *The Biggest Loser* aim to help people change their appearance (and health) through weight loss. NBC/Photofest

Remember that perceptions of artifacts (and physical appearance in general) can change over time. To illustrate, when the late British politician Margaret Thatcher carried a handbag, it was at first perceived as a sign of weakness, but with her rise to prime minister, the handbag came to be a symbol of tremendous power (Givhan, 2013).

Space and Environment

Believe it or not, you also send nonverbal messages by the spaces that surround you and your communication partners. We examine three factors here: proxemics, territoriality, and environment.

Proxemics

Ben's first job involved a coworker Lucas, who was a close talker—a person who stands very near when speaking to others. "During shifts when I'd be on with this guy, I'd always have to try to find some excuse to be away from the counter," Ben said. "If we were both behind the counter together, he'd talk so close that I'd end up completely backed into a corner, with the counter digging into my back, just hoping for someone to rob the place so there'd be an excuse to get out of the situation" (Edwards, 2013). Ben's intense discomfort with Lucas was due to **proxemics**, the way we use and communicate with space.

Professor Edward Hall (1959) identified four specific spatial zones that carry communication messages (see Figure 4.2).

▶ *Intimate* (0 to 18 inches). We often send intimate messages in this zone, which is usually reserved for spouses or romantic partners, very close friends, and close family members.

FIGURE 4.2

ZONES OF PERSONAL SPACE The four zones of personal space described by Edward Hall indicate ranges that generally apply across cultures.

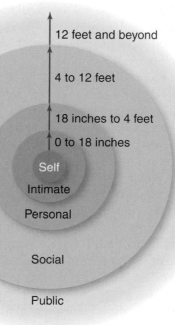

12 feet and beyond

4 to 12 feet

18 inches to 4 feet

0 to 18 inches

Self

Intimate

Personal

Social

Public

COMMUNICATIONACROSSCULTURES

What Nurses Wear

It might be strange to think that just a few decades ago professional women with college degrees were expected to show up for work wearing nipped-waist dresses, frilly aprons, and white linen caps. For more than 100 years, variations on this theme signified a woman trained in the medical profession. "The nurse's cap," writes nursing historian Christina Bates (2012), "is one of the most evocative garments ever associated with an occupational group" (p. 22). Well into the twentieth century, nurses' uniforms separated the nurses from the doctors—and coincidentally the ladies from the men—in the health care field. But they also served as important signifiers. Prior to the opening of the first nurses' colleges in the 1830s, nursing was left largely to religious orders and untrained mothers, wives, and sisters. The adoption of a uniform—however odd it may seem today—served to provide some status to the young women who emerged from these nursing schools, separating them from the women who went before them (Bates, 2012).

Today such ensembles are limited, for the most part, to sexy Halloween costumes, but most nurses still wear a uniform of sorts: usually a simple pair of hospital scrubs in any of a number of colors or prints. In contrast to the nurse uniforms of yore, these simple and practical ensembles are for the most part gender-neutral. But even these seemingly nondescript items convey meaning. Research shows that the choice of color or print of scrubs can have an impact on patients' perceptions about a nurse's competence. Among adult patients who were asked to comment on a variety of nursing uniforms, white scrubs were perceived as indicative of higher levels of professionalism, attentiveness, reliability, empathy, and six other traits than were colored or print scrubs. But among children and adolescents, there was little if any discernable difference in the way they perceived different uniforms for nursing professionals (Albert, Wocial, Meyer, Na, & Trochelman, 2008).

Of course, uniforms are not limited to the nursing profession. Police officers, sports teams, military and paramilitary organizations, and of course many schools have dress requirements that are much more strict than those that govern what today's nurses wear to work. By dressing in uniform, members of these groups convey messages about who they are, what their role is, and to which group they belong.

THINK ABOUT THIS

❶ Do you think that nurses' uniforms became less gendered as more men entered this traditionally female profession, or do you think men began to think more seriously about the field as the old frilly uniforms gave way to more androgynous scrubs?

❷ Why do you think the color of nurses' uniforms had such an impact on adults' perceptions? Why might it have had less of an impact on younger patients? Do you think that those younger patients' perceptions will change as they age?

❸ Consider the traditional nurse's uniform in a few different contexts. How is it that a uniform that indicated professional prestige 100 or even 50 years ago now seems so blatantly sexist?

❹ The traditional nurse's uniform sent a very concrete message about the woman wearing it in terms of her job and her qualifications. What message, if any, do modern scrubs send? Is the meaning of scrubs concrete or abstract?

► *Personal* (18 inches to 4 feet). In the personal zone, we communicate with friends, relatives, and occasionally colleagues.

► *Social* (4 to 12 feet). The social zone is most comfortable for communicating in professional settings, such as business meetings or teacher–student conferences.

► *Public* (12 feet and beyond). The public zone allows for distance between interactants at, for example, public speaking events or performances.

EVALUATING**COMMUNICATION**ETHICS

THINK ABOUT THIS

The Job Killer Tat

You're a few years out of college, working at a public policy think tank that specializes in childhood education research. It's a great position with lots of room for advancement and the ability to be active in an area that really interests you. What's more, the organization is growing rapidly and looking to fill new positions. When your manager mentions that they're seeking someone who can work with policymakers in the state capitol, and asks if you know anyone, you immediately think of your friend Dave. This position is essentially Dave's dream job, and he's more than qualified, having dual majors in early childhood education and communication and having worked freelance as a grant writer for nonprofit organizations. You pass Dave's résumé on to your manager and wish your buddy good luck.

When Dave shows up at your office for an interview, you are astonished. He has forgone a traditional suit and tie and is wearing a short-sleeved collared shirt that reveals the full arm sleeve of tattoos that he has been cultivating since he was about sixteen years old. You had mentioned to Dave that the office environment is very professional and that the position would require him to interact with lobbyists, lawyers, and lawmakers on a regular basis. You know that your boss will not think well of his decision not to cover up his tattoos—or even attempt to find a suit. You're worried that your boss will think you've wasted his time with a candidate who is less than serious and you're angry at Dave for possibly insulting your organization's sensibilities (and for possibly making you look like a fool for recommending him). What do you do?

❶ Why might Dave have failed to consider the professional context of the interview? Could his own professional experience as a freelancer have changed his definition of "professional attire"?

❷ If you could rewind the situation and start over, would you offer Dave more clear directions on how to dress or would you not recommend him at all?

❸ Knowing what you know about Dave's skills and education—and knowing that he would adapt his behavior as directed—would you hire Dave? Or is his failure to figure out what was appropriate ahead of time a deal breaker?

Your personal space needs may vary from the forgoing space categories. These vary according to culture too; Hall "normed" these zones for different cultures around the world. How close or distant you want to be from someone depends on whom you're dealing with, the situation, and your comfort level. You might enjoy being physically close to your boyfriend or girlfriend while taking a walk together, but you probably don't hold hands or embrace during class. Gender also plays a role. Research says that groups of men walking together will walk faster and typically leave more space between themselves and others than women will (Costa, 2010). But regardless of your personal preferences, violations of space are almost always uncomfortable and awkward and can cause relational problems (Burgoon, 1978).

Proxemic messages are not limited to the real world. In the online virtual world *Second Life*, you create your own space in which you and your avatar move. Avatars use proxemic cues to send relational messages and structure interaction, much as people do in real life (Antonijevic, 2008; Gillath, McCall, Shaver, & Blascovich, 2008).

Territoriality

Closely related to proxemics is **territoriality**—the claiming of an area, with or without legal basis, through continuous occupation of that area. Your home, your car, and your office are personal territories. But territories also encompass implied ownership of space, such as a seat in a classroom, a parking space, or a table in a restaurant. Few people like anyone encroaching on their territory. If you're a fan of *How I Met Your Mother*, then you know that nothing good can come from taking the booth that Ted and his crew have unofficially claimed.

Territoriality operates in mediated contexts as well. Just as we do with physical spaces in the real world, we claim our social networking pages by naming them and decorating them with our "stuff," we allow certain people ("friends") access, and we "clean up" our space by deleting or hiding comments. Research shows that young people are more adept at managing their space on Facebook than are their parents (Madden & Smith, 2010). Some clean up their wall regularly, deleting status updates and wall posts as often as they make them. Others take social media "vacations" or "breaks" or simply deactivate their accounts when they are not online so "friends" cannot see their wall, post anything on it, or tag them in photos while they're metaphorically not around (Boyd, 2010).

Environment

Any home designer or architect knows that humans use space to express themselves. The layout and decoration of your home, your office, and any other space you occupy tells others something about you. For example, the way you arrange your furniture can encourage interaction or discourage it; the décor, lighting, and cleanliness of the space all send messages about how you want interactions to proceed. Even the scent of a space impacts communication: customers stay in stores longer and rate the store higher if the aroma is pleasant (as in the scent of chocolate in a bookstore) (Doucé, 2013). Professors who have neat, clean, attractive offices are rated by their students as more friendly, trustworthy, and authoritative (Teven & Comadena, 1996).

Color also matters. Hollywood location scouts negotiated with Juzcar in southeastern Spain to paint all the bone-white Andaluz stone buildings baby blue to film the feature-length version of *The Smurfs* there. The blue color was so unique—and clearly signaled the popular movie—that tourists flocked there. Although the producers agreed to repaint the buildings white after the filming, the townspeople left them blue because the tourist trade had relieved their unemployment woes (Herman, 2013).

The environment's power to affect communication may explain, in part, the success of shows like *Extreme Makeover: Home Edition* and *Renovation Raiders*. In transforming dreary or cluttered spaces into warm and vibrant rooms, the best makeovers reflect not only a family's practical needs but also its unique personalities and interests. That's because the designers understand that environment communicates to others about who we are.

Touch

Touch is the first communication we experience in life. A newborn baby is soothed in the arms of her parents; she begins learning about herself and others while reaching out to explore her environment. **Haptics** is the use of touch to send messages. We hug our loved ones in happy

CONNECT

Territoriality can have an impact on group communication, as we generally feel more in control of situations on our own turf (Chapters 9 and 10). Think about this the next time a professor breaks you up into random groups. Do you enjoy moving across the room from your usual seat, or do you prefer your group members to come to you? Chances are good that a new "territory" will affect your communication.

● **MANY PEOPLE** favor "their" spots, which can include a favorite table at the bar, a preferred spot in the lecture hall, or a usual seat in the car. CLIFF LIPSON/CBS /Landov

and sad times, we reassure others with a pat on the back, and we experience intimacy with the caress of a romantic partner.

There are as many different types of touches as there are thoughts about and reactions for being touched. The intimacy continuum (Heslin, 1974) provides insights into how our use of touch reflects our relationship with a communication partner:

▶ *Functional-professional touch* is used to perform a job. How would your dentist perform your root canal if he or she didn't touch you?

▶ *Social-polite touch* is often a polite acknowledgment of the other person, such as a handshake.

▶ *Friendship-warmth touch* conveys liking and affection between people who know each other well, as when you hug your friends or offer your brother a pat on the back.

▶ *Love-intimacy touch* is used by romantic partners, parents and children, and even close friends and family members. Examples include kissing (whether on the mouth or cheek), embracing, and caressing.

▶ *Sexual-arousal touch* is an intense form of touch that plays an important part in sexual relationships.

Another classification system for touch distinguishes among a dozen different kinds of body contact (Morris, 1977). Table 4.2 illustrates these types of contact in connection with the intimacy continuum.

TABLE 4.2

HOW PEOPLE TOUCH

Type of Contact	Purpose	Intimacy Type
Handshake	Forming relational ties	Social-polite
Body-guide	A substitute for pointing	Social-polite
Pat	A congratulatory gesture but sometimes meant as a condescending or sexual one	Social-polite or sexual-arousal
Arm-link	Used for support or to indicate a close relationship	Friendship-warmth
Shoulder embrace	Signifies friendship; can also signify romantic connectiveness	Friendship-warmth
Full embrace	Shows emotional response or relational closeness	Friendship-warmth
Hand-in-hand	Equality in an adult relationship	Friendship-warmth
Mock attack	An aggressive behavior performed in a nonaggressive manner, such as a pinch meant to convey playfulness	Friendship-warmth
Waist embrace	Indicates intimacy	Love-intimacy
Kiss	Signals a degree of closeness or the desire for closeness	Love-intimacy or sexual-arousal
Caress	Normally used by romantic partners; signals intimacy	Love-intimacy or sexual-arousal
Body support	Touching used as physical support	Love-intimacy

Clearly, touch powerfully affects our relationships. It is one factor related to sustained liking in healthy marriages (Hinkle, 1999). Our reassuring touch also lets our friends know that we care and serves to regulate social interactions, as when beginning or ending an interaction with a handshake. However, not all touch is positive. Bullying behaviors like kicking, punching, hitting, and poking are inappropriate forms of touch, unless inside a boxing ring.

Gauging the appropriate amount of touch for a given situation or relationship is also critical for communication. For example, dating partners usually expect touch, but someone who wants "too much" (such as constant hand-holding) can be perceived as needy or clingy. Withholding touch communicates a message of disinterest or dislike, which can damage a relationship, whether with a friend, a romantic partner, or a colleague. Obviously, it's important to adjust touch to individual expectations and needs (and culture, as we explain later in the chapter).

Time Orientation

Imagine you're late for a job interview. If you are the interviewee, you've probably lost the job before you have a chance to say a word—your lateness sends a message to the employer that you don't value punctuality and his or her time. If you are the interviewer, however, it can be completely acceptable for you to keep the interviewee waiting. In fact, by making the person wait, you assert your status by clearly conveying that you have control.

Chronemics is the use of time in nonverbal communication—the ways that you perceive and value time, structure your time, and react to time. Your *time orientation*—your personal associations with the use of time—determines the importance you give to conversation content, the length or urgency of the interaction, and punctuality (Burgoon et al., 1989). For example, when you are invited to someone's home in the United States for dinner, it's acceptable to arrive about ten minutes after the time suggested. It shows consideration for your host not to arrive too early or too late (and possibly ruin the dinner). Similarly, spending time with others communicates concern and interest. For example, good friends will make plans to spend time together even when it's inconvenient.

In our personal lives, deciding the timing of a message can be tricky. How long do you wait after you've met someone to send that person a Facebook friend request or an invitation to connect professionally on LinkedIn? How long do you wait to text or call someone you met at a party to see if he or she might want to go out on a date? Right after you've left the party may seem too eager, but a week later may suggest you're not really interested. Research shows that we do use people's response rate (how quickly they return e-mails, texts, etc.) as an indication of interest and immediacy, but the situation and context also make a difference (Döring & Pöschl, 2009; Kalman & Rafaeli, 2011; Kalman, Ravid, Raban, & Rafaeli, 2006; Ledbetter, 2008).

Influences on Nonverbal Communication

Pick any individual nonverbal behavior—let's say a kiss. A kiss can mean lots of different things in different places, between different people in different situations. A kiss is a friendly manner of greeting between the sexes and with friends

CONNECT

Are you punctual or habitually tardy? Do you evaluate others on their use of time? Does it vary when you are in friendship situations versus professional situations? In Appendix A we illustrate the ways to prepare for an interview so that your use of time is viewed positively.

AND YOU?

What kind of message does it send if you are habitually late to class? What about showing up late to work? On the other hand, what kind of message is sent by showing up early for a party or to pick up a date?

of the same sex throughout much of southern Europe and Latin America. This is not necessarily the case in the United States and Canada, where kissing tends to be reserved for immediate family, romantic partners, or very close friends. In India, public kissing of any sort has only recently become acceptable (Harris, 2013). You might kiss your romantic partner differently in front of your family members than you would when you're alone. Indeed the very definition of *how* you kiss your partner might range from rubbing noses to exchanging saliva (Berliet, 2013). And if you're sending an e-mail to your eight-year-old niece, you might end it with a big wet kiss, signaled by the emoticon 😘. Clearly, culture, technology, and the situation all serve as powerful influences on our nonverbal behavior.

Culture and Nonverbal Communication

When Mike and his friends visited a beach in Qingdao, China, they were surprised to see a woman emerge from the sea wearing gloves, a wetsuit, and a neon-orange ski mask. Another mask-wearing bather told them, "A woman should always have fair skin; otherwise people will think she is a peasant" (Levin, 2012). The tanning booths and self-tanning creams popular in the United States are clearly not important to beach lovers in China because different cultures view physical appearance differently. Relatedly, if you've ever traveled abroad, you may have been advised that certain nonverbal gestures that are entirely acceptable and quite positive in the United States (for example, "A-OK" or "thumbs up") are deeply insulting and crude in other parts of the world (Matsumoto & Hwang, 2013).

As these examples illustrate, nonverbal communication is highly influenced by culture. Culture affects everything from touch to facial expressions including time orientation and notions of physical attractiveness (see Chapter 5). For example, in the United States, people tend to make direct eye contact when speaking to someone, whether a colleague, a supervisor, or a professor. Similarly, in the Middle East, engaging in long and direct eye contact with your speaking partner shows interest and helps you assess the sincerity and truth of the other person's words (Samovar, Porter, & Stefani, 1998). However, in Latin America, Japan, and the Caribbean, such sustained eye behavior is a sign of disrespect.

Similarly, culture affects the use of touch. Some cultures are **contact cultures** (for example, Italy) (Williams & Hughes, 2005) and depend on touch as an important form of communication. Other cultures are **noncontact cultures** and are touch-sensitive or even tend to avoid touch. Latin American, Mediterranean, and Eastern European cultures, for example, rely on touch much more than Scandinavian cultures do. Public touch, linked to the type of interpersonal relationship that exists and the culture in which it occurs, affects both the amount of touch and the area of the body that is appropriate to touch (Avtgis & Rancer, 2003; DiBiase & Gunnoe, 2004; McDaniel & Andersen, 1998). Social-polite touch, for example, involves a handshake between American men but a kiss between Arabic men. And some religions prohibit opposite-sex touch between unmarried or unrelated individuals.

Sex and gender also influence nonverbal communication. Women usually pay more attention to both verbal and nonverbal cues when evaluating their partners and deciding how much of themselves

● **WHILE THE** "thumbs up" is a friendly sign in America, it's considered rude and offensive in certain parts of the Middle East. Maridav/Shutterstock

they should reveal to those partners, whereas men attend more to verbal information (Gore, 2009). Women also engage in more eye contact, initiate touch more often, and smile more than men (Hall, 1998; Stewart, Cooper, & Steward, 2003).

Such differences are not necessarily biologically based. For example, mothers may use more varied facial expressions with their daughters because they believe that women are supposed to be more expressive than men or because their childhood environment presented them with more opportunities to develop nonverbal skills (Hall, Carter, & Hogan, 2000). Adult gender roles may also play a part. Since women are expected to look out for the welfare of others, smiling—as well as other affirming nonverbal behaviors—may help women meet situational, gendered expectations (Hall et al., 2000). This may also help explain why women exhibit greater sensitivity to nonverbal messages. They tend to exhibit more signs of interest (such as head tilts and paralinguistic encouragers like "uh-huh" and "ah") and also decode others' nonverbal behaviors more accurately, particularly those involving the face (Burgoon & Bacue, 2003).

Mediated Nonverbal Communication

At a conference, a colleague told an interesting story about nonverbal communication in mediated contexts. She asked her students to submit their assignments via e-mail by midnight on the date they were due. At 1:00 A.M., she received a frantic note from her student, Aaron, explaining that a computer malfunction had prevented him from sending his speech outline until then. As Aaron typically provided quality work and never missed deadlines, our colleague was not concerned and did not intend to penalize him. So she simply wrote back "Got it" to quickly reassure him that she had received his outline. When she later saw Aaron in class, he said her short response made him worried that she was annoyed about his lateness. "If you had used a smiley face, I would have known what you meant," Aaron said.

When you speak with someone face to face, you've got a number of nonverbal codes at your disposal. Even on the phone, where you have no visual cues, you can use *paralinguistic cues* (vocal tone, rate, pitch, volume, sighs) to offer information. But when you send an e-mail, IM, or text message, many of the nonverbal channels you rely on (eye contact, paralanguage, and so on) are unavailable. However, people have developed a series of creative substitutions for nonverbal cues: capital letters to indicate shouting; creative use of font sizes, colors, and typefaces to provide emphasis; random punctuation (#@*&!) to substitute for obscenities; and animations, figures, diagrams, and pictures to add visuals to messages (Gayomali, 2013). Punctuation (or the lack of it) can help readers "hear" the intonation of what is being said (many people say that they "hear" their friend's texts or posts in that friend's "voice").

As Aaron noted in our example, some individuals expect others to use emoticons in mediated texts to help clarify meaning—whether to express emotion or to signal that something we say is a joke (Walther, 2006). Emoticons can also strengthen the intensity of a message, add ambiguity (was that *really* a joke?), or indicate sarcasm (Derks, Bos, & von Grumbkow, 2008).

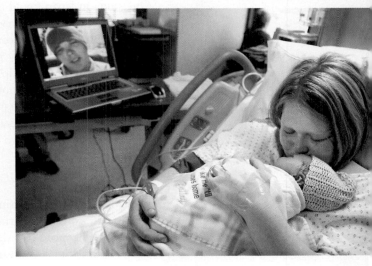

● **TECHNOLOGY HAS BECOME** so advanced that a father stationed in Iraq is now able to witness his child's birth in the United States—via webcam! AP Photo/ The Advocate Messenger, Clay Jackson

WIREDFORCOMMUNICATION

War Games Without Weapons, Sometimes Without Words

It's probably no surprise that soldiers benefit from virtual reality training offered in computerized war games. But soldiers abroad need to learn to dodge more than bullets: in different cultures, they need to learn to navigate different norms and rules of nonverbal communication.

American soldiers stationed in Iraq, for example, have discovered the hard way that gestures that are innocent in the United States can be quite offensive in Iraqi culture (and vice versa). For example, showing the soles of your feet is considered rude in Iraq; proximity while speaking, head bowing, and handshakes can also lead to misunderstanding. In one instance, an Iraqi man gestured at a female soldier by rubbing his fingers together. He was indicating friendship; she thought he was making a lewd sexual gesture.

This is where Tactical Iraqi, a virtual reality game created for the U.S. military, comes in handy. *Wired* magazine reports that "players navigate a set of real-life scenarios by learning a set of Arabic phrases, culturally relevant gestures and taboos. . . . A speech-recognition system records and evaluates the responses. Accurate responses allow the soldier to build a rapport with other characters and advance to the next level" (Cuda, 2006). The point is to help soldiers understand the Iraqi gestures, as well as to know how Iraqis are likely to perceive gestures that are considered innocent in the United States.

Interestingly, the game, though intended for soldiers, has no weapons or combat of any kind. It focuses instead on mutual understanding, with soldiers attempting to gain the trust of their companions in order to rebuild war-torn communities. The game's technical director, Hannes Vilhjalmsson, notes the power of nonverbal communication in this process: "I got a kick out of removing the weapons and replacing them with gestures" (Cuda, 2006). The success of such games has led the U.S. military to invest even more in simulation games—dubbed "first-person cultural trainers"—that help prepare troops for intercultural communication (Drummond, 2010).

THINK ABOUT THIS

1 Do you think soldiers can learn communication skills from a video game? Do you think this method of training would be more or less effective than classroom instruction?

2 Why is establishing competent communication so important for soldiers in Iraq? Do you think such training would have been more or less important for soldiers in Europe during World War II?

3 The company that created Tactical Iraqi is considering a civilian version of the game. Would it be useful to engage different cultures in the United States in virtual reality play? How might its technological format affect its usefulness for various co-cultures (age, education, socioeconomic status, and so on)?

AND YOU?

Have you ever taken an online or distance-learning course? Were you happy with the instruction and the amount of interaction? It is challenging to both present and respond nonverbally in courses offered online. What are the most effective ways to do this, based on your experience?

One study in Japan found that college students use positive emoticons as a "flame deterrent"—to try to prevent emotional misunderstandings that might upset others (Kato, Kato, & Scott, 2009). Since we can't hear voice inflection or see facial expressions in many mediated situations, effective use of the keyboard and computer graphics can help to create a sense of nonverbal immediacy. This can be particularly useful in relationship formation and maintenance; for example, a dating Web site that used avatars to restore nonverbal cues improved perceptions of the effectiveness of online interaction so that participants exchanged more information and had a stronger desire to pursue a relationship (Kotlyar & Ariely, 2013).

The Situational Context

Dancing at a funeral. Raising your Starbucks cup to toast your professor. Making long, steady, somewhat flirtatious eye contact with your doctor. Wearing a business suit to a rock concert. Do these situations sound strange or potentially uncomfortable? The situational context has a powerful impact on nonverbal communication.

Recall from our model of competent communication (Chapter 1) that the situational context includes spheres like the place you are in, your comfort level, the event, current events, and the social environment.

Now imagine dancing at a wedding, toasting your friend's accomplishment, flirting with an attractive friend, or wearing a business suit to a job interview. In each instance, the situational context has changed. Situational context determines the rules of behavior and the roles people must play under different conditions. Competent communicators will always consider the appropriateness and effectiveness of nonverbal communication in a given context.

Two of the primary factors involved in situational context are the public–private dimension and the informal–formal dimension. The **public–private dimension** is the physical space that affects our nonverbal communication. For example, you might touch or caress your partner's hand while chatting over dinner at your kitchen table, but you would be much less likely to do that at your brother's kitchen table or during a meeting at city hall. The **informal–formal dimension** is more psychological, dealing with our perceptions of personal versus impersonal situations. The formality of a situation is signaled by various nonverbal cues, such as the environment (your local pub versus a five-star restaurant), the event (a child's first birthday party or a funeral), the level of touch (a business handshake as contrasted with a warm embrace from your aunt), or even the punctuality expected (a wedding beginning promptly at 2:00 P.M. or a barbecue at your friend Nari's house going from 6:00 P.M. to whenever) (Burgoon & Bacue, 2003). Competently assessing the formality or informality of the situation affects your use of nonverbal communication—you might wear flip-flops and shorts to hang out at Nari's, but you probably wouldn't wear them to a wedding and certainly wouldn't wear them on a job interview.

If your nonverbal communication does not appropriately fit the public–private and formal–informal dimensions, you'll likely be met with some nonverbal indications that you are not being appropriate or effective (tight smiles, restless body movements, gaze aversion, and vocal tension).

BACK TO ▶ Pixar Animation Studios

At the beginning of this chapter, we considered how animators at Pixar use elements of nonverbal communication to tell elaborate stories in films like *Up* and *WALL-E*. Let's reconsider some of the ways nonverbal codes operate in these and other films.

▶ The directors of *Up* used simple visual cues to highlight the characters so their appearance provides insights into their personalities. Carl is very squarish in appearance, so he's perceived as boxed in, in both his house and his life. Eight-year-old Explorer Scout Russell is round and bouncy—like Carl's balloons, reflecting his optimistic, energetic personality. These nonverbal elements carry subtle yet influential messages.

▶ Animators study human kinesics to make decisions about how their animated characters should move. To animate the aged Carl, they studied their own parents and grandparents and watched footage of the Senior Olympics.

If Carl moved like eight-year-old Russell, the credibility of the film would be compromised.

▶ It takes talented voice actors to bring a script to life. The veteran actor Ed Asner breathed life into Carl, delivering not only his lines, but also believable vocal cues—grunts, sighs, speaking through clenched teeth—that made those lines more human and real. But for the roles of young Ellie and Russell, the directors chose nonactors who would give genuine, unpolished performances full of childish energy—the goal was for them to sound more like real children than actors reading from a script.

THINGS TO TRY ▶ Activities

1. LaunchPad for *Real Communication* offers key term videos and encourages self-assessment through adaptive quizzing. Go to **bedfordstmartins.com/realcomm** to get access to:

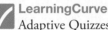 **LearningCurve** Adaptive Quizzes.

▶ Video clips that illustrate key concepts, highlighted in teal in the Real Reference section that follows.

2. Record a new episode of your favorite scripted television show. Try watching it with the sound turned all the way down (and closed captions turned off). Can you guess what's going on in terms of plot? How about in terms of what the characters are feeling? Now watch it again with the sound on. How accurate were your interpretations of the nonverbal behaviors shown? How successful do you think you would have been if it were an unfamiliar show, one with characters you don't know as well?

3. Shake up your clothing and artifacts today. Wear something completely out of character for you, and consider how people react. If you normally dress very casually, try wearing a suit, or if you're normally quite put together, try going out wearing sweatpants, sneakers, or a T-shirt; if you're normally a clean-shaven man, try growing a beard for a week, or if you're a woman who never wears makeup, try wearing lipstick and eyeliner. Do you get treated differently by friends? How about strangers (such as clerks in stores) or any professionals (such as doctors or mechanics) with whom you interact?

4. Observe the nonverbal behaviors of people leaving or greeting one another at an airport or a train station. Do you think you can tell the relationship they have from their nonverbal behaviors? Describe the variety of behaviors you observe, and categorize them according to the codes and functions detailed in this chapter.

5. Try smiling (genuinely) more than you usually do—and with people you might not usually smile at. See what happens. Do you feel differently about yourself and others? Do others respond with more smiles of their own? (A group of thirty of our students tried this one day and reported back that they thought they had made the whole campus a happier place—though there were a few people they encountered who remained their solemn selves.)

6. Play with text-to-speech features on your computer. Compare the way the machine reads a passage of text to the way you would read it. Do you have a choice of voices from which to choose, and is there one you prefer? Would you rather listen to an audiobook performance by a noted actor or a computer-generated voice reading the same material?

A Study Tool

Now that you have finished reading this chapter, you can:

Describe the power of nonverbal communication:

▶ **Nonverbal communication** is the process of signaling meaning through behavior other than words. It is often spontaneous and unintentional, and its meaning may be ambiguous (p. 94).

▶ When **channel discrepancy** occurs, words and actions don't match, and nonverbal behaviors are more likely to be believed than verbal ones (p. 96).

Outline the functions of nonverbal communication:

▶ Nonverbal communication reinforces verbal communication in three ways: **repeating** (mirroring the verbal message), **complementing** (reinforcing the verbal message), and **accenting** (emphasizing a part of the verbal message) (p. 97).

▶ Nonverbal cues can be used for **substituting** or replacing words (p. 97).

▶ Nonverbal communication also functions as **contradicting** behavior, conveying the opposite of your verbal message (pp. 97–98).

▶ Nonverbal cues also serve an **interaction management** function (p. 98) by which they are used to **regulate** verbal interaction (p. 98).

▶ A feeling of closeness, or **immediacy**, can be created with nonverbal behaviors (p. 99).

▶ Individuals with good nonverbal communication skills may practice **deception**, with good or bad intentions (pp. 99, 101), when they attempt to use nonverbal behaviors to convince others of something that is false.

Describe the set of communication symbols that are **nonverbal codes**:

▶ **Kinesics**, the way gestures and body movements send various messages, includes **emblems** (movements with direct verbal translations in a specific group or culture), **illustrators** (visually reinforcing behaviors), **regulators** (interaction management cues), **adaptors** (unconscious release of bodily tension), and **affect displays** (indications of emotion) (pp. 101–103).

▶ Seven primary facial expressions are inborn and are recognizable across all cultures: sadness, anger, disgust, fear, interest, surprise, and happiness (pp. 103–104). **Masking** is a facial management technique whereby we replace an expression of true feeling with one appropriate for a given interaction (p. 104).

▶ **Oculesics** is the study of the use of the eyes in communication settings (p. 104).

▶ How we pause, the speed and volume of our speech, and the inflections we use are vocalized nonverbal messages called **paralanguage** (p. 105), including **pitch** (vocal variation that gives prominence to certain words or syllables), **tone** (vocal modulation that expresses feelings of moods), **volume** (how loud or soft words are spoken), and a variety of other factors.

▶ **Vocalizations** are paralinguistic cues that give information about the speaker's emotional or physical state, such as laughing, crying, or sighing (p. 107). **Back-channel cues** are vocalizations that signal vocally but nonverbally that you do or don't want to talk (p. 107).

▶ Physical appearance and **artifacts**, accessories used for decoration and identification, offer clues to who we are (p. 107).

▶ **Proxemics,** the way we use and communicate with space, depends on the cultural environment and is defined by four specific spatial zones: intimate, personal, social, and public (pp. 107–108).

▶ **Territoriality** is the claiming of an area, with or without legal basis, by regular occupation of the area (pp. 110–111).

▶ The use of touch to send messages, or **haptics**, depends on the relationship with the communication partner (pp. 111–113).

▶ **Chronemics** is the perception of and use of time in nonverbal communication (p. 113).

Illustrate the influences culture, technology, and situation have on our nonverbal behavior:

▶ **Contact cultures** are more likely to communicate through touch, whereas **noncontact cultures** may tend to avoid touch (pp. 114–115).

▶ Gender influences communication with behaviors traditionally associated with femininity, such as smiling, often perceived as weak (p. 115).

▶ In mediated communication, capitalization, boldfaced terms, and emoticons are used as nonverbal cues (p. 116).

▶ Competent nonverbal communication relates to the situation; the **public–private dimension** is the physical space that affects our nonverbal communication, and the **informal–formal dimension** is more psychological (p. 117).

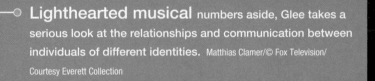

Lighthearted musical numbers aside, Glee takes a serious look at the relationships and communication between individuals of different identities. Matthias Clamer/© Fox Television/ Courtesy Everett Collection

5

Communication and Culture

If you were trying to imagine a group that clearly reflects the diversity of the United States, it might look a bit like the cast of *Glee*. At once a scathing satire of high school life and a joyful celebration of music, *Glee* debuted in May 2009 to rave reviews and an immediate audience following. It was also a charming—and often troubling—exploration of intercultural and co-cultural communication and relationships. The diverse characters conformed to stereotypes in many ways—there was Rachel, the ambitious diva; Kurt, the self-assured and fashionable gay teen; Santana, the mean-spirited cheerleader; and Puck, the insensitive jock. But the show also dealt with real communication issues and challenges in almost every episode, including bullying, teen pregnancy, and death and grief (particularly when Cory Monteith, the actor who played Finn, passed away in 2013). It also explored the way differences in religious beliefs, personal lifestyles, and social status affect group bonding.

There's no doubt that individuals from different co-cultures respond well to seeing people like themselves represented on television. But *Glee* was never a sweet take on multiculturalism: Sue Sylvester, cheerleading coach turned principal, pointed out the differences between team members and openly, viciously mocked them. Her mean-spiritedness not only provided the show with zinging laughs and a definable "bad guy" but also acknowledged the real struggles that teens from just about every co-culture must face. "That's real life," noted Kevin McHale, who played Artie. "It's not like, oh, you need to be sensitive. High school is not always sensitive" (McLean, 2011).

While Sue Sylvester considered the glee club to be the lowest form of high school life, Jane Lynch (the actress who played Sylvester) has a clear sense of why the show's celebration of misfits struck such a chord. "*Glee* presents this idealised [sic] world where no matter who you are or how different you are from the 'norm,' you're going to get supported in this glee club," says Lynch. "And you're going to be held up as unique, and you're going to be loved for it" (McLean, 2011).

After you have finished reading this chapter, you will be able to

○ Define and explain culture and its impact on your communication

○ Delineate seven ways that cultural variables affect communication

○ Describe the communicative power of group affiliations

○ Explain key barriers to competent intercultural communication

○ Demonstrate behaviors that contribute to intercultural competence

As episodes of *Glee* demonstrate, communication among individuals of different races, sexes, religions, and so on can be messy—but it can also be exciting, challenging, enlightening, and enjoyable. To be part of any team, or to be a good neighbor and an informed citizen, you need to understand this essential communication process. Whether you're looking to learn how to better communicate with your older relatives, understand the way your roommate's faith plays out in her communication, or contemplate current national debates surrounding issues like immigration, this chapter aims to help you better understand cultural differences *and* similarities to increase your competence in intercultural encounters. We begin with an overview of culture. Then we explore cultural variations and group affiliations as well as the challenges and opportunities that intercultural communication offers.

Understanding Culture

As you'll recall from the communication competence model (Chapter 1), your encounters with others occur within overlapping situational, relational, and cultural contexts. **Culture** is a learned system of thought and behavior that belongs to and typifies a relatively large group of people; it is the composite of their shared beliefs, values, and practices. Although we might commonly think of culture as a person's nationality, it applies to any broadly shared group identity. In this section, we investigate how culture is learned, how it affects our communication, and why learning how to communicate in different cultures is so important.

Culture Is Learned

Culture is not something you're born with; it is something you learn through communication. As children, you observe the behaviors of your parents, siblings, and extended family members. For example, they teach you how to greet guests in your home, whether to make direct eye contact with others, and what words are polite rather than inconsiderate. Later you observe the behaviors of your teachers and your peer groups. You learn what types of conversational topics are appropriate to discuss with peers rather than adults; you learn the nuances of interacting with members of the same or opposite sex. You also listen to and observe television, movies, and various forms of advertising that reflect what your culture values and admires.

Through these processes, you acquire an understanding of what constitutes appropriate behavior. This is the framework through which you interpret the world and the people in it—your **worldview** (Schelbert, 2009). Much of your worldview is not obvious. For example, many of your nonverbal behaviors (like gestures, eye contact, and tone of voice) occur at an unconscious level (Hall, 1976). You have learned these behaviors so well that you don't even notice them until someone else behaves in a manner that doesn't meet your expectations. For example, you may not realize that you routinely make eye contact during conversation until someone fails to meet your gaze. Your use of language carries more obvious cultural cues; speaking Italian in Italy enables you to fully participate in

● **DO YOU EXTEND** a hand or bow to greet others? It probably depends on what you were taught by older relatives as a child. (left) © Design Pics Inc./Alamy; (right) Knauer/Johnston /Getty Images

and understand the Italian way of life (Nicholas, 2009). Language can also teach you the traditions of your culture as evidenced by prayers of your faith, folk songs of your grandparents, or patriotic oaths you make (such as the U.S. Pledge of Allegiance).

Culture Affects Communication

Just as we learn culture *through* communication, we also use communication to *express* our culture. Our worldview affects which topics we discuss in personal and professional settings, as well as how we communicate nonverbally. It also affects the way we perceive others' communication.

In the United States and many Western cultures, a popular worldview often equates thinness with beauty; this perception is reflected in the messages we communicate. Media tabloids, as well as personal comments on YouTube, are filled with judgments about celebrities and their weight. Following the birth of Prince George, Kate Middleton, the Dutchess of Cambridge, emerged from the hospital with a visible postbirth "baby bump," and a frenzy of public debate ensued (Britney, 2013). Interestingly, some of the same tabloids that praised Middleton for showing off her "bump" (Fuller, 2013) later also gushed at the quick loss of her pregnancy weight (Baez, 2013). Media personalities themselves

CONNECT

You frequently communicate your worldview when you present yourself for strategic purposes (Chapter 2). For example, if you are meeting your significant other's parents for the first time or attending a job interview, you will likely present yourself in a manner that expresses key elements of your culture— perhaps bowing or shaking hands, using formal language, or dressing in a particular way.

AND YOU?

Reflect on how you learned your general culture. In what ways was it directly imparted to you? What role did communication with parents, caregivers, siblings, and other important people in your life play in this process?

often join the public conversation too. Kim Kardashian and Jessica Simpson, for example, have lashed out via Twitter at weight-related criticisms ("Don't Call Me Fat," 2013), but they also share in the celebration when they lose weight and express frustration when they don't ("Jessica Simpson," 2013).

In many other cultures, worldviews about weight and physical attractiveness differ greatly. Jessica Simpson herself discovered this when she traveled around the world for VH1's series *The Price of Beauty* (Hinckley, 2010). She found, for example, that in Uganda, larger women are considered desirable, and so they prepare for marriage in a "fattening hut." This cultural practice expresses to the people of Uganda the importance for women of *gaining* weight, much like the U.S. tabloids express to Americans the value of *losing* it.

Intercultural Communication Matters

The fact that people from different cultures perceive the world quite differently can lead to misunderstandings, anger, hurt feelings, and other challenges when they interact. This is why communication scholars invest a great deal of time and effort to study and write about **intercultural communication**, the communication between people from different cultures who have different worldviews. Communication is considered intercultural when the differences between communicators are so substantial that they can create different interpretations and expectations (Lustig & Koester, 1993).

The answer to addressing intercultural misunderstanding is *not* to limit yourself to interactions with people who perceive things exactly like you. In this mobile society, you study, play, and work with people who are different from you on a number of levels. Let's now consider why studying intercultural communication matters so much.

A Diverse Society

The United States is a diverse country with a population that reflects a range of ethnic, racial, and religious backgrounds. Different regions of the country (and sometimes different neighborhoods in the same city) have distinct cultures as well (see Figure 5.1). You have a unique cultural background and communication style that differ in some ways from those of others. So, to function as a member of such a diverse society, you need to be able to communicate appropriately and effectively with a wide variety of individuals. Two key parts of this process include understanding your own cultural expectations for communication and respecting those of others.

Mobility

You and your family may have moved to a new community while you were growing up, or perhaps other families moved into your hometown. Whether due to shifts in the economy and employment (Goudreau, 2013) or international immigration (Taylor & Cohn, 2012), the people around you are likely to be changing.

● **WHETHER YOU'RE** volunteering for the Peace Corps in another country or just going to a different part of your home state, it's important to be sensitive to cultural differences when communicating. Courtesy of the Peace Corps

THEN & NOW
A snapshot of the nation

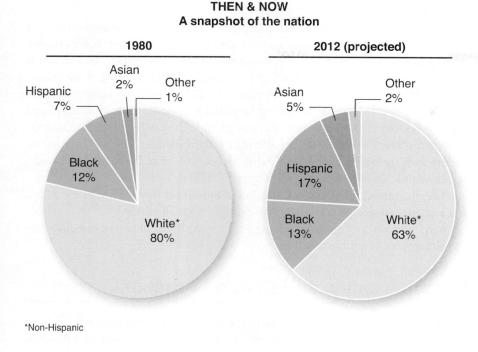

1980

Hispanic
7%

Asian
2%

Other
1%

Black
12%

White*
80%

2012 (projected)

Asian
5%

Other
2%

Hispanic
17%

Black
13%

White*
63%

*Non-Hispanic

FIGURE 5.1

U.S. CENSUS DATA INDICATING INCREASED DIVERSITY IN THE NATION

Source: U.S. Census Bureau; numbers have been rounded.

As such, you must be ready to address cultural differences—not just between nations but also between regions, states, and cities. Even if you don't physically encounter many people from outside your community, you will almost certainly communicate with new people at some time or another through media.

Mediated Interaction

Clearly, mediated communication is changing the way we experience the world and broadening the range of people and groups with whom we regularly interact. In the United States today, some 70 percent of American adults use broadband (high-speed Internet) at home (Zickuhr & Smith, 2013). In addition, 63 percent of adult cell phone owners access the Internet via their phones or tablets (Duggan, 2013). We communicate electronically more and more each year, and now more than one generation of adults worldwide are "digital natives" who have grown up with these technologies (Joiner et al., 2013; Prensky, 2012). Through the Internet, we connect not only with far-off family and friends but also with individuals from around the country—or around the world—when we participate in online gaming, watch YouTube videos, or comment on others' blogs.

In addition to the newer media technologies, more traditional media also enable exposure to people from different cultures. Calls to customer service centers are answered in other parts of the country or on the other side of the world. Radio stations bring international music and news right to your car. And television offers glimpses of cultures we might not be a part of—including British situation comedies on BBC America, soccer games broadcast from South America, and foreign films presented on the Independent Film Channel. American TV programming also has increasingly diverse casts.

AND YOU?

How long have you lived in your current location? Are people in your community treated differently based on their status as a new or established member in the community? How might your response change based on your own level of involvement in the community?

Diverse Organizations

Any job you take will involve some degree of intercultural communication. A teacher may have students whose families are from different parts of the country or from other countries entirely; an entrepreneur must understand how different groups respond to her product and her marketing campaigns. Being aware of how culture affects communication is especially crucial to business communication across borders (Busch, 2009). During negotiations, for instance, you may need to know how hard to push a client to commit and when to be silent. The increasingly global reach of organizations also means that managers need to be effective leaders with increasingly multicultural workforces (Mazur, Boboryko-Hocazade, & Dawidziuk, 2012; Okoro & Washington, 2012).

Clearly, intercultural communication is important in your life as a student, as a citizen, and as a professional. The culture in which you live (or were raised) has particular ways of communicating in the world. We illustrate these now by examining seven cultural variations.

Communication and Cultural Variations

It is one thing to notice cultural differences; it is quite another to be able to *explain* them. *Why*, for example, might Germans seem very blunt and direct as they speak, whereas the Japanese may seem never to get to the point? Scholars have identified seven major communication variations[1] across cultures: high- and low-context cultures, collectivist and individualist orientations, comfort with uncertainty, masculine and feminine orientations, approaches to power distance, time orientation, and value of emotional expression (Hall, 1976; Hofstede, 1984, 2001; Matsumoto, 1989).

These seven variations are often treated like opposites, so you may think that your culture must be one or the other. However, these variations actually play out along a spectrum: your culture may be masculine in some ways and feminine in others. Also, within any culture, there is great variance among different groups in terms of where they fall on the spectrum. Finally, there are always differences among individuals as well—some people are more like their dominant culture than others. With these caveats in mind, let's consider each variation more closely.

High- and Low-Context Cultures

Our culture strongly affects how direct we are in our use of language and how much we rely on other, nonverbal ways to communicate. Individuals in **high-context cultures** (including Japan, Korea, China, and many Latin American and African countries) use contextual cues—such as time, place, relationship, and situation—to interpret meaning and send subtle messages (Hall, 1976; Hall & Hall, 1990). A Japanese person who disagrees with someone, for example, may say something indirect, such as "Maybe" or "I'll think about it," or she may not

CONNECT

If you are from a low-context culture, you may wonder how to decode communication from a high-context friend or colleague. The key lies in developing strong listening skills (Chapter 6). By participating in *active listening*, you can look for opportunities to select and attend to nonverbal messages or contextual clues that will help you understand the message your friend is encoding and sending.

---

[1]Geert Hofstede referred to these variations as cultural *dimensions*—largely psychological value constructs that affect the way people think about and perform communication behaviors.

real communicator

NAME: Vanessa Gonzalez
OCCUPATION: Marketing and Admissons Director

If you had asked me who "I" am and what groups I belong to at the beginning of my college career, I could have answered you without a second thought: I'm Latina, I'm an American, I'm a first-generation college student, I'm studious, and I love to travel. But my experiences with intercultural communication—in college, and now in my job—really shook up these categories for me and taught me a great deal about communication with others.

My current job is with a college-preparatory high school in the United States that sponsors an International Academy. The position requires a combination of marketing and intercultural skills. I work to attract students from many different countries to the Academy, which is, as one might expect, culturally diverse. The on-campus housing provides a secure living environment for international students while giving them the opportunity to interact with others from all over the world. But not only international students benefit from this experience. The school also offers enriching classes and extracurricular activities for domestic students to help them to widen their cultural experiences. One program pairs international students with domestic students so that international students can become oriented to the school, and domestic students can learn more about another culture.

One of the most exciting parts of my job is the opportunity to travel internationally. Recently I visited schools in South Korea, Vietnam, and Thailand, where I participated in recruiting fairs and met with students and their families. As you might guess, I encountered several cultural variations. One that stood out to me was the different ways that students interact with their parents. In South Korea, students are expected to have a strong sense of independence at a relatively young age

(compared to U.S. students). By their early teens, students often have their own flat or a private area of the family home. In this living situation, they are expected to take responsibility for their studies with little parental oversight. In Vietnam, on the other hand, students are more closely watched over by their parents, who are concerned with guiding not only their academic success but also their overall happiness. When meeting students of both these cultures, I kept this information in mind so that I knew whether to bring the parents fully into the recruitment discussions or if I should interact more directly with the student.

Other international experiences have shown me how to navigate cultural variations that I may not expect. For example, while studying abroad in India in college, I found myself at a hotel where the hot water for the showers wasn't working. When I called down to the front desk, the hotel manager assured me that he would address the issue. Still, several trips down to the front desk later, the water remained cold! It finally dawned on me that his quiet gestures indicating "yes" actually meant "no": "No, there will not be any hot water today." It was up to me—the listener—to decode all of the contextual cues that pointed to this response, despite my own upbringing in a low-context culture (where the manager would likely have said: "Our hot water heater is broken but will be fixed by 6 A.M. tomorrow").

At the International Academy, I similarly need to be sensitive and help students from high- and low-context cultures adapt (especially high-context cultural students, who are not always used to responding to blunt questions). Our teachers also need to adapt their methods to be sure their students understand them. It's incredible to watch such a diverse group grow comfortable with their surrounding and with their fellow students, picking up new ways to communicate and learn.

say anything at all. The communication partner must understand the message solely from clues of disagreement in the *context,* such as the fact that the person is silent (or hesitates to speak). People from a high-context culture also tend to attribute a communication partner's behavior to factors related to the situation rather than to an individual's personality. For instance, instead of assuming that someone who remains silent is rude, they might think that the individual didn't respond because the situation called for restraint and politeness.

A **low-context culture**, by contrast, uses very direct language and relies less on situational factors to communicate. The United States, Canada, Australia, and many northern European countries tend to have a low-context style. In the United States or Germany, for example, it would seem normal for someone to disagree by saying openly, "That's not right" or "I'm sorry, but I don't agree with what you are saying." Although people from high-context cultures would likely think such directness disrespectful, people from low-context cultures tend to believe it is rude to be unclear about what you think. In fact, researchers have found that Americans often find indirectness very confusing and may even interpret Japanese silence or a response like "I'll think about it" as agreement (Kobayshi & Viswat, 2010). Table 5.1 compares high- and low-context styles.

Collectivist and Individualist Orientations

An Arab proverb says that you must "smell the breath" of a man in order to know if he can be trusted. But in the United States, Americans get very uncomfortable when other people stand "too close" to them. Americans also tend to knock on a closed door before entering and usually ask the person inside if it's OK to enter or if she would like to join the group for lunch. But in Lesotho (a tribal culture

TABLE 5.1

A COMPARISON OF HIGH- AND LOW-CONTEXT CULTURES

High-Context Cultures	Low-Context Cultures
• Rely on contextual cues and nonverbal signals for communicating meaning	• Rely on direct language for communicating meaning
• Avoid speaking in a way that causes individuals to stand out from others	• Admire standing out and getting credit
• Usually express opinions indirectly	• Construct explicit messages
• Usually express disagreement by saying nothing or being verbally vague	• Usually express disagreement clearly
• Tend to find explanations for behaviors in the situation	• Tend to find explanations for behaviors in individuals
• Admire relationship harmony	• Admire eloquence and very direct verbal messages

in South Africa), people's rooms often have no doors at all; people go in and out freely, and if someone sees you, they will grab you and assume you want to have lunch with the group. Such differences in the value of personal space and independence versus belonging and group loyalty illustrate our second cultural value: collectivist and individualist orientations.

Individuals from **collectivist cultures** perceive themselves first and foremost as members of a group—and they communicate from that perspective (Triandis, 1986, 1988, 2000). Collectivist cultures (including many Arab and Latin American cultures as well as several Asian cultures, such as Chinese and Japanese) value group goals and emphasize group harmony and cooperation. Communication in such cultures is governed by a clear recognition of status and hierarchy among group members, and loyalty to the group and the honor of one's family are more important than individual needs or desires (Wang & Liu, 2010). In addition, collectivist communicators are generally concerned with relational support; they avoid hurting others' feelings, apologize, and make efforts to help others to maintain the group's reputation and position of respect (Han & Cai, 2010). For example, if an individual attending a business meeting discovers a financial error, she will not likely mention who made the error, nor will she call attention to her own success in discovering it. Instead, she will emphasize the group's success in correcting the error before it became a problem for the company.

Conversely, **individualist cultures** value each person's autonomy, privacy, and personal "space." They pay relatively little attention to status and hierarchy based on age or family connections. In such cultures, individual "self-esteem" is important, individual initiative and achievement are rewarded, and individual credit and blame are assigned. Thus, an individual who notes an error—even one by her superiors—will probably be rewarded or respected for her keen observation (as long as she presents it sensitively). The United States is a highly individualist culture—American heroes are usually those celebrated for "pulling themselves up by their bootstraps" to achieve great things or change the world. Other Western cultures, such as Great Britain, Australia, and Germany, are also at the high end of the individualism scale.

Comfort with Uncertainty

Cultures also differ in the degree of anxiety that individual members tend to feel about the unknown. All cultures, to some degree, adapt their behaviors to reduce uncertainty and risk, a process called **uncertainty avoidance**. Cultures that are more anxious about the unknown are said to be *high uncertainty avoidance cultures*—people from these cultures strive to minimize risk and uncertainty. In high uncertainty avoidance cultures (such as in Portugal, Greece, Peru, and Japan), communication is usually governed by formal rules to satisfy a need for absolute truth, correct answers, and stability. People value consensus and have little tolerance for differences of opinion. By following social rules and minimizing dissent, they reduce uncertainty and anxiety in prescribed communication situations (Gudykunst, 1993).

In contrast, cultures with a higher tolerance for risk and ambiguity (like Sweden, Denmark, Ireland, and the United States) are considered *low uncertainty avoidance cultures* (Hofstede, Hofstede, & Minkov, 2010). Their lower level of

AND YOU?

To what degree do you identify with an individualist or collectivist culture? How might the answer to this question be complicated if the family you grew up with identifies strongly with one dimension but the larger culture in which you were raised strongly identifies with the other?

CONNECT

Just because people from cultures like those in the United States and Ireland have a greater acceptance for uncertainty than others doesn't mean that they are entirely comfortable with the unknown. In fact, members of low uncertainty avoidance cultures will engage in *passive*, *active*, and *interactive strategies* to reduce uncertainty when dealing with a new relational partner (Chapter 7); similarly, they will seek opportunities to learn about a new organizational culture so that they can *assimilate* competently (Chapter 11).

anxiety about the unknown means that these cultures are comfortable with a variety of communication styles, are more tolerant of differences of opinion, and have fewer formal rules for behavior (Hoeken et al., 2003).

Masculine and Feminine Orientations

The masculinity or femininity of a culture refers to the way an entire culture (including both men and women within the culture) values and reflects characteristics that have traditionally been associated with one sex or the other. Thus, a **masculine culture**—sometimes referred to as an *achievement culture*—places value on assertiveness, achievement, ambition, and competitiveness (Hofstede, Hofstede, & Minkov, 2010). Men and women in such cultures also usually make clear distinctions between the sexes, such as expecting more aggressiveness in men and more passivity in women.

Highly **feminine cultures**—sometimes referred to as *nurturing cultures*—place value on relationships and quality of life. Such cultures prize affection, friendliness, and social support between people over assertiveness. Scandinavian cultures (such as Sweden and Norway), as well as Chile and Portugal, tend to rank high in femininity, whereas Mexico, Japan, and Italy tend to be high in masculinity.

When discussing masculine and feminine orientations, remember that individual men and women *within* each culture vary in how they may value masculinity and femininity (Tripathy, 2010). For example, Japan ranks as a highly masculine culture, yet in recent years many Japanese men have been embracing a less restrictive view of masculinity. Analysts note that these men may communicate in ways that are gentle, shy, or sensitive (Faiola, 2005).

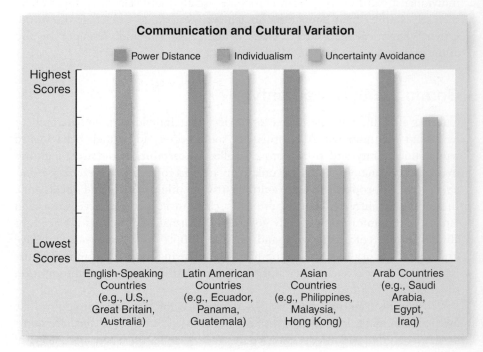

FIGURE 5.2

COMMUNICATION AND CULTURAL VARIATION
Source: Adapted from Hofstede, Hofstede, & Minkov, 2010.

Approaches to Power Distance

The critically acclaimed film *Slumdog Millionaire* is about Jamal, a Mumbai teen who grew up in the city slums and became a contestant on the Indian version of *Who Wants to Be a Millionaire?* Jamal endures brutal police interrogation on suspicion of cheating because the show's producers cannot imagine that he could know so much. This may seem shocking to some people in the United States, where upward mobility is a value and underdogs become folk heroes. Why?

It has to do with a culture's ideas about the division of power among individuals, a concept known as **power distance**. In India, social status is far more stratified than in the United States. The caste system—formally outlawed in 1950 but still lingering in India's culture—placed individuals, families, and entire groups into distinct social strata. That meant that the family you were born into determined who you could associate with and marry and what job you could hold. Those born into the lowest tier (the untouchables) were considered subhuman, even contagious, and were ignored by higher castes of people. Individuals generally accepted their place in the caste system. Even today, the idea that one's social status is set in stone lingers (Bayly, 1999).

Status differences in a culture result in some groups or individuals having more power than others. But a person's position in the cultural hierarchy can come from sources besides social class, including age, job title, or even birth order. In *high power distance cultures* (like India, China, and Japan), people with less power accept their lower position as a basic fact of life. They experience more anxiety when they communicate with those of higher status. And they tend to accept coercion as normal and avoid challenging authority. People in *low power distance cultures* (such as the United States, Canada, Germany, and Australia) tolerate less difference in power between people and communicate with those higher in status with less anxiety. They are more likely to challenge the status quo, consider multiple options or possibilities for action, and resist coercion.

Figure 5.2 shows how different types of cultures vary in their value of power distance, as well as how they differ on the other cultural dimensions of individualism and uncertainty avoidance.

Time Orientation

When you are invited to someone's home for dinner, when is it appropriate to arrive? Early, the exact time of the invitation, or twenty minutes (or even two hours!) later? **Time orientation**, or the way cultures communicate about and with time, is an important—yet frequently overlooked—cultural dimension (Hall, 1959).

Many Western cultures (such as the United States and Great Britain) are extremely time-conscious. Every portion of the day is oriented around time—including time for meals, bed, meetings, and classes. Even sayings express the importance of time: *time is money, no time to lose, wasting time* (Mast, 2002). But in many Latin American and Asian cultures, time is fluid and the pace of life is slower. Arriving two hours late for an invitation is perfectly acceptable.

● **HYACINTH BUCKET** of the British sitcom *Keeping Up Appearances* epitomizes monochronic culture: she holds friends and neighbors to strict social appointments and tracks them down if they're so much as seconds past due. © BBC. Courtesy Everett Collection

● DURING *FAMADIHANA*, the Malagasy people of Madagascar embrace their ancestor's bones, literally, and love for each other and their culture, figuratively. © Gideon Mendel/CORBIS

An American businessperson might get frustrated and give up after spending six months working on a deal with a Japanese company, when the Japanese may be wondering why the Americans quit so soon when they were all just getting to know each other!

A key cultural distinction operating here is whether cultures are monochronic or polychronic (Gudykunst & Ting-Toomey, 1988; Hall, 1976; Victor, 1992). **Monochronic cultures** treat time as a limited resource. Such cultures (including the United States, Germany, Canada, and the United Kingdom) use time to structure activities and focus on attending to one person or task at a time; they value concentration and stick to schedules. In monochronic cultures, people line up to wait their "turn"—to see a professor at office hours, to check out at the grocery store, to get into a concert. **Polychronic cultures** are comfortable dealing with multiple people and tasks at the same time. Seven or eight people all crowding around a stall and shouting out their needs at a mercado in Mexico is expected, not rude. Polychronic cultures (such as in Mexico, India, and the Philippines) are also less concerned with making every moment count. They don't adhere as closely to schedules, are less likely to make or attend to appointments, and change plans often and easily.

Even Web-based communication can be affected by such differences in the perception of time. One study found that people from polychronic cultures were less bothered by download delays than were people from monochronic cultures (Rose, Evaristo, & Straub, 2003).

Value of Emotional Expression

In Chapters 14 and 16, we discuss the importance of emotionally connecting to your audience and appealing to their emotions (*pathos*). However, it's essential to understand your audience's comfort with emotional expression. A culture that favors understatement may be suspicious of a highly dramatic speaker. You would want to ensure that your verbal and nonverbal communication is logical, credible, and competent for the context while attempting to touch their hearts.

In the central highlands of Madagascar, Rakotonarivo Henri is dancing with the bones of his grandfather. Accompanied by five brass bands, Henri and others on this island in the Indian Ocean emerge from family crypts with cheerful emotion. Amid joyful singing and dancing, they openly express their feelings to one another—and the dead—in a ritualistic ceremony called the *famadihana*, or the "turning of the bones." The ritual is meant to celebrate their ancestors, pass on the rituals and stories to the next generation, and publicly show how they love one another (Bearak, 2010).

One thing that people from all cultures share is the ability to *experience* emotion. But *expressing* emotions (including which emotions under which circumstances) varies greatly. In some cultures, emotional expression is associated with strength, whereas in others it is associated with weakness. Sometimes emotional expression is seen as chaos and other times as an identification of and processing of problems (Lutz, 1996).

Many collectivistic cultures (for example, Arab cultures) often use **hyperbole**—vivid, colorful language with great emotional intensity (and often exaggeration). Individualistic cultures (particularly English-speaking) tend toward **understatement**, language that downplays the emotional intensity or importance of events (often with euphemisms) (Wierzbicka, 2006). Consider, for example,

what about you?

Each of us has values about what is important and appropriate in interacting with others. Often these values reflect the larger culture in which we have been raised, but our opinions may also vary widely as individuals. This scale should give you a sense of how closely your own values relate to the larger cultural differences discussed in this chapter. For each of the statements that follow, write the number that most closely matches your opinion: 5 = strongly agree; 4 = agree; 3 = unsure; 2 = disagree; and 1 = strongly disagree.

_____ 1. People should say what they think clearly and directly.

_____ 2. My own goals in life are not as important as my family's or community's hopes for me.

_____ 3. Change results in uncomfortable stress in life.

_____ 4. It is important to work hard to get ahead professionally, even if relationships might suffer.

_____ 5. Children shouldn't be expected to provide for the old-age security of their parents.

_____ 6. It is important to plan carefully for the future.

_____ 7. People should keep their emotions to themselves.

_____ 8. If you disagree with someone, you should speak up.

_____ 9. People should take care of family before themselves.

_____ 10. Risk-taking is foolish; it is better to follow the regular path.

_____ 11. People should try to be the "best" at whatever they do.

_____ 12. Students should feel free in class to disagree with their teachers.

_____ 13. It is important to be on time to appointments.

_____ 14. People should grieve quietly rather than make a big scene.

_____ 15. You shouldn't have to guess what someone means.

_____ 16. If someone in my group or family fails, we all feel the shame.

_____ 17. I hate situations in which I do not know how I am supposed to act.

_____ 18. Men and women are just different; there is nothing wrong with that.

_____ 19. It is fine to question the views of people in authority.

_____ 20. You should make a schedule and keep to it.

_____ 21. Colorful language and exaggeration are signs of personal weakness.

Add your scores here to assess which way you lean in your cultural values:

#1, 8, 15: _____ low-context (9–15); high-context (3–8)

#2, 9, 16: _____ collectivist (9–15); individualist (3–8)

#3, 10, 17: _____ high uncertainty avoidance (9–15); low uncertainty avoidance (3–8)

#4, 11, 18: _____ masculinity (9–15); femininity (3–8)

#5, 12, 19: _____ low power distance (9–15); high power distance (3–8)

#6, 13, 20: _____ high time orientation (9–15); low time orientation (3–8)

#7, 14, 21: _____ devalue emotional expression (9–15); value emotional expression (3–8)

the difference between describing a military battle by saying "the river ran red with the blood of the slaughtered" versus "there were a number of casualties." A particularly striking example of understatement comes from the United Kingdom and Ireland—three decades of bombings and violence by paramilitary groups in Northern Ireland is a period referred to simply as "the Troubles" (Allan, 2004).

We've seen that communication in different cultures varies along continuums in seven key ways. Yet within these broadly defined cultures, we all vary our communication in more specific ways based on the many groups to which we belong or with which we identify, as we see in the next section on group affiliation.

Understanding Group Affiliations

Ellen DeGeneres is an American, a woman, and a baby boomer. She is white. She is a Californian and also a Southerner. She is a lesbian, a vegan, an animal rights activist, and an environmentalist. She is also a successful entertainer and very wealthy. All of these characteristics—and many others—form DeGeneres's unique identity. These attributes also make her a member of various groups. Some of these groups might be formal (as expressed by her affiliations with various animal rights groups). However, most are informal, reflecting the more general ways in which we all group ourselves and others based on particular characteristics. Thus, Ellen is a member of the white community, the southern community, the wealthy community, the entertainment community, and so on.

You too have multiple aspects to your identity, including the many groups to which you belong. Of course, some of your group memberships may be more important to you than others, and these group affiliations powerfully shape your communication—and affect how others communicate with and about you. In this section, we'll consider these facts by examining co-cultural communication as well as social identity theory and intergroup communication.

● **IN WHICH** groups can Ellen DeGeneres claim membership? WENN/Newscom

Co-Cultural Communication

As we discussed in Chapter 1, **co-cultures** are groups whose members share at least some of the general culture's system of thought and behavior but have distinct characteristics or attitudes that unify them and distinguish them from the general culture. As you saw in our example about Ellen and as Figure 5.3 shows, ethnic heritage, race (or races), gender, religion, socioeconomic status, and age form just a few of these co-cultures. Other factors come into play as well: some co-cultures are defined by interest, activities, opinions, or by membership in particular organizations (for example, "I am a Republican" or "I am a foodie").

Our communication is intrinsically tied to our co-cultural experience. For example, a **generation** is a group of people who were born during a specific time frame and whose attitudes and behavior were shaped by that time frame's events and social changes. Generations develop different ideas about how relationships

The Cultural Context

FIGURE 5.3

THE MULTIFACETED
NATURE OF CO-CULTURES

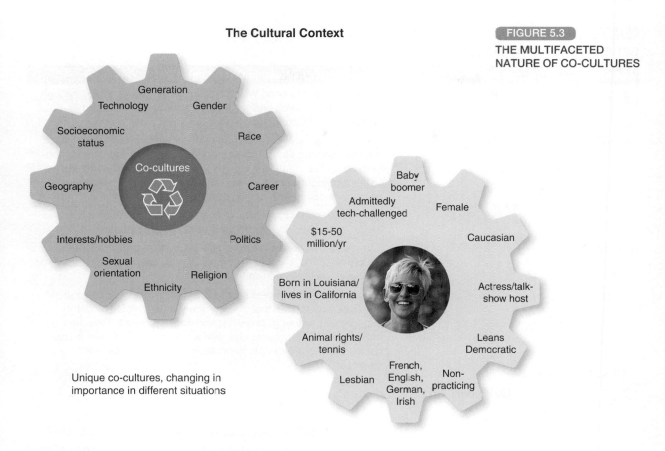

Unique co-cultures, changing in importance in different situations

work, ideas that affect communication within and between generations (Howe & Strauss, 1992). For example, Americans who lived through the Second World War share common memories (the bombing of Pearl Harbor, military experience, home-front rationing) that have shaped their worldviews in somewhat similar—though not identical—ways. This shared experience affects how they communicate, as shown in Table 5.2.

Similarly, the interplay between our sex and our gender exerts a powerful influence on our communication. *Sex* refers to the biological characteristics (that is, reproductive organs) that make us male or female, whereas **gender** refers to the behavioral and cultural traits assigned to our sex; it is determined by the way members of a particular culture define notions of masculinity and femininity (Wood, 2008, 2011). Recall from Chapter 3, for example, that we can use differences in our language styles to express differences in gender identity (Tannen, 2009, 2010).

So, are we destined to live our lives bound by the communication norms and expectations for our sex or gender, our generation, our profession, our hobbies, and our other co-cultures? Hardly. Recall the concept of *behavioral flexibility* discussed in Chapter 1. This concept notes that competent communicators adapt their communication skills to a variety of life situations. There are contexts and relationships that call for individuals of both sexes to adhere to a more feminine mode of communication (for example, comforting a distraught

AND YOU?

What do you consider to be your group memberships and allegiances? What type of impact, if any, do you think these memberships have on your communication?

TABLE 5.2

GENERATIONS AS CO-CULTURE

Generation	Year Born	Characteristics Affecting Communication
Matures	Before 1946	Born before the Second World War, these generations lived through the Great Depression and the First World War. They are largely conformist with strong civic instincts.
Baby Boomers	1946–1964	The largest generation, products of an increase in births that began after the Second World War and ended with the introduction of the birth control pill. In their youth, they were antiestablishment and optimistic about the future, but recent surveys show they are more pessimistic today than any other age group.
Generation X	1965–1980	Savvy, entrepreneurial, and independent, this generation witnessed the fall of the Berlin Wall and the rise of home computing.
Millenials	1981–2000	The first generation of the new millennium, this group includes people under 30, the first generation to fully integrate computers into their everyday communication.
Pluralist	2001–Current	These digital natives were born into a media-rich, networked world of infinite possibilities that enables them to use digital tools for engagement, learning, creativity, and empowerment. They are the most diverse of any generation and are more likely to have social circles that include people from different ethnic groups, races, and religions.

Source: Taylor & Keeter, 2010; Horovitz, 2012.

family member), whereas other contexts and relationships require individuals to communicate in a more masculine way (for example, using direct and confident words when negotiating for a higher salary). Similarly, a teenager who feels most comfortable communicating with others via text messaging or Facebook might do well to send Grandma a handwritten thank-you note for a graduation gift.

In addition, there is a great diversity of communication behaviors within co-cultures (as well as diversity within larger cultures). For example, your grandmother and your best friend's grandmother may not communicate in the exact same style simply because they are both women, they were born in the same year, or they were both college graduates who became high school English teachers. Similarly, the group typically defined as African Americans includes Americans with a variety of cultural and national heritages. For some, their story stretches back to colonial times; others are more recent immigrants from Africa, the Caribbean, and elsewhere ("Census," 2010). Christians include a wealth of different denominations that practice various aspects of the larger faith differently. Christians also hail from different races and ethnicities, socioeconomic statuses, regions, political views, and so on. All of these intersecting factors affect communication within any given co-culture.

Social Identity and Intergroup Communication

Clearly, our group memberships strongly influence our communication. This is because our group memberships are such an important part of who we are. According to **social identity theory**, you have a *personal identity*, which is your

AND YOU?

Do you consider yourself more of a masculine or feminine individual? (Note that your choice may not align with your biological sex.) Do others communicate with you in ways that support or criticize this aspect of your communication?

WIREDFORCOMMUNICATION

Online Gamers: Women Are Hard-core, Too

The stereotypical view of the gaming community—especially hard-core players—is that it is young and male. But industry reports note that 47 percent of online gamers are female, and that women over age 18 buy far more games than younger men (Entertainment Software Association, 2012). So what are women playing? And do they play differently than men?

Communication researchers studied more than seven thousand players involved in the Massively Multiplayer Online (MMO) game *Everquest II* and found several distinct characteristics related to gender. Although they represented just under 20 percent of the players, female players proved to be more "hard-core"—they played more often and were less inclined to quit the game. Their motivations for playing were different too. Men were more motivated by achievement than were women, whereas women were slightly more motivated than men by social reasons (Williams, Consalvo, Caplan, & Yee, 2009). Interestingly, although both men and women tended to underreport the amount of time they spent playing, women were three times more likely than men to lie about how much they played.

The single biggest difference between the sexes in the study hinged on players' romantic relationships. More than 60 percent of the women in the study played with a romantic partner; less than 25 percent of the men did. Interestingly, male and female players who were in romantic relationships with other players perceived their relationships differently, with men noting less contentment and overall satisfaction with their partners, and women reporting higher levels of overall happiness and satisfaction (Williams, Consalvo, Caplan, & Yee, 2009).

THINK ABOUT THIS

❶ Do you play live games online? Do you consider the gender of the players you compete against when you do? Do you choose to reveal your own gender when you play?

❷ Do you or would you try online gaming with your romantic partner? Explain how you think your communication is (or might be) altered when you share games online.

❸ Consider the discussion of gender as co-culture in this chapter. Why do you think women were so much more likely to underreport the amount of time they spent playing?

---

sense of your unique individual personality, and you have a *social identity*, the part of your self-concept that comes from your group memberships (Tajfel & Turner, 1986). We divide ourselves into "us" and "them" partly based on our affiliations with various co-cultures. The groups with which we identify and to which we feel we belong are our **ingroups**; those we define as "others" are **outgroups**. We want "us" to be distinct and better than "them," so we continually compare our co-cultures to others in the hope that we are part of the "winning" teams.

Studies in **intergroup communication**, a branch of the discipline that focuses on how communication within and between groups affects relationships, find that these comparisons powerfully affect our communication (Giles, Reid, & Harwood, 2010; Pagotto, Voci, & Maculan, 2010). For example, group members often use specialized language and nonverbal behaviors to reveal group membership status to others (Bourhis, 1985). So, a doctor might use a lot of technical medical terms among nurses to assert her authority as a doctor, whereas sports fans use Facebook posts to support their fellow fans, team members, and coaches, and to denigrate those of rival teams (Sanderson, 2013).

CONNECT

In Chapter 2, you learn that the *self-serving bias* holds that we usually attribute our own successes to internal factors and our failures to external effects. Because we want to feel good about our group memberships as well, we tend to make the same attributions. So if your sorority sister gets an A on a difficult exam, you may attribute it to her intelligence; if she fails, you may assume that the exam was unfair.

COMMUNICATIONACROSSCULTURES

The It Gets Better Project

Columnist Dan Savage was stewing. He'd just heard about the suicide of an Indiana teenager, Billy Lucas, who had hanged himself in his grandmother's barn at the age of fifteen. Lucas, who may or may not have been gay, was perceived as gay by his classmates and bullied harshly because of it. Savage felt heartbroken and angry. Nine out of ten gay teenagers experience bullying and harassment, and like most other gay men and women, Savage had endured bullying during his teenage years. But in spite of it, he was now a happy adult with a fulfilling life that included a great career and a loving family. He was frustrated that Billy Lucas would miss out on those things. "I wish I could have talked to this kid for five minutes," Savage wrote in his column. "I wish I could have told Billy that *it gets better*. I wish I could have told him that, however bad things were, however isolated and alone he was, *it gets better*" (Savage, 2010).

It was too late to say those things to Billy Lucas. But Savage knew there were thousands more young people like Billy Lucas, teenagers who were gay or lesbian or simply unsure about their sexuality and who were being targeted and tormented. He knew that those teens are four times more likely to attempt suicide than others—and he believed that it wasn't too late to talk to them. So Savage and his partner sat down in front of their webcam and made a video. They talked about their own experiences at the mercy of bullies and about being isolated from their own parents when they first came out. But they also talked about what comes later: about gaining acceptance, finding places where they weren't alone, and building families and careers. They posted the video to YouTube and encouraged others to do the same. The It Gets Better Project was born.

By November 2013, more than fifty thousand videos had been posted—from straight and gay people, celebrities, and ordinary people from all over the world—and the site had logged more than fifty million views ("It Gets Better," 2013). Suddenly, isolated teens had a place to go to be assured that they were not alone, that they could survive the bullying, and that life would, indeed, get better.

❶ Consider how the It Gets Better Project offers LGBTQ teens who are feeling isolated the opportunity to envision their lives as part of a co-culture. Can the Project help them find peers and role models?

❷ Thank about how technology allows individuals to connect with others who share narrowly defined interests (e.g., graphic novels) or face similar but uncommon challenges (e.g., a specific physical disability). How can connecting with others who share these interests and challenges via the internet enrich their lives?

❸ The Project is aimed at a very specific co-culture—and yet, the videos posted come from people from all walks of life. Is it important for LGBTQ teens to hear messages of encouragement from outside the co-culture? Do the messages posted have value for straight teens as well?

Note: The project does not offer any solutions for dealing with bullies or advise students to engage in conflict with those who abuse them. It simply offers them a peer experience, to show them that they're not alone, and tries to show them that life will go on after the bullying ends.

Our group identification and communication shift depending on which group membership is made **salient**—or brought to mind—at a given moment. For example, students often consider themselves ingroup members with fellow students and outgroup members with nonstudents. However, a group of students at different schools might identify themselves in smaller units. For example, suppose community college students consider themselves outgroups from students attending a four-year university. If all of these students discover that they're rabid fans of the *Hunger Games* trilogy or that they volunteered for Habitat for Humanity, they might see each other as ingroup members while discussing these interests and experiences.

In addition, your group memberships are not all equally salient for you at any given time, and your communication reflects this. For instance, suppose you are a female Egyptian American Muslim from a middle-class family and a straight-A student with a love of languages and a passion for outdoor adventure sports. When displaying who "you" are, you may emphasize your "student-ness" (by wearing your college insignia) and sports enthusiasm (by participating actively in sporting events). Your race, religion, and socioeconomic status don't come as much to the forefront. But remember that other people treat you based on the groups to which *they* think you belong. So someone else might focus on other aspects of how you look or talk and see you primarily as "a woman," "a Muslim," or "an Egyptian."

The ways in which others perceive our social identity influences communication on many levels. In the 1960s, Rock Hudson was a Hollywood heartthrob who kept his identity as a gay man a secret. At that time, audiences would not likely have accepted him in heterosexual romantic roles if they knew that he was not interested in women. Today, straight actors take on gay and lesbian roles (such as Heath Ledger and Jake Gyllenhall in *Brokeback Mountain*). But it isn't certain whether audiences will accept gay and lesbian actors in straight roles. To be sure, the openly gay Neil Patrick Harris has no problem playing the womanizing Barney Stinson on *How I Met Your Mother*. But some actors, including Rupert Everett and Richard Chamberlain, have noted that coming out hurt their careers irreparably, and they have advised young gay actors to maintain their privacy in regard to their sexuality (Connelly, 2009; Voss, 2010).

● **JOHN BOEHNER'S** tearful response upon becoming Speaker of the House in 2011 gained him much media airtime, perhaps because we are prone to criticize open displays of emotion from men. KEVIN DIETSCH/UPI /Landov

Intercultural Communication Challenges

With all of the cultural variations that are possible in the individual and overlapping co-cultures to which each person belongs, it is understandable that communication difficulties sometimes arise. Even with people you know well who are like you in many ways, you can sometimes experience difficulties during communication. Let's look at three of the more pressing intercultural challenges that communicators experience when interacting with others: anxiety, ethnocentrism, and discrimination.

CONNECT

In Chapter 14 on speech delivery, we offer practical tips to help you build your confidence and face the natural anxiety that accompanies a speaking opportunity. Many of these tips are also useful for overcoming anxiety in intercultural encounters. For example, Allison might visualize her success in navigating a foreign city in order to boost her sense of efficacy.

Anxiety

"What if I say something offensive?" "What if I don't know how to behave?" "What if I embarrass myself?" These are just a few of the worries that people sometimes have as they approach intercultural communication encounters. Consider the experience of Allison, an American student about to set off on a semester abroad in China:

> Here I was, standing, in the check-out line of the Chinese market in Rockville, Maryland, listening to the cashier yell at me with an incomprehensible stream of syllables. This was after a rather harrowing attempt to find groceries in the overcrowded store. A year of Chinese wasn't helping me as I stood in front of an entire display of green vegetables, trying to figure out which sign would lead me to my desired product. During all of this, my accompanying friend turned to me and said, "This is how crowded it will be wherever you go in China" (Goodrich, 2007, para. 1).

You can probably imagine Allison's anxiety as she considered her upcoming adventure: if she felt uncomfortable navigating the market just a few miles from her dorm, how would she be able to communicate effectively several thousand miles away?

But for most of us, the more positive experiences we have with those who differ from us, the less intimidated we feel about communicating with someone from another culture. And the less intimidated we feel, the more competent our communication becomes. In fact, one study found that American students who took the risk and studied abroad perceived themselves as being more proficient, approachable, and open to intercultural communication than those who lacked overseas experience (Clarke, Flaherty, Wright, & McMillen, 2009). Even online interactions across cultures may ease anxiety and foster understanding. Digital tools such as Skype, e-mail, and Google Docs enable students in globally connected classrooms to engage in international communication experiences even if physical travel is not feasible (Rubin, 2013).

Although anxiety may be a natural part of any new experience or interaction, it would be unfortunate to allow it to prevent you from experiencing the clear benefits and enrichment gained from intercultural experiences.

● **THE IDEA OF STUDYING** abroad may initially cause you anxiety, but positive experiences in a foreign country can make you a more competent and interculturally sensitive communicator. Ryan Sensenig/Photo Agora

Ethnocentrism

In the fashion world, the gowns worn by prominent trendsetters are always big news. So, when Michelle Obama wore a stunning Naeem Kahm sheath to a state dinner, newspapers and bloggers were bound to comment. But the buzz the following morning was not over what she wore but on how to explain the color of the gown. The gown, described by its designer as "a sterling-silver sequin, abstract floral, nude strapless gown," was a color somewhere between peach and sand.

The Associated Press initially described it as "flesh-colored," but changed it to "champagne" when one editor questioned: "Whose flesh? Not hers" (Phanor-Faury, 2010).

This is a simple and common example of **ethnocentrism**, a belief in the superiority of your own culture or group and a tendency to view other cultures through the lens of your own. Together with intercultural anxiety, ethnocentrism can inhibit our ability to have satisfying intercultural interactions and experiences (Neuliep, 2012). Ethnocentrism can make communication biased: we tend to communicate from the perspective of our own group without acknowledging other perspectives. The offense is often unintended, which further reveals the fact that we sometimes behave in ways that "normalize" one group and marginalize another—without even realizing it. Describing a peach-colored dress as "flesh" colored, for example, insinuates that light-colored skin is the default standard, and that darker skin tones are therefore something "other" or different from the norm. It's also unclear. "While beige may be 'nude' for most white women," noted one commentator, "'nude' for me would be brown" (Phanor-Faury, 2010).

Ethnocentrism is not the same thing as ethnic or cultural pride. It's a wonderful and uniquely human experience to express feelings of patriotism or to experience a deep respect for your religion or ethnic heritage. Ethnocentrism arises when you express a bias on behalf of your own co-cultures—when you treat others as inferior or inconsequential, or ignore them altogether. Carlos, for example, is a proud Catholic for whom the Christmas holidays have great religious meaning. He decorates his home with a nativity scene and sends Christmas cards to family and fellow Christians as December 25 draws near. But he also sends a separate set of "Season's Greetings" cards to his friends who do not celebrate Christmas. He thus shows respect for their traditions while still sharing his wishes for peace and goodwill with them.

Discrimination

Ethnocentrism can lead to **discrimination**—behavior toward a person or group based solely on membership in a particular group, class, or category. Discrimination arises when attitudes about superiority of one culture lead to rules and behaviors that favor that group and harm another group.

Recall from Chapter 2 that *stereotypes* about and *prejudice* toward a particular cultural group may result in discrimination, preventing individuals from understanding and adapting to others (Cargile & Giles, 1996). Yet seemingly positive stereotypes can have similarly discriminatory effects. For example, consider the "model minority" stereotype of Asian Americans that characterizes them as quiet, hardworking, studious, and productive. As Suzuki (2002) points out, these beliefs have led some employers to dismiss Asian Americans' complaints about discrimination in the workplace and have made government

● A BEAUTIFUL GOWN? Yes. A flesh-colored gown? Only if you're white and think ethnocentrically that white skin is the norm for "flesh." Brendan Smialowski/Getty Images

agencies and nonprofit organizations less inclined to support programs to assist lower-income Asian Americans since Asian communities seem largely self-sufficient.

Discrimination can be explained in part by research on intergroup communication. Studies show that we have a biased tendency to treat fellow ingroup members better than we treat members of outgroups (Giles, Reid, & Harwood, 2010). In fact, we even *interpret* ingroup behaviors more favorably than outgroup behaviors. For example, if you discovered that someone in your sorority was caught cheating on an exam, you would likely explain the behavior as an unusual situation brought on by challenging circumstances. But if you heard about someone from another sorority (an outgroup) cheating, you would be more likely to attach a personal explanation, such as "She's dishonest."

Improving Intercultural Communication

As with many worthwhile things in life, you can improve your intercultural communication with effort. Training programs help you become more mindful and considerate in your interactions across cultures and lead to positive changes in your thinking, feelings, and behavior (Landis, Bennett, & Bennett, 2004). Intercultural training generally focuses on three areas:

▶ **Changing thinking (or cognition).** Our thinking changes when we increase our knowledge about cultures and co-cultures and develop more complex (rather than simplistic) ways of thinking about a culture. These moves reduce negative stereotypes and help individuals appreciate other points of view.

▶ **Changing feelings (or affect).** When we experience greater enjoyment and less anxiety in our intercultural interactions, we feel more comfortable and positive about intercultural exchanges.

▶ **Changing behavior.** When our thoughts and feelings are altered, our behavior changes too. We develop better interpersonal relationships in work groups and perform our jobs better when we know what to say and not to say—do and not do. We thus act with greater ease and effectiveness in accomplishing goals.

You don't need to attend a special program or hire a professional intercultural trainer to improve your intercultural communication. You simply need to consider some important points as you communicate with people from other generations, faiths, ethnicities, and so on: be mindful, desire to learn, overcome intergroup biases, accommodate appropriately, and practice your skills.

Be Mindful

As you learned in Chapter 2, being *mindful* means to be aware of your behavior and others' behavior. To be mindful, you must know that many of your communication attitudes and behaviors are so rooted in your own culture that they are unconscious. When someone stands a bit too close to you, you might just sense "something funny." Or you might interpret someone's very direct eye contact as a sign of hostility rather than merely a cultural difference. Of course, not all uncomfortable interactions stem from cultural differences, but being mindful of the possibility gives you a wider range of effective ways to respond.

You should also ask yourself whether you might be interpreting another person's behaviors negatively or positively based on whether the individual shares your group memberships. Part of this mindfulness is practicing **intercultural sensitivity**, or mindfulness of behaviors that may offend others (Bennett & Bennett, 2004). When Luke, who is Catholic, married Caroline, who is Jewish, his mother insisted that the family pictures be taken in front of the church altar and religious statues in the garden outside. This was insensitive to the Jewish side of Caroline's family. Had Luke's mother reflected on how she would have felt if her own religious beliefs had been disregarded in this manner, she might have behaved very differently. Being sensitive doesn't mean giving up your own beliefs and practices, but it does mean not forcing them blindly on others.

Desire to Learn

Learning culture-specific information can be a useful starting point in intercultural communication; knowledge of general interaction patterns common for a particular group can increase your awareness of other ways of communicating. It can also prepare you to adapt—or not adapt—as you consider the many factors influencing an intercultural interaction.

But *how* do you go about learning about another culture or co-culture and its members' communication preferences? Is it okay to ask group members questions or to seek clarification? Do you have to visit a foreign country to learn about that nation's culture? Do you need a close friend within a given co-culture to understand aspects of that co-culture's communication? We encourage you to ask respectful and earnest questions and to experience other cultures in whatever way you are able—whether that means trying foods outside of your own culture, studying the scriptures of another faith, or deciding to study abroad.

In fact, with all the technology available to you today, you can make contact through online communities and social networking groups, even if you can't personally travel around the world. For example, some students have taken to posting videos of themselves practicing a foreign language in order to elicit feedback from native speakers on the quality of their speech and accent. Such attempts to learn more about another culture's language or way of speaking can also be seen in YouTube videos in which American and British children attempt to swap accents and rate each other on how accurate they are.

Overcome Intergroup Biases

Learning about other cultures is a great start to improving intercultural communication. But many scholars also recommend spending time with members of other cultures and co-cultures, virtually and face to face.

AND YOU?
Consider a time you felt competent in learning about another culture or co-culture. What was the situation? How did you gain knowledge about the culture? Did this knowledge cause you to change your behavior or thoughts?

Intergroup contact theory is one prominent idea for addressing intercultural challenges (Allport, 1954). According to this theory, interaction between members of different social groups generates a possibility for more positive attitudes to emerge (Pettigrew & Tropp, 2006). In other words, if you have contact with people who are different from you, you have a chance to understand and appreciate them better. Although contact theory has some support, researchers also find that mindlessly getting people from different groups together can actually backfire and reinforce cultural stereotypes (Paolini, Harwood, & Rubin, 2010). This happened in many U.S. cities during the 1970s and 1980s, when there was a highly controversial effort to racially integrate schools by busing children to schools on faraway sides of their cities. Even staunch proponents of the plan admitted that racial tensions became worse, not better (Frum, 2000).

Part of the problem is that when different groups get together we often engage in **behavioral affirmation**—seeing or hearing what we want to see or hear. In other words, if you think teenagers are lazy, then regardless of how hard your fourteen-year-old cousin studies, you don't see the effort. Instead, you notice his eye-rolling or slumped shoulders, so you still perceive him as unmotivated. We may also engage in **behavioral confirmation**—when we act in a way that *makes* our expectations about a group come true (Snyder & Klein, 2005). Again, if you think your teenage cousin (like all teens) is lazy, you'll more likely give him tasks that do not require much effort. When he, in turn, fails to put in a great deal of effort, you confirm to yourself, "See? I knew he wouldn't try very hard."

So, how do we make successful intergroup interactions more likely? First, intergroup researchers argue that we must have *good-quality contact* with outgroup members, because negative contact can increase the perception of differences (Paolini, Harwood, & Rubin, 2010). But good contact is not enough, because it makes it easy to explain away such positive interactions as unique to the individual or the situation. For example, if you believe that fraternity brothers are simply party boys and you wind up in a study group with a particularly hardworking member of Phi Sigma Phi, you can mentally create excuses: "Ben is the exception to the rule."

Researchers argue that we must have good contact *with people we think are "typical" of their group* (Giles, Reid, & Harwood, 2010). If you attended a few fraternity events and got to see Ben and several of his brothers more regularly in their fraternity setting, you might learn that many of them are serious students and that some of them aren't even into the party scene. We all need to be aware of our *own* behaviors and biased perceptions when interacting with members of other cultures and groups, so we do not simply confirm our existing expectations.

● **GOOD-QUALITY** contact with members of a campus fraternity could serve to counter the bias that frat brothers are nothing more than jocks and partiers. © Jeff Greenberg/PhotoEdit

Accommodate Appropriately

Another way to improve intercultural communication is to adapt your language and nonverbal behaviors. Recall from Chapter 3 that adjusting your language and style of speaking toward the people with whom you are communicating is a process called **accommodation**. On a simple level, you do this when you talk to a child, squatting down to get eye contact and using a basic vocabulary; police officers also do this when they adopt the street slang or foreign phrases commonly used in the neighborhoods they patrol. When speakers shift their language or nonverbal behaviors *toward* each other's way of communicating, they are engaging in **convergence**. We typically converge to gain approval from

EVALUATINGCOMMUNICATIONETHICS

THINK ABOUT THIS

That's Not a Soy Substitute

You and your friend Greg signed a lease for an off-campus apartment—you both wanted the opportunity to cook for yourselves rather than eat in the dining hall every night. In fact, food is actually one of the main reasons that Greg brought up the idea of moving off campus in the first place.

Greg is a strict vegan and does not consume animal products, including meat, dairy, and even honey. You are not a vegan—in fact you're not even a vegetarian—but you've always admired and respected Greg's passion for animal rights, his affiliation with the American Society for the Prevention of Cruelty to Animals (ASPCA), and his hard work to become a veterinarian. Before you and Greg decided to move in together, you had a frank conversation during which he told you that he would be uncomfortable having animal products in the apartment and wondered if you would be willing to eat a vegan diet in your shared space. You thought Greg would make a great roommate and you wanted the situation to work out, so you agreed. Besides, you figured you could always grab a cheeseburger on campus.

The arrangement worked out rather well and you barely think about the food restrictions, except for when Greg's girlfriend Amanda visits. Amanda is well aware of Greg's desires and views but you suspect that she finds them to be ridiculous and insulting. Sometimes you even feel that she's trying to bait you into complaining about Greg's veganism so that the two of you can "gang up" on him in an effort to enact a change of behavior. You tried to stay out of it, but one evening you arrived home to find Amanda alone in your living room, eating a container of pork fried rice—and we're not talking about some sort of soy pork substitute. "Please don't tell Greg," she pleaded. "I told him I'd hang out here until he's done with class tonight and I got hungry. I cannot eat any of that tofu and wheat gluten stuff in your refrigerator so I ordered takeout. Besides, you must think that his restrictions on what we eat here are crazy . . . don't you?"

You feel annoyed by this conversation and want to mention it to Greg, but you also feel that Greg and Amanda's communication and discussions about personal practices and group affiliations are their business. What should you do?

❶ Would this situation be different if it took place in a freshman dorm and Greg was a randomly selected roommate? Would it be ethical for Greg to ask you to follow the same restrictions—and would it be unethical for you to refuse?

❷ What if Greg's reasons for having food restrictions encompassed additional co-cultural factors, such as religion? Would this be a more, less, or equally pressing reason for you to accommodate food restrictions in your home? Why or why not?

❸ How might you structure an ethical response to Amanda or an ethical conversation with Greg based on the suggestions for improving intercultural communication provided in this chapter? How might you be mindful, be empathic, or desire to learn?

● **ALTHOUGH SQUATTING** to speak at eye level with a child is an appropriate accommodation, a senior adult may perceive this behavior as patronizing. Sitting may be more respectful. (left) PhotoAlto/Eric Audras/Getty Images; (right) Clarissa Leahy/ Getty Images

others and to show a shared group identity (Gallois, Franklyn-Stokes, Giles, & Coupland, 1988). Convergence usually results in positive reactions, because if I speak like you, it is a way of saying "I am one of you."

Accommodation is not an absolute, all-or-nothing goal: usually, it involves making small efforts to show that you respect others' cultural and communication behaviors, and you appreciate their efforts to communicate with you. Ramon makes efforts to speak English when he greets his customers at the restaurant where he works, even though it is not his native language and he struggles with it at times. Conversely, many of his regular customers who do not speak Spanish will greet him with the Spanish words they do know ("¡Hola, Ramon! ¡Buenos dias!") and thank him for their meal ("¡Gracias!").

However, it is important to be careful not to **overaccommodate**, which means going too far in changing your language or changing your language based on an incorrect or stereotypical notion of another group (Harwood & Giles, 2005). For example, senior citizens often find it patronizing and insulting when younger people speak "down" to them (slow speech, increase volume, and use childish words) (Harwood, 2000). For Ramon, if his customers were to speak slowly and loudly, or in poorly mangled attempts to communicate in Spanish, Ramon might think they were making fun of him.

Practice Your Skills

Communicators need to use verbal and nonverbal behaviors effectively and appropriately to attain goals and get along in intercultural situations. Sometimes this literally means using the language of another culture well enough to communicate effectively. Sometimes it simply means communicating your interest and appreciation for another person's life experiences and point of view (Chen & Starosta, 1996). Communicators with fewer social skills have more difficulty managing the "different" interactions that intercultural situations demand, so it is important to develop the following skills (Arasaratnam, 2007).

▶ **Listen effectively.** You can't be mindful unless you listen to what people say (and what they don't say). For example, health practitioners first need to listen to what cultural groups say about themselves and their beliefs about what will make them healthy. Then health practitioners need to shape health messages for these specific audiences (Larkey & Hecht, 2010). Knowing when to talk and when to be quiet (so you can listen) is crucial to intercultural encounters.

▶ **Think before you speak or act.** When someone communicates in a way that seems strange to you—not meeting your gaze, for example, or speaking very directly—take a moment to think about whether his or her behavior is a cultural difference rather than evasion or hostility.

▶ **Be empathic.** *Empathy* is the ability to picture yourself in someone else's place in an attempt to understand that person's experience. When you develop empathy, you can change your perceptions and improve your understanding of the ways in which another person's culture affects his or her communication.

▶ **Do the right thing.** Stand up for someone who is being mocked for his or her race, religion, or sexual orientation. Fight for those who don't have a voice. You don't need to be wealthy, established, or powerful to do this. When a friend makes a remark that you see as culturally insensitive, respond with a simple reminder ("That's a rude statement" or "Oh, man, don't talk like that"). You'll send a powerful message without chiding or berating your friend.

BACK TO ▶ *Glee*

 At the beginning of the chapter, we talked about the hit musical comedy television show *Glee,* which depicted the complexity within and between co-cultures and a satirical take on high school life. Let's revisit *Glee,* and see how the show both related to and reflected some of the concepts described in this chapter.

▶ *Glee* reflected culture in the United States in terms of the diversity of the cast as well as in the overarching themes. The members of the McKinley glee club were underdogs not only at their school but also among the other show choirs with which they competed. As part of an individualist, low power distance, and masculine culture, Americans tend to believe that with a level playing field and a lot of hard work, anyone can be successful. *Glee* tapped into this sentiment, following a long tradition of underdog stories.

▶ *Glee* also explored the ways in which cultural differences can threaten, but not necessarily damage, relationships. Kurt and Mercedes were best friends, but their different views about faith posed challenges that threatened their friendship: Mercedes was a devout Christian, while Kurt, a young gay man, had an extremely negative reaction to religion. Through exploration and discussion, the two learned to respect each other's views, even though they did not agree.

▶ Think about social identity. The first impression that most people got of Puck was that of a jock, but he also identified closely with his Jewish heritage. Artie, who used a wheelchair, was often seen as "different," but his acceptance among this new peer group led others to see past his disability and view him as they would any other teen. In addition, the members of the football team and cheerleading squads who also participated in glee club tried to balance expectations of them as athletes and "popular kids" with their participation in the traditionally outgroup glee club.

THINGS TO TRY ▶ Activities

1. LaunchPad for *Real Communication* offers key term videos and encourages self-assessment through adaptive quizzing. Go to **bedfordstmartins.com/realcomm** to get access to:

 LearningCurve Adaptive Quizzes.

▶ Video clips that illustrate key concepts, highlighted in teal in the Real References section that follows.

2. On a blank piece of paper, begin listing all the co-cultures to which you belong. How many can you come up with? How do they overlap? If someone asked you to identify yourself by using only one of them, could you do it? Could you rank them in order of importance to you?

3. Make a list of all the places where you have lived or traveled. (Remember, this does not just mean "travel to foreign countries." Think about trips to other neighborhoods in your city or areas of your state.) Create a bullet-point list to describe the attitudes, customs, and behaviors of each place that seemed to typify the area. How was communication different in each area? How was it similar?

4. Many popular films in the United States are based on foreign language films from other cultures, such as *The Departed* (2006, based on the Hong Kong film *Infernal Affairs,* 2002), *The Tourist* (2010, based on the French film *Anthony Zimmer,* 2005), and *Let Me In* (2010, based on Sweden's *Let the Right One In,* 2008). Watch one such film, as well as the original foreign language film that inspired it. What cultural changes to the story can you detect? How do the nonverbal behaviors of the actors differ?

5. Do a little virtual shopping in the toy department of an online retailer, and use the search options to see what kinds of toys the retailer suggests for girls versus boys. What do these suggestions say about culture, gender, and the ways in which children play? Do these nonverbal messages influence culture, or are they more of a reflection of culture?

Now that you have finished reading this chapter, you can:

Define and explain culture and its impact on your communication:

▶ **Culture** is a system of thought and behavior, learned through communication, that reflects a group's shared beliefs, values, and practices (p. 122).

▶ Your **worldview** is the framework through which you interpret people's behavior (p. 122).

▶ **Intercultural communication** is the communication between people from different cultures who have different worldviews (p. 124).

Delineate seven ways that cultural variables affect communication:

▶ Individuals in **high-context cultures** use contextual cues to interpret meaning and send subtle messages; in **low-context cultures**, verbal directness is much more important (pp. 126–128).

▶ In **collectivist** cultures, people perceive themselves primarily as members of a group and communicate from that perspective; in **individualist cultures**, people value individuality and communicate autonomy and privacy (p. 129).

▶ Our discomfort with the unknown (**uncertainty avoidance**) varies with culture (p. 129).

▶ **Masculine cultures** tend to place value on assertiveness, achievement, ambition, and competitiveness; **feminine cultures** tend to value nurturance, relationships, and quality of life (p. 130).

▶ **Power distance** is the degree to which cultures accept hierarchies among individuals (p. 130).

▶ **Time orientation** is the way that cultures communicate about and with time. In **monochronic cultures**, time is a valuable resource that is not to be wasted. **Polychronic cultures** have a more fluid approach to time (pp. 131–132).

▶ Cultures differ in their expression of emotion. Cultures that embrace **hyperbole** use vivid, colorful, exaggerated language, whereas cultures that value **understatement** use language that downplays emotional intensity (pp. 132, 134).

Describe the communicative power of group affiliations:

▶ **Co-cultures** are groups whose members share some aspects of the general culture but also have their own distinct characteristics (p. 134).

▶ A **generation** is a group of people born into a specific time frame (pp. 134–135).

▶ **Gender** refers to the behavioral and cultural traits associated with biological sex (p. 135).

▶ **Social identity theory** notes that your *social identity is based* on your group memberships. We communicate differently with people in our **ingroups** versus **outgroups** (pp. 136–137).

▶ Studies in **intergroup communication** examine how our group membership affects our interaction, and our social identity shifts depending on which group membership is most **salient** at a given moment (pp. 137–138).

Explain key barriers to competent intercultural communication:

▶ Anxiety may cause you to worry about embarrassing yourself in an intercultural interaction (pp. 140–141).

▶ **Ethnocentrism** is the belief in the superiority of your own culture or group (p. 141).

▶ **Discrimination** is biased behavior toward someone based on their membership in a group, class, or category. People often discriminate based on *stereotypes* and *prejudiced* views of other groups (pp. 141–142).

Demonstrate behaviors that contribute to intercultural competence:

▶ Be mindful of cultural differences and develop **intercultural sensitivity**, an awareness of behaviors that might offend others (p. 143).

▶ **Intergroup contact theory** suggests that interaction between members of different social groups can encourage positive attitudes. However, intergroup biases interfere with this process: **behavioral affirmation** is seeing or hearing what you want to see or hear in group members. **Behavioral confirmation** is acting in a way that makes your expectations about a group come true (p. 144).

▶ Research supports the importance of **accommodation**, adjusting your language and nonverbal behaviors. **Convergence** is adapting your communication to be more like another individual's. If you **overaccommodate**, however, the interaction can be perceived negatively (pp. 145–146).

▶ It is important to *practice* your intercultural skills (pp. 146–147).

> ○—— **A doctor's** ability to effectively listen to a patient can literally mean the difference between life and death. Clarissa Leahy/Getty Images

 LearningCurve can help you master the material in this chapter. Go **to bedfordstmartins.com/realcomm.**

Listening

Listening skills are crucial in medical care situations: doctors must probe patients for information and also work with teams of other medical professionals whose expertise and perspectives can be valuable. This listening process is especially important to older patients, who are more likely to have multiple health issues and to be juggling a variety of medications. Yet some studies suggest that these patients forget anywhere from 40 to 80 percent of what they are told almost immediately and misremember up to half of what they do retain (Sagon, 2013). "In a doctor's office, a lot of people, especially older people, feel pressure to get out because they know the doctor is busy and they're a bit intimidated," explains one such patient, seventy-eight-year-old Bill Allen (Klein, 2013).

Patients who don't listen to their doctors are more likely to misunderstand their doctors' advice, which increases the likelihood of complications and hospitalizations. But poor listening skills aren't limited to patients—doctors are guilty as well. When doctors don't listen to their patients, they are more likely to misdiagnose illnesses. These mistakes are costly: poor communication between doctors and patients is cited in at least 40 percent of medical malpractice suits (Landro, 2013).

The field is seeking to change those statistics. Many hospitals, health care systems, and insurers are requiring doctors to receive special training to improve their communication skills, providing advice and skill-building exercises to help them to listen better to their patients and also to teach them to speak in ways that encourage their patients to listen more effectively (Landro, 2013). Candidates for admission at many of the nation's top medical schools (among them Stanford and UCLA) must demonstrate effective communication skills in a series of short "mini interviews" that test their interpersonal skills and ability to work with others under pressure before they can even be accepted. Those who fail to listen well or who are overly opinionated are considered poor candidates (Harris, 2011).

On elementary school report cards, "Listens well" and "Follows directions" are high praise for young children (Edwards & Edwards, 2009). But somewhere in the years that follow, we stop thinking about listening as a crucial skill. "I listen well" probably isn't a line on your résumé, like being able to speak German or design an app. Yet professors, employers, and medical professionals often define effective listening as a crucial skill. In fact, listening pioneer Ralph Nichols claimed that listening helps us achieve our most basic human need: to understand and be understood (Nichols, 2006).

In this chapter, we examine the nature of listening—how we hear, process, come to understand, and then respond to others' communication. We learn why listening is so important and why we so often fail to listen effectively. And we describe tools and techniques you can use every day to become a more effective and competent listener.

How We Listen

How many times have you realized you weren't really listening to the music on your iPod? You know you heard the music, and you may have sung along, but minutes later, you realize you must have been thinking about something else because you can't recall what you heard.

Hearing and listening are not the same thing. **Hearing** is the physiological process of perceiving sound, the process through which sound waves are picked up by the ears and transmitted to the brain. Unless there is a physical reason why hearing does not take place, it is an involuntary process—you can't turn it on or off. But you can, to some degree, decide what sounds you're going to notice. This is where listening comes in.

Listening is a multidimensional process of recognizing, understanding, accurately interpreting, and responding effectively to the messages you hear. It is much more than just hearing words or being able to recall information (Bodie, Worthing, Imhof, & Cooper, 2008; Janusik, 2005). Listening involves processing what others say and do, paying attention, understanding (Thomas & Levine, 1994), and then creating messages that respond to the speaker and are directed toward achieving goals (Bodie et al., 2012; Janusik, 2005; Wiemann, Takai, Ota, & Wiemann, 1997). In the next section, we examine how this crucial process works.

The Listening Process

The listening process occurs so quickly that we may think of it as automatic, but in fact, listening involves a complex web of skills. It has three very specific components. First, we must have the motivation to pay attention to messages—known as the *affective component* of listening. The *cognitive component* of listening involves selecting a specific message to pay attention to, focusing on it, and understanding it. Finally, the *behavioral component* involves responding verbally and nonverbally to let others know we have remembered and understood what they said (Bodie, 2012; Halone, Cunconan, Coakley, & Wolvin, 1998). We can develop and improve our listening skills by focusing on these three components.

Affective Component

Recall from Chapter 4 that when you display your *affect*, you are showing the positive or negative feelings you have toward something—your attitudes. Similarly, the **affective component of listening** refers to your attitude toward listening to a person or message. For example, if you care about your roommate Brett, you are probably open to listening to him tell you how worried he is about his economics midterm. You may be even more interested if you have a midterm coming up yourself! Being *willing* to listen is an important first step in listening effectively.

However, when you are not motivated to listen, you are prone to "tune out" or only listen halfheartedly. If Brett seems to worry or complain about exams all the time (especially if he gets good grades anyway), then you may not want to hear him go on and on about this again. Or perhaps you are jealous of Brett's good grades. There are many factors that can affect our motivation to listen, including preexisting schemas (Chapter 2) that we have about a person, topic, or situation, and several listening challenges we explain later in this chapter.

Cognitive Component

The **cognitive component of listening** involves the mental processes of selecting messages to focus on, giving them our attention, and then trying to understand them. In the face of competing stimuli—your roommate Brett complaining about his economics midterm while your other roommates stream *The Walking Dead* and you get multiple texts from your parents—you must choose one sound over the others, a process called **selecting**.

Next, through **attending**, you elect to *focus attention* on the communication. If you select Brett's voice (deciding that it's more interesting or important than the sound of *The Walking Dead*), you attend actively to his words and message. Attending is not always easy, however; if your phone keeps chirping at you with new texts, attending to Brett's message may be more difficult.

Suppose that while talking about his midterm, Brett mentions a disagreement he had with his professor over the wording of an essay question. He throws around phrases like "aggregate supply" and "reciprocal demand." You've never studied economics, so you barely understand a word he's saying. **Understanding**—making sense of messages—is a crucial step because it enables you to interpret meaning.

● **THERE'S A BIG** difference between hearing a song on the radio and listening to a friend express concern about a personal issue. (left) Blend Images/Punchstock/Getty Images; (right) Blend Images/Punchstock/Getty Images

CONNECT

As relationships develop (Chapter 7), communication content changes, as do listening behaviors and goals. When you are in the early stages of friendship with someone, you use informational listening to discover hobbies and things you may have in common. But in later stages, critical and empathic listening becomes more important as you seek to analyze, understand, and connect on a deeper level.

COMMUNICATIONACROSSCULTURES

THINK ABOUT THIS

A Quick Lesson in Deaf Etiquette

In the 2013 season of the popular reality competition show *Project Runway*, one of the twelve designers vying for the big prize was Justin LeBlanc. Like the other designers, Justin had high hopes for launching his own fashion line: he was ready and eager to work tight deadlines on the challenges doled out by host Heidi Klum and was grateful for the helpful advice of mentor Tim Gunn and the mostly constructive critiques of the show's three judges. But unlike his fellow competitors, Justin did not look Klum, Gunn, or the judges in the eye when they spoke. Instead, he watched his interpreter, who translated their words into American Sign Language (ASL) for him. LeBlanc is deaf; although he has a cochlear implant, he remains dependent on ASL for most of his communication.

It's not surprising, of course, that Justin—given his passions and interests—wanted to compete in a reality show, particularly one that could launch a successful career in a fiercely competitive industry. Many people were surprised, however, by how the show handled Justin's disability. For the most part, they ignored it by *listening to him*. The producers provided Justin with an interpreter and then, essentially, got out of the way. The interpreter sometimes appeared on camera but was never introduced or identified. Klum, Gunn, and the other contestants looked at Justin when speaking to him, even though he was focusing on their words through the interpreter's signs. As Deaf1 advocate writer Lilit Marcus [herself a Child of Deaf Adults (CODA)] notes, the Project Runway cast and crew did not exclude Justin from the conversation and interaction: they truly listened to him and "clearly got a quick lesson in Deaf etiquette" (Marcus, 2013).

❶ Do you think the hosts and judges of *Project Runway* knew instinctively to look at Justin, rather than the interpreter, or is that a skill they had to learn? If you are not familiar with Deaf culture, what would you instinctively do?

❷ If you are part of Deaf culture, does it please you to see Justin treated this way? Do you think that the hearing cast members were competent listeners?

❸ What is the interpreter's role here? Should she have gotten some kind of billing or place in the story? Why or why not?

❹ Few would advocate turning to reality TV for lessons in etiquette of any kind. How did *Project Runway's* treatment of Justin's disability compare with that of persons with disabilities on other television shows?

When you don't understand something, you need to listen more actively. For example, you might ask Brett questions to learn more about the economics terms or his situation (Husband, 2009).

Behavioral Component

The third component involves *showing* the person that you understand and remember the information given—the **behavioral component of listening**. As a student, you know it's important to recall information from class during an exam, and it continues to count in real-life situations. **Remembering**, or recalling information, contributes to perceptions of competence in interactions far beyond the classroom (Muntigl & Choi, 2010). If you don't recall what happened in your conversation with Brett, he might be annoyed later when he tells you about how his dilemma turned out and you stare vacantly at him. Both your words and your nonverbal behaviors should communicate that you remember.

Responding involves generating feedback or reactions that let others know you've received and understood their message. So when Brett wonders if he should talk to his professor and you say, "Sounds like you think it's the best course of action given the importance of this exam for your grade," it lets him know that you fully comprehend his concern.

Motivated listeners choose to select, attend, understand, remember, and respond—and we call them **active listeners**. **Passive listeners** fail to make those choices; they may misinterpret messages, ignore them altogether, or need information and instructions repeated for them. Passive listeners are often regarded as less competent by the people around them. After all, you probably wouldn't pour your heart out to someone who seems more interested in watching TV than listening to you.

The goal, then, is **listening fidelity**: the match of our thoughts and another person's thoughts and intentions through communication (Beard, 2009; Fitch-Hauser, Powers, O'Brien, & Hanson, 2007; Powers & Bodie, 2003). Active listening plays an important role in achieving this goal.

Personal Listening Preferences

Each day, you spend a lot of time listening to your professors, other students, family members, and friends—more time than you spend reading or writing (as shown in Figure 6.1). Using technology can fuse these categories; for example, when you're reading a post that your friend wrote on your Facebook timeline, you're also "listening" to the message your friend is conveying. Clearly, listening will remain a vital communication skill no matter how technology continues to evolve (Janusik & Wolvin, 2009).

But how, exactly, are you listening? Four distinct preferences, or styles, emerge when it comes to listening—regardless of whether the communication is face to face or through technology (Barker & Watson, 2000; Villaume & Bodie, 2007; Watson, Barker, & Weaver, 1995):

TIME COMMUNICATING

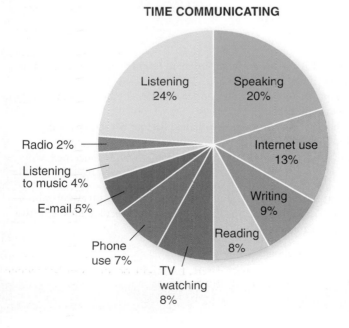

Listening 24%
Speaking 20%
Radio 2%
Internet use 13%
Listening to music 4%
E-mail 5%
Writing 9%
Phone use 7%
Reading 8%
TV watching 8%

FIGURE 6.1

TIME COMMUNICATING
Time spent by college students in communication activity, including personal computer time, multitasking, weekday and weekend time with work, family, friends, and school. Listening to mediated communication channels comprises the most time.
Source: Janusik & Wolvin, 2009.

what about you?

The following statements describe the ways some people think and behave when they are in various listening situations. Please indicate in the space at the left of each item the degree to which you believe the statement applies to you, using the following five-point scale: 1 = not like me at all; 2 = somewhat like me; 3 = neither like me nor unlike me; 4 = somewhat like me; and 5 = very much like me.

_____ 1. I am frustrated when others don't present their ideas in an orderly, efficient way.

_____ 2. I prefer to listen to technical information.

_____ 3. I focus my attention on other people's feelings when listening to them.

_____ 4. When hurried, I let others know that I have a limited amount of time to listen.

_____ 5. When listening to others, I focus on any inconsistencies and/or errors in what's being said.

_____ 6. I prefer to hear facts and evidence so I can personally evaluate them.

_____ 7. When listening to others, I quickly notice if they are pleased or disappointed.

_____ 8. I begin a discussion by telling others how long I have to meet.

_____ 9. I often jump ahead and/or finish the thoughts of speakers.

_____ 10. I like the challenge of listening to complex information.

_____ 11. I become involved when listening to the problems of others.

_____ 12. I interrupt others when I feel pressured by time.

_____ 13. I am impatient with people who ramble on during conversations.

_____ 14. I ask questions to probe for additional information.

_____ 15. I nod my head and/or use eye contact to show interest in what others are saying.

_____ 16. I look at my watch or clocks in the room when I have limited time to listen to others.

Add your scores for the questions here:

Question #   *Score*

1, 5, 9, 13: _____ If greater than 15: You are an action-oriented listener who focuses on tasks and organizes things into themes.

2, 6, 10, 14 _____ If greater than 15: You are a content-oriented listener who carefully evaluates what you hear.

3, 7, 11, 15 _____ If greater than 15: You are a people-oriented listener who listens with relationships in mind.

4, 8, 12, 16 _____ If greater than 15: You are a time-oriented listener who is concerned with efficiency.

Note: Like many people, you may score high on a number of these styles. This may contribute to your behavioral flexibility if you are able to use the listening behaviors that are most effective and appropriate for the person and situation.

Source: Adapted from Bodie, Worthington, and Gearhart (2013).

▶ **People-oriented listeners** have relationships in mind. They tend to be most concerned with other people's feelings, are good at assessing others' moods, and can listen without judging.

▶ **Action-oriented listeners** focus on tasks; they organize the information they hear into concise and relevant themes. They keep the discourse on track, so they're valuable in meetings and as members of teams and organizations.

▶ **Content-oriented listeners** carefully evaluate what they hear. They attend to information from credible sources and critically examine the information from a variety of angles. They are particularly effective when information is complex, detailed, and challenging.

▶ **Time-oriented listeners** are concerned with efficiency; they prefer time limitations on the listening interaction. They favor clear, pertinent information and have little patience for speakers who talk too much or wander off topic.

Although some people show a clear preference for one style over another, about 40 percent of people score high on two or more listening styles (Barker & Watson, 2000). Thus, the best listeners adapt their listening styles to different situations (Bodie & Villaume, 2003). For example, you may be more content-oriented while listening to a political debate so you can analyze the information and make a judgment, more people-oriented when consoling a friend because you care about maintaining the relationship, more action-oriented during a meeting on a group project, or time-oriented when you're working under a tight deadline.

AND YOU?
Consider the examples of listening styles we've given here. Do you favor a particular listening style? Are you able to adopt different styles in different situations?

The Value of Listening Well

As a young man, Dr. Ernesto Sirolli headed to Zambia to work with an Italian NGO (nongovernmental organization) focused on building local agriculture. He had good intentions and dreams of helping the Zambian people, but every project his organization sponsored failed miserably. In a 2012 TED talk, Dr. Sirolli recounts his attempts to teach the Zambian locals to grow Italian tomatoes and zucchini (which they had no interest in doing!). Just when the tomatoes were ripening to perfection, hundreds of hippos emerged from the river and ate absolutely everything. The Italians were shocked; the Zambians smiled knowingly and explained that this is why they don't have agriculture. Sirolli learned a powerful lesson: "Why don't we, for once, instead of arriving in the community to tell people what to do, why don't [we], for once, listen to them?" (TED, 2012). From this and similar experiences the Sirolli Institute developed the Enterprise Facilitation model, which focuses on responsive, person-centered approaches to local economic development through listening to local people's needs, passions, dreams, abilities, realities, and prospects. As a result, more than two hundred fifty communities around the world have successfully implemented locally focused programs for economic development.

As Ernesto Sirolli learned, it pays to listen well. In every aspect of life—from winning at Quizzo to arguing for a pay raise to helping a rural merchant establish a successful trade—listening well is essential to achieve success. Put simply,

● **DAVE RIFE,** owner of fast-food franchise White Castle, poses as a new hire in his own company, listens carefully, and takes directions from a veteran employee.
Jeffrey R Staab/CBS via Getty Images

listening affects more than your ability to communicate: it enables you to live a productive, satisfying, and healthy life (Bodie & Fitch-Hauser, 2010). Let's look at a few specific examples.

Effective Listening Helps Your Career

Effective listening is valued and rewarded professionally. Surveys of *Fortune* 500 company personnel reveal that listening is one of the most important skills that a college graduate can possess (Wolvin & Coakley, 1991) and employers routinely report that effective listening is related to job satisfaction, performance, and achievement of the organization's goals (Flynn, Valikoski, & Grau, 2008; Gray, 2010; Welch & Mickelson, 2013). Employees who are good listeners are seen as alert, confident, mature, and judicious—qualities that result in professional rewards like promotions and pay raises. Employers also value employees who can listen effectively in diverse contexts. For example, a manager expects her assistant to listen carefully to instructions for a project as well as listen for irritation or confusion from a customer. Similarly, employees must listen carefully to others during teleconferences and WebEx meetings despite distractions like background noise or malfunctioning equipment (Bentley, 2000).

Moreover, to be strong leaders, established professionals need to listen to others, make others feel heard, and respond effectively to them (Stillion, Southard, & Wolvin, 2009). The CBS reality series *Undercover Boss* features CEOs who go "undercover" in their own companies. Unrecognized by employees, they listen more than anything—by asking questions, hearing about the reality of work life for people at all levels of the organization, and probing for insights into what works and what doesn't work. In most instances, the CEO returns to make positive changes in the company's operations—and improve communication with the employees as well.

Effective Listening Saves Time and Money

AND YOU?

Can you think of a time when poor listening cost you something? Have you ever missed test instructions? Missed meeting a friend or a team practice? Do you think these lapses reflect the value (or lack of value) you placed on these events?

One reason that professionals value listening skills so much is that good listeners save time by acting quickly and accurately on information presented to them. You comprehend more when you listen well (Rubin, Hafer, & Arata, 2000), so if you actively listen to your instructor's remarks about an upcoming exam, you can save time by studying more effectively.

Businesses lose millions of dollars each year because of listening mistakes alone (Rappaport, 2010). Repeated or duplicated tasks, missed opportunities, lost clients, botched orders, misunderstood instructions, and forgotten appointments can cost companies money—as can failing to listen to customers. A few years ago, the makers of Tropicana orange juice changed its product packaging, and loyal customers deluged the company with irate letters and e-mails. Company officials quickly responded and reverted to the recognizable label (an orange with a straw protruding from it), but they could have avoided the costly fiasco if they had listened to their customers in the first place (Wiesenfeld, Bush, & Sikdar, 2010).

Effective Listening Creates Opportunities

Good listeners don't just avoid mistakes; they also find opportunities that others might miss. A real estate agent who listens to what a young couple is looking for in their first home and comprehends their financial constraints will more likely find them the right home. An entrepreneur who listens to fellow diners at a popular restaurant complain that no place in town serves vegetarian fare might find an opportunity for a new business. Even writing a textbook like the one you are reading involves listening. As authors, we must listen to our peers (who help us decide what topics and scholarship to include), to students (who help us identify what examples and issues in the manuscript are most relevant), and to our editors (who help us make the material more clear and engaging).

● **HOW WILL** your real estate agent help you find your dream home if he doesn't listen to and comprehend your desire for high ceilings and hardwood floors? Juice Images/Punchstock/Getty Images

Effective Listening Strengthens Relationships

Have you ever had a friend who just talked about himself or herself without ever allowing you to share your own thoughts or concerns? Does your roommate or a colleague send text messages or update Facebook while you're talking? They may be hearing, but they're almost certainly not listening. And your relationship may be suffering as a result.

In new relationships, the partners must listen competently to learn more about each other; failure to do this usually results in less attraction and more negative emotions (Knobloch & Solomon, 2002). As your relationships progress, listening remains a top priority. For example, you are more likely to self-disclose to a friend you think is listening to you. Similarly, you can significantly reduce your partner's stress in a challenging situation by letting him or her talk through difficult events while you listen actively (Lewis & Manusov, 2009). Even when a friend verbally "ruminates"—talks over and over again about the same issues— listening supportively can help the person feel more satisfied with the friendship (Afifi, Afifi, Merrill, Denes, & Davis, 2013).

Effective Listening Accomplishes Your Goals

A court stenographer depends on specialized listening skills to record court proceedings accurately. But is he listening differently than, say, the judge or the jury? Does he listen the same way when he is watching a movie, reading Twitter posts, or chatting with friends? Probably not, as each listening situation involves achieving different types of goals. In the sections that follow, we discuss the different ways in which we listen to accomplish our goals and desires. In some

TABLE 6.1

LISTENING GOALS

Type	Description	Strategies
Informational	Listening to understand, learn, realize, or recognize	Listen for main ideas or details; take speaker's perspective; use memory effectively
Critical	Listening to judge, analyze, or evaluate	Determine speaker's goal; evaluate source of message; question logic, reasoning, and evidence of message
Empathic	Listening to provide therapy, comfort, and sympathy	Focus on speaker's perspective; give supportive feedback; show caring; demonstrate patience; avoid judgment; focus on speaker's goal
Appreciative	Listening for enjoyment of what is being presented	Remove physical and time distractions; know more about originator (author, artist, composer); explore new appreciative listening opportunities

situations, you need to listen for information; in others, you must listen for ideas, emotions, or enjoyment. You listen to comprehend, to evaluate, to communicate empathy, and to appreciate (Steil, Barker, & Watson, 1983). And sometimes you listen with all these goals in mind.

CONNECT

When listening for informational purposes, you may ask *primary* and *secondary questions*, which first seek information and then clarify the speaker's message (see the Interviewing Appendix). Secondary questions are particularly useful in job interviews because they show the interviewer that you are an engaged listener who desires to learn more specific information about the position and organization.

Informational Listening

When you listen to a weather report on the radio, attend a lecture, or hear the details of your significant other's day at work, your primary goal is to understand what's being said. Through this process of **informational listening** (sometimes referred to as *comprehensive listening*), you seek to understand a message. As a student, you use informational listening extensively to understand concepts and information your instructors are presenting to you. Anyone giving you directions, providing instructions, or telling a story all require informational listening from you.

Questions are important aids to informational listening. Through *questioning techniques*, you coordinate what the speaker is saying with what you are hearing. Asking such questions signals that you *are* listening; it also indicates to the speaker that you are tuned in and interested. Questions can also help a speaker become more effective by getting to the points that will do the listener the most good.

Critical Listening

Most listening is informational, but we sometimes need to go a step further—to making a judgment about a message we're hearing. When you evaluate or analyze information, evidence, ideas, or opinions, you engage in **critical listening** (sometimes called *evaluative listening*). This type of listening is valuable when you cannot take a message at face value. Most of us probably need to employ this type of listening when considering a big financial purchase, like a car. Don bought his last car from a friend of a friend and failed to ask enough questions about the vehicle's history. If he'd listened more critically, he would have learned the car had been in two accidents.

Critical thinking is a necessary component of critical listening. When you think critically, you assess the speaker's motivation, credibility, and accuracy (Has she presented all the facts? Is the research current?), and ethics (What does she stand to gain from this?). Four tips can help you improve your critical listening abilities:

▶ *Determine the thesis or main point of the speaker's message.* This isn't always easy, particularly if the speaker is rambling on and on without making a point. But you can watch for key words and phrases like "What I'm trying to say . . ." or "The issue is . . ." or "Okay, here's the deal . . ."

▶ *Focus your efforts.* Listening is sometimes hard work. You might need to store up energy. For example, don't head into your three-hour large group lecture after working out or frantically finishing a paper. You may also need to concentrate and avoid distractions.

▶ *Decode nonverbal cues.* As you learned in Chapter 4, nonverbal behavior communicates volumes of information. Your friend might reveal sadness or anger in ways that don't come across in his verbal message; your professor might hint at information that will be on a test by sharing it slowly and loudly or repeating it.

▶ *Use your memory.* If you're in a lecture or on a job interview, note-taking can help jog your memory of what was said. If you're listening to a classmate share concerns about a group project, note-taking might be awkward, so try to make mental associations with her words. For example, if she says, "Benjamin's too controlling," you might think "bossy Benjamin" to remember her complaint.

Empathic Listening

When we engage in **empathic listening**, we try to feel how another person feels. Getting in touch with our own thoughts and feelings is a first step (Wolvin, 2010), but empathic listeners must use this self-knowledge to create a framework that recognizes that the feelings and thoughts of others are probably not identical to their own. Empathic listening requires openness, sensitivity, and caring—and the display of nonverbal immediacy behaviors (see Chapter 4) (Bodie & Jones, 2012).

Through empathic listening, we can provide emotional support for someone in need or comfort someone when tragedy or disappointment strikes (Bodie, Vickery, & Gearhart, 2013; Gearhart & Bodie, 2011). This is particularly important in medical situations. Doctors, nurses, and other health care providers must listen compassionately to the seriously ill. They need to determine the mental and emotional state of the patients and their families to decide how

● **WHEN *MODERN FAMILY*** parents Claire and Phil Dunphy sit their children down for a family meeting or lecture, Haley, Alex, and Luke must listen more comprehensively than they would during casual, everyday interactions with Mom and Dad. ABC/ Photofest

As you assess the credibility of a speaker (Chapters 15 and 16), you are critically listening. You focus, evaluate words and presentation style, and determine the main points. A critical listener listens to what the speaker doesn't say, too; for example, did the speech about oil seepage on the coast account for natural seepage as well as that from oil platforms?

CONNECT

Empathic listening relies on appropriate nonverbal communication (Chapter 4). In addition to paraphrasing messages, you let your partner know you're listening by leaning in, nodding, and making eye contact. Your tone of voice and your vocalizations—like the supporting "mmm-hmm"—also show empathy. The combined effect of your verbal and nonverbal messages tells your partner that you care.

AND YOU?

Whom do you call when you have exciting news or when you're feeling down? What makes this person a good listener? Are you a good listener in return when this person calls you?

much information to disclose to them and when. Empathic listening helps manage the emotions of people confronting adverse events and can help uncover erroneous assumptions contributing to their anxieties (Iedema, Jorm, Wakefield, Ryan, & Sorensen, 2009; Rehling, 2008). As a bonus, when health care providers listen empathically, not only do they help patients reduce anxiety, but also their patients are more satisfied and compliant with treatments (Davis, Foley, Crigger, & Brannigan, 2008).

When you listen empathically, it's helpful to paraphrase the thoughts and feelings being expressed. **Paraphrasing** involves *guessing* at feelings and rephrasing (not repeating) what you think the speaker has said. Empathic listening recognizes and elaborates on others' feelings, giving them some degree of legitimacy without suggesting an answer or solution (Fent & MacGeorge, 2006; Shotter, 2009). Just remember not to overdo paraphrasing; not only does the conversation become awkward, but also the other person may feel ridiculed (Weger, Castle, & Emmett, 2010).

Appreciative Listening

You use **appreciative listening** to take pleasure in sounds. Listening to music, poetry, narrations, comedy routines, plays, movies, and television shows all qualify as appreciative listening goals (Christenson, 1994). Some people find this type of listening so important that they schedule time to do it—that's why we buy tickets to concerts and other performances or tell our family members to not bother us when *The Voice* is on. Appreciative listening can also help relieve stress, unclutter the mind, and refresh our senses. We can't help but wonder if this is why credit card and health insurance companies play classical music while they keep callers on hold for twenty minutes—not that it keeps most of us from being irritated.

Table 6.1 (p.160) offers ideas for accomplishing each of the four listening goals discussed in this section. Yet we all know that competent listening doesn't happen easily, as the following listening challenges illustrate.

Listening Challenges

Maybe you grew up watching and reading about Thomas the Train and his friends; maybe you're a parent enjoying the gang's antics with your preschooler right now. If so, then you know that Thomas and company often have a lot of trouble listening. Thomas gets overexcited about his assignments and ignores essential instructions in his attempts to prove himself independent and "really useful." Gordon and Spencer tend to be overconfident and believe that giving orders makes them seem important, so they devalue the voices of their friends. And Toby is sometimes intimidated by the others (particularly Belle) and shrinks away quietly, before they're even done talking.

Much like these fictional trains, we all fail to listen effectively at times—despite the established benefits of listening well. We may find ourselves unable to listen to someone or something that we find boring. We may have trouble focusing when we have a lot on our mind, are in a rush, or are coming down with a cold. We may want to be supportive, but we feel we have heard the same complaint a hundred times. In this section, we discuss **listening barriers**, factors that interfere with our ability to comprehend information and respond appropriately. We also offer advice for overcoming these barriers (Nichols, Brown, & Keller, 2006).

Environmental Factors

Loud noise, such as sounds we experience at sporting events and rock concerts or when working around heavy equipment, is only one environmental factor impairing our ability to listen (and sometimes hear) (Cohen, 2013). Large groups present another difficulty, as they involve more people competing for your attention. Distractions in your environment—your phone signaling text messages, a baby crying, a train rumbling by your house—can also impair listening. Indeed, local transit systems can be as loud as a rock concert (around 120 decibels) (Childs, 2009). Even the temperature or air quality in a room can be distracting enough to affect our listening.

● **SOMETIMES** we listen for the pure enjoyment of the sound of a jazz artist, a string quartet, or a rock band.
© Herman Leonard Photography LLC

If you know that environmental factors will distract you from a listening situation ahead of time, you can take steps to eliminate distractions. For example, if there's a classroom on your campus that's always cold, even when it's ninety degrees outside, bring a sweater or jacket to that class. Avoid busy public places when planning for an intimate conversation. And if you must attend a lecture with a lot of rowdy people, get to the meeting early and pick a seat closer to the speaker.

Hearing and Processing Challenges

● **LISTENING** is not reserved for those with the ability to hear. These two friends are sharing ideas through sign language. © vikki martin/Alamy

Sometimes difficulty with listening lies not in the environment but in a physical or medical issue. For example, our hearing ability declines with age, affecting our ability to hear words as well as speech tone, pitch, and range (Bellis & Wilber, 2001; Villaume & Brown, 1999). Stereotypes of older adults portray them as unable to engage in normal conversation because of cognitive decline, but the real problem is often that they have to work harder to distinguish sounds (Murphy, Daneman, & Schneider, 2006). Accidents, diseases, stress and anxiety, and physical differences can also cause varying degrees of hearing impairment—for anyone, not just elderly people (Roup & Chiasson, 2010).

Still, hearing loss (even total hearing loss) does not mean that an individual cannot listen competently. Deaf individuals often speak of "listening with their eyes" and research notes that those who cannot hear physically are quite competent at decoding nonverbal behaviors revealing a speaker's emotions (Grossman & Kegl, 2007). In addition, individuals

AND YOU?

We know that manners are culturally bound (rude behavior in one culture may be acceptable behavior in another). Taking into account your culture and co-cultures (including age, gender, and so on), do you find multitasking behaviors—such as updating Twitter while a friend is talking—to be rude or acceptable? Why? How might your answer change if you were older or younger or from a different region in the world?

who use American Sign Language as a primary language also listen to each other and encode and decode messages as do any individuals speaking the same vocal language.

Even someone with perfect hearing can face listening challenges. For instance, a person with *attention deficit disorder* (ADD) may have difficulty focusing on information and tasks, which can make listening challenging. People with *auditory processing disorder*, a learning disability that makes it difficult to process information they hear, must use strategies to focus on and understand spoken information: they might adjust their environment, for example, by always sitting in the front of the classroom or always studying in the quietest section of the library. They might rely more heavily on written or visual cues when learning new information, use paraphrasing to confirm that they've received and processed messages correctly, and focus on only one listening task at a time.

Multitasking

Listening well can be nearly impossible when your attention is divided among many important tasks. **Multitasking**—attending to several things at once—is often considered an unavoidable part of modern life. We routinely drive, walk, cook, or tidy up while listening to music, talking on the phone, communicating on social networking sites, or watching television.

● **YOUR ABILITY** to accomplish tasks would undoubtedly be stretched too thin if you attempted to write a paper, browse Web sites, and carry on a phone conversation simultaneously. Getty Images/Flickr Open

We may believe we're giving fair attention to each task, but research shows that our ability to attend to more complicated chores suffers when we multitask. That's because our ability to focus is limited—we end up shifting our attention between various tasks, which decreases our efficiency and accuracy (Wallis, 2006). If you grew up surrounded by television, PlayStations, and iPods, you may be able to multitask better than people who grew up without such distractions. But regardless of age or experience, heavy multitaskers are less able to switch tasks efficiently and tend to be distracted by irrelevant pieces of information (Ophir, Nass, & Wagner, 2009)

So what are realistic remedies for this listening barrier? One remedy is discipline: vow to silence your cell phone, log out of your social networking site, and refrain from texting for a specified period. Another remedy is to be mindful and considerate of others. You may think it's no big deal to text a friend during a classmate's presentation in your human communication course, but if the roles were reversed, you might take offense or wonder if you were boring your listeners (Mello, 2009; Stephens & Davis, 2009). This point goes for interpersonal interactions, too—if you're texting Rodney or playing Words with Friends with Denise while having lunch with Alex, you might be sending Alex an unintended message that you don't value his company.

Boredom and Overexcitement

It can be hard to listen to a speaker whose presentation is lifeless or whose voice lulls you to sleep or even to a perfectly competent speaker

WIREDFORCOMMUNICATION

Don't Touch That Smartphone

The stack of phones in the middle of the table is buzzing. Three friends, gathered for an after-work drink at a local pub, are anxious. Mike, Jacob, and Elisse had all set their phones to vibrate. Only Karen sits smugly, looking over the menu with a bemused smile, knowing one of the others would soon give in. She'd turned her phone off. There was no way she was paying for dinner tonight. "Phone Stack" is a game of sorts but also a response to the culture of multitasking and technology overload that has pervaded every aspect of our social lives. When a group goes out to dinner or for drinks, phones get stacked in the center of the table, the idea being that they are off-limits. The first person to give in—to answer a call, check in on Foursquare, take a quick look to see who that text is from, or even grab the phone "just to check the time" gets stuck with the bill. The bigger the group is, the higher the stakes (Tell, 2013).

Stepping away from the bings, beeps, and buzzes that connect us to our social networks can be a challenge. But it's also important that we give those in our physical presence our undivided attention—something that's hard to do if you're worried that you might miss some important information coming in on your smartphone. And although it may seem like you can easily attend to the people you're with *and* the people you're online with, you really can't. According to cognitive researchers, the human brain doesn't really multitask—it just divides its attention. That means we're never really paying attention to more than one thing at a time; we're just constantly toggling between tasks (Wallis, 2006). Recent evidence suggests that multitasking doesn't just affect our ability to focus at a specific time—it actually has lasting effects on the way we think and react even when we're determined to focus on just one thing. "The technology is rewiring our brains," notes Nora Volkow, one of the world's leading brain scientists (Richtel, 2010). And although there is some evidence of benefits to multitasking, on the whole, those identified as multitaskers are far less adept at filtering out extraneous information in order to focus on what is important (Richtel, 2010). This important part of the listening process—selecting—suffers when we try to attend to several things at once.

So when you pick up your phone to check out your opponent's hundred-point move in Words with Friends, remember that you are actually ignoring your dining partner's story about her last Words with Friends victory. Oh, and bear in mind that you might wind up picking up the tab, too.

THINK ABOUT THIS

❶ Which is more rude: ignoring a text or ignoring the person in front of you? Which communication transaction should take priority?

❷ Does it bother you when people attend to other things—checking e-mail, Web surfing, and such—when you are speaking to them? Do you check your phone when you are out with friends?

❸ Why is it so hard to ignore a buzzing phone? Is it easier to focus on other things if your phone is out of reach or turned off? Under what circumstances do you turn off your phone?

presenting a boring topic. When something (or someone) seems overwhelmingly dull, we often wind up daydreaming about more interesting things like weekend plans, an intriguing new stranger, or postgraduation plans. Nonetheless, boring information may still be important enough to warrant your attention.

On the flip side, your own overexcitement can distract you from listening effectively, even if the speaker or topic is essentially engaging. If you're consumed by plans for an upcoming vacation, for instance, you may have difficulty listening to a great class lecture.

You can still improve your listening skills in situations where you're experiencing boredom or overexcitement. First, become more conscious about the situation. Think about how *you* would deliver the information being discussed and how you would restructure it or give examples. As you do this, you may find yourself listening more attentively. Second, avoid daydreaming by taking notes. Third, relate information to your own life. To illustrate, if you're sick of listening to a friend complain for the hundredth time about her problems with her mother, imagine how you'd feel in the same situation. Your interest in your friend's problem may perk up.

Attitudes About Listening

You probably haven't spent much time analyzing your attitudes and feelings about the act of listening (who has?). Yet sometimes our attitude is the very thing that causes our listening struggle. Let's examine three examples here.

Talking Seems More Powerful Than Listening

In many Western societies, people tend to think that talking is powerful, so *not* talking must be weak. By not valuing the power of listening, we neglect it. Michael listens to his wife only to plan what he's going to say next; he's not interested in what his wife has to say, only in making *her* listen to *him*. Katrina thinks she already knows what others will say; when her sister is speaking to her, she nods quickly and says, "Yeah, yeah, I know." If Michael and Katrina remembered that listening actually empowers us, they would be more effective communicators.

Listening well doesn't simply mean to stop talking. You have to adjust your speaking-to-listening ratio (talk less and listen more). If a desire to dominate a conversation creeps up on you, remind yourself that through the act of listening, you empower your communication partners to reveal their thoughts, insights, fears, values, and beliefs (Fletcher, 1999). Equally important, you free yourself to comprehend multiple concepts and make more connections between ideas (Dipper, Black, & Bryan, 2005). In the long run, you may even exert more influence in your relationships because, as people come to think you understand and relate to them, they will give *you* more influence.

Overconfidence and Laziness

Randall walked into a status meeting certain that he knew everything that was going to be said. As he sat through the meeting only half listening to his colleagues tossing ideas around, his boss began asking him questions that he was unprepared to answer. Although confident individuals usually understand information better than their less confident peers (Clark, 1989), many people overestimate their abilities to retain and recall information. Thus, *over*confidence like Randall's frequently leads to laziness—failure to prepare or plan for a situation and then failure to pay attention during it.

Listening Apprehension

You may know that many people suffer from public speaking anxiety. But did you know that many people also struggle with concerns about listening? **Listening apprehension** (also called *receiver apprehension*) is a state of uneasiness, anxiety,

CONNECT

Believe it or not, public speakers must listen to the audience to help the audience listen to the speech. Chapter 14 describes the importance of interacting *with* the audience rather than speaking *at* your listeners: are they yawning, looking confused, laughing, or nodding in agreement? By watching for such verbal and nonverbal cues, competent speakers adjust elements of their speaking (rate, pitch, volume, and so on) to meet the audience's needs.

real communicator

NAME: Tammy Lin
OCCUPATION: Physician

Effective listening in medical contexts means give-and-take between doctors and patients with the goal of promoting better health and wellness. As a physician specializing in internal medicine, I think of this daily. For my patients' maximum therapeutic benefit, I must listen closely to them—and they must also listen to me. The answers to patients' questions often lie in their stories, and for me to make an accurate diagnosis, I must actively listen and elicit the necessary information.

I like to think of listening to my patients as a process of discovery. Coming up with an accurate diagnosis and devising an effective treatment plan can be a puzzle. I have to search for as much information as possible about patients' health—such as what they eat and drink, what drugs (prescription and nonprescription) they take, what toxins they may have been exposed to, and what exercise they do (or don't do). This might seem like a simple question-and-answer method, but there are often roadblocks. For example, some patients are incredibly anxious when speaking with a doctor or are too embarrassed to give truthful answers (particularly about issues like diet or mental health). Still other patients seem to withhold information to see how "good" I am at figuring things out on my own. In all of these circumstances, it's up to me to put the patient at ease by opening with generally "safe" questions and easing my way into more difficult topics.

Knowing how to listen is an essential skill that allows me to do my job. With every patient, I focus on giving my full attention, not interrupting, and remaining open to whatever the patient would like to tell me. Nonetheless, my patients also have an obligation to be engaged listeners and honest participants in their own health care. Clearly, it's important that they listen in order to understand the options they have for treatment, and I encourage them to paraphrase the information I've shared. (When patients paraphrase in their own words, it shows that they comprehend what I've said. Asking them to repeat my exact words is not particularly helpful!) I also welcome and encourage questions, letting patients know that no question is too silly or simple. If I'm giving complex instructions (like information on taking a medication at a specific time of day), I either encourage patients to take notes or provide them with written materials they can bring home. Sometimes the process of writing down the information helps patients process and absorb it. Because patients may be distracted during their visit, they may not fully understand or remember what I tell them.

A particularly difficult listening challenge involves sharing and hearing bad news—like the diagnosis of a life-changing or potentially terminal illness. I always anticipate the patients' shock and watch their nonverbal communication to gauge how much information they can absorb at the moment—and what needs to be saved for later. It's simply not beneficial to spew off facts and treatment options to someone who is flushed, breathing rapidly, or crying with her head in her hands. Similarly, I hope that my patients are also monitoring my nonverbal cues in such situations. If I tell a patient that he has type 2 diabetes, for example, I use a serious tone of voice and somber facial expression while maintaining direct eye contact. It's essential that the patient sees me taking this diagnosis seriously so that he is aware of the seriousness of the lifestyle changes he'll need to implement.

The next time you see your doctor, remember that it's a mutually beneficial listening process. For a physician to arrive at an accurate diagnosis and come up with a successful treatment plan, the patient must be prepared to share all of the information related to his or her health situation (for example, current medications, recent life changes, and so on). Before your next visit, write down your questions and don't be afraid to ask about anything you don't understand. Be prepared to listen to your doctor, and help your doctor listen to you.

● **ALEX TRIES** to be helpful in offering Gigi candid advice about her romantic troubles, but her defensive response deters him from sharing his opinion in the future. © New Line Cinema/Courtesy Everett Collection

fear, or dread associated with a listening opportunity. Listening to your boss reprimand you about your job performance, listening to someone else's personal problems, or listening to highly detailed or statistical information can trigger listening apprehension, which compromises your ability to concentrate on or remember what is said (Ayres, Wilcox, & Ayers, 1995).

Students with high listening anxiety have lower motivation to process information in the classroom, which can affect their overall academic performance (Schrodt, Wheeless, & Ptacek, 2000). So it is important to assess your ability to listen effectively and to spend time developing your listening confidence. What do you think about your own listening apprehension? You may have a better idea after you complete the self-assessment on page 156.

The Ethics of Listening

As with other communication activities, you have ethical choices to make with listening situations. Some choices are positive and constructive, leading to more effective listening situations overall. Other choices are less competent; you don't accomplish your own personal or relational goals—and don't contribute anything to the goals of others. Consider the ethics of defensive, selective, and selfish listening as you evaluate the following listening behaviors (Beard, 2009; Gehrke, 2009; Lipari, 2009).

Defensive Listening

In the romantic comedy-drama *He's Just Not That Into You*, Gigi repeatedly misinterprets the behavior of her romantic partners and ignores the advice of her friends. They communicate with her through words and nonverbal behaviors, but she fails to listen and process them effectively. Instead, Gigi constantly makes up excuses to defend herself in order to fend off her feelings of rejection. Gigi is guilty of **defensive listening**, arguing with the speaker (sometimes with aggression) without fully listening to the message. Although defensive listening is an understandable response when there is a history of disrespect or aggression, it is not productive because defensive responses frequently beget defensive comments.

We've all been in situations where someone seems to be confronting us about an unpleasant topic. But if you respond with aggressiveness and argue before completely listening to the speaker, you'll experience more anxiety, probably because you anticipate not being effective in the listening encounter (Schrodt & Wheeless, 2001). If you find yourself listening defensively, consider the tips shown in Table 6.2.

Selective Listening

When you zero in only on bits of information that interest you, disregarding other messages or parts of messages, you are engaging in **selective listening**. At times this may be beneficial, as when you decide to ignore your sister's comment

CONNECT

Selective listening can also be influenced by our attributions—personal characteristics we use to explain other people's behavior. If you believe that your classmate Lara is lazy, you may listen only to messages that support your attribution. Competent communicators avoid selective listening by verifying their perceptions, seeking thoughtful explanations, and moving past first impressions in order to understand communication partners (Chapter 2).

Tip	Example
Hear the speaker out	Don't rush into an argument without knowing the other person's position. Wait for the speaker to finish before constructing your own arguments.
Consider the speaker's motivations	Think of the speaker's reasons for saying what is being said. The person may be tired, ill, or frustrated. Don't take it personally.
Use nonverbal communication	Take a deep breath and smile slightly (but sincerely) at the speaker. Your disarming behavior may be enough to force the speaker to speak more reasonably.
Provide calm feedback	After the speaker finishes, repeat what you think was said and ask if you understood the message correctly. Often a speaker on the offensive will back away from an aggressive stance when confronted with an attempt at understanding.

TABLE 6.2

STEPS TO AVOID DEFENSIVE LISTENING

that you are the "preferred" child in the family and instead just focus on her ideas for planning a happy upcoming holiday gathering.

But selective listening is also common in situations where you are feeling defensive or insecure and can have negative implications. For example, if you really hate working on a group project with your classmate Lara, you may only pay attention to the disagreeable or negative things that she says. If she says, "I can't make it to the meeting on Thursday at eight," you shut off, placing another check in the "Lara is lazy" column of proof. However, you might miss the rest of Lara's message—perhaps she has a good reason for missing the meeting, or maybe she's suggesting that you reschedule.

Selective listening can also be unethical in evaluating impressions of people. Imagine that you're a manager at a small company. Four of your five employees were in place when you took your job, but you were the one who hired Micah. Since hiring well makes you look good as a manager, you might tend to focus on Micah's accomplishments and the positive feedback from others in the organization on Micah's performance. That's great for Micah, but you must be sure to also listen to compliments about other employees, particularly when making decisions about promotions.

A specific type of selective listening is **insensitive listening**, which occurs when we listen only to the words someone says, failing to pay attention to the emotional content. Your friend Adam calls to tell you that he got rejected from Duke Law School. Adam had mentioned to you that his LSAT scores made Duke a long shot, so you accept his message for what it appears to be: a factual statement about a situation. But you fail to hear the disappointment in his voice—even if Duke was a long shot, it was his top choice as well as a chance to be geographically closer to his partner, who lives in North Carolina. Had you paid attention to Adam's nonverbal cues, you might have known that he needed some comforting words.

To improve your communication, particularly when you're feeling apprehensive or defensive, you must take care to acknowledge your selective listening and pay attention to both the verbal and nonverbal aspects of a message. You must not close your ears to competing information just because it makes you uncomfortable.

Self-Absorbed Listening

Self-absorbed listeners hear only the information that they find useful for achieving their own specific goals. For example, your colleague Lucia may seem really engaged in your discussion about some negative interactions you've had with Ryan, your boyfriend. But if she's only listening because she's interested in Ryan and wants to get a sense of your relationship's vulnerability, then she's listening with her own self-interests in mind.

Self-absorbed listening can also be **monopolistic listening**, or listening to control the communication interaction. We're all guilty of this to some degree—particularly when we're engaged in conflict situations. Suppose your grades declined last semester. Your father says, "I really think you need to focus more on school. I'm not sure I want to shell out more money for tuition next semester if your grades get worse." You may not take his advice seriously if all you're doing while he's talking is plotting a response that will persuade him to pay next semester's tuition.

Self-absorbed listeners sometimes hurt others by the way they listen. *Attacking* is a response to someone else's message with negative evaluations ("That was a stupid thing to say!"). *Ambushing* is more strategic. An ambusher listens specifically to find weaknesses in others—things they're sensitive about—and pulls those weaknesses out at strategic or embarrassing times. So if Mai cries to Scott about failing her calculus final and Scott is later looking for a way to discredit Mai, he might say something like, "I'm not sure you're the right person to help us draw up a budget, Mai. Math isn't exactly your strong suit, is it?"

Pseudolistening

When you become impatient or bored with someone's communication messages, you may engage in **pseudolistening**—pretending to listen by nodding or saying "uh-huh" when you're really not paying attention at all. While pseudolistening may help you keep up a polite appearance of listening, one of its downsides is that you can actually miss important information or offend your communication partner and damage the relationship when the pseudolistening is discovered. Pseudolistening is a common trope in television sitcoms—when Homer Simpson or Peter Griffin nod absently (daydreaming about food or some other inappropriate topic) even though they haven't listened to a word their communication partner has said, we find it funny and perhaps a little familiar. But in real life, implying that we have listened when we have not can have disastrous consequences: we miss instructions, neglect tasks that we have implied we would complete, and fail to meet others' needs.

Listening in Context

Chances are, you've recognized bits of yourself or your friends scattered throughout this chapter. We have all, at one time or another, felt defensive, nervous, bored, or lazy and found that we were less effective listeners because of it. But you probably don't feel that way all the time. You might find yourself to be a great listener in certain situations and weak in others. That's because, as with every other part of communication, our listening skills and abilities are affected

● **WHAT MIGHT** Mr. Burns be saying here? Homer Simpson doesn't know because he's pseudolistening. Fox/Photofest

EVALUATINGCOMMUNICATIONETHICS

THINK ABOUT THIS

Listening When You're Sick of Hearing

You were happy to lend your friend Jamie a sympathetic ear as Jamie worked through a difficult breakup earlier this year. You were by Jamie's side when her fiancé moved out; you took care of letting friends know that the romance had ended so she wouldn't have to go through the pain of telling them herself. You even served as a go-between for her and her ex as they sorted through untangling their lives—helping sort through paperwork and forwarding mail for her. And, of course, as a single person yourself, you were there to empathize as Jamie faced the prospect of heading back into the dating world. You agreed to be each other's date when attending parties with all of your coupled-up friends and made plans to check out a speed-dating party together as sort of a gag.

But now, only eight months after the breakup, Jamie is in the throes of a new romance with an attractive coworker. You can't help but feel a bit jealous—you've been single for more than three years; it doesn't seem fair that Jamie should find love so quickly. What's worse is that Jamie insists on spending as much time as possible with this new love—often at the expense of time with you. You want to support and be happy for your friend, but you're finding it very difficult to listen to discussions about day hikes and movie nights and sports outings. You find yourself continually avoiding the subject of dating, and as a result, you notice that Jamie seems less interested in talking to you. Somewhat relieved, you start to avoid talking to Jamie at all. You're not all that surprised when Jamie suddenly asks you why you're mad. But you don't really know what to say. You know why you're avoiding your friend, but you're sort of embarrassed about your reasons. What should you say?

❶ Should you tell Jamie the truth? Is it ethical to hide your true feelings from a friend? What might happen if you just say, "I'm embarrassed to say that I'm feeling a bit jealous. I'm feeling bummed about my own love life, and I miss having you as my similarly single friend"?

❷ What are Jamie's ethical responsibilities here? Has your friend been listening to you? Should Jamie have been able to sense your sensitivity about the situation from the way you've responded?

❸ What kinds of unethical listening behaviors might be at work here? Are you avoiding? Is Jamie ambushing?

by context (Bommelje, Houston, & Smither, 2003). In this section, we examine the ways in which the context of communication influences listening.

The Relational and Situational Listening Contexts

Imagine that you're a shy, introverted person, standing in a crowd of people at a party. You positively hate events like this, vastly preferring interpersonal or very small group activities. Your friend Yvonne asked you to come here, but, as usual, she is late. (You've stopped going to the movies with Yvonne since it's pointless to pay $12 for a ticket when you'll miss the first half hour of the film.) Suddenly, Yvonne calls you and begins a hasty explanation: "I'm sorry I'm late, but. . . ." You may hear Yvonne's excuse, but are you listening?

The situation we're in and the relationship we have with other communicators at any given time have a profound effect on our communication. When you're in an unfamiliar or uncomfortable place or at a formal event (such as a funeral, a wedding, or a professional conference), you may experience the sort of listening apprehension that we discussed earlier. And in some situations, such as a party, background noise can make it hard for you to listen. We've all been in a situation where there are so many people talking or loud music playing that we literally have to scream to be heard. It feels like it takes all of our energy and concentration just to make out a conversational partner's words. Clearly, this kind of situational context can make communication more challenging.

The relational context can also create problems. Take your friend Yvonne. As great a friend as she is, you perceive her chronic lateness as a sign that she doesn't value your time or friendship. So when she tries to explain why she's late for this particular party, you hardly pay attention. You offer no empathy, and you don't think deeply about her message. Perhaps it's another excuse about car trouble or running into an old friend on her way to meet you. But maybe it isn't—and there's something far more serious going on with Yvonne. The only way to find out is to listen actively.

The Cultural Listening Context

In various parts of the United States and abroad, you will encounter listening behaviors different from your own. As you travel or do business across the country or the world, you'll likely find it necessary to understand and adapt to listening differences.

When you think about traits and habits that make someone a "good" listener or a "bad" listener, you're often thinking about how your culture judges listening ability. For example, indirect styles of communication, common in Eastern cultures like China and Japan, require listener-responsible communication that saves face for the speaker. So a listener would be expected not to question the speaker directly, to construct meaning and understanding from the context of the situation, and to accommodate the speaker's needs more than the listener's (Lustig & Koester, 2006). Speaker-responsible listening, common in Western cultures like the United States and Canada, is more direct; the speaker usually tells the listener what he or she wants the listener to know. The listener can ask direct questions without offending the speaker, and both speaker and listener may be assertive without threatening the relationship or making the situation uncomfortable.

In addition to actual listening behaviors themselves, *perceptions* of appropriate listening vary among cultures. One study of competence and listening found that U.S. Caucasians are perceived as expressive listeners who exhibit nonverbal facilitators (like nodding, saying "mmm-hmmm," and the like). Caucasians are also seen as using more questioning techniques to clarify and comprehend the speaker's message. Latinos and Asian Americans are perceived as somewhat less expressive than whites, and African Americans are perceived as the least expressive listeners among these groups (Dillon & McKenzie, 1998). If you are comfortable or aware of only the preferred listening style of your own culture, miscommunication can occur. So Jennifer, a Colombian American, speaking with Jonathan, an African American colleague, might judge Jonathan as an ineffective listener if he

CONNECT

As you learned in Chapter 5, cultures vary in their comfort with emotional expression. Some cultures have a tendency toward *understatement* (downplaying emotion) whereas others favor *hyperbole* (exaggerating emotion). As a competent communicator, you must listen carefully to assess your partner's emotional state and needs based on this important cultural variation.

● **WHEN TWO PEOPLE** from different backgrounds address each other, they must be mindful of the culturally influenced behaviors and expectations that are at play. Jetta Productions/Getty Images

is less expressive than she would hope as she complains about a difficult client. She needs to remember that culture—including gender—is at play in this situation.

In traveling around the globe, you will also find that expressiveness is viewed very differently in different cultures. Whereas many Westerners consider deep feelings private (or to be shared only with intimate relational partners), other cultures, including Hindus in Fiji and the Ommura in New Guinea, do not regard private feelings as sacrosanct; they communicate a variety of emotions to others to build shared experiences (Brenneis, 1990). Table 6.3 shows suggestions for communicating with people of different cultures.

A discussion of culture would not be complete without thinking about how your concepts of masculinity and femininity affect your perceptions of listening competence (Burleson et al., 2011). For example, men in the United States are usually discouraged from expressing intense emotions in public (Brody, 2000). This reluctance to react emotionally to information may give the appearance that men are not listening. Expectations about appropriate feminine behavior encourage women to exhibit *more* verbal and nonverbal feedback when listening, such as nodding and smiling more, and using more encouraging filler words ("Really?" "Oh, wow," "Right"). Most research indicates that an individual's role (being a parent, for example) accounts for more listening differences than the sex of the listener does (Duncan & Fiske, 1977; Johnston, Weaver, Watson, & Barker, 2000). Nonetheless, listening stereotypes are still powerful and make their way into entertainment and advertising at every level. In the episode

● **THE GANG** from *Family Guy* believes that listening—along with the verbal and nonverbal expressions that accompany it—is for women only!

Tactic	Explanation	Example
Recognize cultural differences	When communicating with someone from a different culture, keep in mind that factors such as country of origin, religion, gender, educational level, and socioeconomic status all play into our values and beliefs about communication. If you can, learn about the person's background, and ask questions.	If your future mother-in-law is a devout Catholic from France and you are a nonreligious person from St. Louis, you might want to learn more about French culture and Catholicism; you might ask your fiancée questions about how to get to know Mom.
Clarify behaviors as appropriate	Pay attention to the cultural needs of the listener. If you find that cultural differences are preventing good communication, tell the speaker or be silent to observe context and nonverbal behaviors.	"I don't think I'm understanding you correctly. Can you say that in another way for me, please?"
Adjust to differences	Ask more questions if necessary; ask the speaker to work with you to bridge the gap between cultural differences.	"I'm sure I'm not getting the complete picture. Can you give me an example of the problem to help me understand it better?"

TABLE 6.3

TIPS FOR COMMUNICATING ACROSS CULTURES

"I Am Peter, Hear Me Roar," *Family Guy*'s Peter decides to get in touch with his feminine side and calls his buddy Quagmire "just to talk." He wants to listen to what's going on with his friend and have his friend listen to him in turn. Quagmire is so uncomfortable with this situation that he slams down the phone!

The Technology Listening Context

Anish Patel could have walked across campus to attend his microeconomics course in person. But why bother, when the lecture is streaming live over the campus network? Instead of listening with his classmates in a crowded lecture hall, he watches on his laptop in the comfort of his own apartment (Gabriel, 2010).

Russell Hampton is both a father and the president of a book and magazine publishing unit of Walt Disney Company. When he was driving his daughter and her teenage friends to a play, he listened to their conversation about an actor in a Disney movie and tried to join in the conversation. Suddenly, the girls became very quiet. Russell could see his daughter texting in the rearview mirror and chided her for being rude and ignoring her friends. He later discovered that all three teens were texting each other—so that they could listen to one another without Russell listening to them (Holson, 2008).

As these two examples illustrate, technology can be both helpful and hurtful to the listening process. Anish Patel might listen more effectively in a classroom with the energy of live interaction where questions can be asked and notes compared. But he might also be able to process the lecture more effectively by rewinding and listening again to sections of the lecture without distraction. Russell Hampton might be hurt that his daughter and her friends shut him out of their conversation, but their texts give them a powerful way of listening to one another.

Listening to messages in various technological contexts requires a lot more effort than other forms of communication. For example, when you talk on the phone, you rely on verbal messages as well as vocal nonverbal messages (tone of voice, speaking rate, silences, and so on) because you lack other nonverbal cues such as body movement and eye behavior. But when you read your mom's e-mail or you text your significant other, you often lack both components.

For this reason, you must be sure to listen actively to the cues you do have at your disposal. When your friend Sheila capitalizes a word in a text, she's giving emphasis to a particular point; you can show her that you've listened by making sure to address that particular point. In general, you show your communication partners that you've listened to their Facebook posts when you respond to the questions or concerns that they raised. You're not listening competently if you respond to your father's questions about when you're coming home next with an e-mail that details what you had for lunch. Similarly, you listen well when you enter an online chat and read the sequence of comments before responding (rather than blurting out a response to the first post you see).

And, of course, using technology competently also means taking into account the receiver of your message. Consider how your friend Eddie in Milwaukee would want to hear the news that you've broken up with his cousin whom you've been dating for two years: Through a text message? On Twitter? Over the phone? You'll want to choose the channel that is the most effective and appropriate for the occasion.

BACK TO ▶ The Doctor's Office

At the beginning of this chapter, we talked about the importance of good communication between doctors and patients, as well as the costs of communication breakdowns in the health care field. Let's take a moment to revisit the nature of listening as it relates to patient–doctor interactions.

▶ All communication is transactional, and both parties—in this case, the doctor and the patient—are responsible for it. But the expense of lawsuits and malpractice insurance ultimately puts the pressure on the health care professionals to improve communication in order to avoid costly mistakes. That's why so many hospitals and insurance companies are providing training for doctors. Medical schools are taking the process a step further by weeding out candidates who are poor communicators.

▶ Doctors also bear greater responsibility for communication outcomes because they, at the end of the day, are the professionals and are expected to be adept at every aspect of their jobs. Linda Berstein, who directs a program for improving health care professionals' communication skills, notes, "To be a good doctor, you have to have the ability to listen to the patients and follow their leads" (quoted in Landro, 2013, para. 26). Doctors in the program are trained to ask better questions, to probe for additional information, and to ensure that patients understand their directions.

▶ Age may affect memory, but the situational context plays a role here as well. In a doctor's office, faced with concerns about our health and intimidated by unfamiliar medical terminology, we are more likely to experience listening apprehension, which will affect our ability to process information.

▶ Note the patient's explanation that people might rush out of a doctor's appointment because "they know the doctor is busy." In this case, the relational context is negatively impacting communication. A doctor who implies that she is busy, or perhaps that she has more important patients to attend to, might leave a patient thinking that her case, or her illness, is less important or perhaps not as serious.

THINGS TO TRY ▶ Activities

1. LaunchPad for *Real Communication* offers key term videos and encourages self-assessment through adaptive quizzing. Go to **bedfordstmartins.com/realcomm** to get access to:

 LearningCurve Adaptive Quizzes.   ▶ Video clips that illustrate key concepts, highlighted in teal in the Real Reference section that follows.

2. Describe a time when you listened well. How do you know you listened well? Where were you? Who were you with? What were your goals? Did you adapt

your listening to the situational, cultural, or relational context? What can you learn from this successful listening experience to guide you in future listening challenges?

3. Practice listening with your eyes as discussed in this chapter. When you go to your next class, observe your instructor or whoever is speaking. Form an overall impression of the speaker from nonverbal cues such as body movements, eye behavior, and tone of voice. What emotions do they suggest? Do they match the verbal message being conveyed?

4. As you become a more critical listener, inquire about inconsistencies when you observe them in conversation. For example, if your friend offers you verbal and nonverbal messages that contradict each other, let him or her know. Be careful to avoid being defensive here. Instead of saying, "You're sending me mixed messages," say, "I'm confused about what you mean. You said you were happy with the decision, but you frowned and sighed at the same time."

5. Practice listening styles that are less familiar to you. Some people don't paraphrase well; others are uncomfortable being person-centered. The best way to try this out is to look back at the chapter and think about the discussions that made you feel uncomfortable ("I could never do that"). Then give it a try in a context that might benefit you. For example, if you tend to be an empathic, person-centered listener in group meetings and your meetings always run late because of it, try being a more time-centered or action-centered listener.

6. Keep a log of how you "listen" with technology. Is it easier—or more difficult—for you to select, attend, remember, understand, and respond? Compare your experiences with friends. Do some of your friends or family prefer the technology or do they value face-to-face listening more?

Now that you have finished reading this chapter, you can:

Outline the listening process and styles of listening:

▶ **Hearing** is physiologically perceiving sound; **listening** is the process of recognizing, understanding, and interpreting the message (p. 152).

▶ Effective listening involves three components (p. 152).

  ▶ The degree to which we are willing to listen is the **affective component** (p. 153).

  ▶ The **cognitive component** involves **selecting** (choosing one sound over others), **attending** (focusing on the message), and **understanding** (making sense of the message) (p. 153).

  ▶ The **behavioral component** includes recalling information to communicate—**remembering**—and **responding**, giving feedback (pp. 154–155).

▶ **Active listeners** make choices about selecting, attending, and so on, and are more competent than **passive listeners** (p. 155). **Listening fidelity** is the degree to which the thoughts of the listener agree with the intentions of the source of the message (p. 155).

▶ **People-oriented listeners** listen with relationships in mind (p. 157).

▶ **Action-oriented listeners** focus on tasks (p. 157).

▶ **Content-oriented listeners** carefully evaluate what they hear (p. 157).

▶ **Time-oriented listeners** prefer information that is clear and to the point (p. 157).

▶ Most people develop multiple listening preferences (p. 157).

List the advantages of listening well:

▶ Listening well helps your career, saves time and money, creates opportunities, strengthens relationships, and helps you achieve goals (p. 159).

▶ **Informational listening** is used to understand a message (p. 160).

▶ In **critical listening**, you evaluate information, evidence, ideas, or opinions (pp. 160–161).

▶ **Empathic listening** is an attempt to know how another person feels, often using **paraphrasing** to recognize and elaborate on the other's feelings (pp. 161–162).

▶ **Appreciative listening** is used when the goal is simply to appreciate the sounds, such as listening to music (p. 162).

Identify challenges to good listening and their remedies:

▶ **Listening barriers** are factors that interfere with our ability to comprehend information and respond appropriately (pp. 162–163).

▶ Allergies and crying babies are examples of environmental factors that impair our ability to listen (p. 163).

▶ Hearing loss challenges can be overcome with understanding of nonverbal behaviors (pp. 163–164). Processing challenges (for example, ADD) are faced by many who have normal hearing.

▶ **Multitasking**, attending to several things at once, limits focus on any one task (p. 164).

▶ A boring speaker or topic can be hard to follow, but overexcitement can be distracting (pp. 164–165).

▶ Talking may be regarded as more powerful than listening (p. 166).

▶ Overconfidence may cause us to become lazy and not pay careful attention during communication (p. 166).

▶ **Listening apprehension**, anxiety or dread associated with listening, may hinder concentration (p. 166, 168).

Identify ethical factors in the listening process:

▶ **Defensive listening** is responding with aggression and arguing with the speaker, without fully listening to the message (p. 168).

▶ **Selective listening** is zeroing in on bits of information that interest you (pp. 168–169). **Insensitive listening** occurs when we fail to pay attention to the emotional content of someone's message and just take it at face value (p. 169).

▶ Self-absorbed listeners listen for their own needs and may practice **monopolistic listening**, or listening in order to control the communication interaction (p. 170).

▶ **Pseudolistening** is pretending to listen while not really paying attention (p. 170).

Describe how various contexts affect listening:

▶ Different situations create different challenges (p. 171).

▶ The dynamics of the relationship changes how you listen (p. 171).

▶ The cultural context affects listening behavior (pp. 172–173).

▶ Technology is an important context for listening (p. 174).

Interpersonal
Communication

CHAPTER 7

Developing and
Maintaining
Relationships

CHAPTER 8

Managing
Conflict in
Relationships

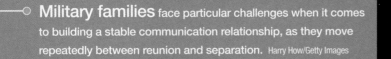

Military families face particular challenges when it comes to building a stable communication relationship, as they move repeatedly between reunion and separation. Harry How/Getty Images

LearningCurve can help you master the material in this chapter.
Go to **bedfordstmartins.com/realcomm**.

chapter 7

Developing and Maintaining Relationships

Mary Marquez is a U.S. Army wife. She's strong; she has to be. For a good part of the year, she manages her job, two teenage sons, the house and its bills and maintenance, and her relationships, all while missing—and worrying about—her husband, Justin. When Justin is home, Mary obviously wants to spend time with him. But as soon as she's feeling comfortable and connected, he's sent off to some other part of the world and she's on her own again.

Mary and Justin are like many other families whose military-related separations put a strain on their communication and relationships. Justin and Mary often don't know when and where Justin will deploy; even when the deployment has been scheduled, dates often fluctuate. This uncertainty puts a strain on every member of the family as they struggle between the independence they must have during the deployment and the connectedness they desire when they are all together (Merolla, 2010b). Some military spouses deal with it by not dealing with it at all—that is, by engaging in arguments about other matters or by shutting down communication completely. But Mary and Justin work on their communication. They hide notes for one another around the house while he is home. When he is away, they plan times when they can connect online, and during those conversations they try to focus on "normal," routine things like talking about their days or discussing a book they are both reading. Mary said these behaviors "made it feel more routine and made it feel like he wasn't so far away" (Sahlstein, Maguire, & Timmerman, 2009, p. 431).

The distance and time zone differences can make connecting in real time difficult, though; when family members miss a connection, it can lead to hard feelings and misunderstandings. For example, one of Mary's friends described how disgruntled her husband became when she and the kids weren't at home waiting for his call.

chapter
outcomes

After you have finished reading this chapter, you will be able to

- Explain key aspects of interpersonal relationships

- Describe why we form relationships

- List ways to manage relationship dynamics

- Describe the factors that influence self-disclosure

- Outline the predictable stages of most relationships

As you learned in Chapter 1, people need to be in relationships with other people: relationships help us meet many needs, such as companionship and intellectual stimulation. Could Frodo of *The Lord of the Rings* have survived without the help of his friend Samwise Gamgee helping to stave off the evil effects of the ring? Of course not! The military family we described here are no different; their relationships are important to their survival, too.

In this chapter, we focus on **interpersonal relationships**, the interconnections and interdependence between communicators. To understand these relationships, we need to be aware of the role communication plays in them. **Interpersonal communication** is the exchange of verbal and nonverbal messages between people who build relationships, share meanings, and accomplish social goals (Burleson, 2010). You engage in interpersonal communication in your most intimate relationships—when you sit down to a heartfelt conversation with your significant other or when you catch up with your best friend. But you also engage in interpersonal communication when you get to know your professor during office hours and when you chat with your new neighbor. Even though your relationship with your friends or significant other is probably more important to you than your relationship with your neighbor, competent communication allows you to meet personal needs, whether it's finding support after a hard day's work or borrowing a hammer.

So let's take a closer look at interpersonal relationships and the communication that takes place in them by examining the types of relationships we form, why we do so, and what happens once we're in them.

Types of Interpersonal Relationships

Martin asks Pete, "Do you know my friend Jake?" Pete responds, "I've met him once or twice." In two short sentences, we gain information about the relationships at play: to Martin, Jake is a friend; to Pete, he's just an acquaintance. We're all involved in multiple relationships, and we distinguish among them in countless ways: acquaintances, colleagues, coworkers, teammates, friends, family members, romantic partners, virtual strangers we see all the time (like a barista or grocery clerk), and so on. Every person has a complex **relational network** or web of relationships that connects individuals to one another. In this section, we focus on family relationships, friendships and social relationships, and romantic partnerships, as well as online relationships.

Family Relationships

For some people, the term *family* refers to immediate relatives who live in the same household. For others, it means a more extended family that includes grandparents, aunts, uncles, and cousins. Still others use the term to describe groups of people with whom they are intimately connected and committed, even without blood or civil ties, like some fraternal organizations or religious communities. But for our purposes, a **family** is a small social group bound by ties of blood, civil contract (such as marriage, civil union, or adoption), and a commitment to care for and be responsible for one another, often in a shared household.

Communication Standard	Examples
Openness	• Share feelings; able to talk when something is wrong • Talk about sensitive issues like sex or drugs
Structural stability	• Everyone listens to and obeys at least one person in the family • Deal with emotional issues when everyone can handle them
Affection	• Be loving and affectionate with one another • Say affectionate things like "I love you"
Emotional and instrumental support	• Help each other; know support will be there • Able to count on each other
Mind reading	• Know what's going on with each other without asking • Understand how the other feels without discussing it
Politeness	• Never be rude or inconsiderate • Never talk back
Discipline	• Have clear rules for family members • Know the consequences for breaking family rules
Humor or sarcasm	• Able to tease other family members • Poke fun at each other, lovingly
Regular routine interaction	• Meet regularly to discuss things • Set aside time to communicate
Avoidance	• Avoid topics that are too personal • Agree to skirt issues that are painful

TABLE 7.1

FAMILY COMMUNICATION QUALITIES

Source: Adapted from Caughlin (2003).

● **THOUGH *MODERN FAMILY*** emphasizes the diversity of forms a family can take, it also suggests that, no matter what type of family you're a part of, the same core communication skills help all family members to support and share with each other. ABC/Photofest

Our first and most basic relationships are with family. From them, we learn communication skills and develop characteristics that affect how we interact with other people throughout our lives. ABC's award-winning *Modern Family* features three Los Angeles families—that of Jay Pritchett and those of his daughter Claire and son Mitchell. Jay and his second wife, Gloria, have a baby son and her teenage son from a previous relationship. Claire and Phil Dunphy have three children, and Mitchell and his partner, Cameron, have an adopted Vietnamese daughter. Although the mockumentary format delivers a lot of laughs, the communication relationships are very solid and serious. The families support the diversity among them and challenges they all face, and they are very involved in each other's lives (see Table 7.1). They teach their children the beliefs, values, and communication skills they need to face life's challenges, to feel loved and secure, and to achieve success both professionally and personally (Ducharme, Doyle, & Markiewicz, 2002). These messages are essential for enriching family life and positively developing younger family members (Canary & Dainton, 2003; Guerrero, Andersen, & Afifi, 2013; Mansson, Myers, & Turner, 2010).

● **OPRAH WINFREY AND GALE KING'S** decades-long friendship illustrates the benefits and joys that can result from a close, caring relationship. Frazer Harrison/Getty Images for AFI

As you learn about interpersonal relationships, remember the competent communication model from Chapter 1. There is no one right way to communicate with friends, family, or romantic partners because competent communication considers relational, situational, and cultural contexts. You may feel comfortable sharing personal information with your father; your friend Julie may not. You and your significant other may develop a communication style that simply wouldn't work for your brother and his girlfriend.

Friendship and Social Relationships

As individuals grow and interact with people outside their families, they establish new, nonfamily relationships. **Friendship** is a close and caring relationship between two people that is perceived as mutually satisfying and beneficial. Friendship benefits include emotional support, companionship, and coping with major life stressors (Rawlins, 1992, 2008). Children who form successful friendships with others perform better academically and demonstrate fewer aggressive tendencies than those who do not (Doll, 1996; Hartup & Stevens, 1997; Newcomb & Bagwell, 1995; Rawlins, 1994; Weisz & Wood, 2005). And secure, stable friendships and family relationships serve to enhance children's ability to process communication behaviors (Dwyer et al., 2010).

Although everyone has a personal opinion as to what qualities a friend should possess, research finds agreement on six important characteristics of friendship (Pearson & Spitzberg, 1990): availability (making time for one another), caring (expressing concern for well-being), honesty (being open and truthful), trust (being honest and maintaining confidentiality), loyalty (maintaining the relationship despite disagreements), and empathy (communicating understanding of feelings and experiences). The extent to which friends share these characteristics helps build the relational context of their relationship (see Chapter 1).

Some of the relationships you call "friendships" might actually be more accurately described as **social relationships**, relationships that are functional within a specific context but are less intimate than friendship. For example, you may have casual work pals with whom you can complain about your boss, people with whom you socialize via your ragtag pick-up hockey team, or a hair stylist you love to visit so that you can engage in celebrity gossip (see

WIREDFORCOMMUNICATION

To Friend, or Not to Friend

Among toddlers on playgrounds, the question "Will you be my friend?" is common. But as we grow older, it's rare that any relationship begins with such formalities. That is, until we get to Facebook. Suddenly, it has become the norm to reach out to people you know—and people you barely know or don't know at all—and invite them to be your "friend" in this virtual environment. These connections can be valuable: for individuals seeking to network, for organizations seeking to promote a business or cause, for groups trying to organize or distribute information to members, and for anyone who wants to share thoughts, photos, or other content, Facebook provides a simple interface and a large and somewhat customizable audience.

Complicating the issue is the fact that each of the social networking site's more than 874 million active users uses it in a different way. Some think of it as a microblog for posting their observations or opinions, or for sharing experiences, whereas others use it as a networking space for making professional, social, or civic connections. Some might post a good deal of personal information for the world to see (photos, favorite causes, political rants, religious statements) whereas others might use it only to keep in touch with close friends and family. Among social media users, 58 percent note that they limit access to their content to "friends only" (Madden, 2012), but deciding who a "friend" is can be difficult. The company's prime mission is "to make the world more open and connected" ("Our Mission," 2013), and in pursuit of that goal, the platform makes it increasingly difficult to maintain just a small network of Facebook friends. So, what starts out as a close circle of friends with whom you might share intimate details of your life is quickly expanded as "friend requests" from acquaintances, colleagues, "friends of friends," and others start showing up in your notifications box.

Of course, you can simply deny friend requests, lock down your privacy settings, and keep your group small. But when you do that, you risk insulting or offending those who seek to connect with you—which can be awkward. How do you deny a friend request from your boss? Your professor? Your nana? On the other hand, if you accept every friend request that comes in, you risk having your information broadcast beyond your intended circle of connections. A time-stamped comment on a colleague's page could reveal that you were not exactly on task at work all day if that colleague is a "friend" of your boss; liking a friend's private photo or relationship status could out him to his family if you—or any of your "friends"—share connections with them.

Recent data suggest that Facebook use may be declining. Teens are largely abandoning the site for other networks (Bercovici, 2013), and more than a quarter of current users note that the site is less important to them than it was a year ago. Among adults who do not use the network, some 20 percent are former Facebook users who have left (Rainie, Smith, & Duggan, 2013). Relatively few former users and nonusers specifically site privacy issues as a key concern, although many have noted that there was too much drama, gossip, and boring, mundane, or negative posts from "friends."

THINK ABOUT THIS

❶ Are you on Facebook? Have you ever rejected a friend request or unfriended someone? How did that affect your relationship with that "friend"?

❷ As discussed in the chapter, the term *friend* is often used to describe people with whom we have social relationships but do not share close, intimate ties. How does Facebook's use (or misuse) of this term affect its meaning?

❸ Do you think that the way you use Facebook has changed over time? Does the way you use it relate to the number of "friends" in your network? Do you post the same way for a large group as you would for a small group?

❹ Other networks have tried to make it easier to separate groups of friends online (Google+, for example, enables users to easily group connections into different "circles"). But Facebook remains the largest and most popular social network. Do you think that Facebook is here to stay? Why or why not?

Markoff & Sengupta, 2011). Indeed, it's likely that the vast majority of your six hundred Facebook "friends" are really social acquaintances. Sometimes, these social relationships can become awkward when one partner assumes too much intimacy. For example, someone you barely know in your religious community might expect to be invited to your wedding, or you might encounter unease if you ask a few coworkers to go to happy hour in a corporate culture that discourages outside socialization (DeKay, 2012).

Romantic Relationships

What ideas, thoughts, and feelings come to mind when you think about romantic relationships? Do you think of romantic dinners, jealousy, butterflies in your stomach? Perhaps you think about sex or about commitment and love (Tierney, 2007).

Love can be used to describe feelings other than romantic ones, including our feelings for our families, friends, pets, or anything that evokes strong feelings of like or appreciation (as in "I love the Chicago Bears" or "I love burritos"). But we typically define **love** within the context of relationships as a deep affection for and attachment to another person involving emotional ties, with varying degrees of passion, commitment, and **intimacy** (closeness and understanding of a relational partner). There are many types of love that can characterize different relationships—or even the same relationship at different times. For example, the love between Anna and Mario, married for fifty-seven years, is probably not the same as when they were first married. Studies involving hundreds of people revealed six categories of love: *eros* (erotic, sexual love), *ludus* (playful, casual love), *storge* (love that lacks passion), *pragma* (committed, practical love), *mania* (intense, romantic love), and *agape* (selfless, unconditional love) (Hendrick & Hendrick, 1992; Lee, 1973). Some relationships may be characterized by only one of these types, whereas others may move through two or more types over time.

The complexities of romantic love can be astounding, but the desire to attain it is as universal as it is timeless. In fact, the value of relationships and the characteristics that comprise love and commitment between two people are fairly consistent regardless of culture. One study found that among Americans, Chinese, Japanese, and Koreans, differences in notions of love were not pronounced, and respondents from all four countries reported that happiness and warmth were associated with love (Kline, Horton, & Zhang, 2005).

Studies show that relational harmony has both physical and psychological benefits, as you can see in Figure 7.1 (Parker-Pope, 2010a). However, research reveals that there isn't one specific path to romantic satisfaction. Dating partners in both long-distance and geographically close relationships enjoy satisfaction through the use of compatible styles of humor and other coping skills to decrease relational stress (Hall, 2013; Vela, Booth-Butterfield, Wanzer, & Vallade, 2013). Same-sex couples in long-term, committed relationships share the same benefits of meaningful commitment (such as life satisfaction and general well-being) as heterosexual couples (Clausell & Roisman, 2009). Cohabitating unmarried couples who see themselves on a trajectory toward marriage enjoy similar satisfaction and well-being as married couples, but those who have

FIGURE 7.1

EFFECTS OF RELATIONSHIP HARMONY
This figure represents some of the benefits that happy relationships might expect.
Source: Parker-Pope, 2010a.

ambiguity about their path or the future of the relationship are more at risk for negative relational outcomes (Willoughby, Carroll, & Busby, 2012).

Online Relationships

Tens of thousands of people around the world play and connect via online games like *World of Warcraft* and *Eve Online*. In fact, the game company Blizzard hosts an in-person gaming convention that draws people from all fifty U.S. states and over forty countries. Although the gamers are certainly drawn to the costume and dance contests and the announcements of new products, they are perhaps even more drawn to the interactions they can have with other gamers. They hang around hotel lobbies talking long after the event is over, illustrating the importance of the relationships they have formed within these online worlds (Schiesel, 2011).

For years, online relationships were considered impersonal, lacking the richness of nonverbal cues found in face-to-face relationships (Tidwell & Walther, 2002). But mediated communicators actually take advantage of the lack of these cues to gain greater control over both their messages and their presentation of self. **Social information processing theory** (SIP) (Walther, 1996; Walther & Parks, 2002) argues that communicators use unique language and stylistic cues in their online messages to develop relationships that are just as close as those that develop face to face—but often take more time to become intimate. Online communicators can develop **hyperpersonal communication**, communication that is even *more* personal and intimate than face-to-face interaction. Freed from the less controllable nonverbal cues (such as appearances or nervous fidgeting), online communicators can carefully craft their messages and cultivate idealized perceptions of each other (Walther & Ramirez, 2009). Indeed, relational partners often feel less constrained in the online environment (Caplan, 2001),

AND YOU?

Do you have any relationships that exist strictly online? Do you consider these relationships different from other ones in your life? Are they more intimate or less?

● **ROMANTIC COUPLES,** regardless of sexual orientation, age, race, or ethnicity, all enjoy similar benefits of being in a relationship: intimacy and commitment. (top left) Mike Powell/ Getty Images; (top right) © John Birdsall/ The Image Works; (bottom left) ZHAO YINGQUAN/Xinhua /Landov; (bottom right) Hola Images/Getty Images

which can lead to the development of rich and meaningful relationships both online and off (Antheunis, Valkenburg, & Peter, 2010; Pauley & Emmers-Sommer, 2007).

Romances and friendships can frequently bud and be maintained through the use of electronic media. More than one-third of U.S. marriages now begin as online matches (Cacioppo et al., 2013); although their initial interactions are entirely electronic—only meeting face to face after a series of messages, e-mails, and perhaps phone calls—the resulting relationships are more satisfying, and the individuals are slightly less likely to separate or divorce once married (Cacioppo et al., 2013). Even established couples maintain long-distance relationships by using electronic media; they tend to communicate greater intimacy than geographically close partners and are more likely to avoid conflict and problematic topics when communicating electronically (Stafford, 2010). Similarly, sharing photos, videos, and stories on Facebook, Twitter, or blogs allows us to share our lives with friends and family in other states and countries. And regular texting, video chats, phone calls, and e-mail messages keep partners close and aware of each other's lives (Bergen, 2010; Maguire & Kinney, 2010; Mansson, Myers, & Turner, 2010; Merolla, 2010a).

Of course, a danger of communicating *solely* online with someone is that it can be difficult to detect whether the information posted is truthful. Photos can be altered and descriptions of one's experiences exaggerated. At the extreme, online relationships might even be outright false. Former Notre Dame linebacker Monti Te'o was the apparent victim of an elaborate relationship hoax. He thought he was developing a romantic relationship with a woman online who turned out to be a fake persona created by an acquaintance. When finally revealed, the hoax created much personal as well as public embarrassment and dismay (Zeman, 2013).

COMMUNICATIONACROSSCULTURES

Boys Need Best Friends, Too

Among adolescent girls, the formation of close, intimate friendships is almost expected. Teenaged girls giggle through the night at slumber parties, whisper secrets during school, and text each other frequently; they make each other friendship bracelets and wear matching clothes that declare their relationships for all the world to see. But what about the boys?

Research indicates that young boys seek the same kinds of intimate relationships that girls do: they want to share deep secrets with their closest male friends and know that they can trust in and count on them. But according to psychologist Niobe Way, boys' relationships are less public—and certainly less celebrated in society—than girls' friendships, primarily because of cultural ideas about what constitutes "masculine" behavior. Way points out that male friendships are often stifled as boys become men, and pressure to conform to gender stereotypes pressures them to adopt the mantle of American maleness: they must be stoic and independent, aggressive and competitive (Way, 2011). "During late adolescence," Way says, "boys begin to lose their closest male friendships, become more distrustful of their male peers, and in some cases, become less willing to be emotionally expressive. They start sounding, in other words, like gender stereotypes" (Way, 2011). This pattern is not limited to American males—similar patterns can be found in Chinese boys' relationships (Le, 2011).

Given the importance of friendship to our overall well-being, this gender disparity should be a grave concern. "Many of the boys in our studies spoke about feelings of loneliness and isolation during late adolescence and how they missed their formerly close male friendships," Way explains. "We heard these patterns of loss and distrust right at the moment in development that the rate of suicide among boys in the United States jumps to become four times the rate of girls" (Way, 2011).

THINK ABOUT THIS

❶ Think about the nature of the friendships you had as a twelve- or thirteen-year-old. Do you have the same sorts of relationships with your best friends now? Do you think that your most intimate relationships are affected by your gender?

❷ Does it bother you that having close friendships is often deemed "feminine" behavior? What does friendship have to do with gender and sexuality?

❸ What benefits of close intimate relationships are American boys missing? In what ways might learning to be more independent and stoic benefit American girls?

Why We Form Relationships

We've already established that romantic relationships are a universal desire, and additional research shows that individuals across cultures value a variety of relationships similarly (Endo, Heine, & Lehman, 2000; Landsford, Antonucci, Akiyama, & Takahashi, 2005). The reasons for forming specific relationships, however, are as individual and complex as each of us and rooted in unique needs and motivations, which may develop and change over time. In this section, we examine the factors of relationship formation, including proximity, attractive qualities, similarity, and personal and social needs.

Proximity

As practical as it sounds, one of the first criteria of relationship formation is simple **proximity**, or nearness. Think about how many of your friends you got to know because they sat next to you in elementary school, lived on the same dorm floor, or worked with you at Applebee's.

Physical proximity was once the most important factor in determining and maintaining relationships. If you were to move away from a neighborhood, switch schools, or change jobs, you would likely lose touch with old friends and eventually make new friends in your new surroundings. But modern technology allows you to interact regularly through mediated channels—*virtual* proximity with those who may be physically quite far away. Nonetheless, if persons are not in physical proximity and fail to establish and maintain virtual proximity—for example, if they avoid social networking or don't have access to a computer, tablet, or smartphone—the chances of forming or maintaining relationships dwindle.

Attractive Qualities

Hollywood movies often deal with troubled relationships, but the movie *Julie and Julia* is different. It revolves around a young blogger attempting to find purpose in her life by cooking her way through Julia Child's famous cookbook. The reality of Child's life—her love of cooking and her marriage to Paul Child—is the refreshing background for the rest of the film (Parker-Pope, 2010b). It depicts not only the exciting beginning of relationships but also the possibility of happy, easy, fun, interesting relationships in which people can remain attracted to one another for a lifetime. The Childs are attracted to one another romantically, intellectually, and socially. You might also be attracted to someone because of a variety of personal qualities that you admire, such as an outgoing personality, sense of fun, intellectual prowess, or simply a warm smile.

As you've learned in earlier chapters, your physical appearance does also play an important role in attracting others, especially in the very early stages of a relationship when first impressions are formed. People who are considered beautiful or attractive are often perceived as kinder, warmer, more intelligent, and more honest than unattractive people, and they have earlier opportunities for dating and marriage (Canary, Cody, & Manusov, 2008).

But before you focus only on physical attractiveness, remember two things. First, beauty is largely in the eye of the beholder, and individual tastes vary due to factors too numerous to discuss here (including cultural standards). For example, among the Padaung tribe of Southeast Asia, women wrap rings around their necks to push down their collarbones and upper ribs, giving the illusion of extremely long necks, considered a sign of beauty and wealth; Western standards of beauty are not the same. Second, our communication affects perceptions of beauty; repeated interaction with others alters our initial impressions of their physical appearance (Canary, Cody, & Manusov, 2008). So your ability to use verbal and nonverbal messages appropriately and effectively probably has a lot more to do with your perceived attractiveness than perfect clothing or the size of your jeans.

Similarity

The notion that "opposites attract" is so common in popular culture that many people take it as an undeniable truth. But despite the popularity of the concept, research shows that attraction is more often based on the degree of *similarity* we have with another person, whether through shared hobbies,

CONNECT

Although culture plays a powerful role in our ideas about physical attraction (Chapter 5), it's important to remember that we all have schemas about attractiveness (Chapter 2). So although you might find Jordan very attractive, your friend Cameron might not because Jordan reminds her of a previously awful romantic partner or because Jordan bears a striking resemblance to her brother.

AND YOU?

Consider someone with whom you share a very close relationship. In what ways are you similar to this person? Are those similarities what attracted you in the first place?

personality traits, backgrounds, appearances, or values (Gonzaga, Campos, & Bradbury, 2007). For example, consider close friends Liza and Cheryl. Liza is an African American student from Denver, a literature major, and a tomboy who loves the Broncos. Cheryl is a white student from Boston, majoring in engineering; she hates sports but follows fashion and rarely steps out of her dorm room without makeup. To an outsider, they seem like a mismatched pair. But ask either of them what they have in common, and they'll roll off a list of similarities: both grew up in urban neighborhoods, attended all-girl Catholic high schools, love indie rock, and take great pride in their ability to quote J. R. R. Tolkien. So long as the relational partners feel that they have much in common, as Liza and Cheryl do, they feel similar and attracted to one another.

Similarity can be closely connected to our perceptions of a person's attractive qualities. We are often attracted to those we think are about as physically attractive as we are. We also tend to think that when we find someone attractive, we must also have similar other qualities. Sometimes two individuals who hail from the same ethnic group (and thus are more genetically similar) tend to help, favor, and form relationships with people from their own ethnic groups (Rushton, 1980). However, more societal acceptance of diverse friendships and romantic relationships is contributing to more pervasive intercultural relationships (Balaji & Worawongs, 2010; McClintock, 2010). And, as people from various cultures interact more and more, they have opportunities to practice relational skills (like self-disclosure and empathic listening) and see many types of similarities in each other (Jin & Oh, 2010).

Personal and Social Needs

In U.S. prisons today, more than twenty-five thousand inmates are serving their time in solitary confinement—removed from the general prison population, isolated in small cells with little human contact (Casella & Ridgeway, 2012). Some activists worry about the harshness of the measure. They hold that human beings form and maintain relationships in order to satisfy basic personal and social needs—companionship, stimulation, meeting goals—and it is cruel to deny those needs (Ramirez, Sunnafrank, & Goei, 2010). Proponents argue that it is this very denial of these needs that makes such punishment effective. In any case, these personal and social needs are key factors for all of us in the relationships we form with others.

● **SENATOR JOHN MCCAIN** cites communication with fellow prisoners of war, even if fleeting, as one of the factors that helped him to survive solitary confinement in Vietnam. © Bettmann/Corbis

Companionship

Humans feel a natural need for companionship and **inclusion**—to involve others in our lives and to be involved in the lives of others. Thus loneliness can be a major motivation behind some people's desire for a relationship. In fact, psychological problems such as anxiety, stress, depression, alcoholism, drug abuse, and poor health have all been tied to loneliness (Canary & Spitzberg, 1993; Segrin & Passalacqua, 2010). Unfortunately, beginning a romantic relationship just for the sake of not being "alone" or confirming a ton of "friends" on Facebook does not mean that you won't be lonely. Finding a meaningful connection and creating an emotional tie with someone, such as by helping a fellow student understand his notes or providing water for a Race for the Cure participant, are ways of overcoming loneliness that lead to high-quality relationships (Hawkley & Cacioppo, 2010).

Stimulation

All people have a need for intellectual, emotional, and physical stimulation (Krcmar & Greene, 1999; Rubin, Perse, & Powell, 1985). Nobody enjoys being bored! So we seek out diversions like television or music. Interactions with others frequently provide multiple types of stimulation at once, which can contribute to our relational satisfaction (Guerrero, Farinelli, & McEwan, 2009).

Consider some of the communication relationships you have formed with various people that provide stimulation over the course of a day. You might go for coffee with that classmate who really makes you laugh. You stop your professor in the hallway to share an interesting story related to your class. You check up on Facebook and decide to "hide" updates from that person who always irritates you. And then you meet up with your significant other, who greets you with a warm hug after a long day. It's also possible, of course, for you to find multiple forms of stimulation in one person.

The innate need for stimulation is what causes many people to feel uncomfortable about solitary confinement. Senator John McCain, recalling the more than five years he spent as a prisoner of war in Vietnam, noted: "As far as this business of solitary confinement goes—the most important thing for survival is communication with someone, even if it's only a wave or a wink, a tap on the wall, or to have a guy put his thumb up. It makes all the difference" (McCain, 2008).

Meeting Goals

Although you may form relationships because of proximity, attraction, or similarity, you might also enter into relationships simply to achieve practical goals. In addition to our psychological needs to alleviate loneliness or obtain stimulation, we have mundane needs for getting through our daily tasks as well as longer-term goals for achieving our life's plans. We often form relationships with people to help us or inform us or give us pep talks to meet these needs and achieve our goals. For example, you might develop a relationship with a classmate because you need someone to help you figure out an assignment or give you advice about your major. If you have dreamed all your life about working in finance, you might seek relationships with influential people in that field through networking via your college alumni group or through an internship.

Of course, people can form relationships to achieve manipulative goals as well, which is the argument that is put forward by those who feel that solitary confinement is justified. When particularly dangerous prisoners are kept in isolation, they are unable to form relationships that might help them to accomplish dangerous goals (such as gang memberships or terrorist networking) (Sullivan, 2006).

Managing Relationship Dynamics

When it comes to relationship advice, you don't need to look far for what seems like "expertise." From the fictional Carrie Bradshaw to the real-life Dr. Phil and from books like *Men Are from Mars, Women Are from Venus* to countless *Cosmo* magazine self-quizzes, popular culture is brimming with advice on managing and

AND YOU?

Do you rely on different relational partners for companionship, stimulation, or goal achievement? Do you have some relationships that provide all three functions?

maintaining healthy relationships. Thankfully, communication scholars explore the way we manage relationships in a far more scientific way. In this section, we rely on that scholarship to explore the dynamics of relationships as they constantly change, grow, and evolve throughout our lives, specifically looking at costs and rewards, reducing uncertainty, and dialectical tensions (Knapp & Vangelisti, 2008; Solomon & Vangelisti, 2010).

Costs and Rewards

Every relationship has advantages and disadvantages for the parties involved. Your close friendship with Arturo may offer companionship and intimacy, but you may also need to accept his negative feelings about your religious beliefs and invest time in working through difficult situations together. **Social exchange theory** explains this process of balancing the advantages and disadvantages of a relationship (Thibaut & Kelley, 1959). Relationships begin, grow, and deteriorate based on an exchange of rewards and costs.

Rewards are the elements of a relationship that you feel good about—things about the person or your relationship that benefit you in some way. There are *extrinsic rewards*, the external advantages you gain from association with another person (such as social status or professional connections); *instrumental rewards*, the resources and favors that partners give to one another (for example, living together to save money); and *intrinsic rewards*, the personally satisfying rewards that result from an exchange of intimacy (for instance, intellectual stimulation or feelings of safety). **Costs**, by contrast, are the things that upset or annoy you, cause you stress, or damage your own self-image or lifestyle. If you find your relationship too costly (for example, there is a lot of conflict, jealousy, or infidelity), you may decide to end the relationship (Dainton & Gross, 2008; Guerrero, La Valley, & Farinelli, 2008).

The social exchange of costs and benefits is inherently complicated. You might wonder, for example, why good-natured Watson sticks out a partnership and friendship with acerbic and belittling Sherlock (in any of the recent

Most of us don't ponder the costs and rewards of our relationships on a daily basis. But when we feel that a relationship involves too many costs, conflict often ensues. As you learn in Chapter 8, we like to feel that we are both giving and receiving in a relationship. So if your roommate Tamara is always leaving her chores for you, you might need to engage in conflict management to balance the relationship.

● **THE HIT SERIES**
Sherlock depicts Watson as an ex-military doctor who finds purpose and excitement in accompanying the famous detective on his various investigative adventures. *Elementary* surprises with a female Watson, a sober companion of ex-addict Holmes who later becomes the sleuth's assistant. (left) © BBC/Courtesy Everett Collection; (right) CBS/Photofest

what about you?

Assessing the Costs and Rewards of a Relationship

Think of a current romantic relationship (or, if you are not in one now, think of a past one). As you assess your partner's traits and behaviors, use a five-point scale for your answers: 5 = strongly agree; 4 = agree; 3 = neither agree nor disagree; 2 = disagree; and 1 = extremely disagree.

_____ 1. My partner laughs at my jokes.

_____ 2. My partner makes appropriate jokes or comments.

_____ 3. My partner is physically attractive to me.

_____ 4. My partner is affectionate.

_____ 5. My partner wears clothes I like.

_____ 6. My partner has a pleasing personality.

_____ 7. My partner and I have similar views about religion.

_____ 8. My partner and I have similar views about children.

_____ 9. My partner shares emotions appropriately.

_____ 10. My partner acknowledges my feelings.

_____ 11. My partner fits in with my friends.

_____ 12. My partner fits in with my family.

_____ 13. My partner and I share similar dreams for the future.

_____ 14. My partner enjoys hobbies and activities similar to mine.

_____ 15. My partner and I agree about career paths.

_____ 16. My partner appreciates my racial and ethnic background.

_____ 17. My partner manages finances well.

_____ 18. My partner appreciates my political views.

_____ 19. My partner overlooks my shortcomings.

_____ 20. My partner is an interesting person.

Scoring: Add your scores together to get an informal assessment of how rewarding or costly you perceive your relationship to be. If you scored between 74 and 100, you perceive your relationship as very rewarding on a number of levels and are likely to value and maintain this relationship; if you scored 47–73, you see both costs and rewards in your relationship and are able to balance these effectively; if you scored 20–46, you perceive your relationship as having more costs than rewards, and you might consider ways to fix or end it.

Note: The importance of certain costs and rewards varies greatly from individual to individual, so the weighting of particular traits (for example, physical attraction or similarity of views) may vary.

Sherlock Holmes television adaptations or the original nineteenth-century novels by Sir Arthur Conan Doyle). But the benefits of the relationship (including intrigue, intellectual stimulation, and a desire to "fix" or help a deeply troubled individual) might just outweigh the costs (such as personal safety, frequent insults, and lack of emotional connection or support).

Reducing Uncertainty

Although we weigh the costs and rewards in all stages of a relationship, at the very beginning we do not have much information to consider. We may have excitement at the prospect of a new friendship to enjoy or romance to explore, but the uncertainty about the other person is also uncomfortable. That's why we need to use a variety of techniques to get to know one another.

According to **uncertainty reduction theory**, when two people meet, their main focus is on decreasing the uncertainty about each other (Berger & Bradac, 1982). The less sure you are of the person's qualities, the way the person will behave, or what will happen, the higher the degree of uncertainty. Thus, reducing uncertainty increases your ability to predict that person's behavior. As two people—college roommates, coworkers, romantic partners—reduce the uncertainty between them, they uncover similarities, become better at predicting what the other will do or say, and thus develop more comfort.

In order to reduce uncertainty and increase the likelihood of a closer relationship, you must obtain information about your new relational partner. If you're a fan of the *Twilight* series, you know that upon first noticing each other at school, Edward and Bella each used several strategies to find out more information about the other. Bella asked her classmates about Edward; she watched how he behaved and made observations about how he presented himself. Eventually, she questioned him directly. Edward, finding his ability to read minds useless on Bella, was forced to employ similar strategies. Unless you too can read minds, you've likely employed those same strategies yourself. Depending on the situation, three types of strategies may work well: passive strategies, active strategies, and interactive strategies.

Passive Strategies

Most college students who live on campus are faced with the prospect of sharing a small space with a complete stranger. When Shawna heard about her new roommate, Ramona, she entered her name and hometown into Google. She quickly found Ramona on Facebook and learned that she is a concert pianist and an avid knitter who sometimes sells her creations through Etsy.com (see Antheunis, Valkenburg, & Peter, 2010).

Shawna engaged in a passive uncertainty reduction strategy. **Passive strategies** involve observing others in communication situations without actually interacting with them. You may also analyze their interactions with others when you believe they are not under a lot of pressure to conform to social roles. Without Ramona knowing it, Shawna had already found out quite a bit about her. Social networking allows us to monitor others with relative ease, but we also use passive strategies whenever we observe others going about their day-to-day business.

CONNECT

It's important to reduce uncertainty in all communication contexts. For example, in Chapter 12 we discuss audience analysis, which allows you to learn about the people who will listen to your speech. By understanding your audience's expectations, learning about their opinions of your topic, and carefully considering their demographics, you can reduce uncertainty and determine the most effective way to reach them.

Active Strategies

Active strategies let you obtain information about a person more directly by seeking information from a third party. For example, Shawna may discover (via Facebook) that she and Ramona have one friend in common. In that case, Shawna might contact this individual to see how much she knows about Ramona. Does she party a lot? Is she neat or messy? Does she snore?

Active strategies can be particularly useful when the information you are seeking could be awkward for a new relationship. For example, Shawna might wonder if Ramona would be uncomfortable having significant others spend the night in their dorm room. Thus, she might chat with the mutual friend to get a sense of Ramona's feelings in order to be prepared to discuss it when they arrive on campus.

Interactive Strategies

Sometimes you will need to find out important information about a relational partner through **interactive strategies**, that is, by speaking directly with that person rather than observing or asking others for information. When "meeting" for the first time (be it in person or virtually), Shawna might ask Ramona what kind of music she likes, what major she is pursuing, and why she chose this particular school. Although direct questioning reduces some uncertainty, it also entails risks. If you ask questions that are perceived as too forward or inappropriate (for example, "What are your political beliefs?"), you might push the person away.

Dialectical Tensions

> **AND YOU?**
>
> Consider your relationship with your oldest friend or with a close family member. Evaluate the ways in which dialectical tensions have manifested themselves in that relationship over the years. Have these tensions shifted over time? Is there one particular tension that continues to crop up?

Weighing costs against benefits and reducing uncertainty are not the only challenges we face in developing relationships. In any relationship, it is common to experience contradictions or opposing feelings about your relational partner and about the relationship itself. When a love relationship becomes serious, for example, one or both partners might find themselves mourning their old, single lifestyle, despite the benefits of commitment.

Relational dialectics theory holds that **dialectical tensions** are contradictory feelings that tug at us in every relationship, whether a newly formed friendship or a committed romantic partnership. These tensions can be external (between the partners and the people with whom they interact) or internal (within their relationship). Of the many possible types, we focus on three internal tensions that dominate research: *autonomy* versus *connection, openness* versus *closedness*, and *predictability* versus *novelty* (Baxter & Simon, 1993). Note that dialectics exist along a continuum; they are not all-or-nothing trade-offs but rather ranges of options that need to be continually negotiated and adjusted (Baxter, Braithwaite, Bryant, & Wagner, 2004). These tensions are natural and normal—experiencing them does not indicate that your relationship is in trouble!

Autonomy Versus Connection

Identical twins Eva and Amelia have always done everything together—from their first breaths of air right on through their college educations. As they grew older, loosening these bonds was a real struggle. Eva remembers bursting into tears at her bridal shower and explaining, "It's just that I've never had a party all to myself before" (see Hazel, Wongprasert, & Ayres, 2006).

In all close personal relationships—family connections, romantic relationships, and friendships—there is a tension between independence (autonomy) and dependence (connection). In other words, we struggle because we want to be our own person while at the same time be fully connected to the other person. This tension can result in hurt feelings. Attempts to express autonomy can be easily misunderstood—children's attempts to express their own identities are often seen as acts of rebellion, whereas romantic partners risk alienating their loved ones when they pursue certain interests alone. On the other hand, we can be seen as nagging when we try to force connectedness on our relational partners: if we drag our partners off to yoga class or a sporting event in which they have no interest, we're more likely to alienate them than to bring them closer.

● **THREE'S A CROWD** (sometimes). Perhaps no familial relationship plays out the delicate balance between autonomy and connection as clearly as that of multiple-birth siblings. Patti McConville/Getty Images

So how might you bridge the gap between autonomy and connectedness? One strategy is to alternate time together and time apart. You might go to yoga with your sister who enjoys it while your romantic partner enjoys a solo evening at home. On Saturdays, however, you and your significant other might try out different local kayaking spots—a shared passion that you engage in together. Or you might manage the tension with the physical space in your home—deciding the décor for the living room together but displaying your comic book memorabilia in your own office hideout.

Openness Versus Closedness

Every superhero from Batman to Superman to The Question knows about this tension. To become close, individuals must share information with their relational partners. However, by disclosing information, they reveal a part of their private selves that then becomes vulnerable. The tension comes as partners strive to find a balance between sharing information (openness) and desiring to keep some things private (closedness). This can be seen in superhero comics and movies when a character like Bruce Wayne wants to maintain close relationships with various love interests but cannot tell any of them about his secret life as Batman. The tension between Batman's duty to Gotham City and duty to his loved ones takes a toll on those relationships.

Without the excuses of double lives, most people need to disclose some private information to those with whom they have relationships in order to facilitate a perception of involvement and deep understanding. Even when we take into account cultural differences (see Chapter 5), relational intimacy is consistently advanced by self-disclosure (as we develop more fully later) (Chen & Nakazawa, 2009). But it is not always a good idea to reveal your every thought to your partner. Contrary to the notion that there should be "no secrets between us," relational dialectics researchers argue that much information might be better left unsaid. The comparison you make in your mind between your current romantic partner and an attractive celebrity is a good example.

Some couples will alternate over time between one or the other ends of the spectrum, such as lots of openness during one phase of their relationship and

● **FOR SOME,** the surprise of breakfast in bed might be enough to shake up the normal routine. For others, it might take zip-lining through a rainforest or backpacking across Asia. Cultura/Matt Hoover Photo/Getty Images

more closedness at other times. Partners who are willing to try to fulfill each other's needs for information while still maintaining their own privacy are more likely to manage this dialectical tension with satisfaction (Baxter, 1990).

Predictability Versus Novelty

Which is more important to relationships, safety and security or excitement and spontaneity? The third dialectical tension is where proponents of relational dialectics theory disagree with the concept of uncertainty reduction that we discussed earlier. Rather than accepting that uncertainty is inherently uncomfortable, dialectics researchers argue that people have a simultaneous need for stability through predictable relational interaction *as well as* a need for new and unexpected experiences in personal relationships. On the one hand, partners seek stable patterns of interaction: Colin and Casey, for example, enjoy the comfort of their evening routine of dinner and television, and their understanding of each others' typical reactions and emotions helps them to know how to support one another and avoid unnecessary upsets. At the same time, being able to almost finish each other's sentences can be too predictable, so some novelty in their interactions is also welcome. This is why Colin might surprise Casey with an unexpected love-note in the lunch she takes to work, or why Casey might spontaneously cook a Thai meal or suggest a vacation to somewhere they'd never thought to go before.

Self-Disclosure and Interpersonal Relationships

Do you remember Angelica from Chapter 2 (p. 57)? You may recall her heavy debt due to her lifestyle (expensive vacations, a new car, a nice apartment, and so on). When she divulges her personal financial mishaps to a friend, she is self-disclosing, revealing very personal information. As you've likely experienced in your own life, self-disclosure has a powerful impact on the development of interpersonal relationships (Samter, 2003). The process of choosing what information to disclose to others and when has long fascinated communication researchers and scholars who note that it is informed by issues as complex as personality type and individual tendencies (Hesse & Rauscher, 2013), situational and relational variables (Frisby & Sidelinger, 2013), and culture (Chen & Nakazawa, 2012). Keeping these variations in mind, we now examine the ways in which the decisions to divulge or withhold personal information affect relationships.

Social Penetration Theory

In many relationships, a primary goal is to increase intimacy, or relational closeness. **Social penetration theory** (SPT) explains how partners move from superficial levels to greater intimacy (Altman & Taylor, 1973). SPT uses an onion as a metaphor to describe how relationships move through various stages: just as you might peel off layers of an onion in an attempt to reach the core or center, a relational partner attempts to reach the most intimate thoughts and feelings at the other partner's "core" (see Figure 7.2).

According to SPT, each layer contains information that is increasingly more private and therefore more risky to divulge to someone else. The outer layer represents aspects of the self that are obvious, such as our appearance, or are surface-level revelations, such as our social categories (male, college student, Texan). Successive layers become more private as partners assess the costs and benefits of the relationship and of disclosing information to each other. If costs exceed rewards, it is unlikely that the partners will move inward toward the more deeply concealed layers. Upon getting to know Jorge, for example, you might find that despite his boisterous exterior, he sometimes suffers from serious bouts of depression, which he manages with medication. But Jorge must choose to reveal this information: it is a part of him that only his closest, most trusted friends know, and he's likely to reveal it only as a relationship becomes more intimate.

FIGURE 7.2

SOCIAL PENETRATION THEORY (SPT) MODEL
According to the SPT model, relational partners peel away successive layers of information about each other as they move toward greater intimacy.

Communication Privacy Management

Communication privacy management theory (CPM) helps explain how people perceive the information they hold about themselves and whether they will disclose or protect it (Petronio, 2000, 2002). CPM explains why Celeste, for example, will boldly share her religious beliefs, whereas Eddie will keep his faith intensely private. CPM theory presumes that people believe they own their private information and need to set up boundaries to control the potential risks that may make them vulnerable (Petronio, 2004).

Two key features of relationships are central to privacy management. First, privacy management is affected by the dialectical tension of openness versus closedness, discussed earlier. You want to share information in order to increase intimacy with your partner, but it may be risky to do so, and maintaining private information is a worthy goal in its own right. Second, privacy management requires cultural, situational, and relational rules or expectations by which people must be willing to abide. For example, it would likely be considered impolite for you to ask your boss about his medical condition because

AND YOU?

Do you post any personal information on social networking sites? What kind of information are you willing to reveal? What kind of information do you consider too private to share in mediated contexts?

that topic is far too private for a work context in many cultures, and you are unlikely to have that level of personal intimacy with your manager. Yet that type of disclosure is expected in close relationships (Derlega, Winstead, Mathews, & Braitman, 2008).

real communicator

NAME: May Hui
OCCUPATION: Entrepreneur/Matchmaker

As a self-professed romantic, I love bringing people together. So, after years of being a sales, marketing, and operations executive for a *Fortune* 500 company, I decided to start my own business to help people with the often challenging dating process.

CatchMatchmaking is not your average dating service; my partner and I use relational communication principles to help singles find a "match" and potentially develop a committed relationship. We create articles and YouTube videos to teach our clients the basics of interpersonal communication. This might seem surprising, but a lot of people don't know what to do on a date; either they haven't had a lot of dating experience or they have had relationships that "went bad" and are afraid of another failure. After we give them advice and coach them, however, they gain confidence and present themselves better. Here's how we do it.

First, we interview clients about their answers to questionnaires they complete online. Like most dating services, we match couples according to preferences for religion, height, income level, common interests, goals, and values. But we find that the profiles people create are often *so* scripted; they might say they are *adventurous*, but when we follow up about their activities, they may not mean that in the same way that a "match" might (for example, *adventurous* = climbing Mt. Everest or *adventurous* = traveling to another town). We go beyond the

adjectives to discover that what clients frequently do, how they behave, and what they really want in a "match" are not what they filled out on their questionnaire.

Second, we coach our clients on the basics of self-presentation. Being nicely dressed and groomed shows your date that you care enough to make yourself attractive. Nonverbal behaviors (making eye contact, leaning in, softening tone of voice, smiling) show warmth and interest in the other person.

Third, we help them overcome awkward dating conversations. In the beginning of a relationship, it is important to ask your partner a lot of questions and get him or her talking. After all, whoever talks more usually says the date was great, so sometimes it is important to talk less about yourself and do more to discover details about the other person. It is also important to self-disclose appropriately; sex, religion, and politics are not the best topics for a first date. Neither are past relationships; if your date asks what happened with your last relationship, don't complain about your past partner or give a bunch of gory details. Instead say, "Yes, I had a relationship that didn't work out, but I learned something and moved on." You can save more details for the third, fourth, and fifth dates.

I absolutely love what I am doing, particularly on days when I hear that two clients have become engaged! The communication classes I took are key to the way I run my organization, and the interpersonal courses are key to the success of my business that brings me so much joy.

If there is a threat to your privacy boundaries (for example, your trusted friend told your secret to someone else), you experience **boundary turbulence** and must readjust your need for privacy against your need for self-disclosure and connection (Guerrero, Andersen, & Afifi, 2013; Theiss, Knobloch, Checton, & Magsamen-Conrad, 2009). Boundary turbulence occurs in mediated situations, too. If you have personal information about someone else, do you have the right to "tweet" that? What about inside jokes or pictures taken at a party—do you have the right to share them with others? Judgments can be made about you based on what your "friends" do on Facebook (Walther, Van Der Heide, Kim, Westerman, & Tong, 2008), and you often alter the kinds of disclosures you make depending on whether or not your parents are Facebook friends (Child & Westermann, 2013) or whether you are messaging friends who are distant versus nearby (Waters & Ackerman, 2011). So you can see how complex privacy management becomes in online communication.

Strategic Topic Avoidance

Certain topics are simply too sensitive for some people to confront openly. One or both relational partners can use **strategic topic avoidance** to maneuver the conversation away from potentially embarrassing, vulnerable, or otherwise undesirable topics (Dailey & Palomares, 2004). Just as in privacy management, there are topics we avoid because we are culturally trained to do so. For example, prior relationships, negative information, dating experiences, money issues, and sexual experiences are largely considered inappropriate for public communication (Baxter & Wilmot, 1985; Dailey & Palomares, 2004; Guerrero & Afifi, 1995). So if a colleague at the office asks about the size of your recent bonus, you could say that it's none of his business, but research shows that you'd be better off to use a less direct avoidance tactic, such as keeping silent, deflecting, giving an unrelated response, lying, or simply ending the conversation (Dailey & Palomares, 2004).

Like other issues related to self-disclosure, there are ethical considerations regarding pursuing and avoiding topics. Is it appropriate for parents to disclose the private details of their impending divorce to their children? They may mean well (for example, they may want to reduce uncertainty for their children), but they may use such strategies unethically (such as if each parent argues for his or her own side of the story in order to be viewed in a better light). In addition, adolescent children may suffer emotionally and view the disclosures as inappropriate (Afifi, McManus, Hutchinson, & Baker, 2007).

Every relationship is unique and, as we have discussed, relational partners may experience different degrees of comfort with disclosure or avoidance at different times. For example, dating couples who are experiencing relationship dissatisfaction have been found to engage in more topic avoidance, often to create some emotional distance (Merrill & Afifi, 2012). On the other hand, people in more satisfying relationships may also use topic avoidance, but as a way to be sensitive to the other person's concerns and accommodate to the other's needs (Dailey & Palomares, 2004). In other words, strategic topic avoidance can have benefits or detriments, depending on how and why the topics are being avoided.

AND YOU?

What topics do you consider strictly off-limits? Are there some topics you are willing to discuss with some people but not with others? How do you inform others of your unwillingness to discuss these topics?

Stages of a Relationship

In *The Descendants*, actor George Clooney plays Matt King, a real estate lawyer suddenly confronted with significant changes in his relationships. He finds his wife near death and learns of her infidelity almost simultaneously; he is suddenly forced to parent his angry daughters; and he is the cousin in charge of selling off family land in Kauai to developers (Scott, 2011). We witness King's relationships in flux, challenged by significant relational events called **turning points** (Baxter & Bullis, 1986)—positive or negative events or changes that stand out in people's minds as important to defining their relationships (for example, stories about "how we met" or detours such as negative disclosures).

A turning point can often move a relationship into a new "stage"—a different set of feelings and communication behaviors that partners demonstrate. Several scholars argue that relationships, as they change over time, progress through several different predictable stages (Knapp & Vangelisti, 2000). During each stage, our communication patterns differ and our assessments of costs and rewards determine whether our relationship will remain at the same stage, move to a closer stage, or shift to one further apart. Figure 7.3 outlines the relational stages we develop in the following sections.

Initiating Stage

In the **initiating stage** of a relationship, you make contact with another person, saying "Hello" or asking for a name. If you think about the number of new people you initiate with on a given day, you won't be surprised to learn that many relationships don't move beyond this stage. Just because you say "Good morning" to the woman who sold you a bagel doesn't mean the two of you will be chatting on the phone later today. But you will likely use your first impression of a person to gauge whether or not you're interested in moving forward with the relationship (Canary, Cody, & Manusov, 2008).

It can be awkward to
verbally indicate that you
want a relationship to end
or to move beyond the initiating stage. You wouldn't
tell a new classmate, "I
don't like you. Stop talking
to me." Luckily, nonverbal
communication helps you
address this issue. You can
indicate like or dislike with
facial expressions, posture,
use of space, or touch
(Chapter 4), hoping this
individual properly
decodes your message.

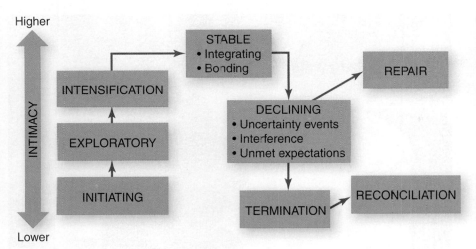

FIGURE 7.3

TYPICAL STAGES OF A RELATIONSHIP It is normal to move between and among stages in different relationships as we become more or less intimate with others.

Exploratory Stage

In the **exploratory stage**, you are seeking relatively superficial information from your partner. You make small talk, asking things like "Were you a fan of *Breaking Bad*?" or "How many brothers and sisters do you have?" You're not likely to reveal anything too deep or personal; you're still testing the waters, so to speak. A number of monitoring strategies are also at work to reduce uncertainty in this stage. In addition to the small-talk questioning we mentioned, you're likely to observe your partner closely in order to learn more about his or her attitudes and behaviors. As in the initiating stage, you'll want to invest further in the relationship if the rewards seem high.

Intensification Stage

The **intensification stage** occurs when relational partners become increasingly intimate and move their communication toward more personal self-disclosures. This stage includes the use of informal address or pet names ("honey," "darling") as well as "we" talk ("We're going to the concert on Friday night, right?" "Where are we going for your birthday next week?"). Relational partners in this stage also understand each other's nonverbal communication to a greater degree and often share their affection with one another ("What would I do without you!") (Knapp & Vangelisti, 2000).

Stable Stage

By the time partners reach the **stable stage**, their relationship is no longer volatile or temporary. They now have a great deal of knowledge about one another, their expectations are realistic, and they feel comfortable with their motives for being in the relationship. Relationships reach the stable stage when uncertainty reduces to the point where partners feel comfortable understanding each other's preferences and goals (Goss & O'Hair, 1988).

● **SUPERSTARS** Jay-Z and Beyoncé Knowles have managed to maintain a stable relationship for years despite the strains and visibility of being a celebrity couple.
BENOIT TESSIER/Reuters /Landov

Two substages occur here. First, we see relational partners **integrating** or "becoming one." You and your roommate Dana now cultivate common friends, develop joint opinions, and may share property. Second, people treat you as a pair—one of you would never be invited to a party without the other one (Knapp & Vangelisti, 2000). If the relationship progresses beyond integrating, **bonding** takes place when two partners share formal, public messages with the world that their relationship is important and cherished. Engagements, weddings, civil unions, and entering into legal contracts (such as buying a house together) are common ways to reveal a bonded romantic couple.

Life's challenges inevitably arise for partners in a stable relationship, so each individual will need to determine if the benefits of the relationship (such as intimacy or companionship) outweigh the costs that these challenges represent. For a few tips on developing and maintaining stable relationships, see Table 7.2.

Declining Stage

Have you noticed your partner criticizing you more often, refusing to talk about issues important to you, getting defensive, or speaking with contempt? If these behaviors are occurring more often than positive behaviors in your relationship, you may be in a **declining stage**, when the relationship begins to come apart (Gottman & Silver, 1999). Three factors typically lead to this stage: uncertainty events, interference (concerning family, work, timing, money, or the like), and unmet expectations.

TABLE 7.2

**STRATEGIES FOR
MANAGING STABLE
RELATIONSHIPS**

Strategy	Examples
Remember what made you interested in the relationship in the first place	• Share inside jokes • Visit favorite places (a coffeehouse where you used to meet)
Spend quality time together	• Share your day-to-day activities • Explore new hobbies and interests
Share tasks and humor	• Plan finances and do chores together • Have inside jokes and laugh together
Be understanding	• Empathize with your partner's concerns, dreams, fears, and so on • Try to see conflict-causing situations from your partner's point of view
Express affection	• Proclaim how important your partner is ("You're a great friend" or "I love you") • Do something nice or unexpected for your partner without being asked
Have realistic expectations	• Don't compare your relationships to others • Accept your partner's strengths *and* weaknesses
Work on intimacy	• Offer supportive, positive messages, particularly during stressful times • Reveal your commitment by showing and sharing that you are invested in the relationship (self-disclosure, make future plans together)

Source: Guerrero, Andersen, & Afifi (2013).

Uncertainty Events

Events or behavioral patterns that cause uncertainty in a relationship are called **uncertainty events**. They may be caused by competing relationships (romantic or platonic), deception or betrayal of confidence, fluctuations in closeness, and sudden or unexplained changes in sexual behavior, personality, or values (Planalp & Honeycutt, 1985). One or both partners are left wondering about the cause of the events and their significance for the relationship. If your romantic partner suddenly starts withholding information from you or a close friend begins engaging in activities that you find offensive, you will experience uncertainty. Uncertainty events may be sudden and very noticeable (betrayal of confidence, for example), or they may be subtle and escape immediate attention (your sister gradually stops returning your phone calls).

Interference

When Patrick becomes involved in a serious romantic relationship, his best friend Dennis feels abandoned. Jason wants to get married, but Nora is not ready. Emma and Leigh find that financial troubles are straining their relationship.

These are just some of the many obstacles that may pop up in a relationship and interfere with its growth. Timing, the family or friends of one or both partners, and problems with work or money can all contribute to the decline of a relationship. Arguing over finances is a frequent reason for couples seeking therapy (Atwood, 2012), and study of one thousand spouses found that 84 percent

EVALUATING COMMUNICATION ETHICS

THINK
ABOUT
THIS

Money, Family, and Paying the Bills

You have a pretty good relationship with your parents, but money has also been a source of conflict with them. You're the first in your family to attend college, and you're working twenty hours a week (and full time during the summer) to contribute toward your living expenses and tuition. You've taken out a hefty amount of money in student loans as well. You know that money is tight for your parents, and you are grateful for the help that they can provide. Your mother, for example, sends generous packages of food, and your father and stepmother pay for your car insurance. But money is still a constant concern for you.

Recently, you discovered that you could qualify for a particular scholarship and a grant—money for college that does not need to be repaid—if you can prove that your income falls below a certain threshold. The only way to make that happen is to declare yourself independent from your parents' care. But that would have some negative financial consequences for them, as they would no longer be able to claim you as a deduction on their tax return. You decide to discuss the issue with your father, hoping that he will see the situation from your point of view, but he does not. In fact, he becomes so angry that he threatens to cut you off altogether—no more car insurance money and no place to live during the summer internship you've arranged near your father's town. He tells you that if you want to be independent, you should be completely independent.

Either way you look at it, your relationship with your father has been affected. If you do declare yourself independent, you will lose his assistance and gain his wrath. If you don't, you will resent him deeply for causing you additional financial stress. You want to repair your relationship with him . . . but how?

1 Can you put yourself in your father's position and empathize with him? What are your responsibilities here as an ethical listener?

2 In light of the information you have gleaned from this chapter, how would you prepare to have a conversation about repairing the relationship no matter which decision you make? What repair tactics could you consider using?

3 Construct a conversation that allows for relationship repair (based on the decision that you make regarding your independence). What might that conversation be like? What communication skills could you use? How will you ensure that the conversation is ethical?

of married couples reported money as a culprit in marital distress ("Money," 2006). Romantic partners or even friends often view money differently because of upbringing, spending habits, and gender (Blumstein & Schwartz, 1983).

Unmet Expectations

Whenever people enter into a relationship, they form ideas about what they think will or should happen; these expectations influence how we (and our partners) send and receive messages. Unrealistic expectations can create problems in a relationship: if Hannah believes that true love means never arguing, she might interpret her boyfriend Liam's criticism of her perpetual tardiness as a sign that they're not meant to be together. Realistic expectations, by contrast, can increase relational satisfaction and improve interpersonal communication (Alexander, 2008). Luisa, for example, has learned that her friend Emily is never going to remember her birthday. It's not a sign that Emily doesn't care; she just isn't good with dates. Instead, Luisa focuses on the kind things that Emily does for her, like sending her funny postcards from her business travel or watching the dogs when Luisa had to leave town for a funeral.

Repair Stage

A relationship in decline is not necessarily doomed to failure: partners may attempt to save or repair their relationship by changing their behavior, interactions, or expectations. If you have a strong commitment to someone else, particularly in a romantic relationship, you often perceive problems as less severe, so you are more likely to reduce conflict and potentially repair the relationship (Miczo, 2008). **Repair tactics** should include improving communication, focusing on the positive aspects of each partner and of the relationship itself, reinterpreting behaviors with a more balanced view, reevaluating the alternatives to the relationship, and enlisting the support of others to hold the relationship together (Brandau-Brown & Ragsdale, 2008; Duck, 1984).

In short, partners hoping to repair a relationship must focus on the benefits of their relationship rather than the source of a particular argument (see Table 7.2 on p. 205); many tips for managing stable relationships also apply to repairing them. Relational partners should listen to each other, take each other's perspective, and remind themselves about the attractive qualities that sparked the relationship in the first place (for example, how Talia can make Greg laugh and how Greg can make Talia feel at ease with her emotions). Partners may also try to increase their intimacy by offering more self-disclosures and spending quality time together (Blumstein & Schwartz, 1983). If a relationship is in serious decline, however, and seems beyond repair, the partners may need to seek professional help or outside support.

Termination Stage

Try as they might, not all relational partners stay together (hence the existence of sad songs and bad poetry). The **termination stage**, or end of a relationship, usually comes about in one of two ways (Davis, 1973). The first is *passing away*, which is characterized by a gradual fade as the relationship loses its vitality, perhaps because of outside interference or because partners don't make the effort to maintain it. Also, if partners spend less time together as a couple, communication and intimacy may decline, leading to dissatisfaction and a perception of different attitudes. This is why romances and friendships sometimes deteriorate when one partner moves away or why marriages and outside friendships change when kids come into the picture. The second way relationships often end is in *sudden death*—the abrupt, and for at least one partner, unexpected termination of a relationship. This might happen if your spouse or romantic partner has an affair, or if you decide that you can no longer tolerate a friend's emotionally manipulative behavior. Communicating your desire to end a relationship can be difficult; some messages useful for terminating romantic relationships in particular are listed in Table 7.3.

Reconciliation

Is there any hope for a terminated relationship? Soap operas and sitcoms say so— but it's true in real life as well. **Reconciliation** is a repair strategy for rekindling an extinguished relationship. Attempting reconciliation entails a lot of risk—one partner might find that the other partner is not interested, or both partners

TABLE 7.3

TERMINATION STRATEGIES FOR ROMANTIC RELATIONSHIPS

Strategy	Tactics	Examples
Positive-tone messages	Fairness Compromise Fatalism	"It's not right to go on pretending I'm in love with you." "We can still see each other occasionally." "We both know this relationship won't work out anyway."
Deescalation	Promise of friendship Implied possible reconciliation Blaming the relationship Appeal to independence	"We can still be friends." "Perhaps time apart will rekindle our feelings for each other." "We have to work too hard on this relationship." "We don't need to be tied down right now."
Withdrawal or avoidance	Avoid contact with the person as much as possible	"I don't think I'll be able to see you this weekend."
Justification	Emphasize positive consequences of disengaging Emphasize negative consequences of not disengaging	"We should see other people since we've changed so much." "We'll miss too many opportunities if we don't see other people."
Negative identity management	Emphasize enjoyment of life Nonnegotiation	"Life is too short to spend with just one person right now." "I need to see other people—period!"

Source: Canary, Cody, & Manusov (2008), pp. 278–286. Adapted with permission.

might find that the problems that pushed them apart remain or have intensified. But research reveals that there are a few tactics that can help the partners mend the relationship (O'Hair & Krayer, 1987; Patterson & O'Hair, 1992):

▶ *Spontaneous development:* The partners wind up spending more time together. Perhaps a divorced couple is involved in their son's school or two ex-friends find themselves helping a mutual friend.

▶ *Third-party mediation:* The partners have a friend or family member mediate the reconciliation.

▶ *High affect:* The partners resolve to be nice and polite to one another and possibly remind each other of what they found attractive about the other in the first place.

▶ *Tacit persistence:* One or both partners refuse to give up on the relationship.

▶ *Mutual interaction:* The partners begin talking more often following the dissolution, perhaps remaining friends after their breakup.

▶ *Avoidance:* The partners avoid spending time together and begin to miss each other.

If you think about couples in popular culture who have broken up and gotten back together—Penny and Leonard on *The Big Bang Theory*, for instance—you can clearly see some of these strategies at work.

AND YOU?

Have you ever been able to restore a relationship that you thought was irreparably damaged? Have you ever ended a relationship but secretly believed that you would repair it at some point in the future?

BACK TO ▶ Mary and Justin

At the beginning of this chapter, we met Mary and Justin, a couple struggling to maintain a close and functional family life during Justin's regular military deployment. Let's consider how they deal with the strains of time, distance, and uncertainty in light of what we've learned in this chapter.

▶ Military spouses often take on the role of single parents, making new rules and routines for interaction with the children when their partners are gone. When the soldier returns, his or her unfamiliarity with these behaviors may strain communication. When Justin is home, he and Mary talk a lot about how they should guide and discipline their sons so that the boys experience consistency—and so that they manage the dialectical tensions of autonomy versus connection.

▶ Depending on what technologies are available (and when), families can talk every day or regularly to keep abreast of one another's lives. They can engage in activities together, even though they are far apart. Mary and Justin like to choose a book that they read independently and then discuss when they have time together. They also pray together at an agreed-upon time, even though they are not connected physically or electronically. These simple but meaningful activities help them to feel a sense of closeness despite the distance.

▶ Sharing family news—whether big ("Doug made the basketball team") or small ("Daniel was home from school today with a bit of a cold")—helps to keep Justin involved in the family's day-to-day activities. Mary and Justin's discussions of their daily lives help them to increase feelings of intimacy.

▶ All spouses may sometimes worry about how much to disclose to their partners. For example, Mary worries that if she discloses her exhaustion at dealing with their son's disrespectful behavior alone, Justin will feel guilty for not being there. However, research shows that healthy self-disclosure between spouses correlates with fewer health problems and higher marital satisfaction (Joseph & Afifi, 2010).

THINGS TO TRY ▶ Activities

1. LaunchPad for *Real Communication* offers key term videos and encourages self-assessment through adaptive quizzing. Go to **bedfordstmartins.com/realcomm** to get access to:

 LearningCurve Adaptive Quizzes.

▶ Video clips that illustrate key concepts, highlighted in teal in the Real Reference section that follows.

2. List one family relationship, one friendship, and one romantic relationship in which you are or have been involved. For each of these relationships, list at least five self-disclosures you made to those individuals, and describe how each revelation advanced relational intimacy. Now list at least five self-disclosures you wish you had *not* made to each of these individuals. Did these inappropriate

self-disclosures increase or decrease your intimacy? Reflect on these lists as you self-disclose in future relationships.

3. Consider a romantic relationship that has ended. Using the stages outlined in this chapter, create a time line of the relationship. Include significant turning points that encouraged the relationship to move into another stage as well as any stages that may have been skipped. Reflect on your level of satisfaction at each stage, and note any changes you would have made at that point. If any stages were omitted from the time line, reflect on why. Based on your experiences in this relationship, did you or will you communicate differently with later romantic partners?

4. As a new romantic relationship begins, keep a journal of the communication events that occur. In this journal, indicate the stage you perceive the relationship to be in (based on the stages in this chapter). List key communication events that increase or decrease attachment in the relationship. Reflect on and include in your journal your level of satisfaction with the relationship and if and how you would like the relationship to proceed.

5. In small groups in your class, discuss how popular culture and films portray interpersonal relationships, considering specifically relationship stages. Discuss communication techniques that the characters might have used to produce different relationship outcomes. Analyze how accurately the communication behaviors of the characters themselves and those they use in their relationships reflect real-life communication episodes.

Now that you have finished reading this chapter, you can:

Explain key aspects of interpersonal relationships:

▶ **Interpersonal relationships**, the interconnections between two individuals, are influenced by **interpersonal communication**, the exchange of verbal and nonverbal messages between people who share meanings and accomplish social goals (p. 182).

▶ We all have a complex **relational network** or web of relationships. We have **family** relationships, **friendship**, **social relationships** romantic partners, and relationships we establish and maintain online (pp. 182–185).

▶ **Love** is a deep affection for another person with varying degrees of passion, commitment, and **intimacy**, or closeness and understanding (p. 186)—and is important to romantic relationships.

▶ **Social information processing theory** explains that virtual relationships develop much like face-to-face contact but the process often takes longer to become more intimate. Online relationships have the potential to develop even more personal and intimate relationships than face-to-face ones, a phenomenon known as **hyperpersonal communication** (pp. 187–188).

Describe why we form relationships:

▶ Relationship formation requires either physical or virtual **proximity**, or nearness (pp. 189–190).

▶ Physical, intellectual, and social attraction motivates relationship formation (p. 190).

▶ Similarity often increases attraction (pp. 190–191).

▶ Humans have a natural need for companionship and **inclusion**—a need to share our lives with others (p. 191).

▶ We form relationships for intellectual, emotional, and physical stimulation (p. 192).

▶ Relationships help us accomplish goals (p. 192).

List ways to manage relationship dynamics:

▶ **Social exchange theory** (p. 193) explains how we balance the advantages and disadvantages in our relationships.

▶ **Rewards** are what make you feel good about the relationship and may be extrinsic, instrumental, or intrinsic. **Costs** are aspects of the relationship that upset you (p. 193).

▶ According to **uncertainty reduction theory**, a relationship priority is to decrease the uncertainty

between partners through the use of **passive strategies**, which involve observing others without actually interacting (p. 195), **active strategies**, which involve seeking information from a third party (p. 196), and **interactive strategies**, which involve communicating directly with the person (p. 196).

▶ **Relational dialectics theory** holds that **dialectical tensions** arise when opposing or conflicting goals exist in a relationship (p. 196).

▶ Individuals may struggle to find a balance between independence and dependence, openness and closedness, and predictability and novelty (pp. 196–198).

Describe the factors that influence self-disclosure:

▶ **Social penetration theory** explains how relational partners move toward intimacy, (p. 199).

▶ **Communication privacy management theory** helps explain how people perceive the information they hold about themselves and how they disclose it (pp. 199–200). **Boundary turbulence** arises when violations make it necessary to readjust the need for disclosure versus privacy (p. 201).

▶ **Strategic topic avoidance** is used to maneuver the conversation away from topics that make people feel vulnerable (p. 201).

Outline the predictable stages of most relationships:

▶ **Turning points** are events or changes important to relationship definition (p. 202).

▶ The **initiating stage** is the first contact (p. 203).

▶ In the **exploratory stage**, there is superficial communication (p. 203).

▶ More self-disclosure occurs in the **intensification stage** (p. 203).

▶ In the **stable stage**, expectations are accurate and realistic. We see partners **integrating**, or becoming one, and **bonding**, sharing messages about their relationship with the world (pp. 203–204).

▶ In the **declining stage**, **uncertainty events**, interference from outside the relationship, and unmet expectations take a toll, though **repair tactics** may reverse the decline (pp. 204–207).

▶ In the **termination stage**, the relationship fades away or is unexpectedly terminated by one partner (p. 207).

▶ **Reconciliation** is a repair strategy for rekindling relationships (pp. 207–208).

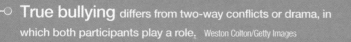

True bullying differs from two-way conflicts or drama, in which both participants play a role. Weston Colton/Getty Images

 LearningCurve can help you master the material in this chapter.
Go to **bedfordstmartins.com/realcomm**.

Managing Conflict in Relationships

Students don't need to be told that kids can be mean. They've all seen a fellow student being harassed, physically or verbally, by a classmate. Some may have even been the target of a bully at some point in their lives. Others may have been the tormenters themselves. And every few months, a news report sounds the alarm about a growing epidemic of bullying: stories of heartbreaking child suicides and chilling school shootings detail the torments some teenagers inflict on others and the lengths to which some victims will go to escape. By 2014, laws or policies against bullying were on the books of each of the fifty states (StopBullyingNow.gov). Many schools adopted "zero tolerance" policies, which prescribe automatic and severe punishments for students who exhibit any violent or bullying behavior (American Psychological Association, 2008).

Is every mean word or act of aggression an example of bullying? Probably not. As Emily Bazelon, journalist and author of the book, *Sticks and Stones: Defeating the Culture of Bullying and Rediscovering the Power of Character and Empathy,* points out, the word *bullying* is itself being abused—applied to any and all acts of aggression or insensitivity that come up between children rather than to long- or short-term patterns of abuse by popular or powerful children over weaker ones. In many cases, incidents labeled as bullying, including fights and online attacks, are really two-way conflicts in which both students play a role (Yoffe, 2013). "Most teenagers can identify bullying," Bazelon notes, "but they can also distinguish it from what they often call 'drama,' which . . . is an accurate and common name for the ordinary skirmishes that mark most children's lives. In fact, it's drama that's common, and bullying, properly defined, that's less so" (Bazelon, 2013).

After you have finished reading this chapter, you will be able to

- Describe the factors that lead to productive conflict

- Identify conflict triggers in yourself and others

- Explain the forces that influence how people handle conflict

- Evaluate and employ strategies for managing conflict in different situations

- Recognize your ability to repair and let go of painful conflict

Dealing with conflict—be it with a romantic partner, a family member, a colleague, a classmate, or an institution—can be hard. Some avoid it altogether, whereas others lash out aggressively, in person or via social media. But there is also a middle ground that falls between covering our ears and posting aggressive comments in a public forum. There are also lots of ways in which we may not only manage conflict but also grow and learn from it. In this chapter, we'll take a look at some of the root causes of conflict and examine the ways in which we engage in conflict with others. We'll then consider productive ways in which to manage conflict and reconcile our relationships.

Understanding Conflict

You've undoubtedly had countless conflicts in your life. But just what is conflict, anyway? **Conflict** is not simply an argument or a struggle: it's an interaction between two or more interdependent people who perceive that they have contradictory goals or scarce resources. In other words, there is conflict when I believe that if you get what *you* want, I cannot have what *I* want.

Scholars like to distinguish between conflict—which is inevitable and sometimes cannot be resolved—and **conflict management**, which refers to the way that we engage in conflict and address disagreements with our relational partners. For example, consider Lisa and Steven Bradley, a couple who seemed to have it all: a beautiful home, four expensive cars, designer clothes, dinner out (or ordered in) every night. But they had a secret: Lisa spent lavishly without consulting Steven, and Steven stewed about it without ever confronting Lisa. Like countless Americans today, even the relatively well-off Bradleys were spending more than they earned, essentially living on credit. Though they rarely fought about it, Lisa and Steven were struggling to keep up with their bills and were on the brink of divorce (Greenhouse, 2006; Oprah.com, 2008).

For Lisa and Steven, the conflict was rooted in differing ideas about money, credit, and financial priorities. And they chose to manage their conflict by avoiding discussion and confrontation, which in this case wasn't particularly helpful. As the Bradleys eventually discovered—and as you'll see throughout this chapter—conflict can be managed either unproductively or productively. Let's examine these two approaches to conflict and consider the costs and benefits of each one.

Unproductive Conflict

If you haven't already guessed, Lisa and Steven's approach to managing their conflict over money was an unproductive one. **Unproductive conflict** is conflict that is managed poorly and has a negative impact on the individuals and relationships involved.

In many respects, our relationships—including those with families, friends, colleagues, and romantic partners—are defined by how we manage conflict. But the damage of unproductive conflict isn't always limited to relationships. Researchers have discovered that when conflict is handled poorly, those involved can experience a poorer sense of well-being at work (Sonnentag, Unger,

& Nagel, 2013), as well as personal health problems, including sleep disruptions (Hicks & Diamond, 2011), emotional distress (Davies, Sturge-Apple, Cicchetti, & Cummings, 2008), mood disorders (Segrin, Hanzal, & Domschke, 2009), heart disease, and immune deficiency (Canary, 2003).

Productive Conflict

Not all conflict is negative, however. In fact, conflict can be as valuable as it is inevitable! Conflict that is managed effectively is called **productive conflict**. We don't always notice the conflicts that we handle productively, as when two people quickly reach a compromise over some issue on which they disagree (like whether to eat at the Olive Garden or Pizza Hut), without argument or confrontation. But productive conflict can also follow unproductive conflict, as when Lisa and Steven, feeling fed up with the debt and realizing that their marriage was in jeopardy, began to confront and work on their financial and relationship problems, cutting their budgets and taking on additional work for more income. By addressing the problem collaboratively—facing the reality of their debt, agreeing on their financial priorities, setting a budget, and making decisions about money together—the couple began both resolving their financial problems and healing their relationship.

It is important to note that productive conflict does not necessarily mean a successful resolution of conflict, but even without resolution, productive conflict can still benefit both parties. Let's look at a few examples.

Productive Conflict Fosters Healthy Debate

To believe that conflict can be productive rather than destructive, you have to actively engage in it. There is no greater intellectual exercise than exploring and testing ideas with another person. And like a sport, it can get competitive, as evidenced by the popularity of debate teams in schools and the media fanfare surrounding political debates during major elections. In fact, active and lively debate allows us to exchange ideas, evaluate the merits of one another's claims, and continually refine and clarify each other's thinking about the issue under discussion; debates on the floors of Congress, for example, allow representatives

Few people enjoy conflict, but avoiding it can have negative consequences. In Chapter 9, we discuss *groupthink*—when groups focus on unity and conflict avoidance rather than openly discussing alternative solutions to problems. If your student organization president makes an irresponsible suggestion on how to spend funds and you and the others keep silent, conflict may be avoided—but at a cost.

● **EVEN WITH MATTERS** as simple as making plans for a Friday night, we may be uncompromising and create unproductive conflict or discuss the options, reach an agreement, and act on it.
conrado/Shutterstock

● **ALTHOUGH IT MAY** have been frustrating and stressful to solve a logic puzzle together under time constraints, this couple in *The Amazing Race* emerged triumphant, feeling all the closer for having managed the pressure and communication challenges successfully. MONTY BRINTON/CBS /Landov

to go on record with their opinions on bills being considered and to try to persuade their colleagues to consider their positions. When government leaders fail to engage in such debates—when they evade questions or block a bill from going to debate on the floor of the legislature—they are formally engaging in the same kind of unproductive conflict avoidance that individuals use when they refuse to discuss difficult subjects. Conflict and healthy debate can also be a useful part of everyday life, as when a couple discusses and evaluates the pros and cons of buying a new car.

Productive Conflict Leads to Better Decision-Making

Healthy debate serves a real purpose in that it helps individuals and groups make smarter decisions. By skillfully working through conflicting ideas about how to solve a problem or reach a goal, we identify the best courses of action. That's because a productive conflict provides an arena in which we can test the soundness of proposed ideas. Suggested solutions that are logical and feasible will stand up to scrutiny during the decision-making process, whereas weaker solutions are likely to be exposed as flawed. So by engaging in productive discussion about your conflict, the real costs and impact of, say, a new hybrid car are revealed, and you are able to come up with a workable solution: you will continue driving your old car while sacrificing this year's vacation and dinners out to put an additional $350 every month into a special savings account toward the purchase of a secondhand hybrid car in one year.

Productive Conflict Spurs Relationship Growth

Differences of opinion and clashing goals are inevitable in any relationship. And that can be part of what keeps our relationships fun and interesting! But how the partners *handle* the disagreements that arise determines whether their bond will grow stronger. As two individuals—be they romantic partners, friends, roommates, or colleagues—work through their disagreements productively, they build on the relationship (Dainton & Gross, 2008). For example, contestant pairs on the CBS reality series *The Amazing Race* face many relational challenges as they race around the globe completing obstacles and quests. Contestants may disagree with how their partner approaches a particular situation (like refusing to ask for directions when lost), or they may get frustrated if the partner loses an important document or forgets to ask the all-important taxicab to wait around until the end of a challenge. Yet most contestants manage to end their race without permanently damaging their relationships; many even cite the race as an experience that improved their communication during highly stressful and intense situations. To paraphrase the German philosopher Friedrich Nietzsche, that which does not kill a relationship can indeed make it stronger.

AND YOU?

Have you ever let a small conflict grow into a bigger one simply because you avoided engaging in conflict management? On the other hand, are there times when avoiding conflict is more productive than trying to address it?

Conflict Triggers

▶ "He was drinking from the milk carton again. I caught him. It's so disgusting—I have to use that milk, too, you know!"

▶ "Is there any point to trying to make plans with Lynette? She's always saying she's too busy to get together."

▶ "I swear, my boss thinks I have no life outside of this organization. Why is he e-mailing me and texting me about my projects on weekends?"

Do any of these scenarios seem familiar? Everyone has a trigger that drives them absolutely mad when it happens, and conflict often ensues. The fact is that conflicts arise for a number of reasons. People often have conflicting goals, beliefs, or ideas; we face competition for scarce resources, such as money or time. We experience misunderstandings, and unfortunately, we lose our tempers. And sometimes we encounter people who are deceitful or uncooperative or who intentionally undermine our efforts to achieve our goals. In the following sections, we'll examine a few common conflict triggers.

Inaccurate Perceptions

Misunderstandings are a common—and regrettable—cause of conflict. For example, in the movie *The Break Up*, partners Brooke and Gary fight over the give-and-take in their relationship. Brooke is frustrated that she frequently accompanies Gary to baseball games (which she does not particularly enjoy), but Gary never takes her to the ballet. Although it may seem that Gary is selfish and uninterested in Brooke's desires, Brooke does have a role in this conflict. Gary points out that Brooke never told him she dislikes baseball—he thought they were mutually enjoying the games—and she never shared her desire to attend a ballet. Had they communicated openly, they could have avoided these perceptual errors altogether and potentially saved their relationship.

Incompatible Goals

Since much communication is goal driven, conflicts are bound to arise when goals are perceived as incompatible (Canary, 2003). On *Grey's Anatomy*, for example, the stable relationship between Callie and Arizona has had a number of challenges. Early on there was the perceived incompatible goal about children: Callie wanted to settle down and start a family, but Arizona was certain that she never wanted to have children. When couples differ on such serious life decisions, it can be extremely difficult to resolve conflict. But even among relational partners who are in agreement on big life decisions, other goals are likely to come into conflict. For example, couples that are committed to having a family have conflicts about the timing, number, and rearing of children.

CONNECT

The best way to account for unusual behavior may be to ask if your perceptions are accurate. In Chapter 7, we discuss *interactive strategies* that help you to reduce uncertainty and get information directly from a person. You might tell a friend, "I sense that you're angry with me because you haven't talked to me today. Am I right?" Such questions allow your friend to clarify perceptions and may eliminate unnecessary conflict.

● **THOUGH CALLIE AND ARIZONA** fall on different sides of the kids or no kids debate, is there a way they might negotiate their opposing goals? ABC/Photofest

Unbalanced Costs and Rewards

Your roommate is annoyed that you keep eating her food; you are annoyed that she doesn't clean the bathroom. Conflict often arises when we are struggling to get a share of some limited resource, such as money, time, or attention. Recall from Chapter 7 that many researchers argue that we treat our interpersonal relationships almost like financial exchanges; we tally up our *rewards* (what we're getting from a relationship) and compare these to our *costs* (what we're putting into the relationship). If we think our costs are outweighing the rewards, then conflict may likely be triggered. For Callie of *Grey's Anatomy*, Arizona's refusal of intimacy after her leg amputation and Callie's increased responsibility for household management are costs of this relationship that lead to much tension and many conflicts.

Provocation

Of course, not every conflict arises out of natural differences between individuals' goals or perceptions. The hard truth is that people can be uncaring or even aggressive at times. Although conflict is indeed a natural part of every relationship, a great many conflicts arise through **provocation**—the intentional instigation of conflict. A wide range of events can spark intense negative emotions in a relationship (Canary, 2003):

> *Aggression.* Aggressive behaviors range from verbal intimidation to physical threats. Fear and defensiveness (along with even more aggression) are common responses to such behavior.

> ▶ *Identity threats.* When someone insults you personally, it can threaten your identity. Threats to identity management range from mild insults ("Man, you have a dirty car") to condescending remarks ("I'll go slowly so you can keep up") to attacks on one's values or religion and racial or ethnic slurs.

> ▶ *Lack of fairness.* When someone uses more than his or her fair share of resources—in families, workplaces, or living situations, for example—it commonly stirs up negative reactions.

> ▶ *Incompetence.* When someone you work with or depend on performs poorly, the person is in a sense provoking conflict. Feelings of anger and resentment occur when a lab partner fails to bring needed supplies or write his or her share of the lab report.

> ▶ *Relationship threats.* When a relationship comes under threat, conflict is likely to arise. If your romantic partner reveals things that suggest he or she has other interests, you feel jealousy, anger, or insecurity. Similarly, a young child may see a new baby sibling as a threat to his relationship with his parents, or you might see a new, talented coworker as a threat to your connection with your boss.

● **ALEC BALDWIN'S** quick temper and aggressive behavior have gotten him into scrapes on numerous occasions. Europa Press/Europa Press via Getty Images

Factors Affecting Conflict

We've just looked at triggers that can cause a conflict to crop up between people. But once a conflict arises, several specific forces can influence how the people involved handle the conflict. We examine these forces next.

Power Dynamics

When one person has power over another, that dynamic can cause one or both of the people to handle conflict unproductively. Power dynamics are often at play in the workplace, where your boss determines the nature of your work and can fire, promote, or transfer you. If you and your boss disagree about some issue at work, your boss may pull rank, saying something like "I'm in charge here." But power dynamics also come into play in more intimate relationships. For example, if you are dependent on your parents for tuition, shelter, food, or anything else, they may use that power to control your behavior, perhaps pressuring you to choose a specific school or major or making bold declarations about how you should spend your time.

In romantic relationships, unhealthy partnerships are often characterized by too much dependence of one partner on the other, control of one partner, and an inability to communicate boundaries, among other things (Canary, Cody, & Manusov, 2008). You can imagine what happens when conflict enters such an unbalanced relationship. In some cases, the partner with more power may engage in activities that make the other partner fearful and compliant, such as bullying or intimidating. Let's say that Chris and Amy are considering purchasing their first home together and that Amy is just starting a freelance writing career. Amy now relies on Chris's full-time job for health insurance and a stable income. In a relationship where power is balanced and healthy, Chris would be supportive of Amy's new venture and would want to come to a mutual decision about the size and type of home they purchase. But if the balance of power is skewed in Chris's favor—either because he is domineering or because Amy refuses to voice her opinions—Chris may engage in some of the tactics we mentioned: saying, for example, "Well, I'm the one *paying* for the house," or "Fine, I guess we'll just keep throwing away money on rent," if Amy suggests that perhaps Chris's top-choice house isn't what's best for them.

It's important to bear in mind that differences in power aren't limited to material resources. In any relationship, one person has power over another if he or she controls something that the other person values. For example, when you are angry with your best friend, you may ignore her, depriving her of the benefit of spending time with you. Some people even withhold physical or emotional affection from their romantic partner as a form of punishment or as a means to try to control their partner's behavior. When the power balance is unequal, conflicts are more likely, and relational partners tend to be less satisfied (Dunbar & Abra, 2010).

Attitudes Toward Conflict

Some people love a good argument. They relish the opportunity to negotiate a new employment contract or debate friends on political issues. Studies show

CONNECT

Cultural context has a strong impact on power dynamics. In Chapter 5, we discuss *high- and low-power-distance cultures*, which differ in their expectations and acceptance of the division of power among individuals and groups. In intercultural group settings—where members and leaders may have different attitudes about power dynamics—it's a good idea to discuss the dynamics openly to make conflict more productive and enhance group communication (see Chapter 10).

AND YOU?

Think of an attitude you
have about conflict that is
making it difficult for you to
talk productively about
disagreements with someone
in your life. For example, do
you believe that discussing
conflict will destroy your
relationship? What steps
might you take to begin
letting go of this
unproductive attitude?

that those who have positive views about conflict spend time imagining conflicts with other people and planning out and rehearsing conflict scenarios in order to achieve positive outcomes and relieve stress (Wallenfelsz & Hample, 2010). Others find conflict uncomfortable and believe it can only lead to hurt feelings or a damaged relationship. This discomfort might lead you to steer clear of conflict entirely or avoid it in situations when you don't think that you will argue very effectively, you don't consider the particular disagreement very important, or you don't believe that the current time or place is appropriate for having an argument.

Some people take their negative views of conflict to the level of a destructive tendency called **taking conflict personally (TCP)** (Hample & Dallinger, 1995). When we take conflict personally, we feel so threatened by conflict that we interpret most disagreements as personal insults or assault. We may also dwell on negative thoughts and feelings of persecution and, if we cannot avoid conflict altogether, may actually lash out aggressively (Wallenfelsz & Hample, 2010). Our attitudes about conflict, whether we embrace or detest it, have an important effect on how we deal with it.

Communication Climate

Another factor that affects how we handle conflict is the **communication climate** (Gibb, 1961)—the general "atmosphere" surrounding how we feel about our communication in different relationships.

What types of climate might you face when engaging in conflict with others? We suggest three possibilities: uncertain, defensive, and supportive. The AMC television series *The Walking Dead* illustrates the ways different climates can affect conflict management.

▶ **Uncertain climates** are those in which at least one of the people involved is unclear, vague, tentative, and awkward about the goals, expectations, and potential outcomes of the conflict situation. Many conditions can create uncertain climates, including unfamiliarity with the people, the surroundings, or the topic at hand. In uncertain climates, communicators are hesitant to take action, and conflict management can bog down. On *The Walking Dead*, small groups of survivors band together in order to survive. Clearly there are innumerable uncertainties in this postapocalyptic world: How will Sheriff Rich Grimes and his people keep out the "walkers"? How will they obtain necessary supplies? And how far are they willing to go to defend their group from others competing for resources like food, weapons, and shelter? This confusion is compounded by the overwhelming fear and hesitation of many of the individual characters who struggle to decide a clear course of action.

▶ **Defensive climates** are those in which the people involved feel threatened. It is an atmosphere of mistrust, suspicion, and apprehension, leading to efforts to control and manipulate others (Forward, Czech, & Lee, 2011). On *The Walking Dead*, survivors in the Grimes camp are always on the defensive: every moment is fraught with anxiety, not only about the zombies who wander up to the gates of their prison camp daily but also about competing groups seeking to overtake them, as well natural threats and concerns like illness and hunger.

▶ **Supportive climates** involve communicators who are open to one another's ideas and feelings. Such climates involve neutral (rather than blame-filled) descriptions of the conflict situation and allow communicators to develop trust and cooperation toward a productive resolution of problems (Forward, Czech, & Lee, 2011). On *The Walking Dead*, supportive climates are hard to find. But individuals—friends, spouses, siblings, and even strangers—do work to manage problems among themselves. When Rich worries that he is failing as a leader and a father, he hangs up his holster to take time to focus on being

CONNECT

The differences among communication climates are often related to language and nonverbal communication (Chapters 3 and 4). In addressing conflict with a friend, you might use few words and avoid eye contact (uncertain climate), raise your voice or speak sarcastically (defensive climate), or offer reassuring touch and speak with a firm but understanding tone (supportive climate).

● **AS THE FEW** escapees of a zombie epidemic band together in the postapocalyptic series *The Walking Dead*, they find themselves in a variety of communication climates: moving from an initial defensive mistrust of one another to a climate of supportiveness to ensure their cosurvival.
© American Movie Classics/ Courtesy: Everett Collection

a father to his son and new baby daughter. Although others in the group want him to step back into his leadership role, they allow him the time to mourn the death of his wife Lori, to repair his relationship with his son Carl, and to bond with his new baby daughter. But when the camp is threatened, they make it clear that he needs to step up as a leader and a defender once again.

How do you move from a defensive or uncertain climate to a supportive one? Your first task is to make sure you know which climate you are experiencing. Your gut instincts can be a credible guide here, but you can also make some formal assessment of the climate situation. What are your past experiences with this topic, this person or group, and these conditions? How did your own communication contribute to the situation? Once you know the climate you are in, you can take steps to move toward a supportive climate. Figure 8.1 offers several communication steps to help you find your way to supportive conflict climates.

Culture and Conflict

Culture and conflict are clearly linked. If we consider how important culture is to our identities and how pervasive conflict is in our lives, we can begin to understand how culture influences and guides our conflict experiences. Differences in cultural values, beliefs, and attitudes can lead to conflict directly, and these differences can also affect how individuals perceive conflict, what their goals are for conflict, and how conflict is handled. Let's examine the influence on conflict of our broad cultural orientations, as well as our co-cultural group memberships.

Cultural Orientation

Research in culture and conflict management often examines differences between individualist, low-context cultures and collectivist, high-context cultures. As you learned in Chapter 5, *individualist cultures* emphasize personal needs, rights, and identity over those of the collective or group, whereas *collectivist cultures* emphasize group identity and needs. In addition, you'll recall that people rely more on

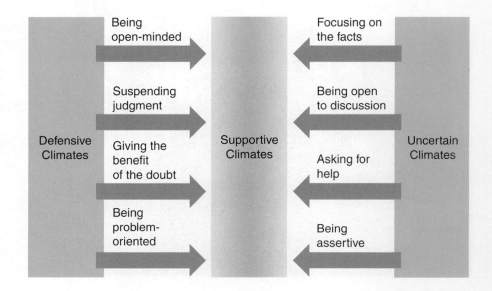

FIGURE 8.1

STEPS TO REACHING A SUPPORTIVE CLIMATE

indirect verbal messages and nonverbal communication than on what is actually said in *high-context cultures*. In *low-context cultures*, people are expected to be more verbally direct and say what they mean.

When applied to conflict, European Americans tend to take an individualist and low-context approach, whereas Latinos and Asians are more collectivist and high context (Ting-Toomey & Oetzel 2002). European Americans, for example, tend to view conflict as a necessary way to work out problems and feel that specific conflict issues should be worked out separately from relational issues. For Latinos and Asians, on the other hand, conflict is perceived as having a negative effect on relational harmony, and conflict issues cannot be divorced from relationships. Indeed, cross-cultural research finds that people living in high-context cultures (for example, India and Thailand) prefer to avoid conflict altogether or give in to the other person's wishes, whereas people in low-context cultures (for example, the United States and Ireland) prefer to engage in conflict more openly and competitively (Croucher et al., 2012). In addition, communication during conflict in individualist, low-context cultures is expected to be clear and direct, whereas in collectivist, high-context cultures, people are supposed to pick up on subtle cues and vague verbal messages (Merkin, 2009). Understanding these important cultural distinctions can help us understand how confusion, frustration, and miscommunication can happen when conflict arises.

Co-Cultures

In the film *The Kids Are All Right*, mothers Jules and Nic are worried about their teenaged son, Laser, who appears withdrawn. They ask him, over and over, if there's anything he wants to talk about. They complain that his friend Clay is a bad influence. They ask him for reasons why he sought out his biological father without telling them. But Laser simply does not want to talk. Although such nagging female/noncommunicative male stereotypes are standard in fiction and film, there is some evidence to suggest that, in fact, women are more inclined to voice criticisms and complaints, and men tend to avoid engaging in such discussions.

● IN *THE KIDS ARE ALL RIGHT,* mothers Jules and Nic and their adolescent son Laser play out the typical imbalance of communicativeness between females and males. MANDALAY/SAINT AIRE/10TH HOLE/ANTIDOTE / THE KOBAL COLLECTION

Differences between men and women reflect one important way that our co-cultures affect how we deal with conflict. Recall from Chapter 5 that **co-cultures** are the groups we belong to with distinct characteristics or attitudes that unify us and distinguish us from the larger general culture. These distinctions often play out in conflict situations. In a classic study of marital conflict, for example, Gottman (1994) found that women tend to criticize and attack their partner's character more than men and that men tend to "stonewall" (refuse to engage) more than women. More recent research also suggests that sex and gender influence satisfaction level with regard to certain conflict management strategies. Afifi, McManus, Steuber, and Coho (2009) found that when women perceived that their dating partner was engaging in conflict avoidance, their satisfaction level decreased, but avoidance did not cause the same dissatisfaction in men.

Age is another co-cultural difference that affects conflict. When faced with a potential argument, younger (under forty) and middle-aged (forty to fifty-nine) adults are more likely to openly argue, whereas older adults (over sixty) prefer to use passive strategies, such as "letting it go" or waiting for the situation to change on its own (Blanchard-Fields, Mienaltowski, & Seay, 2007). These avoidance strategies appear to be beneficial, as older adults experience less negative emotion than their younger counterparts when they deal with social tensions passively (Birditt, 2013). Researchers argue that older people may have learned from experience to recognize when an argument is "just not worth it" and that they may be choosing the strategies that help them manage their own emotional well-being (Charles, Piazza, Luong, & Almeida, 2009). For younger and middle-aged adults, however, conflict situations may more often require direct confrontation (for example, at work or in battles with parents), so passive strategies may be ineffective for them at achieving their goals. These confrontations can take a toll: by middle age, the increase in conflict and interpersonal stress appears to have an especially negative impact on people's well-being (Darbonne, Uchino, & Ong, 2013).

When we think of conflict and culture or co-culture, it is important to remember not to assume that all members of a culture or group reflect the extreme differences. It is also dangerous to assume that differences in culture mean irreconcilable differences in conflict. Competent communication in conflict means understanding and respecting differences while working to "expand the pie" for both parties. Even in the most uncomfortable and frustrating conflict situations, we can learn a great deal about others and ourselves through culture.

Communication Channel

In many communication situations, we don't think much about which available channel we should choose. Not so when it comes to conflict. If you've ever sent flowers as a way of apologizing, left a voice mail on a weekend to let an instructor or colleague know you've missed a deadline, or delivered bad news via a text message, chances are you chose that channel as a way of avoiding engaging in conflict face to face. But conflict and communication channels are often intertwined: conflict can arise from poor channel choices, as we perceive things differently depending on the channel used (see Chapter 2). Even more interesting

---

AND YOU?

Do you see yourself as more of a feminine or masculine individual? In what ways have gender differences influenced the conflicts you've experienced with people whose gender is different from yours?

CONNECT

A lack of nonverbal communication can pose problems when handling conflict via mediated channels (Chapter 4). If you text an apology to your friend, he can't see your facial expressions to appreciate how sorry you are. Emoticons do help display feelings (😊!), but competent communicators must consider if nonverbal communication is the best channel for a particular message. When dealing with conflict, it might be better to speak face to face or over the phone so that nonverbal behaviors such as tone of voice can be decoded.

is the powerful way that channel choice influences conflict management.

Of course, some practical considerations can influence which channel we select to communicate with someone else about a disagreement, such as whether a person lives close enough for us to talk about an issue in person. However, our reasons for choosing one channel over another are often rooted in emotions. If you're intimidated by someone in a conflict situation, you may feel safer communicating with him or her by e-mail than over the phone or face to face. But beware: managing conflict with close friends or romantic partners through electronic channels can come across as insensitive and even cowardly. Just ask those who found out that their relationship was over via a changed "relationship status" on their significant other's Facebook page!

Online Anonymity and Conflict

On a related front, the relative anonymity of electronic communication has emerged as a new factor that influences conflict, particularly in the generation of heated and unproductive electronic exchanges in Internet forums, in e-mails, and through social networking sites (Shachaf & Hara, 2010). Of course, people have long been able to provoke conflict anonymously—for example, prank phone calls were common in the days before caller ID. But the Internet has provided a vast arena for **flaming**—the posting of online messages that are deliberately hostile or insulting toward a particular individual. Such messages are usually intended only to provoke anger and can ignite flame wars between individuals when friendly, productive discussions give way to insults and aggression. In many cases, the root cause of these conflicts is not even a disagreement but one person's misinterpretation of another's message.

Flaming should be distinguished from **trolling**, which is the posting of provocative, offensive, and often false messages to forums or discussion boards in order to elicit from the participants a negative general reaction (Morrissey, 2010). Trolls often use their online anonymity to intentionally stir up conflict and create damage. In the online gaming community, they also purposely disrupt teamwork or try to ruin the gaming experience of others (Thacker & Griffiths, 2012). Research reveals that trolls are typically motivated by boredom, amusement, attention seeking, and revenge (Shachaf & Hara, 2010; Thacker & Griffiths, 2012).

Technological channels are also an arena for even more aggressive conflict behaviors, such as **cyberbullying**—abusive attacks on individual targets conducted through electronic channels (Erdur-Baker, 2010). Researchers point out that traditional face-to-face bullying, although highly unpleasant, is also extremely intimate, and victims can at least find some place or time of refuge. Cyberbullying, by contrast, makes use of text messages, e-mails, and social networking sites to deliver a nonstop stream of cruel messages or photos that may be visible to others for a

● **THE COFOUNDER** of Wikipedia, Jim Wales, allegedly broke up with his girlfriend on his Wikipedia page. Perhaps that wasn't the best choice! © Rick Friedman/ Corbis

AND YOU?

Consider a recent conflict. What channel did you select to communicate with the other person? How did the communication channel affect the quality of the exchange? Did the channel you chose lead to a productive conflict or an unproductive one? Why?

WIREDFORCOMMUNICATION

Locking Down Trolls versus Free Speech

Internet forums are, in a sense, a grand experiment in free speech. A trip to an open forum on just about any topic—from the new iPhone to Edward Snowden's NSA leaks—is likely to yield astute critiques and interesting perspectives—as well as lots of irrelevant, incoherent, offensive, and inflammatory banter. Does the value of the open discourse outweigh the negative impact of vitriol? In September 2013, the editors at *Popular Science* made a tough decision in response to this question and shut down the comments section on the publication's companion Web site. "It wasn't a decision we made lightly," explained online content editor Suzanne LaBarre in a letter to readers. "As the news arm of a 141-year-old science and technology magazine, we are as committed to fostering lively, intellectual debate as we are to spreading the word of science far and wide. The problem is when trolls and spambots overwhelm the former, diminishing our ability to do the latter" (LaBarre, 2013). Indeed, a recent study indicates that comments can influence the way readers perceive the initial post. Specifically, readers exposed to uncivil remarks and personal attacks made in the comments became more polarized than those who were exposed only to civil discourse in the comments section (Anderson, Brossard, Scheufele, Xenos, & Ladwig, 2013).

Although civility in the reader comments are a concern for most Web editors, few have gone the route of *Popular Science*. But many large organizations do try to limit unproductive comment threads by replacing open forums (in which readers are able to comment freely, often anonymously) with moderated forums, which trade complete openness for order. Forum moderators—commonly known as mods—set strict rules for posts, often review all posts before making them public, and have the power to censor or ban specific posts. At *The New York Times*, comments are reviewed by a team of fourteen moderators who eliminate comments that are offensive, off-topic, or simply insubstantial, in order to keep the commentary focused and productive. Webzine Boing Boing similarly deletes posts that moderators find offensive. "It's fun to have disagreements," explains Boing Boing founder Mark Frauenfelder, "but if someone gets nasty, we will kick them out" (Frauenfelder, quoted in Niemann, 2014).

THINK ABOUT THIS

1 Do you participate in Internet forums? Do you prefer moderated or open forums? What makes you prefer one over the other?

2 Which is more important, a free-speech open forum or a managed, productive conflict? Do you think it's necessary to trade off one for the other?

3 Why might a Web site choose to eliminate comments altogether, rather than simply to moderate comments? Can a publication, electronic or otherwise, still host lively debate without offering comment threads alongside the articles it posts?

long time (Patchin & Hinduja, 2011). The perpetrator may not even be known, and the torment can be difficult to escape (Dempsey, Sulkowski, Dempsey, & Storch, 2011). The problem has serious consequences, as victims often experience mental health problems such as depression, loneliness, and low self-esteem; drops in academic performance and loss of relationships with peers at school; and a host of negative emotions, including fear, anger, embarrassment, sadness, and guilt (see Dehue, 2013). An extreme consequence among teens and preteens is evidenced by the suicide of a twelve-year-old Florida girl, Rebecca Sedwick. After a dispute over a boy, a months-long barrage of negative messages ensued, such as "nobody cares about u" and "you seriously deserve to die" (Stapleton & Yan, 2013). Rebecca finally posted on Facebook, "I'm jumping. I can't take it anymore," and the next day she jumped to her death from a tower at a cement plant. Rebecca's story initially even led law enforcement to consider stalking charges against the twelve- and fourteen-year-old "bullies" (Liston, 2013).

In some cases, cyberbullies—so empowered by their anonymity—entirely disregard expectations surrounding particular situational contexts. After seventeen-year-old Alexis Pilkington took her own life, her friends and family set up a Facebook memorial page to remember Alexis and to share their mutual grief. Sadly, alongside messages honoring this young woman's life were lewd, hateful, and inappropriate messages indicating that Alexis "got what she deserved." A family friend summarized the bullies' attempt to create controversy and conflict in such an inappropriate time and space: "Children want to mourn their friend, and there are posts of photos with nooses around her neck. It's disgusting and heartless" (Martinez, 2010, para. 6).

● **SOMETIMES THE** competition for a lone piece of pie can mask larger emotional issues. Alan Richardson/Getty Images

Conflict Styles

Let's consider a common, very simplistic scenario: you are sitting with your sister at the dinner table after a family meal. There's one last piece of Aunt Corinne's homemade chocolate peanut butter pie, and you and your sister both want it. Do you give up easily and just let her have it? Yell at her until she gives up (or until Dad takes it for himself)? Or suggest that you split the pie and each take half? We each have different **conflict styles**, or sets of goals and strategies that we use to manage conflict (Guerrero, Andersen, & Afifi, 2013; Rahim, 1983). Some of us may feel most comfortable with one primary style that we employ in multiple situations, but often it works better when we are able to change our styles to fit the particular situation and parties involved.

In certain types of conflict, such as a competition for a piece of pie, the people involved can resolve the conflict—that is, bring it to an end—in just seconds. But when the conflict is more complex or when a seemingly simple disagreement is a symptom of a larger problem between people, resolving the situation will require more time and thought. If you are resentful of always having to share everything with your sister—your laptop, your PlayStation, the family car, even attention from your parents—your conflict is bigger than a piece of pie. Resolving it may require a more involved approach, such as honest, lengthy dialogue about your resentments and possible ways for each of you to have more things you can call your own. The styles we use for managing conflict, be they simple or complicated, generally fall into one of three basic categories: escapist, competitive, or cooperative (see Table 8.1).

Escapist Styles

People who do not like conflict often use **escapist styles**—they try to prevent or avoid direct conflict altogether or, if they have to engage in it, get it over with as quickly as possible. There are two styles that both involve trying to escape conflict: avoiding and obliging.

TABLE 8.1

CONFLICT STYLES: THE PIE INCIDENT

Type	Description	Examples
Escapist —Avoiding —Obliging	Conflict is avoided or given into; personal goals may not be important; conflict is not seen as a viable alternative	• Postpone the pie debate ("Let's not have dessert now") • Relinquish the pie ("You can have it")
Competitive —Direct fighting —Indirect fighting	Individual goals are pursued; relationship may be threatened, especially if it gets aggressive	• Claim the pie ("That's my piece of pie"; "Oh, no, it's not") • Argue for your right to the pie ("I deserve this pie") • Hint that you'll do something bad if you don't get the pie ("It would be a shame if the pie ended up in the trash")
Cooperative —Compromising —Collaborating	Pursuit of mutual interests; problem-solving approach emphasized; relationship is preserved	• Share the pie • Broker a deal ("I'll do the dishes if you let me have the pie") • Address underlying needs ("Pie means having something special; how else can we each feel special?")

When you are **avoiding**, you do not express your own needs and goals, even if you have a grievance. But before you think this is being selfless, note that avoiders also do not allow others to express *their* needs. Instead, when the potential for conflict arises, avoiders often hide from the person who is angry. When confronted, they may try to change the subject or offer to discuss the issue later ("let's not spoil our nice dinner; we can put the pie back in the fridge and leave it until later"). Avoiding can be beneficial to a relationship in certain situations, such as when a confrontation might hurt the other person or when it would be better to postpone dealing with the conflict until a more appropriate time. Stafford (2010) found, for example, that couples in long-distance relationships may benefit from conflict avoidance because it minimizes differences and maximizes positive interaction. But avoidance strategies may be unproductive if they continually prevent people from dealing with issues that need to be addressed. Research has found that continual avoidance of conflict in families negatively impacts family strength and satisfaction (Schrodt, 2009; Ubinger, Handal, & Massura, 2013).

The other escapist style is **obliging** (also called accommodating or yielding). When you oblige someone, you give in to what he or she wants—that is, you let your sister have the pie! This is an escapist style because, like avoiding, it is a way to get out of having to engage in the conflict. The difference is that when you are obliging, you are at least somewhat concerned about the other person's goals—you would rather "lose" than have the other person be upset with you. Obliging strategies can be effective at preserving relational harmony, particularly when an issue is relatively unimportant (there will be other opportunities for pie) or when giving in shows that you recognize how much the issue really means to the other person (it's her favorite pie and she's had a tough day). Indeed, research shows

COMMUNICATIONACROSSCULTURES

Yours, Mine, and Both of Ours

The sight of a family lighting a menorah alongside their Christmas tree is not all that unfamiliar, of course; nor is the story of one parent who quietly leaves behind his or her own religious faith and allows his or her spouse (and his or her spouse's family and congregation) to take the spiritual lead. For couples of mixed faith, navigating differences in religion can be fraught with conflict, ranging from inconveniences over holidays to misunderstandings with parents and extended families, to troubling arguments over inconsistent messages or values. And yet, a 2008 Pew study found that nearly four in ten American marriages are between spouses of different religious affiliations (Pew, 2008). How do they navigate these potential conflicts?

Many families simply embrace more than one religion: the same Pew study indicates that almost a quarter of Americans attend religious services of more than one denomination or faith (Pew, 2008). Susan Katz Miller, author of *Being Both: Embracing Two Religions in One Interfaith Family*, conducted a survey of parents in interfaith communities, who had enrolled their children in interfaith education programs, and found that for these families, expressing more than one religion had benefits that extended beyond simply resolving conflicting faiths. Interfaith families felt that embracing both religions fostered family unity and gave extended families (especially both sets of grandparents) equal weight. On a more personal level, it prepared children to speak more frankly about their own religious identity and to address outsiders' questions about a last name or skin color that doesn't quite align with society's ideas about religion, ethnicity, and culture. And crucially, Miller points out more than 90 percent of the parents she surveyed chose interfaith communities—sometimes along with memberships in traditional congregations—because they wanted their children to be literate in both religions (Miller, 2013).

For some, the question is not so much a matter of which religion, but how much. The Kellers were both born and raised Roman Catholic, but as adults they are not equally devout—Emma still practices, but husband Bill describes himself as a "collapsed Catholic" who does not believe in God or even in religion. Nonetheless, their children were baptized and will receive the sacraments so important to the Catholic faith. "It's not something we fight about," writes Emma. "Accepted or rejected, our religion gives us a common language, some cultural reference points, and a sense of tradition that we are both comfortable with" (Keller, 2009).

THINK ABOUT THIS

❶ Is the kind of productive conflict described by Miller and Keller possible for people of all faiths? Why might having dual faiths be out of the question for some?

❷ Is every mixed-faith relationship an exercise in compromise of some sort? What sorts of compromises are the Kellers and Millers making? What other ways are there of managing conflicting faiths?

❸ Think about the benefits of interfaith communities described by Miller. Do you think it's really possible to explore alternative faiths while still remaining true to your own? Are there any benefits to adopting one faith over the other?

that people who feel very "close" in their relationships tend to engage more in obliging than do more distant relational partners (Zhang & Andreychik, 2013). However, if you always give in, your sister may learn to exploit you (think about what happens when parents always give in to their child's tantrums!), or you may build up resentment at never getting your own needs met in the relationship.

Competitive Styles

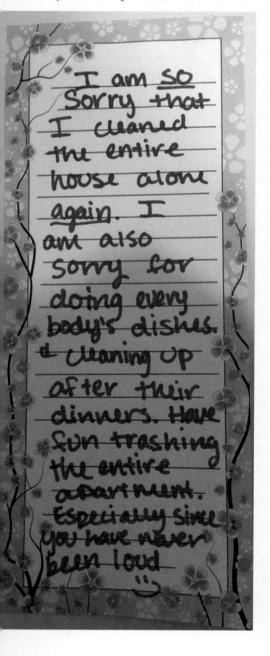

If you decide that you want the pie more than you want to avoid fighting with your sister, you might demand the entire piece for yourself, at your sister's expense. Such **competitive styles** promote the objectives of the individual who uses them rather than the desires of the other person or the relationship.

Engaging openly in competition is **direct fighting** (also known as dominating or competitive fighting). Direct fighters see conflicts as "win or lose" battles—for me to win, you must necessarily lose. Winning arguments involves being assertive—voicing your positions with confidence, defending your arguments, and challenging the arguments of your opposition. Direct fighters are often effective at handling conflicts because they don't let negative emotions like anxiety, guilt, or embarrassment get in the way, and they stand up for what they believe is right. For example, people tend to openly challenge others when they feel the need to defend themselves from a perceived threat (Canary, Cunningham, & Cody, 1988). This would be a valuable strategy if the friend you came to a party with attempts to get behind the wheel of a vehicle after consuming alcohol. Drunk driving is a threat to your own, your friend's, and the public's well-being, and you would probably be well-served to assert yourself competitively in this situation.

On the other hand, the direct fighting style has its downside, particularly for close relationships (Guerrero, Andersen, & Afifi, 2013). Part of the problem is that direct fighting often involves tactics that can be hurtful, such as threats, name-calling, and criticism. What begins as assertiveness can quickly move to **verbal aggressiveness**—attacking the opposing person's self-concept and belittling the other person's needs. For example, if you were to rudely assert to your sister "You're so fat—I would think you'd want to *avoid* pie," you may end up "winning" the pie, but you may well damage your bond with your sister. Indeed, research finds that parents' verbal aggression toward their children can negatively impact relationship satisfaction and is associated with nonsecure attachment styles among young adults (Roberto, Carlyle, Goodall, & Castle, 2009). When verbal aggression is used by supervisors toward their subordinates in the workplace, it can also negatively affect employee job satisfaction and commitment (Madlock & Kennedy-Lightsey, 2010).

Competition doesn't always involve being openly assertive or aggressive. Many competitors instead use a "passive" style of aggression known as **indirect fighting** (Sillars, Canary, & Tafoya, 2004). Your sister might hide the pie so that you cannot find it, or she might leave a nasty note next to it saying "my germs are on this." With indirect fighting, people often want you to know that they are upset and try to get you to change your behavior, but they are unwilling to face the issue with you openly. In most situations, passive-aggressive behaviors come across as hostile and ineffective and usually end up being destructive to relationships. Studies have found that indirect fighting is associated with lower relationship commitment in friendships (Allen, Babin, & McEwan, 2012), reduced satisfaction in romantic partnerships (Guerrero, Farinelli, & McEwan, 2009), and even long-term distress in marriage (Kilmann, 2012).

Cooperative Styles

Of course, one very practical way for you and your sister to manage the pie conflict is simply to split the last piece. That way you at least both get some pie. Conflict styles that aim to benefit the relationship, to serve mutual rather than individual goals, and to produce solutions that benefit both parties are called **cooperative strategies** (Zacchilli, Hendrick, & Henrick, 2009).

EVALUATING**COMMUNICATION**ETHICS

The Accidental Relationship Counselor

You and your sister Ellen are close in age—she's only a year younger than you—and are very close friends. And while it was weird when Ellen began dating your best friend, Steve, during your junior year of high school, over the past few years you've gotten used to them being together. They've been dating for three years now, and you still hang out with them all the time, both individually and as a couple.

But lately you've been noticing that their relationship isn't as close as it used to be. Even though you all commute to the same community college, you've noticed that Ellen and Steve aren't always together the way they used to be. While you and Steve navigated the campus together as freshmen last year, Ellen is tackling her first year at school in a more independent manner. She is making lots of new friends, joining campus clubs, and spending a lot of time away from Steve (and you). While you're happy to see your little sister spreading her wings, you worry about her future with Steve.

Making things worse, Steve is confiding his doubts about the relationship in you—he tells you that he thinks Ellen might be interested in other guys and asks you if she has mentioned anyone in particular. He then mentions that there is girl in one of his classes who he thinks might like him. Meanwhile, Ellen mentions that she's disappointed in the way Steve is handling college. When the three of you had lunch recently, Ellen publicly vented her frustration at Steve: "You still act like you're in high school. You have all the same friends, all the same interests. Don't you want to experience something new?" As awkward as that encounter was, you feel even worse when Ellen later confides to you privately: "I feel like maybe it's time we broke up. What do you think?"

You always knew that the day might come when Steve and Ellen split up, but you never imagined you'd feel so caught in the middle. You know that Steve loves her and wants to stay together, but at the same time you know that Ellen isn't entirely happy in the relationship. What will you do?

THINK ABOUT THIS

❶ You know that both Ellen and Steve rely on you as a friend (and in Ellen's case, as family). How can you maintain your relationships with both of them even as their relationship with each other is falling apart? Is it fair of them to involve you at all?

❷ What outcomes are possible here? Can you provide advice to help them stay together? Should you?

❸ What do you think of Steve mentioning another girl? Would it affect you differently if Ellen were just a friend, and not your sister?

Splitting the pie is one particular cooperative conflict style called **compromising**. In a compromise, the goal is to find the "middle ground" between two (often extreme) positions. Each party gains something (half of the pie) but also gives up something (the other half). Compromises can be arrived at through trading, whereby one partner offers something of equal value in return for something he or she wants. For example, separated parents who must navigate joint custody arrangements might strike compromises regarding time spent with their children. The advantage of compromise is that it lets you and the other person quickly resolve or avert a conflict by agreeing on a decision-making method. However, important relationships can suffer if the people involved are *always* making compromises. That's because compromising means giving up *some* of what you want, even though you're getting a little of something else in return.

To reach a truly win-win solution, in which both parties end up *fully* satisfied with the outcome, requires the **collaborating** style. Collaborators are problem solvers who creatively work toward finding ways to meet the goals of both parties. In order to see how this might be achieved, let's consider an issue more serious than pie, such as this conflict within a family: twenty-year-old Kieran wants to drop out of college to join the Army. His mother is very upset and wants him to continue his education. A number of strategies can help them effectively collaborate.

First, it is important that the discussion *focus on issues*—remain centered on the matter at hand and steer clear of any personal attacks. If Kieran's mother boldly declares, "You are irrational and thoughtless. Who drops out of college with only one year left?" she's getting verbally aggressive and isn't considering the fact that Kieran may well have very good reasons for his decision. Second, it helps to do some *probing*—asking questions that help you to identify each other's specific concerns. If Kieran's mother asks probing questions ("Why do you want to join the Army now when you're so close to graduating?"), she'll get a better understanding of why and how he's come to this decision. Likewise, Kieran will get a better sense of his mother's feelings if he asks similar questions of her ("Why is it so important to you that I finish my degree now?").

Probing helps encourage another important aspect of collaboration—*disclosure*. Kieran, for example, might note that he is concerned about his career—the job market for college graduates in his major is completely flat, and so he sees the Army as a great employment opportunity. His mother might play the role of *devil's advocate*—provide counterpoints and worst-case scenarios—and explain that he'll still have to pay back all his college loans, and that all that expenditure will have amounted to little if he doesn't finish. But Kieran's mother too should be disclosing. She might reveal her own fears ("What if you get hurt or killed?") as well as the hopes she had built for her son to have a college degree ("I want you to have the chance at success that I never had").

Finally, collaborating involves shifting the focus from what your positions are ("I want to leave college to join the Army" and "I want you to stay and finish college") to addressing each other's *underlying needs*. Probing and disclosure may reveal that it is not just about a career opportunity for Kieran but also about his desire to serve his country, to do something noble and just with his life, or to fight for an important cause. His mother's needs may be about her wanting the best life for her son or about keeping him close to her. Once they identify and

what about you?

Self-Assessment on Conflict Management Styles

Each statement that follows illustrates a strategy for dealing with a conflict. Rate each statement on a scale of 1 to 4, indicating how likely you are to use this strategy: 1 = rarely; 2 = sometimes; 3 = often; and 4 = always.

_____ 1. I explore issues with others to find solutions that meet everyone's needs.

_____ 2. I try to negotiate and adopt a give-and-take approach to problem situations.

_____ 3. I try to meet the expectations of others.

_____ 4. I argue my case and insist on the merits of my point of view.

_____ 5. When there is a disagreement, I gather as much information as I can and keep the lines of communication open.

_____ 6. When I find myself in an argument, I usually say very little and try to leave as soon as possible.

_____ 7. I try to see conflicts from both sides by asking questions like: What do I need? What does the other person need? What are the issues involved?

_____ 8. I prefer to compromise when solving problems so that I can just move on.

_____ 9. I find conflicts challenging and exhilarating; I enjoy the battle of wits that usually follows.

_____ 10. Being at odds with other people makes me feel uncomfortable and anxious.

_____ 11. I try to accommodate the wishes of my friends and family.

_____ 12. I can figure out what needs to be done in a given situation and I am usually right.

_____ 13. To break deadlocks, I meet people halfway.

_____ 14. I may not get what I want but it's a small price to pay for keeping the peace.

_____ 15. I avoid hurt feelings by keeping my disagreements with others to myself.

Scoring: The fifteen statements correspond to the five conflict resolution styles. To find your dominant style, total the points in the respective categories. The one with the highest score indicates your most commonly used strategy. The one with the lowest score indicates your least commonly used strategy. If you are a leader who deals with conflict on a regular basis, you may find that you exhibit a blend of styles.

Total:
Collaborating: 1, 5, 7 _____
Competing: 4, 9, 12 _____
Avoiding: 6, 10, 15 _____
Obligating: 3, 11, 14 _____
Compromising: 2, 8, 13 _____

Source: Adapted from Adkins (2006).

respect each other's needs, they can begin to find options and alternative solutions that may address many of them. For example, Kieran's mother might suggest that he join the Army Reserve instead, which would allow him to serve his country while still finishing school, as well as ensuring a career if he wants to go on active duty after graduation. Kieran might also improve his correspondence skills and keep in regular contact with his mother, whenever feasible, while deployed.

Could collaboration be achieved even in the case of chocolate peanut butter pie? If the pie is not that important, then compromising is probably the easiest cooperative strategy. But if the pie conflict is a reflection of some underlying problems with competition or self-worth between you and your sister, then attempts to address each other's needs about "feeling special" or "deserving a treat" may lead you to think of some mutually beneficial things you can do for each other that have nothing to do with pie!

Reconciliation

CONNECT

In Chapter 3, we discuss how to choose our words carefully, since they can often be misconstrued (especially when sent via technological devices!). If you are trying to heal a larger problem with a friend, you should aim to talk to the person face to face—and also think carefully about what you will say beforehand.

Annie and Helen are rivals, each repeatedly trying to show up the other in their attempts to prove how close and loyal they are to their mutual friend Lillian. In the popular film *Bridesmaids*, many hilarious moments emerge for the audience as we follow these characters' outrageous attempts to act as maid of honor for their engaged friend. But for the characters themselves, the conflicts lead to deep feelings of hurt and resentment, as well as relational detachment. To repair their relationships (in time for a happy wedding), Annie, Helen, and Lillian engage in two key forms of communication that help them move past their conflicts: apology and forgiveness. We'll now explore how each of these can help deescalate conflict and push us toward relationship reconciliation.

Apology

When Lillian is missing on the day of the wedding, Helen seeks Annie's help to find their friend. Annie resists, but they are eventually able to work together once Helen begins to admit that she has been behaving badly. To **apologize** is to admit wrongdoing and take responsibility for your own role in the conflict. It can often be difficult to apologize, because it means swallowing your pride and confessing that you did something wrong. Helen hates admitting it, but she acknowledges that she hurt Annie by putting distance between Annie and Lillian. The apology may or may not be accepted (Annie doesn't want to hear it at first), but when we hurt others, acknowledging it and expressing our regret and remorse can go a long way toward repairing the damage (Donnoli & Wertheim, 2012). Annie and Helen do eventually experience a reconciliation that may lead to the beginnings of friendly interactions between them.

An important part of taking responsibility is to recognize how our conflict styles or behaviors might be affecting the other person. **Metacommunication**, or communicating with each other about how we communicate, can help us become more aware of our own communicative missteps in relationships (Acitelli, 2008). Your best friend might tell you, for example, that "When you yell at me, I don't hear what you are saying because I'm so afraid of you." You might respond,

"I don't mean to yell—I raise my voice because I'm not sure that you're listening. In my family, whoever is loudest gets heard." Metacommunication is important because it allows us to step back from whatever the conflict is about and take notice of how we actually communicate during our disagreements. It can help us to identify new ways to handle conflict that are more productive and perhaps even to catch ourselves *before* we are about to deliver hurtful messages.

How do you know when it is time to apologize? Your friend or relational partner may well demand it from you directly, particularly if you've done or said something seriously hurtful (Theiss, Knobloch, Checton, & Magsamen-Conrad, 2009). But your own feelings of guilt might also be a good indicator—guilt is what makes us realize that we have behaved badly, which motivates us to confess and try to repair any damage we may have caused (Behrend & Ben-Ari, 2012). And studies show that you are more likely to be forgiven for relational transgressions or hurtful comments if you sincerely apologize (Bachman & Guerrero, 2006; Morse & Metts, 2011).

Canary and Lakey (2012) argue that when relational breaches are very serious, only a "complete and heartfelt" apology from the offender offers any hope for the relationship to continue. For Annie and Lillian, Annie's destructive meltdown at the bridal shower led Lillian to break off the friendship and disinvite Annie to the wedding. The two are only able to repair their friendship when they both apologize: Annie freely admits that it was her fault (including her "mental problems"), but Lillian also apologizes for acting hastily in the heat of the moment to kick Annie out of the wedding.

There are times, however, when the hurt is too deep even for a sincere apology to be able to repair the damage. In that case, the relationship may end in separation. For it to continue, the offended partner often must be willing to accept the apology and begin to forgive the transgression.

● **LILLIAN AND ANNIE'S** heartfelt apologies are essential to getting their close friendship back on track. Suzanne Hanover/©Universal Pictures/Courtesy Everett Collection

Forgiveness

To **forgive** is an emotional transformation, in which you "let go" and move beyond the conflict or "wrong" that you perceive another has done to you (Waldron & Kelley, 2005). It is not condoning, excusing, or forgetting someone's transgression but reducing the negative reactions to the transgression and engaging in compassion and kindness toward the other person (Toussaint, Owen, & Cheadle, 2012).

After Annie and Lillian apologize to each other in *Bridesmaids*, they begin to joke with each other about their past conflicts and history together as friends. They do not hold grudges about the past but instead just move ahead to their friendship in the future. They express that their relationship will change once Lillian gets married but that they will have a new kind of close friendship. Indeed, scholars argue that forgiveness involves a renegotiation of the relationship, including new expectations and rules for future interactions (Guerrero, Andersen, & Afifi, 2013).

AND YOU?

Consider the most serious situation you've faced in which you had to offer an apology. What events and feelings led up to your decision to apologize? How did you feel before the apology and after? Do you believe that the apology affected the outcome of the relationship? If so, how?

In addition to having relational benefits, forgiveness can also have health benefits. Research shows that forgiveness following interpersonal conflict can reduce the stress load on the heart (Lawler et al., 2003). Having a more "forgiving personality" is also associated with improved cardiovascular functioning (Toussaint & Cheadle, 2009), as well as greater overall mental health and physical well-being (see, for example, Toussaint, Owen, & Cheadle, 2012).

Note, however, that *requiring* an apology or penance from another person before you are willing to forgive may actually have negative consequences. For

real communicator

NAME: Anonymous
OCCUPATION: Police officer

[*Note: Due to security reasons, the officer must remain anonymous.*] I'm a police officer in Chicago. Cops on TV are always running around with their guns drawn or tossing bad guys against brick walls, and although I do some of that, of course, I'd say that over 90 percent of my job is spent communicating with people. And most of that time is about managing conflict.

In my first few years out of the academy, I responded to a lot of domestic disputes. Neighbors call in about other neighbors making too much noise; spouses and parents call in about fighting in the home. These are unproductive conflicts: screaming, destruction of property, and all too often violence. And few things have the potential to escalate unproductive conflict like uniformed men and women coming into your home with guns, right?

The first thing I do is use my eyes to see if physical injuries are apparent or if a crime has been committed. If so, it's a domestic violence situation, and I arrest the perpetrator, taking him or her to jail. The conflict is temporarily resolved. Most of the time, however, these calls are incidents of domestic *disputes*. A crime hasn't been committed. I can't make an arrest. And my job becomes much more difficult. Now I have to manage conflict—through mediation.

First, I don't use any challenging strategies as I might with a drug dealer on the street. I stay nonaggressive (I am, after all, in someone else's home). I try not to lean forward, I stay out of people's faces, and I speak in a monotone. I try to exude calmness, because everyone else in the place is freaking out.

One time, I had a man who simply wouldn't stop screaming at and about his wife: *I hate her! I hate her guts!* As calmly as possible, I asked, "You hate who?" He said, *I hate my wife!* I looked shocked and said, "Sir, you hate your *wife*?" I kept the questions coming. In the academy they call this verbal judo, the sword of insertion. In communication classes, it's called probing. I asked the man simple questions, getting him down to facts, getting him to think about things reasonably, as opposed to thinking about them emotionally.

Sometimes, I'll turn to one party and say, as respectfully as possible, "Listen, I know I don't have a right to ask you to leave your own house, but maybe there's a cousin's place you can go crash at for the night, or maybe you can go take a long walk and cool down." It's not a win-win or lose-lose resolution; it's a separation, a temporary one. It's an escapist strategy, a prevention of further unproductive conflict, a rain check on the situation until a better time, when heads are cooler. Often that's the best I can do. I've got other homes to go to, other conflicts to manage.

one thing, the apology may never come and you may be stuck hanging onto the bitterness. For another, withholding forgiveness until your "conditions" are met may be associated with relationship deterioration (Waldron & Kelley, 2005), and possibly even increased health risks (Toussaint, Owen, & Cheadle, 2012), compared to when you forgive because you feel it is the morally "right" thing to do (Cox, Bennett, Tripp, & Aquino, 2012). It appears that being able truly to let go of the hurt is what provides the most optimism for relationship reconciliation.

BACK TO ▷ Bullies and Drama

 Back at the beginning of this chapter, we talked a bit about school bullying, and the somewhat ill-defined line between conflict and bullying behavior. Let's revisit the topic now that you've explored both the good and the bad sides of interpersonal conflict.

▶ Bazelon talks about the difference between bullying, which involves repeated abuse and a marked power difference, and "drama," which involves more of a two-way interaction. Researchers note that discussions of bullying often suggest "that there are bullies and there are the bullied, but dramas that involve relational aggression often lack a clear perpetrator and victim (Markwick & Boyd, 2011)." The difference between the two is rooted in power dynamics—it's only bullying if one party has some power, be it real or perceived, over the other.

▶ Few people get through high school without some intimate familiarity with bullying—either as a victim, a perpetrator, or a bystander. But most of us manage to get through it, not necessarily unscathed, but without resorting to harming ourselves or others. Learning to manage conflict productively, even (or perhaps especially) when faced with bullying, is an important part of growing up. "Doing this right," Bazelon points out, "means recognizing that there is truth in the old sticks-and-stones chant: Most kids *do* bounce back from cruelty at the hands of other kids. They'll remember being bullied or being a bully; they'll also learn something useful, if painful" (Bazelon, 2013).

▶ In any incident, it is important that the context be considered. But "zero tolerance" policies for bullying and other infractions leave administrators' hands tied when it comes to discipline: students who clearly have no intentions of violence or harm—such as a child whose mother packed a knife in her lunch box to cut an apple—receive the same punishment as a student who brings a knife to school to attack a classmate. Researchers suggest productive policies, ones that encourage student dialogue, inform students about bullying, and empower administrators to consider the context of an incident when assigning blame or doling out punishments, are far more effective than zero-tolerance rules (American Psychological Association, 2008).

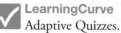 Activities

1. LaunchPad for *Real Communication* offers key term videos and encourages self-assessment through adaptive quizzing. Go to **bedfordstmartins.com/realcomm** to get access to:

✓ LearningCurve Adaptive Quizzes.

▶ Video clips that illustrate key concepts, highlighted in teal in the Real Reference section that follows.

2. The engagement in and resolution of interpersonal conflict are often key factors in romantic comedies (like *Life as We Know It* and *When Harry Met Sally*), as well as in buddy-driven action films (such as *Shanghai Noon* and *The Other Guys*). Try watching such a film, and pay attention to the way in which the principal characters engage in conflict with one another. How does their conflict management lead to relationship growth?

3. For an interesting look at conflict and debate, you need not search further than the U.S. Congress. Debates on the floor of the Senate and House of Representatives are broadcast on C-SPAN and provide an interesting glimpse into the way that conflict and argument shape new laws and policy. In addition to observing how this process works, pay attention to the way that strict rules regarding time and etiquette keep the debate relatively diplomatic. For a comparison of rules in the House and Senate, go to http://www.senate.gov/reference/resources/pdf /RL30945.pdf.

4. Read the advice column in your daily paper or an online magazine. Bearing in mind what you've read in this chapter, consider the nature of the interpersonal conflicts discussed. What are the precursors to the conflicts? What kinds of tactics does the columnist suggest using to manage and resolve the disagreements?

5. This week, if you have a disagreement with a friend, roommate, romantic partner, family member, or boss, identify *one* change you could make to manage and resolve the conflict more productively. For example, could you suggest a compromise? Look for a broader range of promising solutions to your disagreement? Apologize or forgive?

Now that you have finished reading this chapter, you can:

Describe the factors that lead to productive conflict:

▶ **Conflict** is a negative interaction between interdependent people, rooted in disagreement (p. 214).

▶ **Conflict management** refers to how relational partners address disagreements (p. 214).

▶ **Unproductive conflict** is conflict that is managed poorly and that has a negative impact (pp. 214–215).

▶ **Productive conflict** is healthy and managed effectively. It fosters healthy debate, leads to better decision-making, and spurs relationship growth (p. 215).

Identify conflict triggers in yourself and others:

▶ Many conflicts are rooted in errors of perception (p. 217).

▶ Incompatible goals can spark conflict (p. 217).

▶ Conflicts arise when the costs of an interpersonal relationship outweigh the rewards (p. 218).

▶ **Provocation**, the intentional instigation of conflict, arises when one party demonstrates aggression, a person's identity feels threatened, fairness is lacking, someone you depend on is incompetent, or an important relationship is threatened (p. 218).

Explain the forces that influence how people handle conflict:

▶ Power dynamics affect relationships in which there is an imbalance of power (p. 219).

▶ Personal attitudes about whether conflict is good or bad influence whether people engage or avoid dealing with it (pp. 219–220).

▶ People who take most disagreements as personal insults or assault are engaging in a destructive tendency called **taking conflict personally (TCP)** (p. 220).

▶ **Communication climate** varies and may be uncertain, defensive, or supportive (pp. 220–222).

▶ Cultural variations, such as individualism/collectivism and high or low context, and co-cultures, such as gender or age, have a strong influence on conflict (pp. 222–224).

▶ Our reasons for choosing certain communication channels may be rooted in emotions or practical considerations (pp. 224–225).

▶ The Internet provides an arena for **flaming**, hurling hostile, insulting online messages at an individual; **trolling**, posting offensive messages to stir conflict in an online group; and **cyberbullying**, engaging in repeated abusive attacks through electronic channels (pp. 225–227).

Evaluate and employ strategies for managing conflict in different situations:

▶ **Escapist styles** are used to stay away from direct conflict (p. 227). Walking away, changing the subject, or postponing conflict are tactics in the **avoiding** style, whereas giving in to the other person's wishes is **obliging**. Escapist strategies are good for quick resolutions but may leave issues unresolved (p. 228).

▶ **Competitive** styles promote the interests of individuals who see conflict as "win-lose" battles (p. 230). In **direct fighting**, people use assertiveness to argue openly to get their way, which can sometimes lead to **verbal aggressiveness**, or attacks on individuals personally. **Indirect fighting** involves using passive-aggressive tactics to express conflict without engaging in it openly (pp. 230–231).

▶ **Cooperative** strategies benefit both parties (p. 231). With **compromising**, both parties give up something to gain something (p. 232). **Collaborating** involves finding a win-win solution that satisfies all parties. Collaborating involves focusing on issues, asking probing questions and playing devil's advocate, disclosing your concerns, and attempting to address each other's underlying needs (pp. 232–234).

Recognize your ability to repair and let go of painful conflict:

▶ **Apologize**, or openly take responsibility, for your own misbehavior, including using **metacommunication** to talk with each other about your communication behaviors (pp. 234–235).

▶ **Forgive** in order to emotionally move past the conflict and let go of the bitterness and resentment (p. 235).

Group and Organizational Communication

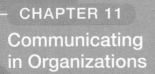

Team Rubicon, a group composed mainly of military veterans, uses skills from deployment to provide disaster **relief.** Photo courtesy of Kirk Jackson, Team Rubicon

When a 7.0-magnitude earthquake devastated Haiti on January 10, 2010, Jacob Wood and William McNulty didn't just watch television in horror. They didn't just say a prayer or make donations to the Red Cross. Instead, they made some phone calls and a couple of Facebook posts, and within three days, they and a small team of fellow veterans were on the ground in Port-au-Prince. As Marine Corp veterans who had served in both Iraq and Afghanistan and who had volunteered in New Orleans after Hurricane Katrina, it was clear to Wood and McNulty that disasters and war zones had a lot in common: limited resources, collapsed infrastructure, a lack of information or communication, populations in chaos, and horrific sights and situations that can grind even the most earnest volunteer to a halt. It was also clear that the skills they honed during their deployments— medical triage, decisive leadership, the ability to quickly assess and respond to a situation, and focus intently on the task at hand—were invaluable, especially during the first few days after a disaster. The group refers to its role as "bridging the gap" between disasters and the arrival of conventional aid (Team Rubicon, 2014).

In the years since, Team Rubicon, the veteran's service/disaster response organization founded by Wood and McNulty, has provided intense, immediate relief in the aftermaths of floods, earthquakes, hurricanes, tornadoes, and other disasters around the world and around the United States. The organization consists of more than fourteen thousand members, most of them military veterans, who mobilize quickly and deploy to disaster-stricken areas and regions on a moment's notice (Team Rubicon, 2014). But in the process of providing relief, Wood and McNulty found yet another gap they needed to bridge. Returning veterans often find it difficult to adjust to civilian life, a reality that was brought into sharp relief when close friend and founding member of Team Rubicon, Clay Hunt, took his own life in March 2012. Once again proving that adaptability and focus are crucial to "bridging the gap," Team Rubicon adjusted its mission to include veteran's services, including suicide prevention, career training, and leadership opportunities.

**After you have finished
reading this chapter,
you will be able to**

- List the characteristics
  and types of groups and
  explain how groups
  develop

- Describe ways in which
  group size, social
  relationships, and
  communication
  networks affect group
  communication

- Define the roles
  individuals play in a
  group

- Explain how a group's
  cohesion, norms, and
  individual differences
  affect group processes
  and outcomes

When three or more people come together, their interactions and relationships—and their communication—take on new characteristics. As you can see in our discussion of Team Rubicon, groups can have a tremendous impact, both on individual members and on those with whom the groups interact. In this chapter, we'll learn more about group communication, how groups operate, and the factors that influence their communication.

Understanding Groups

Your family sitting down to dinner. A group of coworkers having a drink together at the end of a shift. Six exasperated parents sitting in a doctor's office with sick kids. Each of these examples involves multiple people engaged in some activity—and most of us would probably say that these are examples of "groups of people." But are they really groups? We'll explore what it actually means to be in a group, in addition to understanding what types of groups exist and how those groups develop in the first place.

Characteristics of Groups

We consider a collection of individuals a **group** when there are more than two people who share some kind of relationship, communicate in an interdependent fashion, and collaborate toward some shared purpose. When we break that definition down, we can identify three key characteristics:

- *A shared identity.* Members of a group perceive themselves as a group. That is, they share a sense of identity: they recognize other members of the group, have specific feelings toward those individuals, and experience a sense of belonging. People may identify themselves, for example, as members of the student council, a park cleanup crew, a baseball team, or a string quartet.

- *Common goals.* Members of a group usually identify with one another because they have one or more goals in common. Goals may be very specific—coming up with an ad campaign for a new project or organizing a fund-raiser for your soccer team—or they might be more general, such as socializing. In either case, a shared sense of purpose helps define a group, even when there is some disagreement about specific goals or ways of achieving them.

- *Interdependent relationships.* Members of a group are connected to one another and communicate in an interdependent way. Simply put, the behavior of each member affects the behavior of every other member. This interdependence is fostered by the way that group members adopt specific roles and collaborate to accomplish their goals.

Looking back at the examples at the beginning of this section, you can probably guess that your family or a group of coworkers constitutes a group. You share an identity with the other members and have feelings about them (for better or worse); you likely have common goals, and you are interdependent—

that is, you rely on them, and they on you, for love, friendship, or professional accomplishments. This is not the case with the strangers in a pediatrician's office. They might share a goal (seeing the doctor), but they do not interact with each other interdependently, and they do not share an identity. Note that it is not the number of people involved or their location that determines whether people are communicating in groups. Four friends chatting over coffee at your local Starbucks constitute a group; so do twenty mothers who've never met but who contribute regularly to an online parenting forum. In both cases, the individuals are joined by shared goals, shared identity, and interdependence.

Types of Groups

Groups can take many forms. The most common among them are called **primary groups**—long-lasting groups that form around the relationships that mean the most to their members. Your family constitutes one primary group to which you belong; your friends are another.

● **BANDMATES** such as the members of Vampire Weekend must share a sense of identity, communicate interdependently, and collaborate to achieve their shared goal of creating music. Tim Mosenfelder/Getty Images

In addition to primary groups, there are groups defined by their specific functions (for instance, support groups, study groups, and social groups). However, any one of these groups can perform multiple functions. Alcoholics Anonymous (AA), for example, is primarily a **support group**—a set of individuals who come together to address personal problems while benefiting from the support of others with similar issues. But AA is also a **social group**, as membership in the group offers opportunities to form relationships with others. And finally, as a group with a specific mission—to help members manage their struggles with alcohol and addiction—AA is also a **problem-solving group**.

Although all groups are to some degree social, some groups are more task-oriented than others. **Study groups**, for example, are formed for the specific purpose of helping students prepare for exams. Perhaps the most task-oriented and goal-driven type of group is the **team**—a group that works together to carry out a project or to compete against other teams. Sports teams are an obvious example, but teams are also common in large organizations or as subsets of other groups: an Army unit might select a few members to form a reconnaissance team; a community group might nominate a team of individuals to take charge of its annual fund-raiser.

One of the more noteworthy and common types of teams in today's organizations is the **self-directed work team (SDWT)**, a group of skilled workers who take responsibility themselves for producing high-quality finished work (Colvin, 2012; Douglas, 2002). In self-directed work teams, members control their own

AND YOU?

In Chapter 7, we talked about family as an example of interpersonal relationships. Now think about your family as a group. What are the family's common goals? What do the members of your family see as the family's defining traits? How can a change in behavior by one family member affect other members?

WIREDFORCOMMUNICATION

Smart Mobs: What Flash Mobs and Political Protests Have in Common

In 2014, more than four thousand straphangers in New York City—and countless others in twenty-five countries around the world—boarded mass-transit trains in their boxers, briefs, or bloomers for a coordinated "no pants subway ride" (Improv Everywhere, 2014). A seemingly spontaneous dance performance also erupted in 2014 among passengers at a train station in Shanghai—it was to celebrate the Chinese new year and renew interest in Chinese folk traditions. In 2011, Occupy Wall Street demonstrators converged on New York's Zuccotti Park to protest economic policies that they felt were deepening the divide between rich and poor.

What do these stories have in common? They're all examples of smart mobs: large groups of individuals who act in concert, even though they don't know each other, and who connect and cooperate with one another, at least initially, via electronically mediated means (Rheingold, 2002). But smart mobs have two important additional characteristics that a generic social network lacks: a shared goal and a finite time frame (Harmon & Metaxas, 2010). Like all electronic social networks, smart mobs are grounded in a shared desire for communication and rely on affordable devices that offer instantaneous communication. Simply communicating is not enough to make a smart mob—there must be a tangible goal that is organized via mediated communication and achieved quickly and effectively.

There's a difference, of course, between a social movement and an absurd, pants-free subway ride. The latter is what has come to be called a flash mob—a form of smart mob in which people come together for a brief public act that may seem pointless or ridiculous. Even if the goal, often entertainment or artistic expression, seems not-so-smart, flash mobs are still smart mobs: through technology the participants are organized and quickly mobilized to carry out their collective act. Political protests, on the other hand, are largely comprised of activists who may already be connected and organized but use technology—including smart mob demonstrations—as tools for making their political or social goals more visible (Conover et al., 2013). In fact, the term *smart mob* was first identified in 2001, when calls for protest in the Philippines spread via text message, gathering more than a million people to a nonviolent demonstration in Manila within four days. Largely hailed as the world's first "e-revolution," the Manila protests quickly and peacefully brought about the resignation of President Joseph Estrada.

In the years since, social media–fueled revolutions in Tunisia, Egypt, and other Middle Eastern nations—sometimes referred to as "Twitter Revolutions" by media pundits—have bolstered the notion that electronic communications are somehow responsible for modern social movements. This is, most likely, an oversimplification: social movements are usually the culmination of frustrations that have been building for many years, which come to a pinnacle when activists begin to organize. Malcom Gladwell points out that one of the most dramatic political demonstrations in American history started with just four African American college students asking for service at a "whites only" lunch counter in Greensboro, North Carolina, on February 1, 1960; within a month, the sit-ins had spread throughout the South—all without a single text or tweet (Gladwell, 2010). But, even then, the existing media played an important role: newspaper photos of those first four students printed in the Greensboro *Record* inspired others to join them.

THINK ABOUT THIS

❶ Many social movements benefit from social networks, but is it fair to credit electronic communication with bringing about social change? How did groups like the American civil rights movement organize demonstrations? If these groups relied on technology, does that make them smart mobs?

❷ In an effort to quell uprisings in Egypt in 2011, the Egyptian government blocked citizens' access to the Internet, yet protests continued. What does this say about the pervasive nature of electronic communication? What does it say about the role of electronic communication in causing and fueling action?

❸ What is the social value of a flash mob? Is it just something fun that technology makes possible, or might there be important effects for the participants or the audiences?

❹ Is a smart mob really a group, as defined in this chapter? If not, what is it?

management functions, such as arranging their schedules, buying equipment, and setting standards for productivity, quality, and costs. They also conduct their own peer evaluations and coordinate their future plans with management. Their complementary skills and experiences enable the team to accomplish more together than any individual member could achieve independently (Katzenbach & Smith, 1993).

Perhaps the most dramatic impact of self-directed teams is the improved performance and cooperation of employees throughout the organization. Organizations are shifting their structural power and decision making from upper levels to lower levels of management in efforts to implement change and growth and empower employees (Douglas, Martin, & Krapels, 2006). Federal Express and Minnesota-based 3M are among an increasing number of companies that involve employees through work teams. (See Table 9.1 for tips on working in a self-directed work team.).

AND YOU?

In your first job out of college, do you think you would prefer to work as part of a self-directed work team or in a more traditionally arranged team where a manager takes control? What would be the advantages of each?

Models of Group Development

If you've ever become wrapped up in a reality TV show such as *Survivor*, *The Biggest Loser*, or *The Amazing Race*, you know how fascinating and dramatic group interactions can be. In each of these shows, a season typically opens with the forming of a group: cast members start off as strangers but are quickly thrust into a group situation—sharing a living space and working together to accomplish certain tasks. As the season progresses, the group members bond, conflicts erupt, and alliances are forged. In fact, much of the drama in reality television stems from the tensions that arise between cast members as they struggle to work with—or against—one another (and, of course, editing can heighten the drama even more). Research shows that as a group progresses, it goes through several specific stages. Let's look at two different research perspectives on the stages of group development.

TABLE 9.1

SELF-DIRECTED WORK TEAMS: TIPS FOR WORKING COLLABORATIVELY

Action	Considerations
Define a clear purpose for the team	What are the team's goals—short term *and* long term?
Foster team spirit	Build a sense of energy, excitement, and commitment in your team by engaging in team-building activities and events, rewarding members who demonstrate commitment, and identifying new challenges for the team to take on.
Train	Working on a self-directed team may be a new experience for some members. See if your organization can provide training to help members understand and implement the defining practices of self-directed teams.
Clarify expectations	Make sure all members of the team understand what's expected of them in terms of their roles and performance. For example, what functions will each member serve? How, specifically, will the team define "success"?
Set boundaries	Articulate where the team's responsibilities begin and end. If necessary, remind members that they are working in the service of the organization and that they need to stay focused on their specific purpose.

Sources: Capozzoli (2002); Nelson (2002); Rosenthal (2001).

Developing a relationship with a group isn't so different from starting a new interpersonal relationship. In both contexts, we reduce uncertainty about our relational partners so that we feel secure and confident about roles, interactions, and so on. So whether you're beginning a new romance or forging a new student organization, try the passive, active, and interactive strategies that we discuss in Chapter 7 (see pp. 195–196).

Tuckman's Model of Group Development

Tuckman's model states that as groups develop, they progress through five stages: forming, storming, norming, performing, and adjourning. The model proposes that these stages are linear—that is, groups go through them in order over time. Although the model was originally proposed for face-to-face groups, recent research has also applied these stages to how "virtual" teams develop online (Johnson, Suriya, Yoon, Berrett, & Fleur, 2002). Let's look more closely at each particular stage:

▶ *Forming.* When a group first comes together, its members are unsure how to act around one another, nervous about how others perceive them, and unclear on their roles and the group's task. In this **forming** stage, group members try to figure out who will be in charge and what the group's goals will be. The primary purpose of this stage is for group members to learn more about one another and the group's objectives. Once individuals feel accepted, they can begin to identify with the group (Moreland & Levine, 1994).

▶ *Storming.* After forming, group members move into the **storming** stage, in which they inevitably begin experiencing conflicts over issues such as who will lead the group and what roles members will play. Group members also begin to disagree on goals, tasks, and cliques, and other competitive divisions may even begin to form (Wheelan, 2012; Wheelan & Burchill, 1999). The group members must work on mending these differences and resolve conflicts if the group is to continue to function effectively.

▶ *Norming.* During the **norming** stage, group members move beyond their conflicts, and norms emerge among members that govern expected behavior. **Norms** are recurring patterns of behavior or thinking that come to be accepted in a group as the "usual" way of doing things (Scheerhorn & Geist, 1997). During this stage, group roles also solidify based on individual member strengths, and a leader may emerge. In addition, group identity grows stronger as members realize the importance of their roles within the group and the need to cooperate to accomplish goals.

▶ *Performing.* Once the group has established norms, the action shifts to accomplishing their tasks. During the **performing** stage, members combine their skills and knowledge to work toward the group's goals and overcome hurdles. This stage is characterized by high levels of interdependence, motivation, and clarity in delegation of team member tasks.

▶ *Adjourning.* Many groups—though clearly not all—eventually disband. For groups whose project or task has come to an end, there is an **adjourning** stage (Tuckman & Jensen, 1977). The group members reflect on their accomplishments and failures as well as determine whether the group will disassemble or take on another project. Some groups choose to celebrate their achievements with a final get-together, what Keyton (1993) calls a **termination ritual**. Members may also opt to maintain friendships even if they will no longer be working together.

AND YOU?

Think about your experience as part of a group to which you no longer belong—an old job, your high school class, or a club that you're not a part of anymore. Did the group go through all five phases described here?

Gersick's Punctuated Equilibrium Model

Although Tuckman's model represents a linear view of group development, other scholars have argued that groups do not necessarily follow sequential "stages" of development. Gersick (1988), for example, argues instead that groups progress in a **punctuated equilibrium** process. This means that groups experience a period of inertia or inactivity until they become aware of time, pressure, and looming deadlines, which then compel group members to take action.

As a student, a pattern of procrastination followed by bursts of activity may sound familiar to you. Research confirms that it is common to procrastinate on class assignments, especially when working in groups when there is a perceived diffusion or share of responsibilities (Karau & Williams, 2001). Gersick (1988) suggests that groups often procrastinate (and, in reality, waste time) until the critical halfway point of a project. Then, when they hit this midpoint transition and realize that their original plan isn't coming together, they focus their energy on completing the project and mobilizing their efforts. Gersick argues that groups go through this in a cyclical fashion, with long periods of inactivity followed by spurts of intense activity and change (Chidambaram & Bostrom, 1996), and that this pattern almost becomes a habit or routine (Gersick & Hackman, 1990).

● **BILL AND TED** procrastinate until they need the help of a time machine to finish their report in cult classic *Bill and Ted's Excellent Adventure.* © Orion/Courtesy Everett Collection

real communicator

NAME: Jack MacKenzie
OCCUPATION: Media Research Professional

As executive vice president of a national media research consulting firm, I know the importance of understanding group dynamics. Our office is made up of teams that work together to provide valuable information about marketing and design for a diverse client base. These clients include broadcast networks, cable channels, Internet start-ups, and video game producers, as well as product providers of everything from apple juice to mobile phone features.

Our research is conducted by two teams of highly qualified people. The quantitative team crunches the data and the qualitative team focuses on the majority of the in-person interaction with consumers (meaning interviews and focus groups). These groups work together as an even larger team to generate the feedback we give clients. Obviously, it is important that they work together smoothly.

Our teams are mainly self-directed, meaning that they take the responsibility for producing high-quality work without a lot of supervision. My part in encouraging this outcome is to hire independent, efficient, and responsible employees. If I'm successful in picking the right candidates, then I don't need to step in and supervise too closely. Some of the skills I would say are most important for self-directed work teams are flexibility, ability to process and analyze information, mindfulness of fair treatment of others, and a sense of what responses are appropriate in any given situation.

Another important aspect of self-directed teams is that teammates are able to figure out their roles and arrange their workflow based on work style and intellectual or emotional compatibility. As team members work together, they negotiate responsibilities, demonstrate their strengths, and rely on one another to get the job done in the most efficient way possible. If you've ever worked in groups at school, work, or in your community, you may have experienced some frustrating behavior: group members not listening, hogging the floor, or not doing their share of the work. I remind my teams that a lot of people pay more attention to what comes out of their mouths than what comes into their ears and that they should be doing the opposite. *Listening* is what makes a good consultant—and a good team member.

Research consulting is a fast-paced business that requires the ability to listen, acquire information, and share that information with clients—all within a team setting. One of the most rewarding parts of my job is hearing that a client has found one of our teams so helpful that the client has requested to work with the same group for further research and analysis. When this happens, I know the team has functioned very well.

I've studied generational groups at length: Millennials, GenXers, Baby Boomers, and the emerging Pluralist Generation. I enjoy opening the eyes of our clients to seeing the world through a generational lens—how to understand generational transition and how it affects program development and revenue streams. On a personal note, the results of this research are comforting to me. I have confidence in the young adults who are going to lead us in the future; I understand where they are coming from and where they will lead us. Perhaps because of this, society makes more sense to me than it does to other people.

My job does not get old. Conducting research on human behavior and attitudes necessarily means the information is changing every day. Sharing that information with our clients and helping them make smart business decisions with our information is very rewarding.

We should point out, however, that not all groups experience the critical transition that gets them to mobilize and adapt their behavior successfully (Okhuysen & Eisenhardt, 2002; Okhuysen & Waller, 2002). Thus, it might be wise from the beginning of a group project to take note of the inactivity or procrastination your group is experiencing so that you can help spur action earlier and avoid a stressful rush or failure to finish the project by the deadline.

Complexity of Group Communication

When you chat with an instructor in her office, you probably speak freely and informally. The two of you may exchange questions and comments rapidly, interrupt one another, and prompt each other for more information. But when you sit with that same professor in a classroom full of other students, the nature of your communication changes; you might be expected to raise your hand, defer to other students who are already speaking, or not ask questions at all.

What has changed? Why is the nature of your communication so different in the classroom from the way you converse in her office? In this section, we'll take a look at how complex group communication can be, depending on the number of individuals involved, their relationships, and their patterns of interaction.

Size and Complexity of Groups

As you'll recall from Chapter 1, dyadic communication refers to interactions between just two people (a dyad). When a third person joins the interaction, the dyad becomes a small group. Scholars generally agree that small group communication involves at least three members (Bormann, 1990), with a maximum of fifteen to twenty-five members (Sosha, 1997). Some communication scholars argue that in order to effectively perform tasks within classrooms or work projects, five to seven members may be optimum (Cragan, Wright, & Kasch, 2008). The basic logistics of communication—the need to take turns speaking and listening, for example—grow more complex the larger a group gets, creating the need for more structured exchanges among members.

AND YOU?

When you work independently, do you work in a linear fashion or does your pattern of activity resemble the punctuated equilibrium model? Does that behavior change when you work in a group?

● **WHEN YOU'RE** chatting with a professor during office hours, you are the focus of your professor's attention. However, in the classroom, you have to respect that other students want to speak as well! (left) © Bob Mahoney/The Image Works; (right) AP Photo/Damian Dovarganes

COMPLEXITY OF GROUP RELATIONSHIPS Each time a person is added to a group, the number of relationships increases substantially.

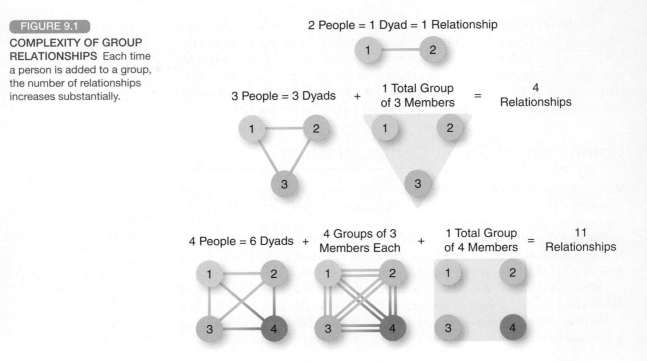

Specifically, the bigger the group, the more its communication takes on the following characteristics:

▶ *Interaction is more formal.* Group communication simply cannot work in the same kind of informal way that dyadic communication occurs, due to the need to include more communicators in the discourse. Individuals participating in a group may feel the need to obtain permission to speak, and they may also be reluctant to interrupt a speaker.

▶ *Each member has limited opportunities to contribute.* Participants may want or be required by a leader to share "floor time" with other group members. Such time constraints can inhibit the quality and quantity of their contributions. Even without a formal leader, in larger groups a few members tend to dominate much of the talk, while the less assertive members tend to remain quiet.

▶ *The communication becomes less intimate.* The greater the number of participants is, the less comfortable participants feel self-disclosing or voicing controversial opinions.

▶ *The interaction consumes more time.* As more participants are invited to contribute or debate, and there are more opinions possible, the interaction takes longer to complete.

▶ *Relationships become more complex.* As more participants are added, the relationships become more complex. In the dyad, of course, there is only one relationship—that between person 1 and person 2. But as shown in Figure 9.1, add another person, and you now have four potential relationships—between persons 1 and 2, 1 and 3, 2 and 3, and all three together. The number of relationships multiplies further with each additional participant!

The Formation of Cliques

In the comedy series *The Big Bang Theory*, geniuses Leonard and Sheldon are roommates and close friends. Sheldon, the quirky theoretical physicist, is extremely socially awkward and rarely takes kindly to new people or situations. Inevitably, when Leonard starts dating their neighbor, Penny, Sheldon has a difficult time adapting to his friend's new time commitments. In fact, he even winds up trying to trail along on Leonard and Penny's dates and frequently interrupts them when they wish to enjoy time alone. Even if you've never behaved quite like Sheldon, perhaps you've felt like he does—you love hanging out with your best friend, but whenever her boyfriend is around, you feel like you might as well be invisible. That's because your presence has changed the nature of the communication from dyadic to group communication, but the other two people haven't adjusted their communication behavior. They've remained a dyad that leaves you the lone outsider.

As a group's size increases, small subgroups of individuals often begin to bond together within the group, forming **cliques** (or coalitions) (Wilmot, 1987). Cliques are a common part of group life—they're a fixture in middle school and high school. You have your marching band kids, your football players, the art students, and so on. Many people think that they will escape cliques once high school ends, but this is rarely the case. In college, you might form cliques with others in your major, your dorm, or a particular organization. In office settings, members of cliques or coalitions typically sit next to each other in meetings, eat lunch together, share similar opinions, and support one another's positions.

When cliques take shape in a group, communication becomes more challenging because members are no longer dealing only with other individual members. Rather, they must navigate relationships and figure out how to communicate with entire subgroups. In addition, **countercoalitions**, in which one subgroup positions itself against another on an issue, can leave anyone who isn't affiliated with a subgroup in a very awkward position.

This tendency for members of groups to organize themselves into coalitions or cliques can have consequences for those who find themselves left out. **Social ostracism** is the exclusion of a particular group member (or members)—for example, when one clique or coalition limits the amount of information they share with a particular member and exclude him or her from group activities and the decision-making process (Kameda, Ohtsubo, & Takezawa, 1997). Ostracism can also occur in virtual groups, such as online work teams or Facebook friendship networks. In online environments, exclusion may occur through more subtle signals, such as reduced message frequency or an overall lack of responsive communication (Cramton, 1997; Williams, Govan, Croker, Tynan, Cruickshank, & Lam, 2002).

Rejection by one's peers can lead to anxiety, anger, and sadness, as targets of ostracism feel a decrease in belonging, control, and self-esteem (Williams, 2001; Wittenbaum, Shulman, & Braz, 2010). However, responses to social ostracism vary. Research on gender differences (Williams & Sommer, 1997), for example, has found that females who are ostracized are more likely to compensate, that

CONNECT

As you learn in Chapter 5, we define ourselves by our group memberships, with a tendency toward favoring our *ingroup* members and comparing ourselves to (and sometimes excluding) *outgroup* members. Although it may be a natural tendency to form cliques with those who share our affiliations, competent communicators must remember to be inclusive of various groups and co-cultures—particularly in team and organizational settings.

● **STUART FROM** *The Big Bang Theory* wants to be part of the gang, but often ends up feeling ostracized. MONTY BRINTON/CBS/Landov

AND YOU?

If you've ever been bullied or witnessed bullying, you know that social ostracism can be a powerful—and hurtful—force. But is excluding someone from communication always aggressive or malevolent? Consider situations in which you may have excluded a group member from communication, either in person or online. What were your motives, and how did it affect communication in the group?

AND YOU?

Have you ever been excessively quiet or shy in a group? Do you consider this behavior social loafing or do you feel that the situational or relational context is primarily to blame? Why?

is, work harder to be part of the group. Males, on the other hand, tend to engage in a practice called **social loafing**, which we discuss next.

Social Loafing

On many education and learning blogs, you can find students and instructors complaining about one of the most dreaded assignments of all time: the group project. At first glance, doesn't it seem that group projects should be easier than working solo? There are more minds with whom to try out ideas and share in the work. But what we all dread is having group members who don't pull their own weight. The fact is, in a group, people may become prone to social loafing—failing to invest the same level of effort in the group that they'd put in if they were working alone or with one other person (Karau & Williams, 1993). In almost every group situation, from your high school yearbook committee to cut-throat competitions like *Survivor*, there are always a few individuals who manage to make it through to the end simply by keeping their heads low and letting their teammates do most of the work. Clearly, social loafing affects both participation and communication in groups (Comer, 1998; Shultz, 1999).

Despite the negative connotation of the word *loafing*, it's not always due to laziness. When a person fails to speak up because he or she feels shy around a lot of people, the person is engaging in social loafing. Social loafing also results from the feelings of anonymity that can occur in larger groups, where it is more difficult for an individual member's contributions to be evaluated. Thus a member may put in less effort, believing that nobody will notice that he or she is slacking or, conversely, that he or she is working hard. If group members perceive an inequality in individual effort, conflict can and often does emerge, harming team morale. Social loafing even occurs in online groups and teams (Piezon & Ferree, 2008): members of an online discussion group, for example, may post messages or photos that are unrelated to the group's topic or they may not respond at all to a request for everyone's opinion on an idea.

Scholars argue that there are several practices that can help to manage your group's productivity and prevent or reduce social loafing (Cox & Brobrowski, 2000; Latane, Williams, & Harkins, 1979; Van Dick, Tissington, & Hertel, 2009):

▶ *Establish objectives and performance goals.* Make the schedule clear to all team members so everyone is aware of deadlines. Clarify what each member's individual responsibility is. You may even consider putting everything in writing, akin to a contract, so that there's no confusion about who should be taking care of what.

▶ *Establish individual accountability.* At the beginning of a project, be sure that all team members understand that they are expected to carry out their duties responsibly. This will establish the importance of each person's future performance. Also discuss how members will be evaluated and the consequences of social loafing or poor performance (Cox & Brobrowski, 2000).

▶ *Encourage team identity and ownership.* Early on in the process, promote team unity by coming up with a group name or symbol. Take the time to get to know each other and build social bonds and trust. This will help foster more team loyalty. Encourage team members to take pride and ownership in their work—which will also promote dedication to the cause.

what about you?

Are You a "Social Loafer"?

Do you exert less effort on a task when participating in a group than you would if you were performing it alone? If so, you may be a social loafer. A major complaint about group work involves dealing with free-riding behavior: resentment about group members who don't do their fair share or who even undermine the overall group goal. With your last group experience in mind, use the following five-point scale to determine if you were a social loafer: 5 = extremely like me; 4 = somewhat like me; 3 = neither like nor unlike me; 2 = somewhat unlike me; and 1 = extremely unlike me.

_____ 1. I arrived on time for group meetings and stayed until the end.

_____ 2. I showed enthusiasm about group activities.

_____ 3. I showed a positive attitude toward fellow group members.

_____ 4. I participated in planning the project/activity.

_____ 5. I volunteered for tasks appropriate to my expertise.

_____ 6. I contributed regularly to group discussion.

_____ 7. I put forth effort equal to or greater than that of my group members.

_____ 8. I delivered my contributions in a complete fashion.

_____ 9. My fellow group members perceived me as agreeable.

_____ 10. My fellow group members perceived me as thorough.

_____ 11. My fellow group members perceived me as dependable.

_____ 12. My fellow group members perceived me as conscientious.

_____ 13. I met all deadlines.

_____ 14. I asked for help from others when needed.

_____ 15. I supported the contributions of other group members.

_____ 16. I was open to suggestions from others.

_____ 17. I gave credit to others for their suggestions and contributions.

_____ 18. I made positive adaptations to the differences of group members.

_____ 19. I tried my absolute best.

_____ 20. I shared credit/blame for the outcome of our group.

_____ Add your scores together to get an informal assessment of social loafing.

74–100 You are NOT a social loafer. You carry your weight in a group and reinforce the contributions of others. People value you and your contributions.

47–73 You may be a social loafer in certain group situations. With your last group experience, you were probably frustrated but not sure how to make it better. In the future, be sure you are communicating support and involvement, and show respect for others so that each person feels that he or she has a useful role to play.

20–46 Social loafer! In group situations, people are likely to see you as apathetic and may even resent you. Whenever you join a group in the future, you should work harder to do your fair share and show support for all your group members.

Source: Adapted from Maiden & Perry (2011).

▶ *Stay in contact.* If a miscommunication occurs between members, be sure to discuss it right away. Ambiguity and confusion will only encourage members to become less connected with the group and more likely to engage in social loafing.

Group Networks

Just as a group's size and social relationships influence the complexity of communication within the group, so do networks. **Networks** are patterns of interaction governing who speaks with whom in a group and about what. To understand the nature of networks, you must first consider two main positions within them. The first is *centrality*, or the degree to which an individual sends and receives messages from others in the group. The most central person in the group receives and sends the highest number of messages in a given time period. At the other end of the spectrum is *isolation*—a position from which a group member sends and receives fewer messages than other members.

A team leader or manager typically has the highest level of centrality in a formal group, but centrality is not necessarily related to status or power. The CEO of a company, for example, may be the end recipient of all information generated by teams below her, but in fact only a limited number of individuals within the organization are able to communicate directly with her. Her assistant, in fact, may have a higher degree of centrality in the network, because she must interact with so many people in the organization. As you might imagine, networks play a powerful role in any group's communication, whether the group is a family, a sports team, a civic organization, or a large corporation.

In some groups, all members speak with all others regularly about a wide range of topics. In others, perhaps only a few members are "allowed" to speak directly with the group's leader or longest-standing member about serious issues. In still other groups, some members may work alongside one another without communicating at all. There are several types of networks, including chain networks, all-channel networks, and wheel networks (see Figure 9.2) (Bavelous, 1950).

Chain Networks

In a **chain network**, information is passed from one member to the next in a sequential pattern. Such networks can be practical for sharing written information: an e-mail, forwarded from person to person along a chain, for example, allows each person to read the original information from other prior recipients. But this form of group communication can lead to frustration and miscommunication

FIGURE 9.2

GROUP COMMUNICATION NETWORKS

Source: Adapted with permission from Scott (1981, p. 8).

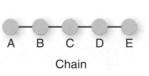

Chain

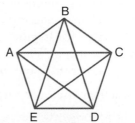

All-Channel   Wheel

when information is spoken, as the messages can easily get distorted as they are passed along. Person A tells person B that their boss, Luis, had a fender bender on the way to work and will miss the 10:00 A.M. meeting. Person B tells person C that Luis was in an accident and will not be in the office today. Person C tells person D that Luis was injured in an accident; no one knows when he'll be in. You can imagine that Luis will be in a full-body cast by the time the message reaches person G!

All-Channel Networks

In an **all-channel network**, all members interact with each other equally. When people talk about roundtable discussions, they're talking about all-channel groups: there is no leader, and all members operate at the same level of centrality. Such networks can be useful for collaborative projects and for brainstorming ideas, but the lack of order can make it difficult for such groups to complete tasks efficiently. Imagine, for example, that you're trying to arrange to meet up with a group of friends. You send out a mass e-mail to all of them, to determine days that will work, and you ask for suggestions about where to meet. The recipients each hit "reply all" and share their responses with the whole group. By using an all-channel network, the entire group may learn that Friday is not good for anyone, but Saturday is. However, only a few people have suggested favorite spots, and there's no consensus on where to go. That's where wheel networks come in.

Wheel Networks

Wheel networks are a sensible alternative for situations in which individual members' activities and contributions must be culled and tracked in order to avoid duplicating efforts and to ensure that all tasks are being completed. In a **wheel network**, one individual acts as a touchstone for all the others in the group; all group members share their information with that one individual, who then shares the information with the rest of the group. Consider the preceding example: as the sender of the initial e-mail, you might take on a leadership role

● **THE COPYEDITING TEAM** in a newsroom works as a wheel network. All of the copy editors report to one copy chief, who regulates the copyediting style. AP Photo/Herbert Knosowski

and ask everyone just to reply to you. Then you could follow up with a decision about time and place to meet and send that out to everyone else. Wheel networks have the lowest shared centrality but are very efficient (Leavitt, 1951).

Understanding Group Roles

When we communicate in groups, we tend to fall into particular roles, much like playing different parts in a play. These roles influence the process and outcomes of group interaction. Let's look closely at three types of roles—task, social, and antigroup.

Task Roles

In some cases, a role is defined by a task that needs doing, and a person is asked or appointed to fill it (or he or she volunteers). Such **task roles** are concerned with the accomplishment of the group's goals—specifically, the activities that need to be carried out for the group to achieve its objectives. For example, your role on a committee charged with organizing a campus Zumba party might be to post advertisements for the event in key locations around campus, in the student newspaper, and on the university Web site.

Task roles can also be specifically related to the group's communication; for instance:

▶ An *information giver* offers facts, beliefs, personal experience, or other input during group discussions ("When the College Republicans posted their ad in the student lounge, they had good attendance at their event").

▶ An *information seeker* asks for input or clarification of ideas or opinions that members have presented ("Jeff, are you saying you don't think we would get good attendance on a Thursday night?").

▶ An *elaborator* provides further clarification of points, often adding to what others have said ("I agree with Ellie about getting Spike to DJ the event—he has a huge following in town").

▶ An *initiator* helps the group move toward its objective by proposing solutions, presenting new ideas, or suggesting new ways of looking at an issue the group is discussing ("How essential is it that we schedule our event for the last Thursday of the month? If we moved it a week later, we wouldn't have to compete with the Homecoming festivities").

▶ An *administrator* keeps the conversation on track ("OK, let's get back to the subject of when to schedule the event") and ensures that meetings begin and end on time ("We've got five minutes left; should we wind up?"). This role appears in online groups, too, where forum administrators (also known as moderators or masters) coordinate and sometimes screen the members' comments.

Social Roles

Some roles evolve to manage how people in the group are feeling and getting along with each other; such roles are called **social roles**. For example, in a college dormitory, one student might unofficially fill the role of "hall parent"—mentoring freshmen, listening compassionately to people's problems, and making everyone feel secure. Consider these additional examples of social roles (Anderson, Riddle, & Martin, 1999; Benne & Sheats, 1948; Salazar, 1996):

▶ A *harmonizer* seeks to smooth over tension in the group by settling differences among members and working out compromises when conflict arises ("There is only one communal TV lounge per floor, so can we plan on reserving the first-floor lounge for people who want to watch the football game on Sunday, and leaving the second floor free for people who want to watch the Golden Globe Awards?").

▶ A *gatekeeper* works to ensure that each member of the group gets a chance to voice their opinions or otherwise contribute to discussions. ("Tonya, we haven't heard from you yet on the issue of overnight guests in our dorm. What are your thoughts?").

▶ A *sensor* expresses group feelings, moods, or relationships in an effort to recognize the climate and capitalize on it or modify it for the better ("I feel like tempers are getting a little short right now—maybe we ought to break for dinner, and meet back here in an hour to continue this discussion when we're all feeling less hungry?").

Each member in a group can play task and social roles, and the roles can be official or unofficial. For example, Evelyn is the dorm's resident advisor, officially tasked with maintaining harmony among the students who live there. But Mike is also an unofficial harmonizer because he has a knack for mitigating tensions between people. Mike also has a lot of ideas for events, so he frequently finds himself acting as an initiator during meetings. Members like Mike can move into or out of such personal or task roles depending on whether the role is needed and whether others in the group are willing to fill it.

Antigroup Roles

Unlike task and social roles, **antigroup roles** create problems because they serve individual members' priorities at the expense of group needs. You've probably seen evidence of these antigroup roles in the groups you belong to:

▶ A *blocker* indulges in destructive communication, including opposing or criticizing all ideas and stubbornly reintroducing an idea after the group has already rejected or bypassed it ("None of the dates any of you proposed will work for the party. It really needs to be five weeks from today, as I said earlier").

▶ An *avoider* refuses to engage in the group's proceedings by expressing cynicism or nonchalance toward ideas presented or by joking or changing the subject ("Well, whatever, I'm guessing it's not a big deal if this party doesn't even happen, right?").

▶ A *recognition seeker* calls attention to himself or herself by boasting or by going on and on about his or her qualifications or personal achievements

CONNECT

Competent leadership can address problematic antigroup roles. As you learn in Chapter 10, a *directive leader* might lay out tasks to thwart a distracter; a *supportive leader* might thank each member for his or her contributions, preventing a recognition seeker from claiming the glory. Leaders have the power to affect norms and roles by encouraging group members to make productive contributions.

("I planned a gathering for a women's studies group last year, and it went really well. People still talk about it! So trust me on this one").

▶ A *distractor* goes off on tangents or tells irrelevant stories ("Does anyone know what happened on *Game of Thrones* last night? I missed it").

These antigroup roles are not limited to face-to-face group communication—you've no doubt run into a few distractors, blockers, or recognition seekers in online forums. Online groups are also often disrupted by *trolls*—individuals who intentionally insert irrelevant and inflammatory comments into the discussion in order to stir up controversy.

Antigroup roles obviously add to the dysfunction of a group (Wilson & Hanna, 1993). For instance, a *blocker* who acts superior to other team members and criticizes the members' ideas may harm group morale and productivity. To mitigate the impact of these antigroup roles, members can revisit the norms the group has established and make the changes needed to improve group communication (for example, "All ideas get a fair hearing"). People fulfilling certain task or social roles can also help. For instance, if you're a gatekeeper, you can prompt an avoider to contribute her opinion on a proposal that the group has been considering. Research also indicates that positive and proactive responses to avoiders and blockers can help establish individuals as leaders in their organizations (Garner & Poole, 2009).

Role Conflict

Imagine that you work at a local retail store and you've been promoted to store manager. As part of your new role, you will have to manage staff members who are working as individual contributors at the store. In this new role, you'll be managing several close friends who you used to work alongside as regular staff. That's where things might get complicated: as manager, you'll have to evaluate staff members' performance, and how can you give a good friend a poor performance review and still remain friends?

Role conflict arises in a group whenever expectations for a member's behavior are incompatible (Baxter & Montgomery, 1996). Role conflict can make group communication profoundly challenging. For the manager who must evaluate a friend—especially a friend whose performance could be better—there is rarely a perfect option. You might give candid constructive feedback to your friend on his performance while trying to constrain the damage to your friendship by saying something like "I hope you know I'm offering this feedback as a way to help you improve. As your friend and manager, I want to see you do well here." A less ethical approach, of course, would be to defer to your friend's feelings instead of to your responsibility as manager—essentially, to spare his feelings by giving him a better review than he deserves.

Status

Groups also form around—or are defined by—status. Status is like a social currency, unequally distributed within groups, which gives some members more

AND YOU?

Have you ever been in a leadership role in a group of friends? Have you ever been subordinate to a friend in a group situation? Did any conflict arise and, if so, how did you resolve it?

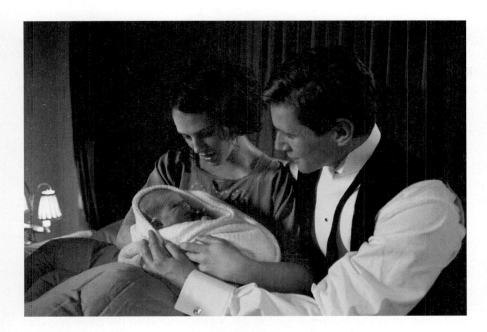

power than others. In some groups, status is formally defined by a clear hierarchy: the military, for example, operates on a hierarchy of leadership with officers outranking enlisted troops. But status is also informally conferred: a charismatic or especially competent military recruit may emerge as a leader and gain status among her peers even if she does not outrank them. That kind of perceived status—based not in any kind of formal rules but instead on peoples' perceptions of one another—can be potent.

A number of factors have been shown to increase perceptions of status. For example, status can be gained through having access to material resources or information that other group members do not have (Poole & Hollingshead, 2005). Similarly, physical attractiveness has been known to enhance a group member's status (Webster & Driskell, 1978, 1983). Gender may play a role, too, as males have traditionally had higher status and participation rates and greater access to resources and information than females (Carli, 1999; Ellyson, Dovidio, & Brown; Smith-Lovin, Skvortz, & Hudson, 1986). Of course, as mentioned in the foregoing military example, people can also *earn* status through their own competence or communicative effectiveness as they participate in the group.

Within groups, those with higher status are given more opportunities to make contributions toward completing the task, their suggestions are often evaluated more positively, and they exert greater influence over lower-status members (Berger, Wagner, & Zelditch, 1985). Perceptions of higher status can lead to those group members having greater influence even if they don't have any formal power. The "popular kids" at a high school, for example, may have more influence on school events than the elected student council. All of these vagaries are at play in the popular British period drama *Downton Abbey*, which depicts the goings-on at a stately manor house in the early twentieth century. The Granthams, the aristocratic family that lives in the home, have a high status conferred on them not only by wealth but also by noble title. Within the family, the men are afforded more status than the women, who cannot inherit the estate

Status is often pertinent in the workplace—especially between supervisors and supervisees. To settle well into a company's *organization culture*, it's necessary to carefully foster this relationship. In Chapter 11, we give tips on how to interact with a supervisor or supervisee in a professional and courteous way.

and are limited in their ability to make decisions. Status also separates the family from the "downstairs" staff, who lack fortune or title, but who consider their status superior to those who work in factories or on the local farms.

Group Climate

In addition to the complexity of group interaction and the roles that group members play, group communication is also strongly affected by the overall "climate" or collective atmosphere in the group. Specifically, group members are affected by the level of the group's cohesion, the norms that emerge for their behavior, clarity of goals, and their differences as individuals. In the sections that follow, we explore each of these factors in more detail.

Cohesion

Cohesion is the degree to which group members bond, like each other, and consider themselves to be one entity. A cohesive group identifies itself as a single unit rather than a collection of individuals, which helps hold the group together in the face of adversity. In fact, cohesion is an important factor in generating a positive group climate, in which members take pride in the group, treat each other with respect, develop trust, feel confident about their abilities, and achieve higher success in accomplishing goals. Such positive climates can also foster optimism and confidence in the face of obstacles. A self-confident, cohesive group tends to minimize problems, eliminate barriers, and cope well with crises (Folger, Poole, & Stutman, 2001). In general, cohesive groups perform better than noncohesive groups on decision-making tasks (for example, selecting a course of action more quickly and making more informed choices) (Carless & DePaola, 2000; Welch, Mossholder, Stell, & Bennett, 1998). Nonverbal communication is also influenced by group cohesion; Yasui (2009) found that cohesive group members often repeat and build on one another's gestures.

You can determine group cohesion in several ways. If you take a look at how the participants feel about their own membership in the group, you'll see that the more satisfaction and fulfillment members feel, the more cohesive they are. Members of a cohesive group are also enthusiastic, identify with the purposes of the group (Tekleab, Quigley, & Tesluk, 2009), and tell outsiders about its activities. Even positive, constructive argumentation (as opposed to verbal aggressiveness) can be a sign of group cohesion (Anderson & Martin, 1999). Finally, consider how well the group retains members. A cohesive group will retain more members than a noncohesive group.

Gouran (2003) offers several practical suggestions individuals can use for increasing cohesion and fostering a more positive group experience:

▶ Avoid dominating other group members.

▶ Stay focused on the tasks the group must accomplish.

▶ Be friendly.

▶ Show sensitivity to and respect for other members.

CONNECT

In Chapter 3, we discuss *jargon*, vocabulary unique to a specific hobby or profession. Jargon helps build group cohesion because it connects members to one another. A group of police officers, for example, might speak about *perps* (perpetrators), *vics* (victims), *collars* (arrests), and *brass* (supervisors)—terms that their mechanic or physician friends would not use. This use of language helps officers bond as a group.

COMMUNICATIONACROSSCULTURES

The International American Pastime

The typical major league baseball team has a full roster of players and a substantial staff of coaches who work with players on specific skills. There's the general manager, a bullpen coach, a batting coach, a bench coach, and strength and conditioning coaches. There's a bevy of trainers and coordinators. And, sometimes, there's a language coach.

In 2012, more than a quarter of the players in Major League Baseball (MLB) were foreign-born (Associated Press, 2013). Many of them arrive in American locker rooms with much fanfare but with few or no English skills. In order to succeed as part of a team, however, it's crucial that they be able to communicate with their teammates and coaches, both on and off the field. The finite rules and language of the game, along with the formal nonverbal signals teams develop to communicate on the field, help to create a clear code of communication. For Asian players, most of whom are drafted straight out of the Japanese leagues, like Yu Darvish, Hiroki Kuroda, and Wei-Yin Chen, translators are essential. They have long accompanied players on the field during practices and assisted them in interviews, and in 2014, new MLB rules solidified translators' roles in their organizations by allowing them to accompany coaches onto the field during games for on-field conferences (Associated Press, 2014).

But the new rule may have limited impact on the many Latino players in the league. Because most Spanish speakers have at least a few bilingual teammates who can translate for them, and because most spend some time in the farm system, where they can pick up a somewhat functional, if limited, English vocabulary (what one reporter called "Baseball English"), most Spanish speakers do not have team-provided translators (Andriesen, 2007; Associated Press, 2014). It's unclear whether this less formal mode of communication is sufficient. Yankees closer Mariano Rivera admits that, early in his career, there were times when he was completely lost when "talking" with his coaches. "You nod your head yes, but you have no idea what they are saying" (Riviera, in Associated Press, 2014, para. 2).

The answer may be for the game to become more bilingual. The San Diego Padres, like many other organizations, offer English language classes to help players who are not fluent in English. But the team also takes the opposite approach: they teach basic Spanish to their staff. "It's something I thought was important to make us efficient when dealing with players when we're going to the Dominican [Republic] or with our players who are just coming here and don't have command of the English language yet," said Padres Director of Player Development Randy Smith (Brock, 2010). The next step might be targeting players long before they get to the big leagues: in 2013, Major League Baseball announced a pilot program that will provide English language classes and other educational support for prospects in the Dominican Republic (Sanchez, 2013).

THINK ABOUT THIS

❶ How important is it to have all the players on a team speak the same language? Would having a single language policy increase group cohesion? What might the downsides of such a policy be?

❷ Who is responsible for developing a shared code when coaches and players speak different languages? How might the rules of communication be worked out between individuals who speak different languages?

❸ What other cultural differences might inhibit communication on a professional sports team? How does multiculturalism and globalization affect other sports?

❹ Is it fair to provide translators for Asian players but not for Latinos? Why or why not? Should all members of the organization be tasked with learning a second language or just the ones who don't speak English?

▶ Demonstrate that you value others' opinions.

▶ Cooperate with other members rather than compete with them.

Clearly, cohesion offers groups tremendous benefits, but unfortunately there is also a downside. Too much cohesion can actually cause the group to be unproductive. For example, if you and the other members of your study group enjoy each other's company so much that you talk and laugh together about everything *but* the course material, you'll never get your work done, which will hurt your goal of doing well on the exam! In addition, if your group members wish to maintain their cohesion at all costs, they may fail to question or criticize each other's knowledge or ideas, even if they are incorrect. In this scenario, you could all end up with the wrong understanding of some key concepts that will be on your exam. In the next chapter, we'll also see that excessive cohesion and the failure to express disagreement play a key part in groupthink, a serious problem in the group decision-making process. We now turn our attention to group norms.

Norms

As you saw earlier in the chapter, over time a group will develop norms. Norms emerge within the group and are imposed by members on themselves and each other; they may not be stated outwardly, but they direct the behavior of the group as a whole and affect the conduct of individual members. In a business environment, norms might dictate the kinds of topics that can be expressed in a meeting (Should non-task-related conversation be interjected? Are jokes appropriate?). In an online group, norms might evolve to govern the use of foul language, negative comments, or criticism. For example, a recent study showed that established members of an online anorexia support group allow new members to share pro-anorexic statements in order to establish that they are ill. In time, however, these members are initiated into the group norm that prohibits such unhealthy and negative statements (Stommel & Koole, 2010).

Some norms have a negative impact on communication. For example, suppose a group permits one member to dominate the conversation or allows members to dismiss an idea before discussing its pros and cons. A group with these norms will have difficulty generating enough diverse ideas to make informed decisions. If you find yourself in a group with unproductive norms like these, consider modifying them—this is possible if you approach the task diplomatically (Brilhart & Galanes, 1992). The following three-step process can help:

1. *Express your loyalty and dedication to the group, to show that you have the group's best interests at heart.* For instance, "I've been a member of this school committee for two years now and have hung in there during the tough times as well as the good times. I want to see us be the best we can be."

2. *Cite specific examples of the behavior you find harmful to the group's effectiveness.* To illustrate, "When we didn't take time to explore the pros and cons of the special-ed funding strategy that came up last month, we ended up making a decision that we regretted later."

3. *Ask other members for their opinions about the problem norm you've identified.* If others feel that the norm is still warranted, they may advocate keeping it ("Well, there are some situations where we don't have as much time as we'd like to consider the merits of an idea. During those moments, we need to be able to move ahead with a decision quickly").

With respectful, productive discussion, the group may decide to maintain the norm, change it under specific conditions ("We'll have someone play devil's advocate when time allows"), or abandon it entirely.

Clarity of Goals

Think of the worst group meeting you've ever attended. How would you describe that meeting? Was the conversation disorganized? Unproductive? Confusing? Did you leave the meeting with a bad feeling about working with the group again in the future? Often such a poor communication climate is caused by the group's lack of a clear goal to begin with. To communicate productively and promote a positive atmosphere in any group, members need goal clarity: that is, they must understand what the group's purpose is, what goals will help the group achieve its purpose, how close the group is to achieving its goals, and whether the activities members are engaging in are helping the group move toward its goals.

Goals vary considerably from one group to another. For example, a team in one of your classes may have the simple goal of completing a fifteen-minute in-class exercise and reporting the results to the rest of the class. An urban beautification fund-raising committee may have the goal of collecting $4,000 for new landscaping at a neighborhood park.

One effective way to make sure your group has clear goals is to encourage the members to define them as a group. When members take part in establishing goals, they feel more committed to and excited about achieving those objectives. Research shows that a group is more likely to reach its goals when those goals are communicated in terms that are specific ("Raise $4,000 by the end of March"), inspiring ("Imagine our neighborhood becoming a community of choice for young families"), and prioritized ("We'll need to focus on this goal first and then this other one next") (O'Hair, Friedrich, & Dixon, 2007).

▶ *Enable group members to prepare.* Each group member should have a clear idea of what he or she is to be working on and should prepare accordingly. Send an agenda and any relevant assignments to team members in advance of any meetings.

▶ *Use time productively.* Avoid unnecessary meetings—don't meet just for the sake of meeting. In any meeting situation—be it a face-to-face, sit-down meeting or a telephone conference calls, be sure to establish clear goals in advance to keep the meeting on task.

As you learn in Chapter 1, *goal achievement* is an important function of communication in all contexts. Just remember that although it's important for a group to keep the end goal in sight, competent communicators are flexible—they try to maintain interdependence while being open to various ideas on achieving goals. They also recognize that the goal itself may change as group members share ideas and present solutions to problems.

● **JUST AS ANY** Girl Scout troop sets personal and group goals for the cookie-selling season, your groups can productively divvy up responsibilities to make sure you achieve your aims. © Matt Slocum/AP

Once your group begins working toward its goals, encourage yourself and your fellow members to talk regularly about the decisions you're making and the actions you're taking to ensure that these all support progress toward the goals.

Individual Differences

Members of a group may share norms, goals, and cohesion with their fellow members, but they also each bring personal differences that can strongly affect the communication climate. Let's examine how cultural factors and communication apprehension—which vary by individual—affect our ability to communicate in groups.

Cultural Factors

As you've learned throughout this book, culture has a big impact on how we communicate. Cultural diversity can have a particularly significant impact on group processes and outcomes (Thomas, Ravlin, & Wallace, 1996). When a group has culturally diverse members, that diversity can have benefits (such as enabling the group to produce a wide array of viewpoints) as well as challenges (including misunderstandings between members).

As we discussed in Chapter 3, cultures in English-speaking nations such as the United States, Great Britain, and Canada are largely individualist and low context, valuing personal accomplishment, self-esteem, and direct communication. As such, people in individualist cultures want their own opinions heard and appreciated, and they are likely to express them clearly and openly. In a collectivist and high-context culture, people value cooperation and group harmony, as well as indirect expression. They allow group norms (rather than their own personal goals) to have the largest influence on their behaviors and thoughts (Triandis, Brislin, & Hul, 1988). Not surprisingly, this difference can present a challenge when members of these cultures are working together in groups. People from individualist cultures will likely more openly vocalize their disagreement with the others and try to persuade each other, whereas the collectivists may feel "bulldozed" as they stifle their own objections for the good of the group. Conflict also occurs because of these differences in members' attitudes and basic orientations to problems (Tjosvold, 1992).

Communication Apprehension

The next time you're sitting in your communication classroom or logging on to a discussion forum in your online course, take a peek around. Is there someone who never speaks up or raises a hand? Perhaps you're assuming that this person has nothing to say or that he or she is a social loafer. Maybe you're right. But it's also possible that this individual feels uncomfortable participating in group conversation even when his or her contribution would clearly help the group. People who are fearful or nervous about speaking up in groups are experiencing **communication apprehension** (CA). We discuss CA more fully in Chapter 14, because this anxiety is particularly common in public speaking situations, but it can affect collaboration in groups as well. Particularly in newly formed groups, individuals experiencing high levels of communication apprehension are less likely to participate; they produce and share fewer ideas with

AND YOU?

Have you ever misunderstood another member of a group you were involved in because of cultural differences? If so, how did you and the other person deal with the misunderstanding?

team members, make less significant contributions to the group discussions, and perceive group discussions as less positive than do members of the team with low levels of communication apprehension (Comadena, 1984; Jablin, Seibold, & Sorensen, 1977; Jablin & Sussman, 1978; Sorenson & McCroskey, 1977). Team members experiencing communication apprehension are also less likely to be perceived as leaders (Hawkins & Stewart, 1991). Within the work environment, those with high levels of communication apprehension prefer to work independently, engage in more listening and observation than action during group interactions, and respond less favorably to change and evolving task demands (Russ, 2012).

What explains this communication apprehension? Scholars have identified several causes (Schullery & Gibson, 2001):

▶ *Lack of self-esteem.* When individuals doubt the worth of their contributions, they may decline to speak up in a group. Fear of being wrong, of being mocked, or of creating a bad impression can further lead to communication apprehension.

▶ *Status differences.* Group members who hold a relatively low position in the group's social or political hierarchy may avoid disagreeing with their superiors in the group because they fear retribution from the more powerful persons.

▶ *Unbalanced participation.* When a group member—or a small number of group members—dominates the conversation in a group, the less aggressive members may retreat from communicating. This strongly influences how decisions are made in the group.

Some simple techniques can help a group address communication apprehension among members. For example, to ease self-esteem problems, consider starting a group meeting by having each member tell the member to the left what he or she appreciates about that person. To neutralize status differences, have members sit in a circle and invite lower-status members to speak before higher-status ones. To rebalance participation, suggest a norm that calls for everyone to weigh in on ideas presented in the group. Or look for members who are holding back and invite them specifically to contribute their views.

You may be wondering how communication apprehension manifests or changes in the somewhat anonymous world of online groups. Indeed, the online environment affords those with high communication apprehension more anonymity and less social risk (Curtis, 1997; Ward & Tracey, 2004), and shy individuals tend to report less communication apprehension during discussions conducted online rather than face to face (Hammick & Lee, in press). However, research relating to the impact of communication apprehension in online contexts is mixed and has produced inconsistent findings (Flaherty, Pearce, & Rubin, 1998; Hunt, Atkin, & Krishnan; 2012; McKenna, 1998; Patterson & Gojdycz, 2000). Studies reveal that shy and apprehensive college students self-disclose much less on Facebook, are less self-expressive, and have fewer friends (Hunt et al., 2012; Sheldon, 2008). But regardless of the channel (traditional or online), communicatively apprehensive individuals are more reticent to participate in groups.

CONNECT

If you suffer from communication apprehension in groups, you're probably aware of the negative effects it can have on your social and professional life. Luckily, there are many practical strategies for dealing with apprehension, as we discuss in Chapter 14. Check out our tips on desensitizing yourself, visualizing your success, and taking care of yourself in anxiety-producing situations.

EVALUATING**COMMUNICATION**ETHICS

Sketchy Behavior

You have recently formed a comedy troupe with four other friends: Calvin, Eddie, Meredith, and Sylvia. Your first live show with the group is in just a few weeks, and your group has written and rehearsed five sketches. But you and Calvin have had doubts about one sketch, written by Eddie and Sylvia, since day one. Rather than voice your concerns, you and Calvin have been trying to come up with an alternative sketch. During a late-night session, the two of you come up with an idea for a sketch that in your opinion outclasses the one you've been having problems with.

It is now a few days before the show, and the two of you have decided, independent of the other members, that the weaker sketch needs to be changed in favor of the one you've written. You are concerned about how this will look and have a nagging feeling the other members are going to perceive your writing of this sketch as a selfish way to push your work over that of your teammates, but you feel strongly that the new sketch will make the show a greater success. Calvin suggests that you present your sketch to Meredith, since she was not involved in writing either sketch. "If we convince Meredith that our sketch is the stronger one," Calvin reasons, "we'll be able to point to her opinion as a truly objective opinion—she's got no agenda."

You're pretty certain that Meredith will prefer your sketch, not only because you feel it is better but also because it features a role that Meredith would love to play. And you know that if you talk to Meredith beforehand, you'll have a clear majority in favor of your sketch should the decision be put to a vote. But is this ethical?

THINK ABOUT THIS

❶ What role did group communication play in this scenario? Might cliques have been involved? What were other communication options?

❷ Is it unethical to attempt to gain Meredith's vote even if you honestly believe that it's in the best interest of the group?

❸ What ethical implications arise from approaching Meredith with the new sketch? Should the sketch be presented to the entire team at the same time? Is it fair to tempt Meredith with a juicy role in exchange for her vote?

Assertiveness and Argumentativeness

Although people who experience communication apprehension are *less* likely to speak up in groups, there are also people whose traits make them *more* likely to speak up. Have you noticed when working on class projects that some members of your group always seem to voice their opinions boldly or never seem to be afraid to speak out when they disagree with group members? These are likely to be students with assertive and argumentative personalities. **Assertiveness** refers to the use of communication messages that demonstrate confidence, dominance, and forcefulness to achieve personal goals. For example, you are being assertive when you openly tell your group members, "I want an 'A' on this project, so I would like us all to work as hard as possible to make this happen." Some people have a greater tendency than others to use such assertive messages. **Argumentativeness** is a particular form of assertiveness, in which a person tends to express positions on controversial issues and verbally attack the positions that other people take (Infante & Rancer, 1982)—in other words, people who are argumentative tend, not surprisingly, to argue, and they often even enjoy it! But note that to be "argumentative" and not "aggressive" means that you refute the other people's *positions on issues*—you do not attack them personally!

What effect do assertive or argumentative people have on group interaction? Highly argumentative group members are likely to be more dominant and, hence, play a significant role in group decision making (Limon & La France, 2005). In meetings, for example, individuals who are more argumentative are perceived as more credible communicators (Infante, 1981), and within small groups they are more often perceived as leaders (Schultz, 1980, 1982). Interestingly, research has found that leadership appears to be most strongly associated with higher levels of argumentativeness *in combination with* lower levels of communication apprehension (Limon & La France, 2005).

You might think that group harmony would suffer when people openly assert or argue their positions, but argumentativeness can actually reinforce cohesion within a group (Anderson & Martin, 1999). This is because group members are advocating for the solutions that may be most helpful at accomplishing the group's tasks. Indeed, in most group situations, assertiveness and argumentativeness are perceived as constructive traits (Infante, 1987). It is important to remember, however, that we must distinguish these constructive forms of speaking up with the destructive tactic of "verbal aggressiveness" that we discussed in Chapter 8 as a negative, hostile way of handling conflict.

● **INITIALLY IN** *Pitch Perfect*, Aubrey leads the Bellas with an overwhelming assertiveness that leaves little room for any of the other a capella girls' input. Ultimately, the key to the group's success lies in a more balanced participation that allows for shared ideas and cooperation.
Universal Pictures/Photofest

BACK TO ▶ Team Rubicon

At the beginning of the chapter, we were introduced to Team Rubicon, a team of military veterans who provide disaster relief. Let's consider what we've learned in this chapter, and how it applies to the experience of these inspiring veterans.

▶ The name "Team Rubicon" sends two messages. "Team" speaks to the small, cohesive nature of military units. "Rubicon" is taken from the phrase "crossing the Rubicon," a military metaphor that dates back to classical Rome and refers to making a commitment to a difficult course of action from which there is no turning back. By establishing its goals right in the group's name, Team Rubicon makes both its goals and its means clear. Although the organization has many members, it consists of many small teams that are able to adjust plans and adapt tactics to administer immediate aid in the most dire of circumstances.

▶ The only people who can truly understand what combat veterans are going through are other veterans. Team Rubicon draws on this unique bond, as well as the specialized skills of veterans, and the group's impact comes in the form of small, platoonlike groups that share a goal and a purpose. That unity, identity, and cohesiveness mean a lot. "It is a brotherhood—or a sisterhood," explains Danielle Harrington, an Army reservist and Team Rubicon volunteer who joined hurricane relief efforts in New York in 2012. "It is nice to be around like-minded people, who have the same values and the same ethos" (Harrington, in Hameed, 2012, 2:30).

▶ In military organizations, roles are assigned to each group member with a clear hierarchy of leadership and designated task roles. These roles are easily adapted to emergency situations, when decisions must be made and actions taken quickly and effectively. That's a large part of Team Rubicon's success. But it is also true that the decisions involved in civilian jobs, higher education, and family life might seem unimportant or insignificant to men and women returning from life-and-death situations. This lack of purpose can be devastating for veterans, especially when coupled with depression or post-traumatic stress. Through career training programs like the Clay Hunt Fellowship, Team Rubicon hopes to help veterans adapt their very specific skills to nonemergent situations, while continuing to find purpose, community, and self-worth through service.

 **THINGS TO TRY** Activities

1. LaunchPad for *Real Communication* offers key term videos and encourages self-assessment through adaptive quizzing. Go to **bedfordstmartins.com/realcomm** to get access to:

   ✓ **LearningCurve** Adaptive Quizzes.

   ▶ Video clips that illustrate key concepts, highlighted in teal in the Real Reference section that follows.

2. Consider a group to which you belong—your communication class, your family, your religious community, and so on. Draw a chart that depicts members of the group and the patterns of communication among them. What kind of network does the group most closely resemble?

3. Read up on the history of some influential but now defunct music group (such as the Beatles, Public Enemy, or Nirvana). Did the group go through all the stages of group development outlined in this chapter? How did the group determine roles and establish norms? How did members deal with conflict? How did the eventual disbanding of the group play out?

4. Consider the adjourning phase of group development for a group you were part of that disbanded—Scouts, a sports team, the school newspaper staff—and think about what aspects of the group made for the hardest good-bye from the group. Are high-performing groups hardest to leave? Groups with the clearest established norms? What sorts of closing rituals have you experienced?

5. The telephone game, passing a message from person to person, is fun simply because of the inevitable message distortion that gets revealed at the end. Can you think of a time when a message was passed to you from an indirect source that you discovered to be blatantly wrong? Maybe it was bungled homework instructions or a wrong meeting time or place. Given these sorts of problems, what type of workplace might function best with a chain network?

6. Analyze the group dynamics from five of your favorite television shows. See if you can identify the various social and antigroup role types in each of the groups.

7. Next time you work in a group, pay attention to how the group works. Does the activity follow a linear model, or is the activity punctuated by periods of inertia and periods of intense activity? How does the group activity pattern differ from your own behaviors when you work alone?

Now that you have finished reading this chapter, you can:

List the characteristics and types of groups and explain how groups develop:

▶ A **group** is a collection of more than two people who have a shared identity, have common goals, and are interdependent (p. 244).

▶ **Primary groups** are long-standing and meaningful groups, such as family groups (p. 245).

▶ Specific-function groups include **support groups**, **social groups**, **problem-solving groups**, and **study groups** (p. 245).

▶ A **team** is a task-oriented group, and a **self-directed work team** is a group with responsibility for producing high-quality finished work on its own (p. 245, 247).

▶ Groups often develop through five specific stages: **forming**, **storming**, **norming** (**norms** are recurring patterns of thought or behavior), **performing**, and **adjourning** (pp. 248–249). A **termination ritual** takes place in the adjourning stage of group development where the group chooses to celebrate its achievements with a final celebration (p. 249).

▶ Some groups show patterns of **punctuated equilibrium**, in which procrastination and inactivity are followed by bursts of inactivity and change (p. 249).

Describe ways in which group size, social relationships, and communication networks affect group communication:

▶ The bigger the group, the more interaction becomes formal, less intimate, more time-consuming, and complex and the less opportunity members have to contribute (pp. 251–252).

▶ **Cliques** (coalitions)—small subgroups—may emerge within larger groups, making communication more challenging. Members of cliques often engage in **social ostracism**, when particular group members are ignored or excluded from participating in the group. A **countercoalition**—a subgroup positioned against another subgroup—may leave unaffiliated members in an awkward position (p. 253).

▶ Group members are often prone to **social loafing**, giving less effort and making other group members pick up their slack (pp. 254–255).

▶ **Networks** are patterns of interaction governing who speaks with whom in a group. The member who sends and receives the most messages has the highest degree of centrality; at the other end of the spectrum is isolation (p. 255).

▶ In a **chain network**, information is passed from one member to the next rather than shared among members (pp. 256–257).

▶ In an **all-channel network**, all members are equidistant and all interact with each other (p. 257).

▶ In a **wheel network**, one individual is the touchstone for the others (pp. 257–258).

Define the roles individuals play in a group:

▶ **Task roles** involve accomplishment of goals and include information giver, information seeker, elaborator, initiator, and administrator (p. 258).

▶ **Social roles** evolve based on personality traits and members' interests and include harmonizer, gatekeeper, and sensor (pp. 258–259).

▶ **Antigroup roles** put individual needs above group needs and include blocker, avoider, recognition seeker, distractor, and troll (pp. 259–260).

▶ **Role conflict** arises when expectations for behavior are incompatible (p. 260).

▶ Group members with higher status have more power and influence within the group (pp. 260–261).

Explain how a group's cohesion, norms, and individual differences affect group processes and outcomes:

▶ **Cohesion**, how tightly group members have bonded, helps hold the group together in the face of adversity and helps to create a positive climate (pp. 262, 264).

▶ Norms direct the behavior of the group, sometimes negatively, requiring modification (pp. 264–265).

▶ Goals should be specific, arrived at by group decision, clearly defined, supported with the necessary resources, and able to be monitored (pp. 265–266).

▶ Individual differences can create communication challenges in groups—including cultural factors and varying levels of **communication apprehension**, or nervousness about speaking up. Group members also vary in their **assertiveness**—their tendency to use communication openly to accomplish their goals, and their **argumentativeness**—a trait characterized by advocacy for or defense of positions along with the refutation of the positions that other people take (pp. 266–269).

Captain Ray Holt may not have the easiest police squad to command, but his leadership skills make him a respected and effective head of the team. FREMULON/DR. GOOR PRODUCTIONS/3 ARTS ENTERTAINMENT/UNIVERSAL TV/Kobal Collection

LearningCurve can help you master the material in this chapter.
Go to **bedfordstmartins.com/realcomm**.

chapter 10

Leadership and Decision Making in Groups

Captain Ray Holt is finally in charge: as the new commanding officer on *Brooklyn Nine-Nine*, he arrives at his post intent on making the precinct into one of the best in the NYPD. But the motley crew of detectives he inherits may not fit the bill. His two top detectives, the fiercely competitive Amy Santiago and the immature yet effective Jake Peralta, are continually at odds with each other. The mysterious Rosa Diaz doesn't even try to control her temper. Holt's old friend and new second-in-command, Sergeant Terry Jeffords, is on desk duty after, upon becoming a father, he found himself suddenly—and comically—risk-averse.

But Holt is undeterred. He advises his staff that he has high expectations: regulations are to be followed; paperwork is to be properly filed. With his no-nonsense style and an imposing presence, he does not seem like a man to be trifled with. But that doesn't stop the childish Peralta: when Holt insists he wear a necktie, Peralta responds by wearing one around his waist.

But before long, Peralta is wearing that tie, Jeffords is back in action, and Diaz is managing to smile at juries during testimony. Holt earns their respect, loyalty, and even obedience, not by laying down a hard line but by explaining himself. When Peralta asks why it took him so long to get his own command, Holt succinctly explains that it had to do with his coming out twenty-five years earlier. "The NYPD was not ready for an openly gay detective," Holt says. "But then, the old guard died out, and suddenly they couldn't wait to show off the fact that they had a high-ranking gay officer. I made captain. But they put me in a public affairs unit. I was a good soldier. I helped recruitment. But all I ever wanted was my own command. And now, I've finally got it, and I'm not going to screw it up" (*Brooklyn Nine-Nine*, 2013).

chapter outcomes

After you have finished reading this chapter, you will be able to

- Describe the types of power that effective leaders employ

- Describe how leadership styles should be adapted to the group situation

- Identify the qualities that make leaders effective at enacting change

- Identify how culture affects appropriate leadership behavior

- List the forces that shape a group's decisions

- Explain the six-step group decision process

- List behaviors to improve effective leadership in meetings

- Demonstrate aspects of assessing group performance

Wat makes a leader? Power? Experience? Decisiveness? In this chapter, we continue our discussion of group communication by examining two additional processes that often emerge in groups: leadership and decision making. These two processes are tightly interrelated: a group's leader affects how the group makes decisions, and the decisions a group makes affect how the leader operates. When leadership and decision making work together in a constructive way, a group stands the best possible chance of achieving its goals. To understand how these processes influence a group's effectiveness, let's begin by taking a closer look at group leadership.

Understanding Group Leadership

It's a word that's constantly tossed about in political campaigns, highlighted on résumés, and used in book titles and biographies. But just what is *leadership*? Scholars have grappled with the task of defining leadership for many years.

Two key terms that show up in many definitions over the years have been *direction* and *influence*. That's because in its most essential form, **leadership** is the ability to direct or influence others' behaviors and thoughts toward a productive end (Nierenberg, 2009). This capacity for influence may stem from a person's power or simply from group members' admiration or respect for the individual. Because influence involves power over others, let's take a look at power—what it is and where it comes from.

Five Sources of Power

If you've ever seen the classic Steven Spielberg film *Jaws*, you know that it is, on the surface, the tale of a small coastal town being terrorized by a nasty, man-eating shark. But at the heart of the tale is the interaction among a group of men, each of whom bears or takes some responsibility for ridding the waters of the treacherous animal. First, there's the town's mayor, whose main priority is protecting the local economy. Second, there's the town's new chief of police, who's thrust into the story when the first body washes ashore. Also playing a role are Matt Hooper, a young marine biologist who studies sharks, and Quint, the war-scarred local shark hunter. Over the course of the film, each man demonstrates leadership that is firmly rooted in the nature of the power he possesses.

Researchers have identified five types of power—legitimate, coercive, reward, expert, and referent (French & Raven, 1959).

- ▶ **Legitimate power** comes from an individual's role or title. The president, the supervisor at work, and the coach of a team all possess legitimate power as elected or appointed leaders. In *Jaws*, the elected mayor of Amity Island, Larry Vaughn, has some degree of legitimate power, as does Martin Brody, the chief of police, though his power is subordinate to the mayor's authority.

- ▶ **Coercive power** stems from a person's ability to threaten or harm others. A harsh dictator who keeps his people under threat of violence or economic hardship holds such power, but so does a boss who threatens to dock or

 QUINT, CHIEF BRODY, and Matt Hooper each bring something different to the shark-hunting mission and derive their power from different sources. © Universal Pictures/Courtesy Everett Collection

demote employees if they step out of line. In *Jaws*, the mayor—whose primary concern is protecting the town's tourist-dependent economy—uses this kind of power to influence or override decisions made by the police chief: he hired Chief Brody, and he can fire him.

▶ **Reward power** derives from an individual's capacity to provide rewards. For example, your boss might offer all the people in your department a paid day off if they work late three nights in a row on an important project. In the film, the mayor relies on reward power: hundreds of local fishermen set out to catch the shark in hopes of winning a monetary reward.

▶ **Expert power** comes from the information or knowledge that a leader possesses. Expert power is divided in *Jaws*. Faced with any other kind of homicide, Brody's credentials as a former New York City police officer might have given him a fair amount of expert power, but as a newcomer without fishing experience, he gets little respect from the islanders. Matt Hooper, who studies sharks, fares a little bit better. But Quint, who has decades of shark-hunting experience, quickly emerges as the true expert, garnering the respect of his crewmates.

▶ **Referent power** stems from the admiration, respect, or affection that followers have for a leader. The popular kids in your high school may have had the power to influence other students' style of dress or way of behaving simply because others admired them. In *Jaws*, Quint demonstrates this kind of power: when he relays his story as a survivor of the USS *Indianapolis*, which sank in shark-infested waters during World War II, Brody and Hooper gain a new sense of understanding of, and admiration for, Quint's obsession with killing sharks.

It's important to note that these types of power are not exclusive of one another; indeed, most leaders wield several, if not all, of these types of power.

Consider the instructor for your course. He or she demonstrates legitimate power as your teacher but may also exercise reward and expert power, providing you with some extra credit and offering valuable information, respectively. As another example, Quint demonstrates legitimate power as captain of his own

COMMUNICATIONACROSSCULTURES

THINK ABOUT THIS

Leaning In versus Gender Judo

Making up 50 percent of the population and 47 percent of the workforce (U.S. Census Bureau, 2012), women are outperforming men in terms of earning college and advanced degrees (Associated Press, 2011; Perry, 2013). But when you look at the highest levels of corporate and public sector leadership, it's clearly still a man's world: in January 2014, a mere 23 of the CEOs of *Fortune* 500 companies were female and the United States Congress had only 99 women (79 out of 435 in the House of Representatives). Leaving aside the reasons for the underrepresentation of half the population in corner offices, consider the communication challenges that women working in male-dominated industries face. What's it like to be the lone woman at the boy's club? And how do women overcome preconceived notions of masculine versus feminine leadership styles?

Facebook CEO Sheryl Sandberg struck a chord with women when she suggested that females in leadership roles take a firmer stand in advocating for themselves—and, by extension, for all women. Her 2013 book *Lean In: Women, Work, and the Will to Lead* encouraged women to stop underestimating themselves and act like men, to stop worrying about appearing "bossy," and to simply be the boss. The phrase "lean in" took hold in the public imagination as stylistic shorthand for women to push themselves outside of their comfort zone and to make the same demands that men typically do. By "leaning in" instead of "pulling back," Sandberg argued, women would be playing by the same rules as men, allowing themselves to be as ambitious—and successful and well compensated—as their male colleagues. When outnumbered in the boardroom, Sandberg explained, it is even more crucial for women to demand their seat at the table.

But other women in similar situations have noted that it may be easier—and more effective—to use more traditional feminine communication techniques when dealing with an entrenched masculine culture. Joan C. Williams interviewed 127 highly successful women and found that adopting masculine communication styles often backfired. "If you're too feminine," Williams explains, "you're perceived as incompetent. But if you're too masculine, you're seen as difficult to work with." Williams suggests what she calls "gender judo" (judo being the Japanese martial art of the "gentle way," which involves overcoming your opponent by using his own momentum to overpower him). In practice, it means reminding men of traditional feminine roles (like that of a mother, daughter, or teacher) with which they are comfortable and using those roles to exert authority. "Be warm Ms. Mother 95 percent of the time," explained one executive "so that the 5 percent of the time when you need to be tough, you can be" (quoted in Williams, 2014).

1 How do these tactics reflect the concept of behavioral flexibility discussed in Chapter 2?

2 Which of these tactics seems more ethical? If adopting a masculine style of leadership—for example, being "bossy"— has proven problematic for women, is it fair for them to rely on stereotypical, gendered leadership roles to communicate?

3 Don't men bear some of the responsibility for ensuring that they communicate competently and ethically with their female supervisors, colleagues, and staff? Do workplaces need to become, essentially, more feminine?

4 Sandberg's work is directed primarily at women in leadership roles. How does her advice affect women with less power? Is Williams's advice more or less salient to women lower on the organizational chart?

vessel as well as expert and referent power. Note also that individuals gain power only if others grant it to them. That's true to some degree even of coercive power: for example, Brody could have chosen to quit his job early on rather than to acquiesce to the mayor. Thus group members often decide to allow a particular individual to lead them.

Shared Leadership

With so many sources of power, it's not surprising that in some groups several individuals take on leadership roles, each drawing from different sources of power. Thus leadership can be shared by a few members of the group who divvy up the power and take control of specific tasks. For example, imagine that your sorority is planning a trip to Jazz Fest in New Orleans. As chair of the social committee, you take care of organizing the group for the event—publicizing the trip and recording the names of individuals who are interested in going. Another sorority sister, Eva, takes care of booking a block of hotel rooms in the French Quarter and negotiating a group rate. Lily, the chapter president, gets in touch with the sister chapter at Louisiana State University to arrange to meet up. Meanwhile, Keisha, your chapter's community outreach chair, organizes a fundraiser on campus in the hope of raising money for Habitat for Humanity in New Orleans so that your sorority may present the organization with a generous check during your visit.

When the talents and powers of each group member are leveraged through shared leadership, members feel more satisfied with the group process and more motivated to perform (Foels, Driskell, Mullen, & Salas, 2000; Kanter, 2009). As a result, the group is more likely to achieve its goals. Probably for these reasons, many businesses and professional organizations in the United States are moving toward a shared-leadership model, whereby people at lower levels of an organization carry out leadership and decision-making responsibilities (Krayer, 2010).

Group Leadership Styles

What is the best way to lead a group? Should you accept input from the members or rule with an iron fist? Do you focus mainly on the task at hand or help resolve relationship problems? It turns out that there is no one "best" style of leadership. Rather, scholars argue that effective group leaders, whether they're leading alone or sharing power with someone else in the group, adapt their leadership styles to the needs of the group or the situation at hand. Five possible styles are discussed here—directive, supportive, participative, laissez-faire, and achievement oriented—each of which works best under different conditions (Gouran, 2003; Pavitt, 1999).

Directive

A **directive leader** focuses on the group's tasks and controls the group's communication by conveying specific instructions to members. This style works best when members are unsure of what's expected of them or how to carry out their responsibilities. Directive leaders can move their group in the right direction by charting next steps in the group's tasks and clarifying the group's goals, plans,

Shared leadership is at the heart of the self-directed work team we describe in Chapter 9, where sharing leadership goes beyond improving group member motivation to allow members to set standards for the group, conduct peer evaluations, bring in new members, and coordinate plans with management. The end result is often goal achievement and a sense of cooperation rather than divisive competition among members.

● *LAW AND ORDER'S* Lieutenant Van Buren never leaves her detectives hanging; she gives them specific and thorough directions for every step of a case. ©NBC/Photofest

and desired outcomes. For example, the leader of a police squad—like Ray Holt, discussed in the chapter opener—would instruct his team specifically as to how they should handle their paperwork or follow complicated regulations.

Supportive

A **supportive leader** attends to group members' emotional and relational needs. This style is especially helpful when members feel frustrated with their task or with each other. Supportive leaders might stress the importance of positive relationships in the group, reminding members of the group's importance, and expressing appreciation for members' talents and work ethic. Consider Tim Gunn of *Project Runway*. As a leader and mentor figure to the aspiring designers, he helps them not only visualize their designs and talk through their frustrations but also encourages team members to communicate with each other, listen to each other, and "make it work." He is always profuse in his praise, and even when a particular design doesn't impress him, he is encouraging and positive in his criticism.

Participative

A **participative leader** views group members as equals, welcomes their opinions, summarizes points that have been raised, and identifies problems that need discussion rather than dictating solutions. This style works well when group members are competent and motivated to take on their tasks but also benefit from their leader's involvement and feedback. Participative leaders do give some assistance and support to group members, but unlike directive or supportive leaders, they tend to guide and facilitate group discussion rather than giving direct instructions or motivational messages. Many online topic forums and blogs are moderated by participative leaders—they allow discussion among members of the group to take off in many directions, and they contribute right along with everyone else. But they also step in when needed to remind inappropriately contributing members of the purpose of the discussion or the accepted rules of discourse.

Laissez-Faire

The **laissez-faire leader**, whom some call a "hands-off" or delegating leader, is the leader who gives up some degree of power or control and gives that power to team members. This style is the absence of involved leadership—the leader trusts others to handle their own responsibilities, does not take part in the group's discussions or work efforts, and provides feedback only when asked. Parks Director Ron Swanson of *Parks and Recreation* is a hilarious parody of this style of leadership—he is a die-hard libertarian who believes that his role as a government employee is to "do as little as possible." Although it may seem like a *lack* of leadership, the laissez-faire leader can actually be effective, particularly with

mature or experienced groups, where just checking in occasionally and seeing if the group has questions is all that is warranted. Ron Swanson is able to remain hands off because he delegates responsibility to his supercompetent deputy director, Leslie Knope.

Achievement Oriented

An **achievement-oriented leader** sets challenging goals and communicates high expectations and standards to members. This style works best when group members are highly skilled and are eager to produce great accomplishments. In addition to setting lofty goals, such leaders encourage outside-the-box thinking, compare the group with other high-performing groups, and keep members focused on tangible outcomes. *Parks and Recreation*'s Leslie Knope has an achievement-oriented style of leadership. She identifies an ambitious goal and then does everything in her power to make that goal happen. Her ambition is often initially at odds with her apathetic coworkers and reluctant community. But her commitment, enthusiasm, and optimism are infectious, and she usually ends up inspiring everyone around her to help pitch in to make it happen.

Leadership Qualities

When leaders are able to adapt their styles to the needs of the groups they guide, they can enhance the productivity and satisfaction of group members in their day-to-day activities. But there are also leaders who have unique qualities that enable them to effect change on a larger scale—be it reforming a school, turning a small company into a huge, multinational corporation, coaching a winning sports team, or inspiring a massive social movement. Let's examine some of these unique qualities.

what about you?

What Type of Leader Are You?

Leadership is the ability to direct or influence others toward a productive end. Leadership behaviors can vary from person to situation. Use the following five-point scale to find out which style(s) of leadership you exhibit: 5 = extremely like me; 4 = somewhat like me; 3 = neither like nor unlike me; 2 = somewhat unlike me; and 1 = extremely unlike me.

_____ 1. I ask a lot of questions to find out what others know.

_____ 2. I usually know or find out the facts and delegate work to group members early on.

_____ 3. I have high expectations and expect everyone to contribute positively.

_____ 4. I watch the emotional reactions of group members to be sure I don't hurt anyone's feelings.

_____ 5. I think that my group members should be able to make their own decisions.

_____ 6. I ask questions and encourage others to participate so they will contribute their ideas.

_____ 7. I organize the group's notes and agenda, paying less attention to individuals.

_____ 8. I figure everyone should share responsibility for making the group successful.

_____ 9. If people aren't participating, I'll reach out to find out why.

_____ 10. I don't give a lot of feedback to group members; they should know what they are doing.

_____ 11. When a problem arises in a group, I present it and then sit back and listen to everyone's responses.

_____ 12. I am comfortable explaining the overall project and then assigning others to specific tasks.

_____ 13. I expect everyone to have high standards for success.

_____ 14. I pay attention to personal problems that may affect the working environment.

_____ 15. I find that group members will be more successful if I just check in on them occasionally.

Sum your answers for the question numbers that follow, noting the areas with the highest score:

_____ (#1, 6, 11) You are a participative leader.

_____ (#2, 7, 12) You are a directive leader.

_____ (#3, 8, 13) You are an achievement-oriented leader.

_____ (#4, 9, 14) You are a supportive leader.

_____ (#5, 10, 15) You are a delegating leader.

A mix of high numbers (12–15) indicates a diverse leadership style; as we point out in this chapter, adapting your leadership style to suit your group's needs is an essential leadership skill.

▶ *Vision.* A principal at a failing high school might have an idea in her mind of what her school would look like if it were functioning more effectively. She might envision students who are engaged in cooperative projects, an active PTA organization, a new library or computer lab, or mentoring partnerships with members of the surrounding business community. **Visionary leaders** are able to picture a new or different reality from what currently exists and consider the bigger, long-range picture of the group's or organization's future (Sashkin & Burke, 1990). They do not just consider how best to reach certain goals, but they also question the very goals themselves and are able to empower group members to take some risks, explore possibilities, and develop creative ideas (Uhl-Bien, 2006). Of course, when leading groups on a day-to-day basis, such questioning may stall the ability to move forward on basic tasks. But when attempting major reforms or trying to get to the root of serious problems, having this kind of vision is a key ingredient of leadership effectiveness (Bennis & Nanus, 1985).

▶ *Charisma.* Although vision may be important for many kinds of leadership, other leaders may be effective because they have an engaging personality and dynamic speaking style. **Charismatic leaders** are vibrant, likable communicators who generate a positive image among their followers. Their charisma can motivate people and make them respond receptively to their leader's ideas (Bono & Ilies, 2006; Cherulnik, Donley, Wiewel, & Miller, 2001). The principal, for example, might at a town meeting speak enthusiastically about the school and her plans, compliment the community, and maybe even tell some tasteful jokes. Her dynamism could help motivate her faculty, her students, their parents, and community leaders to embrace and work toward her goals.

▶ *Initiative.* Our principal may have vision or charisma (or both), but to make major reforms at her school, she is also likely to need the initiative and energy to make these changes a real possibility. **Transformative leaders** see change, adaptation, and growth as the means for groups and organizations to survive. They spark change not only by *having* a new vision but also by conveying that vision clearly to others, showing real passion for the work ahead, and energizing the group toward meeting the goals set forth in the vision. If the principal is able to change her school from a failing one to a highly successful one (that is, to bring reality in line with her vision), she would have to ensure that things actually happen—for example, that her incentives or programs actually make students and teachers work harder and that the hard work results in higher levels of engagement and performance. As Northhouse (2012) explains, "transformational leadership involves an exceptional form of influence that moves followers to accomplish more than what is usually expected of them" (p. 169).

You have likely noticed that many of our most celebrated leaders, like Martin Luther King, Jr., Alice Paul, Winston Churchill,

CONNECT

All types of leaders—visionary, transformative, and charismatic—must have the ability to persuade others to their plan or way of thinking. They must be able to speak persuasively (Chapter 16) in a way that resonates with their audience.

● **ACTIVIST CELEBRITIES** like environmentalist Leonardo DiCaprio use their charisma to bring about social change and awareness for causes. JIM RUYMEN/UPI/Landov

EVALUATING COMMUNICATION ETHICS

Leading the Interns

You are currently working as an editorial assistant at a reputable music magazine, and among your responsibilities is leading a group of young, aspiring summer interns. You find this task especially rewarding because, as a college student, you suffered through a mind-numbing internship in order to get your foot in the door, so you hope that you can make this internship rewarding for the students in your department.

Back when you were an intern, you worked with an assistant named Bradley, who was in a position similar to the one you're in now. Bradley always seemed to pass off his boring, menial tasks—such as filing, answering his boss's e-mail, and setting up appointments—to the interns so that he could sit and listen to new records in an attempt to further his career in rock criticism. You and the other interns were willing to take on just about any task in order to get a good recommendation, but you always slightly resented Bradley, feeling that he had used you and others in your group.

Since you started working long hours at your assistant job, however, you've wondered if Bradley actually had the right idea. Like Bradley, you aspire to be a music critic, and the mundane tasks of your job are beginning to frustrate you. Such tasks are, however, part of your job description—they are what every assistant does.

You want to have time to talk to writers, to write or edit copy, and to be able to sit in on pitch meetings. Bradley kept you from such experiences as an intern because you were too busy fetching lattes for his boss. The problem is, now you need to get lattes for your own boss, and this is keeping you from gussying up your own portfolio. Yet here are new, young interns willing and eager to do anything to get ahead, perhaps even taking over those menial tasks. What should you do?

THINK ABOUT THIS

❶ Was Bradley wrong, or was he just doing what any aspiring journalist would do to free up his time? Do you have a greater understanding for his struggle in light of your own position?

❷ Is it OK to pawn your work off on unpaid college students, even if they're willing to do it?

❸ As the group's leader, do you have a responsibility to these interns to ensure that they get the most from their internship experience?

❹ Looking back at your own internship, is possible that it was more valuable than you think? What might you have learned about the business while answering the boss's e-mails or filing his completed work?

and Mahatma Ghandi, possess all three of these qualities. Dr. King, for example, had a clear vision for the United States and eloquently articulated his seminal "I Have a Dream" speech. He was also charismatic—a gifted writer and speaker with a magnetic personality and a presence that inspired Americans to join him in demanding equal rights for all citizens. And, finally, he was a transformative leader: he motivated those inside the movement to work hard for civil rights, while changing the way others thought about race, rights, and equality. In a similar vein, our effective high school principal may exhibit vision, charisma, and initiative as she successfully transforms her school.

Unethical Leadership

Competent leadership requires more than the ability to adapt your leadership styles to your group or exhibit the effective qualities of vision, charisma, and initiative. Competent leaders also hold both themselves and the group accountable for achieving their results, and they treat all group members in an ethical manner.

However, some leaders use unethical tactics to try to acquire and keep control over an entire group or individual members within a group. As you'll recall from Chapter 8, some people use verbal aggressiveness to try to get what they want or to "bully" others in online environments. Unfortunately, unethical leaders may also make use of such **bullying** tactics, which include harsh criticism, name-calling, gossip, slander, personal attacks, or threats to safety or job security (Smith, 2005). Bullying can also include offensive gestures, ignoring, withering looks, or even just a sarcastic tone of voice. In group situations, a leader might withhold needed information from group members, exclude them from meetings, or insist on unrealistic deadlines or expectations. Unfortunately, such unethical tactics can prove effective for some leaders. Take chef Gordon Ramsay on the reality TV series *Hell's Kitchen*. Aspiring chefs are split into two teams that are pitted against each other in challenges while also preparing and serving dinner to a roomful of diners. Ramsay is very particular about how he wants the food to taste and look. If something is not up to par, he often screams profanities at the contestant responsible for the mistake, showing no qualms about insulting contestants' appearance, ethnicity, or professional background. Although his anger and derogatory statements are usually met by a grim "Yes, chef," and although he may gain the respect of some of the contestants, some do tire of being abused on a regular basis and break down or walk out. And although Ramsay has been very successful with his aggressive, bullying style of leadership, few would consider his outbursts to be ethical.

Although Gordon Ramsay's bullying behavior is aggressive and potentially harmful, it is, at least, transparent. There is little guessing as to what he wants from his staff or why he punishes them. But some unethical leaders might use more sinister means to manipulate their subordinates. Consider, for example, a crime lord who speaks with sweetness and praise but who intimidates by hinting at violent consequences for those who would challenge his control in a particular community. On a smaller scale, a supervisor might manipulate employees by pretending to favor one employee's position while also making a "backroom" deal with an opposing employee. Such maneuvering reflects an unethical leadership style known as **Machiavellianism**, named for sixteenth-century philosopher Niccolò Machiavelli, who advised rulers to use deceit, flattery, and other exploitative measures strategically to achieve their desired ends (Becker & O'Hair, 2007; Christie & Geis, 1970). Machiavellian leaders in groups may, like bullies, have some success in exerting power and control but at a cost—they are liked less and have less credibility (Teven, McCroskey, & Richmond, 2006).

It's also important to be aware that the very talents and qualities mentioned earlier that make leaders effective can also be used for unethical purposes. Some leaders use their charisma or transformative power for self-serving purposes (O'Connor et al., 1995; Yukl, 1999) or in pursuit of a vision that is morally reprehensible. Consider, for example, Adolf Hitler and Osama Bin Laden. Both of these men held visions that were destructive and hateful, and they possessed the personal charisma to motivate others to work toward their vision—resulting in some of the most notorious acts of evil in human history.

In many organizational contexts, bullying behaviors can escalate to illegal harassment, communication that hurts and offends, creating a hostile environment. Victims of bullying may find our tips in Chapter 11 (p. 329) helpful for dealing with such unethical behavior in a group, in an organization, or even in an interpersonal relationship.

● **MACHIAVELLIAN MOBSTER** Don Corleone from *The Godfather* may outwardly seem like a calm family man, but consider the consequences of not taking him up on one of his "offers you can't refuse." The Everett Collection

Culture and Group Leadership

As you'll recall from Chapter 3, culture can strongly shape the way people interact. Let's look at two issues—gender and cultural variations—that prove to be particularly powerful factors when leading a group.

Gender and Leadership

Would you vote for a female presidential candidate? A 2013 poll shows 86 percent of Americans think the country is ready to elect a woman president. And nearly 75 percent think the country will elect one in 2016 (Fox, 2013). But why the concern over a leader's biological sex? Is there really a difference between men and women as leaders?

With a few key exceptions, research has provided little support for the popular notion that men and women inherently lead differently, although the idea has nonetheless persisted. For example, we might assume that men would have a masculine style of leadership, emphasizing command and control, whereas women would have a feminine style of leadership, emphasizing more nurturing relationship environments. Some research has indeed suggested that feminine leaders think of organizations as webs of relationships, with leaders at the center of the web, in contrast to the more traditionally masculine view of organizations as pyramids with a leader at the top. Feminine leaders may also view the boundaries between work and personal life as fluid and may communicate their understanding of employees' need to balance professional and personal obligations (Helgesen, 1990; Mumby, 2000; Rosener, 1990). However, meta-analyses (which examine the combined results from many different studies) have found that men and women do not differ in overall leadership effectiveness (Eagly, Karau, & Makhijani, 1995). In fact, one study (Rutherford, 2001) even notes that men and women's leadership styles are often dictated by factors *other* than sex and gender, such as the general communication style of the group or organization.

Cultural Variations

Two additional leadership factors are the variations we see among cultures, such as whether they are high or low context or value high or low power distance. You may recall that people from high-context cultures (such as Japan) tend to communicate in indirect ways, whereas those from low-context cultures (like the United States) communicate with more verbal directness (Hall, 1976). Imagine, for example, a manager tasked with keeping a team on target to meet a very tight deadline. A leader from a high-context culture might simply present a calendar noting due dates and filled with tasks and competing projects; she would rely on her team to get the point that the deadline is in trouble and expect team members to offer solutions. A leader from a low-context culture, on the other hand, would be more likely to clarify the situation directly: "I'm moving the deadline earlier by two weeks; that means you'll need to accelerate your work accordingly." The ways in which group members respond will also be influenced by culture: group members from a high-context culture might communicate in a similarly indirect way with their leader ("We have some concerns

about the new deadline"), whereas those from a low-context culture would be more direct ("Sorry, we can't make the new deadline").

Power distance is another cultural difference that affects how groups may communicate with their leaders. As we learned in Chapter 3, *power distance* is the extent to which less powerful members of a group, be it a business organization or a family, accept that power is distributed unequally. In a high power distance culture, the members are not likely to challenge their leader's opinions or authority. This means that a leader who wants all members to offer their ideas at a meeting might need to make a special effort to encourage everyone to participate in the discussion. In contrast, in a culture with low power distance, members are likely to offer their opinions and disagree with the leader without much prodding.

Decision Making in Groups

On January 28, 1986, the blue skies above Cape Canaveral in Florida seemed to be ripped open when the U.S. Space Shuttle *Challenger* suddenly exploded shortly after liftoff. One of the worst disasters in NASA history (the second being the explosion of the *Columbia* seventeen years later), it claimed the lives of seven astronauts. Investigation into the tragedy found that faulty fittings (called O-rings) had failed during takeoff, causing the explosion. But a large part of the blame for the disaster was laid on communication failures within NASA. Prior to launch, there had been some concern among NASA engineers that the O-rings might fail, but the shuttle launched in spite of these concerns.

How could a collection of such brilliant minds have committed such a grave error? Although some faulty leadership may have played a role, there were many people involved in the exchange of information as well as in the final decision making. Indeed, decision making in a group is more complex than decision making by one leader or between just two people, and thus it is important to examine the forces that influence the group decision-making process. In the following sections, we examine each of these topics in detail, looking at the *Challenger* disaster specifically as an example of what can go wrong in group decision making.

Groupthink

The *Challenger* disaster is often pointed to as a classic example of **groupthink**—a problem in which group members strive to maintain cohesiveness and minimize conflict by refusing to critically examine ideas, analyze proposals, or test solutions (Janis, 1982). After the disaster, NASA engineers testified that the climate at NASA made them reluctant to voice their concerns if they couldn't back them up with a full set of data (McConnell, 1987). Indeed, the Rogers Commission (1986), which investigated the disaster, noted that had safety concerns been more clearly articulated—and had NASA management been more receptive to concerns raised by engineers from various departments—it is unlikely that *Challenger* would have launched that day.

As you learned in Chapter 8, engaging in productive conflict fosters healthy debate and leads to better decision making. Unity and cohesion are important for groups to operate effectively, but if these qualities are taken to an extreme—that is, if they become more powerful than members' desire to evaluate alternative courses of action—the group can't generate enough diverse ideas to make smart decisions (Miller & Morrison, 2009; Park, 2000). This appears to have been the case at NASA in the 1980s. In a more receptive group climate, a productive conflict over the O-rings might have revealed the problems that the engineers sensed but couldn't quite voice specifically. The following are some symptoms of groupthink that you should be aware of in your group interactions:

▶ Participants reach outward consensus and avoid expressing disagreement so as not to hurt each other's feelings or appear disloyal.

▶ Members who do express disagreement with the majority are pressured to conform to the majority view.

▶ Tough questions are ignored or discouraged.

▶ Members spend more effort justifying their decisions than testing them.

● **SOMETIMES VOICING** dissent is more important than group unity. If the engineers at NASA had shared their concerns, the *Challenger* disaster might not have happened. © Bettmann/ Corbis

One important way to prevent groupthink is to encourage dissent among members and manage it productively (Klocke, 2007). In fact, some of the same practices for handling interpersonal conflict discussed in Chapter 8 can help you deal constructively with disagreements in a group. For example, frame conflicts as disagreements over issues or ideas, not as evidence of a weak character or some other personal shortcoming in particular members. To illustrate, when someone in the group expresses a dissenting viewpoint, don't say, "It's clear that you aren't as dedicated to our cause as I had hoped." Instead, say something like "It looks like we have some different ideas circulating about how to handle this new problem. Let's list these ideas and talk about the possible benefits and risks of each of them." A recent study by Aakhus and Rumsey (2010) supports this point by noting that productive conflict can generate more supportive communication for members of an online cancer support community than simply expecting members to keep dissenting opinions private.

Forces That Shape Group Decision Making

Experts have identified three forces—cognitive, psychological, and social—that strongly affect how groups and their leaders discuss and arrive at decisions (Hirokawa, Gouran, & Martz, 1988). All of them appear to have played some role in the *Challenger* disaster.

Cognitive Forces

Cognitive forces consist of group members' thoughts, beliefs, and emotions. These affect how everyone in a particular group perceives, interprets, evaluates, stores, and retrieves information, which in turn influences the group's decisions. NASA officials who made the fateful decision to launch the *Challenger* shuttle apparently discounted the credibility of key information available to them at the time, and they drew incorrect conclusions from the data. They also wrongly believed that the shuttle system was sound, which made them overly confident in their ability to have a successful launch.

Psychological Forces

Psychological forces refer to group members' personal motives, emotions, attitudes, and values. In the *Challenger* disaster, lower-level NASA decision makers had initially recommended postponing the launch until the day warmed up. But when higher-ups pressured them to reverse their recommendation, they caved in—perhaps because they were worried about losing their jobs if they didn't go along.

The decision makers also changed their attitudes about which criteria to use for postponing a shuttle launch. Previously, NASA rules dictated that a launch wouldn't take place if anyone doubted its safety. But with the *Challenger*, the rule had changed: the launch would proceed unless someone presented conclusive evidence that it was unsafe. Engineers hesitated to express their inconclusive qualms, and so the launch proceeded.

AND YOU?

How do cognitive, psychological, and social forces affect decision making in the groups in which you're currently involved? Have these forces ever caused your group to make a poor decision? If so, how?

Social Forces

Social forces are group standards for behavior that influence decision making. In the *Challenger* disaster, engineers were unable to persuade their own managers and higher NASA officials to postpone the launch. They tried to prove that it was *unsafe* to launch rather than take the opposite (and possibly more effective) tactic: showing that no data existed to prove that the launch was *safe*. Part of the difficulty may have been some loyalty to or pride in the NASA identity. With so many years of successes in the space program, many members may have felt that no project of NASA's could *be* unsafe.

The Problem-Solving Process

As the *Challenger* disaster illustrates, group decision making is complicated and affected by social forces that can hamper communication—sometimes with tragic results. How can groups come to better decisions? To make decisions, groups and their leaders often go through a six-step process (Dewey, 1933). To illustrate these steps, consider EcoCrew, a group of sixteen environmentally active students at a West Coast community college who wish to resolve environmental problems in their community.

Identifying the Problem

The EcoCrew group has scheduled its first meeting in the student union lounge. Susan, the group's founder, is the designated leader. Deciding to adopt a participative leadership style, Susan invites each person to give his or her perception of the problem the group will set out to address before debates or questions occur. Members pipe up with a number of issues and activities they'd like the group to address. One suggests the elimination of plastic bags from campus shops; another wants to address littering on the beaches.

By inviting members to voice their concerns one at a time, Susan is providing an opportunity for the group to identify and define several problems. Once all the members have presented their views, Susan encourages the group to discuss the various proposed definitions of the problem and agree on one that EcoCrew can productively address. The group decides that litter, both on campus and on the nearby beach, is the most immediately troubling environmental issue.

Having defined the problem it wants to address, EcoCrew has gotten off to an effective start. According to researchers, many groups don't spend enough time identifying the problem they want to tackle (Gouran, 2003). Without a clear, agreed-on problem to address, a group can't work through the rest of the decision-making process in a focused way.

Analyzing the Problem

Having decided to tackle litter cleanup as its primary mission, EcoCrew begins to analyze the problem. Susan suggests that members each carry a diary for a week and note how much litter they see and where. When the group meets again the following week, all members agree that the two biggest litter problems in the area are on the beaches and in the wooded areas surrounding the campus parking lots. Several members note that the trash cans on the beaches are not being emptied

CONNECT

Brainstorming and clustering can help you in both public speaking and small group settings. When choosing a topic, both strategies allow you to generate ideas based on your interests, your audience's interests, and your time constraints (Chapter 12). In a group, brainstorming and clustering allow you to identify and discuss solutions from a variety of perspectives to ensure that the solution meets the needs of the group.

often enough by city sanitation workers, causing trash overflow to be blown onto the beach by the ocean wind.

Generating Solutions

Once the EcoCrew team has identified and analyzed the problem, the next step is to come up with a solution. Susan starts asking for ideas from the group and writes them down on a whiteboard to be evaluated later.

This technique, called **brainstorming**, encourages members of a group to come up with as many ideas as possible without judging the merits of those ideas at first. The intent is to prompt fresh thinking and to generate a larger number of potential solutions than a group might arrive at if members evaluated each idea as it came up. As the EcoCrew members throw out idea after idea, the whiteboard grows dense and colorful with possibilities (see Figure 10.1).

Once the members have run out of new ideas, they'll need to narrow down the list. To help them focus on the one or two strongest ideas, Susan invites them to define the criteria that eventual solutions will have to meet. First, Susan reminds them that the primary goal would be to reduce litter on the beach. Another member, Wade, then points out that at this point, the group has no budget, so it needs to limit its initial efforts to tasks that have little or no cost. Another member, Larissa, notes that because the group has a relatively small membership, it should focus on things either that the group can manage on its own or in which the group could encourage nonmembers to participate. The group concludes that an acceptable solution must meet these key criteria.

● **WRITING DOWN** any ideas that your team has on a whiteboard can be a great way to get the creative juices flowing. Punchstock/Getty Images

FIGURE 10.1

SUSAN'S WHITEBOARD

- More trash cans!
  - Can we provide these?
  - Get the city to provide?
- Covered trash cans that keep litter in—wind-resistant?
- Increase city sanitation pickups!
  - Letter writing/e-mail campaign?
  - Contact the mayor?
- Beach cleanup?
  - Massive volunteer beach cleanup event
  - Monthly volunteer beach cleanup?
- Antilitter advertising? "Don't pollute!"
  - Flyers/posters would create more litter.
  - Permanent signs/billboards? $$$$

Evaluating and Choosing Solutions

Once EcoCrew has generated its list of possible solutions, group members have to evaluate the pros and cons of each idea to consider how well it meets the criteria the members have defined. For example, one member, Kathryn, points out that the lack of funding makes replacing the garbage cans out of the question and would make an antilitter advertising campaign difficult, if not impossible. Wade notes that organizing a beach cleanup would cost next to nothing: they could all volunteer to get together to pick up garbage and clean up the beach. Larissa adds that if they get the word out, they'd also be able to attract additional volunteers—and potential new members—from outside the group to participate. Thus the group decides to launch a monthly beach cleanup: a regular social event to raise awareness of the group, encourage non-members to participate and new members to join, and involve little to nothing in terms of cost.

Implementing the Solution

Implementing a solution means putting into action the decision that the group has made. For EcoCrew, this means making plans for the regular beach cleanup. The group focuses first on logistics—setting dates and times. One member, Allison, volunteers to act as a liaison with the county sanitation department to see if it can provide trash bags and picks for the volunteers and to arrange for the sanitation trucks to pick up the trash once it's been bagged.

Larissa adds that, with a bit of legwork, the group could turn the cleanup into a large community event; she volunteers to arrange for an end-of-day gathering and to see if she can get her mother's sandwich shop to donate food. Wade notes that he can probably get his roommate's band to entertain free of charge as well.

Assessing the Results

● **AFTER THEIR BEACH** cleanup, the EcoCrew team needs to assess the results. The first question should be: "Was the beach cleaner after our event?" © 2007 Getty Images

Once a group has implemented its agreed-upon solution, members should evaluate the results. Evaluation can shed light on how effective the solution was and whether the group needs to make further decisions about the problem at hand. For EcoCrew, it will be helpful to assess the first event in terms of how well it met the three key criteria:

▶ Was the beach cleaner at the end of the day as a result of the group's efforts? Before-and-after photos of the beach reveal a very successful cleanup.

▶ Did the event wind up costing the members any money? Thanks to the donations of local restaurants and supplies provided by the county sanitation department, along with free advertising via social networks, the event cost the group absolutely nothing.

▶ Did the event attract volunteers from outside the group? Fifteen nonmembers participated in the cleanup, among them several schoolchildren who attended with their parents.

By revisiting these criteria, the group is able to tweak its plan for the following month's cleanup event. Larissa suggests that the members pitch in a few dollars to place an ad in the local paper thanking the volunteers and donors and announcing the date of the next cleanup. Wade follows up by suggesting that the group make a pitch at the nearby schools to get more local families involved. Kathryn volunteers to submit a brief story about the cleanup, along with photos of the event and the results, to the campus newspaper. And Susan suggests holding a raffle at the next event, with half the proceeds paid out in prizes and half retained by the group, to get a small budget started to cover future ads and expenses.

Leadership in Meetings

EcoCrew was able to identify a problem, create a solution, and implement it very successfully. Much of the planning and implementation took place in meetings. Group leader Susan was able to direct the discussion and manage the deliberations in ways that kept the group focused and invited input from all participants. Indeed, meetings—be they face to face, over the phone, online, or through a combination of media—are an integral part of many group activities. But they are not always successful, and the failure of a meeting often rests on the shoulders of the group leader.

Consider Julia, a freelance Web designer who works from a home office. On Friday, Julia received an e-mail from her biggest client, Jacob, asking her to phone in to a meeting with the sales team to discuss marketing materials related to the launch of the new Web site she's designing for his skateboard manufacturing company. Struggling with several competing deadlines, Julia dreaded spending an hour or two listening to a group of people she'd never met discuss parts of the project with which she had little to do. But she reluctantly confirmed that she could take part in the meeting the following Monday.

After spending the better part of Monday morning reviewing her design for the project and outlining a few ideas for ways it could be teased into the marketing campaign, Julia dutifully dialed in to the conference room at the designated time, only to find herself placed on hold for twenty minutes before the meeting began. What followed was equally frustrating: Jacob spent the better part of an hour describing all aspects of the site to the team of salespeople, who were entirely unfamiliar with the project. Julia—who was responsible only for creating the look and functionality of the Web site and had nothing to do with content or sales—sat miserably watching the clock, grateful that at least the team couldn't see her as she scribbled angry doodles and notes to herself.

Meetings can be integral to group decision making, but they can often be unproductive and frustrating. Ineffective meetings are one of the top time wasters cited by workers: one survey of more than thirty-eight thousand workers worldwide found that people spend more than five working hours per week in meetings, and about 70 percent of the respondents felt that most meetings weren't productive (Microsoft, 2005). In this section, we'll analyze meetings from a communication perspective and consider how they can be best used to arrive at better decisions and solutions. We'll discuss how technology has

AND YOU?

Consider the six steps to problem solving we've just discussed. If Susan, the leader of EcoCrew, had chosen a different leadership style, would this have affected how the problem-solving steps were carried out? If so, how? What has your experience been in solving problems in groups with different types of leaders?

CONNECT

Planning a meeting can be similar to planning a speech, particularly regarding audience analysis (Chapter 12). In both contexts, you must be aware of the expectations and goals of others involved (your audience or attendees): Why are they present? Why should they listen to you? How is the meeting or speech relevant to them? In addition, you need to consider the situational context for the event (location, room setup, and so on) in both contexts to ensure that it won't inhibit communication.

changed meetings—and how it hasn't. Most important, we'll show that effective leadership is crucial to conducting effective and productive meetings.

Planning Meetings Effectively

Let's consider all the reasons why Julia found the meeting we've just described so frustrating. First, it was a bad time: she was struggling to meet deadlines and really didn't want to stop working to sit in on a meeting. Worse, she probably didn't really have to be there either—the client was using the meeting to inform the sales team about the site as a whole, not to discuss Julia's design. Further complicating the issues were the meeting's late start, Julia's unfamiliarity with the sales force, and a medium—speakerphone—that limited Julia's communication with the team. Put simply, the meeting was poorly planned.

Proper planning is crucial for successful meetings. Making a few decisions beforehand and taking steps to clarify goals and logistics for the team can lead to more effective decision making during the meeting itself. There are several steps that group leaders can take to plan meetings more effectively.

Justify the Meeting

Before calling a meeting, a group leader should consider what he or she wants to accomplish and assess whether a meeting is even necessary to meet that goal. If there are no clear goals for a meeting, it's impossible for any goals to be met as a result of it. The leader also needs to ensure that only those whose presence is necessary in order to meet the goals or who would truly benefit from attending are included.

In many cases, meetings can be avoided altogether or made smaller and more efficient by asking team members to contribute information ahead of time or simply picking up the phone to ask someone a question when one arises (Conlin, 2006).

Clarify the Purpose and the Participants

If a meeting is necessary, it is the responsibility of the leader to clearly articulate the goals of the meeting and the roles of everyone who is to attend. Think back to Julia's situation. Her client, Jacob, wants to get his sales force interested and excited about the launch of the Web site. Getting the sales force together to view the beta version and get feedback on it might seem like a good way to brainstorm ideas for marketing. But Jacob failed to clarify what he wanted to accomplish at the meeting and what Julia's role would be. He might have made a more efficient use of Julia's time by discussing elements of the design with her prior to the meeting or asking her to outline a few key features for him to use in the meeting without her actually attending.

Set an Agenda

President Dwight D. Eisenhower noted, "I have often found that plans are useless, but planning is indispensable." Creating a plan is a valuable phase in decision making, even if the plan itself isn't followed to the letter in the end. Setting an agenda is crucial.

Meeting with sales team to discuss marketing strategies for new SlickBoards Web site.

Date: March 24, 2015
Time: 10:00 A.M.–12:00 P.M. (EST)
Location: Conference Room 2. Call-in number 555-555-0823.

AGENDA

I.   Welcome
   A. Quick introduction of core team working on Web site
   B. Introduce purpose of meeting—to discuss the marketing strategies for the new SlickBoards Web site
II. Why do we need a new SlickBoards Web site?
   A. Overview of our current Web site and its deficiencies
   B. Present the concept of the new Web site, why we needed a revamp, and how it improves on the old site
III. What will be on the new SlickBoards Web site?
   A. Outline all the new information about the products that will be on the Web site and how it will increase sales
   B. Explain how clients will be able to customize their SlickBoard directly on the new Web site
IV. How should we market this new Web site?
   A. Discuss the focus of the marketing campaign: What's the message?
   B. Brainstorm how to get the message out
   C. Distill list of ideas; assign roles
V.   Conclusion and follow-up
   A. Take any questions or concerns
   B. Establish next meeting time and what should be accomplished by then

FIGURE 10.2

JACOB'S AGENDA Although Jacob's meeting agenda is very well organized, there is no indication that Julia needs to be present for it or that she plays a role in this meeting.

An **agenda** for a meeting should detail the meeting's subject, goal, logistics, and schedule. It should list or include any materials that participants would need to have read or reviewed in advance of the meeting so that everyone arrives with the appropriate background on the issue. Think of your agenda as a checklist—an essential component of meeting success (Gawande, 2009). A sample agenda for Jacob's meeting is provided in Figure 10.2.

Managing Meetings Effectively

So you now see that meetings can go well—or they can go horribly off track. During a meeting, the leader is responsible for managing the discussion in ways that help the group communicate while remaining focused on the meeting's goal. The following steps can help.

Arrive Prepared

When running a meeting, it's crucial that the leader has done the preparation we described previously. As the leader, if you've planned properly, you are fully aware of your goals for the meeting and familiar with all the background information you'll need. If you can't articulate a goal for the meeting, you probably shouldn't call the meeting at all (*Business Week*, 2005).

Keep the Group Focused

Participants often contribute relevant information during meetings, but they also often get off track. When a member brings up a topic that's not on the agenda or goes off on a tangent, the leader should politely interrupt by simply noting, "We're getting off the subject here," which can bring the group back to the main focus of the meeting (*Business Week*, 2005).

Keep an Eye on the Time

Nobody likes wasting time sitting through a long meeting when a short one would do. Group leaders need to be aware of time constraints to keep their meetings running efficiently and to respect the time pressures on the other members. When large groups are involved or when the agenda includes many topics or issues, it can be helpful to impose *time limits* on certain components of the discussion. When a decision must be made, taking an informal vote on a decision— a tactic called a **nonbinding straw poll**—can help move the group forward.

Manage Distractions

● **ALTHOUGH DR. MINDY LAHIRI** and her colleagues often disagree about how best to run their practice, they're able to work through disputes to manage a well-respected office known for strong patient care. Jordin Althaus/©Fox/Courtesy Everett Collection

Unfortunately, even the best of us can easily become distracted. In particular, the use of cell phones during meetings can really harm group productivity: checking e-mail or texts (or surfing the Web!) is totally inappropriate and often offensive to colleagues. Research shows that cell phone use impacts the way group members perceive individual communication competence (Tolman, 2012). Thus, it's essential that your group comes up with a policy regarding proper etiquette and behavior during its meetings, particularly in regard to cell phone use.

Manage Conflict

As you saw in Chapter 8, the best decisions are usually those that have come from productive conflict (Kuhn & Poole, 2000; Nicotera, 1997). When group members deal with conflict productively, they ask clarifying questions, respectfully challenge one another's ideas, consider worst-case scenarios, and revise proposals as needed to reflect new information and insights. This process leads to sound decisions because it enables group members to generate the widest possible range of ideas as well as test each idea's pros and cons. An idea that survives this rigorous process has a better chance of succeeding in action.

The other advantage of productive conflict is that the group members who have a hand in exploring and arriving at a decision will feel a greater sense of ownership over the decision, which leads to greater commitment. Thus, decisions made through productive conflict have a greater chance of being implemented. That's a good thing, since even the most brilliant decision is useless unless a group puts it into action.

real communicator

NAME: Aaron Tolson
OCCUPATION: Dancer, Choreographer, Instructor

I jump feet first into my work. I am a tap dance instructor, performer, and choreographer, and—together with my voice—I use my feet to champion the art form, promote it worldwide, and share it with others.

Tap is my life. I choreograph, produce, and direct a number of programs and shows, as well as perform and teach around the United States and internationally. As a teacher, I take the role of directive leader, as students come to me from all over the world for instruction on how to learn the art of tap. This type of dance is very popular throughout Europe and also in Russia and in Japan, so I have the pleasure of working with a varied group of international students. Beyond my dance expertise, I also share my own stories of failings and successes in order to help my students navigate the complex (and sometimes difficult) world of professional dance.

I read my classes for their learning style, observe their nonverbal behavior, and adapt my leadership approach accordingly. The pace and tempo of the classes vary, as well as my leadership behaviors. For example, with older students I'm less sarcastic and with younger groups I use more humor.

I've been interested in dance since the age of ten. I also ran track and was able to get a track scholarship to college, where I earned an undergraduate degree in communication. During my time there, I also focused on looking for opportunities to dance wherever I could. By my senior year, I landed a place in the New York Shakespeare Festival tap program, Funk U!

After college, I became a company member in Manhattan Tap. My big break came when I was chosen for a featured role in *Riverdance*. I toured with *Riverdance* for six years as a soloist and dance captain of an extremely talented and motivated group. We performed at Radio City Music Hall, on Broadway, at NBA games, and on stages around the world.

Having become a leader in the tap community, I was made national spokesman for SóDança, a professional dancewear company. Since I was chosen for my expertise, I appreciate the opportunity to try out their tap shoes and offer ideas to make them even better. I've even gotten the chance to help design a pink shoe that represents my daughter. I met my wife when choreographing her tap number for the Miss America Pageant, so I have dance to thank for the two most important ladies in my life.

In an effort to enhance and develop tap opportunities for aspiring dancers, I helped to create Speaking in Taps, a preprofessional company designed to teach youth, as well as Tap2You, a program that offers classes and tap competitions (which I started with a business partner, Derick Grant). Through all these endeavors, I strive to emphasize the rhythm, musicality, and timing of tap with a strong focus on performance and education. I hope to inspire others to do what I did: jump feet first into a dancing career.

For this reason, making decisions by **consensus**—group solidarity in sentiment, belief, or decision—is often a better approach than making decisions by majority vote. According to the consensus approach, everyone must agree on the final decision before it can be implemented. It takes more time than deciding by majority vote, but it can be a powerful way to enhance feelings of ownership and commitment from group members. One caution, however, is to be careful to encourage *genuine* consensus, rather than allowing group members to silence their opposition in order to preserve group harmony!

Summarize Periodically

As a group explores and settles on decisions, it's important that someone (a leader or any member) regularly summarize what has happened. Summaries provide members with opportunities to confirm, correct, or clarify what has occurred so far during the conversation. Summaries thus help ensure agreement, formation of next steps, and how members are to carry out their designated tasks.

Follow Up

After the meeting has concluded, group members should implement their decisions and take stock of the results as well as the experience of working together. A simple follow-up e-mail that details the decisions reached at the meeting can ensure that everyone comes away with the same perceptions and is aware of what each person must do to keep the group moving toward its goal.

Using Meeting Technology Effectively

Technology has changed the nature of meetings in both positive and negative ways. Obviously, the ability to set up virtual meetings through teleconferencing and Internet videoconferencing makes it possible for groups to collaborate over long distances. That's how Julia, the freelance designer, is able to "attend" a meeting with her client and his sales staff without leaving home. Such virtual links can be beneficial for a team that needs to actively communicate about some issue or problem. But it also can be ineffective; the fact that everyone *can* be included doesn't necessarily mean that everyone *must* be included. Julia, for example, did not need to sit in on the meeting with the sales team: she had little to add and gained nothing by being there. Further, the ability to share information with team members quickly and efficiently via e-mail and file sharing has enabled teams to avoid some meetings altogether (Conlin, 2006). Julia and Jacob, for example, might have e-mailed a link to the beta version of the site to the entire sales team rather than having a meeting to discuss it in the abstract.

WIREDFORCOMMUNICATION

THINK ABOUT THIS

Leadership. With Lasers.

Hands-on managers usually like to make some kind of personal connection with all their employees. But how can they do it when employees are spread across several offices, in different cities, even in different countries?

Evernote CEO Phil Libin uses technology to bridge the gap. Huge video monitors, along with webcams, are installed in high traffic areas of both the corporate headquarters in Mountainview, California, and studio office in Austin, Texas. But the monitors are not there for videoconferencing. The idea was to create, essentially, a window from one office to the other to connect the two spaces in a way that would encourage casual chats between coworkers in different places. The connection, Libin explains, helps to foster a cohesive atmosphere between the main office and the satellite studio. "We very specifically wanted to avoid the feeling that if you're not working at headquarters, you're in a second-place office" (Libin, quoted in Bryant, 2012, para 26).

But encouraging interconnectedness between his scattered employees wasn't quite enough for Libin. He wanted a way to be in both offices, even when he couldn't be in either one. And so, enter the robots: Libin can log into "his anybot," a six-foot-tall, mobile "telepresence" (think of a Segway with an iPad on top) and take a virtual stroll around the office, carrying a live feed from his webcam. The robot serves as his eyes and ears and allows him to have casual conversations with employees he meets as he drives his robotic avatar around. Libin also points out that the robot has a laser pointer. "You can shoot lasers, which is just good design," he explains. "You shouldn't build a robot without a laser" (quoted in Bryant, 2012, para. 28).

As a programmer turned CEO, it's probably not surprising that Libin is so eager to embrace technology. But just as he's brought in some new electronic wizardry, he's also gotten rid of some conventional technology. Specifically, employees at Evernote do not have phones on their desks. Because the work they do generally does not involve phone calls, the company discourages chatter in the work space; employees can chat on their company-provided cell phones just by walking to a quiet area. "If you have a phone at your desk, it's just sitting there and you're kind of encouraging people to talk on it. . . . If you're at your desk, you should be working. And that's actually worked really well. I don't think anyone misses phones. Even though it's one big room, it's actually fairly quiet because no one is sitting there talking at their desk" (quoted in Bryant, 2012, para. 12).

1. What advantage does a mobile robot offer over a simple phone call or a video chat? Is it a tool or a toy?

2. What does the use of a robot say about Libin's leadership style? Do you think it's effective?

3. Does the idea of a constant live video stream between two offices seem inviting or invasive to you? Do you think such a channel would encourage competent communication?

4. What kinds of companies do you think are more likely to be early adopters of technology like robots or virtual windows? Do you think their employees would be more receptive than those in other sorts of businesses? Do the same factors affect the acceptability of removing former technology, like phones?

But is there a difference between face-to-face meetings and virtual meetings? Research indicates that face-to-face teams perform better initially. However, once the group is established, virtual teams actually do better at brainstorming, whereas face-to-face teams perform better on tasks that require negotiation or compromise (Alge, Wiethoff, & Klein, 2003; Salkever, 2003). Savvy team leaders, then, will bring their teams together for face time early in the process, if possible, so that team members can get to know one another and get a sense of the others' styles and personalities. But as the teams develop, electronically mediated communication—especially e-mail—can often take the place of face-to-face group meetings.

Evaluating Group Performance

Groups that intend to work together and meet on a regular basis should evaluate their decision-making performance periodically. By assessing how well the group makes decisions, achieves its goals, and solves problems, a group can identify and address areas needing improvement. Regular and consistent assessment helps ensure quality and improvement (Beebe, Mottet, & Roach, 2012). When evaluating your group's performance, it's helpful to assess the group's overall effectiveness as well as the performance of individual members and leaders.

Kowitz and Knutson (1980), scholars with extensive research on evaluating groups, recommend assessing three aspects of a group's performance: the informational, procedural, and interpersonal considerations.

Informational Considerations

Ask yourself whether your group is working on a task that requires everyone's expertise and insights. If not, the group doesn't actually need to be a group! In this case, it should select a different task or assign just one or two members to deal with the current task.

● **THINK ABOUT** whether each group member's expertise is necessary to achieve a goal. If not, those members don't need to be present. Jon Feingersh/Getty Images

If the task does require contributions from all members, how well is the group doing on this front? For example, are members conducting needed research and inviting one another to share information during group gatherings? Does the group know when it needs to get more data before making a decision? Does the group analyze problems well? Come up with creative solutions? Offer opinions respectfully? Elaborate on problems, concerns, and solutions?

By regularly assessing these aspects of information management in your group, you can identify where the group is falling short and address the problem promptly. For instance, if you notice that the group rushes to make decisions without getting all the facts first, you could say something like "I think we need to find out more about the problem before we take action."

Procedural Effectiveness

How well does your group coordinate its activities and communication? Key things to evaluate on this front are how the group elicits contributions, delegates and directs action, summarizes decisions, handles conflict, and manages processes. For example, do some members talk too much while others give too little input? If so, the group needs someone to improve the balance of contributions. Simply saying something like "Allie, I think we should hear from some other people on this subject" can be very effective. Or does your group tend to revisit issues it has already decided on? If so, you can expect many members to express frustration with this time-wasting habit. A leader or another member can steer the group back toward its current task by saying something like "OK, what we've been talking about is . . ." or "I'm not sure revisiting this previous decision is helping us deal with our current problem."

Interpersonal Performance

How would you describe the relationships among the members of your group while everyone is working together to accomplish a task? If these relationships are strained, awkward, or prickly, the group probably won't function effectively. Observe how group members behave on the following four fronts:

▶ Do they provide *positive reinforcement* for one another—for instance, by showing appreciation for each other's contributions and hard work?

▶ Do members seem to feel a sense of *solidarity* with one another—for example, by sharing responsibility for both successes and failures?

▶ Do members *cooperate freely* with one another, fulfilling the responsibilities they've agreed to shoulder and pitching in when needed?

▶ Do members demonstrate *respect* for one another—for example, by keeping disagreements focused on the issues at hand rather than on personal character?

If you can answer yes to these four questions, your group scores high on interpersonal performance.

CONNECT

As you evaluate interpersonal performance, you are essentially determining what type of climate your group has developed. As we discuss in Chapter 8, supportive climates—in which individuals are open to and supportive of one another's ideas—often have an advantage in being effective and achieving goals.

Individual Performance

One of the most important assessments you can make is about yourself and what predispositions you bring to the group. According to Keyton and Frey (2002), **grouphate** is the extent to which you detest (or otherwise feel negatively about) working in groups. To assess grouphate, group members are asked a series of questions about the degree to which they like or dislike working in groups:

▶ I like working in groups.

▶ I would rather work alone.

▶ Group work is fun.

▶ Groups are terrible.

▶ I would prefer to work in an organization in which teams are used.

▶ My ideal job is one in which I can be interdependent with others.

To what extent to you agree or disagree with each of these questions? Your basic orientation to group interaction can influence your communication. It is not always easy to work with others but it is a fact of organizational (and academic) life. This process of self-introspection will foster personal growth and learning.

Conversely, your group can also benefit from systematic assessments of team members. Simple evaluation forms can be created and used to evaluate team members on a variety of qualities. For example, you can rate your team members on the quality of their contributions. Specific questions pertaining to a team member could include the following:

▶ Was the team member prepared for meetings and well informed?

▶ Did the team member meet individual responsibilities and deadlines?

▶ Was the team member respectful and tactful with fellow team members?

▶ Did the team member listen to, understand, and follow the group's discussions?

▶ Were the team member's comments relevant and well timed?

▶ Was the team member open-minded?

▶ Did the team member deal with conflict appropriately and effectively?

Both self-assessment and peer evaluations can provide information that can benefit the group by identifying areas of concern or deficiency and suggest specific areas for improvement. This information will only help improve the group process and decision making. In sum, assessment is healthy for the life and success of a group.

BACK TO ▶ *Brooklyn Nine-Nine*

At the beginning of this chapter, we took a look at Captain Ray Holt, the fictional commanding officer at a New York police precinct on the sitcom *Brooklyn Nine-Nine*. Let's take a look at Holt's leadership in light of what we've learned in this chapter.

▶ In the NYPD, there is a clear hierarchy of legitimate power. As commanding officer, Captain Holt has authority over all of his detectives, but even a captain must defer to the chiefs who outrank him. For Holt, that meant "being a good soldier" and working in the public affairs office for many years. Although that job did not align with Holt's career goals, it helped the department to meet other goals: having a gay (and African American) captain in a high-profile role helped the department to change its image and improve recruitment.

▶ Holt's power is rooted not only in his rank as captain (legitimate power) but also in his experience as a veteran officer who knows how to solve major cases (expert power). As commanding officer, he also has coercive and reward power—he can reward or punish his detectives based on their performance. His personal story, too, affords him an additional degree of referent power: over the course of his long career, Holt overcame prejudices within the department and played a central role in changing the face of the NYPD, something his young, diverse squad might have taken for granted.

▶ In a police squad room, there is an expectation of a directive style of leadership—supervisors lay out clear instructions, and officers are expected to follow those instructions. But Holt knows that, despite their hijinks, his detectives are capable and competent. For this reason, he can take a more achievement-oriented approach, setting goals and providing guidance for meeting those goals.

THINGS TO TRY ▶ Activities

1. LaunchPad for *Real Communication* offers key term videos and encourages self-assessment through adaptive quizzing. Go to **bedfordstmartins.com/realcomm** to get access to:

 LearningCurve Adaptive Quizzes.   ▶ Video clips that illustrate key concepts, highlighted in teal in the Real Reference section that follows.

2. Arrange an interview with the chair, president, or director of an organization to determine how the various groups within the organization operate. How closely do these groups conform to the decision-making process discussed in this chapter? Report what you have learned to the class.

3. Create a chart that lists the four leadership styles described in this chapter (directive, participative, supportive, and achievement oriented). Evaluate the leaders of each of the different groups in which you participate—your boss at work, your professors, your resident assistant in the dorm—in terms of their leadership style. Where do they fall on your chart? Do some fit more than one category? Do some fit none of the categories?

4. Select a city, state, or campus problem that is relevant to the members of your class. Form a group to solve the problem using the six-step decision-making process described in this chapter.

Now that you have finished reading this chapter, you can:

Describe the types of power that leaders employ:

▶ **Leadership** is the ability to influences others' behaviors and thoughts toward a productive end (p. 274).

▶ **Legitimate power** comes from an individual's role or title (p. 274).

▶ **Coercive power** stems from the ability to threaten or harm others (pp. 274–275).

▶ **Reward power** is derived from the ability to bestow rewards (p. 275).

▶ **Expert power** comes from the information or knowledge an individual possesses (p. 275).

▶ **Referent power** stems from the respect and affection that followers have for a leader (p. 275).

Describe how leadership styles should be adapted to the group situation:

▶ A **directive leader** gives specific instructions (pp. 277–278).

▶ A **supportive leader** attends to members' emotional and relational needs; (p. 278).

▶ A **participative leader** views members as equals, inviting collaboration; (p. 278).

▶ A delegating leader, whom some call a "hands-off" or **laissez-faire leader**, allows group members to carry out tasks on their own; (pp. 278–279).

▶ An **achievement-oriented leader** sets challenging goals and has high expectations; (p. 279).

Identify the qualities that make leaders effective at enacting change:

▶ **Visionary leaders** envision the long-range future (p. 281).

▶ **Charismatic leaders** use an engaging personality and dynamic communication style (p. 281).

▶ **Transformative leaders** energize others and make real changes (p. 281).

▶ Unethical leadership behaviors include **bullying**, the use of aggressive tactics, and **Machiavellianism** or leadership by manipulation (p. 283).

Identify how culture affects leadership behavior:

▶ Masculine leadership—valuing hierarchy and control—and feminine leadership—valuing relationships and nurturing (p. 284).

▶ Leaders from high-context cultures tend to make suggestions rather than dictating orders or imposing solutions (p. 284).

List the forces that shape a group's decisions:

▶ **Groupthink** occurs when members avoid challenging the group's ideas or decisions (p. 286–287).

▶ **Cognitive forces** are members' thoughts, beliefs, and emotions (p. 287).

▶ **Psychological forces** refer to members' personal motives, goals, attitudes, and values (p. 287).

▶ **Social forces** are group standards for behavior that influence decision making (p. 288).

Explain the six-step group decision process:

▶ Identify and define the problem (p. 288).

▶ Analyze the problem (pp. 288–289).

▶ Generate solutions by **brainstorming**, coming up with as many ideas as possible; then identifying the criteria that solutions will have to meet (p. 289).

▶ Evaluate and choose a solution (p. 290).

▶ Implement the solution (p. 290).

▶ Assess the results (pp. 290–291).

List behaviors to improve meetings:

▶ Assess whether the meeting is necessary, ensure that those present are necessary, ask for information in advance, articulate goals, and set an **agenda** (pp. 292–293).

▶ To manage the meeting, arrive prepared; keep the group focused; keep an eye on the time, perhaps using a **nonbinding straw poll** manage distractions; manage conflict; summarize periodically; consider making decisions by **consensus,** and follow up (pp. 293–296).

Demonstrate aspects of assessing group performance:

▶ Informational considerations.

▶ Procedural effectiveness (p. 299).

▶ Interpersonal performance (p. 299). Avoid grouphate, or negativity toward working in groups (p. 300).

Though Zappos has nearly 15,000 employees, it's managed to keep its warm, welcoming culture with core values like "Create Fun and a Little Weirdness." © James Leynse/Corbis

✓ **LearningCurve** can help you master the material in this chapter.
Go to **bedfordstmartins.com/realcomm**.

Communicating in Organizations

Where did you get those shoes? If they arrived on your doorstep just thirty-six hours after you clicked on them, chances are they came from Zappos.com. The company, founded in 1999, has earned a reputation for not just offering customers a huge selection of clothing and accessories but also for providing a user-friendly at-home shopping experience, complete with free returns. So, when your favorite classic black Chuck Taylors start wearing out, you don't need to leave the house: just go back to Zappos, click a few buttons, and a fresh new pair is on its way to you. That's one reason Zappos CEO Tony Hsieh called his management book *Delivering Happiness*.

But it's not the only reason. The company's core business, Hsieh says, has been rooted in what he calls the "Three Cs": clothing, customer service, and company culture. And it's the last item on the list that Hsieh feels is the most important: "Our belief is that if we get the culture right, most of the other stuff—like delivering great customer service or building a long-term enduring brand or business—will just be a natural by-product" (Hsieh, 2013, para. 2). For Zappos, the challenge was taking what started as a small, family-like culture to scale as the company grew into a large, thriving organization with close to fifteen thousand employees. That meant formulating a list of core values—such as "Build a Positive Team and Family Spirit" (#7), "Create Fun and a Little Weirdness" (#3), and "Pursue Growth and Learning" (#5)—and using those values as a framework for decision making at every level (Zappos, 2014). Those values, developed with input from Zappos employees, have served as an articulation of the spirit of the company; Hsieh notes that he has hired and fired employees based on those core values (Nisen, 2013).

Hseih's commitment to culture doesn't end at the corporate office. Zappos recently unveiled a new corporate headquarters in downtown Las Vegas that is designed not to rival the sprawling, city-unto-itself model of the famed Googleplex or Apple campuses, but to become a vital part of the surrounding community.

After you have finished reading this chapter, you will be able to

- Describe and compare approaches to managing an organization
- Describe ways in which organizational culture is communicated
- Contrast relational contexts in organizations
- Identify the challenges facing today's organizations

The management at Zappos takes a particular interest in developing a culture within and around the company that shapes communication. Culture and communication play an important part in all **organizations**, groups with a formal governance and structure. You see this in action every day: your college or university, student groups, fraternity, religious community, volunteer organizations, and state and local governments are all actively involved in the process of communicating messages about themselves and their members. This is why we stress that **organizational communication**, the interaction necessary to direct an organization toward multiple sets of goals, is about more than meeting agendas and skills or getting along with moody bosses. It is at work in your life *right now* (Eisenberg, Goodall, & Trethewey, 2013). So it's important that we understand these organizations and how we communicate in them. In this chapter, we'll look at several approaches to managing organizations, issues related to organizational culture, important contexts for communicating in organizations, and common issues facing organizations today.

Approaches to Managing Organizations

For as long as humans have been working together toward shared common goals, we've been trying to figure out how to organize ourselves to achieve success. Whether we're talking about effective ways to build a castle, establish a town in the wilderness, or run a factory, preschool, or student government, it's useful to learn the various approaches to managing organizations. Over the centuries, these approaches have changed quite dramatically, and the changes have had important implications for how people in organizations work together and communicate. In the following sections, we'll take a quick trip through time to see how this evolution has played out, beginning with the classical management approach and moving on to the human relations, human resources, and systems approaches.

Classical Management Approach

In the classic children's novel *Charlie and the Chocolate Factory*, Charlie, an impoverished youngster, wins a tour through the most magnificent chocolate factory in the world, run by the highly unusual candy maker Willy Wonka (originally portrayed in films by Gene Wilder and later by Johnny Depp). As Charlie tours the factory with a small group of other children, he sees an army of small men called Oompa Loompas. Each Oompa Loompa is charged with performing a specific task: some do nothing but pour mysterious ingredients into giant, clanking candy-making machines; others focus on guiding the tour boats that ferry the children along rivers of sweet liquid. Still others work only on packing finished candies into boxes as the candies come off the assembly lines. You could almost compare the chocolate factory to a car and each worker to a specific part with a specific job—seat belt, brakes, steering wheel, and so on.

To Charlie, the factory might be a novelty or a curiosity, but to organizational communication scholars, it's a pretty clear example of the **classical management approach**—an approach that likens organizations to machines

● **WHETHER YOU'RE** part of a fraternity trying to rush new members or part of Greenpeace's efforts to save the oceans, your organization must communicate its beliefs and goals to the outside world. (top, left) Elena Rooraid/PhotoEdit, Inc.; (top right) © Yuriko Nakao/Reuters/Corbis; (bottom, left) © Bob Rowan; Progressive Image/Corbis; (bottom, right) © JimYoung/Reuters/Corbis

with a focus on maximizing efficiency. Not surprisingly, classical management reached its peak during the Industrial Revolution in the nineteenth century—a time when factories and machinery were proliferating rapidly in various parts of the world, particularly Europe, North America, and Japan.

Classical management depends on two central ideas, both of which have strong implications for communication. The first is a **division of labor**, or the assumption that each part of an organization (and each person involved) must carry out a specialized task in order for the organization to run smoothly. This is exactly what you see in *Charlie and the Chocolate Factory:* each worker has a very specific job, and there is little reason for individual workers—or groups of workers on different tasks—to communicate with one another. Classical management approaches also favor **hierarchy**, which refers to the layers of power and authority in an organization. To illustrate, in Willy Wonka's chocolate factory, Willy has the most power to control the working conditions, rewards, and other aspects of life for all the creatures who work in the factory. His team of lower-level "managers" (such as the head of the Oompa Loompas) has somewhat less power. And the assembly-line workers themselves have almost no power at all. As illustrated, communication in such situations usually flows from the top (management) down to the bottom (the lowest-level workers). It's unlikely that a worker pouring chocolate would contact Willie Wonka to make suggestions for improving the factory.

Human Relations Approach

If reading about the classical management approach makes you want to protest that you're a person, not a cog in a machine, you're not alone. Critics of such organizational practices became more vocal during the Great Depression and World War II, times characterized by massive social and economic changes in the United States. For example, scholars Eric Eisenberg, Bud Goodall, and

> **AND YOU?**
> Are you involved with or familiar with any organizations that favor hierarchy and a division of labor? What are the pros and cons for communication in such organizations?

● **THESE OOMPA LOOMPAS** from *Charlie and the Chocolate Factory* are responsible for rowing a boat down the chocolate-filled river and not much else!
© Warner Brothers/Courtesy Everett Collection

Angela Trethewey (2013) discuss the work of Mary Parker Follett (1868–1933), a Boston social worker who developed new and seemingly radical ideas about leadership, community, and communication. She believed that "only cooperation among people working together in groups under a visionary leadership produced excellence in the workplace, the neighborhood and the community" (Eisenberg, Goodall, & Trethewey, 2013, pp. 77–78). That was a far cry from the classical management approach. Follett and others set the stage for the **human relations approach** to management, which considers the human needs of organizational members (enjoying interpersonal relationships, sharing ideas with others, feeling like a member of a group, and so on).

The benefits of this approach came into sharper focus in the 1930s when Harvard professors Elton Mayo and F. J. Roethlisberger conducted an experiment at Western Electric's Hawthorne plant in Cicero, Illinois, in order to discover why employees were dissatisfied and unproductive. The researchers separated workers into two different rooms. In one room, the researchers slowly increased the amount of light; in the other, the amount of light was held constant. Much to the researchers' surprise, both groups of workers showed an increase in productivity, regardless of the amount of light they were exposed to. Why? It turns out that the employees were motivated by the increased attention they were receiving from management rather than the increased amount of light (Eisenberg, Goodall, & Trethewey, 2013).

In organizations managed with the human relations approach, managers express more interest in their employees (for example, asking them how they are doing or giving them praise). They provide incentives for good work and emphasize that "we're all in this together," so employees have a greater sense of belonging to a larger cause or purpose. Organizational members are also encouraged to interact with each other on a more personal level, allowing for greater satisfaction and connectedness with the organization.

Human Resources Approach

The human relations approach was an improvement over the classical one in terms of considering that workers' personal needs are important for their satisfaction and productivity. But it fell short of valuing employees' own perspectives and goals regarding the organization. Thus, the **human resources approach** takes the basic ideas of human relations and goes one step further. Specifically, it considers employees as assets to the organization who can be fulfilled by participating and contributing useful ideas (Eisenberg, Goodall, & Trethewey, 2013; Miller, 2009).

In Chapter 16, we will introduce you to Abraham Maslow and his hierarchy of needs, which asserts that people must fulfill basic needs (such as obtaining food and shelter) before they can achieve higher needs (such as finding friendship, love, and enjoyable work). As you will discover, Maslow's work is particularly useful when discussing persuasive speaking, but it has also had a powerful impact on communication in organizations. For example, managers learned that their workers would be more productive if management allowed them to fulfill their higher-level needs (such as self-worth) in addition to their lower-level needs (such as worker safety). And when given more responsibility and autonomy to achieve their own goals, they perform better and remain motivated, which benefits both the employees and the organization (Eisenberg, Goodall, & Trethewey, 2013).

The human resources approach can also be applied to other organizational situations. Imagine that you're a new member of a synagogue, and your rabbi notices that you have a knack for working with kids. He or she might motivate you to fulfill your potential by volunteering with the Hebrew school class each week. You feel proud of your accomplishments in helping the kids, and your synagogue's educational mission is also being served. Everyone wins.

The Systems Approach

You can see that the human relations and human resources approaches to management have had a huge impact on the plight of organizational members. No longer is an employee a "cog in the machine" as in the classical approach; an employee is now a person with feelings and ambitions who is a valuable, contributing member of an organization. But there is another approach to management that is less concerned with the uniqueness of individual needs or organizational goals and instead focuses on the interconnectedness of the parts of an organization. The **systems approach** views an organization as a unique whole made up of important members who have interdependent relationships within their particular environment (Monge, 1977). Much like an ecosystem in which plants, animals, and weather patterns all affect one another, so too do the members of an organization, as well as outside forces in the environment: all affect each other and the organization as a whole.

Figure 11.1 shows how a college or university works as a system. Its members include faculty, students, office staff, financial aid staff, and the bursar, all of whom have relationships and interactions with one another. The college exists within an environment, which includes other systems that directly affect it. These other systems might be the city and state where the college is located, the legislature that sets tuition, local employers who offer students full-time or part-time jobs, the families that the students come from or live with, and the high schools that supply many of the students.

Two of the most important components of organizations as systems are openness and adaptability. **Openness** in a system refers to an organization's awareness of its own imbalances and problems. Using our university example, let's say that our college begins receiving messages from local elementary schools that the university's student teachers seem poorly prepared for the classroom. The university has two choices: it can ignore this feedback about the health of its program, or it can look to correct the problem, perhaps restructuring its elementary education program with feedback from local educators, professors, students, and government and policy representatives. The latter choice clearly helps the organization move forward by allowing for change and growth in light of changing times and circumstances. This ability to adjust is known as **adaptability**.

● **THE HUMAN RESOURCES** approach takes into consideration your needs and interests. Tim Klein/Photodisc/Getty Images

AND YOU?

Think of a situation when an organization you belonged to was faced with criticism. Was the organization open to suggestions for change, or was it closed off from such discussions? What was the end result?

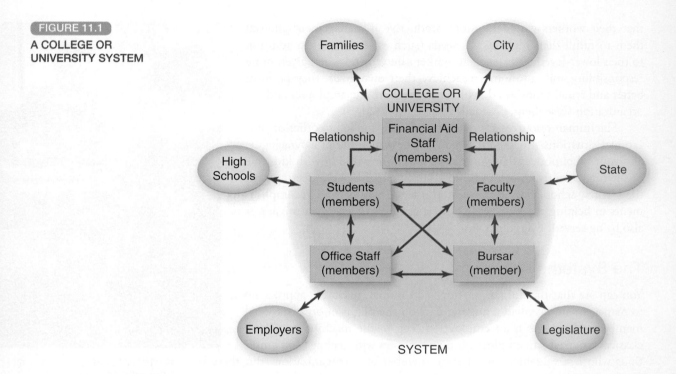

And at the heart of it all is communication. If everyone involved in the system, from students to professors to principals, keeps to themselves and never voices concerns or ideas, the system can become closed and collapse under the weight of its own problems.

Communicating Organizational Culture

The management approaches you learned about in the preceding section can cause one organization to feel quite different from another. If you were working in a nineteenth-century factory that valued classical management, you probably wouldn't have team birthday parties or picnics the way you might under the management of the human resources approach, which values individuals. Yet understanding how different organizations come to have such different atmospheres is more complex than simply understanding their management styles. We must come to understand **organizational culture**, an organization's unique set of beliefs, values, norms, and ways of doing things (Harris, 2002). Of course, *communication* plays a pivotal role in both the shaping and expression of organizational culture. We'll explore how in the sections that follow, looking at the popular Trader Joe's grocery store chain.

Organizational Storytelling

Do you enjoy food shopping? We often don't. The lines are long, the store lighting is glaring, and there's always someone who leaves a cart in the middle of the aisle so that you can't pass. But if you're lucky enough to live near a Trader Joe's, you might have a very different experience when purchasing groceries: employees smile and recommend their favorite salsa, food prices remain reasonable despite nationwide increases, and the colorful South Seas décor gives the place a bold, fun appearance. This is because Trader Joe's has developed an organizational culture that values a friendly, neighborhood feel while offering quality food from all over the world at seemingly reasonable prices.

One of the ways that Trader Joe's forms and ensures its cultural values is through **organizational storytelling**, the communication of the company's values through stories and accounts, both externally (to an outside audience) and internally (within the company). An organization telling a story isn't so different from a parent telling a story to a young child. Just as fairy tales and children's books teach kids important lessons, like the dangers of talking to strangers, organizational stories help would-be customers and potential members answer the question "What is this company all about?" or "Why should I support or join this organization?" They also help employees and current members of an organization understand why they work for a company or support a particular organization (Aust, 2004; Boje, 1991). James and Minnis (2004) also note that when the organization is a for-profit business, "Good communicators use storytelling to sell products, generate buy-in and develop and cultivate corporate culture" (p. 26).

What Trader Joe's stories communicate and shape its organizational culture? First, consider the store's South Pacific ambiance: the employees wear Hawaiian shirts, and hand-lettered signs feature tropical icons like palm trees and coconuts. Trader Joe's also tells stories of its ability to acquire fine merchandise at low prices—someone with really nice penmanship takes the time to write puns on a giant chalkboard ("Leaf it to us to give you your favorite bagged salads"). Trader Joe's Web site and newsletter (*Trader Joe's Fearless Flyer*) present fun drawings, facts about the company, and cleverly written highlights of featured products. (Is anyone up for some Spanish gazpacho soup or Lemon Raspberry Zinger Bundt cake?)

In addition, like many successful organizations, Trader Joe's makes use of metaphors in its storytelling. A *metaphor* is a figure of speech that likens one thing to something else in a literal way, although there is no literal connection between the two (Jacobs & Heracleous, 2006). Trader Joe's metaphor is, essentially, "We are a ship." The employees at Trader Joe's are all crew members, including the captain (store manager) and the first mate (assistant store manager) (Lewis, 2005). Each member is essential to keeping the ship running, which makes for friendly employees and happy customers.

Trader Joe's also makes use of stories about **organizational heroes**, individuals who have achieved great things for the organization through persistence and commitment, often in the face of great risk (James & Minnis, 2004; Schulman, 1996). Trader Joe's employees and would-be customers alike all learn about "Trader Joe" himself, a Stanford University M.B.A. graduate named Joe Coulombe who opened a chain of Pronto Market convenience stores in the Los Angeles area during the 1950s. In the 1960s, 7-Eleven stores invaded southern California, threatening to crush Joe's

AND YOU?

Think about a store that you shop at frequently. What messages do the store layout and décor send customers? Does the store offer any literature or brochures about itself? Does it have a Web site? If so, what do these media communicate about the organization?

● **AT TRADER JOE'S,** employees always have bright smiles—and plenty of tasty food recommendations. Andy Kropa/Redux

business. Rather than admit defeat, Coulombe changed his tactics: trusting that the burgeoning airline industry would entice more Americans to travel—and that those Americans would want to find the foods they enjoyed abroad once they were back home—Coulombe began stocking imported foods other convenience stores didn't carry. Thus began the first Trader Joe's in 1967 (Hoover, 2006).

real communicator

NAME: Kibibi Springs
OCCUPATION: Marketing Communication Professional

I know a lot about organizations. Not only did I work for major corporations for years as an employee, but I also continue to work with them now as a consultant on programs to improve organizations. Although lots of consultants claim to be able to improve performance and profitability, the work I do focuses on changing the *culture* and overall wellness of the organization. Basically, we teach professionals how to redesign their habits and communication skills to improve their quality of life within the structure of the organization and within the framework of a healthy lifestyle. When they learn to engage in low-stress, healthy behaviors, they—seemingly miraculously!—become happier and more productive.

As I ascended the corporate ladder, I found that I couldn't be happy if my job was my whole identity. I'd seen so many people lose their health, their families, and even their sanity because they had no work–life balance. I decided to become an entrepreneur and help those people. I had an undergraduate degree in communication and then earned a master's in consumer and organizational psychology where I focused on the intersection between rising organizational health care costs and the health impacts of uncivil behavior in the workplace. With this combination of strengths, I have been able to work with companies to enact large and small "culture change programs."

Most companies today are concerned about their culture. They want to find and retain good workers. They want to be productive and creative. They want (and need) to adapt to a changing world and new technologies. Younger organizations that come to me are usually in touch with these goals; they ask for help in sustaining the positives and the strong dynamics. I work with both management and employees to develop more sustainable lifestyle habits and more collaboration and relationship skills—which can even include emotional intelligence training.

Bigger, older organizations often come to me in crisis. Things have gone wrong and they are not sure why. In these cases, I have to analyze the entire organization to find the root(s) of the problem. The good news is that they came to me—which means they are open to change! If even one person in the organization says, "We are really bad at 'x'; we need some help," it is an indication that they are willing to take steps to improve the situation. I often start with management in these situations, interviewing them about goals and culture and looking for the commonality of the core groups. Once I have an understanding of the current culture, I teach them how to be more positive, how to relax, how to ask questions, and how to listen. I help them choose behaviors that advance their personal and professional goals within the framework of a healthy lifestyle—and enable them to pass these on to their workforce.

I encourage everyone to find an organization that employs the whole person—one that is positive about its people as well as its products.

Learning About Organizational Culture

Could someone who dislikes people, Hawaiian shirts, and exotic foods find a successful career at Trader Joe's? According to Cohen and Avanzino (2010), **organizational assimilation** is the process by which newcomers learn the nuances of the organization and determine if they fit in. Studies suggest that successful assimilation is often based on a newcomer's ability to figure out and make use of behaviors that will be appropriate and effective in a given organization (Mignerey, Rubin, & Gorden, 1995). Typically, new organizational members are quite motivated to get these behaviors figured out because the uncertainty of not knowing what to do or say can be challenging (Cohen & Avanzino, 2010). Organizations understand this as well and generally seek to help. That's why religious organizations often have new-member classes and employers often have an orientation program to acquaint newcomers with the organization.

At Trader Joe's, for example, new employees are subject to the group "huddle," when all staff members at the store come together in a circle to share information and introduce themselves, perhaps noting where they're from or how long they've been with Trader Joe's. The idea is to make each new employee feel like part of the team (or in this case, crew) and to get to know everyone.

Similarly, an additional perk of working for Trader Joe's is the free samples. Employees are always encouraged to try new products and even make up recipes for everyone to try (Lewis, 2005). This is one way that employees become actively engaged with the products: they feel personally connected to the products and can make heartfelt recommendations to customers, thereby furthering Trader Joe's value of a friendly, interactive shopping experience.

CONNECT

Strategies that help reduce uncertainty in interpersonal relationships (Chapter 7) can also help in new organizational settings. At a new job, you might use *passive strategies* to learn whether joking with peers is acceptable; *interactive strategies*, like asking where to find office supplies; or *active strategies*, like asking a colleague how your new boss reacts to difficult situations. Such strategies help you assimilate faster and more comfortably.

Relational Contexts in Organizations

In the third season of the HBO show *Girls*, the main protagonist, Hannah Horvath, gets an office job. Quitting her position as a Brooklyn barista, she starts freelancing in "advertorial"—ads that also have editorial content—at *GQ Magazine*. However, during her first few days, she struggles to navigate the company's organizational culture. When chatting with a friendly colleague, she's told not to let the others hear her say she "works" at *GQ*—since she's not a full-time employee. In a meeting, she dominates the discussion and shoots down the one idea of another, more established colleague—who later tells her outright that he doesn't like her. And in an especially uncomfortable scene, she tells her new supervisor that she doesn't plan to be there for long, because she wants to be a "real" writer. (Her supervisor, unsurprisingly, is not impressed.) Though Hannah's faux pas are humorous, it *can* be confusing to understand and establish professional relationships if one hasn't worked in an organizational environment before. In the following sections, we'll look more closely at the most common professional relationships.

● **HANNAH HORVATH** in *Girls* is thrilled to start work at *GQ*—but manages to quickly offend a new colleague, along with her supervisor. Craig Blankenhorn/© HBO/Courtesy Everett Collection

Supervisor–Supervisee Relationships

Few relationships are parodied as often as the relationship between supervisors and the people they manage. Think of Homer Simpson reporting to Mr. Burns or the gang on *The Office* dealing with the iconic (and awkward) manager Michael Scott. We often enjoy portrayals of the "bad" boss or the "crazy" boss who causes employees to sit around the lunch table complaining, even though in real life, most bosses are fairly reasonable people. Perhaps we find pleasure in these portrayals because supervisors, inherently, have power over us. Bosses negotiate our salaries and approve our vacation time; they might determine our hours or whether we get promoted. There are supervisory roles in nonworkplace situations as well. Your priest may require you to attend premarital counseling sessions before he will agree to marry you and your fiancé; you have to get your student government president to approve your idea for this year's budget before you can actually plan to do anything with that money. And to achieve anything worthwhile with your supervisor, the two of you must be communicating regularly. The supervisor–supervisee relationship is an important ingredient in maintaining employees' commitment to the job and organization (Jablin, 1987; Teven, 2007a).

If you're involved in a professional, community, or student organization where people are reporting to you, don't be a Mr. Burns! You should know how to get the most out of your conversations with the people you supervise. Often you can improve communication by following just a few simple steps:

► Schedule adequate time for important conversations. For example, if you are the president of a student organization and you need to speak to the treasurer about his messy bookkeeping, don't do it in the ten minutes you have between classes. Set up an appointment to allow adequate time to discuss the problem and generate solutions.

► Ask supervisees for suggestions and ideas. For example, if you're working as a manager in a bank, you might ask the tellers for suggestions to make the work schedule more equitable.

► Demonstrate that you're listening when a supervisee is speaking to you, giving appropriate verbal and nonverbal responses, such as paraphrasing what you're hearing and nodding.

Even if you manage several people, you almost certainly report to a supervisor yourself—and it's important that you be able to communicate competently in this context as well. You can certainly follow the guidelines regarding listening and avoiding distractions that we mentioned earlier, but there are a few additional points to consider when you're the person with less power:

► Spend some time thinking about what you'd like to say to your boss. What are the main points you want to make? What do you hope to achieve through this discussion? It's embarrassing to start talking with a supervisor only to realize that you forgot what you wanted to say.

CONNECT

In addition to the tips we list here, competent communication with your boss will also include competent use of nonverbal communication (Chapter 4). Be sure to make appropriate eye contact, avoid fidgeting, and use an appropriate tone of voice. Shifty eyes, rapid movements, or a sarcastic tone can make you come across as guilty, hostile, or anxious—not desirable when discussing a difficult situation with your manager.

▶ Then spend some time *rehearsing* what you want to say to your manager. You might even ask a friend or family member to rehearse the conversation with you so that you can hear yourself speak.

▶ When you speak with your manager, try to avoid being emotional or hurling accusations such as "You always . . ." or "You never. . . ." It's typically more productive to be specific and logical and to ask for clarification: "When you removed me from the Edwards project, I took that to mean that you didn't think I was capable of handling it. Am I misunderstanding something?"

Mentor–Protégé Relationships

One important relationship in organizations is between mentor and protégé. A **mentor** is a seasoned, respected member of an organization who serves as a role model for a less experienced individual, his or her **protégé** (Russell & Adams, 1997). Research shows that mentoring actually provides a number of key benefits for everyone involved (Jablin, 2001). For one thing, it accelerates the protégé's assimilation into the organization and its culture, which helps the newcomer become productive faster and thus helps the organization meet its goals (particularly in reducing the number of members leaving an organization) (Madlock & Kennedy-Lightsey, 2010). Protégés win too: in one study, protégés reported that mentors helped make their careers more successful by providing coaching, sponsorship, protection, counseling, and ensuring they were given challenging work and received adequate exposure and visibility (Dunleavy & Millette, 2007). Protégés experience greater job satisfaction, and the mentors benefit by receiving recognition as their protégés begin to achieve in the organization (Kalbfleisch, 2002; Madlock & Kennedy-Lightsey, 2010).

Many colleges and universities set up mentorships for incoming students in order to help them adjust to life at the college or perhaps even life away from home. In many cases, second-, third-, or fourth-year students agree to be "big brothers" or "big sisters" to help the newcomers figure out campus parking, where to get a decent sandwich between classes, or which professors to take or avoid. First-year students may then become mentors themselves in future years. As you can imagine, the communication between mentor and protégé changes over time in this example. At first, the protégé may rely quite heavily on the mentor, since everything in the college environment is new and perhaps somewhat frightening. However, as the first-year student adjusts and begins to feel comfortable and self-assured, he or she will rely less and less on the mentor. By the next fall, the protégé may well be on an equal par with the mentor, and the relationship may have turned into a friendship or may have dissolved entirely. Understanding that mentor–protégé relationships go through four distinct stages—initiation, cultivation, separation, and redefinition—can help both

CONNECT

For competent communication in the evolving relationship between mentor and protégé, you need to understand key aspects of the relational context—history, goals, and expectations—discussed in Chapter 1. As a protégé, you might be uncomfortable if your company mentor asked you for professional advice; it might be equally awkward to ask your mentor for advice on searching for a new job when you first meet. Such communication defies expectations.

● **WITH COLLEGE MENTORING** programs, older students help new arrivals to acclimate, from navigating an unfamiliar campus to completing those first daunting class assignments.
© Marty Heitner/The Image Works

AND YOU?

Have you ever been involved in a mentoring relationship? If so, did you find that this relationship benefited you in any way? Did it benefit your organization as well? How would you describe the changes in communication that took place over the course of the relationship?

parties adjust to these natural changes. See Table 11.1 for more on these stages and the communication that takes place during each.

If you are new to an organization—be it a community college, a house of worship, or a job—and a mentorship interests you, you can see if the organization has a formal program. If such a program does not exist, you can still find a mentor, albeit in a more informal way. Consider the following tips (Kram, 1983):

▶ Ask your peers (colleagues, members of a congregation, and so on) to recommend individuals who might be interested in serving as a mentor.

▶ Identify people who have progressed in the organization in ways that interest you and determine whether one of them would make a good mentor.

▶ Build rapport with someone you think would be an effective mentor. Ask if he or she would like to sponsor you in a mentor–protégé relationship. Explain why you think he or she would be a good mentor, and describe your qualifications as a protégé—such as your ability to learn or to cultivate networks quickly.

Peer Relationships

One of the most fun aspects of watching the television show *Grey's Anatomy* is keeping track of the web of relationships among the staff at Seattle Grace Mercy West Hospital. Workplace friendships, secret crushes, full-fledged romances, and bitter resentments could definitely keep your night interesting! Yet these interactions also interest us as scholars because such **peer relationships** reveal the

TABLE 11.1

STAGES IN MENTOR–PROTÉGÉ RELATIONSHIPS

Stage	Communication Goal	Mentor Responsibilities	Protégé Responsibilities
Initiation	Get to know one another	• Show support through counseling and coaching • Help protégé set goals	• Demonstrate openness to suggestions and loyalty to the mentor
Cultivation	Form a mutually beneficial bond	• Promote the protégé throughout the organization (for example, by introducing him or her to influential people) • Communicate knowledge about how to work best with key people and what the organization's culture is	• Put new learning to use (for example, by forging relationships with influential people) • Share personal perspective and insights with mentor
Separation	Drift apart as protégé gains skill	• Spend less time with protégé	• Take more initiative in the organization • Strive for development or promotion
Redefinition	Become peers	• Occasionally provide advice or support as needed	• Stay in touch with mentor at times if additional advice is required

importance of **peer communication**, communication between individuals at the same level of authority in an organization. Researchers, management coaches, and popular magazines warn that Americans are spending more and more time in the workplace, leaving less time for outside personal relationships. Yet we all need friends and confidants. So where do we find them? You guessed it—in the organizations we devote time to, particularly the organizations we work for. Research, however, seems to say some contradictory things about whether or not this phenomenon is healthy.

In a survey of more than five million workers over thirty-five years, 29 percent of employees say that they have a "best friend" at work (Jones, 2004). This statistic matters: out of the approximately three in ten people who state that they have a best friend at work, 56 percent are engaged with, or enjoy, their work, whereas 33 percent are not engaged. Only 11 percent are actively disengaged and negative about their work experience. On the other hand, of the seven in ten workers who do not have a best friend at work, only 8 percent are engaged, whereas 63 percent are not. The remaining third of employees without a workplace best friend are actively disengaged from their work (Gallup, cited in Jones, 2004). These findings have powerful implications for employers: having a workplace best friend makes workers seven times more likely to enjoy their work and consequently be more productive. Perhaps this is the thinking behind organizational initiatives to help employees get to know one another—office picnics, hospital softball teams, and school Frisbee and golf tournaments.

But there's also a potential downside to these workplace intimacies. One is that the relationships may not actually be so intimate after all. *Management Today* warns that professional friendships are often based on what is done together in the workplace. Although that may be beneficial for finding personal support on work-related issues, the friendship can easily wither and die when the mutual experience of work is taken away ("Office Friends," 2005). Privacy and power also come into play, since sharing personal details about your life can influence how others see you in a professional setting. For example, Pamela, an insurance broker from Chicago, did not want her colleagues or boss to know that she was heading into the hospital to have a double mastectomy in order to avoid breast cancer. But she did tell her close friend and colleague, Lisa. When Pamela returned to the office, there was a "get well soon" bouquet of flowers from her boss waiting on her desk. Lisa had blabbed; Pamela felt betrayed and had the additional burden of her colleagues' knowing this private, intimate detail about her life (Rosen, 2004). It's also important to remember that friendships in the workplace—and all organizations—are going to face trials when loyalty and professional obligations are at odds.

Please don't take this to be a warning against making friends in the organizations to which you belong. Relationships with colleagues and other organizational members can be both career enhancing and personally satisfying; many workplace friendships last long after one or both friends leave a job. But it's

● THE *GREY'S ANATOMY* surgeons spend so much time at Seattle Grace Mercy West Hospital that their work life *is* their social life—and what results is a complex web of peer relationships. © ABC/Photofest

When communicating with peers in organizations, remember *communication privacy management* (Chapter 7), which helps you understand how people perceive and manage personal information. You may decide that certain topics, such as your romantic life, are off-limits at work. You must determine for yourself what is private in different relationships—and it's also wise to consider the cultural expectations of your organization before sharing.

important to be mindful as you cultivate such relationships. The following tips can help (Rosen, 2004):

▶ *Take it slow.* When you meet someone new in your organization (be it your job or your residence hall association), don't blurt out all of your personal details right away. Take time to get to know this potential friend.

▶ *Know your territory.* Organizations have different cultures, as you've learned. Keep that in mind before you post pictures of your romantic partner all over your gym locker for the rest of the soccer team to see.

▶ *Accept an expiration date.* Sometimes friendships simply don't last outside of the context in which they grew. You may have found that you lost some of your high school friends when you started college; this point is also particularly true for friendships on the job. Accept that life sometimes works out this way and that no one is to blame.

EVALUATINGCOMMUNICATIONETHICS

More Than Friends at Work

You've begun to notice that two colleagues at work, Cheryl and Michael, are spending an inordinate amount of time together, and you suspect that they may be romantically involved—or at least engaged in a very strong flirtation. They work together on several projects, so it's natural that they spend a lot of time together, but you—along with a few of your colleagues—are beginning to be annoyed by the amount of time the two spend in one or the other's office, chatting about personal and other nonwork issues and generally goofing off during working hours. Both of them are beginning to fall behind on their work, and their slacking off is affecting the performance of your entire department. You've approached Michael about it, noting that "people are beginning to notice" how much time he spends with Cheryl. They cooled it for a few days after that, but gradually, they returned to their old behavior.

Personally, you don't have a problem with the two of them having a relationship outside the office. Although the company has a policy requiring employees to disclose any romantic relationships between coworkers, you think the policy is an invasion of privacy and you don't agree with it at all. But you also know that they're goofing off is starting to affect their work: both are missing deadlines, forcing others on their team to work harder. Making matters worse, their behavior has become a hot topic of gossip around the water cooler, distracting other members of your team from getting their work done.

You've considered speaking to your boss, who works on a different floor and isn't aware of Cheryl and Michael's day-to-day behavior, or even talking to human resources about it. But you're reluctant to "rat them out," especially because you're not even sure that the two are actually romantically involved. What should you do?

THINK ABOUT THIS

❶ What's the real issue here, Cheryl and Michael's relationship or their behavior? If they acted more professionally at work, would the status of their romantic relationship matter?

❷ How does your opinion of the company policy on dating at work factor into your decision? Does the impact of your coworkers' flirtation change your opinion of the policy?

❸ What other approaches could you take to get Cheryl and Michael to change their behavior? Is going over their heads your only option?

Challenges Facing Today's Organizations

Diversity is a word you likely hear a lot nowadays. We use it throughout this book to highlight the importance of understanding and respecting people from various co-cultures with experiences different from our own. But you also hear about companies needing to "diversify" and the importance of tailoring messages to a "diverse" audience. What does it all mean? It means that today's organizations need to branch out and be open to new ideas and experiences. They must make use of new communication technology and address colleagues and other organizations worldwide. Organizational members must find ways to balance the multitude of pressures for their time and must learn to be tolerant of each other's differences and behave competently and respectfully at all times. We examine these important issues in the sections that follow.

Workplace Conflict

Today's diverse workplace requires employees to be able to work with a variety of colleagues who may differ in culture, religion, race, ethnicity, age, gender, and sexual orientation (Lämsä & Sintonen, 2006). In addition, most jobs require employees to work in actual teams (Devine et al., 1999), which entails close interaction with others who have different personalities, ideas, interests, and goals. When people work closely together, conflicts may arise, which can have negative effects on performance, productivity, and the workplace climate (Kolb & Putnam, 1992). Although not all conflict is bad, if it is handled poorly it can foster tension and animosity. According to Gottman (1994), unconstructive reactions include the following:

> CONNECT
>
> Conflict such as criticism, contempt, and stonewalling can arise in other types of interpersonal relationships (Chapter 8) as well. Remember to use cooperative strategies (such as focusing on the issue and considering options and alternatives) to deal with these types of issues.

- ► *Criticism* involves attacking another's personality or character rather than focusing on his or her bothersome behavior. Since organizations value accountability and can blame individuals for any failures or problems, they can be a magnet for criticism. Although criticism isn't necessarily bad in itself, it can become a problem when it becomes pervasive and brings about more harmful behavior.

- ► *Defensiveness* is a self-protective response to another's actions or accusations. Since people have an inherent need to protect themselves, they may lie (perhaps even to themselves) to avoid facing consequences or to cover up mistakes (Knapp, 2008). When something goes wrong in an organization, people often deny responsibility, make excuses, and counterattack (Gottman, 1994). These reactionary behaviors can be very harmful to workplace relationships, even destroying friendships.

- ► *Contempt* includes communicating with truly negative intent. It may include insults, sarcasm, name-calling, ridicule, hostile humor, and/or body language such as rolling one's eyes. The end target is to make the person feel rejected or excluded from a community. Not only is contempt harmful for the workplace, but it also negatively affects people's health and well-being.

- ► *Stonewalling* often follows contempt and involves creating physical and/ or psychological distance from people (or the larger organization) by being unresponsive to efforts to communicate—in other words, withdrawing (Gottman & Levenson, 1992). Other stonewalling behaviors include giving others the silent treatment and disconnecting from the organization in a social manner.

What should you do if you are witness to these types of negative behaviors in an organization—or, worse, are dealing with them yourself? These tips may help you get past interpersonal conflict in a constructive way.

▶ Stop conflicts before they even start. If you are interacting with another person and feel that he or she is behaving in a way that might lead to conflict (such as sending brusque e-mails or ignoring your advice), either give this person the benefit of the doubt or gently bring up your concerns.

▶ If you do find yourself in conflict with another, try to talk to the person one-on-one in a nonthreatening manner. Focus on the specific behavior at hand and try to find a solution or compromise to work more smoothly together in the future.

▶ If you can't get past the conflict, consider bringing in a mediator (such as a supervisor or human resources representative) so that you can both air your concerns in a neutral setting.

Communication Technology

Advances in communication technology—including instant messaging, professional and social networking sites, and videoconferencing—enable members of organizations to communicate more easily, particularly with clients and colleagues who work offsite or in home offices. But they've also introduced new challenges for organizations.

First, there's the question of figuring out which channel is most appropriate for a particular message in an organizational setting. We discussed this point in earlier chapters—you might, for example, text a friend an apology if you're too embarrassed to call her. But there are additional ethical and legal considerations when choosing channels in organizations. If you're a manager, you simply cannot fire someone in an e-mail with the entire department copied. Rather, you would need to have a private face-to-face meeting—or perhaps a phone call if the employee works elsewhere in the country or the world. This is an illustration of **media richness**, the degree to which a particular channel is communicative (Daft & Lengel, 1984, 1986).

Media richness theory suggests that people must consider the number of contact points a particular channel offers for a message (Montoya, Massey, Hung, & Crisp, 2009). Face-to-face communication is the richest because it allows for verbal and nonverbal contact. Speaking on the phone is slightly less rich because it allows for verbal contact and some limited nonverbal contact (tone of voice, rate of speaking, and so on) but removes the opportunity to communicate with body movements. Text messages are even less rich because they lack most nonverbal cues and need not be responded to immediately. The level of richness people expect in their communication vehicles depends on their goals. So if you need to tell the treasurer of your student organization that your meeting has been moved to a different room, you can just text her. However, if you needed to discuss the fact that you noticed a $250 discrepancy on the books, you'd have better communication with a face-to-face conversation.

Research shows that most people do make conscious decisions about which communication vehicle to use based on the situational and relational contexts. Table 11.2 offers a look at various organizational goals and people's perceptions about the most competent channel for achieving those goals.

With such a variety of communication technologies available to organizational members to keep in close contact with one another, it should come as no surprise that people wind up using technology to achieve personal goals as well. Twenty years ago, employees might get in trouble if they spent too much time

WIREDFORCOMMUNICATION

Working Here, There, and Everywhere

When Marissa Mayer took over as CEO at the struggling Internet company Yahoo, it was not surprising that she would implement some of the organizational techniques used at her wildly successful former company, Google. She provided each employee with a new smartphone and free meals. And in a controversial step, she put an end to the company's work-at-home policy: she wanted employees to be collaborating face to face on projects, which meant bringing everyone back into the office. Telecommuting, she explained, was "not what's right for Yahoo right now" (Mayer, quoted in Tkaczyk, 2013, para. 4).

Yahoo was not the first, or the last, company to shift gears on telecommuting: Hewlett-Packard—once a trailblazer in telecommuting—began bringing more workers back into the office to facilitate brainstorming and teamwork almost a decade ago (Holland, 2006), and other companies, like Best Buy, Zappos, and Aetna, have followed suit (Rampell & Miller, 2013).

Reactions to the move were mixed. Mayer, a new mother as well as a new CEO, had a nursery built next to her office at Yahoo so she could take her baby to work. It seemed hypocritical, complained some critics, to deny other parents the option to work at home near their own children. Some worried that employees who used to work well at home would be less productive when faced once again with the distractions of a busy office environment.

But others point out that Mayer was hired to bring the kind of energy and innovation that define Google to its failing competitor, and much of that innovation is spurred by the communication environment at the Googleplex—a sprawling campus designed to keep employees happy while they collaborate and interact face to face (Rampell & Miller, 2013). And, of course, many noted that there is no one-size-fits-all solution, and that different workers, and different types of work, require different policies and norms for where and when and how people should work (Fayard, 2013).

Mayer herself acknowledged that there were trade-offs in both situations. "People are more productive when they're alone," she explained a few months after the announcement. "But they're more collaborative and innovative when they're together" (Mayer, quoted in Tkaczyk, 2013, para. 6).

THINK ABOUT THIS

❶ Mayer's assertion suggests that prioritizing creativity over productivity is "right for Yahoo right now." Must there be a trade-off between productivity and creativity? What factors would influence a company's decision to maximize one over the other?

❷ The change in policy at Yahoo was big news, prompting commentary and blowback far beyond the business pages. Why was a change in human resources policy such big news? Does Mayer's gender play a role?

❸ What does your ideal work situation look like? Do you envision a career spent working at home, in a collaborative office environment, or in some other kind of setting? Do you think Yahoo will be a more or less attractive place to work in the future?

● **IF YOU HAVE** something sensitive to discuss with a colleague, it's better to do so in a face-to-face conversation rather than with a text message. (left) Image Source/Punchstock/Getty Images; (right) GoGo Images/Punchstock/Getty Images

making personal phone calls on the job. So consider how much more distracting it can be to have the ability to bank online, text your romantic partner, and read your brother's blog during the day. Sixty-nine percent of workers admit that they access the Internet at work for non-work-related purposes, and many of them are quite busy on social networking sites like Facebook (Schweitzer, 2007). Richard Cullen of the Internet filtering company SurfControl, for example, states that Facebook alone may be costing Australian businesses $5 billion a year due to decreased worker productivity (West, 2007). What's more is that organizations aren't just concerned about *when* you're updating your status, but also about *what* you're posting—particularly whether or not you're posting comments about the organization or individuals associated with it. Consider, for example, the 2011 case of Natalie Munroe, a high school English teacher who was suspended and faced termination over unflattering comments she made about her students on her personal blog. The blog was relatively anonymous—Munroe never used her full name or identified individual students—and was only followed by nine friends and family members. In addition, the vast majority of posts had nothing to do with the school, the students, or the teaching profession (Werner, 2011). But as with many other high-profile social networking suspensions and terminations, organizations have a keen interest in the way employees represent them in the virtual world.

TABLE 11.2

EMPLOYEE SURVEY OF APPROPRIATE COMMUNICATION CHANNELS FOR ORGANIZATIONAL TASKS

Task	By E-Mail	By Phone	In Person
Edit or review documents	67%	4%	26%
Arrange meetings or appointments	63%	23%	12%
Ask questions about work issues	36%	17%	44%
Bring up a problem with one's supervisor	6%	6%	85%
Deal with sensitive issues	4%	9%	85%

Source: Pew Internet & American Life Project Email at Work Survey, April–May 2002; *N* = 1003; margin of error = ± 3%.

Concerns over employee Internet use have led many organizations to an increase in workplace **surveillance**, or monitoring of employees to see how they're using technology (Ball, 2010; Lucero, Allen, & Elzweig, 2013; Williams, 1993). On some levels, monitoring seems to make sense, particularly when employees are spending time on questionable non-work-related activities. Yet it still raises several important ethical questions: Does monitoring constitute an invasion of employees' privacy? Should workers accept monitoring as a fact of organizational life? These questions are stimulating important research and lively debates in legal circles, but no one seems to have a clear answer. One thing seems obvious, however: in any organization, you'll be much more productive if you limit the amount of time you spend using communication technologies for personal matters.

And what happens if work intrudes on your online life—for example, if your supervisor attempts to "friend" you on Facebook? Although we mention this situation in Chapter 7, it bears repeating. In many work situations this might be an unprofessional move on the part of your supervisor, so business professionals would recommend that you ignore this request (Peluchette, Karl, & Fertig, 2013). Most workplace environments understand that their employees prefer to keep their professional and personal lives separate. However, if you feel that you *must* accept the friend request, you can and should take advantage of your privacy settings to limit what your supervisor can see.

Globalization

Daily direct flights to locations around the world, instant messaging and videoconferencing, international wire transfers—we're living in an age where the other side of the world is an instant message away. Globalization is the buzzword in today's society—you hear it on the evening news, read about it in magazines and newspapers, and see the evidence of it in your everyday life. If you've bought something with a "Made in China" sticker or if you've recently seen a foreign film at your local theater, you've experienced the effects of globalization. **Globalization** is the growing interdependence and connectivity of societies and economies around the world.

Globalization is especially evident in the business world. Increases in communication technology and the convenience of travel have allowed companies to expand their labor force beyond geographical boundaries. More often than not, when you call customer service for help on the DVD player you bought in the United States, the person who picks up the phone is in India. More and more services are being outsourced to developing countries, where wages and operating costs are lower. Take Kenneth Tham, a high school sophomore in California. Most afternoons, he signs on to an online tutoring service, TutorVista. His tutor is Ramya Tadikonda, a twenty-six-year-old mother in Chennai (formerly Madras), India. TutorVista's president, John J. Stuppy, thinks that in this day and age, global tutoring makes the most sense because it makes "high-quality, one-on-one tutoring affordable and

● **HAVE YOU EVER** bought something in the United States with a "Made in China" label? That's globalization at work! Tom Grill/Getty Images

accessible to the masses" (Lohr, 2007). This example highlights a few of the benefits of globalization. U.S. companies benefit from the lower costs of operating in developing countries, and people in those countries benefit from better-paying jobs and a higher quality of life.

Although globalization has torn down some of the barriers to legitimate commerce between countries, it has also made unethical labor practices easier. **Human trafficking**, the recruitment of people for exploitative purposes, is an example of the darker side of globalization. As wages rise in countries that have grown past the early stages of development, there is a need for even cheaper labor to be shipped in from even poorer countries, such as Cambodia and Bangladesh. Workers are lured in by shady labor brokers with false promises of high wages. The workers pay their brokers huge sums of money for this opportunity, only to work for paltry sums of money and often in unsavory working conditions. The story at Local Technic, a Malaysian company that makes cast aluminum bodies for hard disk drives, is a typical example of the forced labor that has increased with globalization. An unnamed executive at Local Technic admits that most of the company's guest workers have been duped into working there. He insists it's not the company's fault: sleazy brokers promise more than the company can afford. However, once the workers arrive and find out they've been taken for a ride, they can't quit, because under Malaysian law, they have had to sign multiyear contracts and surrender their passports to their employer. The parts made at Local Technic are used in virtually every name-brand machine on the market, thus implicating companies like Western Digital that have used components made by Local Technic. Although Western Digital is a member of the Electronics Industry Citizenship Coalition (EICC), which aims to improve industry working conditions, its relationship with Local Technic sends a conflicting message (Wherfritz, Kinetz, & Kent, 2008).

Globalization is a powerful force, and its impact on organizations is undeniable. However, without clear global labor laws, unethical practices such as human trafficking are difficult to control and police.

Work–Life Balance

Diane is a single mom with a seven-year-old son. She works forty hours a week as a receptionist in a medical office and is currently completing class work to become a dental hygienist. She is also the "room parent" for her son's second-grade class and is frequently called on to help bake for classroom celebrations and to chaperone class trips. Luis is a nineteen-year-old sophomore at a state university. He is working two part-time jobs to help meet the cost of tuition and is taking six classes with the hopes of graduating one semester early.

These two individuals have different lives, different goals, and different constraints. Yet they have one thing in common: they are sinking under intense pressures from the organizations in their lives. But their pressures are not just a matter of time management. Diane and Luis also must also manage their **emotion labor**—their display of the appropriate emotions that satisfy organizational role expectations (Miller, Birkholt, Scott, & Stage, 1995). Diane must maintain a cheerful demeanor with patients at the medical office and be supportive to her son's teacher. Luis must show respect for his professors as well as the customers at his job. Controlling or maintaining particular

COMMUNICATIONACROSSCULTURES

Work–Life Balance: Around the Globe and Around the Block

If you're like most Americans, chances are that when you consider a job or career, you think not only about salary but also about benefits. As we learned in this chapter, some of the most appealing companies to work for offer enticements like flexible work hours, in-house dining, child care, and even laundry services. These kinds of perks are relatively new, still largely unexpected, and rare enough that the companies offering them are able to fill their staff rosters with the best talent. But what about the most basic benefit of any job—time away from the job?

Two weeks of vacation time is standard in most U.S. companies—but it's not guaranteed. There are no laws in the United States requiring employers to give their employees any paid vacation time or paid holidays. According to recent studies, the average private sector worker in the United States receives only about nine paid vacation days per year and six paid holidays; almost one in four U.S. workers has no paid time off at all. Of course, most successful U.S. companies do offer vacation time to employees, even if they are not required by law to do so. But lower-wage workers typically receive fewer paid days off (seven on average) than higher-wage workers (an average of thirteen) (Ray, Sanes, & Schmitt, 2013; Ray & Schmitt, 2007).

In other rich nations, things are quite different. Workers in the United Kingdom are guaranteed twenty-eight vacation days per year; in Austria and Portugal, workers get twenty-two vacation days in addition to thirteen paid holidays. Canadians enjoy a minimum of ten vacation days and nine holidays. In some of these nations, employers are even required to provide a little extra pay to help with vacation expenses (Ray, Sanes, & Schmitt, 2013; Ray & Schmitt, 2007).

THINK ABOUT THIS

❶ Does it surprise you that vacation time is not mandated in the United States but is mandated in most other wealthy nations? Do you think that Americans would be more or less productive if they had more vacation time?

❷ Consider the cultural variations discussed in this chapter and in Chapter 3. How is the largely masculine, individualist culture of the United State reflected in U.S. policies on and attitudes toward vacation time?

❸ What are your expectations for paid time off from work? Do you expect to be paid for holidays like Independence Day and Thanksgiving? Are your feelings about religious holidays different from your expectations for national holidays?

---

emotions is important, but over time it can become stressful for employees and can lead to burnout (Maslach, 1982; Teven, 2007b). **Burnout** is a sense of apathy or exhaustion that results from long-term stress or frustration. Burnout hurts its victims as well as the organizations and communities they belong to, as it can lead to negative self-evaluations and emotional exhaustion (Hallsten, Voss, Stark, & Josephson, 2011; Maslach, 1982).

Many workplaces are aware of the dangers of burnout and implement programs to assist employees with **work–life balance**, which involves achieving success in one's personal and professional life. Such programs include flexible work arrangements, paid vacation, and onsite child care. In addition, more and more companies are recognizing that they must top their competitors in offering new and creative work–life options in order to recruit the best job candidates.

Yet even in seemingly supportive work environments, many employees are still unable to balance their work and their personal life. For some, this is a choice: "I never go on vacation," says New York City real estate agent Ellen

● **BURNOUT IS THE HARMFUL** result of prolonged labor and stress, as well as a reminder of how vital it is to strike a manageable balance between work and life. © Jens Büttner/epa/Corbis

Kapit. "And when I do, I have my computer, my Palm, my e-mail, and my phone with me at all times" (Rosenbloom, 2006). For employees like Kapit, choosing the organization over other areas of life may be a sign of ambition, pride, guilt, a sense of overimportance, or simply a love of work, according to Ellen Galinsky, president of the Families and Work Institute (as cited in Rosenbloom, 2006). Yet it can also be a sign of fear. In the most recent annual August Work and Education poll, Gallup reports that 43 percent of U.S. workers exhibit widespread concern about having their benefits reduced and feeling less secure in their jobs (Gallup, 2013). The sad truth remains that in far too many workplaces, there is an unspoken rule that if you take a vacation, put your family first, or have outside interests that take up a lot of time, you are not committed to the organization.

So if you're feeling burned out or on the verge of collapsing from organizational pressure, what should you do? This question is at the forefront of a great deal of research in sociology, psychology, business, and communication. Here are a few tips that various scholars, medical doctors, and other professionals find helpful (Mayo Clinic, 2012):

▶ *Keep a log.* Track everything you do for one week, including school- and work-related activities. Note which activities are nonnegotiable (such as taking a mandatory math class), and decide which other commitments matter the most to you. Consider cutting commitments that are not fulfilling or necessary.

▶ *Manage your time.* Organizing your life can help you feel more in control of your circumstances. Set up specific times to study, work, and have fun—and try your best to stick to your schedule.

▶ *Leave work at work.* Be mindful of the boundary between work and home. Even though you might have the technology to connect to anyone at any time from virtually anywhere, make a conscious decision to separate work from personal time. When you're with your family, for instance, keep your laptop in your briefcase or backpack.

▶ *Nurture yourself.* Set aside time each day for an activity that you enjoy, such as watching a particular TV show, working out, or listening to music.

▶ *Get enough sleep.* Enough said!

Sexual Harassment

There are days when none of us want to be at work or at school, particularly when the weather is nice or there's some other fun activity to take part in. Imagine, however, if your main reason for not wanting to head to class or to your job is fear. For many women and men around the world, a fear of being bullied or harassed in the workplace, on campus, or in other settings is far too common. **Harassment** is any communication that hurts, offends, or embarrasses another person and creates a hostile environment. It can take many forms, such as antagonizing people about their sex, race, religion, national origin, sexual orientation, age, or abilities (Federal Communications Commission, 2008).

One particularly offensive type of harassment is **sexual harassment**, which the U.S. Equal Employment Opportunity Commission (EEOC) (2011) defines as follows: "Unwelcome sexual advances, requests for sexual favors, and other

what about you?

○ Are You Off Balance?

1. Which statement best describes you after you leave work for the day?
   A. I don't think about work again until I arrive the next morning.
   B. I usually check my work e-mail before bed.
   C. I check my work e-mail or make calls three or four times during the evening.

2. A big project requires you to stay late to meet a deadline. You think to yourself:
   A. "This is happening way too much. I'll have to talk to my supervisor about it."
   B. "Oh, well, I'll take off a little early next week to make up for it."
   C. "I wonder if Bud, the night watchman, will bring me a sandwich like he always does."

3. Which statement best describes what you usually do on vacation?
   A. I kick back, relax, and savor the time off.
   B. I check in with my organization at least once so that people know I'm available.
   C. I continue to check my e-mail because you never know when an emergency might arise.

4. It's Tuesday, and you arrive home at 5:30 P.M. How do your housemates or family react?
   A. They say hello and discuss dinner plans.
   B. They act surprised—they never know if you'll be on time or not.
   C. They wonder if you've been fired because you're home so very early.

5. What are you most likely to do to manage your time at home?
   A. I organize chores and write to-do lists.
   B. I try to run errands on days off from work or school.
   C. I tackle chores and errands one at a time as needed.

If your answers are mostly A's: You're leading a fairly well-balanced life—congratulations! You may, however, need to give your organization more priority now and then, particularly during time-sensitive projects.

If your answers are mostly B's: You're striking a great balance! Keep up the good work.

If your answers are mostly C's: You're likely headed toward burnout. Consider some of the strategies we discuss to find more balance.

Source: CNN.com/living (2008). Adapted with permission.

Cultural differences, like those discussed in Chapters 3, 4, and 5, can lead to perceptions of harassment when communicators fail to remember the cultural context. Gestures that are entirely appropriate in one culture might be considered offensive elsewhere. The same can be said for verbal messages such as commenting on an individual's appearance. Companies and communicators should take time to clarify perceptions and adapt messages in order to avoid miscommunication.

verbal or physical harassment of a sexual nature . . . when it is so frequent or severe that it creates a hostile or offensive work environment or when it results in an adverse employment decision (such as the victim being fired or demoted)." Specific conduct that can create such an environment may include sexist remarks, embarrassing jokes, taunting, displays of pornographic photographs, and unwanted physical contact such as touching, kissing, or grabbing. Additionally, organizations are also observing new instances of sexual harassment with an increase in the use of computer-mediated communication in the workplace (Ritter, 2014).

How big a problem is sexual harassment? Well, over 90 percent of *Fortune* 500 companies have reported cases of sexual harassment (Keyton, Ferguson, & Rhodes, 2001), and in fiscal year 2011, the EEOC (2012) received 11,364 complaints of sexual harassment. In addition, the American Association of University Women Educational Foundation notes that nearly two-thirds (62 percent) of two thousand college students surveyed in 2005 said that they had been subject to sexual harassment in college (National Organization for Women [NOW], 2006). Women are most commonly the victims of sexual harassment, but men can also experience its negative effects. In fact, 17.6 percent of the charges filed with the EEOC in 2013 were complaints from men (2012). In addition, three-quarters of lesbian, gay, bisexual, and transgendered (LGBT) students report that they have experienced incidents of sexual harassment on campus (NOW, 2006). These statistics are clearly problematic, but what is even more challenging is that victims often feel shame and embarrassment, preventing many of them from filing official complaints. For example, only 7 percent of students say that they reported sexual harassment to a member of their college or university; LGBT students in particular report that they are extremely angry and embarrassed by their experience (NOW, 2006). Still other victims fear that they will lose their jobs if they speak out—particularly if they are harassed by a boss or other individual with power (Vijayasiri, 2008; Witteman, 1993).

Sexual harassment costs organizations millions of dollars every year and robs individuals of opportunities, dignity, and sense of self-worth. For this reason, organizations have instituted official codes of conduct and clear definitions and penalties for sexual harassment. Many even offer training to educate organizational members. For example, some programs discuss gendered communication, noting that women socialized in feminine nurturing are more likely than men to disclose personal information in the workplace. Men, who tend to be more private about personal information at work, may interpret that behavior as flirting and may respond with a sexual advance. Similarly, men may use smiling, extensive eye contact, and touch as signals that they are sexually attracted to someone, whereas many women use these same nonverbal behaviors to demonstrate their interest in a conversation topic and their support of the person who is speaking (Berryman-Fink, 1993). By understanding and being aware of such communication differences, incidents can be prevented before they happen. Nonetheless, when incidents do occur, victims should recognize that the law is on their side; they should feel empowered to take action against an illegal act. If you are a victim of sexual harassment—or even if you think you might be—consider the following communication strategies:

▶ Clearly and firmly tell the harasser that his or her advances are not welcome.

▶ Immediately report the incident to someone who can assist you: a trusted professor, a counselor, or your boss. If the harasser is your boss, you can contact a representative in your organization's human resources department.

▶ Document each incident in writing. Include a description of the incident, the date, the person or persons involved, and any action you took.

▶ If anyone else in the organization witnessed the harassing behavior, have each witness verify the details of the incident and add that information to your documentation.

Likewise, be careful not to inadvertently behave in a harassing manner yourself. For example, if a friend e-mails a dirty joke or pornographic photo to you at work, *don't forward it to anyone else in the organization*. It's not appropriate under any circumstances. And if your organization is like many, it may well fire you on the spot.

BACK TO ▶ Zappos

At the beginning of the chapter, we took a look at how Zappos endeavors to create a corporate culture that is based on core values. Let's revisit the culture at Zappos now that we've learned a bit more about the way organizations shape, and are shaped by, communication.

▶ Hsieh calls culture the company's "No. 1 priority" (Hsieh, 2013, para. 2). But a nice place to work won't remain a nice place to work for very long if the company fails to grow and be profitable. For that reason, the company's core values reflect not merely worker-centric ideas like pursuing "weirdness" or building team spirit but also bottom-line realities like "do more with less" and "deliver WOW through service."

▶ The company also places a premium on communication (see core value #6, "Build Open and Honest Relationships with Communication"). The new headquarters is designed to foster face-to-face communication with central entrances and corridors where top corporate officers, including Hsieh, work not in posh corner offices but in an open-plan, common work space in full view of coworkers and anyone taking a tour of the space (Spillman, 2013).

▶ One key issue facing large companies today is the debate over flexible time and work-at-home policies. At Zappos, the goal is clearly on keeping employees in a face-to-face environment where they can interact with one another spontaneously.

▶ Another level being explored at the company is the importance of becoming part of the surrounding community. Hsieh envisions a downtown lifestyle that enables Zappos employees to meet and work off campus as much as they do at the office.

▶ Although Zappos is taking clear and committed steps toward cultivating its organizational culture, the company recognizes that culture doesn't form overnight. Hseih feels that the process can take anywhere from five years to a lifetime. "It's not a two-year execution and you're done" (Hsieh, quoted in Nisen, 2013, para. 4).

THINGS TO TRY ▶ Activities

1. LaunchPad for *Real Communication* offers key term videos and encourages self-assessment through adaptive quizzing. Go to **bedfordstmartins.com/realcomm** to get access to:

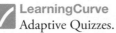 **LearningCurve** Adaptive Quizzes.

▶ Video clips that illustrate key concepts, highlighted in teal in the Real Reference section that follows.

2. Compare two organizations that you belong to or have regular contact with (such as a social organization, a volunteer organization, or a company). Describe the type of management approach at these two organizations. Also think about how the two organizations differ in their organizational culture. Be specific about how their values, artifacts, slogans, or assimilation practices vary.

3. Workplace comedies and dramas typically play off situations that really arise in organizational settings. Watch a few episodes of such workplace sitcoms as *Parks and Recreation* and *Workaholics* or workplace dramas like *Grey's Anatomy* and *The Newsroom* and reflect on the different organizational contexts shown. What are the supervisor–supervisee relationships like? Are there any mentor–protégé relationships? What about peer relationships? How do these various relationships affect the way the organization functions?

4. In this chapter, we talked about some of the challenges that today's organizations face, including work–life balance, sexual harassment, and communication technology. Does your organization—be it a college or university, a club or campus organization, or a business—also tussle with some of these challenges? What challenges are specific to your organization? How might your organization minimize or adapt to some of these challenges?

Now that you have finished reading this chapter, you can:

Describe and compare approaches to managing an organization:

- **Organizations** are groups with a formal governance and structure (p. 306).
- **Organizational communication** is the interaction necessary to direct an organization toward multiple sets of goals (p. 306).
- The **classical management approach** focuses on how to make an organization run efficiently. This approach is dependent on two main ideas: the **division of labor**, the assumption that each part of the organization has a specific function, and **hierarchy**, the layers of power in an organization (pp. 306–307).
- The **human relations approach** considers the human needs of organizational members (pp. 307–308).
- The **human resources approach** also values employees as assets to the organization who can be fulfilled by participating and contributing useful ideas (pp. 308–309).
- The **systems approach** views an organization as a whole in which all members have interdependent relationships. Two key components of this approach are **openness**, an organization's awareness of its problems, and **adaptability**, an organization's allowance for change and growth (pp. 309–310).

Describe ways in which **organizational culture** is communicated:

- Through **organizational storytelling**, the communication of the organization's values through stories to the organization's members and to the outside world (pp. 310–311).
- Using **organizational heroes**, the people who achieve great things for the organization (pp. 311–312).
- Through **organizational assimilation**, the process by which people "learn the ropes" of the organization (p. 313).

Contrast relational contexts in organizations:

- In supervisor–supervisee relationships, the supervisor has power over the supervisee (pp. 314–315).
- In mentor–protégé relationships, the mentor is a respected member of the organization and serves as a role model for a less experienced individual, the protégé (pp. 315–316).

- **Peer relationships** are the friendships that form between colleagues at an organization as a result of peer communication, communication between individuals at the same level of authority (pp. 316–318).

Identify the challenges facing today's organizations:

- Given workplace diversity (of background, culture, and personality), conflict can often arise. If it results in behavior such as criticism, defensiveness, contempt, or stonewalling, then it must be dealt with so that colleagues can continue to work together effectively and peacefully (pp. 319–320).
- Although the wealth of new communication technology has enabled easier communication, there is the added challenge of figuring out which channel to use, taking into consideration **media richness**, the degree to which a particular channel is communicative (pp. 320–321).
- The proliferation of communication technology has increased organizations' use of workplace **surveillance**, or the monitoring of employees to see how they're using e-mail, the Internet, and instant messaging (p. 323).
- **Globalization**, the growing interdependence and connectivity of societies and economies around the world, reduces barriers between countries for business (p. 324). However, unethical practices such as **human trafficking**, the coercion of people into exploitative situations, are also a result of globalization (p. 324).
- Employees engage in **emotion labor**, displaying outward emotions that their organizational duties require, or they take on too many responsibilities or work long hours, often resulting in **burnout**, a destructive form of stress (pp. 324–325). Many struggle with **work–life balance** to find a balance between their work and personal lives (pp. 325–326).
- **Harassment** is any communication that hurts, offends, or embarrasses an individual, creating a hostile environment. One common type is **sexual harassment**, unwanted verbal or physical conduct of a sexual nature that affects an individual's employment, interferes with work performance, or creates an intimidating, hostile, or offensive work environment (pp. 326–329).

Apple fans became accustomed to Steve Jobs releasing new devices or services with a dynamic and instructional keynote. Justin Sullivan/Getty Images

chapter 12

Preparing and Researching Presentations

Since the early 1980s, Macintosh users have sung Apple's praises with a level of enthusiasm and devotion usually reserved for favored sports teams. The lead cheerleader, however, was always the late Steve Jobs, the company's founder and former CEO. Whenever Apple launched a new product or service, Jobs was there, dressed in his trademark black turtleneck and beat-up sneakers, to introduce it.

Jobs was always intimately familiar with the company's products, making him, in many ways, the ideal person to present Apple's latest inventions. Many of the most revolutionary innovations at Apple were created from his own ideas and his frustrations with existing technology. A virtual music store where customers could legally download music for as little as a dollar a song, and then carry them around in their pocket on a device smaller than a deck of cards? That was Jobs's idea. A mobile phone with only one button, a touchscreen, and the ability to add on a seemingly infinite number of applications? Jobs again (Sonnenfeld, 2011).

Jobs was well known for his effective and appropriate use of presentation aids. In many cases, his topic—be it the iPhone, iPad, iPod, or Mac—*was* the presentation aid. But because of his familiarity with his subject—and because he was always sure to be prepared for his speaking event—he was never entirely dependent on those aids. Indeed, when Jobs took the stage in a crowded hall of rabid Mac fans eager to hear about the new iPhone 4 in 2010, the WiFi connection became overwhelmed, and Jobs was unable to connect. But he didn't panic. "He's so well prepared that he knew what was coming next," noted Carmine Gallo, author of *The Presentation Secrets of Steve Jobs*. "It didn't bring the whole presentation to a halt" (cited in Wailgum, 2010, para. 4).

A public figure is expected to speak well, but few public figures—or people in general—are naturally gifted at public speaking. Luckily, the ability to speak appropriately and effectively in a public environment can be learned, developed, and improved. Steve Jobs may have made the process look easy, but think about how ineffective his speeches would have been had he relied entirely on his cool presentation aids without preparing ahead of time.

As you will learn in this chapter, the initial groundwork of becoming a confident, competent speaker and developing strong presentations lies in preparation—namely, clarifying the purpose of your speech, analyzing your audience, choosing an appropriate topic, conducting research, and taking responsibility for your speech. Yet before we even address these issues, you might be wondering why public speaking matters. Here's why it is so important.

The Power of Public Speaking

Jack has what his Irish mother called the gift of blarney. He is an eloquent conversationalist who dominates the discourse in business meetings and at cocktail parties. But put him in front of an audience and he'll panic. Jack's ability to charm friends and colleagues, impress potential dates, and talk his way out of parking tickets disappears completely once the atmosphere changes from informal to formal and his conversational partners are reduced to a more passive audience.

Public speaking always includes a speaker who has a reason for speaking, an audience that gives the speaker attention, and a message that is meant to accomplish a specific purpose (O'Hair, Stewart, & Rubenstein, 2012). It is an incredibly powerful form of communication that has, in fact, changed the world. From the ancient philosophers, who taught debate skills for use in the courts of ancient Greece, to nineteenth-century American abolitionists, who argued to end slavery in the United States, public speakers have charted the course of civilization. Ideally, we should all strive to be informed and conscientious citizens who understand the role of public speaking within a democracy and feel compelled to speak in public on topics that matter to us. Just think about what Jack could do if he used his powers of persuasion on a larger and more formal scale.

Learning how to speak publicly can also play a powerful role in *your* personal and professional life, giving you an edge over less skilled communicators and putting you in a leadership role (Ahlfeldt, 2009; O'Hair & Stewart, 1998). Companies and personnel managers all over the United States have stated that public speaking is one of the most important skills a potential employee can possess (Bianca, 2013; National Association of Colleges and Employers [NACE], 2013).

What if you feel anxious about public speaking? First of all, realize that you are not alone: 75 percent of people experience pounding hearts and sweaty palms when they think about getting up in front of an audience (Richmond & McCroskey, 1998). Second, recognize that through patience and practice, you can counter some of this anxiety, if not conquer it altogether. Completing a course in communication is a great first step (Zabava, Ford & Wolvin, 1993) as is following the advice we lay out here.

This chapter and the chapters that follow show you how to approach public speaking calmly and pragmatically. The first step lies with preparation, the focus of this chapter. The next step focuses on organization, which we will talk about in Chapter 13. Then in Chapter 14, we will discuss the causes of public speaking anxiety and offer techniques to manage any concerns you may have. For now, know that being concerned about giving a speech is natural, but preparation and solid effort can enable you to conquer your nervousness and make you a successful speaker (Bodie, 2010; Schroeder, 2002).

AND YOU?

Have you ever experienced the power of a speech? Think about a specific presentation that you've seen—be it a watershed national event or a more personal experience such as a eulogy at a loved one's funeral. What about the speech stirred your emotions?

Clarifying the General Purpose of Your Speech

In many real-life situations, choosing a topic and purpose for a speech is not a difficult task. You speak because you volunteered—or were forced—to speak on a specific topic for which your expertise is relevant to the situation. For example, you are a public health nurse giving a community presentation on the importance of early screening for breast or prostate cancer. In other cases, the parameters for a speech are quite general: a high school valedictorian or keynote speaker, for example, has to write a speech that both honors and inspires a large group. The possibilities for such speeches are endless. This communication class may provide a similar challenge—finding a speech topic and purpose that fit within your instructor's guidelines, which may range from very specific ("give a five-minute speech defending the constitutional right to free speech") to quite vague ("give a persuasive speech").

Speaking assignments usually fit within one of three general purposes: informative, persuasive, and special occasion.

Informative Speeches

In our information society, managing and communicating information are keys to success (Berrisford, 2006). *Informative speeches* aim to increase your audience's understanding or knowledge by presenting new, relevant, and useful information. Such speeches can take a variety of forms. They might explain a process or plan, describe particular objects or places, or characterize a particular state of affairs. You can expect to give informative speeches in a variety of professional situations, such as presenting reports to supervisors or stakeholders, running training sessions for a company, and teaching in formal education classes.

Consider the TED Talk given by Sarah-Jayne Blakemore, a cognitive neuroscientist, in June 2012 regarding the social and cognitive development of the adolescent brain, in which she also highlights the newest brain imaging technology that tracks how the brain develops in this critical life phase. Through her direct, informative, and engaging style, Sarah connects with her audience and introduces a potentially confusing and challenging topic clearly, complete with attention-grabbing anecdotes, statistics, and humor. A brief excerpt from her presentation is offered in Sample Speech 12.1.

SAMPLE SPEECH 12.1

The Mysterious Workings of the Adolescent Brain

Sarah-Jayne Blakemore

Fifteen years ago, it was widely assumed that the vast majority of brain development takes place in the first few years of life. Back then, 15 years ago, we didn't have the ability to look inside the living human brain and track development across the life span. In the past decade or so, mainly due to advances in brain imaging technology such as magnetic resonance imaging, or MRI, neuroscientists have started to look inside the living human brain of all ages, and to track changes in brain structure and brain function. So we use structural MRI if you'd like to take a snapshot, a photograph, at really high resolution of the inside of the living human brain, and we can ask questions like, how much gray matter does the brain contain, and how does that change with age? And we also use functional MRI, called fMRI, to take a video, a movie, of brain activity when participants are taking part in some kind of task like thinking or feeling or perceiving something. •

Many labs around the world are involved in this kind of research, and we now have a really rich and detailed picture of how the living human brain develops. This picture has radically changed the way we think about human brain development by revealing that it's not all over in early childhood, and instead, the brain continues to develop right throughout adolescence and into the 20s and 30s.

Adolescence is defined as the period of life that starts with the biological, hormonal, and physical changes of puberty and ends at the age at which an individual attains a stable, independent role in society. (Laughter) It can go on a long time. (Laughter) • One of the brain regions that changes most dramatically during adolescence is called prefrontal cortex. So this is a model of the human brain, and this is prefrontal cortex, right at the front. • Prefrontal cortex is an interesting brain area. It's proportionally much bigger in humans than in any other species, and it's involved in a whole range of high-level cognitive functions, things like decision making, planning, planning what you're going to do tomorrow or next week or next year, inhibiting inappropriate behavior—so, stopping yourself from saying something really rude or doing something really stupid. It's also involved in social interaction, understanding other people, and self-awareness. MRI studies looking at the development of this region have shown that it really undergoes dramatic development during the period of adolescence.

• Blakemore defines structural MRI and functional MRI by relating them to a photograph and a movie—two things her audience members are familiar with.

• Blakemore uses humor to connect with her audience.

• Here Blakemore uses a visual aid, a model of the human brain, to explain a difficult concept and to help orient her listeners.

Source: From TED Talk by Sarah Jayne Blakemore, "The Mysterious Workings of the Adolescent Brain," June 2012. Retrieved from http://www.ted.com/talks/sarah_jayne_blakemore_the_mysterious_workings_of_the_adolescent_brain

Persuasive Speeches

Persuasive speeches are very common in daily life and are a major focus of public speaking classes (R. Smith, 2004). *Persuasive speeches* are intended to influence the attitudes, beliefs, and behaviors of your audience. Although they often ask for a *change* from your audience, persuasive speeches can also reaffirm existing attitudes, beliefs, and behaviors: a politician speaking at a rally of core constituents probably doesn't need to change their minds about anything, but she uses persuasive speaking nonetheless to get them excited about her platform or energized for her reelection campaign. In other cases, persuasive speech is a more straightforward call to action. In Sample Speech 12.2, for example, the entertainer and human rights activist Ricky Martin urges members of the international community to step up efforts to put an end to human trafficking. A United Nations goodwill ambassador, Martin offers both facts and statistics related to this global crime, outlines efforts to combat it, and calls for support.

● **AS A MUSICIAN,** Ricky Martin uses melody and lyrics to move his audience. As an activist, he harnesses the persuasive power of statistics as a call to action. Matt Jelonek/WireImage/Getty Images

SAMPLE SPEECH 12.2

Speech at the Vienna Forum

RICKY MARTIN

As a musician, activist, and universal citizen, I thank the United Nations Global Initiative to Fight Human Trafficking for allowing the Ricky Martin Foundation to share our commitment to end this horrible crime. Since this modern-day form of slavery has no geographical boundaries, the truly international reach of this unprecedented forum is an essential platform to combat this global nightmare.

My commitment toward this cause was born from a humbling experience. In my 2002 trip to India I witnessed the horrors of human trafficking as we rescued three trembling girls [who were] living on the streets in plastic bags. Saving these girls from falling prey to exploitation was a personal awakening. ●

I immediately knew the Foundation had to fiercely battle this scourge. That was six years ago. . . . Since then the Foundation expanded and launched People for Children, an international initiative that condemns child exploitation. The project's goal is to provide awareness, education, and support for worldwide efforts seeking the elimination of human trafficking—with special emphasis on children.

This unscrupulous market generates anywhere from $12 to $32 billion annually, an amount only surpassed by the trafficking of arms and drugs. . . . My hope is to secure every child the right to be a child through a not-for-profit organization conceived as a vehicle to enforce their basic human rights in partnership with other organizations, socially responsible corporations, and individuals. . . . ●

● Note how Martin effectively uses a real-life, personal experience to awaken his audience to the horror of the situation.

● Here Martin lays out facts about this international crime and clearly describes his persuasive goal for his speech.

I am certain that our voices, together with the power of other organizations that work against this horrible crime, will continue to galvanize efforts to prevent, suppress, and punish human trafficking.

Changing attitudes and human behavior is difficult, but never forget that multiple small triumphs over a long period of time are tantamount to social change.

As a foundation that supports the objectives of this historic forum that aims to put this crime on the global agenda, be certain that:

We will continue to tell the world that human trafficking exists; we will keep educating the masses; and we will keep working on prevention, protection and prosecution measures in our campaigns to alleviate the factors that make children, women and men vulnerable to the most vicious violation of human rights.

Human trafficking has no place in our world today. I urge you to join our fight. React. It's time. •

Source: From "Speech at the Vienna Forum" by Ricky Martin, United Nations Global Initiative to Fight Human Trafficking, February 13, 2008. Retrieved from www.ungift .org/ungift/en/vf/speeches/martin.html

● Note how Martin ends his speech with a call to action to join the fight against human trafficking.

Special-Occasion Speeches

Special-occasion speeches use the principles of both informative and persuasive speaking for occasions such as introducing a speaker, accepting an honor or award, presenting a memorial, or celebrating an achievement. Almost certainly at some point in your life you will be called on to deliver a speech at a wedding, a toast at a retirement party, or a eulogy at a funeral. Special-occasion speeches are frequently delivered on the world stage as well. In 1993, for example, basketball star and coach Jim Valvano gave what is widely considered one of the most inspiring speeches in sports history when he accepted the ESPY award, a mere eight weeks before he passed away from cancer. His hopeful message, in which he encourages listeners to never give up, served as the inspiration for the V Foundation, which has raised $100 million to fund cancer research nationwide. We can see in Sample Speech 12.3, an excerpt from Coach Valvano's ESPY speech, that uplifting ideas can work well at an occasion like the acceptance of such an important award.

● **COACH VALVANO** takes the ESPY ceremony as an opportunity to share some personal wisdom and persuade the audience of how important it is to live life fully.
Getty Images

● Valvano reveals humility by stating how honored he is to be compared to tennis champion Arthur Ashe—who strove to raise awareness and funds for AIDS research before succumbing to the disease in 1993.

SAMPLE SPEECH 12.3

1993 ESPY speech

COACH JIM VALVANO

I can't tell you what an honor it is to even be mentioned in the same breath with Arthur Ashe. • This is something I certainly will treasure forever. But, as it was said on the tape, and I also don't have one of those things going with the cue cards, so I'm going to speak longer than anybody else has spoken tonight. That's the way it goes. Time is very precious to me. I don't know how much I have left and I have some things that I would like to say. Hopefully, at the end, I will have said something that will be important to other people too.

But, I can't help it. Now I'm fighting cancer, everybody knows that. People ask me all the time about how you go through your life and how's your day, and nothing is changed for me. As Dick said, I'm a very emotional and passionate man. I can't help it. That's being the son of Rocco and Angelina Valvano. • It comes with the territory. We hug, we kiss, we love. When people say to me how do you get through life or each day, it's the same thing. To me, there are three things we all should do every day. We should do this every day of our lives. Number one is laugh. You should laugh every day. Number two is think. You should spend some time in thought. Number three is you should have your emotions moved to tears, could be happiness or joy. But think about it. If you laugh, you think, and you cry, that's a full day. That's a heck of a day. You do that seven days a week, you're going to have something special. . . . •

I just got one last thing, I urge all of you, all of you, to enjoy your life, the precious moments you have. To spend each day with some laughter and some thought, to get your emotions going. To be enthusiastic every day and as Ralph Waldo Emerson said, "Nothing great could be accomplished without enthusiasm," to keep your dreams alive in spite of whatever problems you have. • The ability to be able to work hard for your dreams to come true, to become a reality. . . .

"Don't give up, don't ever give up." That's what I'm going to try to do every minute that I have left. I will thank God for the day and the moment I have. . . .

Cancer can take away all my physical abilities. It cannot touch my mind, it cannot touch my heart and it cannot touch my soul. And those three things are going to carry on forever.

Source: From ESPY Speech by Coach Jim Valvano, "Don't give up. Don't ever give up," March 4, 1993. Retrieved from http://www.jimmyv.org/about-us/remembering-jim /jimmy-v-espy-awards-speech/

• As is common in award speeches, Valvano pays homage to his family—in this case, his parents.

• Valvano encourages the audience with three simple, inspirational things they can do to make every day count.

• Valvano makes an emotional appeal to the audience.

Analyzing Your Audience

As you will quickly discover, **audience analysis**—a highly systematic process of getting to know your listeners relative to the topic and the speech occasion—is a critical step in the speech preparation process (O'Hair, Stewart, & Rubenstein, 2012; Yook, 2004). Because you are asking the audience members to accept your message—to learn new information; to change their attitudes, beliefs, or behaviors; or to recommit themselves to a cause or organization—it is important for you to understand them. You must consider not only their expectations but also the unique situational factors affecting them, as well as their demographic and psychographic background and their potential reactions to your speech. Gaining this understanding will be crucial to choosing and shaping a topic that will resonate with them.

AND YOU?

Have you ever attended a speaking event where the speaker did not behave appropriately for the occasion? How did it make you feel as a listener?

Analyzing expectations in a speaking situation may seem difficult, but you frequently do this work in other communication contexts. As we learn in Chapter 7, relational partners must address each other's expectations in order for the relationship to grow. Similarly, the speaker must remember the audience's expectations for the speaking occasion (level of formality or appropriate language, for example) in order to be competent and successful.

Considering Audience Expectations and Situational Factors

People naturally bring different sets of expectations and emotions to a speech event (O'Hair, Stewart, & Rubenstein, 2012). And as with other forms of communication discussed in this book, competent public speaking involves understanding and acknowledging the expectations of your communication partners—in this case, your audience.

Audiences are likely to have expectations about your speech based on the speaking situation, their cultural norms for public speaking, and even their knowledge about you as an individual or as a speaker. For example, think about the types of expectations you bring to a wedding toast. Would you expect a best man to say the bride is untrustworthy because she cheated on her taxes last year? This would clearly defy tradition and cultural expectations. Similarly, as we learned from some Russian colleagues, an American businessperson giving a speech in Moscow might defy audience expectations by coming right to the point when informing them about a particular technology. In Russia, audiences expect speeches to favor storytelling rather than direct fact sharing.

Audiences can also be influenced by a variety of situational factors that you cannot always plan for. Be aware of issues such as the time of day of your speech, events happening in the outside world, or the comfort and attractiveness of the room. These issues do matter when attempting to hold an audience's attention. Even the size of the audience is a relevant situational factor, as large (more than forty members) or small audiences may demand more or less interpersonal interaction, depending on your topic. To be a competent speaker, you should consider all of these factors when preparing your speech.

Considering Audience Demographics and Psychographics

Although understanding audience expectations and situational factors is an important component of audience analysis, it is only one of the important steps. You should also consider your audience's *demographics* and *psychographics*. **Demographics** are the quantifiable social categories of groups of people. Your analysis might identify statistics for audience members' gender, socioeconomic status (including income, occupation, and education), religious and political affiliations, family status (married, single, divorced, partnered, with children, without children), age, and ethnic background. Other statistics that might be relevant include student enrollment status (full time or part time), student residential status (living on campus or off campus), major area of study, or the geographical regions your fellow students hail from. In addition to understanding their demographic categories, it can be important to analyze your audience's **psychographics**, their psychological qualities such as attitudes, values, lifestyles, behaviors, and interests (Kotler & Keller, 2011; Paul, 2001). Marketing researchers are particularly interested in psychographics, as having such information allows them to more effectively market products to specific targets. To learn about people's psychological profiles, researchers closely monitor Internet traffic, discussions, and trends on social networking sites to see what people think about topics ranging from health and fitness to parenting.

Understanding demographics and psychographics can lead speakers to topics that will be of interest and will carry meaning for specific audiences. For example, one of the most easily quantifiable and useful demographic statistics to consider is the age range of your audience. If you have a good sense of how old most of your audience members are, you'll be able to choose a topic that is relevant to concerns of their generation and ensure that the examples and anecdotes you use in your speech will resonate with the age groups you are addressing.

As we learned in Chapter 5, some audience characteristics will be more *salient*—or significant—in some speaking situations than in others. For example, if your audience members are mostly Latina women in their fifties who have survived breast cancer, their status as survivors is not likely to be salient if you are informing them about the importance of maximizing their annual contributions to their 401(k) plans before retiring in the next fifteen years. But if you are persuading a group to contribute money to the American Cancer Society in order to support new research campaigns, their experience fighting cancer should be firmly in your mind as you develop and deliver your speech.

Now, you're probably thinking, "How can I possibly know all of the demographics and psychographics of my audience members?" You're right, of course. You can't necessarily know that the woman who sits three rows back on the left side of the classroom is an engineering major from a Lithuanian, middle-class family with a part-time job who enjoys tending her virtual garden on Farmville and buys organic produce. But you can look for some general traits and trends. For example, most school Web sites make data available on factors like age, race, gender, and religion and often provide information on the percentage of students receiving financial aid, the number of students living on campus versus those who commute, full-time versus part-time students, and so on. You can also pay attention to general opinion polls on your proposed topic or consider the types of topics your classmates discuss in class or on social media sites.

There are some limitations of demographic and psychographic information that deserve mention here. Sometimes speakers—including politicians and advertisers—mistakenly apply stereotypes to demographic groups or overgeneralize about common opinions and beliefs of group members. And, in some cases, the results of demographic and psychographic data collection can be flawed or even downright wrong (Sprague, Stuart, & Bodary, 2010). Because of this, it's important to be mindful in the way you use this information. For example, your class may be 75 percent Catholic, but that doesn't *automatically* mean that they'll be interested in a speech related to the Church. Additionally, they may not agree with the official positions of the Church (for example, a majority of Catholics favor birth control and a very large percentage of them practice it).

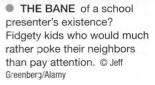
● **THE BANE** of a school presenter's existence? Fidgety kids who would much rather poke their neighbors than pay attention. © Jeff Greenberg/Alamy

AND YOU?

Have you ever found yourself feeling disconnected from a speaker, be it a course instructor or a politician, because he or she failed to consider your age, gender, interests, or lifestyle? Conversely, have you ever found a speaker particularly effective because he or she did consider such factors?

● **ANGELINA JOLIE** often dons stylish all-black outfits in her role as an activist, but she alters her image based on the audience and context: formal wear for a press conference, casual clothes for field work. (left) ROGER L. WOLLENBERG/UPI/ Landov; (right) AP Photo/Boris Heger, UNHCR

That's why it's important to anticipate how your particular audience members might respond to your speech—even before you officially choose your topic and conduct your research.

Anticipating Your Audience's Response

As speech instructors, we openly confess that we get tired of hearing speeches on gun control, abortion, and euthanasia. These topics are surely worthy of thoughtful public discourse, but we've heard the same arguments over and over, and we're interested in learning about new topics. All audience members feel this way from time to time. You may be required to attend meetings at work that have nothing to do with your projects or your job; you may sit through a sermon at your house of worship that feels unrelated to your life experiences. When you are the speaker, it's always useful to remember these experiences and to do your best to ensure that you don't cause your audience to react the same way! Considering a few practical points, and adapting your speech accordingly, can certainly help:

▶ *Consider audience motivation.* Is your audience choosing to listen to your speech or are they required to attend? Voluntary audiences tend to be motivated to listen because they have *chosen* to hear what you say. The audience members in your class, however, are usually required to listen—and some of them may be entirely unmotivated to do so. Therefore, you must work to choose a relevant, engaging topic that they will care about and to engage them with your delivery skills (a topic we'll address in Chapter 14).

▶ *Seek common ground.* Do you and your audience members share certain opinions or experiences with one another? If so, you can capitalize on this **homogeny**—or sameness—by delivering a message that will keep their attention. For example, when his university changed its taxation policies for graduate students receiving stipends, Eduardo delivered a presentation informing his fellow students of the steps they would need to take to ensure proper tax withholding. It didn't matter that the students hailed from assorted fields and departments because they were all stuck dealing with the same confusing tax questions.

what about you?

Assessing Your Audience Analysis

Before you prepare your presentation, you must be sure you have sufficiently considered your unique audience. Complete the following questionnaire prior to each presentation to make sure that your research and planning address your audience's needs, interests, backgrounds, and so on. Depending on the presentation, some factors may be irrelevant. Don't panic if you can't discern every single trait, but you should have a sense of many or most.

Mark the number that most closely matches your feelings of preparedness regarding each statement: 5 = extremely confident; 4 = somewhat confident; 3 = unsure; 2 = somewhat unconfident; and 1 = extremely unconfident.

_____ 1. I know the ages of my audience members.

_____ 2. I am aware of the socioeconomic status of my audience members.

_____ 3. I know the family status (marital status, children) of my audience members.

_____ 4. I know the religious affiliations of my audience members.

_____ 5. I know the political affiliations of my audience members.

_____ 6. I know the ethnic background of my audience members.

_____ 7. I know how familiar my audience members are with my presentation topic.

_____ 8. I know the gender of my audience members.

_____ 9. I am aware of the sexual orientation of my audience members.

_____ 10. I am aware of how my audience members view me.

_____ 11. I know that my topic will be interesting to my audience.

_____ 12. I have identified ways to motivate my audience to listen.

_____ 13. I have carefully considered which aspects of my topic will interest my audience.

_____ 14. I have learned about the interests and life situations of my audience members.

_____ 15. I have considered my audience's expectations for my presentation.

_____ 16. I have considered the situational factors surrounding the delivery of my presentation.

Add your numbers together here: _____

Results

64–80: high confidence in audience analysis
33–63: medium confidence in audience analysis
32–16: low confidence in audience analysis

Generally, the lower your number, the greater is the need to revisit the audience analysis coverage in this chapter and seek more information about your audience members.

▶ *Determine prior exposure.* Audience members' interest in your speech may differ greatly depending on whether or not they have previously been exposed to your ideas and arguments. Having a general sense of what they know about the topic—and how they have reacted to it in the past—will help you prepare. For example, if your informative speech on the Paleo diet went over well with your classmates, then it's reasonable to think that they might be interested in hearing a persuasive speech on the health and financial benefits of a diet with fewer dairy products.

▶ *Consider disposition.* As noted earlier, your audience's preexisting attitudes toward a particular message—or even toward you as a speaker—can have an impact on how they receive your speech. If you are a company executive informing employees that they will not be receiving an annual pay raise, you can assume your audience will be angry with the message (and may well dislike you as a speaker). You would be well advised to focus on areas of agreement, seek common ground, and attempt mutual understanding rather than sweeping changes in attitudes. (We will address how to adjust your speech to receptive, hostile, and neutral audiences in Chapter 16).

As was the case on gathering demographic and psychographic information on your audience members, you may wonder exactly *how* you go about finding information to anticipate your audience's reaction to your speech. Luckily, there are a few steps you can take that may yield incredibly helpful information.

▶ *Observe people.* People-watching is a hobby for some but a must for speakers! You can learn a lot by casually observing those around you. How do they react to topics discussed in class—particularly if the topics are controversial? What types of speakers do they seem to respond to?

▶ *Get to know people.* This may seem like common sense, but you'd be surprised how often students complete a course without making personal connections. Talk to a few people who sit next to you in class or engage with discussion forums in your virtual course. Ask questions. Learn more about your classmates' hobbies, life situations, and other factors that might help you develop an effective speech.

▶ *Survey and interview your audience.* You might also want to assess your audience on a more formal level. After receiving approval from your instructor, you might develop and distribute a short questionnaire to determine your classmates' opinions on a topic you're considering for your speech. Or you might talk with several members of a student organization to get feedback on your topic before you deliver your speech at the next group meeting.

▶ *Use the Web.* Do a Web search for opinion polls on your topic, especially polls that gauge the views of college students or other key demographic groups in your audience. Examine the kind of attention the issue has been getting on campus or in the local media (such as the school's newspaper or Web site).

All of the information you gain about your audience members—from their expectations and situational constraints to their demographics and possible reactions—sets the stage for you to move forward in developing an effective and appropriate speech. The next step is choosing your topic.

When surveying and interviewing your audience to help anticipate their response to your speech, it's important to develop the most useful questions possible. For example, you'll want to consider whether to ask *open, closed,* or *bipolar questions* to get the information you need. And you'll want to avoid unethical directed, leading, and loaded questions. See the Interviewing Appendix for more information.

real communicator

NAME: Matt Schermerhorn
OCCUPATION: Sports Manager

Imagine spending your day walking around the stadium during a Major League Baseball game talking to fans. That's my job—I get paid to watch baseball! Of course, it's only a small part of what I do in sports management for a Major League Baseball team. As you may know, those of us in this exciting field do everything from managing teams to managing events, sports venues, and recreation. It's a privilege to get to wear so many hats.

Everyone in my field shares a lifelong love of sports. But even if you consider yourself a particular sport's greatest fan, your passion may not be enough to land a sports management position. It's a tough market. I interned in sports management for my college baseball team while I was getting my degree in communication, along with studying the business, legal, and marketing aspects of sports management. My internship and my communication degree got me my position—everyone else in my work group had a previous contact on the team.

I'm on the special events and promotions team where my communication skills get put to use in the planning and research for our public presentations. I think public speaking is the greatest skill you can have—not just in terms of giving speeches in front of large groups but also giving a "pitch" to the senior executives who are deciding on sponsorship and offering short, "feel-good-about-our-team" messages to community groups or charitable organizations.

Even social media marketing promotions require me to understand my audience and plan my message accordingly. Twitter is huge for us; it's currently our most efficient way to reach the general public in terms of news distribution. We don't just tweet randomly, however; tweets that come from the franchise have to be professionally crafted (though this certainly doesn't imply that they're dull or boring!).

Lots of planning and research go into all the events that support a major league team. We solicit and manage sponsors and help them design the best promotions for their product. Again, audience analysis is key; we can't afford to look bad because someone chose an image or a word (in an attempt to be creative or funny) that offends or annoys a client or the fans. The in-game entertainment that we provide fans is carefully researched and organized, too. As I go around the stadium on game day, I constantly assess whether or not our entertainment is engaging the diverse crowd members. I get feedback from teens and seniors, families and singles, and people of various ethnic backgrounds; I adjust our next presentation or event accordingly, whether it is directed to the sponsors or the fans.

There are so many communication skills I rely on in this job from public speaking, to interviewing, to project leadership and group team building. I feel fortunate to have such a diverse, interesting, and fun job. I know I'm selling my company every day and I never stop learning.

Choosing Your Topic

Choosing a topic can seem like a daunting task, but it doesn't have to be. As noted, you'll want to consider the audience's expectations for the speech and topics that will interest them, taking their demographics and psychographics into account. In this course, you may have some guidance in that your instructor

● **CHOOSING** a topic from among numerous ideas and interests will call for some thinking and writing. Get creative! © Radius Images/Alamy

may give you a specific assignment. Be certain of your instructor's expectations for your speech, asking questions if necessary, to ensure that your topic and speech are appropriate. In searching for a good topic, you might try two proven strategies for generating ideas: considering personal interests, and brainstorming and clustering.

Finding a Topic That Intrigues You

It's hard to give a persuasive speech about something you don't find particularly inspiring or an informative speech on a topic you know nothing about. Finding a topic that is interesting to you will prove useful, making you more motivated to research, refine your ideas, and generate audience enthusiasm.

But when you have a variety of interests, it can be hard to pinpoint one to speak about. One way to get started is to write up a list of topics that interest you. For example, take a look at the variety of interests listed in Table 12.1. Creating a thorough and detailed list of topics that interest you (or even others) can be a great tool for stimulating speech ideas.

Brainstorming and Clustering

Once you've determined a very general topic—from your interests or an instructor's assignment—you'll need to start amassing information, thinking creatively, and considering problems and solutions related to your topic. This is a process known as **brainstorming**.

In brainstorming, you might consider using a technique for identifying potential topics called **clustering** (R. E. Smith, 1993). It begins with a core idea from which the writer branches out into a web of related thoughts and ideas. Rather than generating a list of ideas, clustering "spills" ideas in a visual way. To

TABLE 12.1

PERSONAL INTEREST TOPICS

Personal Experiences	Controversial Issues	Current Events	Hobbies	Beliefs and Values
Camping trips	Gun control	The economy and new job prospects	Rock climbing	Social justice
Life-threatening event	Smoking bans	National debt	Hiking	Environmentalism
Education	Animal testing	Sporting events	Cycling	Supernatural events
Organizations	Immigration	Musical performances	Camping	Humanitarianism
Accomplishments	Prayer in public schools	Acts of terrorism	Cooking	Spirituality
Military service	Internet privacy	Cyberbullying tragedies	Online gaming	Mysticism
Volunteer work	National health care	Global warming	Auto restoration	Retribution

Source: O'Hair, Stewart, & Rubenstein (2007), tab. 7.4, p. 98. Adapted with permission.

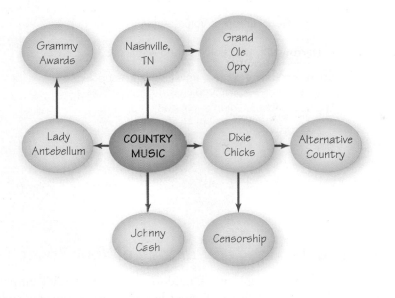

FIGURE 12.1

EXAMPLE OF A WEB OF ASSOCIATIONS PRODUCED BY CLUSTERING Thinking about "country music" can lead to numerous possible speech topics.

begin, simply write a main word or phrase in a circle; then create a web or collection of ideas inspired by the nucleus word or phrase. See Figure 12.1 for a sample of clustering for the nucleus phrase *country music*. As the process continues, you'll be struck by some concepts that might be suitable topics for your speech. In a sense, it's like Googling your own brain, starting out with a word or concept and branching to form a web of links to related thoughts.

Narrowing Your Topic

Now that you have searched for potential topics, it's time to make a choice. Your goal is to select the topic that best meets the following three criteria:

1. Is it a topic you are interested in and know something about?

2. Does the topic meet the criteria specified in the assignment?

3. Is it a topic that your audience will find worthwhile?

Once you are satisfied that your topic meets these criteria, you can begin to consider how to break down your topic further so that it is more specific and manageable. This will aid you a great deal in your research (a topic we will discuss later in this chapter) because it is considerably easier to find information on a specific topic (traditional Jewish foods served for Passover) than an extremely general one (the Jewish faith). One way to narrow down your topic is to break it up into categories. Write your general topic at the top of a list, with each succeeding word a more specific or concrete topic. As illustrated in Figure 12.2, you might begin with the very general topic of volunteering and then narrow the topic down a step at a time until you focus on one particular volunteer program (for example, Read to a Child) and decide to persuade your listeners about the advantages of offering personal time to read to a local elementary school child.

NARROWING YOUR TOPIC Start with a general idea and become increasingly specific until you have a manageable topic for your speech.

General topic: Volunteering

Narrow slightly: Volunteering with kids

Narrow further: Volunteering with grade school children

Narrow further: Volunteer literacy programs for grade school children

Narrow further: Read to a Child

Determining the Specific Purpose of Your Speech

Once you've narrowed your topic, you'll need to zero in on a specific purpose for your speech. Ask yourself: "What is it about my topic that I want my audience to learn, do, consider, or agree with?" A **specific purpose statement** expresses both the topic and the general speech purpose in action form and in terms of the specific objectives you hope to achieve with your presentation.

Let's consider an example. Imagine again that you are giving a persuasive speech on volunteering. Your general purpose and specific purpose might look like this:

> **Topic:** Volunteer reading programs
>
> **General purpose:** To persuade
>
> **Specific purpose:** To have audience members realize the importance of reading with local elementary school children so that they sign up for a volunteer reading program such as Read to a Child

There is an additional level of specificity to consider when preparing your speech. It is called the *thesis statement*—you're probably familiar with this term from high school or your college composition course. We help you understand and develop your own thesis in the next section.

Your thesis statement helps you stay focused on your goals for communicating with others in a public speaking situation. But staying focused on goals also matters in communication contexts such as running a meeting. As we discussed in Chapter 10, clearly stating the purpose of your meeting and organizing your agenda around it helps everyone stay focused and makes you more likely to achieve your goals.

Developing a Thesis Statement

Once you have homed in on your topic, general purpose, and specific speech purpose, you can start to encapsulate your speech in the form of a **thesis statement**, a statement that conveys the central idea about your topic. The thesis statement must clearly summarize what you want the audience to get out of your speech, but is not the same thing as your specific purpose statement; as noted, it is more specific. Revisiting the example about volunteer reading programs, note how your thesis statement works with your general purpose and specific speech purpose and how it expresses the core idea that you want your listeners to walk away with:

TABLE 12.2

GENERATING A THESIS STATEMENT

Topic	General Purpose	Specific Purpose	Thesis Statement
Low-carbohydrate diets	To inform	To inform listeners about low-carbohydrate diets so that they can make good decisions about their own eating habits	Before choosing to start a low-carbohydrate diet, it is important to have a thorough understanding of how carbohydrates affect your body and what the possible benefits and risks of the diet are so that you can make an informed decision about your health.
Study-abroad programs	To persuade	To have listeners realize that studying abroad is an exciting opportunity and encourage them to consider spending a semester taking classes in another country	Studying abroad is an amazing opportunity to learn about another culture, to enhance your educational experience, and to make yourself more appealing to prospective graduate schools and employers.
My grandparents	To honor an amazing couple on their fiftieth wedding anniversary (special occasion)	To celebrate with my family and my grandparents' friends in light of this happy milestone in their lives	In big and small ways, my grandparents have shared their fifty years of love and commitment with their family, their congregation, and their students, having been dedicated teachers for three decades.

Thesis statement: Volunteers who read with local elementary school children through programs such as Read to a Child improve young lives by enhancing children's self-esteem and expanding their possibilities for academic success.

Can you see how the thesis statement works? Offering a solid thesis statement your audience will remember long after your visual aids have faded from their minds will help you achieve your general purpose and your specific purpose: to persuade your listeners to get out there and read with local kids. For additional examples of thesis statements, see Table 12.2.

Researching the Topic

Anyone can make a speech. A *good* speech, however, should offer listeners something new, some information, insight, perspective, or idea that they didn't have before. Such original thoughts are usually the product of both deep reflection and careful research.

In a speech, research is information that helps support the points that you make, strengthening your message and credibility. For many students, the prospect of researching for a speech or presentation might seem boring, overwhelming, or both—and it can be. But if you are working with a topic that intrigues you and you approach your research in a practical way, the research process can be better than you think.

CONNECT

The type of information you choose for your speech should be influenced by its general purpose. If you are persuading your audience (Chapter 16) or giving a speech for a special occasion, try using personal anecdotes to touch your audience emotionally. When informing your audience (Chapter 15), make sure that your use of anecdotes illuminates your topic and doesn't persuade the audience to think a certain way about it.

Types of Information to Consider

A wealth of material is available to enliven your speech and make it more effective. Listeners respond well to a range of compelling information, so try to include a variety of supporting materials in your speech, including testimony, scholarship and statistics, anecdotes, and quotations.

Testimony

When you need to prove a point about which you are not an authority, incorporating the voice of an expert into your speech can lend it some validity. **Expert testimony** is the opinion or judgment of an expert, a professional in his or her field. Opinions from doctors, coaches, engineers, and other qualified, licensed professionals serve as expert testimony. In a speech about knee surgery, for example, you might cite an orthopedic surgeon when explaining the difference between arthroscopy and knee replacement surgery. **Lay testimony** is the opinion of a nonexpert who has personal experience or witnessed an event related to your topic. In a speech on weather disasters, you could provide the testimony from a witness who survived a tornado.

Scholarship and Statistics

If you can bolster testimonies with hard numbers and facts, you'll be more effective as a speaker. **Scientific research findings** carry a lot of weight with audiences, particularly if your topic is related to medicine, health, media, or the environment. For example, in a speech about educational television programs, a speaker might point out that studies have found that children who watched *Sesame Street* as preschoolers were more likely to enjoy elementary school and to achieve higher grades even in high school (Huston & Wright, 1998).

Statistics—information provided in numerical form—can also provide powerful support for a speech, sometimes more than words. Statistics reveal trends, explain the size of something, or illustrate relationships. They can be made more meaningful when paired with or made part of *factual statements*—truthful, realistic accounts based on actual people, places, events, or dates. For example, when speaking about domestic violence, you might use a combination of statistics and factual statements to back your statement that a person is more likely to be killed by a family member or close acquaintance than a stranger:

> Out of 13,636 murders studied in the United States, 30.2% of the victims were murdered by persons known to them (4,119 victims), 13.6% were murdered by family members (1,855 victims), 12.3% were murdered by strangers (1,676 victims), and 43.9% of the relationships were unknown (investigators were not able to establish any relationship). (U.S. Department of Justice, 2010)

Although accuracy is important, we must note that specific numbers and percentages are cumbersome to speak aloud and can be easily forgotten by your audience. Remember that your visual aids can give the specifics while you round numbers and percentages aloud.

Anecdotes

Although facts and statistics are useful for gaining credibility, they can also be boring and easily forgotten. An effective way to breathe life into them, and into your speech in general, is including personal details that give faces to statistics and facts and make them part of a memorable and cohesive story. **Anecdotes** are

COMMUNICATIONACROSSCULTURES

No Longer a Victim

In 2002, a fourteen-year-old girl named Elizabeth Smart was kidnapped from her Utah bedroom at knifepoint. She was held by her captor, a Salt Lake City street preacher and panhandler, and repeatedly raped for nine long months. When she was finally discovered, rescued, and returned to her family, many wondered how she could ever reclaim her life. Had Smart chosen to retreat into a quiet, private life, few would have questioned her decision.

But Elizabeth Smart did not retreat. She faced her abuser in court and testified against him. She returned to school and finished college. She traveled to Paris on a mission for her church. She grew up, got married, and found a career that is more like a calling: she decided to use her experience to shed light on the tragic reality of human trafficking and crimes against children. She became a commentator for ABC News, offering insights into the lives of abducted children, and penned a memoir. She also became a public speaker, one who can attest to the true costs of these crimes, and who speaks as few others can about real steps that might make it harder for children to be victimized—and easier for victimized children to escape.

As a woman of faith dealing with this heinous crime and seeking to prevent others like it, Smart has had to carefully consider the ways in which some of the cultural norms that shaped her life may have impacted her ordeal. In particular, she explained how negative perceptions of premarital sex can be easily mistranslated by children who are victims of sexual abuse. Speaking at a forum on sex trafficking at Johns Hopkins University in 2013, Smart spoke about how she remembered the words of a teacher who, in advocating abstinence, had compared sexual activity to chewing gum. "I thought, 'Oh, my gosh, I'm that chewed up piece of gum. . . . Nobody rechews a piece of gum, you throw it away.' And that's how easy it is to feel like you no longer have worth, you no longer have value," Smart said (Dominguez, 2013). Although her own church takes care to clarify this is not the case, noting that "victims of rape, incest, or other sexual abuse are not guilty of sin," and advising victims, "If you have been a victim of any of these crimes, know that you are innocent," in Smart's young mind, she was unable to get past the idea that the rape had made her worthless (Church of the Latter Day Saints Gospel Library, 2013, para. 7). As a speaker, Smart seeks to correct that misconception, advocating for more practical education for children to empower them to fight for their lives and to understand that victimization does not change how important they are. "If you're given choices, if you're given skills, if you're given permission to fight back," Smart explained, "you don't have to do what other people tell you" (Fox News, 2013).

THINK ABOUT THIS

❶ How does adversity inspire public speaking and, indeed, public life? Why might a victim of a crime choose to speak out? Why might he or she choose not to speak publicly?

❷ What kind of supporting evidence would you look for if you were researching a speech on human trafficking? Should a victim like Elizabeth Smart be expected to present the same kinds of evidence as you would? Why or why not?

❸ Is Elizabeth Smart's religious faith an important cultural element surrounding this discussion? Why or why not?

brief, personal stories that have a point or punch line. The preceding statistics on murder would be greatly enhanced if they were paired with one or two personal stories that bring them down to a more intimate and relatable level. Anecdotes can be pointed or emotionally moving; they can also be humorous or inspiring. When used well, they add a personal and memorable element to your speech.

Quotations

You can also call on the words of others to lend your speech a sense of history, perspective, and timeless eloquence. *Quotations*, repeating the exact words of another person, are usually most effective when they are brief, to the point, and clearly related to your topic. You might quote a historical figure, a celebrity, a poet, or a playwright. For example, in a speech about motivation, you could quote Michelangelo: "The greatest danger for most of us is not that our aim is too high and we miss it but that it is too low and we reach it." Your sources do not need to be famous—you may be motivated to quote a friend or family member: "My grandfather always told me, 'An education is never a burden.'" Be sure to point out the source of your quote and, if necessary, explain who the person is or was.

Researching Supporting Material

Of course, the facts, statistics, anecdotes, and other supporting material that you want for your speech won't come out of thin air. Now that you've got your list of ingredients for your speech, you'll need to do some shopping—that is, you'll need to go out and find the material. Here's how.

Talk to People

If you're looking for testimony, narratives, real-world examples, and anecdotes, you'll need to start talking to people. You may be looking for experts in a particular field or people who have had firsthand experience with an event or occurrence, which can be a challenge. You can try networking with people you know, as well as searching online resources.

You can also talk to people via **surveys**, which involves soliciting answers to a question or series of questions related to your topic from a broad range of individuals. Conducting a survey can give you a sense of how a group of people view a particular event, idea, or phenomenon. For example, if you are giving an informative speech on the ways text messages get misinterpreted, you might randomly select students on campus and ask them how often their text messages resulted in misinterpretations or conflicts. Results from surveys can be discussed to back up your points. Just remember to consider the credibility of your survey results. For example, did you make sure that the sample of people you surveyed was representative of the larger population of students?

● **SURVEYING LOCAL FARMERS** about the effects of factory farming and mass-produced food on their livelihood will likely give you some interesting insights and quotations to use in your speech. SMIRNOV VLADIMIR/ITAR-TASS/Landov

Search the Literature

Published literature lets you reach beyond your own knowledge and experience and can be a valuable resource for supporting material for your speech. If you're giving a speech on hip-hop music, for example, you're likely to find some great material in the pages of a magazine like *Vibe*. If you're looking for studies on mental health issues affecting emergency personnel after the Boston Marathon bombings, you might search through newspaper articles or scholarly journals such as the *Journal of the American Medical Association (JAMA)*.

Most current publications are available in searchable databases in libraries; some can even be accessed online or via a tablet or smartphone apps (though you may have to pay a fee to download complete articles). Such databases give you access to a wealth of stored information. The Internet Movie Database (www .imdb.com), for instance, is a great example of a commonly used database, and its comprehensive information on film, television, and video games is entirely free.

Another type of secondary resource is a **directory**. Directories are created and maintained by people rather than automatically by computers. Because human editors compile them, directories—like the *American Library Directory Online*—often return fewer links but higher-quality results. Directories guide you to the main page of a Web site organized within a wider subject category. You can also access useful literature through **library gateways**—collections of databases and information sites arranged by subject, generally reviewed and recommended by experts (usually librarians). These gateway collections assist in your research and reference needs because they identify suitable academic pages on the Web. In addition to scholastic resources, many library gateways include links to specialty search engines for biographies, quotations, atlases, maps, encyclopedias, and trivia.

Make the Most of Online Research

Twenty years ago, the first stop on any research mission would have been the library. Today, the Internet puts a massive amount of information at your fingertips. In fact, nearly half of all college students are using their smartphones and tablets to do research for their class assignments (Parker, Lenhart, & Moore, 2012). Navigating the vast sea of information—not to mention misinformation—available on the Internet can be daunting and, without wise searching, a waste of time. A solid knowledge of search tools can therefore make your searches more fruitful and efficient.

An Internet **search engine** is a program that indexes Web content. Search engines such as Google, Yahoo!, and Bing search all over the Web for documents containing specific keywords that you've chosen. Search engines have some key

● **WE RELY HEAVILY** on the Internet for our research needs. In fact, *to google* has become a legitimate verb in our everyday language. Courtesy of Google

WIREDFORCOMMUNICATION

The Library in the Sky

"Funny how something that used to be such a commonplace part of research now seems like a special occasion" (Romans, 2011, para. 2). So says a veteran scholar regarding a trip to the library, something he made a pact with himself to do at least once a week in order to supplement his mostly online research with older but important literature.

Wandering the stacks at the library does have a certain romantic feel to it. But is it practical? The digitizing of books, newspapers, and journals has effectively removed the walls between centuries of content and end users. If, for example, you want to write an informative speech on the history of your hometown, you could quickly enter the name of your town into any number of digital archives and access a wealth of news articles and literary references to it in major newspapers dating back several centuries (*The New York Times* digital archive, for example, goes back to 1851). You might find stunning photos of your town from the Associated Press or Corbis photo archives (you can search them for free). The Library of Congress Archive has an ever-growing online collection, where you might find photos, posters, letters, and artifacts. And you'll be able to search through more books than any brick-and-mortar library could possibly hold, thanks to a somewhat controversial project started by Google.

The Google Books Library Project, which aims to "make it easier for people to find relevant books—specifically, books they wouldn't find any other way such as those that are out of print," offers searchable digital scans of millions of books through partnerships with major public and university libraries around the world (https://www.google.com/googlebooks/library/). For books in copyright, Google will provide links to sources you can purchase them from, as well as libraries from which you can borrow. Books no longer in copyright (most books more than ninety years old are in the public domain) can be viewed in full; you even can download a pdf of the entire book. So if a writer stumbled through your town on the way to the California gold rush in 1849 and wrote about it in a novel, a poem, or work of nonfiction, you can find out what he or she thought about it.

Google Books remains somewhat controversial: a class-action lawsuit on behalf of copyright holders, in fact, is pending (Bosman, 2013). But for researchers—or anyone who is just a little intellectually curious, really—there is no denying that the ability to access primary sources quickly, from anywhere, and often for free opens new doors of discovery and allows even the most casual Web surfer to stumble onto texts that were out of reach, or perhaps just languishing unnoticed on library shelves, for decades.

It is interesting to note, however, that old-fashioned, brick-and-mortar libraries, although undergoing tremendous changes in terms of the way they house and deliver information, remain a crucial link in offering access to all kinds of intellectual property. A recent survey by Pew Research revealed that even as they embrace new technologies, Americans still look to public libraries for their casual reading and information needs. More than three-quarters of those surveyed felt that library services like book lending, reference librarians, and access to computers and the Internet were "very important." It seems that, even as armchair research becomes the norm, we still love that feeling of wandering the stacks.

THINK ABOUT THIS

❶ Primary sources are of particular importance to historians, who rely on firsthand accounts of events and phenomena to gain understanding of a particular period. What kinds of primary sources would be helpful when researching your hometown's history? How might they be used in a speech?

❷ Some see the digitizing of content as great way to level the intellectual playing field. But how level is it? Google Books is free, but many archives are not, and many Americans still don't have access to the Internet at home. How can access be further democratized? Should it be?

❸ With so much information going digital, what is your opinion on the role of brick-and-mortar libraries today? Do you think they are more important or less important than they once were? What kind of help can librarians provide?

advantages—they offer access to a huge portion of publicly available Web pages and give you the ability to search through large databases. But they frequently return irrelevant links, and they don't index the "invisible Web"—databases maintained by universities, businesses, the government, or libraries that cannot always be accessed by standard search engines. If a search engine fails to produce useful results, try a **metasearch engine**—a search engine that scans multiple search engines simultaneously. Metasearch technology delivers more relevant and comprehensive results than a search engine. Another great resource is a **research search engine**, which will search only for research published in academic books, journals, and other periodicals. One of the best research search engines is Google Scholar (scholar.google.com) as it has a wide variety of resources. For example, if you type, "binge drinking" into Google Scholar, the search engine will identify about 58,200 scholarly results.

Evaluating Supporting Material

Once you've gathered a variety of sources, you must critically evaluate the material and determine which sources you should use. After all, your credibility as a speaker depends largely on the accuracy and credibility of your sources, as well as their appropriateness for your topic and your audience.

Credible Sources

In today's media, anyone can put up a blog or a Web page, edit a wiki, or post a video to YouTube. (This is why many instructors forbid students to use supporting material from Wikipedia.) What's more, a large and growing number of opinion-based publications, broadcasting networks, and Web sites provide an outlet for research that is heavily biased. Consequently, it is always worth spending a little time evaluating **credibility**, the quality, authority, and reliability, of each source you use. One simple way to approach this is to evaluate the author's credentials. This means that you should note if the author is a medical doctor, Ph.D., attorney, CPA, or other licensed professional and whether he or she is affiliated with a reputable organization or institution. For example, if you are seeking statistics on the health effects of cigarette smoke, an article written by an M.D. affiliated with the American Lung Association would be more credible than an editorial written by a high school French teacher.

A credible source may show a trail of research by supplying details about where the information came from, such as a thorough list of references. In newswriting, source information is integrated into the text. A newspaper or magazine article, for example, will credit information to named sources ("Baseball Commissioner Bud Selig said . . .") or credentialed but unnamed sources ("One high-ranking State Department official said, on condition of anonymity . . .").

The Internet poses special problems when it comes to credibility due to the ease with which material can be posted online. Check for balanced, impartial information that is not biased, and note the background or credentials of the authors. If references are listed, verify them to confirm their authenticity. Web sites can be quickly assessed for reliability by looking at the domain, or the suffix of the Web site address. Credible Web sites often end with .edu (educational institution), .org (organization), or .gov (government).

CONNECT

The sources you cite in your speech are part of your *self-presentation* to your audience (Chapter 2). If your sources are outdated or from your cousin's blog, you will present a self that says, "I am unprepared and I didn't research my topic thoroughly." Conversely, if you offer statistics, facts, and stories from a variety of current, reliable, and compelling sources, you present yourself as trustworthy, prepared, and competent—and your audience is more likely to consider what you're saying.

Up-to-Date Sources

In most cases, you'll want to use the most recent information available to keep your speech timely and relevant. Isaiah, for example, is speaking to a group of potential clients about his company's graphic design services. If, during his speech, he makes reference to testimonials from satisfied clients in 2012 and earlier, the audience may wonder if the company has gone downhill since then. For this reason, always determine when your source was written or last updated; sources without dates may indicate that the information is not as timely or relevant as it could be.

Naturally, one exception to this rule deals with historical or classic speech or research topics. If you are researching a speech to inform your audience about the achievements of early twentieth-century pilot Amelia Earhart, for example, you should feel free to use quotations and statistics from her heyday.

Accurate Sources

When compiling support for your speech, it is important to find accurate sources—sources that are true, correct, and exact. A speaker who presents inaccurate information may very well lose the respect and attention of the audience. There are several ways to help ensure that you are studying accurate sources. In addition to being credible and up-to-date, accurate sources are exact, meaning that they offer detailed and precise information. A source that notes that 54 percent of Americans over age sixty-five now have access to the Internet (Pew Internet, 2013) is more accurate than a source that states that about half of senior citizens have such access. The more precise your sources, the more credibility you will gain with your audience.

Compelling Sources

Support material that is strong, interesting, and believable is considered to be *compelling* information. This kind of information helps your audience understand, process, and retain your message. A speaker might note that 3,331 people were killed and 387,000 people were injured in motor vehicle crashes involving a distracted driver in 2011. Two of the most significant causes of distracted driving are phone calls and text messaging, with 69 percent of U.S. drivers between the ages of eighteen and sixty-four reporting that they talked on the phone while driving in the month before the survey and another 31 percent of the same demographic noting that they had read or sent messages (text or e-mail) while driving during the same time period (CDC, 2013). Now those are some compelling statistics!

To be compelling, your supporting material should also be *vivid*. Vivid material is clear and vibrant, never vague. For example, in a speech about cyclical cicada invasions in the Washington, DC, area, Ana might reference a source describing these bugs as large insects, about one and a half inches long, with red eyes, black bodies, and fragile wings; she might also use a direct quotation from a resident who notes that "there were so many cicadas that the ground, trees, and streets looked like they were covered by an oil slick." Such vivid (and gross) descriptions of information interest listeners. Look for clear, concrete supporting details that encourage the audience to form visual representations of the object or event you are describing.

Ethical Speaking: Taking Responsibility for Your Speech

As a responsible public speaker, you must let ethics guide every phase of planning and researching your speech. Being an ethical speaker means being responsible: responsible for ensuring that proper credit is given to other people's ideas, data, and research that you have incorporated into your presentation, as well as being responsible for what you say (and how you say it) to your audience. Let's review, starting with what happens when you fail to cite your sources properly: plagiarism.

Recognizing Plagiarism

Plagiarism is the crime of presenting someone else's words, ideas, or intellectual property as your own, intentionally or unintentionally. It is a growing problem and is not limited to the written word—or to students (Park, 2003). In August 2012, *Time* columnist and CNN host, Fareed Zakaria, was suspended over an allegation of plagiarism involving a column he wrote on gun control. Zakaria had not cited his sources correctly and later apologized, acknowledging that he had made a mistake. Despite the fact that he was ultimately reinstated, Zakaria certainly suffered the consequences of his actions, particularly an unforgettable blow to his image as a journalist (Haughney, 2012).

Most universities and colleges have clear definitions of plagiarism and enforce strict penalties regarding the issue—your school's plagiarism policy may even be included on your class syllabus. If so, *read this document carefully*. The syllabus is like your contract with your professor; by enrolling in the course, you have agreed to follow it.

Despite the problems associated with plagiarism, many students, writers, and speakers remain unsure of how, when, or why they must credit their sources. In fact, many people are shocked to find that they can be guilty of plagiarism with a seemingly unimportant error, like simply failing to include quotation marks or mistakenly deleting one little footnote when completing a paper or speech. To avoid making the same mistake, keep careful track of where all your material comes from and document it properly. In Chapter 13, we will explain how to document your sources in your speech; for now, we will focus on the important role of taking accurate and thorough notes during the research phase.

> **AND YOU?**
> How do you feel about the fact that even unintentionally using someone else's words, ideas, or intellectual property is still plagiarism? Does it seem unfair that you might suffer severe consequences (such as being expelled) even if you do something without intent? Why or why not?

Taking Accurate Notes

The noted historian Doris Kearns Goodwin was accused of using passages from three other books in her own work without proper attribution. After settling with the wronged authors and making corrections to her book, Kearns explained that the misrepresentation had been the result of a crucial error she had made during the note-taking phase. "Though my footnotes repeatedly cited [another author's] work, I failed to provide quotation marks for phrases that I had taken verbatim, having assumed that these phrases, drawn from my notes, were my words, not hers" (Goodwin, 2002, para. 3).

EVALUATINGCOMMUNICATIONETHICS

Didn't I Already Say That?

You met Alex in your speech communication class and formed a fast friendship when you realized that you both were from New Orleans. You are listening to Alex deliver a speech about growing up in the aftermath of Hurricane Katrina. His speech is compelling, and you are enthralled by his detailed account of how his parish changed in the years after that devastating storm. Having gone through many of the same experiences, you find yourself nodding in agreement with much of what he says. But when he closes with a passage about the lessons the storm taught him—from keeping up his car insurance to counting his blessings—it seems eerily familiar. In fact, it's an almost verbatim copy of a status update you posted to your own Facebook page on Thanksgiving Day, the semester before you met Alex. When you get back to your dorm room and pull up your Facebook history, you realize that a mutual friend, Elliot, had been moved by your post and reposted it to his own page. Alex must have seen it there, because he used it almost wholesale, changing only minor details, like the names of your family and your elementary school.

You are angry—on many levels. You poured your heart into that post, and although it was only about a hundred words, it took you a good deal of time to write and rewrite until it captured exactly how you were feeling. Now you feel like someone has stolen not only your work but your feelings as well. Even worse, you saw that the class was moved by Alex's—*your*—conclusion, and you're certain he's going to get a good grade based at least in part on something you wrote. And because your privacy settings are pretty tight, the passage won't come up on a standard Web search so you know it's unlikely that he'll get caught unless you say something. What do you do?

❶ Is what Alex did plagiarism? Do you even "own" the content you create and post on Facebook?

❷ How is your friend Elliot "sharing" your status different from what Alex did? Does it matter how the content was "shared"? Was your name credited in Elliot's post?

❸ How will you deal with this instance of plagiarism? Should you alert your instructor? Confront Alex? If you were the instructor, how would you handle the situation?

As this example shows, keeping track of all your outside material and its sources can be challenging, which is why taking accurate notes is so critical. To keep yourself organized, consider using note cards to keep track of references separately. Or place all of your references and source material into an electronic document, such as a word processing file or a note-taking application on your smartphone or tablet. For example, many of our students use the basic Note feature that comes standard on the iPad to stay organized and they've also had good experiences with free, platform-agnostic apps. A particularly popular app called Evernote allows you to create and save notes in organized folders; you can even "clip" full Web pages, annotate them to highlight the information you need, and save them as entries for later use, as shown in Figure 12.3.

Regardless of the format you choose, your entry should contain or highlight the quote or material you want to use, along with pertinent information, such as author name, publication information (title, volume, publisher, location, date), and relevant page or paragraph numbers from the source. In addition, each entry should note whether the material is copied *verbatim* (word for word) or *paraphrased* (put into your own words). When you have completed your

ARTICLES

Illinois's Glen Carbon Centennial Library was named Library Journal's 2010 Best Small Library in America.

LITERACY-RICH ENVIRONMENTS:

Reading and Writing at Home

Which will your child learn first: to read or to write? Most children develop these skills at the same time. The following are some things you can do to help your children become readers and writers:

Read aloud every day.
- Set aside a regular time for reading that your children can count on.
- Find other times to read; for example, when you're waiting at the doctor's office.
- Read aloud the items you use in daily life: food labels, directions for baking a cake, and birthday cards.
- Listen to your child pretend to read a book from memory.

Have plenty of children's books around your home.
- Keep books where children can reach them.
- Go to the library regularly.
- Look for secondhand books at yard sales and thrift shops.
- Encourage family and friends to give books as gifts.

Stock up on writing and drawing supplies.
- Store things to write on: paper, pads, and a chalkboard.
- Store things to write with: crayons, markers, pencils, and chalk.
- Store supplies for making books: cardboard, a stapler, a hole punch, and laces.
- Save items to cut and paste: junk mail, catalogs, coupons, and old magazines.
- Keep magnet letters on the refrigerator.
- Store alphabet stamps and a stamp pad.

These are great tips for anyone practicing reading with kids--I should mention this in my speech

Source: "Reading and Writing at Home" (n.d.) Reading is Fundamental, retrieved from http://www.rif.org/us/literacy-resources/articles/reading-and-writing-at-home.htm

Paraphrased: Plan a regular reading time, keep books around, and visit the library

FIGURE 12.3

IF YOU PREFER to do online research, Evernote can help you to keep record of your sources and annotate them with notes for your speech. http://www.rif.org/us/literacy-resources/articles/reading-and-writing-at-home.htm

research, you'll be able to shuffle or copy and paste these individual cards or entries as you develop your speech without losing track of their sources.

You'll also need to keep a **running bibliography**—a list of resources you've consulted. There are various styles of organizing these resources (including styles dictated by the Modern Language Association, American Psychological Association, and so on), so make sure to ask your instructor what his or her preference is if you're required to hand in this document. Regardless, all styles generally require you to list the following information:

▶ The complete name of each author or origin of the source if no author is named ("National Science Foundation Web site," or "*New York Times* editorial")

▶ The title and subtitle of the source (article, book chapter, Web page) and of the larger work in which it appears (magazine, newspaper, journal, book, Web site)

▶ The publication date of the source; for Web sources, date of publication and date of access; for journals, volume and issue numbers

▶ For books, publisher and city of publication; for Web resources, the complete URL

▶ Page numbers for the material used and for the entire work being cited

We present an example of a running bibliography in APA style in Figure 12.4.

FIGURE 12.4

SAMPLE RUNNING BIBLIOGRAPHY IN APA STYLE

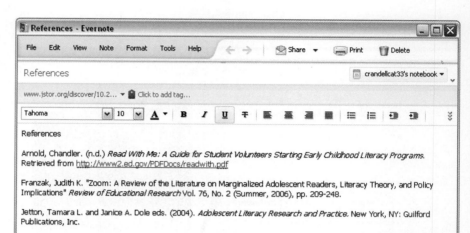

● **ALTHOUGH THE** First Amendment allows anyone to step up on a soapbox and say whatever he or she wants to say, it's still important to refrain from unethical or derogatory speech. ©NMPFT/DHA/SSPL/The Image Works

Speaking Ethically and Responsibly

Your responsibility as a speaker goes beyond simply giving credit to others' work; you need to take responsibility for what *you* say.[1] If you use inflammatory, hurtful, or hateful language, even quoted and cited from another source, you will bear the brunt of the audience's reactions.

The First Amendment to the U.S. Constitution guarantees every citizen the right to free speech, but not all speech is ethical. As a public speaker, you are responsible for providing your audience members with all of the necessary information for them to make accurate, appropriate decisions about you and your message. The speeches by Chinese leader Deng Xiaoping, who tried to intimidate Chinese citizens into revealing the whereabouts of leaders of the unsuccessful 1989 student uprising in Tiananmen Square in Beijing, were unethical and coercive. In addition, it's important to recognize that the right to free speech in this country is not without limits. As Supreme Justice Oliver Wendell Holmes wrote in 1919, the Constitution "would not protect a man falsely shouting fire in a theater and causing a panic" (*Schenck v. United States,* 1919). Speech that endangers people—for example, speech that incites riots, advocates the unlawful overthrowing of the government, or causes unnecessary panic—would not only be ethically questionable but might be illegal as well (*Gitlow v. New York*, 1925; *Schenck v. United States*, 1919).

Although everyone has different standards for ethical communication, the qualities of dignity and integrity are universally seen as core to the idea of ethics. *Dignity* is feeling worthy, honored, or respected as a person; *integrity* is

---

[1]Much of this discussion was inspired by the work of Michael Josephson, founder and president of the Joseph and Edna Josephson Institute of Ethics in Marina del Rey, California.

incorruptibility, the ability to avoid compromise for the sake of personal gain (Gudykunst, Ting-Toomey, Sudweeks, & Stewart, 1995). Basic rules for ethical speaking require that we adhere to four principles: we should strive to be trustworthy, respectful, responsible, and fair in our speeches (Day, 1997).

▶ *Trustworthiness* refers to being honest with your audience about the goal of your message and providing accurate information.

▶ By treating people right, you are showing *respect*. In public speaking, respect is shown by focusing on issues rather than on personalities, allowing the audience the power of choice, and avoiding excluding the audience in discussions.

▶ As a *responsible* public speaker, it is your job to consider the topic and purpose of the speech, evidence and reasoning of the arguments, accuracy of your message, and honest use of emotional appeals.

▶ Ethical public speakers must be *fair* by presenting alternative and opposing views to the audience. A fair speaker will not deny the audience the right to make informed decisions.

BACK TO ▶ Steve Jobs

 At the beginning of this chapter, we talked about how the late Steve Jobs's careful preparation and intimate knowledge of his projects enabled him to be a powerful public speaker on behalf of his company. Let's take a look at his presentation skills in light of what we've learned in this chapter.

▶ Clearly, Steve Jobs enjoyed technology. But he also knew the importance of preparation and practice. If he relied entirely on presentation aids, he would have fallen flat during inevitable technical glitches. His research and preparation shined brighter than this presentation technology.

▶ Jobs also knew his audience. His audience of Apple fans was always eager to hear what he had to say and see what he had to show. He didn't bother talking about competing products, because he knew the crowd was more interested in hearing about Apple products.

▶ Prior exposure played a role in the way Jobs presented his products. The original iPod, launched in 2001 along with the iTunes Store, was a revolutionary device, and Jobs's presentation was full of surprises for his audience. When introducing later iterations of the device, Jobs focused only on new features and options.

▶ The company also limits prior exposure by maintaining a high level of secrecy about products in development. When Jobs introduced a *new* product, there was little chance that the crowd had already heard anything more than rumors about it beforehand, which affected how Jobs presented information to the audience.

THINGS TO TRY > Activities

1. LaunchPad for *Real Communication* offers key term videos and encourages self-assessment through adaptive quizzing. Go to **bedfordstmartins.com/realcomm** to get access to:

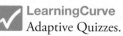 **LearningCurve** Adaptive Quizzes.   ▶ Video clips that illustrate key concepts, highlighted in teal in the Real Reference section that follows.

2. Think back to a memorable speech you've witnessed, either in person or through the media. What kind of speech was it? Was the speaker trying to inform, persuade, or celebrate? Was he or she successful in that endeavor? Did the speech change the way you felt?

3. Tune in to a few news pundits—for example, Bill O'Reilly, Rachel Maddow, Randi Rhodes, or Rush Limbaugh—on the radio, on television, or online. Listen carefully to what they say, and consider how they back up their statements. Do they provide source material as they speak? Can you link to their sources from their online blogs? How does the way they back up their points or fail to back them up influence your perceptions of what they say?

4. Take a look at your school's policy on plagiarism. Does your school clearly define what acts constitute plagiarism? How harsh are the punishments? Who is responsible for reporting plagiarism? How is the policy enforced?

5. The next time you read something—a magazine article, a political blog, a work of nonfiction, a chapter in a textbook—take time to think about the research presented in it. What kinds of research did the authors do? How do they back up their statements? What kinds of research materials do they include?

Now that you have finished reading this chapter, you can

Describe the power of **public speaking** and how preparation eases natural nervousness.

Identify the purpose of your speech:

▶ *Informative speeches* aim to increase the audience's understanding and knowledge of a topic (p. 337).

▶ *Persuasive speeches* are intended to influence the beliefs, attitudes, and behaviors of an audience (p. 339).

▶ *Special-occasion speeches* are given at common events (like weddings and funerals), and many of us will deliver such a speech at some point in time (p. 340).

Conduct **audience analysis**:

▶ It is important to understand and appreciate your audience's expectations for the speech as well as key situational factors (p. 342).

▶ Knowing **demographics**, the quantifiable characteristics of your audience, and **psychographics**, psychological measures, will help you identify topics that the audience would be interested in learning about (pp. 342–344).

▶ You will want to anticipate your audience's response by considering their motivation, seeking common ground (**homogeny**), determining prior exposure, and considering disposition (pp. 344, 346).

▶ You can learn about your audience by observing people, getting to know people, conducting interviews and using surveys, and using the Web (p. 346).

Choose an appropriate topic and develop it:

▶ Speak about something that inspires you (p. 348).

▶ Use **brainstorming** and **clustering** to amass information, think creatively, and consider problems and solutions related to your topic (pp. 348–349).

▶ A **specific purpose statement** expresses the topic and the general speech purpose in action form and in terms of the specific objectives you hope to achieve with your presentation (p. 350).

▶ Narrow your topic and write a thesis statement, a summary of your central idea (pp. 350–351).

Support and enliven your speech with effective research:

▶ Include **expert testimony**, the opinion of an authority, or **lay testimony**, opinion based on personal experience (p. 352).

▶ **Scientific research findings** carry weight in topics on medicine, health, media, and the environment; **statistics**, information in numerical form, can clarify your presentation (p. 352).

▶ Anecdotes, relevant personal stories, bring the human experience to the speech (pp. 353–354).

▶ **Surveys** will add the point of view of a larger range of people (p. 354).

▶ Use databases to find material, such as **directories**, **library gateways**, **search engines**, **metasearch engines**, and **research search engines**. (pp. 355, 357).

Cull from among your sources the material that will be most convincing:

▶ Take time to evaluate the **credibility**—the quality, authority, and reliability—of each source you use (p. 357).

▶ Up-to-date information convinces the audience of its timeliness (p. 358).

▶ Citing accurate and exact sources gains audience respect (p. 358).

▶ Compelling information is influential and interesting (p. 358).

Give proper credit to sources and take responsibility for your speech:

▶ Avoid **plagiarism**, presenting someone else's intellectual property as your own (p. 359).

▶ Keep accurate track of all your references to avoid unintentional errors (pp. 359–360).

▶ Keeping a **running bibliography**, the list of resources you've consulted, will free you from having to write the same information over and over (p. 361).

▶ Honor the basic rules for ethical speaking (pp. 362–363).

Although the President of the United States is the sole figure to deliver the State of the Union address, he works with a whole team of writers and advisors behind the scenes to put the final speech together. Photo by Pete Souza/The White House via Getty Images

LearningCurve can help you master the material in this chapter.
Go to bedfordstmartins.com/realcomm.

chapter

13

Organizing, Writing, and Outlining Presentations

The Constitution of the United States of America makes a simple demand of the president. "He shall from time to time give to the Congress Information of the State of the Union, and recommend to their Consideration such Measures as he shall judge necessary and expedient" (art. 2, sec. 3).

For much of our nation's history, the State of the Union address was a lengthy letter to Congress read to members of the Senate and House by a congressional clerk. But over time it has evolved into an elaborate and highly politicized annual affair that allows the president to present major ideas and issues directly to the public: the Monroe Doctrine (James Monroe, 1823), the Four Freedoms (Franklin D. Roosevelt, 1941), the War on Terror (George W. Bush, 2002), and the economic overhaul (Barack Obama, 2013) were all detailed for the American people during State of the Union addresses (Amadeo, 2013; Longley, 2007).

And so each January, White House speechwriters face the daunting task of addressing both Congress and the nation with a speech that outlines what is going on in foreign and domestic policy in a way that flatters the president and garners support for his agenda for the following year. To make the task even more difficult, speechwriters must also navigate a deluge of requests from lobbyists, political consultants, and everyday citizens eager to get their pet project, policy, or idea into the president's speech. "Everybody wants [a] piece of the action," lamented former White House speechwriter Chriss Winston. "The speechwriter's job is to keep [the speech] on broad themes so it doesn't sink of its own weight." Matthew Scully (2005), one of President George W. Bush's speechwriters, concurred: "The entire thing can easily turn into a tedious grab bag of policy proposals."

After you have finished
reading this chapter,
you will be able to

○ Organize and support
your main points

○ Choose an appropriate
organizational pattern
for your speech

○ Move smoothly from
point to point

○ Choose appropriate and
powerful language

○ Develop a strong
introduction, a crucial
part of all speeches

○ Conclude with the same
strength as in the
introduction

○ Prepare an effective
outline

Imagine that you are building a bridge, a skyscraper, or even a house. You might have ambitious blueprints, but before you can build it, you need to form a solid foundation and develop a structurally sound framework. Any architect will tell you that even the most exciting and lofty designs are useless without these two crucial components. Skimp on either one and your structure will crack, shift, or collapse.

Building a speech follows a similar process. Whether you are writing a national address for the president of the United States or a five-minute class presentation, you will be unable to make your point if your speech is not structurally sound. As we discussed in Chapter 12, you begin with your idea and then build your foundation with research and a clear thesis statement. The next step is to develop your framework—the overall structure of your presentation. In this chapter, we'll focus on organizing all of your ideas and information into a clear and practical framework and integrating them into a well-written speech. Let's begin by considering the main points of your speech.

Organizing Your Speech Points

You've got your purpose, your research, and your thesis. But before you begin writing, it's best to organize your ideas—to set out the points you want to make, examples you plan to use to support them, and the basic order in which you want to present them. And you will want to do all of this *before* you write your introduction or conclusion. In this section, we'll focus on identifying your main points and developing your supporting points, in addition to considering useful ways to arrange those points and connect them in your speech.

Identifying Your Main Points

First and foremost, you must determine the **main points** of your speech, which are the central claims that support your specific speech purpose and your thesis statement (which you learned about in Chapter 12). That is, you need to identify and organize key ideas that will lead the audience members to accept or think about what you are asking them to do, believe, or consider.

Before you begin developing your main points, you may be wondering how many you will need in your speech. Because each speech is unique, there is no easy answer, but the general rule is that audiences have trouble remembering more than three or four main points. This guideline will serve you well for the purposes of your human communication course, but always check with your instructor if you have questions.

With this in mind, let's consider how main points work in action. Suppose you're giving a persuasive speech advocating for listeners to resist the temptation of texting while driving. What key points do you think will influence your listeners to see the immediate dangers of this behavior? Perhaps they would be motivated to do so if they knew the scope of the problem:

Main Point 1: Driver distraction, specifically mobile phone use while operating a motor vehicle, is a growing problem in the United States.

You'd likely further your argument by acknowledging the attempts governments and organizations have made to combat the problem:

> **Main Point 2:** Although many states have passed laws that ban mobile phone use while driving, these restrictions have not been particularly effective at solving the problem.

Finally, you might propose that the most promising solution lies with individuals making commitments to drive without distractions:

> **Main Point 3:** The only way to prevent distracted driving is to not drive while distracted! Each of us in this room has an obligation to be part of the solution by silencing our mobile phones in the car or even by making a public pledge not to text and drive.

Note that each main point includes only one major idea. This prevents you from overwhelming your audience with too much information and makes it easier for you to supply the examples, testimonies, statistics, and facts to back up each point. When in doubt about developing your main points, ask yourself "Does this point prove my thesis? Does it help me achieve my specific purpose?" If you can confidently answer yes, then you're on the right track.

Supporting Your Main Points

Each main point—as well as your speech as a whole—is fully fleshed out with the use of **subpoints** that provide support for the main points. Subpoints utilize your research to back up your main points in the same way that your main points back up your thesis statement and specific purpose; you can use a similar test to check their usefulness, asking yourself, "Does this bit of information back up my main point?" For example, three subpoints under our main point about driver mobile phone use as a growing traffic safety threat might be:

► In 2010, texting while driving increased 50 percent, and two out of ten drivers say they've sent text messages or e-mails while behind the wheel (CBS News, 2011)).

► The risk of a crash is 23.2 percent greater when texting while driving versus driving when not distracted (Gardner, 2011).

► Each day in the United States, more than nine people are killed and more than 1,060 people are injured in crashes that are reported to involve a distracted driver (National Highway Traffic Safety Administration, 2014).

Like main points, subpoints may—and often should—be backed up with more information, referred to as sub-subpoints.

Well-chosen supporting points will naturally fall under your main point in a clear hierarchy of ideas, forming the basic outline of your speech. Each main point should be supported by a number

CONNECT

When deciding which types of material to use to support your speech points, keep the cultural context in mind (Chapters 1 and 5). Cultural variables affect the type of research to which audience members respond. For example, if your audience consists of concerned parents of teenagers, they will likely be responsive to statistics and facts about teen driving distraction.

● **THINK OF YOUR MAIN POINTS** and subpoints as Russian *matryoshka* dolls— each sub-subpoint should nest inside a subpoint, which should nest inside your main point. Comstock/Jupiter Images

FIGURE 13.1

HIERARCHY OF POINTS Note how many sub-subpoints support a smaller number of subpoints. Each subpoint supports the main point. And the main point supports your thesis.

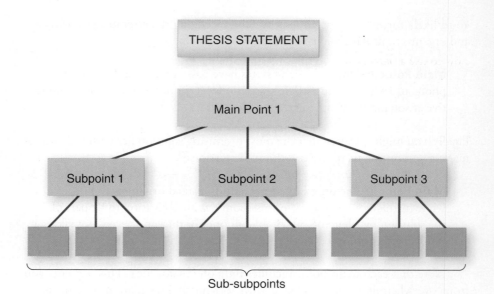

of coordinating subpoints, each carrying equal weight, as well as sub-subpoints that carry less weight. The resulting structure reflects a pyramidlike hierarchy of ideas: a foundation of many sub-subpoints supports a structure of fewer but larger subpoints, which in turn supports a few main points, which together support the thesis statement and ultimately your specific purpose. This structural hierarchy of points, depicted in Figure 13.1, ensures that you've presented a coherent and sturdy argument in support of your thesis and specific purpose. Later in the chapter, we'll show you how to use an outline to detail this hierarchy of points in a text format, but next we'll consider helpful ways to arrange your points.

Arranging Your Points

Think about creating a Facebook photo album of your recent trip to Europe. How would you arrange all of your pictures? You could work chronologically, simply uploading individual photos to one album in the order in which they were taken. Alternatively, you might arrange them by topic with separate albums for specific cities or countries visited or by types of activities (like one album for historical sites visited and another album for silly photos with friends).

You have similar options when preparing a speech. During the process of sorting out your main points and subpoints, you are taking the initial step of arranging your ideas in some sequence. Here are some common arrangements, or patterns, to consider.

Chronological Pattern

Often it makes sense to organize your points according to time: what happened first, second, and so on. A **chronological pattern** presents the main points of a message forward (or backward) in a systematic, time-related fashion. For example, you might use a chronological presentation when speaking about the development of Picasso's style over the course of his life. A chronological

AND YOU?

Organizing your main points and subpoints for a speech may seem overwhelming, but you've likely done this type of work before. Good, clear writing—whether an academic paper or an important letter—requires similar organization. Think of a particular piece of writing you were nervous about—a term paper or a private message to a potential romantic partner. What was the purpose of your writing? How did you go about organizing your main points?

organization can be especially effective when analyzing a step-by-step process, such as a presentation on the stages of grief or how to use a particular smartphone application.

Topical Pattern

Also known as a *categorical pattern*, the **topical pattern** is based on organization into categories, such as persons, places, things, or processes. Thus you might use it to describe the various departments in an organization, the characteristics of a successful employment interview, or the reasons for giving a charitable contribution to a specific organization.

One key concern when selecting this approach is the sequencing of topics, that is, which topic to offer first, second, and so on. Depending on the circumstances, you might choose an ascending or descending order, for example, according to increasing or decreasing importance, familiarity, or topic complexity. The **primacy–recency effect** can offer some guidance in that it notes that audiences are most likely to remember points you raise at the very beginning (primacy) or at the very end (recency) of a message, indicating that you might place your strongest point first or last so that your audience members keep it in mind long after the end of your presentation.

● **DECIDING HOW** to organize your speech, like figuring out how to display family photos on a wall or arranging pictures from a recent trip in a Facebook album, can be tricky because there are so many options to consider: you can do it chronologically, topically, or even spatially.
© Caro/Alamy

Spatial Pattern

The geographical or **spatial pattern** arranges main points in terms of their physical proximity in relation to each other (north to south, east to west, bottom to top, left to right, outside to inside, and so on). As an organizational pattern, it is most useful when describing objects, places, or scenes in terms of their component parts. For example, you might describe the physical layout of the Mall in Washington, D.C., using a spatial pattern.

Problem–Solution Pattern

If you're trying to call an audience to action to address a particular problem, the **problem–solution pattern** of organization can be especially effective. This pattern involves dramatizing an obstacle and then narrowing alternative remedies down to the one that you recommend. The message is organized to focus on three key points:

1. There is a problem that requires a change in attitude, belief, or behavior.

2. A number of possible solutions might solve this problem.

3. Your solution is the one that will provide the most effective and efficient remedy.

Topics that lend themselves to this pattern include business, social, economic, and political problems for which you can propose a workable solution. For example, the persuasive speech described earlier about convincing listeners not to text while driving follows this pattern. The first main point established the problem, the second point described the ineffectiveness of current government efforts to address the issue, and the third point proposed a solution—that listeners themselves make the pledge not to text while driving.

Cause–Effect Pattern

With the **cause–effect pattern**, you attempt to organize the message around cause-to-effect or effect-to-cause relationships. That is, you might move from a discussion of the origins or causes of a phenomenon (for example, rising fuel costs) to the eventual results or effects (increases in the cost of airplane tickets). You can also work in reverse, starting with a description of present conditions and then examining apparent or possible causes. The choice of

---

EVALUATING**COMMUNICATION**ETHICS

THINK ABOUT THIS

The Ethics of Using Research

Six years ago, you and a group of dog-loving friends and neighbors cleaned up an abandoned lot and created "Central Bark," a public dog run. With the help of an online fund-raising campaign and the city's permission, members of the group installed fences, lighting, benches, and a fountain and organized volunteers to ensure the site is clean and cared for. But a few weeks ago, a child was bitten by a dog while walking near the park. Now local residents are concerned that the park is a danger to public safety; there have been calls to ban all dogs from the space. In hopes of keeping the dog run open, your group has asked you to come up with a few key arguments, backed up with solid research, to present to the local civic association at its next meeting.

Like others in the neighborhood, you want to keep dangerous animals out of the park, but you also know that this is the first incident in or around the park since the organization began managing the dog run, and the dog involved was unleashed and outside of the dog run when the event occurred. You also know that although the animal's owner did make use of the dog run, he is not a member of your group and did not have the dog licensed or up to date on its shots.

You believe that the dog run is a valuable part of the neighborhood, not only because it provides pet owners with an enclosed place to let their dogs play but also because, before your group created its partnership with the city, the park was an unused, derelict lot. Going through old news coverage, you find that prior to the dog run opening, the lot was a known location for drug transactions and the site of several assaults. There have been no such crimes recorded there since your group took over the lot six years ago. You are delighted by these statistics and believe that they prove that the improvements your group made to the lot—including the addition of lighting, fences, and increased foot traffic—have actually made the area safer than it was before. But then read further statistics that show that, during the same time frame, drug-related crimes have plummeted across the board in your town—not only at the lot location. You are pretty sure that if you just present the data for the location, you may be able to persuade the board to keep the park open, but you also know that your data may be flawed. What do you do?

1 Just how flawed is your data? Is it possible that the improvements to the lot really have had an impact on crime at that specific location? How might you find out?

2 What other ideas might you propose in order to ensure that dog attacks don't happen again? How can you ensure that only responsible dog owners use the park? What kind of evidence would you seek to support your proposals?

3 Bearing in mind that a child has been injured, is it possible that the park really should be closed? What kind of research should you conduct to obtain unbiased information on how dog runs like Central Bark impact public safety?

strategy is often based on which element—cause or effect—is more familiar to the intended audience: if you're talking about fuel prices, for example, it might be best to start with the cost of gasoline—a very familiar expense—and work backward from there. The cause–effect pattern of organization is especially useful when your purpose is to get your audience to agree with or understand your point rather than to call people to action.

Narrative Pattern

Speakers often tie their points together in a way that presents a vivid story, complete with characters, settings, plot, and imagery. This is called a **narrative pattern**. However, most speeches built largely on a story (or a series of stories) are likely to incorporate elements of other organizational arrangements. For example, you might present a story in a cause–effect design, in which you first reveal that something happened (such as a small aircraft crash) and then describe the events that led up to the accident (the causes).

● **WHEN ORGANIZING** your speech in a narrative pattern, put your feet in a storyboard artist's shoes. Visualize your outline as a storyboard, and think of your speech points as scenes. The Kobal Collection at Art Resource, NY

Motivated Sequence Pattern

The **motivated sequence pattern**, created more than seventy years ago by the noted public speaking scholar Alan Monroe, is a five-step plan for organizing a speech that can be useful in a variety of contexts. Based on the psychological elements of advertising, the motivated sequence pattern includes five phases: attention, need, satisfaction, visualization, and action. Monroe argued that these five steps motivate listeners and may be modified to suit the desired outcome of your speech. Presentations that lend themselves to the motivated sequence include persuasive presentations, inspirational speeches, graduation addresses, speeches advocating social change, and motivational talks. For a more detailed discussion and examples of Monroe's motivated sequence, please see pp. 487–488 in Chapter 16.

Connecting Your Points

When you're pulling together, supporting, and arranging your points, you may find yourself falling into what we like to call the "grocery list trap." Essentially, this is where your speech begins to seem like a thorough list of good but seemingly unrelated ideas. So, how do you move smoothly from one point to another? The key lies in your use of transitions, signposts, and internal previews and summaries.

Transitions

Transitions are sentences that connect different points, thoughts, and details in a way that allows them to flow naturally from one to the next. Clear transitions cue the audience in on where you're headed with the speech and how your ideas

AND YOU?

Clearly, transitions help to clarify messages and keep them flowing in oral and written forms of communication. But do transitions function similarly in mediated communication contexts? For example, how might you transition between points and ideas via text message or instant message?

and supporting material are connected. They also alert your audience that you will be making a point. Consider the following examples of transitions:

▶ "I've just described some of the amazing activities you can enjoy in our National Parks, so let me tell you about two parks that you can visit within a three-hour drive of our campus."

▶ "In addition to the environmental benefits of riding your bike to school, there are some fantastic financial and health benefits that you can enjoy."

Notice how the transitions in both examples also serve to alert your audience that you will be making a point that you want them to remember. Transitions are, therefore, essential to making your points clear and easy to follow.

COMMUNICATIONACROSSCULTURES

THINK ABOUT THIS

Evidence, Popular Culture, and the "*CSI* Effect"

"We've got a match." If you've ever watched *CSI* or any of its several spin-offs, you know that those words are usually the clincher in a comparison of evidence from the murder scene to something belonging to a suspect—be it DNA, carpet fibers, or bullets. The popular procedural drama is based on the premise that stalwart and brilliant teams of forensic scientists can and will work tirelessly to find and present evidence that indisputably solves crimes.

In fact, most of the evidence presented by the show's crime scene investigators is far from indisputable, and the show's portrayal of forensic science is sometimes closer to science fiction than science fact. Fiber evidence, for example, can be examined for possible connections, but no scientist would be able to testify under oath that a specific fiber came from a specific vehicle. Only DNA evidence really comes close to what most scientists would consider mathematical certainty (Toobin, 2007). The show also misleads juries about the technology available to prosecutors—much of the technology shown is beyond the reach of most departments or simply does not exist—as well as the time frame for obtaining results (Toobin, 2007). Mike Murphy, the Las Vegas coroner whose lab was the inspiration for the original *CSI* show, explains that "people expect us to have DNA back in 20 minutes or that we're supposed to solve a crime in 60 minutes with three commercials. It doesn't happen that way" (Rath, 2011).

Some legal scholars worry that the popularity of shows like *CSI* may bias juries in several ways. There is a possibility that jurors who follow the shows believe they have developed some level of expertise about forensic evidence or, at the very least, some expectation that the kinds of evidence presented on *CSI* will be available for every case, a theory that has become known as the "*CSI* effect." Although there is no evidence that watching such programs has any impact on trial outcomes, there are some indications that watching these shows may influence the way jurors perceive the quality of police work in investigations as well as their behavior during deliberations (Rath, 2011; Thomas, 2006).

❶ Do you watch police procedurals like *CSI*? How realistic do you think they are? Does popular culture have an impact on how individuals perceive evidence or detective work? Do you think you would be a more sophisticated juror than someone who doesn't watch such shows?

❷ If you were on a jury in a criminal trial, what would your expectations for evidence be? Would you be willing to convict someone based on a fiber sample, even if the expert witness described it as "similar" rather than "a match"?

❸ Do you think that shows like *CSI* have an ethical responsibility to depict forensic science more realistically? Or is it the audience's responsibility to separate entertainment from reality?

Signposts

Effective speakers make regular use of **signposts**, key words or phrases within sentences that signify transitions between points. Think of signposts as links or pivot points at which you either connect one point to another ("similarly," "next," "once again,") or move from one point to a related but perhaps opposing or alternative point ("however," "on the other hand").

▶ "*Another way* you can help to fight puppy mills is to boycott pet stores that sell animals from disreputable sources."

▶ "*The third problem* with our current emergency room system is that there simply isn't enough money to fund our ERs."

● **DIRECT THE AUDIENCE** from one point in your speech to the next with signpost words or phrases, such as "similarly" or "on the other hand." Jonathan Larsen/Veer

Table 13.1 details various examples of signposts and considers how they function effectively to achieve a specific purpose.

Internal Previews and Internal Summaries

Like a good map that shows travelers points along the way to their destination, **internal previews** prime the audience for the content immediately ahead. They often work best in conjunction with **internal summaries**, which allow the speaker to crystallize the points made in one section of a speech before moving to the next section. For example:

▶ "So far, I have presented two reasons why you should visit the dentist annually. First, it prevents gum disease. Second, it also helps you avoid tooth decay. Now I will address my third point: regular visits to the dentist will benefit your overall good health."

▶ "Now that I have explained what asthma is and the two main types of asthma, allergic and nonallergic, I will discuss what you can do to avoid an asthma attack."

By first summarizing and then previewing, the speaker has created a useful transition that gracefully moves the speech forward while offering audiences an opportunity to synthesize the information already received.

Using Language That Works

Now you know quite a bit about identifying, supporting, arranging, and moving between the main points of your speech. But to describe and explain the points themselves, you must make competent language choices that bring your ideas to life right before your audience's eyes. The words that you choose for your speech are clearly powerful, so it's important to think about them *now*, in the preparation and writing stages, so that you can eventually incorporate them into your actual presentation.

TABLE 13.1
USEFUL SIGNPOSTS

Function	Example
To show comparison	Similarly In the same way In comparison
To contrast ideas, facts, or data	On the other hand Alternatively In spite of
To illustrate cause and effect	It follows, then, that Consequently Therefore Thus
To indicate explanation	For example In other words To clarify
To introduce additional examples	Another way in which Just as Likewise In a similar fashion
To emphasize significance	It's important to remember that Above all Bear in mind
To indicate sequence of time or events	First, Second, Third Finally First and foremost Once Now, Then Until now Before, After Earlier, Later Primarily
To summarize	As we've seen Altogether Finally In conclusion

Source: O'Hair, Stewart, & Rubenstein (2012), p. 189. Adapted with permission.

Part of using language your audience understands involves a careful consideration of *jargon*—technical language specific to a particular industry, organization, or group (see Chapter 3). Jargon might be useful among a very homogenous group, but it can alienate audience members in other settings. A doctor might use medical jargon when addressing colleagues but needs to use everyday terms when addressing other groups.

Respect Your Audience

As noted earlier, communication involves not only what we say but also how others perceive what we say. Most audiences are composed of both men and women from many different cultures, races, religious backgrounds, lifestyles, and educational levels. Therefore, it is important to use unbiased and appropriate language that makes the entire audience feel included and respected.

Keep It Simple

Albert Einstein once advised, "Make everything as simple as possible, but no simpler." This applies to language: speakers and writers who use unfamiliar or inappropriately complex language are not as effective as those who speak directly and in terms that their audience can readily understand and interpret. You don't need to "dumb down" your points; just make your points in a language that is clear, simple, and unambiguous so that your audience can follow what you are saying. In addition, there is no speaker quite as dreaded as the long-winded speaker who repeats the same points or uses six examples where one would suffice. (Admit it—we've all sat through speeches like this!) If you keep your speech short and to the point, you'll have a better chance of reaching your audience with your intended message.

Use Vivid Language

Language paints a picture for an audience. The more vivid your terms, the more audience members can use their imaginations and their senses. For example, if you say you have a car, your listeners get a common, forgettable fact. If you tell them that your father drove a faded orange 1972 Volkswagen Beetle with a dent in the left fender and a broken taillight, you'll give them a very clear and memorable picture of this vehicle. You may assume your great, eye-catching slides and props will paint the picture for you, but you must not forget that words count—often even more than your Power-Point slides.

Incorporate Repetition, Allusion, and Comparisons

In 1851, American abolitionist and women's rights activist Sojourner Truth delivered an effective and memorable speech at the Women's Convention in Akron, Ohio. The speech known as "Ain't I a Woman?" is effective not only because of its powerful message about the evils of slavery and the mistreatment of women but also because Truth's passionate use of language helped make a lasting impression on her listeners. Consider, for example, her use of repetition, allusion, and comparisons. (See Sample Speech 13.1.)

Repetition

Repetition—saying compelling terms, phrases, or even entire sentences more than once—can help increase the likelihood that the audience will remember what matters most in your speech. In Truth's speech, she repeats "Ain't I a woman?" several times. This repetition highlights each of the injustices she feels and influences audience members to consider Truth deserving of the rights and privileges withheld from her.

Allusion

An *allusion* is making a vague or indirect reference to people, historical events, or concepts that an audience will recognize in order to give deeper meaning to the message and possibly evoke emotional responses. Allusions can also provide grounded context that goes beyond what you are saying directly. In Truth's

AND YOU?

Have you ever been part of an audience that had to sit through a speech when the speaker failed to use language the audience easily understood? Do you remember anything important from this speech—or even its main point? How did you feel during the speech?

● **AUDIENCE MEMBERS** wouldn't conjure up this clear and memorable a picture in their minds unless it was painted with vivid language by the speaker. © ilbusca/istockphoto .com

CONNECT

In Chapters 4 and 14, you learn about nonverbal aspects of speech such as rate, pauses, tone, volume, and pitch. In many cases, these factors can help you use repetition effectively. For example, if you repeat a phrase with an upward inflection of voice followed by a pause, you will help the audience anticipate the next line and enhance their retention of your main points.

I Sell the Shadow to Support the Substance.
SOJOURNER TRUTH.

● Notice how Truth encourages the audience to extend this existing belief about women to her, as she too is a woman.

● Truth invokes religious stories that are familiar to the audience members in her effort to persuade them.

SAMPLE SPEECH 13.1

Ain't I a Woman?

SOJOURNER TRUTH

Well, children, where there is so much racket there must be something out of kilter. I think that 'twixt the negroes of the South and the women at the North, all talking about rights, the white men will be in a fix pretty soon. But what's all this here talking about?

That man over there says the women need to be helped into carriages, and lifted over ditches, and to have the best place everywhere. Nobody ever helps me into carriages, or over mud-puddles, or gives me any best place! And ain't I a woman? Look at me! Look at my arm! I have ploughed and planted, and gathered into barns, and no man could head me! And ain't I a woman? I could work as much and eat as much as a man—when I could get it—and bear the lash as well! And ain't I a woman? I have borne thirteen children, and seen most all sold off to slavery, and when I cried out with my mother's grief, none but Jesus heard me! And ain't I a woman? ●

Then they talk about this thing in the head; what's this they call it? [member of the audience whispers "intellect"] That's it, honey. What's that got to do with women's rights or negroes' rights? If my cup won't hold but a pint, and yours holds a quart, wouldn't you be mean not to let me have my little half measure full?

Then that little man in black there, he says women can't have as much rights as men, 'cause Christ wasn't a woman! Where did your Christ come from? Where did your Christ come from? From God and a woman! Man had nothing to do with Him.

If the first woman God ever made was strong enough to turn the world upside down all alone, these women together ought to be able to turn it back, and get it right side up again. And now they is asking to do it, the men better let them. ●

Obliged to you for hearing me, and now old Sojourner ain't got nothing more to say.

Source: From Sojourner Truth, "Ain't I a Woman?" speech delivered at the Women's Convention in Akron, Ohio, May 1851. Retrieved from http://www.feminist.com /resources/artspeech/genwom/sojour.htm

"Ain't I a Woman?" speech, for example, she uses allusion with the words "If the first woman God ever made was strong enough to turn the world upside down all alone, these women together ought to be able to turn it back, and get it right side up again." She is alluding to the biblical figure Eve, who ate the forbidden fruit from the tree of the knowledge of good and evil, and upset the harmonious balance between God and humankind. Truth does not take time to explain this story; she knows that her audience will understand her reference and uses allusion to add power and emotion to her message.

Comparisons: Similes and Metaphors

One of the most common and useful tools in public speaking is the figure of speech known as the *simile*. A simile uses *like* or *as* to compare two things. Truth uses a simile to conjure up the images of her strength and fortitude when she states "I could work as much and eat as much as a man—when I could get it—and bear the lash as well!"

Like similes, *metaphors* liken one thing to another, but in a literal way, even though there may be no literal connection between the two. A metaphor presents the comparison as a statement of fact—it does not contain the word *like* or *as*—but it is not expected to be taken as a fact. You might use a metaphor, such as "The fog was a heavy blanket over the city," to add imagery to your speech.

Writing a Strong Introduction

CONNECT

Like a lead paragraph of a news story that hooks in readers, the introduction to your speech must accomplish four crucial tasks: grab your audience's attention, introduce your purpose and topic, offer a preview of your main points, and give your listeners a sense of who you are and why they should want to hear what you have to say. Recall the "primacy" part of the *primacy–recency effect* discussed earlier in this chapter. Your introduction is the first thing your audience will hear; it therefore sets the tone and the stage for the rest of your speech.

Your speech introduction is the first impression you give your audience. But introductions are important in other contexts as well. The Interviewing Appendix shows how your résumé and cover letter give a potential employer an introduction to you and your abilities. If your résumé has typos or other errors, your first impression will be less than stellar—just as a disorganized or inappropriate speech introduction leaves a negative impression with your audience.

Capture Your Audience's Attention

Finding a creative, attention-grabbing opening can be a struggle, but in the end it will be well worth the effort, for your first words can and do make a big impression on your audience (Hockenbury & Hockenbury, 2009). If you open with something as boring as "Hi, my name is . . ." or "Today I'm going to talk about . . . ," your audience may conclude that there's nothing more interesting to follow. In many cases, it is a good idea to finalize your introduction after the bulk of your speech is complete. This can be an advantage because you will approach your introduction armed with your main points and your supporting material—and probably a few ideas on how to make it lively! Consider the following suggestions.

Use Surprise

It is likely that during research on your topic, you came across a fact, statistic, quote, or story that truly surprised you. Chances are that such information will likewise come as a surprise to your audience. A startling statement uses unusual

AND YOU?

Take a look at your research. Of all the evidence you have gathered for your speech, what jumps out at you? Did you come across any statistics that shocked you? Did you encounter any individuals whose stories touched you—with humor, sadness, or surprise? Think about how any of the statistics, facts, anecdotes, and quotes you've gathered might be worked into an effective introduction.

or unexpected information to get an audience's attention. For example, in a speech on sleep deprivation, you might begin your speech as follows:

> Did you know that every semester, university students are legally drunk for one week straight? Yet despite feeling drunk, they never drink a drop of alcohol. During finals week, students at the University of Oklahoma sleep an average of five hours per night. Sleep deprivation—getting five hours or less of sleep per night—can affect reaction time and mental sharpness. After being awake for seventeen hours straight, a sleep-deprived person has the reaction time and mental sharpness of someone with a blood alcohol concentration of 0.05, which is considered legally drunk throughout most of Europe.

Tell a Story

As discussed in Chapter 12, anecdotes can be useful illustrations for your speech. Real-world stories can be particularly effective when worked into your opening, where they can make audiences feel invested in a person before they even know what your thesis is. For example, Miriam thinks her audience will tune out if she simply informs them that she's going to discuss the secret costs of credit cards. But what if she opens with a story? For example:

> A few months ago, my friend Monica—not her real name—decided that she positively *needed* to own a pair of Jimmy Choo boots. Now, I'll admit, these were some amazing boots: black leather, calf-high, four-inch heels. But they cost—are you sitting down?—$895.00. Like most of us, she didn't have that kind of cash lying around, so she bought the boots on credit and figured that she would pay them off month by month. Despite the fact that she diligently puts $50 toward her payment each and every month, it's going to take Monica 102 months—more than eight years—to pay for those boots. In addition, she'll pay over $750 in interest, which is almost as much as the boots cost in the first place!

By telling a story, Miriam puts a familiar face on her subject; she's also caught the attention of anyone who's ever had the experience of really wanting something they couldn't afford—which is pretty much anyone!

Start with a Quote

Leading with a quotation is a convenient and interesting speech opening. Quotes can connect you as a speaker to real people and real situations. For example, Kenneth is preparing an informative speech on Alzheimer's disease. In his opening, he uses a quote from former president Ronald Reagan, who passed away in 2004 after a ten-year struggle with the disease:

> "I now begin the journey that will lead me to the sunset of my life." That's how Ronald Reagan, upon learning he would be afflicted with Alzheimer's disease, described the illness that would eventually rob him of the eloquence, wit, and intelligence that had defined him as an actor, politician, and president. I'm here today to talk about the tragedy of Alzheimer's disease.

Use quotes worth using.	Don't quote something that you could say or explain more effectively in your own words; paraphrase instead, with an attribution to the original source.
Use relevant quotes.	Even the prettiest bit of prose is useless if it doesn't support your points.
Include a clear attribution.	Whether you're quoting Shakespeare or your six-year-old nephew, it's important that audiences know who said what.
Is the quote from a notable source?	Cite not only the author in your speech but also the date and the work in which the quote appeared, if relevant.
Double-check for accuracy.	You do not want to misquote anyone in your speech, so it's important that you proofread your copy against the original. If you've used an online quote source, it is wise to double-check the quote against additional sources known to be reliable because many online quotes fail to provide accurate source information.

TABLE 13.2

USING QUOTES WISELY

Quotations can come from familiar sources, like Reagan, or from everyday people. Table 13.2 offers tips for using quotes wisely.

Ask a Question

Posing a question is a great way to get the audience's attention and to make people think. Rather than simply presenting some bit of information, posing a question invites listeners to react, in effect making them participants in the speech.[1] For example, "Would you leave your child in a room full of anonymous strangers? No? Then why would you allow your child to participate in online chats?" Here again, saying something startling can add to the effect: not only have you gotten your listeners' attention by saying something provocative, but you've also asked them to internalize what you've said and to react to it. As a result, they're likely to be more interested in and open to what you're about to say.

Make Them Laugh

Humor is another effective way to begin your speech. Usually, humor that is brief, relevant to your topic, and makes a point is most effective. (And when it's well done, humor helps you and your audience members relax!) For example, consider this opening, which makes the audience laugh but is clearly tied to the main topic of the speech on the effects of multitasking: "I find that the key to multitasking is to lower your expectations. Sure, I can do two things at once—if I do them poorly! Today, I want to talk about the hazards of multitasking."

---

[1]Asking questions is an effective way of gaining participation in many communication contexts; see O'Hair, O'Rourke, and O'Hair (2000).

Introduce Your Purpose and Thesis

Whether you capture your audience's attention with stories, questions, or quotations, it is *essential* that your introduction also clearly establishes what your speech is about and what you hope to achieve by speaking. You do this by incorporating your thesis statement. Imagine that you just caught your audience's attention with the description of a fun-filled and active day: kayaking on a pristine lake, hiking in a rain forest, rock climbing on a craggy coastline, and so on. You would then introduce your thesis: "All of these activities—and many more—are available to you in one of our nation's most diverse protected spaces: Olympic National Park. I hope to persuade you to visit and to take advantage of all this park has to offer."

Preview Your Main Points

Another key goal for your introduction is to provide a preview of the main points that will be covered in the body of the speech, in the order that you will talk about them. For example, if you are giving a speech about why students should enroll in an art course, you might say: "There are two reasons why every college student should enroll in an art course. First, it provides students with a creative outlet, and second it teaches students useful and creative ways of thinking about their own subjects of study." Audiences prefer to listen to speakers who are prepared and have a plan the audience can follow; by previewing, you offer a mental outline that your listeners can follow as they attend to your speech.

Connect with Your Audience

Another goal for your introduction is to establish a relationship with your listeners, providing them with a sense of who you are and why they should listen to what you have to say. Like participants in an interview, the members of your audience will come to your speech with three points in mind. They will be curious about the nature of your speech—will it be boring, interesting, or inspiring? They'll also be wondering what they will get from it— will the speech be worth their time and attention? Finally, they will be curious about you as a speaker— will they like and trust you? Your introduction should provide enough information to allow the audience to make accurate assumptions about your speech and about you.

One way that a speaker can establish a relationship with the audience is to demonstrate why listeners should care about the topic. First, make sure that you verbally link the topic to the audience's interests. You should also try to appeal to your listeners' personal needs—let them know what's in it for them. For example, a college recruiter speaking at a high school might talk about what his school offers prospective students. He might also touch on recent local or national events to show the relevance of the school's curriculum.

Writing a Strong Conclusion

There's a reason why courtroom dramas like TV's *Suits* almost always include footage of the hero lawyer's closing statements. When a wealth of evidence, testimony, and facts have been presented, it's easy for juries (and television audiences) to get bogged down in the details and lose track of the bigger, more dramatic picture. For any speaker, it is important to end a presentation with a compelling and pointed conclusion. Once again, the "recency" part of the primacy–recency effect reminds us that the conclusion is the *last* thing the audience will hear in your speech, and it is likely what they will remember most. As such, a speech conclusion must address a number of functions.

● **WHETHER IN THE TV** show *Suits* or a real-world courtroom, one of the most crucial moments in a trial is the closing statement. It's the lawyer's last chance to make his or her case to the jury. Christos Kalohoridis / © USA Network / Courtesy Everett Collection

Signal the End

Your conclusion should alert the audience that the speech is coming to a close. You might use a transitional phrase, such as "In conclusion," "Finally," or "Let me close by saying. . . ." Such phrases serve as signposts, telling audiences that you're about to conclude and asking for their full attention one last time. Remember to keep it brief. Audiences do not like to be overwhelmed with a lot of new information at the end.

Reinforce Your Topic, Purpose, and Main Points

The conclusion of your speech is the last opportunity you'll have to reinforce the topic and purpose of your speech as well as to remind your audience about the key points you want to live on in their memories. In other words, competent speakers should reiterate this essential information so that listeners are able to mentally check off what they have heard and what they should remember. For example, "Today, I discussed the benefits of seeing your physician for an annual physical, even if you're young and feeling fine. Not only can this simple visit offer peace of mind and help to prevent costly medical conditions in the future, but it may also save your life if you have an underlying medical problem that requires early diagnosis and treatment."

Make an Impact

Your conclusion should be memorable and interesting for your audience members, a culmination of all your efforts to develop your points and share your research. Several techniques discussed in the section on introductions can be useful for memorable conclusions as well.

Quotations

To wrap up a speech, speakers often use quotes from historical figures, writers, philosophers, or celebrities. Take care in choosing a quote so that you leave the audience with something to think about. For example, if you are concluding a speech that illustrates the importance of friendships, you might quote the writer Edna Buchanan: "Friends are the family you choose for yourself" (www.ednabuchanan.com). A strong quotation helps make an unforgettable impression.

real communicator

NAME: Chad Ludwig
OCCUPATION: Brand Marketing/Digital Entertainment Executive

The next time you play a game or watch a video online, think of me. Most of my days are spent marketing games and other digital entertainment. My job is dynamic—just like the games themselves—and involves working with diverse audiences: financial stakeholders (investors or company executives), product teams (developers, creative talent, programmers), media (TV, online, social, e-mail, etc.), PR & Promotion executives, and, most importantly, the customer (you!). In a nutshell, I craft messages to convey targeted ideas to each audience, employing the bedrock skills of organizing and writing material. But unlike a speech that's over in a few minutes, my messages reverberate for weeks or months in the form of television advertisements or a "viral" speech (like the ones I produce for YouTube).

I've been involved in the launch of video games from Disney's *Toontown* to *Cars* to *Pirates* and beyond. A lot of time, effort, and planning goes into a successful marketing campaign: knowing the audience and understanding the audience's needs, establishing goals, crafting specific messages, carefully timing the advertisements, and reinforcing a central message throughout the effort (e.g., through Facebook and Twitter). In my experience, there are four key organizational components to successful campaigns: get the audience's attention (Why should I watch this ad when I could be taking a nap?), establish the context (What is this game? What makes it interesting?), give people a reason to care about the product (Why should I buy this game or spend time playing it?), and, most importantly, provide a call to action (How do I purchase this game?).

One of the challenges in all these steps is to use appropriate and effective language and visuals. When I worked on *Pirates*, we thought our promotions should feature sword fighting the undead enemy. However, our initial research with ten- to fourteen-year-olds revealed that they liked ship battling more, so we changed our promotions accordingly. The main point of our campaign (*Pirates* is an exciting, fun game) remained the same, but we tweaked all sorts of details for the audience and the media we were using.

Working in digital content requires that I collaborate early and often with our teams so that we can successfully introduce a great product and sustain consumer enthusiasm for months or even years. Games are not packaged goods that are only purchased once; the content is the basis for an ongoing consumer relationship and my colleagues and I reinforce our key positioning statements throughout that effort. With so many people involved, both the message and the players need to be organized and continually tuned to customer feedback to maximize our ability to communicate effectively.

Statements and Questions

In some types of speeches, it can be especially effective to end with a statement or question that drives home your main point. This rhetorical device is important for conclusions because you want to emphasize the points you made during your speech and have the audience feel connected to your ideas. For example, you might end a speech explaining how to change the oil in your car with a simple statement that sums up your thesis: "Remember, the best way to protect your car is to change the oil every three thousand miles—and it's something you can do yourself."

A Final Story

Stories can be as effective for conclusions as they are for introductions. Stories should always tie in to your speech topic, be relatively short, and make a related point. For example, if you are advocating a college-level foreign-language requirement for your college, you might tell this well-known tale: "Mother Mouse was crossing the street with her three children. She got about halfway across when she saw a cat, ready to pounce upon them. The cat and Mother Mouse eyeballed each other for several minutes. Finally, Mother Mouse let out an enormous 'WOOF!' The cat ran away. Mother Mouse turned to her children and said, 'NOW do you see the advantage of a second language?'"

Reference the Introduction

A final suggestion for creating a strong conclusion is to remind the audience of how you began the speech. If you told a dramatic, powerful story in the introduction, finish it or add a new insight in the conclusion; if you asked a question, answer it. For example, if you began your persuasive speech about cyberbullying with a story about the tragic suicide of Tyler Clemente (who jumped from New York City's George Washington Bridge after being bullied in September 2010), you might say: "We must never forget Tyler Clemente and the other young lives cut short by senseless bullying. Who knows? Your best friend, your younger brother, or your son could just have easily been on that bridge that fateful September evening."

Challenge the Audience to Respond

Whether you are giving an informative or persuasive speech, as the speaker you must consider what you want your audience to *do* with the information you are providing. According to O'Hair, Stewart, and Rubenstein (2012), in an informative speech, you should challenge your audience members to make use of the information. You may extend an invitation to your listeners: "Please join me on Wednesday evening for a town hall meeting on this subject. Our local congressperson will be there to listen to our concerns. I will have the sign-up sheet in the back of the room for you at the end of my presentation."

In most persuasive speeches, the challenge will come through a **call to action** that asks listeners to act in response to the speech, see the problem in a new way, or change their beliefs, actions, and behavior (O'Hair, Stewart, & Rubenstein, 2012). For example, "Sign this petition. In doing so, you will make a difference in someone's life and make our voices heard" or "Don't forget to vote next Tuesday!"

AND YOU?

What kind of impression would you want to leave your audience with? What is the one thing you'd like people to remember about you and your speech?

Outlining Your Speech

At this point, you have all of the building blocks for a successful speech. Now you're ready to pull all of your hard work together in the form of an **outline**—a structured form of your speech content (Fraleigh & Tuman, 2011). An effective outline helps you confirm that your points are arranged clearly and properly, ensures that you've cited your all-important research, and assists you in your

WIREDFORCOMMUNICATION

Bullets on the Brain

There is something sinister in the world of public speaking. You've undoubtedly been exposed to it, at work or at school. It's probably in your home computer. But it's not a virus. You probably paid to have it there. And according to one of the nation's leading experts, it's making all of us stupid.

Edward Tufte is a professor of political science, computer science and statistics, and graphic design at Yale University and has been academia's most influential voice on the subject of the visual display of information for over two decades. He is an expert on the use of graphs and visual aids to explain all types of information, from train schedules to empirical data. He uses computers all the time to crunch numbers and present quantitative information. But Tufte is no fan of presentation software (such as Microsoft PowerPoint, Apple Keynote, Google Presentations, and Prezi). The problem, Tufte (2003) explains, is that programs like PowerPoint force presentations into an outline format, with little development beyond a series of bulleted lists. Because a typical slide contains a mere forty words—about eight seconds of reading—presentations become a succession of short, boring lists of facts, presented out of context and with little room for evaluation.

Of course, current software programs offer you the opportunity to do more than just present bulleted lists. They can add real visual interest to a speech, enabling you to easily share photographs, cartoons, charts, and graphics with an audience. If your presentation includes a lot of data, the use of a few simple graphs can help you to quickly convey quantitative information, rather than just rattling off numbers that your audience is likely to have a hard time visualizing. The problem comes in when presenters rely on the program to design the content of their speeches rather than to enhance it. Tufte finds that a program's format "routinely disrupts, dominates, and trivializes content" (Tufte, 2003).

The best remedy? Make sure you've got good content and only use visual displays that really convey meaning. A solid graph, for example, doesn't just present numbers: it helps the audience to understand the numbers you are presenting. As one tech writer, drawing on Tufte's work, explained, "When you're putting together a chart, you're trying to show one of four things with the data you have: a *relationship* between data points, a *comparison* of data points, a *composition* of data, or a *distribution* of data" (Henry, 2012). Most importantly, remember that pictures may be pretty, but content is still king. "If your numbers are boring, then you've got the wrong numbers," Tufte writes. "If your words or images are not on point, making them dance in color won't make them relevant."

THINK ABOUT THIS

❶ The use of visuals during lectures and presentations is nothing new—instructors and presenters made use of overhead projectors and slide shows for decades before computers arrived on the academic scene. Why is Tufte being so hard on speakers who use them now?

❷ We've spent much of this chapter talking about the importance of outlining and of communicating your final outline clearly to your audience. How is that different from presenting your outline in slide form?

❸ Are there some subjects or types of speeches that lend themselves to software presentations? Are there others that don't?

speech delivery. (In fact, many instructors require students to turn in a formal outline before the presentation. Be sure to check on your instructor's preferences.)

You may already be familiar with the basics of outlining from your high school courses or from your college composition class. We'll refresh you with a discussion of the essentials of outlining before we move to types of outlines and the heart of this section: the preparation and speaking outlines.

Essentials of Outlining

In every phase of outlining, basic guidelines will help you structure and prepare your speech. A solid outline will clearly reveal the structure of your arguments and the hierarchy of your points.

▶ *Use standard symbols.* What an outline does, essentially, is put the hierarchy of points visualized in Figure 13.1 (p. 370) into a text format. To do this, outlines generally use roman numerals, letters, and standard numbers to indicate different levels of importance in the hierarchy.

   I. Main Point

     A. Subpoint

     B. Subpoint

       1. Sub-subpoint

       2. Sub-subpoint

If you need to break down the sub-subpoints even further, you may use lower-case letters (a, b, etc.) to create sub-sub-subpoints.

▶ *Use subdivisions properly.* It is basic logic that a whole of anything—a sandwich, a doughnut, or an outline heading—can never be split into fewer than two pieces. Therefore, as you divide your ideas from main points to subpoints, remember that each numbered or lettered entry must come in a series of at least two points: if you have a I, you must have a II; if you have an A, you must have a B; and so on.

▶ *Separate the parts of your speech.* It is typically helpful to label your introduction, conclusion, and even your transitions to distinguish them from the body of your speech (your main points and supporting subpoints).

▶ *Call out your specific purpose and thesis.* Many instructors want students to include this pertinent information at the top of the outline, so check with your instructor to determine his or her preference. You may feel that you already know this information by heart, but it can be helpful to see it at the top of your outline page, ensuring that all of your main points support the purpose and thesis. Also, you may wind up tweaking them a bit as you work your way through the outlining process.

▶ *Cite your sources.* As discussed in Chapter 12, it is extremely important to give proper citations in your speech. As you work on the outline, you should always mark where a specific point requires credit. Directly after the point, either insert a footnote or a reference in parentheses; once

CONNECT

The ability to outline complex information into manageable steps is useful beyond public speaking. Chapter 9 covers task roles in groups, which involve people organizing the activities that help achieve a group's goals. If you and your siblings want to plan a huge celebration for your parents' twenty-fifth wedding anniversary, you should outline all of the steps needed to make it happen: creating a guest list, contacting and comparing venues, sending out invitations, and so on.

● **ALTHOUGH HOMER SIMPSON** typically eats a whole doughnut in one big bite, he does, on occasion, split it up. Even he knows you can't split it into less than two bites. © 20th Century Fox/Photofest

you complete the outline, arrange the references in order on a separate sheet headed "Works Cited," "Notes," or "References." Citations can be presented in a variety of formats, including styles dictated by such organizations as the Modern Language Association (MLA) and the American Psychological Association (APA). See Figure 13.2 for a sample of how

FIGURE 13.2

REFERENCES (in APA Style)

References

American Academy of Sleep Medicine. (2010, February 15). Sleep problems and sleepiness increase the risk of motor vehicle accidents in adolescents. *Science Daily*. Retrieved from http://www.sciencedaily.com/releases/2010/02/100215081728.htm

Breus, M. J. (2013). Quality sleep, quality relationship. In *Sleep Well with Michael Breus, PhD ABSM*. Retrieved from http://blogs.webmd.com/sleep-disorders/2013/07/quality-sleep-quality-relationship.html

Centers for Disease Control and Prevention. (2008, February 28). CDC study reveals adults may not get enough rest or sleep. Retrieved from http://www.cdc.gov/media/pressrel/2008/r080228.htm

Centers for Disease Control and Prevention. (2011). Insufficient sleep is a public health epidemic. Retrieved from http://www.cdc.gov/Features/dsSleep

Farberov, Snejana. (2013). Sleep-deprived new mom who killed a nanny and injured a toddler when she ran a red light while driving one day after giving birth is sentenced to just 48 hours in prison. *Daily Mail*. Retrieved from http://www.dailymail.co.uk/news/article-2338271/Christina-Padilla-Sleep-deprived-new-mom-killed-nanny-injured-toddler-ran-red-light-day-giving-birth-sentenced-just-48-HOURS-jail.html

National Sleep Foundation. (2013). International Bedroom Poll: Summary of findings. Retrieved from http://www.sleepfoundation.org/sites/default/files/RPT495a.pdf

St. Lawrence University. (2007, December 1). All-nighters equal lower grades. *Science Daily*. Retrieved from www.sciencedaily.com/releases/2007/11/071130162518.htm

Skerritt, P. D. (2011, January 12). Your health at work: Sleep deprivation's true workplace costs. *Harvard Business Review*. Retrieved from http://blogs.hbr.org/your-health-at-work/2011/01/sleep-deprivations-true-workpl.htm

Zamosky, Lisa. (2011). Having trouble sleeping? In *WebMD: Sleep Disorders Health Center*. Retrieved from http://www.webmd.com/sleep-disorders/features/having-trouble-sleeping

FIGURE 13.3

MIND MAPPING can be a great way to organize your ideas if you prefer a more visual style of outline.

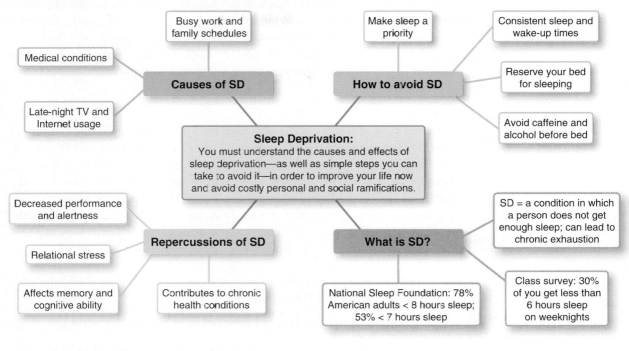

you might handle references in APA format. Your instructor may have his or her own preferences about how to handle citations, so when in doubt, ask.

▶ *Give your speech a title.* Once all of your ideas and points are organized on paper, you can give your speech a catchy title that captures its essence. You might also consider using a provocative question as the title or part of a memorable quotation that you will use in the body of the speech.

At every phase of development, you should review your outline for sound organization. When reviewing, you should see a clear hierarchy of points reflected in each tier of your structure. A weak link in the outline—an unsupported argument, an unrelated point—reveals an overall weakness in the way you've presented and defended your thesis. A solid outline shows not only how well you've organized your material but also how each point is supported by two or more subpoints, making a stronger case for your thesis statement. It also shows the scope and validity of your research by detailing your evidence with complete citations.

If sitting in front of a blank Word document and typing a formal outline feels too overwhelming, you might want to take advantage of some of the free outlining and mind-mapping applications and tools available online. For example, SimpleMind (available on your desktop and for Apple or Android devices) allows you to create a visual mind map, creating and connecting your hierarchy of points in colored circles. Take a look at Figure 13.3 to see how such an application might help you get started on your outline.

Styles of Outlines

There are three basic approaches you can take to outlining your speech, which vary according to the level of detail. All three formats—sentence outlines, phrase outlines, and key-word outlines—can be valuable tools in developing and eventually delivering your speech. In most cases, you'll move from one format to another as you progress from preparing your speech to actually delivering it.

Sentence Outline

The first type of outline is the **sentence outline**, which offers the full text of what you want to say in your speech. Sentence outlines are generally used as you develop and prepare early drafts of your speech because they help you become more comfortable with all aspects of your speech; they are typically not ideal for your actual presentation because many speakers wind up reading directly from the outline, missing out on valuable eye contact with the audience. Consider the following example from Sample Speech Outline 13.1 (see p. 394) regarding sleep deprivation:

II. There are many causes of sleep deprivation, according to the Centers for Disease Control and Prevention.

   A. Busy work and family schedules contribute to sleep deprivation.

      1. As college students, many of us are trying to handle full-time course work and full- or part-time jobs to help pay for tuition, in addition to maintaining relationships with loved ones.
      2. New parents are often incredibly sleep deprived as they attempt to adjust to life with an infant as well as those infamous nighttime feedings.
      3. Shift workers (including police officers, nurses, pilots, and so on) often have trouble establishing good sleep habits because their schedules change frequently and they are sometimes required to work the night shift.

   B. Late-night television and Internet use can interfere with the ability to fall asleep or can prevent individuals from adhering to a bedtime schedule.

   C. The use of caffeine and alcohol can also make it difficult to fall asleep and stay asleep.

   D. Some medical conditions—including insomnia and obstructive sleep apnea—also make sleeping incredibly difficult.

Phrase Outline

A **phrase outline** takes parts of sentences and uses those phrases as instant reminders of what the point or subpoint means. Consider the following example:

II. Many causes of sleep deprivation (CDC)

   A. Busy work and personal lives

      1. Students struggling with school and work

2. New parents adjusting to baby schedule

3. Shift work disrupting sleep

B. Use of TV or computer late at night

C. Use of caffeine and alcohol

D. Medical conditions—insomnia and sleep apnea

The phrase outline is often preferred because it offers speakers a clear road map of their presentation with reminders of key points and phrases while also allowing speakers to deliver a speech rather than simply read it.

Key-Word Outline

A **key-word outline** is the briefest possible outline, consisting of specific "key words" from the sentence outline to jog the speaker's memory. This type of outline allows the speaker to maintain maximum eye contact with the audience, though the speaker must be *extremely* familiar with the content of the speech. An example of a key-word outline is as follows:

II. SD causes (CDC)

A. Family and work

1. College students

2. New parents

3. Shift workers

B. Television and Internet

C. Caffeine and alcohol

D. Medical conditions—insomnia, apnea

From Preparation Outline to Speaking Outline

In most public speaking situations, you will use the basics you've learned to create two outlines. The first is a **preparation outline** (sometimes called a *working outline*), a draft that you will use, and probably revisit and revise continually, throughout the preparation for your speech. The function of a preparation outline is to firm up your thesis statement, establish and organize your main points, and develop your supporting points. It should also help you "map out" the relationships between your main points and supporting points. From the preparation outline, you will eventually develop a **speaking outline**, or *delivery outline*, which is your final speech plan, complete with details, delivery tips, and important notes about presentational aids (which we will discuss in Chapter 14).

● **AS YOU DEVELOP YOUR SPEECH,** you'll transition from a more detailed preparation outline to a speaking outline that will equip you for the actual presentation. DWaschnig/ Shutterstock

An important element of speech preparation is the ability to establish your speech topic, thesis, main points, supporting points, and transitions. You can assess your ability to recognize these elements in the following preparation outline for an informative speech on Obsessive-Compulsive Personality Disorder (OCPD).

Instructions: Place the numbers of the elements listed here into the following organizational outline.

Topic: _____   Thesis: _____

    I. (main point) _____

       A. (subpoint) _____

       B. (subpoint) _____

       C. (subpoint) _____

       D. (subpoint) _____

       E. (subpoint) _____

(transition) _____

    II. (main point) _____

       A. (subpoint) _____

       B. (subpoint) _____

       C. (subpoint) _____

       D. (subpoint) _____

1. I've presented the five signature symptoms of OCPD and will now examine the condition's suspected causes.
2. Adopting a miserly spending style toward both self and others.
3. Perfectionism that interferes with task completion.
4. There are five primary symptoms of OCPD.
5. OCPD.
6. Faulty parenting.
7. Heredity.
8. OCPD is a treatable mental illness that often goes unrecognized due to lack of information or confusion about the symptoms and causes.
9. Harsh punishment/meager rewards.
10. Preoccupation with details, rules, lists, order, organization, or schedules to the extent that the major point of the activity is lost.
11. Recognize the symptoms and causes of OCPD to identify proper help.
12. Medical professionals generally agree on four major causes for OPCD.
13. Stubbornness and inflexibility about matters of morality, ethics, or values.
14. Significant event/circumstance that triggers OCPD.
15. Inability to discard worn-out objects even when they have no sentimental value.

Answers: Topic: 5; Thesis: 8, Main Point I: 4, Subpoints I-A-E: 2, 3, 10, 13, and 15; Transition: 1: Main Point II: 12; Subpoints II-A-D: 6, 7, 9, 14.

You may find a sentence outline works well when working on your preparation outline; as you move toward a final speaking outline, it's best to switch from a sentence format to a phrase or key-word approach (or a combination of the two). To do this, look at your full sentences, and pull out key words, phrases, or headers that will jog your memory and serve as guideposts as you speak. Sample Speech Outline 13.1 shows the full progression from preparation outline to speaking outline.

Your speaking outline should also include **delivery cues**, brief reminders about important information related to the delivery of your speech that are for your eyes alone. You'll likely want to include reminders to show a presentation aid or speak slowly at the beginning of the speech, when you are the most nervous. We'll discuss more about delivery in Chapter 14. Table 13.3 offers a variety of delivery cues that may be helpful to you.

Another important aspect of your speaking outline is that it should contain notes for your **oral citations**, the references to source materials that you mention in the narrative of your speech. After a sentence or phrase in your outline, you might simply place the source in parentheses so that you remember to give credit. For example, the key words "SD-financial costs (Skerritt, HBR)" should

TABLE 13.3

USEFUL DELIVERY CUES

Delivery Cue	Purpose	Example That May Appear in Your Outline
Transition	A segue from one topic or idea to another; might be a simple reminder that you're changing tone here or a specific example or story that takes the speech from one topic to another	• [TRANSITION] • [TRANSITION: Use dog story!]
Timing and speaking rate	A reminder to use a specific speaking rate, either for emphasis or to quell anxiety	• [Slow down here] • [Speed up here] • [Repeat for emphasis]
Volume and nonverbal behavior	A reminder to raise or lower your voice at particular points in your speech or to use particular gestures or body movements for emphasis	• [Louder] • [Softly] • [Thump on podium] • [Count out on fingers]
Sources	Sources for cited material	• [Dowd, M. (2007, May 23). Pass the clam dip. *The New York Times*.]
Statistics	Statistics for reference, with source	• [U.S. Census Bureau: 64% of voting-age citizens voted in 2004, 60% in 2000]
Quotations	Exact wording of a quotation you plan to use	• [Dwight D. Eisenhower: "I've always found that plans are useless, but planning is indispensable."]
Pronunciations	Phonetic reminders for difficult-to-pronounce names or words	• [Hermione (her-MY-uh-nee)] • [Kiribati (kee-ree-BAHSS)]
Visual aids	Reminder when to incorporate particular visual aids	• [Census chart] • [Show model]

Source: O'Hair, Stewart, & Rubenstein (2012), tab. 13.2, p. 211. Adapted with permission.

prompt you to say: "Sleep deprivation costs businesses more than $3,000 per employee annually, in terms of lowered productivity, according to a report by Patrick Skerritt in *The Harvard Business Review*." For material quoted word for word from the source, the oral citation must clarify that the material is in fact quoted rather than your own expression ("As Skerritt notes, 'This doesn't include the cost of absenteeism—those with insomnia missed an extra five days a year compared to good sleepers'"). In such instances, you will likely want to use full sentences in your outline, rather than key words or phrases, to ensure that you do not misquote or misrepresent your source.

Finally, you should choose a comfortable format for using your speaking outline in front of your audience. You may transfer the outline to note cards, which will enable you to flip through notes quickly; alternatively, you might create virtual note cards on your smartphone or tablet, or you might prefer to use a standard-size sheet of paper. In many classroom situations, your instructor will indicate the preferred format.

AND YOU?

How do you outline? Do you think of an outline as a hard-and-fast map, written before you begin writing and strictly adhered to throughout the process? Or do you start with a rough outline, revising and refining the organization as you move through the writing process?

SAMPLE SPEECH OUTLINE 13.1

From Preparation Outline to Speaking Outline

Title: Sleep It Off: Understanding the Dangers of Sleep Deprivation
General Purpose: To inform
Specific Speech Purpose: To inform my audience about the dangers of sleep deprivation so that they may take appropriate steps to avoid this troubling medical issue.
Thesis Statement: You must understand the causes and effects of sleep deprivation—as well as simple steps you can take to avoid it—in order to improve your life now and avoid costly personal and social ramifications.

Sample Preparation Outline •

Introduction

I. Do you ever feel like you're struggling to juggle relationships, work, and classes? Many of us do, and often enough, the first thing we cut out of our busy daily routine is sleep. •

II. For better or worse, the human body needs an adequate amount of sleep to function properly, and my research indicates that we simply aren't getting enough of it.

III. You must understand the causes and effects of sleep deprivation, as well as simple steps to take to avoid it, to improve your life now and avoid costly personal and social ramifications. •

IV. Today I will speak about sleep deprivation. I will begin by explaining what it is, before moving on to its causes and effects, and examining simple solutions to the problem. •

• Note that the speaker uses a sentence outline style throughout the preparation outline.

• The speaker opens with an attention-getting question and offers a response that the audience will likely relate to.

• Thesis statement

• Preview of main points

Transition: So what exactly is sleep deprivation?

Body

I. In a personal communication with Dr. Arkeenah Jones, a family physician, on March 15, 2013, she noted that sleep deprivation is a condition in which a person does not get enough sleep, which can lead to chronic exhaustion. •

        ● Main point 1

    A. The National Sleep Foundation's 2013 Bedroom Poll notes that 78 percent of American adults polled sleep less than eight hours per night, with 53 percent getting less than the minimum recommended seven hours sleep per night.

    B. The results of the survey I passed out last week reveal that 30 percent of people in this very classroom get less than six hours of sleep on weeknights.

Transition: By a show of hands, how many people in this room *like* to sleep? • I thought so. If we enjoy sleeping so much, why are we not getting enough of it?

        ● The speaker keeps her audience involved in the speech by asking questions.

II. There are many causes of sleep deprivation, according to the Centers for Disease Control and Prevention. •

        ● Main point 2

    A. Busy work and family schedules contribute to sleep deprivation.

       1. As college students, many of us are trying to handle full-time course work and full- or part-time jobs to help pay for tuition, in addition to maintaining relationships with loved ones. •

        ● The speaker continually makes her topic relevant to the audience.

       2. New parents are often incredibly sleep deprived as they attempt to adjust to life with an infant as well as those infamous nighttime feedings.

       3. Shift workers (including police officers, nurses, pilots, and so on) often have trouble establishing good sleep habits because their schedules change frequently and they are sometimes required to work the night shift.

    B. Late-night television and Internet use can interfere with the ability to fall asleep or can prevent individuals from adhering to a bedtime schedule.

    C. The use of caffeine and alcohol can also make it difficult to fall asleep and stay asleep.

    D. Some medical conditions—including insomnia and obstructive sleep apnea—also make sleeping incredibly difficult.

Transition: As we've seen, busy schedules, overuse of media, the intake of alcohol and caffeine, and medical conditions can all cause sleep deprivation, • but why does sleep deprivation truly matter so much?

        ● The speaker effectively uses an internal summary in her transition to her next main point.

        ● Main point 3

III. Sleep deprivation can have negative effects on the health and safety of individuals and the community at large. •

    A. According to Lisa Zamosky, a health columnist for the *Los Angeles Times* and writer for WebMD, sleep deprivation is linked to poor concentration and lack of energy.

1. Sleep deprivation decreases workplace productivity, at a cost of more than $3,000 per employee annually, as noted by Patrick Skerritt in the *Harvard Business Review*.
2. Sleep deprivation is a leading cause of automobile accidents, especially among adolescent motorists, according to a February 15, 2010, report by the American Academy of Sleep Medicine. •

B. Dr. Michael J. Breus, "The Sleep Doctor" of WebMD, also notes that sleep deprivation causes relational stress.

1. In my own life, I certainly find that I argue more with friends and family when I'm exhausted than I do when I'm well rested. •
2. The results of the survey I conducted indicate that 55 percent of the members of this class find that "arguing with a loved one" is a problematic outcome of not getting enough sleep.

C. Dr. Arkeenah Jones notes that sleep deprivation affects memory and cognitive ability.

1. In fact, a Centers for Disease Control and Prevention study noted that 23.2 percent of sleep-deprived individuals report difficulties with concentration. Similarly, 18.2 percent report difficulty remembering information.
2. Dr. Pamela Thatcher, a psychology professor at St. Lawrence University, conducted a study in which she discovered that students who pull all-night study sessions typically have lower GPAs than those who do not.

D. Sleep deprivation can contribute to chronic health conditions, including depression, obesity, and diabetes, according to the Centers for Disease Control and Prevention.

Transition: So far, we've discussed the common causes of sleep deprivation as well as their negative—and potentially tragic—effects. At this point you may be wondering how to avoid sleep deprivation altogether. I will discuss several suggestions now. •

IV. You can avoid sleep deprivation with a few simple changes to your daily routine.

A. Make sleeping a priority in your life, along with your other commitments.
B. Have consistent sleep and wake-up times, even on weekends.
C. Don't watch television, play on your laptop, or even study in bed. Try to reserve your bed for sleeping.
D. Don't drink alcohol or consume caffeine too close to bedtime.

Transition: Regulating your schedule and developing good habits are essential for preventing sleep deprivation.

Margin notes:

• The speaker continually uses oral citations to give credit to her sources.

• The speaker builds credibility by noting that she too is prone to the effects of sleep deprivation.

• The speaker transitions to her final main point with an internal summary and an internal preview.

Conclusion

I. Sadly, a realization about the dangers of sleep deprivation came too late for Christine Padilla, a new mother who ran a red light while fatigued and driving only thirty-three hours after giving birth. Padilla struck a nanny pushing a toddler in a stroller, killing the forty-one-year-old woman and seriously injuring the little boy, according to a report by Snejana Farberoy in *The Daily Mail.* •

II. As you've seen today, sleep deprivation is a concerning problem for individuals and communities.

    A. It has many causes ranging from busy schedules and media use to caffeine and alcohol consumption and medical problems.

    B. Its effects can be devastating, as I've detailed in this speech.

    C. Luckily, many of us can prevent sleep deprivation by making simple changes to our daily routines. •

III. Now go get some rest . . . after all of today's speeches are over, that is! •

> • The speaker signals the end of her speech with a tragic story that drives home her main points.

> • The speaker reiterates her main points.

> • The speaker uses a memorable statement and humor to end her speech.

Sample Speaking Outline

Introduction [Speak slowly! Look at audience!]

I. Juggling commitments? Many give up sleeping.

II. We need sleep; research = we don't get enough.

III. Be informed about sleep deprivation (SD) to improve life and prevent negative consequences. •

IV. I will discuss SD: what, causes, effects, prevention. •

Transition: What is SD?

> • Thesis statement. The speaker is so familiar with her speech purpose and thesis that she only needs a brief reminder.

> • Key-word preview of main points.

Body

I. SD = not enough sleep; can lead to chronic exhaustion (Dr. Arkeenah Jones, personal communication, March 15, 2013) •

    A. 78% of American adults sleep <8 hours per night, and 53% sleep <7 hours per night. (National Sleep Foundation's 2013 survey) •

    B. 30% of people in class sleep <6 hours on weeknights. (my survey)

Transition: *Like* to sleep? Then why not sleeping? [**Smile, encourage audience response**]

II. SD causes (CDC) •

    A. Family and work

        1. College students—course work, jobs, relationship

        2. New parents—crying, hungry babies

        3. Shift workers—trouble with consistent schedules

    B. Television and Internet

> • Main point 1

> • The speaker retains a bit more detail in this subpoint in order to keep her statistics straight.

> • Main point 2

C. Caffeine and alcohol

D. Medical conditions—insomnia and obstructive sleep apnea

Transition: Causes: schedules, media, alcohol/caffeine/medical conditions. Who cares?

• Main point 3

III. SD has negative effects for individuals and community. •

A. Decreases performance and alertness (Lisa Zamosky, health columnist for the *Los Angeles Times* and writer for WebMD)

1. Decreases workplace productivity; costs >$3,000 per employee annually (Patrick D. Skerritt, *Harvard Business Review*)

2. Causes auto accidents, especially teens (American Academy of Sleep Medicine, February 15, 2010) •

• The speaker makes sure that her oral citations are clear throughout the speaking outline.

B. Causes relational stress (Dr. Michael J. Breus, "The Sleep Doctor" for WebMD)

1. True for me!

2. 55% of class fights with loved ones from SD (my survey)

C. Affects memory and cognitive ability (Dr. Jones)

1. 23.2% report difficulties with concentration; 18.2% report difficulty remembering info. (CDC)

2. All-nighters lead to lower GPA. (Dr. Pamela Thatcher, psychology professor at St. Lawrence University)

D. Chronic health conditions—depression, obesity, diabetes (CDC)

Transition: Discussed causes and effects. How to prevent SD?

• Main Point 4

• In an earlier practice, the speaker noted her tendency to read directly from notes, preventing useful interaction with the audience.

IV. Daily routine changes • **[Don't read as list. Look up!]** •

A. Prioritize sleeping

B. Consistent sleep and wake-up times

C. No TV/Internet in bed; just sleep

D. No alcohol/caffeine close to bedtime

Transition: Changes in routine and good habits prevent SD.

Conclusion

• The speaker uses effective delivery cues throughout her speech. Here she reminds herself to use a visual aid.

I. Christine Padilla, fatigued mother driving 33 hours after birth, kills nanny and severely injures toddler. (Snejana Farberoy, *Daily Mail*, 2013) **[Show image of crash]** •

II. SD is concerning problem for individuals and communities.

A. Causes: busy schedules, media use, alcohol/caffeine/medical problems

B. Devastating effects

C. Mostly preventable with simple changes

III. Get some rest!

BACK TO ► The State of the Union Address

As this chapter shows, organizing, writing, and outlining your speech are crucial steps in eventually delivering an effective presentation. Recall our discussion of White House speechwriters preparing the State of the Union address from the beginning of the chapter. What considerations and challenges will affect their organization and outlines? How will their organization influence their audiences' perceptions of the speech?

► Ideas will come in from every direction, so planning and organization are key. David Frum, a former White House speechwriter, observed that "the planning for the next State of the Union really begins the day after the last State of the Union" (as cited in Jackson, 2006).

► Speechwriters need to bear in mind that they are writing for two different—albeit not mutually exclusive—audiences. Chriss Winston (2002) points out that members of Congress and Washington insiders judge the speech primarily on its policy content, whereas everyday Americans tend to look for leadership qualities and their own values in the president. The challenge lies in choosing content and language that speak to both groups.

► The key to avoiding what Matthew Scully (2005) refers to as a "tedious grab bag of policy proposals" lies in the skillful use of transitions. Instead of jumping from point to point, speechwriters need to find and build unifying themes among the many policies under discussion. Thus George W. Bush's speechwriters were able to draw connections between such issues as cloning and war by focusing on the overall theme of human dignity and human rights. These connections allowed for natural transitions from one issue to the next (Scully, 2005).

► Creating unified themes is also crucial to keeping the content (and length) of the speech from spiraling out of control. President Bill Clinton was known for long State of the Union speeches that detailed many policy proposals, while President George W. Bush preferred to stick to big ideas. President Barack Obama chose in his second term to use current events, including major storms and shootings, to advance his agenda items, such as climate change and gun control legislation.

THINGS TO TRY ► Activities

1. LaunchPad for *Real Communication* offers key term videos and encourages self-assessment through adaptive quizzing. Go to **bedfordstmartins.com/realcomm** to get access to:

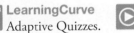

✓ LearningCurve Adaptive Quizzes.

▶ Video clips that illustrate key concepts, highlighted in teal in the Real Reference section that follows.

2. Take a look at the outline of this chapter in the Contents (p. xxix). Do you see a clear hierarchy of points and subpoints? Within the chapter, how are transitions used to move from point to point? How might the techniques used in this chapter work in your speech?

3. Read a famous or familiar speech (such as Martin Luther King's "I Have a Dream" speech) or watch one online. (A great site to consider is TED, which offers inspirational speeches about "ideas worth spreading." See ted.com.) Next, create an outline for your chosen speech. Can you follow a clear sequence of points? Do the subpoints support the speaker's main points?

4. When creating the outline for your speech, write each main point on a separate index card. Spread the cards out on a table and then pick them up in the most logical order. Does this order match the order of your outline? How did you choose to arrange the topics—spatially, chronologically, or topically?

5. Establishing a relationship with the audience is important when giving a speech. Make a list of all of the possible members of your audience. How do you plan to connect with all members of the audience? Pretend you are giving a speech at your old high school. Will your introduction affect the seniors the same way it will affect the principal?

6. Pick a general topic and try to come up with several different attention getters for that topic. Here's an example for the topic "dogs":

▶ Tell a funny story about your dog.

▶ "Did you know that the human mouth contains more germs than a dog's mouth?"

▶ "In my hometown, there is a dog that walks upright like a human because he does not have any front legs."

▶ "Did you know that approximately 10 million unwanted dogs are euthanized annually in the United States?"

Try this with a topic such as your favorite food, favorite vacation spot, or some other appealing topic.

Now that you have finished reading this chapter, you can

Organize and support your main points:

▶ Identify your **main points**, the central claims that support your specific speech purpose and your thesis statement (p. 368).

▶ **Subpoints** support your main points using all of the statistics, stories, and other forms of research you discovered on your topic (pp. 369–370).

Choose an appropriate organizational pattern for your speech:

▶ A **chronological pattern** presents main points in a systematic, time-related fashion (pp. 370–371).

▶ A **topical pattern** is based on categories, such as person, place, thing, or process (p. 371). The **primacy–recency effect** argues that audiences are most likely to remember what comes at the beginning and end of messages (p. 371).

▶ A **spatial pattern** arranges points according to physical proximity or direction from one to the next (p. 371).

▶ The **problem–solution pattern** first presents an obstacle and then suggestions for overcoming it (p. 371).

▶ The **cause–effect pattern** moves from the cause of a phenomenon to the results or vice versa (pp. 372–373).

▶ The **narrative pattern** uses a story line to tie points together (p. 373).

▶ The **motivated sequence pattern** uses a five-step plan to motivate listeners: attention, need, satisfaction, visualization, and action (p. 373).

Move smoothly from point to point:

▶ Build strong **transitions**, sentences that connect the points so that topics flow naturally (pp. 373–374).

▶ Use **signposts**, key words or phrases that signify transitions (p. 375).

▶ **Internal previews** prime the audience for the content immediately ahead (p. 375).

▶ **Internal summaries** crystallize points in one section before moving on (p. 375).

Choose appropriate and powerful language:

▶ Consider your audience when you choose your words (p. 376).

▶ Use simple, unambiguous words (pp. 376–377).

▶ Be concise (p. 376).

▶ Use vivid language (p. 377).

▶ Use repetition, allusion, similes, and metaphors to make a lasting impression (pp. 377–379).

Develop a strong introduction, a crucial part of all speeches:

▶ Grab listeners' attention with surprise, a good story, a quote, a question, or humor (pp. 379–381).

▶ Introduce your purpose and thesis (p. 382).

▶ Preview your main points to provide a mental outline for your audience (p. 382).

▶ Establish a relationship with the audience (p. 382).

Conclude with the same strength as in the introduction:

▶ Signal the end to ask for listeners' full attention, and wrap up quickly (p. 383).

▶ Reiterate your topic, purpose, and main points (p. 383).

▶ Make a final impact with a memorable closing quote, statement, question, or story (pp. 383–385).

▶ Challenge the audience to respond with a **call to action**—what you hope they will do in response to the speech (p. 385).

Prepare an effective outline:

▶ The **outline** puts the hierarchy of points into a text format (pp. 386–387).

▶ The hierarchy of points for a strong outline will show each point supported by two or more subpoints (p. 387).

▶ There are three essential styles of outlines (from most detailed to sparest): **sentence outline**, **phrase outline**, and **key-word outline** (pp. 390–391).

▶ Write a **preparation outline** (or working outline) to organize and develop your speech (p. 391).

▶ The **speaking outline** (or delivery outline) is your final speech plan (p. 391).

▶ Add **delivery cues**, brief reminders about important information, to your speaking outline (p. 393).

▶ **Oral citations**, references to source materials to be included in your narrative, should also be in your speaking outline (pp. 393–394).

Britain's King George VI overcame a stutter to lead the nation in a time of war—and also inspired a young boy, who grew up to pen "The King's Speech." Popperfoto/Getty Images

LearningCurve can help you master the material in this chapter. Go to **bedfordstmartins.com/realcomm**.

chapter

14

Delivering Presentations

On September 3, 1939, Britain's King George VI took to radio waves to inform an anxious Great Britain that the nation was, for the second time in a generation, at war. "In this grave hour," the king began, "perhaps the most fateful in history, I send to every household of my peoples, both at home and overseas, this message, spoken with the same depth of feeling for each one of you as if I were able to cross your threshold and speak to you myself."

Given the opportunity, it's quite possible that he would have preferred to address each of his subjects in that very personal manner rather than via a live radio broadcast. George VI—born Albert Frederick Arthur George, and known to those closest to him as Albert—had suffered since childhood from a crippling nervous stammer (more commonly called a stutter on this side of the Atlantic). Second in line for the throne, he only became king after his elder brother, the dashing Edward, famously abdicated the British throne in order to marry an American divorcée in 1936. Thus Albert was thrust into a position of leadership that he didn't want but was bound by duty and honor to fulfill. And less than three years into his unexpected reign, the reluctant king was called upon to address the nation as it plunged once again into war.

Albert managed to address the nation with surprising grace. He was not perfect, but he managed to get through the speech and deliver his message to a frightened and uncertain public. One listener was David Seidler, a young British boy who had evacuated to the United States before the Blitz and who, like the king, suffered from what he describes as a "profound" stutter. "I heard these wonderful, moving speeches, and had heard that he had been a terrible stutterer," Seidler recalls. "If he could cure himself, it gave me hope" (Horn, 2010). Seidler grew up to become a screenwriter and penned the Academy Award–winning film *The King's Speech*. Seidler, who overcame his stutter as a teenager, accepted his Oscar "on behalf of all the stutterers in the world. We have a voice. We have been heard" (Seidler, 2011).

After you have finished
reading this chapter,
you will be able to

- Identify and control
  your anxieties

- Choose a delivery style
  best suited to you and
  your speaking situation

- Employ effective
  vocal cues

- Employ effective
  visual cues

- Connect with your
  audience

- Enhance your words
  with effective
  presentation aids

- Make efficient use of
  your practice time

Many people feel anxious about delivering speeches—and some manage to avoid it. But consider the nervousness and challenges that King George and David Seidler managed to overcome in the process of finding their voices. As their stories illustrate, with the right tools and plenty of practice, even the most nervous or challenged individuals can become accomplished and engaging speakers. In this chapter, you'll learn the basics of effective speech delivery that will help you connect with your audience and deliver an effective presentation. We begin by acknowledging the nervousness you may naturally experience before moving on to key methods of delivery, guidelines for effective delivery and presentation aids, and tips for practicing your speech.

Understanding and Addressing Anxiety

Comedian Jerry Seinfeld once joked, "According to most studies, people's number one fear is public speaking. Number two is death. . . . This means to the average person, if you go to a funeral, you're better off in the casket than doing the eulogy" (as cited in Peck, 2007). Although Seinfeld's statistics are not accurate (Dwyer & Davidson, 2012), it's true that speechmaking can cause **public speaking anxiety (PSA)**, the nervousness we experience when we know we have to communicate publicly to an audience (Behnke & Sawyer, 1999; Bippus & Daly, 1999). Although we might think of PSA as an emotional challenge, it often manifests itself with real physical symptoms, including a rapid heartbeat, erratic breathing, increased sweating, and a general feeling of uneasiness. (To determine your own level of PSA, visit an online quiz at www.jamescmccroskey.com/measures /prpsa.htm.)

For some individuals, however, this nervousness goes far beyond giving a speech and extends to such essential speaking tasks as answering a question in class, meeting new people, interviewing for a job, or voicing an opinion. The late communication scholar James McCroskey (1977) calls this **communication apprehension (CA)** because it is a more general "fear or anxiety associated with either real or anticipated communication with another person or persons" (p. 78). Yet speaking up or speaking out can clearly enhance personal opportunities and career prospects. In fact, "being a poor speaker is the principal reason people don't make it into the executive ranks" (Ligos, 2001).

But don't despair! Whether you suffer from PSA or even the more general CA, you can learn to control your nervousness. In more severe cases, you might consider meeting with a trained counselor. For less disruptive symptoms, you might simply find comfort in the fact that nervousness is a natural part of life— and that it can actually spur you on to do your best (in the case of a speech, this may mean preparing more thoroughly and practicing more diligently). You may also benefit from the advice we offer here on identifying your anxiety triggers and building your confidence.

Identifying Anxiety Triggers

Before you can conquer your nervousness, you need to identify it. Just what has you so frightened? Research, as well as our personal experiences, points to several key factors, including upsetting experiences, fear of evaluation, and distaste for attention (Ayres, 2005; Bodie, 2010).

Upsetting Experiences

Anna forgot her line in the second grade school play, and the audience laughed. They thought it was adorable, but to Anna, the experience was devastating. It's fairly common for a negative experience in our past to shape our expectations for the future, but it's important to remember that it's never too late to learn or improve personal skills. Anna needs to think about other skills that she has mastered, despite her initial nervousness: she was anxious the first time she drove a car, for example. With practice, she was able to master it—even though she failed her first road test. She needs to approach public speaking with the same kind of "try, try again" attitude.

Fear of Evaluation

Anna's anxiety about public speaking may not be about speaking but about being *evaluated* on her speaking abilities. We all feel this way from time to time, but Anna must remember that her instructor will consider other aspects of her speech preparation, including her organization and research. In addition, she should recall that she's not under the intense scrutiny that she imagines. In most public speaking situations, the audience wants the speaker to succeed. In fact, research shows that audiences are usually far less aware of a speaker's nervousness than the speaker is (Sawyer & Behnke, 2002). Keeping the presentation in this perspective will help Anna to feel less anxiety.

● **PUBLIC SPEAKING** anxiety manifests itself both psychologically and physically, but it can be overcome by identifying the triggers of the anxiety and building confidence. Blend Images/Veer

Distaste for Attention

Alonzo loves to sing in the car, in the shower, and at concerts. But he refuses to sing a solo in his church choir because being the center of attention makes him feel incredibly uncomfortable. Although he may be able to avoid singing a solo, he will likely have to speak publicly at some point. He can minimize his discomfort with being the center of attention by thinking of his speech as an opportunity to communicate with a group rather than to perform. In other words, if he were to give the best-man speech at his brother's wedding, he'd be communicating with a group of family members and close friends rather than putting on a performance. Similarly, when giving a speech for his human communication course, he's part of a group—nervous speakers with similar hopes of succeeding.

Building Your Confidence

Most people can cope effectively with periodic bouts of public speaking anxiety by applying the following advice, which can also be employed for more general cases of communication apprehension.

> ► *Embrace your anxiety.* Anxiety can have positive effects, such as driving you to be more prepared and giving you energy. For example, anxiety over forgetting your speech's main points might cause you to prepare with solid notes. By thinking about what might go wrong, you can come up with simple solutions for just about any scenario. In addition, that jolt of adrenaline

Since many people are apprehensive about speaking publicly, we might assume that communication apprehension (CA) is limited to this context. However, throughout this book you learn that anxiety can occur in many contexts. Some people experience high levels of CA in interpersonal relationships (Chapter 7) whereas others get anxious when working in groups (Chapter 9). And still others find that interviews (Interviewing Appendix) trigger CA. The techniques in this chapter are useful in all situations where CA occurs.

what about you?

Personal Report of Public Speaking Anxiety

Directions: Following are statements that people sometimes make about themselves in the context of delivering a speech. Indicate whether or not you believe each statement applies to *you* by marking whether you strongly disagree = 1; disagree = 2; neutral = 3; agree = 4; or strongly agree = 5.

_____ 1. While preparing for giving a speech, I feel tense and nervous.

_____ 2. I feel tense when I see the words "speech" and "public speech" on a course outline when studying.

_____ 3. My thoughts become confused and jumbled when I am giving a speech.

_____ 4. I get anxious when I think about a speech coming up.

_____ 5. When the instructor announces a speaking assignment in class, I can feel myself getting tense.

_____ 6. My hands tremble when I am giving a speech.

_____ 7. I am in constant fear of forgetting what I prepared to say.

_____ 8. I get anxious if someone asks me something about my topic that I don't know.

_____ 9. I perspire just before starting a speech.

_____ 10. I notice my heart beating fast when I start my speech.

_____ 11. I experience considerable anxiety while sitting in the room just before my speech starts.

_____ 12. Certain parts of my body feel very tense and rigid while giving a speech.

_____ 13. Realizing that only a little time remains in a speech makes me very tense and anxious.

_____ 14. I do poorly on speeches because I am anxious.

_____ 15. I feel anxious when the teacher announces the date of a speaking assignment.

_____ 16. When I make a mistake giving a speech, I find it hard to concentrate on the parts that follow.

_____ 17. During an important speech, I experience a feeling of helplessness building up inside me.

_____ 18. I have trouble falling asleep the night before a speech.

_____ 19. I feel anxious while waiting to give my speech.

_____ 20. While giving a speech, I get so nervous I forget facts I know.

Scoring: Add your scores together for statements 1–20 to assess your level of public speaking anxiety: high anxiety: 80–100; moderate anxiety: 41–79; low anxiety: 20–40.

Source: Adapted from McCroskey (1970).

you feel before starting to speak can also be a source of energy to make your points with enthusiasm—use it!

▶ *Desensitize yourself.* Sometimes the best way to get over something is to "just do it." You address your fear of public speaking by making attempts to get up in front of a crowd in less threatening situations, like asking a question in class or at a community meeting. You might even try singing karaoke with friends—nobody expects you to be any good at it, anyway, and it might be fun!

▶ *Visualize your success.* Research shows that people with high speech anxiety tend to concentrate on negative thoughts before giving their speeches (Ayres & Hopf, 1993). In order to reduce those thoughts (and their accompanying anxiety), it's important to spend time imagining positive scenarios and personal success, a technique known as **performance visualization** (Ayres, 2005; Ayres & Hopf, 1993). Performance visualization allows you to define situations and reduce uncertainty (Honeycutt, Choi, & DeBerry, 2009), so go ahead and imagine yourself standing before your audience with confidence and grace—and it just may happen.

▶ *Take care of yourself.* In order to be productive, remember to take care of yourself in the days leading up to your speech: get enough rest, budget your time effectively to make room for your speech practice sessions, try to eat a light meal before the presentation, and try relaxation techniques (such as deep breathing, yoga, a calming walk, listening to one of your favorite songs, and laughing with friends).

▶ *Be prepared!* As we've mentioned—and as we'll discuss throughout this chapter—adequately preparing for your speech will increase the likelihood of success and lessen your apprehension (Smith & Frymier, 2006). Research demonstrates that confidence does come through preparation and skill building, which means that conducting thorough research, organizing your points, and preparing a useful outline will help you achieve a positive outcome (Schroeder, 2002).

▶ *Rehearse your delivery.* Ask a few friends or family members to observe your speech. (This is particularly useful if you are giving an in-person speech and have a strong preference for mediated communication, like texting or Facebook messaging. Sometimes just practicing in front of people will take the edge off your nervousness.) Also, try recording a few practice sessions first. Ask the same friends to critique your delivery and improve with their feedback in mind.

▶ *Challenge yourself.* We ultimately learn and grow as individuals by pushing ourselves to accomplish things that we have not tried or felt confident with before. Instead of viewing your speech event as something to dread, reframe your thoughts and view it as an opportunity to gain new a valuable new skill!

CONNECT

Chapter 2 discusses *self-efficacy,* or your ability to predict your likelihood of success in a given situation. If you believe that you cannot succeed at giving a speech, asking someone for a date, or interviewing for a job, you're more likely to avoid such communication. In any of these examples, performance visualization can help you manage your thoughts so that you can achieve your goals.

● **MEDITATING OR PRACTICING** yoga can help you learn to relax your muscles and focus your attention. © Blend Images/Alamy

WIREDFORCOMMUNICATION

THINK ABOUT THIS

Facing Your Public Speaking Fears in Virtual Reality

Picture yourself at a podium in front of a huge audience. The people in the audience look bored, even sleepy. As you stand before them, every yawn, cough, and shuffle of their feet echo in the vast auditorium. You struggle to make eye contact with one person or another, but their responses seem far off, their expressions disconnected from everything you are doing and saying.

This may sound like a very real situation—or a very realistic nightmare. In fact, it's a virtual reality simulation designed to help individuals suffering from public speaking anxiety overcome their fear. Companies specializing in virtual reality therapy (VRT) use three-dimensional imaging software, video footage, and sometimes mechanized props that simulate movement to create artificial representations of stress-inducing environments. Clients wear helmets, and motion sensors allow them to interact with the virtual reality environment. "It's a therapist's dream," notes one psychologist who has used the simulations to treat certain social anxieties. "To help people deal with their problems, you must get them exposed to what they fear most" (Lubell, 2004).

The effectiveness of VRT on public speaking anxiety seems promising. A 2012 study showed that VRT participation was equally as effective as standard cognitive-behavioral therapy (CBT) but that participants were more likely to continue with VRT treatment than with CBT. And at the one-year follow-up session, VRT participants had maintained their improvement (Safir, Wallach, & Bar-Zvi, 2012). Nonetheless, there have been no large-scale, scientific studies of the available VRT programs (Lubell, 2004). Even so, it does offer individuals a chance to test their skills in front of an audience in a very private and constructive way.

❶ Do you think virtual reality simulations would be helpful aids in preparing for public speaking? Whom might they help more, individuals with moderate speech anxiety or severe speech anxiety?

❷ What are the benefits of practicing in front of a virtual audience? How would it compare to a real one?

❸ What aspects of the public speaking situation do you think a VRT simulation could effectively simulate? What aspects would be impossible to capture?

With a more realistic understanding of the role of anxiety—and with these tips for addressing it in mind—let's move on to the various methods of delivery that you may confront over the course of your life as a student, professional, and citizen.

Methods of Delivery

You might think of a great speaker as someone who is eloquent yet also sounds as though he or she is speaking without having prepared a written speech. Although that's possible in certain situations, most speakers spend time preparing in the ways we've already discussed in Chapters 12 and 13—writing a speech and preparing an outline of some sort. Deciding just how to prepare for your speech affects, and is affected by, your choice of delivery style. We'll examine four specific delivery options and the potential benefits and pitfalls of each.

Speaking from Manuscript

If you've watched the president of the United States deliver the annual State of the Union address, you may have noticed that he alternates between two teleprompter screens as he reads his speech. That's because he's delivering a speech from manuscript. When you speak from manuscript, you write your entire speech out and then read it word for word from the written text because your allegiance is to the words that you have prepared. Speaking from manuscript is common for presidential speeches because they are quite long and will likely be quoted and interpreted extensively afterwards. A mistake in the delivery of such a speech might not merely embarrass the president but may also affect world events. Manuscript delivery is useful in any situation where accuracy, time constraints, or worries about misinterpretation outweigh the need for a casual and natural delivery style.

However, manuscript delivery also has a number of downsides. First, it's time-consuming, involving tremendous skill and practice and countless rewrites to get the written message exactly right; this makes it a better fit for a president (who has a team of speechwriters at his disposal) than a college student. Second, the static nature of reading from a written speech—whether from a manuscript or a teleprompter—limits your ability to communicate nonverbally with movements, facial expressions, gestures, eye contact, and vocal variety. As you'll learn later in this chapter, planning and rehearsal are crucial for overcoming these tendencies when delivering a speech from manuscript.

Speaking from Memory

Speaking from memory is an ancient public speaking tradition referred to as **oratory**. In this style of speaking, you prepare the speech in the manuscript form as just described but then commit the words to memory.

Oratory delivery is fairly uncommon today as a form of public speaking, as it is both time-consuming and risky. A speaker who forgets a word or phrase can easily lose his or her place in the speech, panic, and never recover. But even if every line is delivered perfectly, the very nature of memorization can create a barrier between speaker and audience. Having memorized the speech and rehearsed without an audience, the speaker tends to deliver it as if the audience wasn't there. Such a speech can therefore end up feeling more like a performance, a one-man or one-woman show, rather than a communication that engages with the audience.

Speaking Spontaneously

Impromptu speaking refers to situations where you speak to an audience without any warning or preparation. (Talk about public speaking fears!) When you are unexpectedly called on to speak in class or in a business meeting, or you are suddenly motivated to give a toast at a party, you must speak impromptu. The secret to excelling at impromptu speaking is to understand that it's never entirely spontaneous; if you are always prepared to give a speech unexpectedly, no speech is entirely unexpected.

One major aspect of preparation is the ability to think on your feet: when called on to speak unexpectedly, begin by first acknowledging the person who introduced or called on you, and then repeat or rephrase the question or issue. This will give you a moment to focus on the topic and quickly construct a plan.

● **SPEAKING FROM** manuscript is a fitting method of delivery for TV newscasters such as Brian Williams, for whom accuracy and time constraints are critical. Bill Greenblatt/UPI

CONNECT

In an impromptu speaking situation you should be aware of the relational, situational, and cultural contexts in which you are communicating (Chapter 1). This knowledge will help you tailor your speech to be appropriate and effective, whether you're giving a toast at a friend's wedding, surrounded by her religious family members, or at an international meeting of a professional association, surrounded by colleagues.

● **NO PUBLIC SPEAKERS** must think on their feet as much as debaters. These political candidates must not only present and defend their sides of key issues but must also anticipate and address what their opponents might say. AP Photo/Robert F. Bukaty

Usually you'll want to choose a simple format easily applied to the topic, such as noting advantages and disadvantages or cause and effect.

Another way to prepare for spontaneous public speaking is listening to others. Determine if you have some personal application of a point or an example that a speaker has made that either substantiates or refutes another speaker. Most audiences enjoy hearing speakers tell a brief story that illustrates a point that another speaker made or a theme that an event uses.

Speaking Extemporaneously

Have you witnessed those calm, collected speakers who seem to be making it up as they go along in a surprisingly organized manner? They are likely practicing **extemporaneous speaking**.

When you speak extemporaneously, you plan the content, organization, and delivery well in advance, but instead of writing the entire speech out word for word, you speak from an outline of key words and phrases or speaking aids, such as PowerPoint or Prezi virtual canvas. Extemporaneous speaking involves delivering your speech in an impromptu style, even though the speech is neither spontaneous nor unrehearsed. Most speakers favor extemporaneous delivery because they can fully prepare and rehearse their presentations while economizing on time because they need not determine in advance the exact words that they want to use.

One downside to extemporaneous speaking is that it's difficult to use precise timing or wording, and speakers can easily get off track, become wordy or repetitive, or exceed their allotted time.

So what's the secret to succeeding at extemporaneous speaking? You can achieve success and confidence through practice and preparation. Consider the following points:

● **WILL FERRELL** and his costars ad-libbed much of *Anchorman*, not unlike what you will do when speaking extemporaneously. Dreamworks/ Photofest

▶ *Prepare well in advance.* You can begin preparing for an extemporaneous speech as soon as you decide on a topic. Think about some possible points you want to make and how you might support them.

▶ *Don't forget the outline!* As mentioned in Chapter 13, your key-word or phrase outline keeps you focused but gives you lots of flexibility with your word choice.

▶ *Practice truly makes perfect.* Actors or musicians don't always give the exact same performance, but they do practice a lot. When you get really familiar with a script or a musical composition (or a speech), you may indeed memorize parts of it, but a little bit of it will change each and every time, allowing for a more natural delivery.

Guidelines for Effective Delivery

Everything from selecting a topic and researching information to outlining your presentation is a prerequisite to the big moment: actually delivering your speech. In this section, we'll take a fresh look at a point that we've emphasized throughout this book: how you say something is as important as what you say. That is, audiences receive information not only from the actual words that you speak but

● **EFFECTIVE SPEAKING**
is a crucial skill. Whether
you're a sports star giving
a press conference or a
climbing instructor giving a
safety demonstration, you
need to know how to deliver
your words in an articulate
and expressive manner. (top
left) Streeter Lecka/Getty Images;
(top right) JJ/Getty Images; (bottom left)
© Chris Kleponis/Zuma/Corbis; (bottom
right) © Jeff Morgan education/Alamy

also through two channels of nonverbal communication: the vocal and the visual. These channels directly impact your ability to connect with your audience whether you are presenting to a small group, a large audience, or even in an online environment.

Effective Vocal Delivery

Actor Seth Rogen is the rare comedian who uses a monotone voice to great comic effect—his delivery of zinging punch lines in a flat, unchanging tone adds an extra layer of irony to films like *This is the End* (2013), *Paul* (2011), and *Pineapple Express* (2008). But listening to him deliver a long speech in the same style would likely lull you to sleep. By using varying aspects of your voice, you can engage your audience as well as convey confidence and trustworthiness. Through practice, you can learn to control the elements of vocal delivery, which include pitch, volume, rate, pauses, pronunciation, and articulation.

Vary Your Pitch

To be an effective public speaker, you must make use of the range of vocal sounds that the human voice is capable of producing. These variations of sound range from high to low—like musical notes—and are known as *pitch*. You speak in a **monotone** (like Seth Rogen or Ben Stein) when you do not vary your pitch at all, and a monotonous speaker can be painful for listeners. So how do you ensure that you are using your pitch effectively? One way to practice is to record yourself speaking ahead of time to determine if there are places where you need to use more energy and extend your pitch levels.

Adjusting Your Speaking Rate and Volume

Speakers can use vocal cues to signal to the audience what needs their attention. Just as we use boldface and italic type in the pages of this book to emphasize certain words and phrases, as a speaker you can use audible cues to emphasize certain points.

How fast or slow you speak is known as your **speaking rate**, and it can also be a key factor in effective speaking. You want to speak slowly enough that your audience is able to hear and absorb what you say but quickly enough to capture the urgency and importance of what you are saying. Typically, if you speak faster, compared with surrounding material, you signal your enthusiasm for the content, and the audience's interest will follow. When you slow down, your rate signals a degree of seriousness and concern. You would deliver a persuasive call-to-action speech at a faster pace in order to show and elicit enthusiasm. You would deliver a tribute or dedication, such as a eulogy, at a slower pace to demonstrate sincerity and seriousness.

Changes in *volume*—how loudly or quietly you speak—can also be used to emphasize certain points. What do you want to stand out from your speech for the audience to remember? Is it a statistic, a name, or a product? Think about giving one word or phrase in every few sentences some "punch." This differentiates the word or phrase from its context.

Using Pauses for Effect

Because many speakers believe that their entire goal is to talk, they pause too infrequently. The truth is that good speakers do not fill every second of a speech with words. Taking a moment between statements, words, or phrases adds drama by giving the audience time to reflect on what you have said and anticipate what will follow. For example, in Martin Luther King Jr.'s famous "I Have a Dream" speech, King's use of pauses, combined with rhetorical tools like repetition, helped to build drama and anticipation as he delivered his speech.

Speaking Clearly and Precisely

One of the quickest ways to lose credibility with your audience is to mispronounce a word—especially a word that is specifically related to the subject of your presentation. **Pronunciation** is the correct formation of word sounds. Many words in the English language are frequently mispronounced, to the point that individuals are not even aware that they are saying these words incorrectly! Presidential mispronunciations in particular are fodder for late night talk show hosts. Take, for example, George W. Bush's mispronunciation of the word *strategy* ("strategery") or Barack Obama's mispronunciation of *corpsman* ("corpse man") that you've likely heard about.

AND YOU?

How do you react when you hear speakers with an accent that is different from yours? Do you find them difficult to understand, or do you make assumptions about them based on the way they speak? How might your own accent be an advantage or disadvantage in your next speaking situation?

But even if presidents occasionally err in their pronunciation, they frequently articulate well. **Articulation** is the clarity and forcefulness with which the sounds are made, regardless of whether they are pronounced correctly. To speak clearly, even if incorrectly, is to be articulate. All speakers strive to be articulate, but there are several ways in which we routinely sabotage our efforts (O'Hair, Rubenstein, & Stewart, 2012).

When a speaker omits certain sounds in a word, runs words together, and speaks so softly that a listener can hardly hear, the speaker is guilty of **mumbling**. Most people mumble either because they are in a hurry, because they suffer from communication apprehension, or because they are not prepared to speak clearly.

Audience perceptions about a speaker's skills can also be affected by **accents**, patterns of pronunciation that are specific to a certain upbringing, geographical region, or culture. Although the word choices of individuals from different cultures may vary from time to time, the greatest difference you hear is in their emphasis on syllables and rhythm while speaking. In the United States, southern speakers tend to drawl (use a slower pace) and elongate vowel sounds. Speakers from the Northeast tend to omit sounds from the middle of words such as *park*, whereas Midwesterners sometimes insert an "r" sound into words such as *wash*.

Effective Visual Delivery

In the same way that a monotone can lull an audience to sleep, so can a stale, dull physical presence. This doesn't mean that you need to be doing cartwheels throughout your speech, but it does mean that you should look up from your note cards once in a while. Otherwise, you'll be little more than a talking head, and your audience will quickly lose interest. What's more, effective visual cues—like dressing appropriately, using effective eye behavior, incorporating facial expressions and gestures, and controlling body movements—can enhance a presentation, helping you clarify and emphasize your points in an interesting and compelling way.

Dressing for the Occasion

If you're like most people, you probably hop out of bed in the morning, open your closet, and hope that you have something decent and clean to wear to work or class. However, on the day of your speech—just like the day of a job interview or an important date—you don't want to leave your appearance to chance.

According to image consultant Diane Parente (2013), the way you dress is essentially your visual résumé; it can either help to present you as competent and prepared or as disheveled and unprepared. Indeed, research indicates that attractive people are more persuasive (Chaiken, 1979; Davies, Goetz, & Shackelford, 2008). However, that doesn't mean that you need to have Hollywood-perfect hair or an expensive wardrobe to be an impressive speaker. Rather, you can signal authority and enhance your credibility by dressing professionally in neat clothing—like a pair of black pants or skirt with a button-down shirt or a simple sweater (Cialdini, 2008; Pratkanis & Aronson, 2001). You should certainly avoid looking overly casual (for example, wearing flip-flops and a tank

CONNECT

Recall from Chapter 4 that *artifacts*—accessories carried on the body for decoration or identification—send powerful messages about you. If you're not sure whether or not to cover up your tattoos or keep your tongue ring in, consider your topic, the occasion, your own comfort level, and what you can glean as the comfort level of the audience. And don't forget that your instructor can offer valuable advice and guidance as well.

COMMUNICATIONACROSSCULTURES

You Sound Like You're From . . .

English may be a common language, but each of us actually speaks it somewhat differently. A sweet southern drawl, for example, sounds markedly different from the rapid clip of a native New Yorker, and neither accent sounds much like the midwestern voice of the anchor on the nightly news. For better or worse, our dialects carry with them certain baggage. When we open our mouths to speak, we are conveying not only the specific message we intended to share but often also a wealth of information about who we are.

Whether we recognize it or not, most of us speak with some sort of regional accent, which is intrinsically tied to the place where we live. Our speech is also affected by ethnic background and socioeconomic status—what linguists call social dialect (Wolfram & Schilling-Estes, 2006). In any case, we might be judged harshly based on the way that we speak: Americans, for example, tend to perceive midwestern accents as the most "correct," whereas strong southern and New York City accents are perceived as signs of lower intelligence (Preston, 1998). Such perceptions are common in almost every culture. In the United Kingdom, BBC business reporter Stephanie McGovern notes that her northern accent, which is perceived in England as being "common" or "working class," elicits a strong reaction from viewers as well as others in the industry. "I've had tweets questioning whether I really did go to university," McGovern says, "because surely I would have lost my accent if I did; a letter suggesting, very politely, that I get correction therapy; and an e-mail saying I should get back to my council estate [the British term for a public housing project] and leave the serious work to the clever folk" (McGovern, quoted in Duell, 2013).

That's why many people whose jobs require public speaking go to great pains to shed their regional accents. Many of them head to speech coaches like the late Sam Chwat, the "speech coach to the stars" whose clients included the actors Robert DeNiro and Julia Roberts, as well as a host of corporate executives and public figures who need to unlearn their hometown accent—or learn a new one (Woo, 2011). Chwat, a speech pathologist who had shed his own thick New York accent in order to avoid confusing his clients, told *The New York Times* in 2010, "I have seen a notable rise in the number of self-referred corporate execs who are trying to retain their competitive edge within their corporations, be clearly understood by customers or clients who typecast or stigmatize them by their speech patterns" (as cited in Roberts, 2010). Although he made his living recognizing, learning, and teaching the varied nuances of different accents, Chwat didn't feel that having an accent, any accent, was a bad thing. "There is no direct instruction for public speaking and standard articulation," he noted, "and there is no penalty for speaking with an accent" (as cited in Roberts, 2010).

THINK ABOUT THIS

❶ What type of accent do you have? How do you feel it is perceived by others from different regions in the United States or even abroad?

❷ Why do most newscasters tend to speak with a midwestern accent? Why might that accent be considered the most neutral?

❸ If a speaker has a strong regional accent, should he or she try to lessen it when speaking publicly? Are there any public speaking situations where a strong regional accent might be beneficial?

❹ Can you recognize social dialects within your own region? What perceptions do they carry?

top) unless a casual appearance is crucial to your presentation. Indeed, you might look a little silly demonstrating surfing positions on your surfboard in a tie or dress. The key is to dress appropriately for the image you wish to present, given your topic and your audience.

Using Effective Eye Behavior

It's likely you've heard some questionable advice about looking at your audience members while giving a speech: "Just look over their heads at the wall" or (worse) "Just pretend your audience is naked and don't stare." Not only are these suggestions awkward, but they are ineffective as well because competent speakers are aware of the power of their eye behavior.

As we noted in Chapter 4, eye behavior is a crucial aspect of nonverbal communication that can be both effective and appropriate when a communicator considers the cultural context in which he or she is communicating with a relational partner. For example, in the United States and many other Western cultures, a lack of eye contact can make a speaker seem suspicious or untrustworthy, making direct eye contact one of the most important nonverbal actions in public speaking as it signals respect and interest to the audience (Axtell, 1991). But how can a speaker make and maintain eye contact with a group of individuals?

One way is to move your eyes from one person to another (in a small group) or one section of people to another (in a large group), a technique called **scanning**. To use it, picture yourself standing in front of the audience, and then divide the room into four imaginary sections. As you move from idea to idea in your speech, move your eye contact into a new section. Select a friendly-looking person in the quadrant, and focus your eye contact directly on that person while completing the idea (just make sure you don't pick a friend who will try to make you laugh!). Then change quadrants and select a person from the new group. Tips for using the scanning technique are offered in Table 14.1.

TABLE 14.1

TIPS FOR SCANNING YOUR AUDIENCE

Work in sections	Do not scan from left to right or right to left. Always work in sections and move randomly from one section to another.
Avoid the "lighthouse" effect	You'll look like a human lighthouse (or a lawn sprinkler) if you simply rotate your upper torso from left to right while you talk, looking at no one person in particular.
Look people in the eye	Avoid looking at people's foreheads or over their heads; look them in the eye, even if they are not looking back at you.
Focus for a moment	Remember to pause long enough on an individual so that the person can recognize that you are looking directly at him or her.
Don't jump away	If someone is not looking at you, stay with the person anyway until you've finished your thought. Then move on to another.
Divide large groups	If the audience is too large for you to get to everyone, look at small groups of two or three people sitting together.

Incorporating Facial Expressions and Gestures

Have you ever seen a cartoon in which a character's face contorts with the jaw dropping to the floor or the eyes bugging out? The animator certainly gets the point across—this character is either entirely surprised or seriously confused. Your facial expressions, although not as exaggerated as those of a cartoon character, serve a similar purpose: they let your audience know when your words arouse fear, anger, happiness, joy, frustration, or other emotions. The critical factor is that your expressions must match the verbal message that you are sending in your speech. As a competent communicator, you are unlikely to smile when delivering a eulogy—unless you are recounting a particularly funny or endearing memory about the deceased.

Like facial expressions, gestures amplify the meaning of your speech. Clenching your fist, counting with your fingers, and spreading your hands far apart to indicate distance or size all reinforce or clarify your message. What is most important is that your gestures are appropriate and natural. So if you want to show emotion but you feel awkward putting your hand over your heart, don't do it; your audience will be able to tell that you feel uncomfortable.

Controlling Body Movements

In addition to eye behavior, facial expressions, and gestures, your audience can't help but notice your body. In most speaking situations you encounter, the best way to highlight your speech content is to restrict your body movements so that the audience can focus on your words. Consider, for example, your **posture**, or the position of your arms and legs and how you carry your body. Generally, when a speaker slumps forward or leans on a podium or desk, rocks back and forth, or paces forward and backward, the audience perceives the speaker as unpolished and listeners' attention shifts from the message to the speaker's body movements.

How do you prevent such movements from happening, particularly if you're someone who fidgets when nervous? One useful technique is called **planting**. Stand with your legs apart at a distance that is equal to your shoulders. Bend your knees slightly so that they do not lock. From this position, you are able to gesture freely, and when you are ready to move, you can take a few steps, replant, and continue speaking. The key is to plant following every movement that you make.

Connecting with Your Audience

It is through vocal and visual delivery that speakers are able to interact with their audiences—that's what makes public speaking different from just writing a good presentation. When you compose an essay, you write it and it goes off to the reader; it's a linear model of communication (as discussed in Chapter 1). But speaking before an audience is more than just providing information through words; it's an interaction between speaker and audience.

Indeed, gifted speakers like Ronald Reagan and Bill Clinton were always aware of this and became known for their ability to deliver even the most formal speeches in a style that felt conversational, personal, and connected. That's because both were able to use their words, voices, and gestures to convey the way they felt about a subject. They also spoke directly to their audiences in a way that

EVALUATING**COMMUNICATION**ETHICS

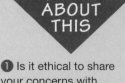

Judging Speeches

At the beginning of this chapter, you read about the struggles that people with physical challenges (such as King George VI) face when delivering speeches. But how do culture and ethics collide when it comes time actually to judge or assign a grade to a presentation?

Imagine that your speech class is engaging in peer evaluation. In groups of six, you practice delivering your speech before the final presentation to the entire class. You will evaluate your group members' speeches twice—and a portion of your grades will be determined by the improvement they make between the first two practice speeches and then between the final rehearsal and the delivery before the entire class.

One woman in your group, Evelyn, has cerebral palsy, a neurological disorder that permanently affects body movements and muscle coordination. It can have a diverse number of symptoms, but Evelyn struggles most with slurred speech, balance, and exaggerated reflexes. Evelyn is quite comfortable talking about her disability and appears to be a confident speaker. Yet as she talks, you find it somewhat difficult to understand her speech. Because many of her words are slurred, you feel like you're missing a few main points. And as much as you try not to, you find the fact that she sways when she speaks and that she must grip the back of her chair for balance somewhat distracting.

You feel bad making these comments to Evelyn on her first evaluation, and so you focus your remarks on improvements she can make on the outline. But you're worried about how the rest of the class will react to Evelyn and even what sort of grade she might get from your professor. You're now facing your second round of evaluations for Evelyn.

1 Is it ethical to share your concerns with Evelyn? Or is it more appropriate to keep quiet in this situation?

2 Would you feel differently offering Evelyn critical feedback in an online peer assessment situation? Why or why not?

3 Imagine instead that Evelyn is not a native speaker of English and you find her accent difficult to understand. Is it ethical to address these concerns when judging her speech?

4 If you have been reading this scenario under the assumption that you don't have any physical challenges, imagine you have a speech challenge or suffer from a chronic illness. Does this influence your critique of Evelyn's speech?

felt unrehearsed and sincere. Let's now take a look at the way our words converge with our vocal and visual delivery to establish such a connection with the audience. We'll also consider the ways we can adapt our delivery to suit the audience's needs and expectations.

Expressing Emotion

If you do not feel passion for what you are talking about, you can be sure that your audience will not feel it either. One of your responsibilities is to ensure that, throughout your speech, the audience feels the same emotions that you do for your subject matter. Many Americans, regardless of their political affiliation, felt an intimate connection to President Obama when he addressed the media in the immediate aftermath of the Sandy Hook Elementary School shootings in December 2012. While remaining authoritative and in control, he also expressed his grief in a way that rang true to everyone watching or listening. He wasn't just speaking as a president that day but as a parent. When an audience feels that a speaker is simply acting, they may question the sincerity of the message.

Adapting to Your Audience

One common mistake speakers make is to speak to—or even at—the audience, rather than to speak *with* the audience. As discussed earlier, in Western cultures, this generally means making and maintaining eye contact. But it also means listening to audience reactions, paying attention to listeners' body movements, and continually gauging their responses to what you say and do so that you can make adjustments to your speech as you go

● **PRESIDENT RONALD REAGAN** earned his reputation as a gifted public speaker by recognizing the interaction between speaker and audience and presenting himself as approachable and self-assured. © Wally McNamee/CORBIS

along. For example, if you observe audience members frowning or squinting, it may be a sign of misunderstanding. You can take this as a cue to slow down or emphasize key points more explicitly. Alternatively, if you notice your audience members responding with smiles, focused eye contact, or even laughter, you probably want to maintain the style of speaking that produced such a positive reaction.

Creating Immediacy with Your Audience

As you learned in Chapter 4, immediacy is a feeling of closeness, involvement, and warmth between people as communicated by nonverbal behavior (Mehrabian, 1971; Prager, 2000). We often think of immediacy as being an important facet of close interpersonal relationships. This is certainly true—but it is also an important component of building trust in the relationship between the speaker and the audience (Andersen, 1979).

Speakers enhance their immediacy with their audience by following many of the guidelines we have already set forth in this chapter: establishing and maintaining eye contact with audience members, smiling, moving toward the audience, using inclusive gestures and posture, speaking in a relaxed or conversational tone or style, and using humor. Research clearly shows that audiences respond favorably to speaker immediacy in a variety of settings (Christophel, 1990; Frymier, 1994; Teven, 2007a, 2007b, 2010; Teven & Hanson, 2004). However, as is the case with interpersonal relationships, immediacy is a two-way street. Audiences help to foster this feeling of closeness and trust by listening actively, responding with eye contact, nodding, and offering nonverbal indications of agreement, surprise, confusion, and so on.

Additional Guidelines for Online Speech Delivery

There are special points to keep in mind when you are delivering a speech for an online course. All of the points we've already made largely still apply (for example, dressing appropriately and looking up from your notes), but you should also consider the following tips for an effective presentation:

real communicator

NAME: Tonya Graves
OCCUPATION: Singer and Actress

When I went to college to study communication in New York State many years ago, I never dreamed that I'd have a career as a singer and actress in Central Europe. But on my first night in Prague, I went to Agharta Jazz Club and met the acclaimed Czech blues guitarist Luboš Andršt. He invited me onstage to sing and I've been singing and acting ever since.

Singing and acting involve many of the same delivery skills that I used in my communication courses, particularly my introductory public speaking course. I have to overcome anxiety (also known as stage fright) sometimes in addition to building my confidence before a performance. I tend do that by paying attention to my breath and by imagining a receptive, engaged audience. Finally, as with giving a speech, I have to practice enough to feel confident and prepared, but not so much that my performance becomes mechanical or lifeless.

Blues, jazz, swing, funk, soul, dance, and pop music—I love them all! My first album was a lovely tossed salad of music. When I sing this variety in a given performance, I need to adjust my voice and facial expression to both the style and the lyrics so that my passion for the music comes across as appropriate and also conveys the emotional message I'm trying to send.

An effective performance depends on the situation, too. If I'm in front of a live audience, like in a jazz club, I'm very intent on establishing immediacy with the audience by making eye contact with real people (and, no, I don't imagine them naked! That's terrible advice!). This helps me feel more comfortable and also ensures that the patrons feel connected to the performance. On the other hand, when I'm in a recording studio, I imagine my audience and adjust my voice intensity to make up for the lack of personal contact. I imagine this is much like what today's students do when they prepare to give a speech in an online course in which the "audience" is an iPhone camera. My delivery is even more complex when I create a music video, as in the single "39 Reasons" (check it out on YouTube); my orange dress and blue scarf were designed to move and "float," accenting my thirty-nine reasons to sing the blues. Everything about my performance—from how I dress to how I prepare to how I deliver—is all part of delivering Tonya Graves to the world!

▶ *Be clear about your assignment.* Different instructors have different requirements for online speeches. Some may require you to assemble your own audience and record the speech; others may expect you to stream to a live audience via Skype or a similar program; still others may allow you to record your speech by yourself and submit it. *Always check on your instructor's preferences.*

▶ *Be mindful of speaking rate and volume.* These factors are particularly important when recording presentations for online delivery since you won't be able to adjust as you go based on your audience's nonverbal appearance of comprehension or confusion. Be sure that your volume is sufficient to be picked up clearly by your video recorder or microphone.

▶ *Note the location of your video camera.* Your camera is the "eyes" of the audience; they'll see what it sees. Make sure that your background (for example, a wall in your home or dorm) doesn't have a lot of distracting elements on display. Also adjust your zoom lens to capture the upper half of your body as well your presentation aids. If you and your aids are too close to the camera, the audience may feel claustrophobic; if the camera is too far away, the audience may strain to comprehend your facial expressions or the writing on your poster.

▶ *Involve your audience.* Even if you don't have an audience that is physically present, you can still create a sense of immediacy by establishing eye contact with the camera, smiling, using inclusive gestures and posture, speaking in a conversational tone, and using humor. Ultimately, be yourself!

▶ *Take your presentation seriously.* Just because your audience is remote or self-assembled doesn't mean that your topic, your audience, and the occasion aren't important or worthy of respect.

Effective Presentation Aids

Bill Gates is a technology buff, to be sure. He is the man behind Microsoft, the company that invented the ubiquitous presentation software, PowerPoint. So when he gives speeches on behalf of the Bill and Melinda Gates Foundation, it's not surprising that he uses PowerPoint slides to graphically display information on changing death rates from malaria in poor countries and the impact of mosquito netting, vaccines, and other preventatives. But Gates also thinks outside the technological box when it comes to presentation aids: "Malaria is, of course, spread by mosquitoes," he tells the crowd. "I've brought some here," he adds, as he opens a jar to let a small fleet of (uninfected) insects fly around the auditorium. "There's no reason only poor people should have the experience" (Gates, 2009). This simple presentation aid got the audience's attention and made the fight against malaria familiar to all those who have ever swatted a mosquito off their arm on a summer evening.

Like Gates, today's speakers online and in person have many tools to create dramatic visual presentations that enhance their words and deepen the audience's understanding of the topic. We'll explore how presentation aids work in the sections that follow.

● **BILL GATES** was certainly thinking outside of the box — or the jar! — when he released mosquitoes into the auditorium to aid a presentation on malaria. Fernando Castillo/LatinContent/Getty Images

AND YOU?

Think back on a variety of different public presentations you've witnessed—speeches by fellow students, presentations by instructors, political debates, and so on. What is the most effective use of a visual aid that you have encountered? What is the least effective? Why?

The Function of Presentation Aids

Although presentation aids can be a valuable asset to a speech, heightening an audience's interest and helping you convey technical information, these aids should *supplement* your speech, not substitute for it. Sure, you may have a moving video or shocking image to share with the audience. But if you don't connect it to a thoroughly researched topic, as part of a well-organized speaking outline and effective delivery, then it will fall flat. To be truly useful, presentation aids must enhance your speech, accomplishing three goals:

▶ *Help listeners process and retain information.* Effective presentation aids can increase an audience's ability to retain information by highlighting key points in addition to helping the audience see relationships among concepts, variables, or items. Always make a point, refer to the presentation aid, direct the listeners' attention to where you want them to focus, and then restate, reiterate, or rephrase what you have said.

▶ *Promote interest and motivation.* Properly used presentation aids can engage your audience members or at least get their attention. If you show terms, photographs, statistics, tables, and other items that truly reinforce your spoken message, the audience will be more likely to go along with you.

▶ *Convey information clearly and concisely.* Effective presentation aids can help simplify complex material. There is no comparison between the amount of time it would take you to read a series of figures versus showing them on a table, graph, or chart. A good visual can present a lot of information in a clear, concise, and simple matter, saving the speaker's time for interpretation and elaboration.

Types of Presentation Aids

Students often ask, "What type of visual aid should I use for my speech?" The answer to that question is never entirely straightforward because it depends on your topic, the needs of your individual speech, the constraints of your speaking time and location, the demands of an in-person versus an online presentation, and a myriad of additional factors. What we can share, however, is a look at the dominant types of presentation aids and their general purposes for speakers. We begin by considering props and models before moving on to media clips and images, graphs and charts, posters and transparencies, flip charts and marker boards, and presentation slideware.

Props and Models

Some things, people, places, or processes are difficult to describe with only words and gestures. An object, or **prop**, removes the burden from the audience of having to imagine what something looks like as you speak. For instance, if you are giving an informative speech on the way to tune a guitar, you might find it difficult to explain the process without demonstrating the procedure on an actual guitar. Adjusting a tuning key to show how it affects the pitch of a given string would be an effective visual (and audio) aid.

If a prop is large and cumbersome or too small to be easily viewed by your audience members (particularly for online speeches), then consider using a **model**, an appropriately scaled object. One of our past students brought in a small-scale model of the Soviet nuclear submarine the *Kursk* to demonstrate how the vessel tragically encountered problems, exploded, and sank.

Be mindful and considerate when selecting and using props and models in your presentation. One of us had a student give a speech on ocean pollution using a live fish in a bowl as a prop. He poured the contaminants he was discussing into the bowl, and his classmates (and instructor) were understandably horrified and distraught when the fish died. The speaker made a powerful point through this prop, but he was entirely inconsiderate of the speaking situation and his audience's expectations in addition to unethically contradicting his premise that we should save ocean wildlife.

Similarly, avoid objects that may be dangerous or even illegal, such as firearms, knives, chemicals, and so on. (You would be surprised to know about some of the scary props we've seen students try to use over the years, ranging from weapons to unfriendly dogs.) Think safety first!

Media Clips and Images

Images, as well as film, television, Internet video clips, interviews, and podcasts, can add another dimension to and stimulate interest in your speech by providing vivid illustrations or clarifications of topics that are difficult to capture with words alone. A speaker informing an audience about reconstructive surgery for cleft palate, for example, might show a photograph of a child born with the condition as well as postsurgical photos, rather than just trying to describe the condition and outcome. When choosing media clips and images, keep a few points in mind:

▶ Make sure that your speaking site is equipped with the equipment you will need to make your selection viewable to your audience.

▶ Keep your video clips short (say, one to two minutes maximum, depending on the length of the speech).

▶ Don't overwhelm your audience with ten illustrations or photographs when two or three would suffice.

▶ Make sure photographs are properly edited and cropped. Your goal is to draw your audience's attention to a specific aspect of the photograph and not overwhelm them with background information.

Graphs and Charts

When you're delivering a speech rich in statistics, data, and facts, visual aids can be indispensable presentation tools (see Figure 14.1). You can actually cut your presentation time drastically and increase your listeners' interest by pointing to some figures on a graph rather than

● **AN INTERESTING PROP** can be a helpful visual aid. This speaker might have trouble illustrating certain muscles and nerves in the human body without a model. Susana Gonzalez/AFP/Getty Images

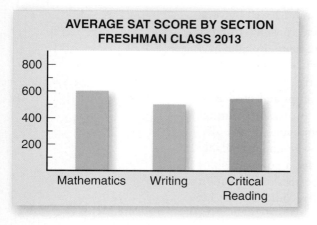

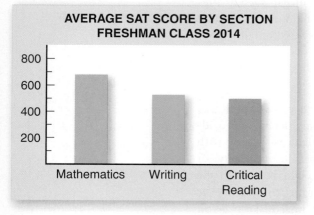

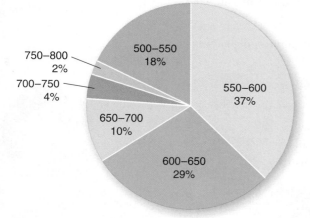

FIGURE 14.1

SAMPLES OF EFFECTIVE GRAPHS Bar graphs use bars of varying lengths to make comparisons. Pie charts depict the division of a whole.

reading them aloud, number by number. Graphs take several different forms. **Bar graphs** show the relationship of two or more sets of figures. A figure comparing a freshman class's average SAT scores by section, for example, is well illustrated with a bar graph. **Pie charts** show percentages of a circle divided proportionately; for example, a university admissions office uses a pie chart to reveal the percentage of freshman students scoring in a particular range on the SAT. A pie chart should ideally have from two to five segments; under no circumstances should it have more than eight since it will become difficult for the audience to read: if you have too many categories, you can add the smallest ones up and present them in a single segment.

Posters and Transparencies

Posters and transparencies provide a large, physical display of key words or images that can be a useful way for you to guide your audience's attention (especially if your speaking site is not suitable for computer display). For example, if you are informing your audience about the magnitude of the D-Day invasion of World War II, you could position one poster showing the very young faces of the soldiers alongside another showing the enormous coastline of beaches and cliffs at Normandy. As you ask your audience to look from the soldiers to the beaches, they can better imagine what it must have been like to run toward those cliffs in the midst of gunfire.

Transparencies are clear plastic sheets that are used with a projector to display text and images on a screen. Like posters, they are a useful means of showing large text or images to an audience, but they can be carried in a folder or briefcase and are often lower cost and easier to make than having posters professionally printed. Verify that your speaking site is equipped with a transparency projector or request one if that is possible. Then purchase low-cost transparency sheets at an office supply store and print or photocopy your color and black-and-white pages.

When designing posters and transparencies, it's often helpful to keep a few key points in mind:

▶ Use large and legible print so that your audience members (particularly online audience members) don't strain to understand your visual aid. For transparencies, this usually means choosing at least a twenty-point font.

▶ Use vivid colors to make your posters and transparencies more appealing.

▶ Avoid cramming more than one main idea or main point into a poster or transparency sheet unless it has a very specific purpose to enhance your meaning (for example, a collage of photos of missing and exploited children in your area).

▶ Put the transparency sheets and poster pages in order of use, and number them in case they get shuffled.

▶ If possible, use a pointer and stand near the poster to limit excessive movement.

▶ When using transparencies, try to stand near the screen instead of standing at the projector with your back to the audience.

Flip Charts and Whiteboards

Flip charts and whiteboards, which are still common in professional settings, have a distinct advantage for displaying words and ideas over posters and transparencies: they can invite and organize audience participation. For example, when presenting a new health insurance plan to a group of managers, a human resources representative might open the speech by asking the managers, "What aspects of health insurance matter most to your employees?" The audience members may respond with comments like "flexibility" or "low copays," which the speaker can jot down on the flip chart or board. He can then refer to each priority as he addresses them in his speech.

Whiteboards and flip charts are also valuable when you wish to "unfold" an idea, step by step, before an audience, such as a coach using a board to break down a certain defense or offense.

Collboards allow a speaker and audience members (whether in a professional or educational setting) to interact using digital pens and interactive whiteboards (Alvarez, Salavati, Nussbaum, & Milrad, 2013). This technology may therefore be a useful alternative to flip charts and whiteboards for getting a high level of audience interactivity or showing your audience how an idea or process unfolds.

Just remember that your use of flip charts and boards should never be distracting. In other words, your audience may become irritated if you're constantly flipping back and forth between pages or running around to point to multiple different diagrams on the board.

Handouts

Handouts are particularly useful when your audience benefits from specific information shared in or related to your presentation at a future point. For example, if you're seeking to persuade your classmates to utilize your campus career services office, you might have a single-page handout with pertinent information, like the Web address, office hours, contact information, services, upcoming events, and so on.

In a face-to-face class, be sure to distribute your handouts at an appropriate time. You do not want to create any unnecessary distractions with noise from shuffling papers! Unless you want your audience to follow along during

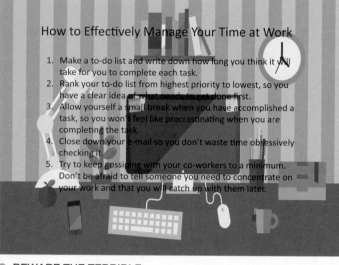

How to Effectively Manage Your Time at Work

1. Make a to-do list and write down how long you think it will take for you to complete each task.
2. Rank your to-do list from highest priority to lowest, so you have a clear idea of what needs to get done first.
3. Allow yourself a small break when you have accomplished a task, so you won't feel like procrastinating when you are completing the task.
4. Close down your e-mail so you don't waste time obsessively checking it.
5. Try to keep gossiping with your co-workers to a minimum. Don't be afraid to tell someone you need to concentrate on your work and that you will catch up with them later.

● **BEWARE THE TERRIBLE** PowerPoint slide! A long bulleted list of all your speaking points on a distracting background is a surefire way to detract from your speech and lose your audience's attention. Blooma/ Shutterstock

some part of your speech, it's often best to distribute your handouts at the end of your speech, but check to see if your instructor has any preferences.

Presentation Slideware

Sitting through hours of slides from your Aunt Sonja's vacation is boring. Sitting through a slide show that essentially repeats your speech outline can be positively unbearable.

Presentation slideware (such as Microsoft PowerPoint, Apple Keynote, and Prezi), when used appropriately, allows you to have a one-stop home for lots of different presentation aids without having to awkwardly move back and forth between media. However, presentation slideware is frequently misused by speakers who plug meaningless text or pointless visuals into slides without considering how to keep the audience's attention. You may, in fact, be familiar with the phrase "death by PowerPoint" (DuFrene & Lehman, 2004).

Too often speakers allow their slides to dominate their presentations, attempting to wow the audience with their technical proficiency rather than focusing on interesting points or well-researched evidence. We often warn our students that the fancier and more detailed the digital presentation, the more suspicious we are of the information being presented.

If you decide to use presentation software in your speech, here are some tips for developing effective slides:

▶ Become familiar with all of the features and options of your specific software before you begin to plug in your presentation information.

▶ Use as few slides as possible. More is not always better! In fact, research by cognitive scientist Carmen Simon suggests that audience members remember an average of four slides from a twenty-slide, stand-alone, text-only PowerPoint presentation ("The ubiquitous PowerPoint," 2013).

▶ Ensure that each slide addresses only one topic or idea for simplicity and clarity.

▶ Use a minimal amount of text. Research indicates that restrained and very direct use of bullet points can positively affect audience recall of information (Vogel, Dickson, & Lehman, 1986), whereas irrelevant information on slides actually reduces learning (Bartsch & Coburn, 2003).

▶ Make sure the font is large enough for easy viewing (we suggest forty-point type for titles and twenty-point type and above for all other text), and be sure to spell-check those visible words.

▶ Use only design elements that truly enhance meaning. (No cheesy graphics, please.)

- ▶ Be prepared to give the same speech without slides in case of a technology glitch. Having backup handouts or transparencies is one idea, but in any case, make sure your presentation is effective even without your slides.

- ▶ Prepare and practice in advance! As we will discuss in the next section, you will need to give yourself enough time to organize, reorganize, edit, and feel comfortable moving between slides.

Practicing Your Speech

If there's one key to developing skill as a public speaker, it's practice. Practice transforms nervous public speakers into confident ones and good public speakers into great ones, particularly when speakers pay attention to four important points: remembering the speaking outline, practicing with presentation aids, simulating the speaking situation, and practicing the actual delivery.

Remember Your Speaking Outline

By now you know the benefits of creating a speaking outline consisting of key words and phrases. Now it's time to practice from it. Review your speaking outline to make sure that all of your key words and phrases work as prompts—if you can't remember that the letters "SD" stand for "sleep deprivation," for example, you might need to write that term out.

Practice Using Presentation Aids

Recall our discussion in Chapter 12 of the annual keynote presentations of the late Steve Jobs. Clearly, Jobs rehearsed his presentations, including his use of presentation software and other technological aids—in fact, he knew it all well enough to work around it when inevitable technological glitches arose. When practicing with your presentation aids, consider the following tips:

- ▶ *Eliminate surprises.* If you're using any kind of technology, practice with it long before you deliver your speech. A video or audio clip that didn't download properly may stall or disrupt your presentation.

- ▶ *Test the facilities in advance.* Be proactive. Will your speaking site's wireless connection be fast enough to stream a clip from Netflix of YouTube? You'll rest easier if you test it out beforehand. Likewise, you should do sound checks for video and audio clips to make sure that the entire audience can see and/or hear them.

- ▶ *Write notes to yourself.* In your outline, make sure that you provide delivery cues to let yourself know when to move to the next item or when to show an image or play a clip. This will help you avoid rushing ahead to get to a particular aid, as well as ensure that you don't forget any.

- ▶ *Rehearse any demonstrations with a partner.* When your presentation aid is actually a live prop (for example, a student in your own class), you'll need to practice with this person in advance of the presentation.

▶ *Have a backup plan.* What will you do if something malfunctions during your speech? If a video clip won't play, can you tell it as a story? You might have a handout prepared for your audience members, just in case your software doesn't work.

Simulate the Situation

You already know that few people can simply walk up to a podium for the first time and deliver a perfect speech. Seasoned public speakers often look and sound great in large part because they've done it before and done it often. Exposing yourself to some of the more unnerving aspects of public speaking—for example, an audience or a self-recording—through simulation can help you become more comfortable. For example:

▶ *Create similar conditions.* Think about the room in which you'll deliver your speech: what is its size, space, and layout? Keep these things in mind as you rehearse—or even better, arrange to rehearse in the room where you will be speaking. Awareness of these conditions will help you practice eye contact, movement, gestures, and your use of notes.

▶ *Practice in front of someone.* Try practicing in front of someone or, preferably, a few people. One method for getting over anxiety about speaking in front of an audience is to "practice upward": practice first in front of one friend, then two, then three, and so on, until you are comfortable speaking before a fairly large group.

▶ *Keep an eye on your time.* Use the timer on your phone to stay on target with your allotted speech time. You might even keep track of how much time you spend on each point, particularly if you have a tendency to go into a lot of detail early on or to rush at the end.

Practice Your Delivery

In any speech, your objective should be to communicate a message to an audience. If your message is clear, the audience will connect with it; if it's buried in a sea of mumbling or if it's forced to compete with distracting body movements, the audience will miss your point. As you practice, you can improve the aspects of delivery you studied in this chapter and concentrate on your message.

▶ *Focus on your message.* Concentrate on the way that you express an argument, paraphrase a quotation, or explain a statistic. If you focus on your message, the right delivery will usually follow naturally.

▶ *Use mirrors cautiously.* Conventional wisdom has advocated rehearsing in front of a mirror in order to practice eye contact, maximize facial expressions, and assess gestures and movement. But you won't have mirrors when you deliver the speech; they can also make you feel self-conscious, distracting you from your message.

▶ *Record a practice session.* Recording your performance will allow you to get a sense of how well you project your voice, articulate your points, and use nonverbal cues.

▶ *Ask for feedback.* See if you can find a person or two to listen to your speech who will give you an honest and constructive critique of your performance. Ask what they remember most about your presentation. Did they focus mostly on your content, or were they distracted by your postures, gestures, or stammering? Were your presentation aids helpful, or were they distracting or confusing?

AND YOU?

After you have practiced in front of one or more friends, family members, or classmates, consider their feedback. Was anything about the feedback surprising? Did they note the strengths and weaknesses that you expected them to pick up on, based on your own self-assessment? If not, how might you incorporate their feedback into your next practice session?

BACK TO ▶ *The King's Speech*

At the beginning of the chapter, we talked about Britain's King George VI, or Albert, who was thrust into a position that demanded public speaking skills even though he struggled with a challenging stutter. Let's think about Albert's journey, as well as that of David Seidler, who was inspired by Albert's story and eventually brought it to the screen with *The King's Speech*, in light of what we've learned in this chapter.

▶ Albert struggled with his stammer for years and was only able to get it under control after prolonged, and somewhat experimental, speech therapy. Fortunately, by the time he was unexpectedly crowned king, he had made great progress. Had his position as a royal prince not required him to speak publicly, he might have avoided speech therapy. He was prepared to speak, even though he did not wish to do so, and never expected to have to do so—at least not as king.

▶ As a king in the early twentieth century, Albert had to contend with emerging media—particularly radio—when giving speeches. Although he still had to contend with the transactional nature of public speeches (in which he must interact with and adjust to the audience), radio gave him the opportunity to gain confidence and practice: the audience's feedback is limited in radio's linear model of communication.

▶ The audience plays a role in the success of any speech, and it is likely that British citizens, facing the uncertainty of world war, *wanted* the king to succeed. As actor Colin Firth (who portrayed the king in David Seidler's *The King's Speech*) noted, "People knew this man was facing his demons just by speaking to them. I think there was a sense that it cost him something. They found it valiant" (CBS News, 2010).

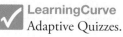 **THINGS TO TRY** Activities

1. LaunchPad for *Real Communication* offers key term videos and encourages self-assessment through adaptive quizzing. Go to **bedfordstmartins.com/realcomm** to get access to:

LearningCurve Adaptive Quizzes.

Video clips that illustrate key concepts, highlighted in teal in the Real Reference section that follows.

2. *The King's Speech* centers on Albert's address to the British people on September 3, 1939, at the outbreak of World War II, audio recordings of which are available online. Listen to them, and consider how you would have received the king's message if you were a British citizen at that time. What do you think of his delivery? Do you think your knowledge of his struggles with stammering affect the way you rate his delivery?

3. While in class, select a partner and give a one- to two-minute impromptu speech on a topic of your choice. Your partner will write down both negative and positive feedback to share with you, and you will do the same in return. Then team up with another pair of partners. You and your original partner will take turns giving the same speeches again, incorporating improvements suggested by your partner the first time around. The new partners in your group will likely give both negative and positive feedback. Listen carefully and apply their advice. Now add another pair of partners to your group, for a total of six people, and give your speech one last time. Think of the feedback from all three sessions. If you received the same negative feedback more than once, you know where further improvement is needed. Did you feel more confident giving your speech the third time than you did the first time?

4. Pay attention to how you meet people and the general first impression you receive from them. Ask yourself what makes you feel the way you do about the person. Does the person make you feel comfortable by smiling at you, looking you in the eye, or coming across as sincere? If you can pinpoint the reasons for your own first impressions, you can better understand what an audience expects from a speaker and adjust your own behaviors in order to make a good impression.

5. When practicing a speech, pay attention to your gestures and body movements. Practice once using movements that you feel are appropriate and comfortable; then practice in front of a friend, and ask how appropriate your movements actually look. Are you using too many gestures? Too few?

6. Search YouTube for a segment with a speaker giving a speech or visit TED talks (the topic does not matter). Turn off the volume so you can only see (not hear) the speech. Analyze the physical speech delivery of the speaker. Make lists of the problems with his or her speech delivery and of things the speaker does well (for example, maintains eye contact). Then watch the speech again, this time with the volume on. Listen carefully to the speaker's vocal delivery (such as pitch, rate, and volume). What do you notice about the speaker's voice? Compare your lists and note all of your observations as you prepare for your own speech.

REAL REFERENCE → A Study Tool

Now that you have finished reading this chapter, you can

Identify and control your anxieties:

▶ **Public speaking anxiety (PSA)** is the nervousness we experience when we know we have to communicate publicly to an audience (p. 404).

▶ **Communication apprehension (CA),** fear or anxiety associated with communication, is a common barrier to effective delivery (p. 404).

▶ Common anxiety triggers include upsetting past experiences, fear of evaluation, and distaste for attention (pp. 404–405).

▶ Confidence comes from being prepared, desensitizing yourself, visualizing success (particularly through **performance visualization**), taking care of yourself, and lots of practice (p. 407).

Choose a delivery style best suited to you and your speaking situation:

▶ Speaking from manuscript is helpful when you need to get the details 100 percent correct but can be static and dull (p. 408–409).

▶ Speaking from memory, referred to as **oratory**, doesn't invite rapport with the audience and is rare today (p. 409).

▶ Speaking spontaneously—when you're asked to speak with no warning beforehand—is known as **impromptu speaking** (pp. 409–410).

▶ **Extemporaneous speaking** makes the speech look easy and spontaneous, but it's actually based on an outline of key points and practice, practice, practice (pp. 410–411).

Employ effective vocal cues:

▶ Use *pitch* to vary your sound range and avoid a monotone (p. 412).

▶ Cue the audience as to what's important by adjusting your **speaking rate** and *volume* (pp. 412–413).

▶ Add drama to the speech by pausing for effect (p. 413).

▶ Speak clearly and precisely: use proper **pronunciation**, practice careful **articulation**, and avoid **mumbling** (pp. 413–414).

▶ If you have an **accent**, be aware of how it might influence your audience (p. 414).

Employ effective visual cues:

▶ Dress appropriately for the speaking occasion (pp. 414, 416).

▶ Make brief eye contact with almost everyone, using the technique known as **scanning** (p. 416).

▶ Facial expressions and gestures must match the verbal message of your speech (p. 417).

▶ Maintain a steady, confident **posture** by positioning your legs at a distance equal to your shoulders, with slightly bent knees, in the stance known as **planting** (p. 417).

Connect with your audience:

▶ Share your passion for the topic with your audience through effective use of emotion (pp. 418–419).

▶ Gauge the audience response and adapt to it (p. 419).

▶ Generate immediacy with your audience (p. 419).

Enhance your words with effective presentation aids:

▶ Effective presentation aids help listeners process and retain information, promote interest and motivation, and convey information clearly and concisely (p. 422).

▶ Based on the needs of your presentation, you can choose among helpful presentation aid types, including **props** and **models**, media clips and images, graphs and charts (including **bar graphs** and **pie charts**), posters and transparencies, flip charts and whiteboards, handouts, and presentation slideware (pp. 422–427).

Make efficient use of your practice time:

▶ Make sure the key words in your speaking outline are meaningful prompts (p. 427).

▶ Do a run-through with your presentation aids (particularly the electronic ones), and try to simulate the actual speaking conditions (pp. 427–428).

▶ Focus on the message (p. 428).

Dr. Neil deGrasse Tyson shoulders a hefty load: educating the public about astrophysics. His flair for informative speaking has earned him widespread praise. Bryan Bedder/Getty Images

LearningCurve can help you master the material in this chapter. Go to **bedfordstmartins.com/realcomm.**

Informative Speaking

As a noted astrophysicist and the director of the Hayden Planetarium at the American Museum of Natural History, it's not surprising that people enjoy asking Dr. Neil deGrasse Tyson questions: What happens if you get sucked into a black hole? Why was Pluto demoted to "dwarf planet" status? What is surprising, however, is that people recognize Tyson at all. After all, scientists—even noted scientists—are not often celebrities, and unless you're a fan of the television show *The Big Bang Theory*, astrophysics is a field that seems far removed from everyday life. Yet Tyson has, in many ways, become the face of science today, having written several bestselling books and given lectures around the country. He also hosts the PBS series *NOVA science-NOW* and has made appearances on *The Daily Show*, *The Colbert Report*, and *Jeopardy! Time* magazine voted him one of the one hundred most influential people in the world, and *People* crowned him the "sexiest astrophysicist alive" (Lemonick, 2007). He has more than 250,000 Facebook fans and over 1.25 million followers on Twitter.

Tyson's popularity is rooted in both his cosmic expertise and his communication skills, which have been recognized by NASA, the Rotary International, and the science advocacy group EarthSky. He has a particular knack for presenting the vast mysteries of the universe in ways that laypeople can understand. During a presentation at the University of Texas, for example, Tyson noted, "We have no evidence to show whether the universe is infinite or finite," before explaining that astrophysicists can only go so far to calculate a horizon—similar to the horizon line viewed from a ship at sea. He then continued that comparison: "Yet a ship is pretty sure that the ocean goes beyond the horizon of the ship, just as we are pretty sure the universe extends beyond our particular horizon. We just don't know how far" (Tyson, 2009).

Tyson recognizes the challenge of informing the general public about complex scientific and cosmic issues that researchers devote decades to understanding: "It was not a priority of mine to communicate science to the public," Tyson says. "What I found was that enough members of the public wanted to know what was going on in the universe that I decided . . . to get a little better at it so I could satisfy this cosmic curiosity" (cited in Byrd, 2010).

After you have finished reading this chapter, you will be able to

○ Describe the goals of informative speaking

○ List and describe each of the eight categories of informative speeches

○ Outline the four major approaches to informative speeches

○ Employ strategies to make your audience hungry for information

○ Structure your speech to make it easy to listen to

Like Neil deGrasse Tyson, the best informative speakers share information, teach us something new, or help us understand an idea. Clearly, Tyson has a talent for informative presentations. He knows how to analyze his audience members and tailor his presentations to engage them quickly. He organizes his information clearly and efficiently so that listeners can learn it with ease. And he presents information in an honest and ethical manner. In this chapter, we'll take a look at how you can use these same techniques to deliver competent informative speeches in any situation.

The Goals of Informative Speaking

As you'll recall from Chapter 12, the purpose of **informative speaking** is to increase the audience's understanding or knowledge; put more simply, the objective is for your audience to learn something. But to be a truly effective informative speaker, your presentation must not only fill your listeners' informational needs but also do so with respect for their opinions, backgrounds, and experiences. In addition, you want to be objective, focusing on informing (not persuading) your audience, and ethical. In this section, we examine these goals and investigate ways that you can ensure that your speech remains true to them at every phase of development and delivery.

Meeting the Audience's Informational Needs

Effective speakers engage their listeners because they have made the effort to understand the needs of their audience members. In informative speaking, the object is for your audience to learn something *new*, so you want to avoid delivering a long list of facts that are already common knowledge. Understanding your listeners' needs also involves choosing an appropriate topic and making that topic relevant to your listeners. Let's take a look at these points using "malware" as an example.

▶ *Gauge what the audience already knows.* Estimating the knowledge level of the audience helps determine where to begin, how much information to share, and at what level of difficulty the audience can understand and still maintain interest. If your goal is to inform an audience of fellow students about malware, for instance, you might assume that they have some experience with annoying computer viruses but that they may not know how to detect or remove malware from their own computers. In that case, your tasks would involve describing the types of malware (like Trojan horse viruses, adware, spyware, and so on), the functions of malware (for hackers), steps to prevent malware from disrupting their lives, and what to do if their computers are affected.

▶ *Decide on an appropriate approach to the topic.* Involving your listeners through the appropriate use of language and presentation aids gives them the impression that you have fine-tuned the speech just for them. You might present the story of the 2012 security breach at the City College of San

Francisco, in which malware illegally transmitted personal data from up to one hundred thousand students to overseas hackers. Be sure to consider the different types of sources at your disposal: visual images, personal accounts, statistics, and expert testimony. These sorts of things will captivate your audience and help them remember the new information you are teaching them.

▶ *Make the topic relevant to each member of the audience.* Always specifically connect the subject to the audience by pointing out how it is pertinent and useful to your listeners' lives. For example, you might appeal to your audience members' sense of injustice when you share stories of fellow students who have lost term papers—or worse—finances or personal identity information to malware. You can offer them peace of mind by offering suggestions to prevent hackers from accessing their personal information in the first place and on what to do should their private information be compromised.

Informing, Not Persuading

Informative speaking often serves as the base for persuasive speaking: indeed, persuasive speakers typically use information as part of their attempt to influence audiences to behave in a certain way. But although informative speaking and persuasive speaking are naturally related, it is important to recognize that they differ in one very important way: an informative speech is intended to be **objective**—it presents facts and information in a straightforward and even-handed way, free of influence from the speaker's personal thoughts or opinions. A persuasive speech, by contrast, is expected to be **subjective**—it presents facts and information from a particular point of view.

When delivering an informative speech, then, you must always remain fair to different points of view; if you find yourself presenting only facts, information, or other material that supports your own opinion, you are most likely delivering a persuasive speech. So it is important to examine your process at every step in the development of the speech to ensure that you are being truly objective. Some of the issues you'll need to evaluate are examined in Table 15.1.

Speaking Appropriately and Ethically

Objectivity is not the only ethical consideration you must bear in mind when delivering an informative speech. You must also consider the implications for your audience members of the information you provide (Sides, 2000).

CONNECT

Meeting your audience's informational needs is important in various contexts. When you're running a group meeting (Chapter 10), gauge what your audience already knows and make the content of the meeting relevant. No one wants to sit through a two-hour meeting on details of a situation that the group members already understand. And don't make your topic—the reason you've gathered—seem confusing or irrelevant.

● **WHEN YOU'RE** speaking to an audience that is knowledgeable about your topic, you don't want to bore them with a long list of facts they already know. Tell them something new! Sam Edwards/ Getty Images

TABLE 15.1

INFORMATIVE VERSUS
PERSUASIVE SPEAKING

	Informative Speeches	Persuasive Speeches
Approach	From a perspective of inquiry or discovery; the speaker researches a topic to find out what information exists and shares that information with an audience.	From a perspective of advocating a position or desired outcome; the speaker researches a topic to find information that supports a particular point of view and then tries to convince an audience to change an attitude or take some action based on that point of view.
Objectivity	The speaker reports information objectively, in the role of a messenger.	The speaker argues a case subjectively and speaks from a particular point of view.
Use of facts and information	The speaker sets out the current facts or state of affairs concerning the topic.	The speaker builds a case that he or she is passionate about and includes information that supports his or her favored position.
Expression of opinions	The speaker may provide others' opinions but refrains from giving his or her own.	The speaker provides others' opinions that support his or her own position or viewpoint; the speaker may mention differing opinions only to rebut or discredit them.

First, ethical speakers must choose appropriate topics for discussion. A fellow communication instructor told us that one of her students gave an informative presentation on how to grow marijuana. No matter what your opinion is on the legalization of marijuana, its use is still illegal in most states, so informing your audience about how to grow it its simply unethical.

As we've discussed throughout this book, an ethical speaker has a responsibility to provide an audience with information that is relevant and reliable in a way that is respectful of both the audience and the subject. The types of supporting material you offer (or do not offer) and your motives for speaking on a particular subject reveal quite a bit about you as an ethical speaker.

In addition, ethical speakers must avoid plagiarism by orally citing sources and providing a complete list of references at the end of a speech outline. If your speech misinforms your audience in any way, you are not offering an appropriate or ethical informative speech.

Topics for Informative Presentations

When it comes to choosing a topic for an informative speech, there are countless options. You can speak, for example, about something very concrete, such as a person, place, thing, process, or event; or about something more abstract, such as a concept or phenomenon. In many cases, your topic will fit into more than one category: for example, a speech on the phenomenon of hip-hop music might include descriptions of the genre (thing) as well as of particular bands (people) and performances (events). You might also talk about the way the music developed over time (process). We'll take a look at eight categories for informative speech topics identified by communication researchers Ron Allen and Ray McKerrow (1985) in the sections that follow.

● **FROM LEGENDARY**
movie stars to historic natural
disasters, you can develop
a compelling informative
speech on virtually anything
(or anyone!). (top left) Getty Images;
(top right) © Columbia Pictures/courtesy
Everett Collection; (bottom left) imago
stock&people/Newscom; (bottom right)
TOSHIFUMI KITAMURA/AFP/Getty Images

People

If there's one subject that fascinates most people, it's other people. That's why we might sneak a peek at *In Touch Weekly* or *The National Enquirer* when we're stuck in line at the grocery store (even if we're not that interested in the latest gossip about the Kardashian sisters). It's why you don't rush to end the conversation when your mother says, "You'll never guess what happened to your cousin Leah." The life of another person can certainly make for an interesting informative speech topic. You might lean toward giving a speech about someone who is famous (or infamous)—indeed, audiences are usually receptive to learning about someone who is famous simply because they revere or worship celebrity (Atkinson & Dougherty, 2006; Spitzberg & Cupach, 2008). On the other hand, an obscure but interesting person, such as Dr. Catherine Hamlin (who provided free medical care to young women in Ethiopia), can also be a great speech topic.

The key to giving a successful speech about another person is to focus on the person's human qualities as well as his or her achievements. In addition, you should show not merely what these people did but also *why* and *how* they did it. In other words, give your audience a real sense of who they are or were. To meet this goal, your speech should include anecdotes, quotes, and stories that show the motivations behind their actions. Chapter 12 offers help in adding these speech supports.

Places

Like people, places can be interesting and compelling topics for an informative speech. You might focus on an inspired description of a real but perhaps unfamiliar place (the surface of Mars, the Arctic tundra) or even a fictional one (The Wall from *Game of Thrones* or the desert of Tatooine in *Star Wars*). Even a very familiar place offers opportunities to provide audiences with some new information. For example, you might investigate the oldest building on your campus or in your town and detail some of its history in your speech. This will allow you

CONNECT

Your audience is an important variable to consider as you choose your topic. Your goal in an informative presentation is to meet the audience's informational needs, so you must understand their knowledge and interests. Before you decide to inform your audience about backyard gardening, solicit information about your listeners using the strategies in Chapter 12 (pp. 341–346). If you learn that most of your audience members live in apartments, they probably won't care about gardening in a backyard they don't have.

what about you?

○ Informative or Persuasive?

Speakers sometimes have a hard time clarifying the general purpose of their presentation topic. Does the speech intend to impart information (informative speech) or to suggest a change in attitudes, belief, or behavior (persuasive speech)? Consider the speech topics that follow, marking "I" for those that seem informative and "P" for those that could be persuasive.

_____ 1. How therapy dogs are trained

_____ 2. Why you should add omega fatty acids to your diet

_____ 3. How omega fatty acids modulate inflammatory responses

_____ 4. Title IX harms male athletes and eliminates important programs

_____ 5. Why you should become an organ donor

_____ 6. The importance of restricting handguns

_____ 7. How fracking works

_____ 8. The benefits of volunteer reading programs for at-risk children

_____ 9. How to cut the cable cord

_____ 10. Why athletic scholarships should be banned

Answers: 1. I; 2. P; 3. I; 4. P; 5. P; 6. P; 7. I; 8. I; 9. I; 10. P

not only to describe the place but also to talk about the people who designed and built it and how the building has been changed over the years.

Objects and Phenomena

A third source of ideas for informative speeches consists of objects or phenomena. These speeches explore anything that isn't human, such as living things (like animals, plants, even entire ecosystems), as well as inanimate objects, such as the Egyptian pyramids, Google Glass, pre-Columbian artifacts, or the *Mona Lisa*. Objects can also be imaginary things (light sabers) or hypothetical ones (a driverless car) or even entire phenomena (the El Niño wind patterns in the western United States or citizen journalism). Audiences usually find these types of speeches interesting because they captivate the imagination or because they stress a topic that the audience hadn't previously considered as having an impact on their lives.

Events

Noteworthy occurrences (past and present) are good topics for informative speeches. Our understanding of history is shaped by events—the Revolutionary

EVALUATING**COMMUNICATION**ETHICS

Ulterior Motives

As captain of the school swim team, you've been asked to deliver an informative speech to the school's alumni during homecoming week detailing the team's past three seasons and hopes for the future. You've outlined a short, simple speech that notes individual members' personal bests, team achievements, and the coach's laudable efforts to recruit promising high school athletes. When your coach reviews your speech outline, she asks you to include more about the many scholarships that the school makes available to athletes.

You know that the coach has many motives for asking you to include more information about scholarship money. She's hoping, first and foremost, to convince alumni to support the team financially, in order to entice more financially strapped but talented swimmers to choose your school. But you're feeling torn: you know that most of the money that goes to your school's sports programs is devoted to the larger and more popular basketball program. You're also feeling annoyed because four years ago, the coach recruited you as a high school scholar-athlete with a partial scholarship that she promised would grow to a full scholarship the following year. The full scholarship never materialized, and now you're about to graduate with huge student loans that you had thought you'd be able to avoid when you chose to attend this school over others that courted you.

As team captain, you're proud of your team's record and eager to inform the alumni about it. But you also don't want to give them information that you feel is somewhat misleading. What should you do?

THINK ABOUT THIS

❶ What are the ethical obligations of a speaker in preparing informative presentations? Can you ignore the coach's request and just say what you want to say?

❷ Is the coach's request really an attempt to inform alumni of what the swim program needs in order to persuade them to donate money?

❸ Are your motivations really ethical? Do you want to avoid talking about scholarship money because you think it will never materialize or because you're angry that the coach misled you?

War, the assassination of Abraham Lincoln, the Apollo 11 moon landing, the terrorist attacks on September 11, the 2011 earthquake and tsunami in Japan, and the 2013 Boston marathon bombings. At a more intimate level, events of local significance can also make interesting and compelling topics for speeches. For example, you might develop an informative speech about the upcoming student film festival at your campus.

You can also build an informative speech around important, tragic, funny, or instructive events in your personal life—the day you went skydiving, the day you witnessed a flash mob, the death of a close friend, or the birth of your first child. Just remember that these stories of personal events must be ethical and truthful. One of us had a student lie about being in a car that was hit by a drunk driver to infuse some personal spark in an informative speech about California drunk driving laws. Such exaggeration and fabrication are never ethical!

In addition to helping an audience to understand the meaning of personal, local, and historical single events, a speaker can also explore the social significance of *collections* of events. You might, for example, talk about the significance of dances for Native American tribes, high school football games in your hometown, or the role of weddings, reunions, and funerals in your family.

● **YOUR SPEECH** doesn't necessarily have to be about a historical event. The first time you went skydiving can be just as compelling a topic as the first time man walked on the moon. (left) Digital Vision/Getty Images; (right) NASA-KSC

Processes

A process is a series of actions, changes, or functions that brings about a particular result. Process speeches help an audience understand the stages or steps through which a particular outcome is produced and usually fall into one of two categories. The first type is a speech that explains how something works or develops. For example, you might give a speech detailing how a hybrid car works, how the human brain system processes sound, or how lightning forms. The second type of process speech teaches how to do something: how to knit, for example, or how to sync your data on your mobile devices. For this type of speech, it is often helpful to incorporate props, visuals, or hands-on demonstrations into your presentation.

Concepts

Although people, places, objects, events, and processes are concrete things that we can readily visualize, concepts are abstract or complex ideas or even theories, like "art," "patriotism," "artificial intelligence," or "loyalty," which are much more difficult for us to understand. The challenge of a concept speech, then, is to take a general idea, theory, or thought and make it clear and meaningful for your audience.

Despite the challenge, many worthwhile informative speeches focus on the explanation of a concept. The idea of "ethnocentrism," the belief that one's cultural ways are superior to those of other cultures, would be an informative speech about a concept (Armstrong & Kaplowitz, 2001). You could then make reference to important historical events that were influenced by ethnocentrism: the Holocaust, ethnic cleansing in Bosnia and Rwanda, or the September 11 terrorist attacks.

Issues

An issue is a problem or matter of dispute that people hope to resolve. Informative speeches about issues provide an overview or a report of problems in order to increase understanding and awareness. Issues include social and personal problems

(such as racial profiling, post-traumatic stress disorder, or unemployment) as well as ideas, activities, and circumstances over which opinions vary widely (such as birth control or affirmative action).

Because of the controversial nature of many issues, giving an informative presentation on one can be a challenge, as it can be difficult to keep your own opinions from influencing the speech. But if you keep your focus on delivering a speech that is truly one of discovery, inquiry, and objectivity, then even controversial topics often break down into more manageable components that you can look at objectively. For example, if you were to give an informative speech on stem cell research, you could break all of your information down into groups of basic facts: what the current laws say, where the stem cells come from, how the research is done, and why such research is being conducted. You could also address the controversy over the issue itself by presenting differing opinions from both within and outside the scientific community. If, however, you take a look at the research and plot your speech points but still doubt your ability to describe an issue objectively, you probably should save the topic for a persuasive speech.

Plans and Policies

The final category for informative speeches concerns plans and policies (Allen & McKerrow, 1985). In such speeches, the speaker tries to help an audience understand the important dimensions of potential courses of action (for example, raising fares on commuter trains in your city or eliminating work-study scholarships at your college). Such speeches do not argue for a particular plan or policy; they simply lay out the facts. Like issue speeches, plan and policy speeches can easily evolve into persuasive addresses, so you must be very careful to focus on unbiased facts; if you find yourself unable to keep your opinion from influencing your speech, consider a different topic.

AND YOU?

Would you find it hard to speak in a purely informative manner on certain subjects? Would you be able to speak, for example, in a nonpersuasive way about your religious beliefs? Your favorite film? Or a musical act that you just can't stand?

 **CONNECT**

At this point, you may have many good topics for an informative speech. But if you need more ideas, remember the advice we offer in Chapter 12 on searching for topics. Try *brainstorming* or *clustering*, soliciting ideas from others, or using the Internet to identify possible topics. Always ask yourself: Is this topic interesting to me? Do I know enough about it? Is it a good topic for an informative speech?

Approaches to Conveying Information

Once you have selected a topic for an informative speech, you can develop it in a variety of ways. Here we will briefly describe four major approaches to informative speeches: description, demonstration, definition, and explanation. These approaches will help you develop the most effective way to share information with your audience.

Description

Description is a way of verbally expressing things you have experienced with your senses. Although most speeches use some type of description, some focus on this task more closely than others. The primary task of a **descriptive presentation** is to paint a mental picture for your audience to portray places, events, persons, objects, or processes clearly and vividly. An effective descriptive speech begins with a well-structured idea of what you want to describe and why. As you move through the development process, you emphasize important details and eliminate unimportant ones, all the while considering ways to make the details more vivid for your audience.

Descriptive speeches are most effective when the topic is personally connected to the speaker. Consider the following excerpt from President Barack Obama's April 2013 "They picked the wrong city" speech to honor those killed and wounded in the Boston Marathon bombings. Many people found Obama's description of the youngest victim, Martin Richard, to be particularly moving:

> And our hearts are broken for 8-year-old Martin, with his big smile and bright eyes. His last hours were as perfect as an 8-year-old boy could hope for, with his family, eating ice cream at a sporting event. And we're left with two enduring images of this little boy, forever smiling for his beloved Bruins and forever expressing a wish he made on a blue poster board: No more hurting people. Peace. No more hurting people. Peace.[1]

From these few vivid lines, audience members learn who Martin was and are moved by this young boy's advocacy of peace; they can imagine who he might have become had his life not been cut so short.

● **PEGGY PAUL** demonstrates her resourceful culinary abilities. Courtesy Peggy Paul

Demonstration

Food blogger and editor Peggy Paul was offered the opportunity to appear on *The Rachael Ray Show* after informing the celebrity host that she could prepare a

---

[1]The full text of President Obama's speech on April 18, 2013, can be found at http://www.ajc.com/news/news/national/transcript-obamas-speech-boston-marathon-bombings/nXQRz

WIREDFORCOMMUNICATION

Talk Amongst Yourselves

There is little doubt that technology is changing the nature of classroom lectures. Many instructors embrace new technologies to enhance their lectures—they might incorporate slideware presentations, offer audio or video clips, or use a computer to run a statistical analysis during class. But one professor suggests that the best use of technology might be to eliminate classroom lectures—that is, to provide lectures online in order to free up class time for other kinds of teaching.

Eric Mazur, a Harvard physics professor, believes that the old lecture format, in which teachers speak and students listen and take notes, is not the most effective method for teaching or the most efficient use of classroom time. After research by a colleague showed that thousands of students who had completed the introductory physics course at universities around the country still did not have an accurate understanding of the nature of force (a fundamental concept for the discipline), Mazur was astounded. He administrated the test to his own students and found that they were no different. He began to try different methods for teaching the concept, shook up his lectures, trying different methods for teaching. Then, he explains, "I did something I had never done in my teaching career. . . . I said, 'Why don't you discuss it with each other?'" He was shocked when, after a scant three minutes of classroom chaos, all the students had figured it out. Those who understood the concept were quickly able to defend their explanations of the concept, while those who had it wrong could not and, thus, students taught each other. Why were students so much more effective at conveying a concept that he understood so much more thoroughly? Mazur hypothesizes that it's precisely because they were not experts. "You're a student and you've only recently learned this," he says, "so you still know where you got hung up, because it's not that long ago that *you* were hung up on that very same thing" (Mazur, quoted in Lambert, 2012, para. 7).

Seeing the value in this kind of peer instruction, Mazur began to rethink the need for classroom lectures. Now he presents his lectures online, before class, and saves his valuable class time for working with students. He has them submit their questions online and then addresses them in class. He also has them work together in class—completing problems, discussing questions, and explaining concepts to one another—to clarify what they learned from the lectures. "Think of education as a whole—what is it? Is it just the transfer of information?" Mazur doesn't think so. "Ultimately, learning is a *social* experience. Harvard is Harvard not because of the buildings, not because of the professors, but because of the *students* interacting with one another" (Mazur, quoted in Lambert, 2012, para. 28).

THINK ABOUT THIS

❶ How and why did the lecture become the de facto form of classroom instruction? Why is in-class instruction less common in university settings?

❷ Why might instructors be hesitant to present lectures online? Is it simple resistance to change, or might other factors be involved?

❸ Does the fact that lectures are widely available online, from noted scholars, for free, make them less valuable? Does Mazur's approach make class time more or less valuable?

❹ If students are engaged in peer learning during class, what is the instructor's role? Is he or she considered a facilitator or an instructor still engaged in public speaking in this format?

four-course gourmet dinner in her tiny apartment with just a toaster oven, a microwave, and a hot plate (Annino, 2007). Sound impossible? But what if she showed you? Rachael Ray (and Peggy Paul) caught on to an important truth: often the best way to explain how something works is to demonstrate it.

Demonstration speeches answer "how" questions—how to use a Roku, how to bake a pie crust, how to salsa dance—by showing an audience the way something works. In this case, Peggy used a combination of explanatory narration and physical demonstration to show how she whips up baked apple pork chops, pear and gorgonzola salad, and chocolate hazelnut quesadillas as easily as we make grilled cheese, all the while making use of props, models, and other visual aids.

The key to delivering an effective demonstration speech is to begin with a clear statement of purpose and to follow a very straightforward organizational pattern. In most cases, a chronological pattern works best for a demonstration, with the process broken down into a number of steps that are presented in order of completion. The following steps in the process of decorative painting techniques illustrate a demonstration speech in chronological order. You can imagine the speaker showing each of the three methods.

To demonstrate how to liven up a room with faux paint, you can use three popular types of decorative wall painting: color washing, sponging on, and ragging off.

Color washing hides flaws in the wall and gives it a textured look. First, paint your wall a base color. Next, with short strokes, brush one or more glaze colors loosely over the contrasting base color (show photographs).

The sponging-on technique gives the wall depth and texture with a variable pattern. Apply two or more coats of paint—satin, flat, semigloss, or gloss—on your wall. After the base coat dries, apply a glaze coat using a sea sponge (show sea sponge and photograph).

Ragging off gives the wall a delicate, evenly textured appearance. Apply two base coats of two colors. While the second color is still wet, use a clean dry rag wrapped around a paint roller, and roll it across the wall (demonstrate technique).[2]

Definition

Most informative speeches require that the speaker define a term or clarify an idea at some point (see "Clarifying Concepts" in the next section for more discussion). For some topics, however, the *entire speech* is focused on definitions. The main goal of **definitional speeches** is to provide answers to "what" questions. Such questions as "What is torture?" and "What is marriage?" have prompted heated debate in the halls of Congress (and elsewhere) in recent years, making it clear that an entire speech could easily be devoted to defining such complex ideas. When you define something, you identify its essential qualities and meaning. Following are various ways to do this, and a definitional speech often incorporates more than one of these techniques.

When offering definitions, competent speakers remember that words have *connotative meanings*—emotional meanings—for people (Chapter 3). Consider the words *marriage* and *torture*. Even if you offer clear dictionary definitions of these terms, your audience may have strong attitudes about them that are influenced by their cultural backgrounds. As an informative speaker, you should be aware of the power of connotative meanings while not trying to persuade people to feel differently about terms.

---

[2]We thank Daniel Bernard and Cory Cunningham and their students for contributing the examples featured in this discussion.

▶ An **operational definition** defines something by explaining what it is or what it does. For example, a salsa can be defined by what it is: "A salsa is a condiment, usually made of tomatoes, onions, and peppers, common in Spanish and Latin American cuisine." Alternatively, it can be defined by what it does: "Salsas are most commonly used as dipping sauces for fried tortilla chips, but they also work well alongside grilled fish."

▶ **Definition by negation** defines something by telling what it is not. For example, "A salsa is not the same as taco or piquante sauce."

▶ **Definition by example** defines something by offering concrete examples of what it is. For example, "Salsas include the basic tomato version you get at your local Mexican restaurant, as well as variants made from mangoes, pineapples, or tomatillos."

▶ **Definition by synonym** defines something by using words that closely mean the same thing. For example, "A salsa is basically just a chunky sauce, similar to a chutney in Indian cuisine."

▶ **Definition by etymology** defines something by using the origin of a word or phrase. For example, "Salsa is the Spanish and Italian word for sauce, derived from the Latin word for 'salty.'"

As noted, definitional speeches can take one or more of these approaches to defining a specific term.

Explanation

Explanatory presentations delve into more complexity than the other approaches to conveying information or creating awareness. **Explanatory speeches** answer such questions as "Why?" or "What does that mean?" To make your points in an explanatory speech, you must provide reasons or causes and show relationships among things; you must use interpretation and analysis. To this end, you should keep three main goals in mind: clarifying concepts, explaining the "big picture," and challenging intuition.

Clarifying Concepts

When providing complex explanations, an audience may have difficulty even just understanding the meaning and use of certain terms. So it is important to clarify your concepts. You may find it useful to use one of the definition techniques discussed earlier. In addition, a particularly effective strategy for explanatory speeches is to provide **elucidating explanations**—details that illuminate the concept's meaning and use. Good elucidating explanations do three things. First, they define a concept by listing each of its critical features. For example, notice in the following sentence how the speaker provides succinct illustrations for the concept of rhetoric: "Aristotle described the canons of rhetoric as consisting of *pathos* (appeal to emotions), *logos* (appeal to logic), and *ethos* (appeal to character)." Second, elucidating explanations contrast examples of the concept. For instance, a speaker might suggest that the difference between gun

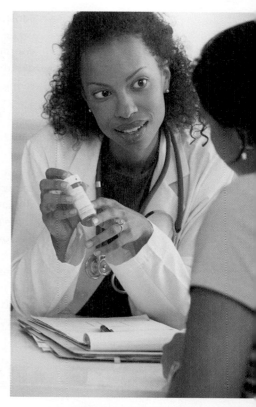

● **DOCTORS ESSENTIALLY** give explanatory speeches to their patients, describing the causes of a medical condition and how it may be treated. Image Source/Getty Images

control and partial gun control is as distinct as night and day. Finally, elucidating examples present opportunities for audiences to distinguish examples from contrasting examples by looking for a concept's critical features—for instance, demonstrating that the most important features of a right-handed person's golf swing are keeping the left arm straight and keeping the head still.

Explaining the Big Picture

Sometimes an idea is difficult for an audience because its complexity makes its main points—the "big picture"—hard to grasp. In this case, speakers should use a quasi-scientific explanation. Just as scientists try to develop models of the world, **quasi-scientific explanations** provide a model or picture of the key dimensions of some phenomenon for a particular audience. These explanations work particularly well for speakers presenting complex topics to laypeople, such as how microchips work, the similarities and differences between levees and dams, or how DNA molecules pass along genetic information. We heard a particularly good quasi-scientific speech explanation in which the speaker explained how radar worked by comparing it to the way an echo works, except that it involves radio waves rather than sound waves.

COMMUNICATIONACROSSCULTURES

Let's Talk About Sex

Few subjects can make an audience as uncomfortable as sex. Religious beliefs, age, experience, and even politics inform not only people's views about sex but also the degree to which they are willing to discuss sexual matters publicly. In many cases, for example, it is unthinkable for Muslims to discuss sexual practices, especially with strangers or in public (El Ahl & Steinvorth, 2006). And in many villages in South Africa, sex is a taboo many women do not—or are told they should not—discuss (le Roux, 2006). And even in cultures without such restrictions, talking about sex is often considered impolite and can make listeners feel embarrassed or uneasy. In diverse populations like the United States, speakers—including health care providers, educators, social workers, and policymakers—must be responsive to the sensitive nature of sexual openness when they speak to audiences.

Some people are already learning how. One of these individuals is Heba Kotb (Raman, 2007), whose weekly television program offers information on sex to women throughout the Middle East. Kotb, who has a doctorate in human sexuality, clinical sexology, and pastoral counseling and is a devout Muslim, remains respectful of her audience's—and her own—religious beliefs by framing her discussion in a religious context, accompanying scientific information about the body with explanations of how Islamic texts address the subject at hand. Indeed, both medical experts and Islamic clerics participate in her show. She also pays careful attention to nonverbal communication: she wears the traditional Muslim headscarf and speaks in a serious tone and uses serious facial expressions. Kotb's sensitive approach, taking cultural taboos, norms, and beliefs into account, seems to allow her to talk more freely about this once forbidden topic.

THINK ABOUT THIS

❶ Kotb's approach to informing women about sex is a far cry from the often lighthearted and humorous approaches used by talk show hosts in the United States. How might her approach to informative speaking be perceived in the United States?

❷ Imagine that you have to give an informative speech about a sexual topic in front of your nursing class. How would you approach the subject? Would you handle it differently if you were speaking in front of your parents? Your religious community?

❸ Does gender play a role in public speaking as well? Would Kotb's message be as well received by her audience if she were a man?

Effective quasi-scientific explanations highlight the main points with such features as titles, organizing analogies, presentation aids, and signposts ("The first key point is . . ."). Good quasi-scientific explanations also connect key points by using transitional phrases (such as "for example"), connectives ("because"), and diagrams depicting relationships among parts.

Challenging Intuition

Some ideas in explanatory speeches may run contrary to what intuition tells us. Consider the polio vaccine, which was tested in 1952 and used an injected dose of an inactive (essentially, dead) polio virus. The notion of using something that makes people sick to prevent people from getting sick is counterintuitive. Imagine how difficult this must have been to explain to patients and worried parents at the time.

If you are giving an informative speech on how vaccines work or another counterintuitive idea, you might want to design your talk around transformative explanations. **Transformative explanations** are designed to help speakers transform "theories" about phenomena into more accepted notions. For your speech on vaccines, you might describe how, by exposing the body to a similar but benign virus (like the dead polio virus), a vaccine essentially teaches the body to defend itself against a specific disease.

Guidelines for Informative Speeches

In Chapters 12 through 14, we provided the basics for developing, preparing, writing, and delivering effective presentations. In this section, we'll take a look at how you can tailor those basic strategies to the needs of an informative speech. Your first goal as a speaker is to get your audience interested in your topic. But you'll also want to make sure that your speech is easy to listen to. It's hard to inform people who are struggling to keep up with you—or wishing they were somewhere else!

● **KIMONOS** are beautiful, but you'll still need to make them relevant to your audience if you really want to draw them in. Christian Kober/ Robert Harding/Newscom

Create Information Hunger

Can you recall a teacher from your past who had the ability to get you interested in a certain subject area? The same techniques work when it comes to public speaking. You want to make your audience hungry for the information you are going to present—get them excited about, or at least interested in, your topic. As you consider a topic for your informative speech, ask yourself, "How will this audience benefit from this information?" If you can't come up with a compelling reason for each person to pay attention to what you say, you need to rethink your topic. Several strategies help you create information hunger, including arousing curiosity and working your topic.

Arouse People's Curiosity

A few years ago, we watched a student inform the audience about kimonos. A kimono is a long, loose Japanese robe with wide sleeves traditionally worn with a broad sash as an outer garment. The speaker defined a kimono, contrasted different types of kimonos, and then demonstrated how to get into one and wear it properly. Although her speech was interesting and her demonstration was effective, in the end we had no idea why we had listened to it! The problem was that although she competently explained the historical and cultural significance of the kimono and gave a detailed demonstration of the process of designing and wearing one, she did little to make the audience interested in the subject as a whole. She might have fared better had she offered some sort of connection between the kimono and the daily lives of the audience. For example:

> Think of your favorite article or ensemble of clothing—that one perfect item or outfit that you just hope you have the occasion to wear. Would you have worn it ten years ago? Will it still be stylish ten years from now? Magazine editors and clothing designers like to throw the word *timeless* around, claiming that some things—the Armani suit, the little black dress—will never go out of fashion. But the truth is that style is a fickle thing, and lapels, hemlines, colors, and waistbands change with the tides. Today, I'm going to talk about an article of clothing that truly is timeless, one that is worn by both men and women and has remained largely unchanged in shape and form for over one thousand years. I'm speaking, of course, about the traditional garment of Japan, the kimono.

Here we've piqued people's interest by asking them first to think about their own experience—about something they own or wish to own. We then draw them into our subject, the kimono, by contrasting it with what Westerners tend to consider "classic" fashion. Such comparisons and personalization of the subject can help keep the audience interested.

Work Your Topic

But what if you can't change the topic? In many real-world situations, you may be asked to explain, define, describe, or demonstrate something that strikes you as boring or irrelevant. A CEO will frequently need to address shareholders with reports of profits and losses, for example, and spokespersons for government agencies are often required to make statements about public policies or current events.

In such cases, the speaker must find the relevance of the subject and establish it for the audience quickly and assertively. If your topic seems somehow disconnected from your audience, it's your job to find the relevance. For example, can you save the audience money or time? Can you help people do something better or improve quality? Even if the benefit is not for the short term, will listening to your speech help them in some way in the future, once they become parents or graduate students or homeowners? Unless you present a clear benefit that people can derive from listening to you, you will not get or keep their attention.

● **PEOPLE USUALLY** groan at the thought of sitting through a boring software presentation, but if the speaker makes it relevant to their needs, they might change their minds. © factoria singular/Alamy

For example, imagine that you are an office manager and need to deliver a presentation to your colleagues explaining how to fill out the company's new expense reports. One way to get them interested in what they might perceive as an unnecessary presentation is to show them that learning how to do this task will benefit them in some way:

> I know it's hard to get excited about something as mundane as filing expense reports. But the good news is that our new electronic transmittal system will get your reimbursements to you faster and more reliably. As you know, it typically takes four to six weeks for an expense report to be routed, approved, and transmitted to accounts payable and another two weeks for accounts payable to cut the check. With this new system, we'll be able to have funds deposited directly to your bank account in as little as ten business days. So with that in mind, let's take a look at how the new system works.

By clearly connecting the subject with the lives and needs of your listeners, you're more likely to have their attention as you demonstrate the less interesting aspects of the process. If you cannot find the subject's relevance, you may need to refine or revise the topic.

Make It Easy

Creating a good informative speech is hard work; listening to one should not be. Your job as speaker is to find and distill a lot of information in a way that is easy for your audience to listen to, absorb, and learn. In short, you need to do your listeners' work for them. There are a number of objectives to bear in mind as you prepare, which we will now discuss.

Choose a Clear Organization and Structure

When people are presented with new information, they need to organize it in their minds in a way that makes sense to them. You can help them in this endeavor by organizing your speech around a clear and logical structure (McCroskey & Mehrley, 1969). Recall from Chapter 13 that there are a number of arrangements for presentations, including chronological, topical, and spatial organizations; problem–solution, cause–effect, and narrative patterns; and arrangements based on motivated sequences. Your choice of organizational pattern will depend on your topic, and every speech will have several organizational options.

For example, if you're planning to deliver a speech on the history of punk rock, you might choose a chronological organization, beginning with mid-1960s' garage bands and following through the 1970s' peak with bands like the Sex Pistols and the Ramones, through the postpunk era, and ending with more modern punk-influenced bands like Green Day and the Libertines. But you also might find it interesting to approach the topic spatially, noting differences between American and British punk, or even causally, demonstrating how the form arose as a reaction to the popular music that preceded it as well as to the economic and political climate of the times. Table 15.2 offers some ideas for using organizational approaches to different informative topics, in addition to

AND YOU?

What techniques can you use to look at a subject and find its relevance to you or your audience? How can these tactics help you create more interesting informative speeches?

● **IF YOUR SPEECH** is on punk rock, you might organize it chronologically, moving from the Ramones to Green Day. (left) Sire Records/Getty Images; (right) Kevin Winter/Getty Images

considering the approaches we discussed earlier (definition, description, demonstration, and explanation).

Emphasize Important Points

Another way to make it easier for your audience to follow and absorb your speech is to clarify what the important parts are. As you learned in Chapter 13, one of the best means to achieve this is by using a preview device and a concluding summary. The preview device tells the audience what you are going to cover ("First, I will discuss X, second, Y, and third, Z"). A concluding summary reviews what the audience heard during the speech ("Today, I talked about X, then showed you Y, and, finally, discussed Z").

Careful and deliberate use of phrases like "The key issue here is . . ." and "I have three main points regarding this piece of legislation" can also signal to your audience that you're about to say something important. In some cases, you might actually highlight what is important by saying so, even telling the audience directly when you're discussing something you want them to remember. This not only supports the organization of your speech but also gives people useful tools for organizing the information as they listen. It's important to make certain, however, that you don't contradict yourself. If you say, "I have one key point to make," and you then list four points of equal importance, you will likely confuse (and annoy) your audience.

Don't Overwhelm Your Audience

Have you ever sat through a lecture or a presentation in which the speaker seemed to give far too much information? Ironically, too many points can make a speech seem pointless, and an overabundance of facts and statistics can make it difficult to follow and impossible to retain. Research shows that receivers' attention and interest levels drop significantly due to information overload. Simply put, too much information overwhelms the audience (Van Zandt, 2004; Wecker, 2012).

Your goal, then, is to keep your presentation as simple as possible so that audiences will find it easy to follow. As you review and rehearse your speech, critically evaluate each and every fact, point, and example—indeed, every

TABLE 15.2

TYPES OF INFORMATIVE SPEECHES, SAMPLE TOPICS, INFORMATIONAL STRATEGIES, AND ORGANIZATIONAL PATTERNS

Subject Matter	Sample Topics	Informational Strategy (definition, description, etc.)	Suggested Organizational Patterns
Speeches about objects or phenomena	• Egyptian pyramids • Pre-Columbian artifacts • *Mona Lisa* • El Niño wind patterns	*Define* and *describe* the object or phenomenon in question. Depending on your specific speech purpose, either conclude at that point or continue with an in-depth *explanation* or a *demonstration* of the object or phenomenon.	You might use a *topical* pattern if you are explaining the categories for Pre-Columbian artifacts. Conversely, you might use a *chronological* pattern if your speech focuses on a historical timeline of the artifacts.
Speeches about people	• Celebrities • Inventors • Athletes • Politicians • British royalty	Paint a vivid picture of your subject using a *description*. Use *explanation* to address the person's or group's significance.	*Narrative* patterns could be useful for speeches about people since stories can include rich details about a person's life. The *chronological* pattern can also be useful to describe someone's life events or achievements.
Speeches about events	• The terrorist attacks on September 11 • The 2011 earthquake and tsunami in Japan • The 2013 Boston Marathon bombings	Use *description* to paint a vivid picture. Use *explanation* to analyze the meaning of the event.	You might use a *chronological* pattern for a topic focusing on events if time or sequence is relevant to your purpose.
Speeches about processes	• How a hybrid car works • How lightning forms • How to sew or knit • How to sync your data on your mobile devices	If physically showing a process, rely on *demonstration*. If explaining a process, vary strategies as needed.	*Cause–effect* patterns of speech organization are helpful in explaining processes of various kinds. Additional patterns of organization could include *spatial* or *chronological*.
Speeches about issues	• Racial profiling • Post-traumatic stress disorder • Unemployment • Police brutality	Focus on *description* and *explanation*.	*Topical* and *spatial* patterns can be particularly useful for speeches about issues (which can easily become persuasive).
Speeches about concepts	• Art • Patriotism • Artificial intelligence • Ethnocentrism • Time travel	Focus on clear *definitions* and *explanations*; the more difficult a concept is, the more ways you will want to define and explain it. Vivid *description* can also be useful.	Consider *topical* organizational patterns for speeches about concepts, as well as the *narrative* pattern. The *spatial* pattern may also work well for your purposes.

Source: O'Hair, Stewart, & Rubenstein (2012), p. 334. Adapted with permission.

word—to make certain that it makes a real contribution to your speech. Eliminate anything that is redundant or tangential. You want to strike a perfect balance by telling your listeners just what they need to know to understand your topic—nothing more, nothing less.

Build on Prior Knowledge

Another way to make your speech easier to listen to and retain is to introduce concepts that are new by relating them to familiar ideas. People are more open to new ideas when they understand how they relate to things they already know about. In an informative speech about successful online fashion businesses, you might discuss the concept of the "virtual model image." Instead of trying on

real communicator

NAME: K. C. Ellis
OCCUPATION: Group Vice President of Client Services, Financial Services Industry

I never dreamed I'd work in financial services when I graduated with my communication degree. I had taken one economics class (accounting) in college and decided finance didn't hold a lot of appeal for me. Then I went to a campus information session where a representative from the company that eventually hired me said they often brought on people who didn't know the difference between a bull and a bear market. They were instead looking for smart, motivated people who could communicate well and had the desire to learn. I went for the interview and got the job.

My firm manages assets for high net worth clients, providing proactive, customized service over the phone and in person. One of my first roles at the firm was to act as a liaison between our clients and our portfolio team. I was tasked with effectively communicating our investment strategy to clients while answering their questions, which could range from complicated investment theory to simple operational requests. Given that each client has a completely different background (in terms of his or her occupation, age, gender, investment experience, etc.), I had to learn how to be flexible in my communication. Through listening to clients, I could find out their depth of knowledge, likes and dislikes, and past experience—and then use this information to provide them with the most helpful, customized answers.

Over my ten years at the company, I've served in a number of roles around the firm: operations, customer service, management, and event planning. I've enjoyed all of them, even the less traditional finance roles. For example, in event planning, I learned valuable skills such as public speaking, negotiation, and managing vendors and onsite staff. Large-scale events require the work of many people—and good communication between them is essential.

Over the past few years, I've moved into a management capacity, and about 25 percent of my time is now spent interviewing potential hires. Despite their different backgrounds (for example, science, business, or academia), the candidates need to have some common communication skills. They must be able to communicate clearly and directly. They must have the ability to explain complex concepts in a simple, understandable way. Above all, they must have empathy—so that they can relay information in a way that best suits the client. Successful portfolio management generally requires investors to be patient and disciplined. Much of what we do is aimed at helping clients stay committed to appropriate, long-term plans. Whether we're interacting with clients through in-person events, written communication (Web sites, articles, and so on.), or phone calls, we're focusing on helping them achieve their goals. The most satisfying part of my job is receiving thanks and appreciation from clients—which makes everything worth it.

clothes in a store (a familiar idea), shoppers can see how certain garments would look on their particular body types. By supplying your measurements online, you can visualize what you would look like in outfits by using the virtual model image (new idea).

Define Your Terms

As discussed earlier, defining your terms is not just for definitional speeches. In any speech, you should choose terms that your audience will know and understand—and provide clear definitions for any words they might not. If at any point in your speech, audience members find themselves wondering what or who you are talking about, you will begin to lose their attention. When a term comes up that requires definition, you must explain it clearly and succinctly before moving on. If you think an audience is familiar with a word but you just want to be sure, you can simply allude to a more common synonym: "People tend to think of rhinoplasties—commonly referred to as 'nose jobs'—as cosmetic in nature, but in fact many are performed to help improve nasal functioning."

Note that definitions are often necessary for proper nouns as well. Audiences may not have a strong background in geography, politics, or world events, so it can be useful to identify organizations and individuals in the same way that you would define a term: "People for the Ethical Treatment of Animals, or PETA, is the largest animal rights organization in the world," or "Colin Powell, a former U.S. Army general and secretary of state under President George W. Bush, noted that. . . ." If you can define and identify terms in a way that is smooth and diplomatic, you will enable audience members who are unfamiliar with them to continue to participate in your presentation, while gaining the confidence of audience members who do know the terms when you explain them accurately.

Use Interesting and Appropriate Supporting Material

Select examples that are interesting, exciting, and clear and use them to reinforce your main ideas. Examples not only support your key points but also provide interesting ways for your audience to visualize what you are talking about. If you are giving a speech about the movie career of Clint Eastwood, you would provide examples of some of his most popular films (*Dirty Harry*, *In the Line of Fire*), his early western films (*Fistful of Dollars*, *For a Few Dollars More*, *Hang 'Em High*), his lesser-known films (*The First Traveling Saleslady*, *Honkytonk Man*), and his directorial efforts (*Gran Torino*, *Million Dollar Baby*, *Mystic River*, *J. Edgar*). You might also provide quotes from reviews of

● **AN ENGAGING SPEECH** on Clint Eastwood's career would include examples that span his many films, from the classic *The Good, The Bad, and the Ugly* to the more recent and highly acclaimed *Gran Torino*. (left) Courtesy Everett Collection; (right) © Warner Bros./Courtesy Everett Collection

his films to show the way Eastwood has been perceived at different points in his career.

When you are offering examples to explain a concept, it's important to choose examples that your audience will understand. Some examples may be familiar enough to your audience that you can make quick references to them with little explanation. If you are giving a speech today on community planning and rebuilding after disasters, you could probably mention Moore, Oklahoma, after the 2013 tornados or Haiti after the 2010 earthquake, and almost any adult member of your audience will get it. But other examples or audiences might require more detail and explanation. For example, if you are giving a speech about conformity, you might wish to use as an example the incident in Jonestown, Guyana, in 1978, when more than nine hundred members of a religious cult committed mass suicide by drinking cyanide-laced punch. As with many aspects of delivering a speech, audience analysis is crucial: if you are speaking to a younger audience, you'll need to offer a good deal of explanation to make this example work. However, an audience consisting mainly of baby boomers, historians, or social psychologists would require little more than a brief reference to "Jonestown" to get the point of the example.

Use Appropriate Presentation Aids

As you will recall from Chapter 14, presentation aids can add value to your speech by helping audiences follow and understand the information you present. Such aids can be especially helpful in informative speeches. For example, in an informative speech about the importance of a person's credit score, the speaker might show (via slides or handouts) sample credit reports. Seeing this information in addition to hearing about it will underscore the importance of your message: everyone has a credit report and a credit score.

Informative speeches also benefit greatly from the use of graphic presentation aids. In a speech describing a process, for example, a flowchart outlining the steps you describe in your speech can help audiences visualize how the process works. Graphs can also be helpful in conveying numerical or statistical information. The combination of hearing your message (the speech content) and seeing your message (through presentation aids) helps the audience retain the content of your informative speech.

Let's take a look at an informative speech by Anna Davis. She chose to inform her audience about how and why social media are being harnessed as a tool to advance social causes and motivate people to act on them.

Anna organizes the speech in a topical pattern: each of her main points is a subtopic or category of the overall speech topic of social media movements. This is one of the most frequently used patterns for informative speeches. Anna's speaking outline and references are included here as well.

● **PRESENTATION AIDS** are especially appropriate in informative speaking because they enable the audience to not only hear about but also to visualize a new topic. Justin Sullivan/Getty Images

Sample Student Informative Speech 15.1

Social Media, Social Identity, and Social Causes

BY ANNA DAVIS

 Watch It Now
To see Anna Davis deliver her speech, go to **bedfordstmartins .com/realcomm**

Anna starts her speech by enthusiastically telling a personal story.

Just before my first year of college, I was excited and nervous about meeting other new students on campus. As soon as dorm assignments were announced, we all began "friending" each other on Facebook and following each other on Twitter. • This is how I found out that my roommate was an obsessive soccer fan and had seen all of Quentin Tarantino's movies. The school also sponsored online forums, allowing me to learn about different student groups and to find like-minded people across campus. For example, I connected immediately with students who share my interest in animal rescue and adoption. These online connections and groups helped my college friendships develop quickly and meaningfully, and gave me a sense of belonging on campus before I even arrived. •

• Anna makes her attention getter *relevant* to the audience by referencing the social media tools that nearly everyone in her class will be familiar with.

Today I'd like to share with you how social media is being used, not only to help students connect but also as a powerful tool to advance social causes and motivate us to act on their behalf. We'll start by looking at a compelling theory of why social media is so uniquely suited to forging connections. Next, I'll review some data on social media's meteoric rise. Finally, we'll see how today's activists are harnessing social media to support an array of social causes to make life better for us all. •

• Anna's personal example helps establish her *ethos*, or credibility. It also relates to her speech thesis, which explains how social media helps everyone answer the question "Who am I?"

Let's begin our conversation about these intriguing developments in communication by considering the underlying reasons why we want to use social media in the first place. What is it that drives us to connect through social media with like-minded people and groups?

• Anna's preview statement organizes her speech. Each section is previewed so listeners can anticipate what is coming.

Anna keeps the audience engaged with animated facial expressions.

Social identity theory offers a compelling answer to this question. First, let me define the concept of social identity. Social identity refers to how you understand yourself in relation to your group memberships. • Michael Hogg, a professor of social psychology at Claremont University, focuses on social identity research. In his 2006 book on contemporary social psychological theories, Hogg explains that group affiliations provide us with an important source of identity, and we therefore want our groups to be valued positively in relation to other groups. • By "affiliations" I simply mean the groups that we join and perhaps link to online.

• By defining technical terms here, Anna can use them later in the speech with the assurance that the audience will understand precisely what she means.

Social psychologist Henry Tajfel—one of the founders of social identity theory—spent years considering how we form our social identities.

• By paraphrasing an expert in the field, Anna helps establish credibility for her speech.

Tajfel believes that the groups to which we attach ourselves, both online and off, help answer the very important question, Who am I? According to Tajfel's 1979 book *The Social Psychology of Intergroup Relations*, we associate with certain groups to help resolve the anxiety brought about by this fundamental question of identity. By selecting certain groups and not others, we define who we are and develop a sense of belonging in the social world. ●

Social media sites such as Facebook provide a platform for this type of social identity formation by offering participants certain tools, such as the ability to "friend" people, groups, and even brands, and to "like" certain posts. The simple act of friending, for example, promotes social affiliation between two individuals, and our Facebook friends are collectively a source of social identity. Because we are proclaiming something important to our groups, announcing that we are in a serious relationship takes on great social significance. As we all know, it's not official until it's "Facebook official."

As you can see, social identity theory gives us insight into the reasons behind the popularity of social media sites: They let us proclaim to ourselves and the world, "This is who I am." Even so, the near miraculous rate of growth of these sites over the past decade is surprising.

According to Marcia Clemmit's 2010 *CQ Researcher* article on social networking, Facebook had over one million members in 2005—just one year after its launch. This growth from zero to a million in one year was quite an impressive feat. Today, according to a May 2013 article on the number of active Facebook users published by the Associated Press, Facebook harbors over 1.16 billion members. ● That's almost four times the population of the United States.

Anna explains the graph while gesturing at the slides.

Like Facebook, Twitter's growth has also been astronomical. Shea Bennett, editor of the Mediabistro-sponsored blog *AllTwitter*, reports in an October 2013 article that Twitter had 218 million active users at the end of June 2013. Like Facebook, its success can be largely attributed to the demand for virtual communities that enable users to connect with one another.

As the data clearly show, people around the world are defining themselves socially and answering the question, "Who am I?" through the use of social media sites. ● And social movement organizations have taken note. Organizations of all kinds are using social media to get their messages across to global consumers and spur their members into action.

While making her point, Anna uses strong eye contact.

Social movements, defined by Princeton.edu as "a group of people with a common ideology who try together to achieve certain general goals,"

● This transition helps listeners prepare for the next main point of Anna's speech.

● To help her audience understand the large numbers she quotes, Anna relates the number of Facebook users to the population of the United States, so the audience can get a sense of just how big 1.16 billion people really is.

● The subtle repetition of the question "Who am I?" relates this main point back to the speech thesis.

When stating facts, Anna refers to her notecards.

range across the political and social spectrum. Consider Occupy Wall Street and the Tea Party. Both of these organizations communicate their messages and build support through social media sites. ● For example, they use Facebook to announce events and link to petitions. In fact, a nonprofit organization called Social Movement Technologies created a Facebook page to help individual social movement organizations get out their message.

But social media is not just being used as a platform for informing the public of a group's mission and activities or even merely to get people to sign petitions. Increasingly, activists are deploying social media to motivate like-minded people to get into the fight.

To get a sense of what this means, consider the recent efforts of a seventeen-year-old skateboarder from St. Cloud, Minnesota. ●

Anna connects to the audience with a real-life story.

For three years, Austin Lee found himself struggling to get support for a skate park in his local community. But when he decided to use Facebook for his cause, things changed nearly overnight. Lee's posting attracted 1,085 members, and even drew a portion of those members to city council meetings on behalf of his cause. David Unze of *USA Today* reported that Lee won the approval—and $500,000—for his skate park (2010). And it all happened within one day of Lee's original posting on Facebook.

So as you can see, if you can use social media to convince people to identify with what you want to accomplish, success is possible. Lee's accomplishment shows us that we not only identify and affiliate ourselves with groups but also are willing to actively work toward accomplishing their goals.

Today I hope I've shown that the skyrocketing use of social media sites over the past decade is no accident. The human desire to develop a positive sense of social identity through group affiliation is one reason for this phenomenon. Capitalizing on this universal psychological drive, social movement organizations are harnessing these technologies to accomplish their goals. Social media sites allow us to communicate, express, and identify with one another in ways that encourage affiliation as well as action. Whether it's a major political movement or a teenager's desire for a local skate park, social media technologies are powerful.

Anna concludes her speech on a warm, personal note.

So as you tweet about new groups or see the next "Facebook official" status update, think about what groups you like, whom you have friended, and what those affiliations may be able to do for you. ●

● Anna uses examples that are well balanced and that do not express a bias.

● Using real examples, such as Austin's, helps Anna's audience imagine and relate to her claims more directly.

● To make her final words count, Anna's concluding statement is memorable and succinct and summarizes her thesis.

References

Associated Press. (2013, May 1). Number of active users at Facebook over the years. *Yahoo! News.* Retrieved from http://news.yahoo.com /number-active-users-facebook-over-230449748.html

Bennett, S. (2013, October 4). How many active users does Twitter have, and how fast is it growing? [Web log post]. Retrieved October 16, 2013, from www.mediabistro.com/alltwitter/tag/twitter-active-users

Brenner, J., & Smith, A. (2013, August 5). 72% of online adults are social networking site users. *Pew Internet and American Life Project.* Retrieved from www.pewinternet.org/~/media//Files/Reports/2013 /PIP_Social_networking_sites_update.pdf

Clemmitt, M. (2010, September 17). Social networking. *CQ Researcher, 20*(32). Retrieved August 17, 2013, from www.cqpress.com/product /Researcher-Social-Networking-v20-32.html

Constine, J. (2012, February 12). Pinterest hits 10 million U.S. monthly uniques faster than any standalone site ever. [Web log post]. Retrieved August 17, 2013, from http://techcrunch.com/2012/02/07/pinterest-monthly-uniques

Hogg, M. (2006). Social identity theory. In P. J. Burke (Ed.), *Contemporary social psychological theories* (pp. 111–136). Palo Alto, CA: Stanford University Press.

Lipsman, A. (2011, August 30). Tumblr defies its name as user growth accelerates. [Web log post]. Retrieved August 17, 2013, from www .comscore.com/Insights/Blog/Tumblr_Defies_its_Name_as_User_ Growth_Accelerates

Madden, M., Lenhart, A., Cortesi, S., Gasser, U., Duggan, M., Smith, A., & Beaton, M. (2013, May 21). Teens, social media, and privacy. *Pew Internet and American Life Project.* Retrieved from www .pewinternet.org/Reports/2013/Teens-Social-Media-And-Privacy.aspx

Occupy Wall Street. (n.d.). In *Facebook* [Group page]. Retrieved August 17, 2013, from www.facebook.com/OccupyWallSt

Social movement. (n.d.). *Wordnetweb.Princeton.edu.* Retrieved from http://wordnetweb.princeton.edu/perl/webwn?s=social%20movement

Social Movement Technologies. (n.d.). In *Facebook* [Group page]. Retrieved August 17, 2013, from www.facebook.com /SocialMovementTechnologies

Tajfel, H., & Turner, J. C. (1979). An integrative theory of intergroup conflict. *The social psychology of intergroup relations*, vol. 33, p. 47.

The Tea Party. (n.d.). In *Facebook* [Group page]. Retrieved August 17, 2013, from www.facebook.com/TheTeaParty.net

Twitter. (2011, March 14). #numbers. [Web log post]. Retrieved from https://blog.twitter.com/2011/numbers

Unze, D. (2010, March 26). Facebook helps spark movements. *USA Today.* Retrieved from http://usatoday30.usatoday.com/news /nation/2010-03-25-facebook_N.htm

Speaking Outline

Anna Davis

Social Media, Social Identity, and Social Causes

General Purpose: To inform
Specific Purpose: To inform my audience members about how social media sites help shape their sense of identity.
Thesis Statement: Today I'd like to share with you how social media is being used, not only to help students connect, but also as a powerful tool to advance social causes and motivate us to act on their behalf.

Introduction

I. **Attention Getter:** How I learned about my roommate via Facebook/Twitter

II. School-sponsored online forums helped me connect with like-minded others.

III. "These online connections and groups helped my college friendships develop quickly and meaningfully, and gave me a sense of belonging on campus before I even arrived."

IV. **Speech Thesis:** Today I'd like to share with you how social media is being used, not only to help students connect, but also as a powerful tool to advance social causes and motivate us to act on their behalf.

    A. Preview main points
    B. Social identity theory
    C. Popularity of social media
    D. How activists harness social media

Body

I. Social identity theory drives us to connect with others.

    A. **Definition:** Social identity refers to how you understand yourself in relation to your group memberships.

        1. Michael Hogg, a professor of social psychology at Claremont University

        2. Group affiliations provide us with an important source of identity, and we therefore want our groups to be valued positively in relation to other groups.

    B. Social psychologist Henry Tajfel. Group affiliations help answer the question, Who am I?

        1. Tajfel's 1979 book *The Social Psychology of Intergroup Relations*. We associate with certain groups to help resolve the anxiety brought about by the question of identity.

    C. Social media sites provide a platform for social identity formation.

1. "Friending" people, groups, and even brands and "liking" certain posts
2. It's not official until it's "Facebook official."
D. Social media sites let us proclaim to the world, "This is who I am."

Transition: Even so, rate of growth surprising.

II. Growth rate of social media sites is astronomical.

A. **[Show slides]** Marcia Clemmit's 2010 *CQ Researcher* article on social networking, Facebook had over one million members in 2005—just one year after its launch.

1. Associated Press May 2013 article put the number of active Facebook users at over 1.16 billion members. Four times the population of the United States.

B. Shea Bennett, editor of the Mediabistro blog *AllTwitter*, in an October 2013 article, listed Twitter at 218 million active users in June 2013.

C. People around the world define themselves socially and answer the question, "Who am I?" on social media sites.

Transition: Social movement organizations have taken note.

III. Organizations of all kinds use social media to get their messages across to global consumers and spur their members into action.

A. Princeton.edu defines social movements as "a group of people with a common ideology who try together to achieve certain general goals."

B. Consider Occupy Wall Street and the Tea Party.

1. Both communicate their messages and build support through social media sites, for example, link to petitions.
2. Nonprofit organization Social Movement Technologies helps individual social movement organizations get out their message.

C. Activists use social media to motivate like-minded people to get into the fight.

D. Example: Austin Lee, seventeen-year-old skateboarder from St. Cloud, Minnesota, wanted a skate park.

1. Facebook posting gathered 1,085 members to group, some even went to city council meetings.
2. David Unze of *USA Today* reported that Lee won the approval—and $500,000—for his skate park (2010).

Transition/Internal Summary: Today hope I've shown you skyrocketing use no accident.

Conclusion

I. Positive sense of social identity through group affiliation drives popularity of social media sites.
II. Social media sites allow us to communicate, express, and identify with one another in ways that encourage affiliation as well as action.
III. Remember the impact of group affiliations when you post online.

BACK TO ▸ Neil deGrasse Tyson

At the beginning of this chapter, we read about astrophysicist Neil deGrasse Tyson, who is widely respected not only as one of the foremost researchers on space but also as one of science's most competent and enthusiastic communicators. Let's consider how his informative presentations measure up to the concepts outlined in this chapter:

▸ Tyson knows his listeners. He understands that while they are not well versed in astrophysics, they are curious about it. He makes abstract topics tangible by using familiar metaphors and examples. When speaking to an audience of fellow astrophysicists, he would not have to take such measures.

▸ Tyson uses effective nonverbal communication in his presentations. He uses appropriate gestures, laughs heartily at his own jokes, moves around the stage rather than gluing himself to a podium, and uses a tone of voice that generates a casual atmosphere. His trademark vests—embroidered with images of the cosmos—indicate his enthusiasm for the subject.

▸ Like everyone, Tyson has personal opinions and beliefs. But when he is speaking informatively, he limits his discussions to facts. In his discussion of the universe noted at the beginning of this chapter, for example, Tyson explains, "None of this is about 'belief.' It's about 'what does the evidence show'?" (Tyson, 2009).

THINGS TO TRY ▸ Activities

1. LaunchPad for *Real Communication* offers key term videos and encourages self-assessment through adaptive quizzing. Go to **bedfordstmartins.com/realcomm** to get access to:

LearningCurve Adaptive Quizzes.   Video clips that illustrate key concepts, highlighted in teal in the Real Reference section that follows.

2. Review Anna's speech on social media movements in this chapter. Into what category does the topic of this speech fall? Which approach or approaches (description, demonstration, definition, or explanation) did the speaker use, and was she successful in using those approaches? Did the speaker prove herself to be reliable and well informed? In what ways did she attempt to create information hunger and make the speech easy to listen to? Was she successful?

3. Informative speeches are everywhere—in your classroom, on the news, and in your community. Watch an informative speech (or read a transcript, available at the Web sites of many government agencies and officials). Apply the concepts you have learned in this chapter to these informative presentations. For example, is the presentation well organized and well delivered? Does the speaker or

author present information objectively? At any point in the speech, do you feel as though the speaker is trying to persuade you to do or believe something? It's important to be a critical listener in order to catch the often subtle differences between informing and persuading.

4. Locate a persuasive speech that you found particularly compelling. Print it out and edit it, removing any and all of the material that you feel is persuasive in nature (for example, the speaker's opinions, any notably biased statements, any evidence that you feel is subjective rather than objective). Does the remainder of the speech hold up as an informative speech? How could you change it to make it a purely informative presentation?

5. Think of a topic that you find excruciatingly dull (for example, balancing your checkbook, studying for a required course you don't like, or taking a summer or part-time job doing something utterly mind-numbing). What would you do if you had to give an informative presentation on such a subject? Based on the information presented in this chapter, can you think of ways to build a presentation on the topic that is informative and interesting? As strange as this task may sound, it is likely that you will have to do something like this at times in your career. (Recall the example from this chapter on informing employees about a new electronic reimbursement system.)

6. Imagine a process you do every day, such as driving a car. Think about how you would explain the process to someone who's never done it or even seen it done before. Consider different ways you could make the level of the presentation appropriate for different audiences. Talking to a child, for example, you might simply say that pressing on the gas pedal makes the car go; you might offer more detail when speaking to adults, explaining how the car works.

Now that you have finished reading this chapter, you can

Describe the goals of informative speaking:

▶ Use **informative speaking** to teach the audience something new (p. 434).

▶ Gauge what the audience already knows to determine where to begin (p. 434).

▶ Find an approach that will engage the audience (p. 434).

▶ Explain the subject's relevance to the audience (pp. 434–435).

▶ Present facts and information in an **objective**, even-handed way, unlike in a persuasive speech, which is **subjective** and presents a point of view (p. 435).

▶ Speak ethically (pp. 435–436).

List and describe each of the eight categories of informative speeches:

▶ People: focus on human qualities as well as achievements (p. 437).

▶ Places: find new aspects of known places or describe the unfamiliar (pp. 437–438).

▶ Objects and phenomena: focus on any nonhuman topic (p. 438).

▶ Events: describe noteworthy events in history or relate a personal experience (pp. 438–439).

▶ Processes: show how something works or teach how to do something (p. 440).

▶ Concepts: explain an abstract idea (p. 440).

▶ Issues: remain objective to report on a social or personal problem (pp. 440–441).

▶ Plans and policies: describe the important dimensions of potential courses of action (p. 441).

Outline the four major approaches to informative speeches:

▶ The **descriptive presentation** paints a mental picture, portraying places, events, persons, objects, or processes (p. 442).

▶ **Demonstration speeches** combine explanatory narration and physical demonstration (pp. 442–444).

▶ There are five categories of **definitional speeches**: an **operational definition** defines something by explaining what it is or what it does; **definition by negation** defines something by telling what it is not; **definition by example** offers concrete examples; **definition by synonym** defines something with closely related words; **definition by etymology** explains the origin of a word or phrase (pp. 444–445).

▶ **Explanatory speeches** answer the question "Why?" with **elucidating explanations**, with **quasi-scientific explanations** or models, or with **transformative explanations** that change preconceptions (pp. 445–447).

Employ strategies to make your audience hungry for information:

▶ Make listeners curious by personalizing the topic and contrasting it to what they know (pp. 447–448).

▶ Present a clear benefit to learning about the topic (p. 448).

▶ Stress the topic's relevance (p. 448).

Structure your speech to make it easy to listen to:

▶ Devise a clear, logical structure (pp. 449–450).

▶ Signal your audience when you're about to say something important (p. 450).

▶ Keep it simple (p. 450).

▶ Relate new ideas to familiar ideas (pp. 452–453).

▶ Define terms your audience may not know (p. 453).

▶ Select interesting examples (pp. 453–454).

▶ Use strong presentation aids (p. 454).

Jamie Oliver accepted his TED prize with a persuasive address on obesity and food education, in which he explained causes, identified solutions, and ended on a personal appeal. Gustavo Caballero/Getty Images

 LearningCurve can help you master the material in this chapter.
Go to **bedfordstmartins.com/realcomm.**

chapter 16

Persuasive Speaking

Suppose you have found a magic lamp with a genie inside. The genie will grant you one wish, but there's a catch: you need to convince him that your wish is worthwhile and that it will have a positive impact on the world. Each year, TED (short for Technology, Entertainment, and Design), an organization devoted to "ideas worth spreading," plays the role of this magic genie. Winners receive $1,000,000 to turn a beneficial and world-changing idea into reality. After months of preparation, TED Prize winners then unveil their wishes and plans at the annual TED conference (TED Prize, 2013).

TED Prize winner and celebrity chef Jamie Oliver presented his wish ("To teach every child about food") at the 2010 conference in Long Beach, California. He opened his speech with a simple statement identifying an important social and medical problem: "In the next 18 minutes when I do our chat, four Americans that are alive will be dead from the food that they eat" (Oliver, 2010, para. 1). Oliver went on to discuss the realities of obesity in the United States and elsewhere, noting the personal health costs as well as the financial costs of caring for people suffering from preventable, diet-related diseases. He then discussed his experiences educating Americans in West Virginia, as part of his *Food Revolution* television program.

Oliver openly considered the causes for the problem he was addressing: a lack of education about healthy food choices at home and in schools; school lunch programs focused on economics rather than on nutrition; a food industry that promotes highly processed, unhealthy foods rather than more costly, healthy options; and confusing or misleading labeling on the foods we buy. He proposed solutions, pointing to successful school lunch programs that could be easily rolled out on a larger scale for a relatively small influx of cash. He also explained how food businesses can—and, indeed, must—be an integral part of the solution.

Oliver ended his speech by reminding his listeners of his personal wish and his goal for speaking that day: to form "a strong sustainable movement to educate every child about food, to inspire families to cook again, and to empower people everywhere to fight obesity" (Oliver, 2010, para. 39).

What do you think of when you hear the word *persuasion*? When we ask students this question, they often mistakenly think of sneaky used-car salespeople and dishonest politicians. They also point to manipulative leaders, like an unscrupulous supervisor at work or a bully at school, who use communication to achieve their own selfish goals while exploiting or harming others in the process. The first two examples might involve people at least *attempting* to be persuasive to sell cars or policies, but their dishonesty certainly involves unethical communication. Examples of exploitative leaders or bullies are a clear-cut description of **coercion**, the act of using manipulation, threats, intimidation, or violence to gain compliance.

Persuasion is none of these things; rather, it is the process of influencing (often changing or reinforcing) others' attitudes, beliefs, and behaviors on a given topic. When done properly and respectfully, it is also a highly ethical practice. Think of all of the important accomplishments that can come from a competent use of persuasion, such as raising money to support victims of natural disasters. Persuasion is also a tool that you use every day, whether you are persuading your roommates to save money by cutting the cable cord or convincing your four-year-old to eat his peas. In this chapter, we will examine the nature and goals of persuasive speaking while helping you consider your audience, the support for your speech, and helpful organizational patterns.

The Goals of Persuasive Speaking

Persuasive speaking is speech that is intended to influence the attitudes, beliefs, and behavior of your audience. Although these three terms may be familiar to you, let's take a moment to examine them in light of how we will think about them in this chapter.

- **Attitudes** are our general evaluations of people, ideas, objects, or events (Stiff & Mongeau, 2003). They are our *feelings* about something, our judgments of good or bad, important or unimportant, boring or interesting, and so on. For example, you might have a positive attitude toward sports and exercise: "Exercising regularly is good."

- **Beliefs** are the ways in which people perceive reality (Stiff & Mongeau, 2003). They are our thoughts about what is true and real and refer to how confident we are about the existence or validity of something: "I believe that exercising results in a healthy body and lifestyle."

- **Behavior** is the manner in which we act or function. It refers to what we *do*, often in response to our attitudes and beliefs (Homer, 2006). For example, if your attitude about exercise is really positive and you believe that it contributes to a healthy lifestyle, you'll probably be motivated to get out there and walk or jog or lift weights.

Speaking to persuade your listeners involves some informative speaking. Just look at any presidential campaign. The candidates all want to inform you about their plans and goals for the nation. However, their primary goal is to use organized and well-developed presentations to influence their audience's attitudes and beliefs about their (or their opponents') suitability for the presidency. And, of course, they want to influence your behavior by getting you to vote for them.

Influencing your audience does not necessarily mean radically changing their attitudes, beliefs, or behavior; it can also mean reinforcing them. For example, when a political party attempts to rally its base, its goal is not to change their faithful listeners' minds but to strengthen their support and get them more actively involved. Of course, to do this effectively, the party must first correctly identify their listeners' existing attitudes and beliefs. In fact, whether your goal is to change or reinforce your audience's attitudes, it is important to use audience analysis (discussed in Chapter 12) to first identify what those attitudes currently are.

Developing a Persuasive Topic and Thesis

An effective topic for a persuasive speech shares some characteristics with an informative one: it should be something that you're interested in, that you know something about, and that is specific enough that you can find a variety of appropriate sources on the topic but not so specific that you can't possibly develop it. When your purpose is to persuade, however, you must also keep a few other points in mind.

First, your topic should be one that people could have reasonable disagreement about or resistance to. Issues such as human cloning, immigration reform, and government wiretapping lend themselves to a persuasive purpose because people hold strongly differing opinions about them. Second, the topic must allow the speaker to develop a message intended to cause some degree of change in the audience. For example, the topic of mandatory smoking bans could seek changes from different audiences who hold very different views: encouraging action (a change in behavior) from people who already agree that smoking should be banned in public or seeking a change in the attitudes of smokers who currently see no problem with smoking in public places.

Once you have determined that a particular topic interests you and can be persuasive, it's time to think about developing your thesis statement. In a persuasive speech, thesis statements are often given as a proposition, or a statement about your viewpoint or position on an issue. There are three types of propositions that we will examine: propositions of fact, propositions of value, and propositions of policy.

Propositions of Fact

If you've ever argued on behalf of something you believed to be true, you've made a **proposition of fact**—a claim of what is or what is not. Persuasive speeches built on propositions of fact commonly involve issues that are open to some interpretation and on which there are conflicting beliefs or evidence. The truth of the

CONNECT

As you consider your audience's attitudes, beliefs, and behavior, don't forget the cultural context (Chapter 1) and their group affiliations (Chapter 5). Your listeners' gender, religious beliefs, socioeconomic status, and ethnicity—as well as their personal experiences—inform their attitudes, beliefs, and behavior. If you fail to respect these factors, you may fail to persuade your audience.

● **IN THE FILM** *Inception*, spy Dom Cobb takes coercion to the next level by manipulating his targets' subconscious minds to extract valuable information. Stephen Vaughan/©Warner Bros./Courtesy Everett Collection

what about you?

Persuasion Resistance Scale

As you listen to other speakers (professors, parents, bosses, friends, classmates), you often—consciously or unconsciously—assess their attempts to persuade you. The extent to which you feel that your behavioral freedom is threatened or that your choices are limited by their persuasive efforts is called your "resistance." To determine your level of resistance, read each statement that follows and indicate how much you agree or disagree: 5 = strongly agree; 4 = agree; 3 = unsure; 2 = disagree, and 1 = strongly disagree.

_____ 1. I resist the attempts of others to influence me.

_____ 2. Being urged to change my views triggers a sense of resistance in me.

_____ 3. I find contradicting others stimulating.

_____ 4. When someone tries to persuade me, I usually think, "I'm going to do the exact opposite."

_____ 5. The thought of being dependent on others aggravates me.

_____ 6. I consider advice from others to be pushy.

_____ 7. I become frustrated when I am unable to make my own decision.

_____ 8. It irritates me when someone points out things that are obvious to me.

_____ 9. I become angry when others try to make choices for me.

_____ 10. Advice and recommendations usually induce me to do just the opposite.

_____ 11. I am content only when I make my own choices.

_____ 12. It makes me angry when another person is held up as a role model for me to follow.

_____ 13. When someone tries to get me to do something, I resist.

_____ 14. It disappoints me to see others easily persuaded.

Add your numbers here: _____

14–28: low resistance   29–55: medium resistance   56–70: high resistance

The higher your resistance, the less likely you are to be persuaded. You may even strengthen an attitude that is contrary to the position of the person attempting to persuade you, because you react so strongly to your choices and freedom being limited. Lower resistance is associated with less perceived threat to your free will and more willingness to change your point of view.

Source: Adapted from Hong & Faedda (1996).

statement may be debatable, but the goal of the speech is clear: you want to align the audience's perception or opinion of the fact with your own. Although it may seem simple to state your belief and back up your points with research that persuades your audience, it can actually be quite challenging. Propositions of fact get at the heart of how you view the world, and your viewpoints may be quite different from how members of your audience perceive reality. Consider the following proposition-of-fact thesis statements:

- ▶ "Single people are as capable of raising happy, healthy, well-adjusted children as are married couples."

- ▶ "Extending unemployment benefits actually hurts, rather than helps, people's ability to survive in a shaky economy."

- ▶ "Eating wheat, even whole wheat, can be dangerous for your health."

Each statement is presented as a fact, yet audiences realize that they are really the beliefs of the speaker, presented for the listeners' consideration, and possibly in conflict with their own. It's important to be tolerant and understanding of people's deeply held beliefs—*even if you ardently disagree with them*—particularly if you hope to get others to see your point of view.

Propositions of Value

Some speeches go beyond discussing what is or what is not and make claims about something's worth. Such evaluative claims are called **propositions of value**. In speeches of this type, you seek to convince an audience that something meets or does not meet a specific standard of goodness or quality or right or wrong. For example:

- ▶ "Torturing prisoners of war is immoral."

- ▶ "The Olympics are becoming less relevant as a sporting event."

- ▶ "Organized religion has done a great deal of good for the world."

Each statement offers a judgment about the overall value of the person, event, object, way of life, condition, or action discussed. Like propositions of fact, it's clear to the audience that these statements of value are not absolute truths but rather the opinion of the speaker. And as with propositions of fact, the speaker must present arguments and evidence that will persuade listeners to align their beliefs and attitudes with the speaker's.

Propositions of Policy

The third type of proposition is concerned with what *should* happen. In **propositions of policy**, the speaker makes claims about what goal, policy, or course of action should be pursued. For example:

AND YOU?

During a campaign season, pay attention to the candidates' speeches and debates, or visit presidentialrhetoric.com to view current and past presidential speeches. How often does the speaker put forth propositions of fact? Of value? Of policy? Does one type of proposition seem to cause more debate or controversy than others?

▶ "LGBTQ individuals should have the same rights as all other Americans."

▶ "Colleges and universities should not consider race when making admissions decisions."

▶ "Any vehicle that gets poor gas mileage (say, less than twenty-five miles per gallon) should be banned in the United States."

In advocating for any of these statements, your task as the speaker would be to persuade the audience that a current policy is not working or that a new policy is needed. Propositions of policy are common during election campaigns as candidates—especially challengers—offer their ideas and plans for what a government should do and how they would do it.

No matter what your topic, and no matter which type of proposition you are advocating, you'll need to know as much as possible about your listeners in order to persuade them effectively. This is the topic of the next section.

Persuading Your Audience

A student once told us an interesting story about audience analysis. At a church service the Sunday after Thanksgiving, her pastor preached on the religious meaning of Christmas (likely in response to the shopping binges known to take place the weekend after many of us eat a little too much stuffing and apple pie). He was hoping to persuade his audience to avoid getting caught up in commercialism, present swapping, and credit card debt. "He was passionate about the topic, and his points were right on," the student said, "but the congregation already agreed with him. It almost felt like he was angry with us or something. It was uncomfortable."

As this story shows, it is crucial to know your audience before developing your speech, as this knowledge will help you tailor your organization, research, and supporting points. It will even help you determine your specific purpose—whether to try to change or to reaffirm the audience's attitudes, beliefs, and behavior. This was the mistake of our student's pastor. He would have benefited from thoroughly understanding his listeners' disposition and needs as well as what is most relevant to them.

Understanding Your Audience's Disposition

According to **social judgment theory** (Sherif, Sherif, & Nebergall, 1965), your ability to successfully persuade your audience depends on the audience's current attitudes or disposition toward your topic, as well as how strongly they feel about their current position.

Let's consider this theory in light of the following example: you are the student government president at a regional college where it is easy for students to visit their hometowns on the weekends. As such, your school has gained a reputation of being a "suitcase" school, making for dull weekends for those students who remain on campus. To address this problem, you propose that the school ban first- and

● **FROM PROPOSING** to improve the quality of campus dining to championing for more money for student events, propositions of policy are common in student government elections.
Image Source Plus/Alamy

second-year students from having cars on campus so that they stick around and invest more in their life at school.

When you speak about this topic, you should think about portions of your audience each having a different possible **anchor position**—their position on the topic at the outset of the speech (Sherif & Sherif, 1967)—about the issue of keeping students on campus. Depending on how strongly the audience members feel about their anchor position, they will also have different **latitudes**, or ranges of acceptable and unacceptable viewpoints, about your topic. These different anchor positions and latitudes might result in three different kinds of audiences for your speech:

● CORETTA SCOTT KING found a receptive audience when she spoke to other like-minded individuals at a press conference on ending the Vietnam War. © Bettmann/Corbis

▶ A **receptive audience** is an audience that already leans toward your viewpoints and your message. These audience members might be residential students who are around on the weekends and wish there was more to do. They probably have a large **latitude of acceptance**; that is, they would find acceptable a wide range of proposals you could make regarding keeping first- and second-year students on campus.

▶ A **neutral audience** falls between the receptive audience and the hostile audience: its members neither support you nor oppose you. Nonresidential commuting students (who are off campus on weekends anyway) might fall into this category. This audience would probably have a large **latitude of noncommitment**, that is, a range of positions that they are not sure about.

▶ A **hostile audience** is one that opposes your message (and perhaps you personally); this is the hardest type of audience to persuade, particularly if you are trying to change people's behavior. In this audience, you'll certainly find first- and second-year students who live on campus but want to spend their weekends away. This audience would likely have a large **latitude of rejection**; that is, they would find unacceptable most proposals that aim to keep students from leaving campus.

So how do you persuade these distinct groups of individuals? Your receptive audience already basically agrees with your position, allowing you to simply reaffirm their current beliefs or perhaps even get them to accept stronger proposals. Your neutral audience may need some more information about the issue: for example, how *exactly* does the student weekend flight impact campus life? Most important, they will need to know why they should care. Perhaps, for example, if there were more to do on campus on the weekends, commuting students would be more interested in getting involved in weekend cultural and social events, strengthening their own attachment to the campus community. Your hostile audience will, of course, require some special consideration. You want these audience members to find you trustworthy and full of goodwill. You want to avoid making them feel as though you're trying to force them to accept your views, as research shows that such behavior will backfire and cause your audience to be less likely to engage with you (Brehm, 1966; Brehm & Brehm, 1981) and less likely to accept your message (Hansmann & Scholz, 2003; McGrane, Toth, & Alley, 1990). Instead, acknowledge their point of view and look for ways to bridge the gap between your beliefs and their beliefs.

Another approach to understanding your audience's disposition is by applying the **stages of change model** (Prochaska, 1994; Prochaska & Norcross, 2001). This contemporary model is often applied in health care settings (for example, to persuade people to stop smoking or use condoms) and it helps predict your audience members' motivational readiness toward modifying behavior. The five stages listed here are precontemplation, contemplation, preparation, action, and maintenance.

▶ In the first stage, *precontemplation*, an individual is not ready to change his or her behavior or possibly may not be even aware that the behavior is problematic. For example, a heavy smoker may not want to quit smoking; she may selectively filter information about the negative health effects of smoking because this information causes anxiety. Hence, a persuasive speaker (for example, a doctor, nurse, or concerned friend) must be able to convince the individual that there is a problem.

▶ In the second stage, *contemplation*, individuals begin to recognize the consequences of their behavior. The smoker might seek information about smoking cessation or smoking-induced health hazards. Individuals usually experience uncertainty and conflict at this stage, so persuasive speakers might help them identify barriers to change.

▶ In the third stage, *preparation*, individuals move to planning and preparing for the changes they have been contemplating. Our heavy smoker might be willing to experiment with small changes, so persuasive speakers might suggest planning a specific day to go "cold turkey" or asking friends to be on hand to provide emotional support.

▶ By the fourth stage, *action*, an individual has made a change and enacted new behaviors, which require a great deal of willpower. The former smoker may be very tempted to pick up a cigarette but she must stay focused on her new, healthy behavior. A persuasive speaker might acknowledge and reward such success and continue to provide emotional support.

▶ In the final stage, *maintenance*, the behavior change is fully integrated into the individual's life and she works to prevent a relapse. The former smoker finds that social reinforcements (such as feeling better and receiving compliments) help her maintain her new, healthy lifestyle. Persuasive speakers should continue to offer support, help to resist temptation, and reinforce messages. Should the former smoker relapse, she goes back to the beginning of the cycle and earlier stages as she attempts to quit smoking again.

When determining whether your audience is receptive, neutral, or hostile or what stage of change they are in, you'll need to conduct a thorough audience analysis to tailor your speech topic and message to them and have a greater chance of being persuasive and have a long-lasting effect on your audience.

FIGURE 16.1
MASLOW'S HIERARCHY
OF NEEDS

Understanding Your Audience's Needs

If you feel that your child isn't getting sufficient or proper instruction in mathematics, you probably aren't going to be too interested in hearing a speech on the importance of raising money for new school football uniforms. That's because that topic doesn't address your personal *needs*, or deficits that create tension. Abraham Maslow (1954), a foundational scholar for how we understand needs, argued that an individual's motivations, priorities, and behavior are influenced primarily by that person's needs. He identified needs in a hierarchical structure of five categories (see Figure 16.1), from low (immature) to high (mature), known as the **hierarchy of needs**.[1]

The theory proposes that the most basic needs must be met before an individual can become concerned with needs farther up in the hierarchy.

1. *Physiological/survival needs:* These are basic survival needs, such as air, water, food, shelter, sleep, clothing, and so on. Even in the short term, if you listen to a speech while you are very hungry, your mind is likely not on the message but rather on getting food.

2. *Safety needs:* These are needs for security, orderliness, protective rules, and avoidance of risk. They include not only actual physical safety but safety from emotional injury as well. When people in a community are concerned with violence and crime, for example, they are less likely to listen to persuasive appeals to increase local arts funding.

3. *Belongingness/social needs:* These needs are centered around interactions with others and include the desire to be accepted and liked by other people and the need for love, affection, and affiliation. These needs are normally met by family ties, friendships, and membership in work and social groups.

4. *Esteem/ego-status needs:* These needs involve validation—being accepted by some group and being recognized for achievement, mastery, competence, and so on. They can be satisfied by special recognition, promotions, power, and achievement.

> **CONNECT**
>
> Maslow's famous *hierarchy of needs* matters in organizations as well. As you learn in Chapter 11, the *human resources approach* to management helps managers to better understand the higher-level needs of their employees, such as self-esteem and personal development, which helps employees to feel more *self-actualized* in their communication (Chapter 2) and motivated to achieve on the job.

[1]Although Maslow's hierarchy of needs has been revised (see Kenrick, Griskevicius, Neuberg, & Schaller, 2010), we have elected to offer the original model as advanced by Maslow given its utility and application to public speaking.

● **MASLOW'S HIERARCHY** of needs is helpful in understanding your audience's needs. For example, it might be hard to convince a group of low-income single mothers to enroll their kids in various costly extracurricular activities. (top left) John Moore/ Getty Images; (top middle) Getty Images; (top right) Josephine Soughan & Simon Pentleton/PYMCA; (bottom left) Izf/Shutterstock; (bottom right) AFP/Getty Images

Unlike the previous three categories, esteem needs are not satisfied internally; they require praise and acknowledgment from others.

5. *Self-actualizing needs:* Needs at the highest level focus on personal development and self-fulfillment—becoming what you can become. Instead of looking for recognition of your worth from others, you seek to measure up to your own criteria for personal success.

The implications of Maslow's hierarchy for persuasive speaking are straight-forward: understanding your audience's needs will help you determine your strategy for persuading your listeners. The message must target the unfulfilled need of the audience, as a need that is already met will not move them, nor will one that seems too far out of reach in the hierarchy. A speech persuading audience members to plant more flowers on an already beautiful campus is unlikely to have much effect; the same appeal to plant flowers on a campus where buildings are in disrepair is also unlikely to get a response, as the audience may be more concerned with those basic infrastructure issues.

Understanding What Is Relevant to Your Audience

Along with appealing to audience needs, you can also persuade listeners—especially neutral listeners—by anticipating their question, "How is this relevant to me?" The **Elaboration Likelihood Model (ELM)** is based on the belief that listeners process persuasive messages by one of two routes, depending on how important—how relevant—the message is to them (Petty & Cacioppo, 1986; Petty & Wegener, 1998; see also Kruglanski et al., 2006). When they are

CONNECT

It will be hard to get your audience to engage in *central processing* if you can't get them to listen to your speech. As you learn in Chapter 6, you need to encourage thoughtful *active listening*. Although your audience certainly bears some of the responsibility, you can help by making sure that you offer relevant, effective supporting material (Chapter 12) and ensuring that your delivery is easy to listen to (Chapter 14).

motivated and personally involved in the content of a message, they engage in **central processing**—they think critically about the speaker's message, question it, and seriously consider the strengths of the arguments being presented. When listeners lack motivation to listen critically or are unable to do so, they engage in **peripheral processing** of information, giving little thought to the actual message and focusing instead on superficial factors, such as the length of the speech or the attractiveness of the speaker.

Whenever possible, you want your audience to engage in central processing, as it produces deeper, more long-lasting changes in audience perspective than peripheral processing does. Audience members who process peripherally

WIREDFORCOMMUNICATION

Interactive Advertising: Persuasion for a Millennial Audience

If you were born between 1980 and 2000, advertisers want you, even if they aren't quite sure what to do with you. They call you the Millennials or the Bridgers or by a variety of generational initials: Generation Y (because you follow Generation X), Generation D (for Digital), and Generation M (for Multitaskers). Your Generation X predecessors (born between 1964 and 1979) were challenging enough, with their tendency to videotape television programs and speed through commercials. But you're even trickier with your TV and video downloads and customized, commercial-free programming. This presents a challenge for advertisers, as well as a wealth of opportunities. They want to reach you, they want to persuade you, and they're just starting to figure out how.

One strategy they are employing is viral marketing—marketing that takes advantage of preexisting social networks. While viral marketing exists offline (where it is better known as a word-of-mouth campaign), it really blossoms online. Advertisers can produce an advertisement and get it in front of millions of potential customers, provided that you find it funny or compelling enough to forward a link to your friends (Elliott, 2010).

Marketers have also tapped into your generation's unprecedented technological know-how to get you involved in the advertising process. User-generated content is persuasive on several levels. Contests for user-generated advertisements can boost interest in a product or service, and the ads themselves can potentially go viral. They also lend an edgy, young image to the product being advertised. Converse sneakers, for example, posted user-generated videos on its Web site, which became an online hit, and MasterCard solicits users to create copy for its ongoing "Priceless" campaign (Bosman, 2006). More recently, advertisers have started trolling through public feeds on Facebook and Twitter, looking for posts related to their products or services. A mobile team responds to such posts, delivering palettes of crunchy goodness to cracker-loving Tweeters (Elliott, 2010). Whether these new tricks of the advertising trade will lure in your Millennial dollars is yet to be determined. But until Generation Z comes along, they'll keep trying.

THINK ABOUT THIS

❶ How many advertisements do you think you encounter in a day? How persuasive do you think they are?

❷ Do you think user-generated content is more persuasive to people in their twenties than traditional advertisements? Do you think it is more persuasive to people in other age groups as well?

❸ When advertisements appear on a Web page, are you annoyed? What kind of Web ad would prompt you to click it?

can certainly be influenced, but because they tend to pay attention to things other than the central message, such as the speaker's reputation or any slogans or emotional manipulation used in the speech (Petty & Cacioppo, 1986), they are less likely to experience meaningful long-term changes in attitudes or behavior.

To put the principles of the ELM model of persuasion into practice, consider the following points:

▶ *Make certain that your message is relevant.* Use language and examples to connect your message to your listeners' lives.

▶ *Be sure to present your message at an appropriate level of understanding.* You can't persuade your audience members if they don't understand the message.

▶ *Establish credibility with the audience.* Show your research, cite experts, and (if relevant) clearly explain your own credentials and experience.

▶ *Establish a common bond with your listeners.* Ensure that they see you as trustworthy. Clearly explain why you support this specific message; if you have a specific interest in it, let them know.

These steps will increase the odds that your persuasive appeal will produce lasting, rather than fleeting, changes in the audience's attitudes and behavior (O'Hair, Stewart, & Rubenstein, 2007).

Strategies for Persuasive Speaking

> When the conduct of men is designed to be influenced, persuasion, kind unassuming persuasion, should ever be adopted. It is an old and true maxim that "a drop of honey catches more flies than a gallon of gall." So with men, if you would win a man to your cause, first convince him that you are his sincere friend. Therein is a drop of honey that catches his heart, which, say what he will, is the great highroad to his reason, and which, once gained, you will find but little trouble in convincing him of the justice of your cause. . . . (Lincoln, 1842, para. 6)

This quote from President Abraham Lincoln truly touches on the important strategies you will need to keep in mind as you persuade your audience, though it was Aristotle who first named the three means of persuasion or **forms of rhetorical proof** that comprise major persuasive speaking strategies. The first, appeal to ethos, concerns the qualifications and personality of the speaker; the second, appeal to logos, concerns the nature of the message in a speech; the third, appeal to pathos, concerns the nature of the audience's feelings. According to Aristotle—and generations of theorists and practitioners that followed him—you can build an effective persuasive speech by incorporating a combination of these factors. We will examine each of these appeals in turn, in addition to considering examples of problematic reasoning that undermine your effective use of ethos, logos, and pathos.

EVALUATINGCOMMUNICATIONETHICS

Emotional Punch or Sucker Punch?

A major retail chain is trying to open a big box store just outside the village, which is proving controversial. As the town board considers allowing the location to be rezoned to accommodate the new store, your communication instructor has asked each student in your class to present a persuasive speech either in favor of opening the store or against it.

Your small college town is known for its charming main street, peppered with small businesses, independent stores, and restaurants. The fact that it's so different from the suburb you grew up in is one of the reasons you chose to attend it. You are concerned that competition from this large store, which will undoubtedly offer lower prices than the local markets, will endanger these small businesses. But you also know that there are a lot of low-income families living in the town who want the jobs, as well as the less expensive merchandise, that a big box store will bring.

Having investigated the company's track record, you find that it does bring jobs but that the jobs are primarily part-time, minimum-wage jobs, with no benefits, and that the overall effect of opening a large store like this will be detrimental to the town's economy as well as its overall charm. However, when you head to a similar store in your hometown to talk to workers and customers, the response you get to the store is incredibly positive. One worker tells you that although she does, indeed, work part time, the second income the job provides on top of his wife's teacher's salary is the only reason he is able to make his mortgage. Another tells you that without this job to supplement her own full-time job as a home health care aide—as well as the low prices she gets on groceries at the store—she would not be able to feed her family.

These comments weigh on you heavily, and you know they would add emotional heft to a speech that supports opening the store. But your other research, which includes economic studies and statistics, has led you to conclude that the store will be bad for the town in the long run. What should you do?

THINK ABOUT THIS

1 What do the opinions of these employees tell you about your research? Are your numbers wrong? Is there really a discrepancy between what employees say and what the numbers tell you?

2 Would it be fair to simply dismiss the evidence your personal investigation produced, simply because you think you know better? Is there a way to include the positive feelings of the employees you talked to without changing your position?

3 Is it possible to find emotional appeals that support the statistical evidence you've gathered? What other people might you speak to about the issue?

4 Is it crucial to include emotional appeals? Are they more or less valuable than other kinds of evidence?

Ethos

If audience members have little or no regard for the speaker, they will not respond positively to persuasive appeals; attitude change in your audience is related to the audience's positive perception of *you*, the speaker, on a personal level (McCroskey & Teven, 1999; Priester & Petty, 1995). Aristotle believed that speechmaking should emphasize the quality and impact of ideas, but he recognized that issues like a speaker's competence, character/trustworthiness, and goodwill also play an important role in how well the audience listens to and accepts the message. He referred to this effect of the speaker as **ethos**, the speaker's credibility.

● **AS HE DEFENDS**
criminals in the courtroom,
Lincoln Lawyer Mick Haller's
credibility and character play
a critical role in whether he
can persuade the jury in his
favor. Saeed Adyani/©Lions Gate/
Courtesy Everett Collection

Part of revealing *ethos*
to your audience is offering an accurate, ethical
presentation of yourself.
As you learn in Chapter
2, *self-presentation* is often strategic—you reveal
or hide particular things
about yourself to achieve a
goal. But if you're giving a
speech on the importance
of safe driving and you
fail to mention that you've
been issued five tickets for
speeding, you aren't being
ethical. Your ethos would
be increased if you shared
your story and the lesson
you've learned from it.

Exactly which elements of a persuasive appeal are based on ethos or
credibility? The first element is competence, or knowledge and experience
with the subject matter. You can evoke
this quality by preparing the speech at
all stages (from research to delivery) by
demonstrating personal acquaintance
with the topic, by revealing familiarity
with the work of experts on your topic,
and by ensuring that your speech is well
organized. The second aspect of credibility is *character* or *trustworthiness*, or
the degree to which a speaker seems
unbiased and fair. A speaker may have
a great deal of knowledge, but if you
think that he or she is trying to deceive you, then you may still not find that
speaker credible. A third element of credibility is communicating *goodwill*, the
degree to which an audience perceives the speaker caring for them and having
their best interests at heart (Teven & McCroskey, 1997). To show goodwill,
you must remember that one of your responsibilities is to help your audience
make informed choices. By giving listeners all the information they need to
make a decision, as well as addressing their needs and expectations relative to
the speech, you show that you have their best interests at heart.

Research does indicate additional ways in which a speaker can utilize
ethos. For example, audiences tend to be more easily persuaded by speakers
who they perceive as being similar to them in background, attitudes, interests,
and goals, a concept known as *homophily* (Wrench, McCroskey, & Richmond,
2008); research also reveals that we trust (and are more easily persuaded by)
speakers we like (Teven, 2008). However, if a speaker is similar to us and very
likeable but unprepared, uninformed, or disorganized (that is, not competent), we probably won't find him or her to be particularly credible. And, as
Frymier and Nadler (2013) explain, when liking and credibility come into
conflict (for example, when we like a source with low credibility), credibility
outweighs liking and we're unlikely to be moved by the speaker's message.

Finally, audiences tend to respond to a speaker's physical attractiveness, which, if evaluated positively, helps a speaker seem more likeable and
more credible (Cialdini, 2008; Yoon, Kim, & Kim, 1998) and can positively
impact attitude and behavior change (Berscheid, Dion, Walster, & Walster,
1971; Chaiken, 1979; O'Keefe, 2002; Widgery, 1974). For example, studies
in advertising and marketing find that physically attractive models are more
effective at selling products than their less attractive counterparts, and the
positive effect of attractiveness on persuasion seems to be greater when models are female and the audience is male (Baker & Churchill, 1977; Teven &
Winters, 2007). Attractiveness does not always lead to persuasion, but it does
seem to matter more if receivers have low involvement or rely on peripheral
processing (Petty & Cacioppo, 1986).

Logos

Many persuasive speeches focus on issues that require considerable thought. Should the United States adopt a national health care plan? Are certain television programs too violent for children? When an audience needs to make an important decision or reach a conclusion regarding a complicated issue, appeals to reason and logic are necessary. Aristotle used the term **logos** to refer to persuasive appeals directed at the audience's reasoning on a topic.

Reasoning is the line of thought we use to make judgments based on facts and inferences from the world around us. This basic human capability lies at the heart of logical proof: when we offer our evidence to our audience in hopes that our listeners will reach the same logical conclusions as we have, we are appealing to their reason. There are two types of reasoning: inductive and deductive.

Inductive reasoning occurs when you draw general conclusions based on specific evidence. When you reason inductively, you essentially start by gathering the specific examples, incidents, cases, or statistics and draw them into a conclusion that ties them all together. For example, if you work at an animal shelter and have been bitten or snapped at several times by small dogs but never by a large dog, then you might conclude inductively that small dogs are more vicious than large dogs.

Deductive reasoning, by contrast, proceeds from the general principle to the specific examples. You begin with a general argument or hypothesis and then see how it applies it to specific cases, incidents, and locations. The most popular way to argue deductively is with a **syllogism**, a three-line deductive argument that draws a specific conclusion from two general premises (a major and a minor premise). Consider this syllogism:

Major premise: All cats are mammals.
Minor premise: Fluffy is a cat.
Conclusion: Therefore, Fluffy is mammal.

The speaker starts with a proposed conclusion or argument and then tests that argument by gathering facts and observations and evidence. Applied to a speech, you might use a syllogism in the following ways:

Major premise: Regular cleanings and visits to the dentist will help keep your teeth in excellent condition and reduce your chances of developing costly medical complications.
Minor premise: The proposed student dental insurance plan is affordable and provides for two free cleanings per year and additional coverage on orthodontics and dental procedures.
Conclusion: Therefore, adopting the proposed student dental insurance plan will keep your teeth in excellent condition and help you avoid costly medical complications.

The extent to which your syllogism is persuasive depends on how well the audience accepts the major premise of your case. If the people in your audience do accept your major premise that regular cleanings and visits to the dentist will

AND YOU?

Think about the last major purchase you made. Now consider the information you had prior to the purchase (advertisements, reviews in the media, advice from others). Did you rely primarily on emotional appeals, ethical appeals, or logical appeals?

COMMUNICATIONACROSSCULTURES

Persuading Across Borders

Actress and activist Angelina Jolie, a goodwill ambassador for the United Nations Refugee Agency, speaks frequently with the desire to raise awareness of and influence policies related to the plight of refugees worldwide. This can be a particular challenge culturally, as some groups in wealthy and stable nations are rather removed from the experiences of refugees and cannot fathom what it would be like to be robbed not merely of one's home but also of one's sense of security, even one's country, by political turmoil or natural disaster.

In one such speech marking World Refugee Day, Jolie explained:

> I'm here today to say that refugees are not numbers. They are not even just refugees. They are mothers, and daughters, and fathers, and sons. They are farmers, teachers, doctors, engineers. They're individuals, all. And most of all they are survivors, each one with a remarkable story that tells of resilience in the face of great loss. They are the most impressive people I have ever met. And they are also some of the world's most vulnerable. Stripped of home and country, refugees are buffeted from every ill wind that blows across this planet (Jolie, 2009).

By evoking American values like family, individualism, and hard work in her appeal for assistance for refugees worldwide, Jolie establishes that helping refugees is an ethical goal that her American audience should commit to. By noting that refugees are mothers, daughters, doctors, teachers, and so on, she engages her audience members' emotions and reminds them that victims are *just like the rest of us*—people with families, professions, and lives that matter.

Jolie follows up by detailing the kindness, generosity, and character she has seen in the refugees she has met during her charitable work. In this way, she puts a human face on the plight of refugees while also establishing her own credibility, showing she is not merely a movie star lending her face to a cause: she is on the ground working for the change she is advocating.

As a global superstar (as well as a spokesperson for an international organization), Jolie must also bear in mind that her audience is rarely culturally homogenous. Whether she is addressing a small group of world leaders (as she did when speaking at a meeting of the G8 in 2013) or a large crowd in the United States, she is aware that her message will be viewed by people all over the world. Some of them may be involved in international efforts for change and awareness; others are simply interested in what she says because she is, after all, a famous actress. Among those stargazers, her example is an inspiration: she effectively combines the important elements of persuasion to shed light on a co-culture that listeners might otherwise have ignored.

❶ Many celebrities (including Ricky Martin, Selena Gomez, David Beckham, and Serena Williams) work with the United Nations as goodwill ambassadors for a variety of specific causes. Why do you think that the United Nations seeks their help? Why would a famous actor or singer be more persuasive than, say, a journalist or a medical doctor?

❷ What kinds of cultural values speak to you in a persuasive speech? Do you think that Jolie's focus on resilience and individuals would be as crucial in a more collectivist culture?

❸ Do many Americans dismiss the plight of refugees as something that is not a problem? Does putting a human face on displaced people make them seem more real? How else might Jolie make a largely American audience feel more connected to refugees?

help keep their teeth in excellent condition and prevent medical complications, then they may believe that the student dental insurance plan that you're advocating is worthwhile and may be inclined to sign up. Hence, your conclusion may be acceptable to them.

● **THE MONTANA METH**
Project persuades with
appeals to reason, emotion,
and credibility. © The Meth Project

Pathos

Another means of persuasion is appealing to the listeners' emotions. The term Aristotle used for this is **pathos**. It requires creating a certain disposition in the audience, often through emotionally charged language and description. For example, consider this statement: "The sight of fishermen slashing and slicing baby seals should send chills through even the numbest and most stoic fur-wearers on earth." Makes your skin crawl, doesn't it?

Although emotion can be a powerful means of moving an audience, emotional appeals may be not effective if used in isolation—particularly if the emotion you arouse is fear (Rothman, Salovey, Turvey, & Fishkin, 1993; Sutton, 1982). In fact, fear appeals are typically only effective if the speaker can get the audience to see that the threat is serious, that it is likely to happen to them, and that there is a specific action they can take to avoid the threat (Boster & Mongeau, 1984; Maddux & Rogers, 1983).

Pathos is typically most effective when used alongside logos and ethos, which offer ways of dealing with and addressing the emotions. For example, consider the Montana Meth Project (2013), "a large-scale prevention program aimed at reducing Meth use through public service messaging, public policy, and community outreach" in the state of Montana. The organization's ads are indeed emotional, graphic, and frightening, playing into viewers' love of family and friends, fear of poor health and degenerating appearance, and sense of shame and horror. A particularly moving print ad depicts an unconscious young woman in an emergency room. It reads, "No one ever thinks they'll wake up here. Meth will change that" (Montana Meth Project, 2013). But the logical appeal is also sound—teenagers who become addicted to methamphetamines will destroy themselves and their loved ones—and the ring of truth enhances the persuasiveness of the emotional appeal. The project's follow-up research shows that the campaign has had overwhelmingly positive results: Teen meth use in Montana has declined by 63 percent, adult meth use has declined by 72 percent, and meth-related crime has decreased by 62 percent since the beginning of the campaign (Montana Meth Project, 2013).

CONNECT

Your word choices have a powerful impact on your audience, as words have different meanings for different people (Chapter 3). Let's say you're persuading your audience to adopt a healthy diet. Some people define healthy as low fat and high fiber, whereas others perceive healthy as an organic, vegan diet. To make sure your audience is on the same page, define how *you* are using the term.

Logical Fallacies

In a predictable scene from any number of movies, TV shows, or actual lives, a teenager argues with her parents that she should be allowed to go to a party because all her friends are going. The exasperated parents roll their eyes and counter, "If your friends were all jumping off a bridge, would you jump too?" In their attempts to persuade the other, both the parents and the child fail miserably. In the eyes of the parents, "All of my friends are going" is not a valid reason why their kid should go to the party, whereas comparing a party to jumping off a bridge makes no sense to the teenager either.

Logical fallacies are invalid or deceptive forms of reasoning. Although they may, at times, be effective in persuading uncritical listeners, active audience members will reject you as a speaker as well as your argument when they hear a fallacy creep into your speech (Hansen, 2002). So be on the lookout for several types of logical fallacies as you listen to a speaker's arguments.

Bandwagoning

When our teenager uses "All of my friends are going" as an argument, she's guilty of using the **bandwagon fallacy**—accepting a statement as true because it is popular. Unfortunately, bandwagoning can sometimes persuade passive audience members who assume that an argument must be correct if others accept it (Hansen, 2002). But credible speakers and critical audience members must be careful not to confuse consensus with fact. A large number of people believing in ghosts is not proof that ghosts exist.

Reduction to the Absurd

When parents counter their daughter's request to go to a party with her friends by comparing it to following them off a bridge, they are doing little to persuade her. That's because they have extended their argument to the level of absurdity, a fallacy known as **reduction to the absurd**. Pushing an argument beyond its logical limits in this manner can cause it to unravel: the teenager sees no connection between going to a party (which is fun) and jumping off a bridge (which is committing suicide).

Red Herring

When a speaker relies on irrelevant information for his or her argument, thereby diverting the direction of the argument, he is guilty of the **red herring fallacy** (so named for a popular myth about a fish's scent throwing hounds off track of a pursuit). If you say, for example, "I can't believe that police officer gave me a ticket for going 70! Yesterday, I saw a crazy driver cut across three lanes of traffic without signaling while going at least 80. Why aren't cops chasing down these dangerous drivers instead?" you would be using a red herring. There may well be worse drivers than you, but that doesn't change the fact that you broke the law.

Personal Attacks

A speaker who criticizes a person rather than the issue at hand is guilty of the ***ad hominem*** **fallacy**—an attack on the person instead of on the person's arguments.

From the Latin meaning "to the man," the *ad hominem* fallacy is a common feature of political campaigns. For example, if a speaker says, "Terry Malone is the better candidate for district court judge because she is happily married, whereas her opponent just kicked his wife out of their house," the argument is focused on the individual and not the person's particular qualifications for the job.

● **POLITICAL RACES** take a turn for the worse and run on logical fallacies when candidates campaign against their opponents with personal attacks. © Mark Makela/In Pictures/ Corbis

Hasty Generalization

A **hasty generalization** is a reasoning flaw in which a speaker makes a broad generalization based on isolated examples or insufficient evidence. For example, suppose Jeff notes in his speech that actor and comedian George Burns smoked for decades and lived to be a hundred years old and then concludes that smoking can't really be that bad. Jeff's claim would be unreasonable (and dangerous) to draw a universal conclusion about the health risks of smoking by the case study of one person. As a speaker, you can avoid this fallacy by providing sufficient evidence and examples that directly relate to the topic and that are representative of the arguments you are advancing.

Begging the Question

Speakers who use the fallacy of **begging the question** present arguments that no one can verify because they're not accompanied by valid evidence. For example, if Amanda notes, "People only watch *True Blood* because *Twilight* is so awesome," she's basing her argument on an unprovable premise (the notion that *Twilight* is awesome—which is a subjective opinion rather than a verifiable fact). If you accept Amanda's premise, you must accept her conclusion. For this reason, this fallacy is often referred to as a *circular argument*.

Either–Or Fallacy

Speakers might try to persuade by using the **either–or fallacy** (sometimes called the *false dilemma fallacy*), presenting only two alternatives on a subject and failing to acknowledge other alternatives. For example, in a speech about local sports teams, Charlie notes, "In this town, you're either a Bears fan or a Packers fan." He fails to acknowledge that there might be fans of other football teams living in the city or individuals who don't care about football at all.

Appeal to Tradition

A local community board informs a merchant group that existing "blue laws" preventing them from doing business on Sundays will continue because they have been on the books since the town's founding. This kind of argument is a fallacy known as an **appeal to tradition**—an argument that uses tradition as proof. When speakers appeal to tradition, they are suggesting that listeners should agree with their point because "that's the way it has always been."

The Slippery Slope

The **slippery slope fallacy** is employed when a speaker attests that some event must clearly occur as a result of another event without showing any proof that the second event is caused by the first. For example, "Video surveillance cameras should not be installed in major metropolitan areas. The next thing you know, the government will be reading our text messages."

real communicator

NAME: Bryan Au
OCCUPATION: Raw organic chef, cookbook author, and spokesperson

Cheeseburger combo meals. Frozen pizzas. Drive-thru fried chicken and microwaveable fried chicken. Get a burrito at the convenience store. Tear off the plastic wrapper. Throw the burrito in the microwave. Press 3. This isn't how college students eat. This is how many people eat. It's SAD—the Standard American Diet.

I advocate the benefits of raw organic food. I recently published a cookbook, *Raw in Ten Minutes*, and I pitch my ideas to agents, publishers, businesses, and TV executives. I deliver persuasive presentations over the Internet, on television shows, in conference rooms, one on one, and in front of thousands of people. I talk about vegan food, and I promote wheat-, gluten-, and dairy-free food. And as you may have already guessed—*what? no cheese? no burgers? no cheeseburgers?*—I run into some very hostile audiences.

Fortunately, I have a background in communication. As an undergraduate, I took a number of communication classes, and the principles and concepts I learned in those classes have been especially valuable to me as a persuasive speaker. For example, as a persuasive speaker, I seek to influence my audience's preexisting attitudes and beliefs toward raw organic food. Those attitudes and beliefs include, but are not limited to, raw food = gross. I try to counteract those beliefs and attitudes, and by doing so, I hope to influence my audience's *behavior*. In other words, I hope to change people's eating habits.

The proposition-of-fact part is easy. Through stories, slides, examples, and statistics, I can persuade my audience that organic food is healthier than overprocessed food. There is, for example, a great bonus feature on the *Super Size Me* DVD that shows a plate of french fries from a certain fast-food restaurant. Those fries have been left out on a counter, unrefrigerated, for a number of months. At the end of those months, the fries look exactly the same. Images like that bolster my propositions of fact.

Because I deal with hostile audiences, it's particularly important that I make appeals to ethos. I need to come across as trustworthy and full of goodwill. I start my presentation with an informal question-and-answer session. People ask me questions, and I ask them questions. *Has anyone eaten any raw food this week? What about a salad?* Through this informal Q&A, I try to demonstrate to my listeners that I'm not trying to force a particular diet on them. I acknowledge their point of view (*hey, I like fast food too!*), and I look for ways to bridge the gap between us. I also appeal to their senses. My raw organic food recipes don't look like lumpy white tofu on a bed of wheatgrass. My recipes look and taste like comfort food.

Finally, with a bridge established between me and my audience, I make a quick little pathos appeal. I dare everyone to give raw organic food a try. Just as I'm daring you.

The Naturalistic Fallacy

The **naturalistic fallacy** originates from G. E. Moore, a British philosopher, in his book *Principia Ethica* (1903); it is an appeal to (or having an inherent bias for) nature saying that what is natural is right or good and that anything unnatural (for example, synthetic or human-made) is wrong or bad. For example, advocating that vaccines are unnecessary on the basis that the human immune system can conquer disease naturally (without medical assistance) fails to regard the fact that vaccines have saved innumerable lives from diseases like polio.

Avoiding these logical fallacies goes a long way toward building ethos with your audience—particularly if the audience is hostile toward your speech topic. You want to rely on facts, research, honest emotion, and your own well-rehearsed presentation to persuade your audience. If you're finding yourself slipping into any logical fallacy to persuade your listeners, you are lacking solid, compelling evidence in that area of your speech.

AND YOU?

What kinds of logical fallacies do you regularly see used in the media? What is your reaction when advertisers, political campaigns, or pundits try to persuade you using faulty logic?

Organizing Patterns in Persuasive Speaking

Once you have a topic, audience research, and thoughts about how to deal with logic, emotion, and competence in your presentation, it's time to organize all of this information. As you will recall from Chapter 13, there are a number of organizational strategies available for your speech; the choice you make depends on your objective, your audience, and your available time. When it comes to persuasive speeches, certain organizational strategies can be particularly helpful, including the problem–solution pattern, the refutational organizational pattern, the comparative advantage pattern, and Monroe's motivated sequence.

Problem–Solution Pattern

As discussed in Chapter 13, when you use a *problem–solution pattern* for your speech, you establish and prove the existence of a problem and then present a solution. When your objective is to persuade, you also need to add a set of arguments for your proposed solution. This format is valuable because it allows you to establish common ground with your audience about the existence of a problem before moving to more delicate matters (your solution). Although audience members may disagree with the evidence and reasoning you use to build your case, your presentation allows for the possibility that they will find the information interesting and plausible. In some cases, an audience may reject a solution that you present but at least leave convinced that "something has to be done."

For example, note in the following outline that the first two main points consider the problem and the third main point offers a solution:

Thesis: Present methods for recycling in our community are inadequate.

Main point 1: The current system for recycling generates low participation by citizens.

Main point 2: Each community in our area has its own recycling plan and system.

Main point 3: Recycling should be a regional, not a local, responsibility.

● **WHEN SPEAKING ABOUT** recycling, you might use the problem–solution pattern to clearly establish the problem before persuading your audience with a solution. RL Productions/Getty Images

A variation on this layout is to use a problem–cause–solution format, making the second point the cause of the problem. This format is often useful because getting your listeners to understand the cause helps them reflect on the problem, and it makes your solution seem plausible or even inevitable. In the following example, the first main point proves the problem, the second main point proves the cause, and the third main point offers a solution:

Thesis: United States presidents should be able to serve more than two terms.

Main point 1: Acceptance of foreign and domestic politics is harmed by changes in administrations.

Main point 2: Historically, our country's greatest periods of weakness have occurred with changes in the presidency.

Main point 3: The American people should choose whether a president is worthy of serving up to four consecutive terms.

This type of format tends to work particularly well when you are presenting a proposition of policy because it often proposes a course of action or a series of steps to achieve resolution.

Refutational Organizational Pattern

If people in your audience have strong objections to a position you are promoting, you will be wise to present, and then refute, their arguments against your main point; it can be an effective way to engage, if not fully persuade, an audience (Allen, 1991; O'Keefe, 1999). In the **refutational organizational pattern**, speakers begin by presenting main points that are opposed to their own position and then follow them with main points that support their own position. Though you can use this pattern when the opposing side has weak arguments that you can easily attack, it is to your advantage to select—and then disprove—the strongest points that support the opposing position (DiSanza & Legge, 2002). This may win over uncertain audience members, or even those in a hostile audience who initially disagree with your stance.

In your first main point, you should present the opposing position. Describe that claim and identify at least one key piece of evidence that supports it. In the second main point, you should present the possible effects or implications of that claim. Your third main point should present arguments and evidence for your own position. The final main point should contrast your position with the one that you started with and leave no doubt in the listeners' minds of the superiority of your viewpoint. For example:

Thesis: Universities are justified in distributing condoms to students free of charge or at reduced prices.

Main point 1: Some parents claim that providing condoms is immoral and encourages casual sex among students.

Main point 2: Sexual relations, regardless of moral values, will occur among students in a college atmosphere.

Main point 3: If condoms are difficult to obtain, sexual activity will result in unwanted pregnancies and sexually transmitted diseases.

Main point 4: Students will engage in sexual relations regardless of whether condoms are available, so it is to everyone's advantage that students have easy access to safe sex methods.

The use of this format with a hostile audience can actually help you build credibility. Having established a sense of respect and goodwill between speaker and audience by acknowledging those points, you can then move on to explain the reasons why you believe, nonetheless, that your thesis is true.

Comparative Advantage Pattern

Another way to organize speech points is to show that your viewpoint is superior to other viewpoints on the topic. This arrangement, called the **comparative advantage pattern**, is most effective when your audience is already aware of the issue or problem and agrees that a solution is needed. Because listeners are aware of the issue, you can skip over establishing its existence and can move directly to favorably comparing your position with the alternatives. With this strategy, you are assuming that your audience is open to various alternative solutions.

To maintain your credibility, it is important that you identify alternatives that your audience is familiar with as well as those that are supported by opposing interests. If you omit familiar alternatives, your listeners will wonder if you are fully informed on the topic and become skeptical of your comparative alternative as well as your credibility. The final step in a comparative advantage speech is to drive home the unique advantages of your option relative to competing options with brief but compelling evidence.

Thesis: New members of our hospital's board of directors must be conflict-free.

Main point 1: Justin Davis is an officer in two other organizations.

Main point 2: Vivian Alvarez will spend six months next year in London.

Main point 3: Lillian Rosenthal's husband served as our director two years ago.

Main point 4: Sam Dhatri has no potential conflicts for service.

Monroe's Motivated Sequence

In Chapter 13, we gave you a brief introduction to Alan Monroe's *motivated sequence pattern* for organizing your speech. It is a time-tested variant of the problem–solution pattern and has proved quite effective for persuasive speaking, particularly when you want your audience to do something—buy a product or donate time or money to a cause, for example. We'll elaborate on Monroe's five-step sequence here:

AND YOU?

Have you ever sat through a lecture or a class where the instructor offered a lesson that affirmed a point of view different from your own? Did the instructor acknowledge differing viewpoints? If so, what was your reaction to hearing the instructor's argument against your belief? Did you respect the speaker more or less for addressing your counterpoints?

Step 1: Attention. The attention step gets the audience interested in listening to your speech. It often highlights how the speech will be relevant to them.

It's two in the morning and you're staring at a blank screen on your computer. You've got a term paper for your history class and a lab report to finish, but these aren't what have you worried right now. It's figuring out your résumé—how to take your work, personal, and educational experiences and cram them all onto one page.

Step 2: Need. This step allows you to identify a need or problem that matters to your audience. You want to show that this issue should be addressed.

Each person in this room will be applying for internships and jobs; such positions are highly competitive. Your résumé, for better or worse, will make a first impression on your potential employer.

Step 3: Satisfaction. The satisfaction step allows you to show your audience the solution that you have identified to meet the problem or need addressed in step 2. This step is crucial, as you are offering the audience members a proposal to reinforce or change their attitudes, beliefs, or behavior regarding the problem or need at hand.

● **WHEN PERSUADING STUDENTS** to utilize their college's career center, use the visualization step in Monroe's motivated sequence to help your audience members picture themselves discussing how to improve their résumés with a college counselor. Photodisc/Punchstock/Getty Images

Visiting our college's Office of Career Services is a great way to get help and direction for your résumé. The professionals employed there will be able to help make your job application materials stand out while making the process seem less overwhelming.

Step 4: Visualization. As its name implies, the visualization step helps your audience see how your proposed solution might play out and how they might benefit.

Instead of sitting up at your computer at 2 A.M., you could be sitting with Tamela, a career counselor, at 2 P.M. as she makes suggestions for formatting your résumé or asks you questions about your past work experiences in order to highlight achievements that you had never even thought to mention.

Step 5: Action. This final step clarifies what you want your audience members to do. This may involve reconsidering their attitudes, beliefs, or behavior.

Make an appointment with a career counselor today. Don't wait—you need those early-morning hours for that history term paper, not your résumé!

Now that you've considered organizational patterns and you have a solid grasp on how to handle persuasive speaking, let's take a look at a sample speech by Elijah Lui. In this speech, Elijah is persuading his audience to recognize the problem of cyberbullying and explaining how listeners can address and prevent it. Organizationally, the speech is arranged along the lines of the problem–solution pattern. Note that Elijah uses a variety of sources to support his arguments. Be sure to check out Elijah's reference list as well as his speaking outline, both of which follow the speech sample.

Sample Student Persuasive Speech 16.1

Preventing Cyberbullying

ELIJAH LUI

Elijah cleans before recording his online speech so that the background isn't distracting.

On the evening of September 22, 2010, Rutgers University freshman Tyler Clementi updated his Facebook status: "Jumping off the gw [George Washington] bridge sorry." According to Lisa Foderaro's report in *The New York Times*, a few hours later Clementi did just that. But what would cause a bright student and talented musician with a promising future to take his own life? A bully with a webcam.

According to a May 21, 2012, report on CNN, Clementi's roommate was sentenced to 30 days in jail, 3 years of probation, 300 hours of community service, and $11,000 in restitution for using a Web cam to view and transmit images of Clementi in an intimate encounter with another young man. Tyler Clementi's story is tragic, but it's not an isolated event. On September 9, 2013, 12-year-old Rebecca Sedwick jumped to her death after allegedly being tormented by two girls on Facebook. A few months earlier, Rehtaeh Parsons, a 17-year-old Canadian high school student, hanged herself after cell phone pictures of her being sexually assaulted were distributed by the alleged attackers. What is going on here? In a word—it's *cyberbullying*. ●

Elijah sits far enough from the camera so that his body movements and gestures can be seen.

My name is Elijah, and I'm here today to confront the growing problem of electronic harassment experienced by Tyler Clementi and so many others. I'll start with a look at the various forms cyberbullying takes and describe the scope of the problem. But I'm not here just to talk about one more social ill; I want to show you how you and your loved ones can stay safe—both by scrupulously guarding your personal information and by actively thwarting cyberbullies. Finally, should you or someone you know become a victim, I want you to be able to respond constructively. ●

 Watch It Now!

To see Elijah deliver his speech, go **to bedfordstmartins.com /realcomm** and watch the sample speech video for Chapter 16. You should critique his topic, preparation, and delivery—so watch carefully!

● Elijah begins his speech with a dramatic example that captures the audience's attention.

● Elijah introduces his topic with a rhetorical question.

● Elijah sets up the organizational pattern of the speech, indicating that he will describe a problem and offer solutions.

As you can imagine from the heartbreaking story I've shared about Tyler Clementi, cyberbullying poses serious mental health risks to the nation's children, teens, and young adults. The Cyberbullying Research Center, a leading resource on the topic, defines *cyberbullying* as "willful and repeated harm inflicted through the use of computers, cell phones, and other electronic devices." • Cyberbullying can take many forms, including posting or sending harassing messages via Web sites, blogs, or text messages; posting embarrassing or private photos of someone without their permission; recording or videotaping someone and sharing it without permission; and creating fake Web sites or social networking profiles in someone else's name to humiliate them. Often these acts are done anonymously.

Recent research paints a chilling picture of the frequency and harm of electronic harassment. According to Hani Morgan, an education professor at the University of Southern Mississippi, the statistics vary widely, but a 2011 report by the National Crime Prevention Council found that 43 percent of teens had been the victims of cyberbullying in the last year. Although most of the research to date has focused on cyberbullying among middle school and high school students, a 2012 study published in the *Journal of School Violence* confirmed that the problem of electronic harassment continues into college. Psychologists Allison Schenk and William Fremouw found that nearly 9 percent of university students had experienced cyberbullying; that means that at least two or three people listening to this speech know what I'm describing because they've felt it. As we have seen with Tyler, Rebecca, Rehtaeh, and too many others, cyberbullying has tragically cut short promising lives. But consequences less dramatic than suicide take a serious toll on cyberbullying's victims. The same study by Schenk and Fremouw reported more symptoms of depression and anxiety, as well as difficulty concentrating, among bullied college students. •

As Professor Morgan explains, the anonymity of unsigned messages and fake user names marks cyberbullying as a dangerous evolution of a long-standing face-to-face bullying problem, but you can take steps to protect yourself. • For one, you can be vigilant about safeguarding your personal information. Our school's information technology office lists the following advice on its Web site. First, never, ever, leave your laptops unattended. Second, keep your account passwords and Social Security numbers completely private. Third, use the most secure privacy settings on your social networking sites. Finally, think carefully about the types of pictures of yourself and your friends that you post online, and restrict views of them to "friends only." Each of these steps can minimize opportunities for bullies to harm or embarrass you in some way.

In addition to zealously guarding your personal information, you can help combat cyberbullying by being a voice against it whenever you

Elijah uses strong eye contact to project confidence.

• Elijah qualifies his source and demonstrates its credibility.

• Elijah begins the body of his speech by ensuring that his audience knows what cyberbullying means.

• Elijah effectively puts his research to work throughout this section, making sure to give credit to his reputable sources.

• Elijah effectively transitions to offering solutions and practical steps avoid cyberbullying.

see it happening. • Several organizations have Web sites that provide information you can use to be part of the solution. The Facebook group Don't Stand By, Stand Up! is a student-led organization formed soon after the suicide of Tyler Clementi. The group urges Internet users to take a stand against cyberbullying by recognizing that bullies—in all forms—rarely succeed in their harassment without the support and attention of bystanders. The National Crime Prevention Council Web site gives specific tips on how to thwart a bully's attempts. The first is to refuse to pass bullying messages along to others—whether via text or photo messaging, social networking, or e-mail—and to let the original sender know that you find the message offensive or stupid. Despite your best efforts to keep your personal information private and speak out against cyberbullying, you may still become a victim.

Online safety expert Parry Aftab's Web site, Stopcyberbullying.org, advises victims to use the "Stop, Block, and Tell" method to respond to bullying behaviors directed against them. Though often taught to younger children, this response makes sense in any case of cyberbullying. After receiving a bullying message, you should first stop. In other words, do nothing. Take five minutes to cool down, take a walk, breathe deeply, or do whatever will help to calm down the understandable anger you are feeling. Then, block: prevent the cyberbully from having any future communication with you. This may mean anything from removing him or her from your social networking site's "friends" list to having your cell phone service provider block the bully from being able to call or text you. The third step is to tell someone about the abuse without embarrassment or shame. For example, you might call campus security or confide in a counselor at the Health and Counseling Center—particularly if the abuse has been going on for a long time and you feel that your self-esteem or relationships have been affected. Similarly, parents of younger children should encourage their children to report any bullying to a trusted adult.

Today we've ventured into the very real—and very dangerous—world of cyberbullying. We've seen cyberbullying's negative impact on people of all ages. We've also seen how you can counter this potentially deadly problem by being vigilant about protecting your personal information and speaking out against cyberbullying. And if you or someone you know experiences cyberbullying, you can react constructively with the Stop, Block, and Tell method. •

Elijah uses appropriate facial expressions to convey the seriousness of his topic.

Cyberbullying isn't just someone else's problem. It's very likely something you need to guard against now or in the future—as a student today or as a parent tomorrow. I urge each of you to make a personal commitment to do your part to combat the problem. Refuse to stay silent in the face of cyberbullying. • Resolve that you will never send or pass along cyberbullying messages of any kind, no matter how harmless doing so might seem. This act

• This transition summarizes the previous point and previews the next one.

• Elijah signals the conclusion of his speech with a summary of his main points.

• Elijah issues a call to action.

alone can make a world of difference in the life of the intended victim. And wouldn't you want someone to take this simple step for you?

We must never forget Tyler Clementi and the other young lives cut short by unnecessary bullying. Who knows? Your best friend, your younger brother, or your son could just have easily been on that bridge that fateful September evening. ●

● By stressing the personal relevance of his topic to his audience, Elijah leaves his listeners with something to think about.

References

Foderaro, L. W. (2010, September 30). Private moment made public, then a fatal jump. *The New York Times*. Retrieved from http://query .nytimes.com/gst/fullpage.html?res=9B07E6D91638F933A0575AC0 A9669D8B63

Hayes, A. (2012, May 21). Prosecutors to appeal 30-day sentence in Rutgers gay bullying case. Retrieved from www.cnn.com/2012/05/21 /justice/new-jersey-rutgers-sentencing/index.html

Hinduja, S., & Patchin, J. W. (2010). *Cyberbullying: Identification, prevention, and response* [Fact Sheet]. Retrieved from www.cyberbullying.us /Cyberbullying_Identification_Prevention_Response_Fact_Sheet.pdf

Martinez, M. (2013, October 28). Charges in Rebecca Sedwick's suicide suggest "tipping point" in bullying cases. Retrieved from www.cnn .com/2013/10/25/us/rebecca-sedwick-bullying-suicide-case/index.html

Morgan, H. (2013, May/June). Malicious use of technology: What schools, parents, and teachers can do to prevent cyberbullying. *Childhood Education, 89*(3), 146–151.

Newton, P. (2013, April 10). Canadian teen commits suicide after alleged rape, bullying. Retrieved from www.cnn.com/2013/04/10 /justice/canada-teen-suicide/index.html

Schenk, A. M., & Fremouw, W. J. (2012, January). Prevalence, psychological impact, and coping of cyberbully victims among college students. *The Journal of School Violence, 11*(1), 21–37.

Stop, block and tell! (n.d.). Retrieved November 1, 2013, from www .stopcyberbullying.org/take_action/stop_block_and_tell.html

Stop cyberbullying before it starts. (n.d.). Retrieved February 9, 2011, from www.ncpc.org/resources/files/pdf/bullying/cyberbullying.pdf

Speaking Outline

ELIJAH LUI

Preventing Cyberbullying

General Purpose: To persuade
Specific Purpose: To persuade my audience to understand and confront the growing problem of cyberbullying.
Thesis Statement: I'm here today to confront the growing problem of cyberbullying experienced by Tyler Clementi and so many others.

Introduction

I.   **Attention Getter:** Relate tragic stories of cyberbullying.

    A.   9/22/10: Rutgers U freshman Tyler Clementi (TC) updates Facebook (FB) "Jumping off gw [George Washington] Bridge sorry." He does. (Forderaro, NYT, Sept. 29, 2010)

    B.   TC's roommate convicted of invasion of privacy. Used web-cam to transmit private images. Clementi's roommate sentenced to 30 days in jail, 3 years of probation, 300 hours community service, and $11,000 in restitution. (Hayes, CNN, May 21, 2012)

    C.   12-year-old, Rebecca Sedwick (RS), commits suicide after Facebook tormenting. (Martinez, CNN, Oct. 28, 2013)

    D.   17-year-old Canadian high school student, Rehtaeh Parsons (RP), hangs herself after photos of her sexual assault distributed by alleged attackers.

II. What is going on here? Cyberbullying (CB)

III. Introduce self.

IV. Will discuss forms and scope of CB; staying safe from and responding to CB.

Body

I.   Forms of CB

    A.   "Willful and repeated harm inflicted through the use of computers, cell phones, and other electronic devices" (CB Research Center)

    B.   Posting/sending harassing messages via Web sites, blogs, texts

    C.   Posting embarrassing photos w/o permission

    D.   Recording/videotaping someone and sharing w/o permission

    E.   Creating fake Web sites/profiles to humiliate

Transition: Recent CB research paints a chilling picture.

II. Scope of CB

    A.   2011 study by Hani Morgan, University of Southern Mississippi: 42% of teens experienced CB.

    B.   2012 study by Allison Schenk and William Fremouw (*Journal of School Violence*)

        1.   Nearly 9% of college students experience CB

        2.   Probably 2 or 3 of you have too

    C.   Consequences of CB

        1.   As in the cases of Tyler, Rebecca, and Rehtaeh, CB can lead to suicide

        2.   In others, symptoms include depression, anxiety, and difficulty concentrating

Transition: CB is a dangerous evolution of face-to-face bullying. You can protect yourself, though.

III. Steps for staying safe from CB

    A. Safeguard personal information (school IT office).

        1. Never leave laptop unattended.
        2. Keep passwords and SSN private.
        3. Use privacy settings.
        4. Post photos with caution.

    B. Be a voice against CB.

        1. Don't Stand By, Stand Up! (formed in honor of TC on FB): bullies don't succeed without help.
        2. Don't pass on CB messages and inform the senders that their messages are offensive/stupid. (National Crime Prevention Council)

Transition: You may still become a CB victim.

IV. Responding to CB: use "stop, block, tell." (Parry Afrlab, July 28, 2009, Frontline interview)

    A. Stop: take 5, cool down, walk, breathe deeply.
    B. Block: prevent communication—remove bully from social networking lists and block cell #.
    C. Tell: campus security, counselor, etc. Children tell parent, teacher, principal.

Transition/Internal Summary: We've seen CB's negative impact and discussed countering CB (privacy, speak out, "stop, block, tell").

Conclusion

I. CB is not someone else's problem.

II. Call to action: make a personal commitment to combat CB.

    A. Refuse to be silent.
    B. Never pass along CB messages.
    C. Voice your concerns at the campus and community levels.

III. Don't forget TC and other CB victims. Your loved one could be next.

BACK TO ▶ Jamie Oliver's TED Prize-Winning Wish

At the beginning of this chapter, we discussed celebrity chef Jamie Oliver's TED speech, in which he presented his wish to educate children about food (Oliver, 2010). Let's consider his speech in light of what we've learned in this chapter.

▶ Oliver has done his share of informative speaking: as a celebrity chef and former star of *Food Revolution*, he gives regular cooking demonstrations that are designed to teach techniques and provide information about food. But this speech, and much of the speaking he does as an activist, is persuasive in nature—he wants to teach people to use the information he provides to change their lives and improve their health, as well as the health of the public at large.

▶ Oliver organizes his TED speech with a problem–cause–solution pattern. First, he identifies the problem, offering startling statistics and compelling personal stories. He then details the causes behind the problem before moving on to solutions, such as giving people the proper information and tools to change their eating behavior and take charge of their lives. He ends with his "wish," his purpose for speaking, hoping to motivate his audience to make it a reality.

▶ Oliver successfully uses presentation aids during his speech: photos of people who are dying from obesity-related diseases, a graphic detailing deaths from diet-related illnesses like type 2 diabetes and heart disease, and, for maximum impact, a wheelbarrow filled with sugar cubes to demonstrate the amount of sugar an average child consumes in five years by drinking just two containers of chocolate milk per day.

▶ Oliver considers his audience when he speaks. He knows that the crowd at his TED speech is receptive to his message; they gave him the award, after all. His message is therefore directed at broad solutions at the institutional level—changes he knows the TED audience can help enact. When speaking to individuals who are less educated about or interested in food and nutrition, he would likely focus on change at the personal level.

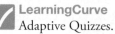 Activities

1. LaunchPad for *Real Communication* offers key term videos and encourages self-assessment through adaptive quizzing. Go to **bedfordstmartins.com/realcomm** to get access to:

✓ **LearningCurve** Adaptive Quizzes.   ▶ Video clips that illustrate key concepts, highlighted in teal in the Real Reference section that follows.

2. Check out a persuasive speech video. You can view one of the persuasive speech videos that accompany this textbook, or you can check one out on YouTube. Listen to and watch the speech critically in light of what you have learned about persuasion. Does the speaker use a clear proposition of fact, value, or policy as a thesis statement? What do you feel the speaker is aiming at—influencing your beliefs, attitudes, or behavior? Maybe all three? Is the speaker's use of rhetorical proofs effective? Consider the elements we have discussed: ethos (character), logos (reasoning), and pathos (emotion).

3. On your next grocery store trip or while waiting in a doctor's office, look through some magazine advertisements (bridal magazines are particularly interesting to search). As you page through the advertisements looking for examples of appeals to ethos, logos, and pathos, consider the following questions:

   ▶ What magazine and ads did you choose to examine?

   ▶ Which form of proof do you find most persuasive? Why?

   ▶ Which form of proof do you find least persuasive? Why?

   ▶ Is there a form of proof used consistently in the ads of the particular magazine you looked at? Why do you think that is?

4. At one point in this chapter, we asked you to think of a time when an instructor presented a viewpoint that went against one of your deeply held beliefs. Now it's time for you to be the speaker.

   ▶ Choose a topic that you feel very passionate about (a controversial topic would work best here).

   ▶ Now imagine that you are presenting the topic to a receptive audience, a neutral audience, and a hostile audience. What do you as a speaker need to do in order to prepare to present your topic to each type of audience? What do you know about your listeners' dispositions? What do you know about their needs? What is most relevant to them?

   ▶ Particularly when dealing with neutral and hostile audiences, what are some ways that you can bridge the gap between your beliefs and those of your audience members? How can you generate goodwill and understanding?

   ▶ Is there a particular organizational pattern that would best suit you, your topic, or your audience? For example, are you sufficiently comfortable with and knowledgeable enough about your hostile audience's counterpoints so that you are comfortable refuting them using the refutational organizational pattern?

Now that you have finished reading this chapter, you can

Define the goals of persuasive speaking:

▶ **Coercion** involves manipulation, threats, intimidation, or violence (p. 466).

▶ **Persuasive speaking** uses the process of **persuasion** to influence **attitudes**, **beliefs**, and **behavior** (p. 466).

Develop a persuasive topic and thesis:

▶ Choose a topic that is controversial and aim to create change in the audience (p. 467).

▶ Thesis statements are often given as a proposition, a statement of your viewpoint on an issue (p. 467).

▶ A **proposition of fact** is a claim of what is or what is not and addresses how people perceive reality (p. 467).

▶ A **proposition of value** makes claims about something's worth (p. 469).

▶ A **proposition of policy** concerns what should happen and makes claims about what goal, policy, or course of action should be pursued (pp. 469–470).

Evaluate your listeners and tailor your speech to them:

▶ **Social judgment theory** holds that your ability to persuade depends on audience members' attitudes toward your topic (pp. 470–471).

▶ A **receptive audience** agrees with you (p. 471).

▶ A **neutral audience** neither supports nor opposes you. A **hostile audience** opposes your message (p. 471).

▶ **Latitude of acceptance and rejection** (or **noncommitment**) refers to the range of positions on a topic that are acceptable or unacceptable to your audience, influenced by their original or **anchor position** (p. 471).

▶ The **stages of change model** helps predict your audience members' motivational readiness and progress toward modifying behavior. The five stages are precontemplation, contemplation, preparation, action, and maintenance (p. 472).

▶ Maslow's **hierarchy of needs** holds that our most basic needs must be met before we can worry about needs farther up the hierarchy (pp. 473–474).

▶ The **Elaboration Likelihood Model (ELM)** highlights the importance of relevance to persuasion and holds that listeners will process persuasive messages by one of two routes: **central processing** (deep, motivated thinking) or **peripheral processing** (unmotivated, less critical thought) (pp. 474–476).

Explain three **forms of rhetorical proof (or classical appeal)**: ethos, logos, and pathos:

▶ The speaker's moral character, or **ethos**, influences the audience's reaction to the message (pp. 477–478).

▶ **Logos** refers to appeals to the audience's **reasoning**, judgments based on facts and inferences (p. 479).

▶ **Inductive reasoning** involves drawing general conclusions from specific evidence; **deductive reasoning** applies general arguments to specific cases (p. 479).

▶ A **syllogism** is a three-line deductive argument, drawing a conclusion from two general premises (p. 479).

▶ **Pathos** appeals to the listeners' emotions (p. 481).

Identify the **logical fallacies**, deceptive forms of reasoning:

▶ The **bandwagon fallacy:** a statement is considered true because it is popular (p. 482).

▶ **Reduction to the absurd**: an argument is pushed beyond its logical limits (p. 482).

▶ The **red herring fallacy:** irrelevant information is used to divert the direction of the argument (p. 482).

▶ The *ad hominem* **fallacy:** a personal attack; the focus is on a person rather than on the issue (pp. 482–483).

▶ A **hasty generalization** is a reasoning flaw in which a speaker makes a broad generalization based on isolated examples (p. 483).

▶ **Begging the question**: advancing an argument that cannot be proved because there is no valid evidence (p. 483).

▶ **Either–or fallacy:** only two alternatives are presented, omitting other alternatives (p. 483).

▶ **Appeal to tradition:** "that's the way it has always been" is the only reason given (p. 483).

▶ The **slippery slope fallacy:** one event is presented as the result of another, without showing proof (p. 484).

▶ The **naturalistic fallacy:** anything natural is right or good; anything human-made is wrong or bad (p. 485).

Choose an appropriate organizational strategy (or **pattern of arrangement**) for your speech:

▶ The *problem–solution pattern* proves the existence of a problem and then presents a solution (pp. 485–486).

▶ The **refutational organizational pattern** presents the main points of the opposition to an argument and then refutes them (pp. 486–487).

▶ The **comparative advantage pattern** tells why your viewpoint is superior to other viewpoints on the issue (p. 487).

▶ Monroe's *motivated sequence pattern* is a five-step process (pp. 487–489).

Interviewees on *The Colbert Report* should expect a few curveballs from the show's satirically minded host, Stephen Colbert. SIPA USA/Jackson/White House/Sipa Press/Newscom

✓ **LearningCurve** can help you master the material in this chapter. Go to **bedfordstmartins.com/realcomm.**

appendix A

Competent Interviewing

Interviews can be scary. Sitting down to speak with someone you don't know—be it a potential employer, a new doctor, a college admissions officer, or a journalist—requires a certain amount of preparation and courage, especially when the person who'll be interviewing isn't even a person at all. That's what guests face when they agree to an interview on Comedy Central's *The Colbert Report* (at least until 2015, when the show will end due to its host's jump to the *Late Show*). Host Stephen Colbert is not a real journalist—he's a character invented and brought to life by the actor and comedian with whom he shares a face and a name. Colbert the character prides himself in being a bully, especially in interviews, where, as one critic explains, he "poses either ridiculous questions on serious topics or earnest questions on ludicrous ones" (Patterson, 2006). In a Colbert Report interview, Colbert always emerges victorious: "I am the only host in America who has never lost an interview. I am 847–and–0, all knockouts" (*The Colbert Report*, 2011).

Such interviews can be especially perilous for politicians—especially for those who agree to sit down with Colbert for his famous "Better Know a District" series. Unlike the show's studio interviews, in which Colbert speaks with authors, academics, celebrities, and government leaders in real time, in front of a live audience, the "Better Know..." series is pretaped, usually on location, and each five-minute comedy segment is edited down from a much longer discussion (some subjects report that the full interviews can take as long as ninety minutes) (Ross, 2007). The final product usually portrays Colbert as the hardball questioner, unconcerned with any answers the interviewee might provide. When he sat down with Seattle's Jim McDermott, for example, he asked the psychiatrist-turned-congressman, "Do you enjoy working with the mentally disturbed, or would you rather be a psychiatrist?" His joke delivered, Colbert moved on before giving McDermott a chance to answer (*The Colbert Report*, 2013).

What would prompt a congressman to submit to an interview knowing well in advance that he will likely be made to look like a fool? And how does an interview like this one relate to other interviews—from serious news features to job interviews? Here we'll take a look at interviews from a communication standpoint—how they relate to other forms of communication, what kinds of factors are at work in an interview situation, and how anyone—from recent college graduates to freshman congressmen and congresswomen, to real and fake news pundits—can improve their interviewing skills.

The Nature of Interviews

Although interviewing is not exactly like grabbing lunch with a friend, the same principles that apply to all forms of communication are also at work in an interview with some important differences.

An **interview** is a transaction that is more structured and goal-driven than other forms of communication. The communication is deliberate and purposeful for at least one of the parties involved and often involves attempts to influence the other(s) (Atlas, 2011; O'Hair, Friedrich, & Dixon, 2011).

▶ *Interviews are planned.* Interviews have a purpose that goes beyond the establishment and development of a relationship. At least one of the parties has a predetermined reason for initiating the interview (for example, to gather information).

▶ *Interviews are goal-driven.* Because a goal exists in advance of the interaction, at least one of the participants plans a strategy for initiating, conducting, and concluding the interview.

▶ *Interviews are structured.* The primary goal of an interview is almost always defined at the beginning of the meeting, something that's rarely true of a conversation with a friend. Interview relationships are more formally structured, and clear status differences often exist. One party usually expects to exert more control than the other.

▶ *Interviews are dyadic.* Like other forms of interpersonal communication, the interview is dyadic, meaning that it involves two parties. In some instances, a "party" consists of more than one person, as when survey researchers conduct group interviews or when job applicants appear before a panel of interviewers. In such situations, even though a number of individuals are involved, there are only two parties (interviewers and interviewees), each with a role to play.

▶ *Interviews are transactional.* Interviews involve two-way communication in which both parties take turns in speaking and listening roles with a heavy dependence on questions and answers. Although most interviews occur face to face, interviews over the phone or via a video conference are also considered transactional discourse. Although the parties take turns in speaking and listening roles, you will recall from Chapter 1 that communicators don't turn themselves off in the listening role; they provide valuable nonverbal feedback.

● **ALL INTERVIEWS,** whether a question-and-answer session with *E!* on the red carpet or a serious job interview, are goal-driven, as well as dyadic and interactive in nature. (left) Roth Stock/Everett Collection; (middle top) © The CW/Courtesy Everett Collection; (middle bottom) ERproductions Ltd./Getty Images; (right) Wavebreakmedia/Shutterstock

Think back to the Comedy Central interviews. They are not only dyadic and transactional but also highly planned. Questions are written ahead of time, based on the interviewee's views and background, and the interviews are structured in a way that helps the company achieve a goal: usually a hilarious spoof on key topics. One key difference is that the interviewee responses are often distorted or cut off—something you wouldn't expect in your own interviews.

Types of Interviews

What type of scene plays out in your mind when you think of the word *interview*? Maybe you start sweating thinking about an upcoming job interview for a position that you really want or maybe you remember interviews for college. But interviewing encompasses much more than just getting a job or getting into the right school. In this section, we look at the different types of interviews that play a role in most of our lives (Stewart & Cash, 2011).

Information-Gathering Interviews

If you watch any crime shows like *CSI* or *The Mentalist*, you've heard people peppered with questions about where they've been, who they've seen, or what they know. The interviewers are trying to obtain *information* from witnesses and suspects (Jundi, Vrij, Hope, Mann, & Hillman, 2013) by collecting attitudes, opinions, facts, data, and experiences through an **information-gathering interview**. We take part in, or are exposed to, the results of such interviews every day; perhaps you've compiled a survey about experiences with campus parking, or maybe you've interviewed your communication professor about career possibilities. In all these instances, the interview serves to transfer knowledge from one party to the other.

AND YOU?

Have you ever imagined interviewing a particular celebrity, political leader, or historical figure? If you were given such an opportunity, what would your goals be for the interview? What kinds of questions would you ask?

Information-gathering interviews can have different variations. Did your computer freak out and delete all of your programs? Have you ever found unauthorized charges on your credit card bill? If so, you are probably intimately familiar with "help desks" or customer service lines. Representatives contacted at these organizations will conduct **service-oriented interviews** or helping interviews designed to cull information and provide advice, service, or support based on that information.

Many television and radio shows involve interviews dealing with politics, crime, governments, the military, international events, weather, and sports. These **media interviews** seek to get information about people and events and sometimes analyze the information or express opinions and emotions. Sports interviews provide a good example. On-field (court) interviews with coaches and athletes capture their emotions in the heat of the win or the defeat, whereas the official postgame interviews provide more predictable, controlled answers. A 2013 on-field interview with Seattle Seahawks cornerback Richard Sherman illustrated the possible pitfalls with court interviews; Sherman's on-air rant against an opponent revealed his personal emotion but overshadowed the team's win that advanced the Seahawks to the Super Bowl. Often media interviews occur in the talk-show format. The Golf Channel's *Feherty* features retired professional golfer and television analyst David Feherty interviewing famous golfers as if they're on *The View, Dr. Phil*, the *Ellen DeGeneres Show*, or the late night shows.

Although all types of interviews involve information gathering to some extent, we'll look next at other types of interviews with unique additional qualities.

Persuasive Interviews

At times the goal of an interview is designed to elicit some change in the interviewee's behavior or opinions. These **persuasive interviews** can involve questions aimed at securing support for or against a particular candidate (political), convincing others to give blood during a campaign (volunteer), or requesting money for an organization or cause (philanthropical).

One type of persuasive interview is the **problem-solving interview**, which attempts to persuade participants to deal with problems, tensions, or conflicts. If you've ever seen an episode of A&E's *Beyond Scared Straight*, you've seen this type of interview in action. In this show at-risk teen offenders are exposed to criminals in prison in an attempt to dissuade them from criminal activity. The teens are asked questions, given information, and helped with formulating a plan or solution to curb their at-risk behaviors.

Problem-solving interviews can also occur in the workplace (such as you and your supervisor meeting to figure out how you can most effectively work from home during snow days) and even in medical situations. Your doctor, for example, may interview you about difficulties in your life that may affect your physical wellbeing; before your appointment, you should prepare

CONNECT

Ethical considerations are important when planning a persuasive interview. As you learn in Chapter 16, there is a difference between persuading people and coercing them with threats. If you're going door-to-door to support a political candidate, remember that your job is to give people information—not to intimidate or belittle them into supporting your candidate. That is clearly unethical communication.

● **TV SHOWS LIKE** A&E's *Beyond Scared Straight* use problem-solving interviews to help at-risk teenagers reevaluate their lives. © A&E/Courtesy Everett Collection

problem-solving questions that will help both you and the doctor to better assess your health (Dwamena, Mavis, Holmes-Rovner, Walsh, & Loyson, 2009) and you should be ready to volunteer information that may help solve the problem (Coulehan & Block, 2006).

Another type of persuasive interview is the **motivational interview**, which elicits change collaboratively. Here interviewers use goal-oriented questioning that's designed to inspire and strengthen personal motivation (Miller & Rollnick, 2013). Showing acceptance and compassion, interviewers can help interviewees become more confident in their ability to make behavioral changes, for example, to lose weight (Wong & Cheng, 2013), deal with pain (Tse, Vong, & Tang, 2013), avoid high-risk drinking and illicit drug use (Kazemi, Levine, Dmochowski, Nies, & Sun, 2013), or quit smoking (Myhre & Adelman, 2013).

Appraisal Interviews

In just about every career—including your academic career—**performance appraisals** are a regular part of reviewing your accomplishments and developing goals for the future. In most corporate environments, a performance appraisal is a highly structured routine dictated by company policies, involving a written appraisal and a one-on-one interview between a supervisor and an employee. But in other less structured performance appraisals, you might meet with your professor to discuss a project or paper or lobby for a change in your grade. Formal appraisals that give only critical, negative feedback do little to improve employee behavior (Asmuß, 2008) and can be very stressful. Effective appraisals will offer insight into strengths as well as weaknesses and help both parties focus on the development of mutual goals for the future (Asmuß, 2013). In other words, if the appraisal interview offers reassurance about what you're doing well and focuses on collaborative goal-setting and continuous improvement, it is less threatening and more useful (Culbert, 2010, 2011).

Exit Interviews

Recruiting and training new people is an expensive process in terms of both time and money, so most organizations want to keep good employees. By conducting **exit interviews** with employees who opt to leave the organization, employers can identify organizational problems—such as poor management style, noncompetitive salary, or weak employee benefits—that might affect employee retention. Your college might conduct an exit interview with you as you graduate to identify the highs and lows of your college experience (and perhaps recruit you for the alumni association).

Exit interviews should be carefully evaluated, as people leaving an organization may hide their true reasons for departing in an effort to put a "positive face" on the situation. Also, interviewers may take that information at face value, reporting more confidence back to the organization

AND YOU?

Do you think of a problem-solving interview as a reprimand or as an opportunity to create needed changes? How can you change the nature of an interview with a negative tone into a more positive experience?

● **AN EXIT INTERVIEW** provides the chance to voice some of the frustrations you experienced as an employee while letting the employer learn about ways to improve the organization in the future. Getty Images/Onoky

● **AFTER EVERY CHALLENGE** on *The Apprentice*, the losing team is subjected to a lengthy questioning by "The Donald" and his advisers to try to figure out what went awry. © NBC/Photofest

than is warranted (Gordon, 2011). In fact, leaving an organization requires people not only to physically disengage but also to deal with feelings of ambivalence and an adjustment in identity as they start to focus on their future (Davis & Myers, 2012). These complexities may not be revealed by a standard exit interview.

Selection Interviews

If you're like most college students, the **selection interview** is probably most relevant to you. The primary goal of a selection interview is to secure or fill a position within an organization and usually involves recruiting, screening, hiring, and placing new candidates (Baker & Spier, 1990; Joyce, 2008). Additionally, members of an organization (for example, university, company, sorority, fraternity, volunteer agency) and candidates evaluate one another by exchanging information to determine if they'd make a good match. Usually both parties want to make a good impression: the interviewer wants to persuade the interviewee about the value of the position or organization, while the interviewee wants to sell his or her unique qualities and abilities.

The **job interview** is the most common type of selection interview in business, government, and military organizations, with the end goal of filling a position of employment (DiSanza & Legge, 2002). Since job interviewing is usually very important to college students, we devote much of this chapter to helping you become more competent in job interviews.

The Format of an Interview

Whether you are interviewing for a job, answering questions for a news reporter, or even watching competitors on a show like *The Apprentice*, you will note the same basic pattern: an opening, the questions, and a conclusion.

The Opening

Late-night talk show host Jimmy Fallon's interviewees are always welcomed with a grand entrance and audience clapping and cheering. But if you're not a movie star plugging your latest project, you probably won't have to worry about this. Whether you are the interviewer or interviewee, your interview will likely begin in a calmer manner, setting the tone for the discourse to follow. As you begin an interview, you should think about three interrelated issues:

▶ The *task:* the nature of this interview and how it will proceed

▶ The *relationship:* whether you like or trust the other party

▶ *Motivation:* what you hope to gain by participating in the interview

CONNECT

The opening of an interview is much like the introduction to a speech. As we discuss in Chapter 13, speech introductions help you achieve four goals: capturing your audience's attention, introducing your purpose, previewing your main points, and connecting with your audience. Openings in both contexts establish the interaction that follows, so your success in engaging your listeners depends on your competency from the start.

EVALUATING**COMMUNICATION**ETHICS

Surveys: Interviewing at Large

Imagine that you are an officer in your college's alumni association, and you have been asked to interview other alumni in order to produce marketing materials that will help increase the number and quality of students applying to your school. Your association wants to show how much graduates enjoyed their school experience and how well they have succeeded in their careers.

You produce a simple one-page survey that asks alumni to rate their school and their postgraduate experience from poor to excellent, which you plan to mail to everyone listed in the alumni register. You are hoping that once all the responses have been tallied, you'll be able to make declarative statements in your marketing materials noting the high percentage of graduates who rate their experience as "excellent." But when you submit your plan and a draft of the survey to the alumni association, you are shot down. "We don't want to hear from everyone," says the alumni president. "We only want to hear from successful graduates who are working at *Fortune* 500 companies or who have made big names for themselves in the sciences."

You are asked instead to create an in-depth survey and conduct it by phone with graduates who have donated more than $1,000 to the school in the past five years. You know that this will skew the results of your survey toward former students who love the school and who have been financially successful since graduating. The association is asking you to present this information as though these students are representative of all students. But you know that although the alumni association depends on successful and wealthy graduates for support, such graduates represent a minority of the students who have attended your school. You know that many students have gone on to successful and fulfilling, if less lucrative, careers in education and the arts. You are concerned that the skewed survey you are being asked to conduct will not paint an accurate picture of the school for prospective students. What are the ethical implications here?

1 Does your plan for a survey of all graduates present a more accurate picture of the school than a telephone survey with only the wealthiest graduates?

2 What about students who attended the school but did not graduate or who are not in the alumni rolls? Would leaving them out skew the results of your survey as well?

3 Does it really matter? Remember, this survey is for material to be used in marketing. Do you think students will infer that quotes from very successful graduates mean that every student at the school goes on to a high-profile, six- or seven-figure salary career?

For example, Eva is doing a telephone survey on student attitudes about parking on campus. The students she calls want to know about the topic of the interview and how long it will take (the task). They want to know something about her and how the information she gathers will be used (the relationship). They want to know how they (or someone else) will benefit from participating in the interview (the motivation). Eva needs to plan what she can say or do at the *start* of the interview that is responsive to these needs (see Table A.1).

The Questions

Once you have set the stage for the interview with an appropriate opening, you need to develop the organizational plan for the body of the interview using questions and answers. The interviewer sets up the structure of the interview by identifying the purpose of the interview and how it will proceed. A response is

● **PROSPECTIVE STUDENTS** on a campus tour should ask their student guides open questions ("What's the social scene like?") and closed questions ("Is the dining hall open on the weekends?") to figure out what student life is *really* like. AP Photo/The News-Gazette, Robin Scholz

solicited from the interviewee, which then prompts reactions from the interviewer, and it just keeps building from there. To have the most effective and most successful interview possible, whether you're the interviewer or interviewee, you need to consider question type, impact, and sequence.

Types of Questions

The path of the interview is largely determined by the types of questions asked. Questions vary in two distinct ways: the amount of freedom the respondent has and how the questions relate to what has happened in the course of the interview.

First, questions vary in terms of how much leeway the interviewee has in generating responses. An **open question** gives the interviewee great freedom in terms of how to respond. Questions like "What's it like being a student here?" and "What issues will influence your vote in this election?" allow the interviewee to determine the amount and depth of information provided. Interviewers often ask open questions when the interviewee knows more about a topic than the interviewer does or to help the interviewee relax (there is no "correct" answer, so no answer is wrong).

In other situations, the interviewer will want a more direct answer. **Closed questions** give less freedom to the interviewee by limiting answers to specific choices. For example, an interviewer conducting a survey of student attitudes toward parking on campus might ask "Do you usually arrive on campus in the morning, afternoon, or evening?" or "Do you use the parking structure or nearby lots?" The simplest form of a closed question is the **bipolar question**, for which there are only two possible responses, "yes" and "no" ("Do you normally eat breakfast?" "Do you own a car?" "Did you vote in the last election?"). To allow for more variation in their answers, interviewees can be asked to respond to a scale, as with the question "How would you rate parking availability on campus?"

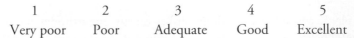

1	2	3	4	5
Very poor	Poor	Adequate	Good	Excellent

Questions also vary in terms of how they relate to what has happened so far in the interview. **Primary questions** introduce new topics; **secondary questions** seek clarification or elaboration of primary question responses. Thus, if interviewing an older family member, you might open by asking "What can you tell me about my family history?" This primary question might then be followed by a number of secondary questions, such as "How did my grandparents meet?" and "How did they deal with their parents' disapproval of their marriage?" Some of the more common forms of secondary questions are illustrated in Table A.2.

Question Impact

In addition to considering question type, interviewers must also consider that the way in which a question is constructed can directly influence the interviewee's

Goal	Description	Example
Clarify the *task*	Orient the interviewee, who may not be well informed about the reason for the interview.	"As you may know, we're looking for ways to increase productivity among our sales associates. I'm hoping you will help me jump-start this initiative."
Define the *relationship*	Make a connection to a third party respected by the interviewee to put him or her at ease.	"I was referred to you by Liam Fitzpatrick, who told me that you've done great work for him in the past."
Determine the *motivation*	Request the interviewee's advice or assistance with regard to a problem.	"Perhaps you can give me insight into the way things work between your division and marketing."

response. A good question is clear, relevant, and unbiased. To create clear questions, consider the following criteria:

▶ Make questions understandable. Ask the classic and simple news reporter's questions of who, what, when, where, why, and how before you proceed to more complex ones (Payne, 1951).

▶ Ensure that the wording of the questions is as direct and simple as possible. For example, asking "For whom did you vote in the last mayoral election?" will get you a more precise answer than asking "How do you vote?"

▶ Keep the questions short and to the point.

Behavior	Definition	Example
Clarification	Directly requests more information	"Could you tell me a little more about the reasons you chose to join the military after high school?"
Elaboration	Extends the request for a response	"Are there any other specific features that you consider important in your search for a new house?"
Paraphrasing	Rephrases the questioner's response to establish understanding	"So you're saying that the type of people you work with is more important to you than location?"
Encouragement	Uses brief sounds and phrases to indicate attentiveness and interest	"Uh-huh," "I see," "That's interesting," "Good," "Yes, I understand."
Summarizing	Pulls together major points and seeks confirmation of correctness	"Let's see if I've got it: your ideal job involves an appreciative boss, supportive colleagues, interesting work, and living in a large metropolitan area?"
Clearinghouse	Asks if you have elicited all the important or available information	"Have I asked everything that I should have asked?"

Source: Adapted from O'Hair, Friedrich, & Dixon (2011).

real communicator

NAME: Cynthia Guadalupe Inda
OCCUPATION: Trial attorney

When I mention that I'm a lawyer, many people are surprised to learn that I spend a great deal of time interviewing people. In fact, I like to think of my job as asking questions and culling information in ways similar to talk show hosts, counselors, and reporters. But before I confuse you, allow me to explain these aspects of my career.

When I was with a district attorney's office for a number of years, my biggest challenge was interviewing many witnesses for the dozens of cases I was assigned in a limited amount of time. In order to do my job effectively, I needed to interview all the witnesses quickly and efficiently—but not make them feel rushed.

The talk show host aspect of my job is putting people at ease during an interview. People are often intimidated by lawyers, so I look people in the eye, smile, and try to be as down-to-earth as possible. (I think I'm this way in real life, so I just have to remember to treat my interviewees as I would my friends and family.) When dealing with Spanish-speaking witnesses, I always conduct interviews in Spanish. This helps to put people at ease because the law doesn't seem as terrifying in one's own language.

The counselor aspect of my job is having empathy for people's situations. I often tell people who are afraid to bring charges or get involved in any way that I understand their fear and reticence. I'll say something like, "I know that there are other things you'd rather be doing; just tell the judge exactly what you are telling me." If an interviewee is very upset, I'll often switch the subject away from the task at hand; I get them talking about themselves instead of the law. They usually relax and it makes it easier to get back to the interview questions.

The reporter aspect of my job is in culling information from my interviewees to focus on what is essential to the case. Preparation really matters here. When I have witnesses on the stand, my questions are targeted toward the achievement of a goal. I ask open-ended questions, but I also have a series of background and clarifying questions to help make my point. When I'm cross-examining a witness, however, my questions are much more closed: I try to ask only questions that call for "yes" or "no" responses. The facts established by the "yes" or "no" answers I'm searching for give less credibility to the opposition's case.

Effective interviewing skills are crucial to my professional success and the well-being of my clients. Interviewing is not all work—I have fun getting to know people and helping them achieve justice.

AND YOU?

Have you ever been asked unethical, biased, or uncivil questions? Did you ever, knowingly or unknowingly, use these types of questions yourself? How can you deal with questions like these if you find yourself in that uncomfortable position?

▶ Phrase questions positively and remain civil (Ben-Porath, 2010). For example, asking "Have you voted in campus student government elections?" is clear and objective; using negative phrasing ("You haven't ever voted in the campus student government elections, have you?") can be confusing and, in some cases, may be unethical and biased (Doris, 1991).

Speaking of ethics, competent interviewers should use questions that are straightforward and avoid hidden agendas. **Directed questions** suggest or imply an answer. If the direction is subtle ("Wouldn't it be so much fun if we all got

Question Behavior	Definition	Example
Leading	Questions that subtly direct interviewees to the correct or desired answer	"Do you take home office supplies like most employees?"
Loaded	Extremely leading questions that almost dictate the correct answer; to be avoided in most cases	"When was the last time you took home supplies from the office?"
Neutral	Questions that allow respondents to choose their answers without pressure from the interviewer's wording	"Do you think the office should provide you with supplies to work at home?"

TABLE A.3

LEADING, LOADED, AND NEUTRAL QUESTIONS

together to paint my apartment this weekend?"), it is termed a **leading question**. Other directed questions are bolder in their biasing effect and are called **loaded questions** ("When was the last time you cheated on an exam?" assumes, of course, that you *have* cheated). Questions that provide no hint to the interviewee concerning the expected response are **neutral questions**—for example, "What is your opinion of the administration on this campus?" (See Table A-3 for more examples of directed questions.)

Question Sequence

The order in which the questions are asked can affect both the accomplishment of the interview's goals and the comfort level of the interviewee. There are three main "shapes" that guide the ordering of questions: the funnel, inverted funnel, and tunnel sequences (Figure A.1).

In the **funnel sequence**, the interviewer starts with broad, open-ended questions (picture the big end of a funnel) and moves to narrower, more closed questions. The questions become more personal or more tightly focused as the interview progresses, giving the interviewee a chance to get comfortable with the topic and open up. The funnel sequence works best with respondents who feel at ease with the topic and the interviewer.

▶ "What do you think about children playing competitive sports?" (general)

▶ "What disadvantages have you witnessed?" (specific)

▶ "What constraints would you advocate for young players?" (very specific)

The **inverted funnel sequence** starts with narrow, closed questions and moves to more open-ended questions. The inverted funnel works best with interviewees who are emotional or reticent and need help "warming up."

▶ "Did you perform a Mozart piece for your piano recital in junior high school?" (very specific)

CONNECT

Even neutral questions can become leading questions if you fail to consider nonverbal communication (Chapter 4). If you grimace, roll your eyes, or change your tone of voice when you ask the neutral question "What, if anything, is your attitude toward fraternities and sororities on this campus?" you are actually asking a leading question (and letting others know your attitude toward the Greek system on campus).

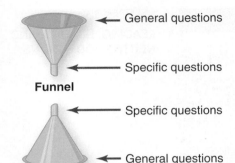

Funnel

General questions

Specific questions

Inverted Funnel

Specific questions

General questions

Tunnel

Questions all at the same level of specificity or generality

FIGURE A.1

FIGURE A.1

FUNNEL, INVERTED FUNNEL, AND TUNNEL SEQUENCES

▶ "What other classical compositions are you comfortable playing?" (specific)

▶ "How did you feel about taking piano lessons as a child?" (general)

In the **tunnel sequence**, all of the questions are at one level. The tunnel sequence works particularly well in polls and surveys. A large tunnel would involve a series of broad, open-ended questions. A small tunnel (the more common form) would ask a series of narrow, closed questions, as in the following example:

▶ "Have you attended any multicultural events on campus?" (specific)

▶ "Have you attended any sporting events?" (specific)

▶ "Have you attended any guest lectures?" (specific)

The Conclusion

Once the purpose of the interview has been achieved, the interaction should come to a comfortable and satisfying close. This phase of the interview is especially important because it often determines the impression the interviewee retains of the interview as a whole.

There are important norms involved when individuals take leave of each other (Knapp, Hart, Friedrich, & Shulman, 1973), so in closing the interview, the interviewer needs to employ both verbal and nonverbal strategies to serve three important functions (Von Raffler-Engel, 1983):

▶ To *conclude*, or signal the end of the interview

▶ To *summarize*, or review the substantive conclusions produced by the interview

▶ To *support,* or express satisfaction with the interaction and project what will happen next

Table A.4 illustrates closing strategies to help you conclude, summarize, and support. As these sample statements indicate, bringing the interview to a close is largely the responsibility of the interviewer. In the next section, we'll look at how this and other responsibilities fall to the interviewer and interviewee.

Understanding Roles and Responsibilities in Interviews

Jan, a thirty-year-old high school biology teacher, is seeking a new career. She can approach this job hunt in two ways. First, she could simply answer advertisements for open positions and hope to be called in for an interview. Alternatively, she

TABLE A.4

CLOSING STRATEGIES

Behavior	Definition	Example
Declare the completion of the purpose or task.	The word *well* signals a close; people automatically assume the end is near and prepare to take their leave.	"Well, I think we've covered a lot of territory today."
Signal that time for the meeting is up.	This is most effective when a time limit was announced in the opening of the interview. Avoid abruptness so the interviewee doesn't feel pushed along an assembly line.	"We have just a few minutes left, so. . . ."
Explain the reason for the closing.	Be sure the reasons are real; if an interviewee thinks you're giving phony excuses, future interactions will be strained.	"Unfortunately, I've got another meeting in fifteen minutes, so we'll have to start wrapping things up."
Express appreciation or satisfaction.	This is a common closing because interviewers have usually received something from the interview (information, help, a sale, a story, employment).	"Thank you for your interest in our cause."
Plan for the next meeting.	This reveals what will happen next (date, time, place, topic, content, purpose) or arranges for the next interview.	"I think we should follow up on this next week; my assistant will call you to arrange a time."
Summarize the interview.	This common closing may repeat important information, solidify agreements, or verify accuracy.	"We've come to three major agreements here today." (List them briefly.)

Source: Labels from Stewart & Cash (2011).

could identify people or organizations that she thinks she'd like to work for and arrange for information-gathering interviews with them. In the first approach, Jan, the job hunter, fills the role of *interviewee*—she answers questions posed by the interviewer. In the second example, Jan acts as the *interviewer*, asking people in various positions for information about potential career paths in their industry. So how are these roles different? How are they similar? Let's find out (Stewart & Cash, 2014).

Responsibilities of the Interviewer

In any interview situation, competent interviewers have at least four responsibilities: they must (1) identify potential barriers, (2) make the interviewee comfortable, (3) ask ethical and appropriate questions, and (4) effectively listen and respond to the interviewee.

Identify Potential Barriers

Before heading into an interview situation, interviewers should take time to reflect on potential barriers that might disrupt the interview. For example, is the space where the interview will take place quiet, private, and fairly neat and organized? Is lighting adequate, are the room and furniture appropriate to the interview purpose, and is enough time allotted to complete the interview satisfactorily? If not, make those adjustments before the interview commences.

Make the Interviewee Comfortable

Interviewees, particularly job applicants and medical patients, are often very nervous in interview situations—and understandably so. A good interviewer should adapt to the situational and relational contexts to help the interviewee feel at ease (Ralston, Kirkwood, & Burant, 2003). It would be effective and appropriate, for example, for an interviewer to smile, make eye contact, and offer a handshake. But be sure to keep these behaviors appropriate to the context; imagine if your doctor entered the examining room and gave you a big hug or if a job interviewer told you about his problems with his partner's parents.

Ask Ethical and Appropriate Questions

Although questions and question sequences can result in productive interviews, it's important to remember that good questions are also ethical and appropriate (and avoid the leading and loaded questions we discussed in the past section). For example, if Erik is a representative from his school newspaper interviewing a biology professor about her recent grant from the National Institutes of Health (NIH), his questions should stick to her research and her plans to implement a new lab on campus. It would be inappropriate and unethical for him to ask how much money she personally will be receiving from the NIH or whether she expects to receive a promotion and salary increase from the university after receiving the award.

On a job interview, certain unethical and inappropriate questions are also illegal. We'll cover these later in this chapter.

Listen and Respond Effectively

The role of the interviewer is not limited to structuring an interview and asking questions. After all, an effective interviewer needs to listen, respond, and evaluate the information that those questions reveal. Throughout the interview, the interviewer should keep both immediate and future goals in mind by making notes (written or mental) during the interview.

Responsibilities of the Interviewee

True, the interviewer is responsible for quite a bit of work in an interview situation, but that doesn't mean that the interviewee is off the hook. As an interviewee, you will benefit greatly by taking on three major responsibilities: (1) clarifying your personal goals, (2) being prepared, and (3) listening and responding effectively.

Clarify and Fulfill Personal Goals

One of the most important things that an interviewee can bring to the interview is a clear sense of personal goals. That is, you should have a clear idea of what *you* want to achieve in the interview; this allows you to look for and

● *CSI: MIAMI'S* HORATIO CAINE indicates that he's finished interviewing a suspect or surveying the crime scene by pausing to put on his trademark sunglasses. Your job interview should also have a simple, comfortable conclusion. © CBS/Photofest

AND YOU?

Have you ever been in an interview where you felt that the interviewer neglected his or her responsibilities? In what ways did the interviewer fail? How would you have handled things differently?

seek out opportunities to advance those aims, such as looking for specific openings in the conversation (Waldron & Applegate, 1998). A job interviewee—whose goal it might be to impress a hiring manager—can seek out appropriate places to give examples of personal energy, drive, and willingness to be a team player. A human resources manager may advance the public relations goals of her organization by selecting the positive information she'll share in a press interview.

Prepare Yourself Responsibly

Your school's career services office and your previous employment situations have likely prepared you for the fact that you'll need to draft a résumé and a cover letter in advance of a job interview. But all interviews benefit from some additional advance planning.

For one thing, you'll want to be well rested and alert. From personal experience, we urge you not to skip meals—more than a few of our students have had growling stomachs during interviews! You'll also want to consider the context and be dressed appropriately for the occasion; this is especially important for official job interviews, where you should match or exceed the dress policy at that place of business. Also remember to plan what you should bring with you to the interview: copies of your résumé to a job interview, for example, or your medical history to an interview with a new doctor.

Listen and Respond Effectively

Just as interviewers must listen and respond effectively, so must the interviewee. For example, in a performance appraisal, carefully consider your answers to your boss's questions. If she asks you to assess what you have accomplished and excelled at, honestly highlight your individual achievements or contributions to your team—without exaggerating.

Shared Responsibilities

Both interviewer and interviewee share in the responsibility to adapt to each other and the interview situation appropriately—in both their verbal and nonverbal communication. If a professor in your department is interviewing you to see if you would be a good fit for your college's honors program, you would typically treat the interview quite formally. For example, you would use professional, formal address when speaking to the professor ("Professor Arisetty" or "Dr. Edmunds"). But if you have known this professor for three years, you baby-sit her children, and she insists that you call her Emilia, you can adapt, feeling free to use her first name and a less strict, more personal style of conversation.

If the interview takes place in a conference room with multiple interviewers, the interviewee can adapt by making appropriate eye contact with each of the interviewers and behaving more formally. But this also depends on the situation. If you are applying to become a barista, for example, and are interviewing on a bench outside the coffee shop, you can consider the situation less formal. In this case, you would also need to avoid distractions from the people and noise around you.

● **THE KIND OF JOB** you're interviewing for dictates how to dress. For an interview with the typically more conservative finance industry, you will need a suit. For an interview at an art gallery, you *might* wear a more casual outfit. (top) Simon Watson/Getty Images; (bottom) © Spencer Grant/PhotoEdit

COMMUNICATIONACROSSCULTURES

Cultural Competence in Social Work

If you ever find yourself struggling—economically, emotionally, or physically—there is someone who can help. In hospitals and schools, for government agencies and nonprofits, social workers are often the point person for individuals in need of health care, mental health services, social support, or simply assistance in navigating large bureaucratic systems such as immigration or the legal system.

The first step in providing this assistance is assessing the problem. Social workers identify client needs, for the most part, by asking questions and listening to answers. In fact, just about every aspect of the social worker's responsibilities depends on skillful interviewing (Kadushin & Kadushin, 2013). A mother who does not wish to leave the hospital after delivering her baby, for example, might say that she does not feel well. But a skilled social worker will explore further to consider other factors that might be impacting the mother's decision, such as postpartum depression, family violence, physical condition of the home, fear of parenting, or lack of social support to care for the child, as well as economic uncertainty. Only if the social worker can identify these concerns will he or she be able to link the mother with resources and services to ensure a healthy and safe situation for the family.

In this role, cultural competence is essential. A social worker seeking to help an undocumented immigrant who is the victim of a crime, for example, will likely face multiple challenges when interviewing a client. Obviously, language barriers can make communication difficult, but such concerns can usually be addressed with the use of an interpreter. However, other cultural factors can profoundly influence the way a client answers questions. Fear of deportation may make the client reluctant to seek assistance, or the client may worry that testifying in court will put his or her job in jeopardy. In cases of sexual assault, in particular, culturally bound gender expectations can make it difficult for some clients to speak frankly about what happened (Clarke, 2014).

THINK ABOUT THIS

1 If you were admitted into a hospital for extended care, would you be able to have a frank discussion with a social worker about your own medical history? What about your sexual history? Do you think your ability to speak about such things is culturally bound?

2 Is it possible for social workers to pay attention to all of the cultural dynamics at play in an interview? How can social workers pay attention to salient cultural factors without resorting to stereotyping their clients based on culture or gender?

3 For social workers, which is more important: asking the right questions or listening to and interpreting answers? How important are follow-up questions?

Culture also plays a profound role in job interview situations (Gardner, Reithel, Foley, Cogliser, & Walumbwa, 2009), affecting both judgments and evaluations (Manroop, Boekhorst, & Harrison, 2013). For example, many people from various ethnic and religious backgrounds find it difficult to brag about their accomplishments at a job interview because their culture frowns on such boastful behavior. Research shows that rather than clearly state a strength ("I have extremely strong organizational skills"), African American interviewees often tell stories about themselves to illustrate their strengths (Hecht, Jackson, & Ribeau, 2003). Researchers also note that European American interviewers often judge story-telling candidates to be "unfocused." Thus African Americans who adapt by directly listing their strengths for a job are perceived more positively in interviews (Hecht, Jackson, & Ribeau, 2003); conversely, a European American interviewer who looks for the message behind the story an interviewee tells has competently adapted as well.

The Job Interview

In one episode of the TV show *How I Met Your Mother*, Marshall goes on a multitude of job interviews. We see him talking to his bathroom mirror before each one, at first saying, "You are confident, energetic," later, "You are flexible on salary; you will not cry," and finally, "You are sad and beaten down." Although you might be able to identify with Marshall's roller-coaster of emotions, you can also recognize that preparing adequately for interviews will make your experiences more successful. In fact, most job interviews involve many of the competent behaviors you have already learned in this text, from audience adaptation to language choice to nonverbal communication (Bloch, 2011).

● **TO AVOID** having the same frustrating experience as Marshall, make sure to follow the advice here to arrive prepared for your interviews. MONTY BRINTON/CBS/Landov

Being aware of these behaviors before you go into the interview will greatly increase your confidence. In the remaining pages of this chapter, we describe how job interviews usually occur and offer solid advice on how to prepare for, engage in, and follow up on the process (Muir, 2008).

Getting the Interview

The first step involves actually getting the interview. This important phase involves three interrelated tasks: locating jobs and doing homework on the organizations, preparing materials to be used in the process (the résumé and cover letter), and building realistic expectations about the interviewing process.

The Job Search

The first element of preinterview preparation involves identifying potential jobs and then researching the field and the organizations. Although there are many strategies for locating jobs, your three best sources are likely to be people you know or manage to meet, placement centers, and discipline-specific job sites.

A great place to start is with family, friends, professors, former employers, and individuals working in your field of interest. You should also plan to network (Brazeel, 2009). **Networking** is the process of using interconnected groups or associations of persons you know to develop relationships with their connections that you don't know. Contact the people you know who work in your field or who might know someone who does, let these individuals know the kind of job you are looking for, and ask for suggestions. You can also make new contacts via social networking services. Use sites like Facebook for more informal networking and sites like LinkedIn for more formal connections. You also can network efficiently through an organization for professionals in your chosen field (many offer student memberships). Whichever connections you make, be sure to remind your contacts of how you met or why you are getting in touch.

CONNECT ▶

Consider the relational context in competent communication (Chapter 1). It is effective and appropriate to respond differently to the same question posed by your doctor, your mother, your boss and your romantic partner. How intimate you are with the person, your relational history, what you know about him or her, and status differences between you have a profound effect on the interview situation.

● **THERE ARE** many different avenues that you can explore when you begin your job hunt. Industry-specific magazines like *Variety*, job placement centers, and employment Web sites are all good places to start. (left) Variety Media, LLC; (top right) Courtesy of careeronestop.org; (bottom right) JOE SKIPPER/Reuters/Landov

Preparing for a job interview is similar to preparing for a speech. In Chapter 12, we suggest studying your audience to know how to present information they'll find useful and interesting; in a job interview, you must do the same. Your goal is to learn about the organization's culture (Chapter 11): Is it a formal or informal place? What does the organization value? This information helps you adapt your communication competently and impress a hiring manager.

Placement centers are another source of jobs. Most college campuses have a centralized placement center where recruiters from major companies come to interview potential employees. And don't forget print media; search for career-specific publications that will help you better focus on your chosen career path, such as *Media Career Guide: Preparing for Jobs in the 21st Century* (Culver & Seguin, 2013).

Finally, start looking for specific job openings. Although general employment Web sites (like Monster.com) can be starting places, they may not yield significant results simply because they attract a large number of applicants (O'Loughlin, 2010); you have less chance of being noticed in a pool of a thousand (or more) than in one of a hundred. A more productive search uses sites that cater to specific industries or even an organization's site (Pearce & Tuten, 2001; Young & Foot, 2005). For example, mediabistro.com and entertainmentcareers.net focus on jobs in the media and entertainment industries, respectively. You can also find job postings on the Web sites for most major companies and organizations (look for links to "Careers" or "Employment"). Consider using job information and posting aggregators (such as LexisNexis) that will let you set criteria or parameters for the types or even geographic locations of positions you want. Doing so will put you in touch with sites that have less traffic and give you a better chance of being noticed.

Prepare Your Materials

Once you've identified potential jobs, you'll need to make contact with the people in a position to hire you. As a job applicant, the crucial first impression you make on a potential employer will likely be via your written materials—a formal cover letter and résumé. In this section, we show you how to prepare these materials so that they communicate the right message about you (Ding & Ding, 2013).

But first, a cautionary note: *before* you send off these written materials, make sure you have cleaned up any searchable information that does not portray you in a favorable light (Brandenburg, 2008; Holson, 2010). If you use social

WIREDFORCOMMUNICATION

Pre-Presenting Yourself: Your Online Persona

Savvy job applicants will always prepare for a job interview by doing a little armchair research—a quick Internet search can reveal lots of insights about potential employers, from benefits to corporate culture. But often young and inexperienced job hunters fail to realize that those little searches can go both ways. As easily as you can Google a company name, a potential employer can also do a search on your name or e-mail address. You might put forth a fantastic résumé and buy the most professional suit for your first interview, but what you've got posted on online chats, blogs, Web pages, MySpace, or Facebook pages might very well be the most important factor in shaping the first impression you make on a potential employer. Research suggests that more than three-quarters of employers Google candidates' names when seeking to fill positions (Levit, 2010).

Consider Brad Karsh, president of a small company in Chicago who was looking to hire a summer intern. When he came across a promising candidate, he did a quick online background check, taking a peek at his Facebook page. There, the candidate described his interests as including marijuana use, shooting people, and obsessive sex. That the student was clearly exaggerating didn't matter. His lack of judgment regarding what to say about himself publicly, Karsh says, took him out of the running for the position (Finder, 2006). Taking a few minutes to find out what's out there on you can yield results. One student reported that upon Googling himself, he found an essay he'd posted on a student Web site a few years prior. The essay was called "Lying Your Way to the Top." Only after he had it removed did he begin getting calls (Finder, 2006).

In addition to cleaning up whatever youthful indiscretions the Internet reveals, savvy candidates will do well to take advantage of the opportunities the Web presents for cultivating an impression that is professional and impressive. Career development expert Chris Perry notes that having no presence at all on the Internet can lead to the impression that you haven't done anything noteworthy. He suggests creating professional profiles on professional Web sites, like LinkedIn and CareerRocket (the latter of which he founded), and posting content there, as well as posting relevant comments to highly read blogs with links back to your own professional sites. As you develop your online presence more thoroughly, it can be helpful to make use of search engine optimization tools that will improve your Google ranking (Levit, 2010). By eliminating content you don't want employers to see, and creating content that you do want to be seen, you can cultivate an online presence that's as impressive as your résumé.

THINK ABOUT THIS

❶ Take a moment to Google yourself. Search not only for your name but also your e-mail address. What comes up?

❷ Do you have a Facebook page or Twitter feed? Think objectively about the impression that your posts to these sites convey. Would you hire you?

❸ Have you been known to comment on news items or blogs in ways that might reveal your personal opinions? Do you consider the material you post on such sites private? Do you think it's ethical for employers to be looking at your postings?

❹ How can you create a better online image for yourself?

networking sites, adjust your privacy settings to ensure that you have not been, and cannot be, tagged in any photographs that you wouldn't want a potential employer to see and that the details of your profile are not visible to anyone other than your approved friends. Perform searches for your name and e-mail address to make sure that any comments you've left on public forums or chat rooms don't come back to haunt you. Consider also asking your friends to search and review your sites for negative information.

The résumé. Begin by pulling together a **résumé**—a printed summary of your education, work experiences, and accomplishments (see Figure A.2). It is a vehicle for making a positive first impression on potential employers. An effective résumé tells just enough about you to make employers believe they may need your skills and experience.

No two résumés look exactly alike, but most résumés should contain the following general information:

▶ *Contact information.* Include both campus and home addresses if necessary, phone numbers, and your e-mail address. Make sure that your voice mail greets callers with a clear, professional message, and check it often. If you have an odd or cute address for your regular e-mail (partygirl@provider .com, numberonedad@provider.net), consider opening another account with a more serious name for all of your professional communication.

▶ *Employment objective.* Be concise and specific about what you're looking for in a position and your career goals. If you are applying for several types of jobs, you should create multiple résumés tailored to specific positions.

▶ *Education.* List the institutions you have attended, their locations, and the dates of attendance. List degrees received (or dates to be received), academic majors, and areas of concentration. Awards and GPA can be listed if they enhance your marketability.

▶ *Work experience.* If your work experiences are all in the same area, list them in reverse chronological order (most recent ones first), focusing on concrete examples of achievement or skills that you have mastered. Explain job functions as well as titles. If, on the other hand, you have had a variety of jobs (for example, waiting tables and being a camp counselor), reverse chronological order may not be very practical. Consider grouping actual employment and volunteer activities together in a way that best matches the job responsibilities you are seeking. Remember that prospective employers read this section carefully to discover how your experience, abilities, and achievements relate to their organization's needs. You can make this easier for them with a clear and organized presentation of yourself.

▶ *Activities.* For employers, participation in a variety of academic, extracurricular, or social activities indicates that you are motivated and get involved. Include activities that are relevant to your career objective, emphasizing accomplishments and leadership roles—and link them clearly together.

▶ *Special skills.* Do you speak fluent Spanish? Are you skilled in a particular programming language? Have you managed a charity race in your community?

SAMPLE RÉSUMÉ

Ellen Ng

111 A Street, Apt. 2C, San Marcos, TX 78666

(555) 375-7111 • ellen.ng@serviceprovider.com

OBJECTIVE

To obtain an entry-level editorial position where I can use my strong writing and editing skills while expanding my knowledge of the publishing process.

EDUCATION

Texas State University, *San Marcos, TX*   *2012–2014*
    Bachelor of Arts, English, May 2014   GPA: 3.7/4.0
    Honors: Recipient, Lorin D. Parkin scholarship (2010); Member, Sigma Tau Delta honor society.

Northwest Vista College, *San Antonio, TX*   *2010–2012*
    Associate of Arts, Liberal and Media Arts (General), May 2012

RELATED WORK EXPERIENCE

Intern, Chronicle Books, *San Francisco, CA*   *Summer 2013*
    Wrote reports on the marketability and publication potential of cookbook proposals and manuscripts. Drafted rejection letters, letters to authors, and letters requesting outstanding permissions fees. Created cost and sales figure spreadsheets. Prepared manuscripts and artwork for production.

Writing Counselor, Writing Center, *Texas State University*   *Fall 2012–Spring 2014*
    Aided students with their academic research papers, résumés, and cover letters. Developed exercises and writing samples to increase college-level writing skills.

Writer/Editor, MyWay in Education, *Hong Kong*   *Summer 2012*
    Created and edited reading comprehension articles and over 300 grammar questions per week for ten different grade levels in accordance with Hong Kong public school standards for company's Web site.

Volunteer, San Antonio Public Library, *San Antonio, TX*   *Fall 2008–Spring 2012*
    Created themed book displays for special events, such as Hispanic Heritage Month and national and international holidays. Read to children ages 3–5 weekly; created activities and games supporting the stories.

OTHER WORK EXPERIENCE AND ACTIVITIES

Waitress/Hostess, Applebee's, *San Marcos, TX*   *Fall 2012–Present*
    Waited tables. Took food orders, brought meals to tables, and cleared tables.

Cheerleader, Texas State Spirit Program, *Texas State University*   *Fall 2012–Spring 2014*

Cashier, Home Depot, *San Antonio, TX*   *Fall 2010–Fall 2011*
    Rang up customer purchases. Assisted in closing up store.

SKILLS AND INTERESTS

Languages: Fluent in English, proficient in written and conversational Mandarin and Cantonese, conversational Spanish

Computer: Word, Excel, PowerPoint, FileMaker Pro, Internet research

Don't be shy—let potential employers know this information. Your skills may be useful to the organization, and your accomplishments show dedication and determination.

▶ *References.* Your references are typically professors, previous supervisors, or anyone else who can confirm your employment history and attest to your work ethic and character. Some organizations want you to include your references (with current contact information) with your résumé, and others will ask for those once you get your first interview (Joyce, 2008). Be sure to include only people who have agreed to serve as references for you.

Once your résumé is complete, take some time to prepare it for electronic submission. Make sure it is readable on all platforms by saving it as a pdf document, so that employers can read it regardless of what type of computer they have. You should also name the file carefully, so that employers will be able to identify it easily. Include your name (or just your last name) in the file title, along with the word *résumé* and perhaps a date (for example, *MartinezRésumé Jan2015.pdf*).

The cover letter.   Whenever you send your résumé to a potential employer, it should be accompanied by a formal **cover letter** (see Figure A.3), a one-page letter indicating your interest in a specific position. The cover letter gives you the opportunity to express how you learned of the position and the organization, how your skills and interests can benefit the organization, and why you are interested in applying for this particular job. The cover letter also serves as a means by which you can demonstrate your written communication skills, so make sure that you use correct grammar, punctuation, and spelling—and proofread carefully!

In many cases, prospective employers accept e-mails as cover letters. So when you e-mail a hiring manager or a human resources representative at an organization, your e-mail should contain the same information as your cover letter. If you are unsure of the protocol, it's always best to be more formal and include/attach an official cover letter along with your e-mail. Be sure to include a subject line (for example, Martinez recruiter position) and to proofread your e-mail carefully before you press Send.

Build Realistic Expectations

The final component of job hunting involves developing realistic expectations about the process. Because only a few résumés will make it through the screening process and you will not be the only candidate called for an interview, you will likely face rejection at least once during the course of a job search—either because there was a better-qualified applicant or because an equally qualified candidate had some advantage (such as a personal contact in the company). Remember that rejection is common—the inevitable result of a tight job market and a less-than-perfect selection process (Fisk, 2010; Hershatter & Epstein, 2010; Lebo, 2009; Luo, 2010). Persistence pays. If you approach the job search intelligently and persistently, you will eventually get a job (Rampell, 2013).

SAMPLE COVER LETTER

111 A Street, Apt. 2C
San Marcos, TX 78666

September 6, 2014

Jane Smith
Director of Human Resources
Roaring Brook Press
A Division of Macmillan
175 Fifth Avenue
New York, NY 10010

Dear Director Smith:

I was excited to see the posting for an editorial assistant position with Roaring Brook Press. I admire your organization's dedication to children and youth, and I would be honored to interview for a position that would allow me to develop my interests in publishing while working on the creative editorial projects that Roaring Brook Press supports.

My publishing experience coupled with my understanding of children's education make me well-suited for an editorial assistant position with your company. I worked as an editorial intern at Chronicle Books in San Francisco, where I maintained author and permissions databases and collated manuscripts and artwork for review and production. I also honed my writing skills through critiquing cookbook proposals and manuscripts based on analysis of the cookbook market.

I have also worked with children in an educational setting. As a volunteer at the San Antonio Public Library, I organized and created informational displays aimed at getting children interested in subjects or cultures unfamiliar to them. I also created games and activities for children based on the books I read to them during story hour. Through this position, I learned how to communicate with children in a creative yet educational way.

I have included my résumé as requested in the job posting, and I can provide references as required. I look forward to discussing my experiences and perspectives with you in person. I can be contacted at ellen.ng@serviceprovider.com or by phone at (555) 375-7111. Thank you for your kind consideration.

Sincerely,

Ellen Ng

Ellen Ng

During the Interview

After a diligent job search, you've finally been called for an interview. Now what? Well, now you impress the socks off your interviewer by making your best first impression, preparing for and anticipating different types of questions, preparing questions of your own, and following up after your interview.

Making a Good First Impression

Salina, who works in the nonprofit world, interviewed a candidate who came forty-five minutes late to the interview. To make matters worse, he explained his tardiness by noting that he had to "run home" to get his mom to help him with his tie. Later, Salina had a phone interview with a young woman who didn't bother to ensure that she had adequate cell phone reception, meaning that the question "What did you say?" dominated the conversation. What these candidates forgot is that the interview is a communication transaction that begins with first impressions and includes situational factors as well as questions.

In any interview, both verbal and nonverbal behaviors contribute to a good first impression. As you prepare for the interview, review your impression-management skills to help your actual performance (Kleinmann & Klehe, 2011). You can also prepare mentally— for example, remembering a personal experience in which you were powerful or took control results in stronger impressions in the interview (Lammers, Dubois, Rucker, & Galinsky, 2013).

In a more practical sense, try to control the things you can at the outset. Give yourself plenty of extra time to get there, so that if something comes up (traffic, a stalled train) you'll still make it on time. Have your clothing ready ahead of time. If it's a phone (or Skype) interview, find a quiet place where you can talk undisturbed and where there are no visual or auditory distractions (Dizik, 2011).

CONNECT

In Chapter 14, you learn that communication apprehension is a general fear of real or anticipated communication with a person or persons. Speaking before an audience causes anxiety for many people—and so does speaking with a hiring manager. To make sure anxiety doesn't adversely affect your communication, try some of our suggestions for building confidence (Chapter 14, pp. 405, 407), such as performance visualization and preparing for the unexpected.

BOX A.1

WHAT *NOT* TO DO AT AN INTERVIEW

The following are real stories about job applicants shared by hiring managers. Needless to say, they didn't get the positions. . . .

▶ "Said if he was hired, he'd teach me ballroom dancing at no charge, and started demonstrating."

▶ "Took three cellular phone calls. Said she had a similar business on the side."

▶ "Man brought in his five children and cat."

▶ "Arrived with a snake around her neck. Said she took her pet everywhere."

▶ "Left his dry cleaner tag on his jacket and said he wanted to show he was a clean individual."

▶ "When asked about loyalty, showed a tattoo of his girlfriend's name."

▶ "After a very long interview, he casually said he had already accepted another position."

▶ "After a difficult question, she wanted to leave the room for a moment to meditate."

Source: Miller (1991). Used with permission.

During the interview, do your best to control your nervousness so that you don't appear hesitant, halting, unsure, or jittery (Ayers, Keereetaweep, Chen, & Edwards, 1998; Tsa, Chen, & Chiu, 2005). As with all competent communication, you should adapt your behavior to be both effective and appropriate. Specifically, sit or stand as the other person directs; lower or raise your vocal tone, rate, and pitch to fit in with the tone and pacing of the other person (DeGroot & Gooty, 2009). Also limit gestures so that you don't distract the interviewer from your words—and relax enough to express genuine smiles (Krumhuber, Manstead, Cosker, Marshall, & Rosin, 2009; Woodzicka, 2008). If you practice with an understanding friend (or even record yourself), you can identify your positive behaviors and minimize any distracting behavior before you go into the interview situation.

If you are still feeling nervous about your first impression, take a look at Box A.1, "What *Not* to Do at an Interview." Even if you wind up failing to make eye contact once or twice or you feel your voice shaking a few times, you can at least say that you weren't the candidate who brought her pet snake to the interview!

Anticipating Common Questions

To discover whether there is a potential match between an applicant and a position, an interviewer typically explores five areas of information as they relate to the specific job:

▶ *Ability.* First, based on the résumé and the interview, questions will assess your experience, education, training, intelligence, and ability to do what the job requires.

▶ *Desire.* Second, questions will focus on your desire or motivation to use your abilities to do a good job by exploring such things as your record of changes in jobs, schools, and majors; reasons for wanting this job; knowledge of the company; and concrete examples of prior success that indicate your drive to achieve.

▶ *Personality.* The third area involves an assessment of your personality and how well you are likely to fit into the position and the organization. Questions are designed to discover your personal goals, degree of independence and self-reliance, imagination and creativity, and ability to manage or lead.

▶ *Character.* A fourth area of judgment is that of character, learning about your personal behavior, honesty, responsibility, and accuracy and objectivity in reports.

▶ *Health.* This is a sensitive topic in interviews; certain questions about your health and medical background are illegal. But if a health issue directly affects your ability to do the job in question, the interviewer may ask. For example, if you are applying for a position at a candy factory, the interviewer may ask if you have a peanut allergy because you would be unable to work in a plant where peanuts are processed.

Some examples of frequently asked interview questions are offered in Table A.5.

● **SOME FIRST** impressions may be memorable, but that probably didn't help this *American Idol* hopeful!

Much as you would practice a speech out loud before officially giving it to a group (Chapter 14), practicing common interview questions aloud (either to yourself or to a willing friend) is a surefire way to increase your confidence in the moment. You may even consider taping yourself in order to get a sense of both your verbal and nonverbal behavior when answering interviewing questions.

<table>
<tr><td>

TABLE A.5

COMMON INTERVIEW QUESTIONS

</td><td>

▶ Tell me about what led you to choose your particular field/your academic major. How satisfied have you been with your choice?

▶ Describe what you understand is required in the position you are applying for. Summarize your qualifications in light of this description.

▶ Why do you want to/did you leave your current employer?

▶ What do you know about our organization that caused you to become interested in us?

▶ Describe something important that you learned from a previous work experience.

▶ Describe a time when you demonstrated initiative in your employment/volunteer position.

▶ Describe a recent project that didn't turn out the way you wanted. How would you make it work if you had another chance at it?

▶ Describe a time when you worked through a difficult coworker situation.

▶ If I gave you this job, what would you accomplish in the first three months?

▶ Are there any questions that you want to ask?

</td></tr>
</table>

Source: Adapted from Greco (1977).

Dealing with Difficult or Unethical Questions

"What fictional character most clearly reflects your outlook on life?" This is an actual question that an interviewer asked a colleague of ours some years ago when she was applying to college. To this day, she remembers the question because she panicked—not because she lacked an answer, but because she wasn't expecting the question. An interviewer might use such unexpected questions to seek insights into the way candidates view themselves or to judge how well they think on their feet. Some questions are simply tricky—they offer a challenge to the interviewee but also a great opportunity to show one's strengths.

Other questions are more than just difficult; they are unethical and sometimes even illegal. Questions that have no direct bearing on job performance and have the potential to lead to discrimination on the basis of race, color, religion, national origin, sex, age, disability, and marital or family status are illegal in the United States. Although an organization whose employees ask illegal questions during employment interviews can be subject to a variety of penalties imposed by the federal government's Equal Employment Opportunity Commission (EEOC), such questions continue to be asked, and applicants must consider how to answer them. There are at least five tactics you can use to respond to illegal questions (Stewart & Cash, 2014). By answering briefly but directly, tactfully refusing to answer, or neutralizing the question, you respond without giving too much information or inviting further inquiry. You can also consider posing a tactful inquiry—that is, asking another question in response—or using the question as an opportunity to present some positive information about yourself. These five strategies are outlined with examples in Table A.6.

Asking Questions of Your Own

Of course, the interviewer should not be the only person asking questions in a job interview. A candidate for any job should arrive at an interview prepared to

what about you?

How Well Do You Interview?

Reviewing your past interviewing behaviors can help you identify where you have excelled and where you need to improve. Using the following five-point questionnaire, evaluate your behaviors in one or more past job interviews: 5 = always; 4 = most of the time; 3 = sometimes; 2 = almost never; and 1= don't know how to do this. Then total your score after completing the questionnaire and see where you fit in.

_____ 1. I dress appropriately for the interview.

_____ 2. I bring a copy of my résumé and a list of references or other relevant material.

_____ 3. I prepare sample answers to questions I am likely to be asked.

_____ 4. I bring notepad and pen but leave electronic devices outside or off and put away.

_____ 5. I greet and make eye contact with the receptionist.

_____ 6. If I need to wait, I sit quietly and patiently (without taking or making phone calls).

_____ 7. I do not chew gum or candy, nor (if I smoke) do I have cigarettes visible.

_____ 8. I make eye contact with the interviewer initially and for a few seconds at a time thereafter.

_____ 9. I firmly shake the interviewer's hand.

_____ 10. I smile and nod appropriately when the interviewer is talking.

_____ 11. I speak loud enough to be heard and keep an even tone to my speech.

_____ 12. I sit upright (not stiffly) and lean slightly forward without crossing my legs.

_____ 13. I listen carefully to the interviewer and do not interrupt.

_____ 14. I avoid frowning and other negative facial expressions.

_____ 15. I answer questions thoroughly.

_____ 16. I speak clearly, avoiding slang.

_____ 17. I check to be sure the interviewer has understood my answer.

_____ 18. I illustrate my answers with specific examples of how I accomplished tasks or managed situations.

_____ 19. If asked, I provide specific examples of the work environment that make me most productive and happy.

_____ 20. When leaving the interview, I smile, shake hands, and thank the interviewer for meeting with me.

74–100 You are likely to make favorable impressions in job interviews by adapting to the situation, preparing yourself and your materials, and monitoring your verbal and nonverbal behavior appropriately throughout the interview.

47–73 You have some strengths in job interviewing but could improve if you spent more time preparing by researching the organization and adapting your verbal and nonverbal behaviors to the situation.

20–46 You probably feel a lot of anxiety as you approach an interview. Work to reduce that anxiety by researching the organization, getting help with your résumé, asking for advice from reputable sources, and conducting mock interviews in which you practice answering behavioral questions with confidence and ease.

TABLE A.6

TACTICS FOR RESPONDING TO ILLEGAL QUESTIONS

Tactic	Sample Illegal Question	Sample Answer
Answer directly but briefly.	"Do you attend church regularly?"	"Yes, I do."
Pose a tactful inquiry.	"What does your husband do?"	"Why do you ask?" (in a nondefensive tone of voice)
Tactfully refuse to answer the question.	"Do you have children?"	"My family plans will not interfere with my ability to perform in this position."
Neutralize.	"What happens if your partner needs to relocate?"	"My partner and I would discuss locational moves that either of us might have to consider in the future."
Take advantage of the question.	"Where were you born?"	"I am quite proud that my background is Egyptian because it has helped me deal effectively with people of various ethnic backgrounds."

Source: Adapted from Stewart & Cash (2011).

ask thoughtful questions about the position and related career paths within the organization, as well as about the organization itself (Johnson, 2010). These questions should indicate that the applicant has done solid homework (your pre-interview research and preparation can shine here) and is able and willing to do a good job for the company.

If you don't have any questions of your own, it often implies disinterest. But avoid focusing on questions about your own compensation and benefits, such as "How much vacation will I get?"—at least not at the first interview. Instead, try to pose thoughtful questions that show your interest while enhancing your understanding of the position and the potential for your future, such as "I noticed in your annual report that you are developing a new training program. If I were hired, would I be in it?" A "final" question that can be very helpful (since it gives you a chance to deal with any hesitations the hiring manager might have) is: "Do you have any questions about my qualifications and abilities to do the job?" And when the interview is wrapping up, be sure to ask what to expect next, such as "What is your time frame for filling this position?"

Following Up After the Interview

You should continue to demonstrate good manners once the interview is over. Thank the interviewer, as well as anyone else you have met within the organization, as you leave. Follow up immediately with a written or e-mailed (or both!) note of appreciation. Thank the interviewer not only for the interview but also for the chance to expand your knowledge of the organization and the industry. Put in writing how excited you are about the chance to work with such a dynamic organization. Send along any support materials that you discussed during the interview (perhaps a writing sample). Since few interviewees remember to send additional materials and a note of thanks, you will certainly stand out.

AND YOU?

Have you ever gone through an interview process to secure a job or admission to college? How prepared did you feel for your first interview? If you could do it again, what would you do differently?

BACK TO ▶ *The Colbert Report*

Back at the beginning of this Appendix, we talked about Comedy Central's *The Colbert Report,* whose satirical "Better Know a District" interviews turn politicians into punchlines. Let's examine the nature of those interviews in the context of what we've learned throughout this Appendix.

▶ Like all interviews, Colbert's interviews are planned and dyadic, but the process of editing them down to just a few minutes makes them less interactive than a real-time interview. Comments and reaction shots are taken out of context, and during editing, Colbert is able to integrate alternative footage that was not part of the actual interview. This gives him an unusual amount of control at the expense of the interviewee.

▶ The format and structure of the interview are also clear to both parties: Colbert's guests are told in advance that he will remain in character and they are asked to play straight against his egomaniacal and satirical alter ego. Participants are well aware that their comments can and will be heavily edited and that much of what they say will be taken out of context.

▶ There's risk in being the butt of a joke, for sure, but in this case, there's also the potential for reward. Politicians might appear on the show to gain exposure for their districts as well as for themselves with Colbert's young, politically active audience. In fact, some research suggests that there is actually a "Colbert Bump"—the host's term for a brief increase in support for politicians following an appearance on Colbert's show (Thompson, 2008).

THINGS TO TRY ▶ Activities

1. LaunchPad for *Real Communication* offers key term videos and encourages self-assessment through adaptive quizzing. Go to **bedfordstmartins.com/realcomm** to get access to:

✓ **LearningCurve** Adaptive Quizzes.

2. Observe a press conference on television. Who is being interviewed? Who is conducting the interview? What is the goal of the press conference? How is control distributed? List five questions that are asked, and label them according to the types listed in this chapter (open, closed, bipolar, primary, and secondary). Did the questioning involve a particular sequence (funnel, inverted funnel, or tunnel)? What did you learn about this interview format by answering these questions?

3. A good source for seeing the subtle differences between legal and illegal job interview questions is at the following job Web site: www.jobweb.com/Interview/help.aspx?id=1343&terms=illegal+questions. Use this site to organize a discussion with your classmates about how you would respond to illegal questions in a job interview. Practice and compare your responses.

4. Assess your goals for employment, and then design (or revise) a résumé for the job that interests you the most. Use the guidelines in this chapter to make it clear and action-oriented. Prepare additional résumés for other positions, keeping in mind that your résumé should highlight the aspects of your training and experience most relevant to each particular position. Discuss your résumé with other students in the class; ask them if your goals are clear. Can they tell what job you are seeking based on the different résumés you show them? Compare your résumé to theirs; although the format may be similar, the content should be unique to you.

5. Create a questionnaire that you will use the next time you visit a physician. Focus your questions on what is already known about your condition and what you want to know about possible treatment. You may also want to ask questions about the training and experience of the physician in a way that will give you the information you want without you seeming contentious. If you have no medical issues, perhaps your questionnaire can be designed for someone else (a child, a friend, or a relative who could benefit from your help).

6. Conduct an in-depth information-gathering interview, and write a four-to-five-page report in which you summarize the information you received. Then comment on what you learned about the interview process. The interview must last at least one hour; the interviewee must be a close acquaintance who is older than you and who must have children (consider interviewing one of your parents). The interview must cover at least two of the following topics:

   a. The person's philosophy of raising children (discipline, finances, making friends, respect for authority, character formation)

   b. The person's political beliefs (political affiliation and commitment, involvement in civic affairs, involvement in government)

   c. The person's religious beliefs, their effect on the person's life, and how these beliefs relate to family life

   d. The person's goals in life and how the person is working to achieve these goals

   e. The person's philosophy of leisure time (ideally how one should spend leisure time versus how this person actually spends it)

Now that you have finished reading this Appendix, you can

Define the nature of interviews:

▶ An **interview** is a transaction between two parties that is deliberate and purposeful (p. 500).

▶ Interviews are planned, goal-driven, structured, dyadic (involving two parties), and transactional (p. 500).

Outline the different types of interviews:

▶ The **information-gathering interview** serves to transfer knowledge from one party to the other (p. 501). **Service-oriented interviews** provide advice or support after getting necessary information (p. 502). **Media interviews** question and analyze people, politics, media, and events (p. 502).

▶ In a **persuasive interview**, questions are designed to change the interviewee's behavior or opinions (p. 502). A **problem-solving interview** deals with problems, tensions, or conflicts (pp. 502–503). **Motivational interviews** are persuasive by eliciting change collaboratively through goal-oriented questions designed to strengthen personal motivation (p. 503).

▶ **Performance appraisals** allow you to review your accomplishments and plan your goals (p. 503).

▶ In **exit interviews**, employers seek to identify organizational problems that might affect employee retention (pp. 503–504).

▶ In a **selection interview**, the primary goal is to fill a position in an organization (p. 504). Selection interviews designed to gain employment are **job interviews** (p. 504).

Describe the three parts of an interview: opening, questions, and conclusion:

▶ An interview should open with the topic and length (the task), something about the interviewer and how the information will be used (the relationship), and who will benefit (the motivation) (p. 504).

▶ Questions and answers accomplish the goals of the interview (pp. 505–506).

▶ An **open question** gives the interviewee freedom to respond in his or her own words (p. 506).

▶ **Closed questions** limit answers to specific choices; **bipolar questions** can be answered with only "yes" or "no" (p. 506).

▶ **Primary questions** introduce new topics; **secondary questions** seek clarification (p. 506).

▶ **Directed questions**, **leading questions**, or **loaded questions** may subtly or even blatantly

influence the answer, whereas **neutral questions** do not hint at a preferred answer (pp. 508–509).

▶ There are three main structures for ordering interview questions: the **funnel sequence**, **inverted funnel sequence**, or **tunnel sequence**, (pp. 509–510).

▶ Interviewers use verbal and nonverbal strategies to conclude and summarize the interview (pp. 510–512).

Devise an interview strategy from the interviewer's point of view:

▶ Consider potential barriers that might be disruptive (pp. 511–512).

▶ Find ways to put the interviewee at ease (p. 512).

▶ Make sure the questions are ethical and appropriate (p. 512).

▶ Remember to listen well and take notes (p. 512).

Prepare for the role of interviewee:

▶ Have a clear idea of what you want to achieve in the interview (p. 512).

▶ Don't arrive tired or hungry. Dress appropriately, and bring any documents you may need (p. 513).

▶ Listen and respond effectively (p. 513).

▶ Share with the interviewer the responsibility of adapting to the situation and the person, being particularly sensitive to cultural differences (pp. 513–514).

Secure job interviews and manage them with confidence:

▶ Locate jobs through networking connections, placement centers, and job-specific sites (pp. 515–516).

▶ **Networking** involves meeting new people through people you already know (p. 515).

▶ Write an effective **résumé** and **cover letter** (pp. 518–520).

▶ Remember that rejection is not uncommon (p. 520).

▶ Impression management involves both verbal and nonverbal behaviors (p. 522).

▶ Come prepared to answer standard questions about your abilities, desire, personality, character, and health (p. 523).

▶ Answer difficult questions honestly but be brief; decline to answer or defuse questions that are unethical (p. 524).

▶ Ask thoughtful questions about the position and the organization (pp. 524, 526).

▶ Follow up with a note of thanks (p. 526).

Today's teens experience more media on a daily basis than their parents did in an entire week. Gary S Chapman/Getty Images

LearningCurve can help you master the material in this chapter. Go to **bedfordstmartins.com/realcomm.**

appendix
B

Understanding Mass and Mediated Communication

Sandie and Chris fell in love during the 1980s, while spending late evenings together watching *Late Night with David Letterman*. Twenty or so years later, their teenage daughter, Abigail, sits in front of a laptop on a Saturday morning, watching streaming clips of Jimmy Fallon sitting behind Letterman's old desk at NBC. She's also monitoring her Facebook page to see if anyone has commented on the picture she created of herself with heartthrob actor Joseph Gordon-Levitt. There are dog-eared copies of her favorite *Hunger Games* books on her bed, and she's reading and posting comments on her blog about the latest film version. Later, she texts her friends to make plans to go to the movies, but not before checking out a few trailers online.

That afternoon, while babysitting her ten-year-old brother, Harry, Abigail spends an hour playing the latest *Legend of Zelda* game with him on their Xbox. Abigail lets Harry play Minecraft on her iPhone while she rewatches her favorite webisodes of *The Lizzie Bennet Diaries* on her laptop. After dinner, she's off to the movies and conscientiously turns off her cell phone—it's the first time she's been disconnected all day.

By the time Abigail goes to sleep, she's experienced more media than her parents did in a week when they were her age. Meanwhile, Chris and Sandie pull up last night's *Tonight Show with Jimmy Fallon* on DVR, grateful that they no longer have to stay up to watch late night television.

Most of us, like Abigail and her family, spend a great deal of time with these interconnecting media technologies, often using two or more simultaneously (Kaiser Family Foundation, 2010; Voorveld & van der Goot, 2013). In this chapter, we look at mass and mediated communication and discuss the blurred lines between the two. We explore the forces that shape how media messages are made, such as the economics of the media industries and the attempts at government influence, and we discuss the potential effects that media have on us as audience members. Finally, we examine the benefits and difficulties that the ever expanding array of media technologies presents for American society, as well as what we can do to cope effectively with our media experience.

The Nature of Media

Although we may talk about "the media" all the time, media are not actually one unified entity. They take many different forms and have many different uses and effects, as we see with Abigail and her family. Some media communicate messages very broadly (such as television), whereas others have more narrowly targeted audiences (ranging from special-interest magazines all the way down to Twitter updates targeting a specific list of followers). But different media also have several qualities in common that distinguish them from face-to-face communication, such as interpersonal or small group interaction.

Defining Mass and Mediated Communication

As we learned in Chapter 1 and have discussed throughout this book, **mediated communication** occurs when there is some technology that is used to deliver messages between sources and receivers. Media may be print (such as newspapers or magazines) or electronic (such as television, radio, or the Internet). But just having our messages mediated does not make communication "mass," as we use many forms of media (phone, e-mail, Facebook, blogs) to communicate in interpersonal, small group, organizational, public, and intercultural contexts. When mediated communication occurs on a very broad scale, we refer to it as **mass communication**. Before the advent of the Internet and social networking, mass communication was characterized by several factors:

▶ First, the types of media that we considered to be mass media had extremely large audiences, typically described in millions (of viewers, readers, listeners, and so on).

▶ Second, the sources of messages tended to be professional communicators. These were people whose livelihoods depended on the success of communication—publishers, actors, writers, reporters, advertising executives, or even the guard at the studio gate.

▶ Third, traditional mass media outlets had less interactivity and opportunity for feedback than other forms of communication, which made it more difficult for sources to know their audience.

 DO THESE LOOK familiar? "Share icons," a common feature of many Web pages, enable the viewer to post and share the page to social media sites, such as Facebook and Twitter. iStock Vectors/Getty Images

These features still apply to many traditional mass media rooted in the publishing, broadcasting, and entertainment industries—but they've also been challenged over the past decade by the increasingly participatory nature of digital communication.

In addition, although traditional mass media are distinct in many ways from the more clearly interpersonal uses of media (such as telephone and e-mail), the changing digital media environment has increasingly blurred the difference between these types of communication. For example, when Abigail posts a status update on Facebook for her friends or forwards a joke over e-mail, her message could potentially wind up being seen by thousands of people—thereby adding a "mass" element to communication that is otherwise mainly interpersonal. Similarly, individual audience members may provide immediate feedback to professional news organizations and TV show creators by posting comments on political and fan blogs—adding interactivity and feedback to what was once a linear form of mass communication.

This merging of traditional mass communication with digital computing and telecommunication technologies is called **media convergence**. Convergence is a critical part of living in a digital media environment, and it affects how mass media content is shaped as well as how mass media messages can influence audiences (Pavlik & McIntosh, 2013).

The Pervasiveness of Media

With broadband Internet access, global satellite technology, and 24/7 news and entertainment content, many of us have mass media content available to us at all times. The average adult spends about 5 hours per day watching TV (Nielsen, 2013) as well as over 5 hours per day on online digital media via computers, smartphones, and tablets (eMarketer, 2013). Children and teens spend about 7.5 hours on a typical day devoted to entertainment media, including TV, movies,

CONNECT

Traditional mass media tended to operate along the lines of the linear model of communication presented in Chapter 1. Messages were sent out and there wasn't much feedback, if any. But emerging technologies provide audiences with increased opportunity for interaction—in fact, many messages depend on audience interaction to become "mass media" messages. Every time you forward a link—or choose not to—you are playing a role in that transaction.

● **IN-FLIGHT BOREDOM** is a thing of the past, as increasingly more airlines equip each individual seat with a TV screen and headset jack, along with basic channels, film rental options, and satellite radio. © Charles Polidano/Touch The Skies/Alamy

computers, cell phone entertainment, video games, music/audio, and print (Kaiser Family Foundation, 2010). Of course, much of this time is spent **media multitasking**—using more than one media type at the same time—and that overlapping usage allows kids and adults to pack nearly 11 hours of content into their daily lives. In fact, in today's digital media environment, it is almost impossible to *escape* media (Pavlik & McIntosh, 2013).

Understanding Mass Media Messages

There are several important factors that help shape the kinds of mass media messages that are made and delivered. In this section, we discuss these key influences, including the economics of a high-risk media industry, the principle of free speech and government regulation, and the role of media bias.

The Business of Media

Media organizations range from tiny production companies to huge international conglomerates (such as Sony) that are parent companies to a number of other large organizations (such as Sony Pictures Entertainment, which itself is the parent company of Columbia Pictures and Screen Gems, among others). Some companies form just for the purpose of making one movie or television show, whereas others, such as Universal and Netflix, oversee, purchase, or distribute thousands of movies and TV programs each year. But all of these companies are businesses—they need to make money to stay in business.

Sources of Revenue

There are two main sources of revenue for the mass media: consumer purchases and advertising. Consumers pay directly for some media messages, such as going to the movies, subscribing to cable, satellite or on-demand online streaming services, and buying magazines, e-books, or DVDs. Advertising dollars also support many of the same media that consumers purchase (magazines, newspapers, cable TV) because purchases alone are not enough to keep these industries afloat. Advertising is also the *sole* support for several other media, including broadcast TV and radio and much of the Internet. Advertising rates are determined mainly by how many people are in the audience (and for how long). For print media, this means circulation size (the number of people who buy or subscribe to newspapers and magazines); for live TV and radio, this primarily means ratings (the number of households that are in the viewing/listening audience for a given time slot, including those who record and watch later the same day). For Web sites and streamed TV content on computers or mobile devices, usage data can get more complicated, but everything gets measured—from unique hits (that is, individual visitors to a site) and the amount of time people spend browsing to people's patterns of

click-through behavior with links. Your "second screen" time matters as well—advertisers want to know, for example, how often while you are watching TV that you also "check in" with an app like Viggle on your mobile device.

Big box office and high ratings are keys to mass media success because mass communication messages are expensive to make and deliver. For example, the production and promotion costs of a half-hour TV sitcom can range from several hundred thousand dollars per episode to several million. Such high investment costs mean that profit can be elusive. In fact, most new TV shows are canceled, few movies become blockbusters, most novels do not become bestsellers, and few albums have strong sales (Vogel, 2011). How, then, do they ever make money? The few blockbuster movies, bestselling books, and hit television shows or albums must make up for all the rest. In economics, this is called **exponentiality**: relatively few items bring most of the income, while the rest add only a little (Vogel, 2011). Across the media industries, about 80 to 90 percent of mass media revenue comes from only 10 to 20 percent of the products made.

Broad Versus Narrow Appeal

For the biggest of the mass media, network television, messages must have very broad appeal to attract the millions of viewers that the networks need in order to sell profitable advertising time. The Super Bowl is such a widely popular event that the cost of advertising is extremely expensive: in 2014, a thirty-second commercial during the Super Bowl cost on average $4 million. But prime-time network TV (ABC, CBS, NBC, Fox, and CW) requires programming that attracts a very large audience on a regular basis. The traditional way for networks to capture broad audiences has been to rely on content that is often described as **low culture**—entertainment that appeals to most people's baser instincts, typified by lurid, sensational images and news stories charged with sex, violence, scandal, and abuse (Berger, 2007). In addition, the networks have relied on programming that doesn't require a great deal of thought or cultural sophistication, leading critics to echo the sentiments of former Federal Communications Commission (FCC) chairman Newton Minow when, in 1961, he first called commercial television a "vast wasteland" (Minow, 1961; Minow & Cate, 2003).

But, wait, you say: there are a lot of popular shows on television right now that are intellectually stimulating, well written, and impressively produced. Scholars agree. Jason Mittel (2006), for example, makes the case that the landscape of television during the last twenty years has actually gotten "smarter." He notes that, although there is much popular content on TV that remains highly conventional, the past two decades have seen a huge increase in critically acclaimed and popular TV shows with **narrative complexity**—complicated plots and connections between characters, a blurring of reality and fantasy, and time that is not always linear or chronological. Beginning with innovative shows like *The X-Files* (1993–2002) and *Buffy the Vampire Slayer* (1997–2003) and continuing with programs like *24* (2001–2010; restarted in 2014), *Doctor Who* (since 2005), and *Game of Thrones* (since 2011), intricate plots, subplots, and "story arcs" weave between stand-alone episodes and continuous serial storytelling (Mittel, 2006). Many of these shows give you a cognitive "workout" because you must think carefully to make sense of what is happening (Johnson, 2005).

What spurred this trend? The explosion of media choices—through cable channels, DVDs, and now online streaming—has allowed audiences to become more demanding, and there is money to be made in meeting that demand (Johnson, 2005). Many of these are *hit* shows, after all. But even without major hits, uniquely appealing shows are possible because of another major industry trend. **Narrowcasting** (also called *niche marketing*) is the process of targeting narrower, more specific audiences. With the diverse array of specialty media

---

EVALUATINGCOMMUNICATIONETHICS

THINK ABOUT THIS

Music Piracy

You and your friend Zach are really into a local band called Spikefish. You've attended their concerts and bought their T-shirts. Spikefish has begun to gather a larger following as well, and their songs are now available to purchase through online music sites, such as iTunes and Amazon. Zach tells you that you don't have to buy the songs—he's found a Web site that allows you to download them for free. Of course, it's illegal not to buy the songs, but Zach says that everybody does it, and as long as you don't download too much too often, you're probably not going to get caught. He gets a lot of his music this way, from struggling new bands like Spikefish as well as mega-successful established artists like U2.

Zach's argument is that you're not really hurting the band by illegally downloading music because it's the corporations—the record labels—that make the real money, and he doesn't care about them. He also says that in some ways, illegal downloading helps the bands—by making people more interested in their music, more likely to attend their concerts, and perhaps more likely to buy some of their music legally in the future. You think that bands deserve to earn the fruit of their labors and talents, and you know that it's wrong to engage in what is clearly illegal conduct. But you also really want your music and it seems so easy to get away with illegal downloading. What should you do? What do you say to Zach?

❶ Does the likelihood of getting caught matter in your decision whether or not to download? Why or why not? Does it matter that illegal downloading is widespread?

❷ What do you think about Zach's argument that stealing from a "corporation" is more defensible than stealing from an individual artist or band? Is that reasonable? And regardless of that, what adverse impacts might there also be for the artists themselves?

❸ Does it make a difference that some bands are struggling new artists, while others are multimillionaires? Why or why not?

outlets, media industries can tap into multiple groups of viewers that, although smaller, are loyal and often passionate audiences (Mittel, 2006). For example, streaming services like Netflix enable shows to generate a loyal fan base. Viewers can watch their favorites repeatedly or "binge" watch—meaning to view episode after episode in one sitting. Fans can also provide reviews or discuss show content online with others. It takes a unique show to withstand this level of viewer scrutiny (Gay, 2014).

Niche programming is also increasingly possible because of sources of revenue besides traditional advertising. Networks can feature advertisers' products within the shows themselves, of course, but even more income is being raised in deals made with international broadcasters and with streaming services like Hulu (Adalian, 2013). Thus, although it's not surprising that a megahit like Fox's *American Idol* (with an average of twelve million viewers each week) pulls in solid advertising revenue (Faughnder, 2014), shows with smaller, dedicated audiences (like FX's *Justified* and PBS's British import *Sherlock*, both with just about four million viewers each episode) can still be profitable (Kissell, 2014).

Of course, narrowcasting doesn't necessarily result in more intellectually demanding or sophisticated content. Many specialty cable channels (such as the youth-oriented MTV) have plenty of low-culture programming (*Teen Mom* perhaps?). But the fact that audiences are now spread across a wide spectrum of specialized entertainment choices (Stelter, 2011) means that the media industries must capitalize on the opportunities presented by digital technologies in order to remain profitable in an increasingly fragmented media landscape.

Minimizing Risk

The desire for an audience often means minimizing risk wherever possible. The TV networks do this in part by promoting content that they believe reflects the cultural and moral values of their audiences. They do extensive audience research, attempting to understand the passions, commitments, values, and relational bonds of viewers and listeners. They also engage in **self-censorship**, carefully monitoring their own content and eliminating messages that might

● **NARROWCAST TV** programs *Justified* and *Sherlock* each have amassed unique and loyal audiences to enable them to compete with more mainstream TV fare. (left) Prashant Gupta/© FX Network/Courtesy: Everett Collection; (right) Colin Hutton/© BBC/Hartswood Filmas/Courtesy Everett Collection

● **RATHER THAN** diminishing her fame, Miley Cyrus's behavior brought her more notoriety. Jeff Kravitz/FilmMagic for MTV/Getty Images

offend their viewers or sponsors. If network executives believe a show's script is too explicit or its message is too morally risky, they may insist on rewrites or prevent the show from airing altogether.

The fear of offending viewers or advertisers does not mean that media avoid controversy. Indeed, controversy can be used to increase ratings. We discussed earlier that lurid, sensational coverage is common across news media outlets, whether about celebrity sex scandals and drug overdoses or political corruption and gruesome murder cases. Entertainment programming can also benefit from controversy—two weeks after singer Miley Cyrus gave a sexually provocative performance at the MTV Music Awards in 2013, the "Wrecking Ball" video she released on YouTube received more than ten million hits in a matter of hours ("Back to Twerk," 2013). And her subsequent appearance hosting *Saturday Night Live* boosted that show's ratings to its highest in months (Alter, 2013). But controversy doesn't always translate into high ratings or long-term success.

Perhaps the most prominent way media industries try to minimize risk is to repeat what has already proven to work. Although they do aim to discover some fresh new idea that will lead to the next big blockbuster or hit TV show, that kind of success is difficult to predict in advance. Media professionals often count on the sure thing: the products or ideas that have *already been* successful. Thus, profitable films—from *Iron Man* to *Toy Story*—are usually followed by a sequel (or two, or three . . .). Popular films are also frequently derived from successful novels (*Hunger Games*), graphic novels and comic book franchises (*The Avengers*), or previously made films (*Carrie, RoboCop*). For television, this means copycat shows (the hugely successful *American Idol* is an Americanized version of the British hit *Pop Idol*) and spin-offs (*Family Guy* begat *The Cleveland Show*). Although some such outings are failures, studios continue to mine familiar stories and characters that they know audiences already know and enjoy.

Free Speech and Media Bias

The infamous 2004 Super Bowl halftime show featured a moment that entered the cultural lexicon as a "wardrobe malfunction" when performer Justin Timberlake pulled off part of Janet Jackson's bustier, exposing her breast. CBS stations around the country faced major fines for indecency. After years of legal battling, CBS eventually prevailed and did not have to pay the fines, mainly because the courts found ambiguity in how indecency rules were being enforced at that time (Denniston, 2012). The debate continues today over how much *right* the government has to fine networks or censor objectionable messages—a controversy rooted in competing interpretations of constitutional law.

The First Amendment

The First Amendment to the U.S. Constitution states, "Congress shall make no law . . . abridging the freedom of speech, or of the press." The principle here is that news media and individual citizens of a well-functioning republic need to be free to criticize their government and speak their views. This means that, even when speech is offensive, the government cannot ban it, punish it, or restrict it, except under very rare circumstances. Interestingly, this doesn't mean that the U.S. government hasn't *tried* to exercise control over media content. But its attempts at regulation are often struck down by the courts as unconstitutional (such as bans on pornography and heavy regulation of political campaign speech). The regulations that U.S. courts allow mostly involve rules about technical issues, such as broadcast signals or ownership of stations and copyright laws. In effect, the U.S. government actually has little direct influence on media *content* compared to the governments of other countries.

Do all of the U.S. media benefit from this protection? The courts have generally held that creative expression *is* protected speech, whether in print, on TV, in movies, or on the Internet. However, the courts have also upheld some content regulations for some kinds of media, particularly broadcasting, as we'll see in the next section.

Electronic Media Regulation

There is an important legal difference between broadcast signals and cable or satellite channels. **Broadcasting** refers to signals carried over the airwaves from a station transmitter to a receiver. For radio, these are the AM/FM stations you might listen to in your car. For television, they are the major networks (ABC, CBS, NBC, FOX, and The CW) and independent local stations. Most cable and satellite companies now carry these signals to you, or you stream their programs over the Internet, so the broadcast TV channels today look just like every other channel on TV or like any show you might watch online.

However, because broadcasting frequencies are limited and because the airwaves themselves are essentially a public resource, the government—through the Federal Communications Commission (FCC)—can regulate which private companies may broadcast over them. In order to keep their broadcasting licenses, broadcasters must agree to serve the public interest. Cable and satellite providers, on the other hand, have not been subject to the same kinds of regulations.

Although the First Amendment right to free speech and press does apply to broadcasters, broadcast television networks and radio stations are subject to some speech restrictions. The courts have held that the government can impose restrictions that serve a "compelling government interest" (that is, the government has a really good reason for doing it, such as to protect children), and only when the regulation is the "least restrictive" way to serve that interest (that is, the government cannot ban all adult TV content just to be able to protect kids from seeing it) (*Action for Children's Television* v. *FCC*, 1991).

Recall the Janet Jackson Super Bowl incident discussed earlier. CBS stations were originally fined because the FCC said that the dance number violated a ban on broadcast **indecency**. *Indecency* legally means "patently offensive . . . sexual or excretory activities or organs" (*Federal Communications Commission* v. *Pacifica Foundation*, 1978), but in practice it means talking about or showing sexual or other bodily functions in a very lewd or vulgar way. This is a very subjective evaluation, of course, which is why broadcasters frequently end up fighting over their fines in court.

● WHEN *SATURDAY NIGHT LIVE* premiered on broadcast network NBC in 1975, the original cast of "Not Ready for Prime Time Players" was relegated to a late-night airtime to allow for its often boundary-pushing sketch comedy. Photofest

The Supreme Court has upheld the government's expressed interest in protecting children from indecent content (*Federal Communications Commission* v. *Pacifica Foundation*, 1978). However, the courts have also said that the ban must be limited only to specific times of day (such as 6 A.M. to 10 P.M.) when children are likely to be in the audience (*Action for Children's Television* v. *FCC*, 1995). Remember that this ban does not apply to cable and satellite channels or to the Internet—so MTV, Comedy Central, and YouTube, for example, could

COMMUNICATIONACROSSCULTURES

The Bechdel Test

Think of the last movie you saw. Now ask yourself three questions:

1. Does the film include at least two female characters that have names?
2. Do these characters ever speak to each other?
3. Do these characters ever speak to each other about anything other than a man?

Chances are, the answer to at least one of these questions will be no. Way back in 1985, cartoonist Allison Bechdel outlined the three preceding simple rules for assessing gender bias (Ulaby, 2008). The "Bechdel Test" (or "Bechdel Rule"), originally a joke in a panel of Bechdel's comic "Dykes to Watch Out For," developed a life of its own, it seems, when people began to realize just how few films were able to meet these three simple criteria. In the thirty years since it was introduced, the Bechdel test has become a popular—albeit not entirely scientific—lens through which to examine bias in film. It has been embraced by feminist scholars, media critics, and most recently, a number of Swedish cinemas that have incorporated the Bechdel test into their film rating system (Associated Press, 2013).

The criteria outlined set a pretty low bar for the inclusion of women in films, and yet a shocking number of popular and critically acclaimed films still fail to clear it. Of the fifty highest-grossing films of 2013, for example, a mere seventeen clearly passed the test; seven barely passed, and the rest failed completely (Waldman, 2014). And of nine Academy Award nominees for best picture in 2014, only three passed (*American Hustle, Dallas Buyers Club, and Philomena*) (Dewey, 2014).

The Bechdel test was never intended to assess the quality of a film or to critique the way films portray women. Many great movies featuring strong female leads (like 2013's *Gravity* or 1998's *Run Lola Run*) fail the test, while some with decidedly unfeminist messages manage to pass (many a movie has been saved on the basis of a conversation about shoes or hair). And, of course, some stories are simply not about women (the plot, setting, and time frame of films like *Twelve Angry Men* or *Saving Private Ryan* would not be expected to support a large female cast). But the test does manage to shine a light on the fact that most Hollywood films are produced primarily for and often centered on men and concerned with male stories.

THINK ABOUT THIS

❶ Do you think that the Bechdel test is a good way of assessing gender bias? What are its limits? Which of the three questions do you think is the most important?

❷ If you changed the test to focus on other populations—for example, asking if there are at least two characters of color that talk to each other about something other than a white person—do you think that fewer or more films would pass?

❸ What does it say about popular media that a set of criteria presented in an offbeat comic could evolve into a test used by scholars and critics alike?

choose to air nudity or use bad language at any time (depending, of course, on whether they think their advertisers or audiences would approve).

Although indecency rules are what you may hear most about, there are also other important areas of media regulation. Much FCC action is directed at how the media corporations conduct their business, such as approving or denying mergers. The FCC has also recently expanded its influence over the Internet, including controversial attempts to limit the control that Internet service providers have over the online traffic that flows through their services.

Media Bias

As you'll recall from Chapters 1 and 2, our own thoughts, opinions, and experiences influence the messages we send as well as the way we interpret the messages we receive. These communication biases are also at work when it comes to mass media. Most scholars agree that media sources—both news and entertainment—express some degree of bias in their viewpoints and in their content. News coverage of a presidential campaign, for example, can be quite different, depending on the political leanings of the network or news organization doing the reporting as well as the personal ideologies of individual reporters, editors, and producers.

In the latter half of the twentieth century, news organizations across the mass media generally expressed commitment to the goal of objectivity—that is, they were primarily concerned with facts and uninfluenced by personal or political bias, prejudice, or interpretation. Although embraced as a laudable goal, both consumers and journalists over the years have questioned whether this goal has been (or even can be) met (Duffy, Thorson, & Vultee, 2009; Figdor, 2010). In any case, today's media are increasingly embracing more partisan news in order to compete in a crowded marketplace (Groeling, 2013; Iyengar & Hahn, 2009). Cable news networks tend to narrowcast to one viewpoint or another in search of higher ratings, and online news sources represent a wide range of ideologically partial reporting—from the *Breitbart* series of Web sites on the right to the *Huffington Post* on the left. Thus the variety of ideologies represented by media today makes it difficult to pin any particular bias on "mainstream" media as a whole.

That does not mean, however, that bias is unimportant. Studies suggest that when presented with coverage of a given issue, partisans of both parties perceive the news to be biased against their own side, especially when they feel a

● **LIBERAL COMMENTATOR** Rachel Maddow and conservative Sean Hannity hail from opposite ends of the spectrum of politicized news coverage, and they are not subtle in their partisanship. (left) The Kobal Collection/NBC-TV/Goldstein, Ali; (right) AP Photo/Fox News Channel, Shealah Craighead

AND YOU?

Where do you get your news? Do you detect any bias on the part of your sources—that is, do you find yourself agreeing or disagreeing with the things they say or write? Is there a difference between news reports and opinion shows?

CONNECT

In Chapter 2, we discuss how schemas help us to make sense of our world. When consuming media, we should remember that messages are usually framed in a way to appeal (or not!) to us. For this reason, it's often a good idea to view news sources from a variety of viewpoints to help form a more fully realized perspective.

CONNECT

As we learned in Chapter 6, the listening process involves a series of decisions about which messages we will select and attend to. This process is especially important in how we process mass media messages—the sheer volume of messages means that media must present appealing, clever, and memorable messages in order to compete for our attention.

strong personal connection to the issue (Matthes, 2013) or to their party identity (Hartmann & Tanis, 2013). In a nutshell, that means we tend to see those with whom we agree as less biased than those with whom we disagree.

Critics on the right *and* the left agree that bias in the media is also a function of the economics and constraints of the news-gathering process itself (Farnsworth & Lichter, 2010). The 24/7 news cycle with multiple technological outlets to fill may lead to overreliance on easy sources—particularly spokespersons for government or interest groups. Journalists must also simplify complex issues and put them into a context that audiences understand (Scheufele & Tewksbury, 2007). **Framing** refers to the *way* issues in the news get presented in order to relate to audiences' existing schemas (Scheufele & Iyengar, 2012). For example, during election campaigns, the news often frames each candidate's actions as though they were maneuvers in a "horse race" (for example, "Will this new revelation pull the candidate ahead? What will the opposition do to try to stay in the lead?"). Such framing is important because public impressions of candidates and campaign events may become a function of who is ahead or behind in the "race," rather than an evaluation of each candidate's detailed positions on issues.

Effects of Mass Media

James gets in trouble at school for trying to kickbox his classmates like they do in video games. Olivia watches a lot of televised high school dramas and worries that appearing too "smart" will make boys not like her. Are media messages influencing the attitudes and behaviors of these kids? We have already seen how audiences and other factors shape media messages. In this section, we will explore the research and theories on how mass media messages might actually shape *us*.

Selectivity and the Active Audience

Do you remember all the commercials you saw last night? Did you read every status update that every one of your friends posted on Facebook? As we discussed in Chapter 6, we make specific choices about which messages we will select and attend to. This selectivity means that audiences are not passive sponges that absorb everything media throw at them. Rather, many communication scholars argue that audiences, even children, are instead active cognitive processors of information (Huston, Bickham, Lee, & Wright, 2007). Being active does not mean, however, that we critically evaluate the messages we see (although we can certainly do that); it means that we look for cues that tell us whether something on TV (or in other media) is interesting, relevant, or otherwise worth noticing (Valkenburg & Vroone, 2004). It also refers to the idea that different people have different reactions and interpretations of media messages (Morley, 2006). The concepts of selectivity and an active audience suggest that media effects are much more limited than we might otherwise believe.

Uses and Gratifications

Rather than looking at what media do *to us*, the **uses and gratifications perspective** focuses on what *we do* with media—that is, the way we make media choices (uses) in order to satisfy our needs and goals (gratifications) (Blumler & Katz, 1974). We might watch comedies or fantasy to escape our troubles at work, or we might search the Internet for updated information on local tornado warnings. In fact, media are competing with ways to meet our needs—when we are feeling lonely, we can get together with friends or phone a family member. Media are also competing with each other—we can check Facebook, watch a beloved TV character, or tune in to our favorite sports commentator (Dimmick, Chen, & Li, 2004).

Of course, what solves loneliness for *you* might just be escape or entertainment to *me*. It's all in the individual's perceptions of the media choices available. For example, studies of gender and video game use find that male college students play for far more hours than do females. Both men and women report that they are motivated to play by the desire to beat the game, but men are more motivated by the value of the game for competition and social interaction with other guys (Greenberg, Sherry, Lacklan, Lucas, & Holmstrom, 2010; Lucas & Sherry, 2004). Women presumably prefer other options for social interaction.

When we come to *expect* that media will serve certain needs, it can lead to **media dependence** (Ball-Rokeach, 1998). Certainly in times of crisis, such as during emergencies like earthquakes, tornadoes, and blizzards, most of us become dependent on media for information and connection to the world. But even without crisis, many people find that they depend on media for specific needs. One national survey found that one-third to one-half of respondents said that they depend on the Internet for in-depth information about health, science, or business issues on a weekly basis (Riffe, Lacy, & Varouhakis, 2008). Some people have become so obsessed with playing online video games that Internet Gaming Disorder was recently included by the American Psychiatric Association as a condition that warrants further research (Internet Gaming Disorder, 2013). This research suggests that what the viewer or listener *brings* to the media experience is important.

Reinforcing Existing Attitudes

One important way in which selectivity limits the effects of media is our tendency to select and evaluate media in a way that confirms our existing views. For example, we often choose our news sources based on whether we anticipate that they will agree with us. In an experimental study of the effects of perceived agreement on news choices, Democrats and liberals preferred CNN and NPR and avoided Fox News, whereas Republicans and conservatives did the opposite (Iyengar & Hahn, 2009). Similarly, when we watch political debates, we tend to interpret our preferred candidate as the winner, and we tend to remember the information that confirms our previous opinions about the candidates.

Increasingly, diverse media outlets make it easier than ever to select and attend only to the entertainment and news messages that already agree with us—political blogs, fan forums, TV and radio analysts, and partisan cable and online news. Some critics lament the fact that we can so easily insulate ourselves from opposing views, arguing that it polarizes us as citizens and is unhealthy for democracy (Sunstein, 2007). But the case can also be made that the ability of audiences to self-filter messages is empowering and is at least better than having others (such as professional media editors or the government) do all the filtering *for* us.

CONNECT

In addition to our news choices, we tend to choose entertainment media that show positive portrayals of our ingroup members (as discussed in Chapter 5). We like to see ourselves presented in media, and narrowcasting is an attempt by entertainment media to capitalize on this tendency by reaching out to different co-cultures.

The Third Person Effect

Another way that selectivity may limit media effects is the fact that we tend to overestimate how much influence media actually have on people. The **third person effect** is a well-documented tendency we have to assume that negative media messages and bias have a much greater influence on *other people* than on ourselves or people we think are like us (Davison, 1983; Sun, Pan, & Shen, 2008). The third person effect can lead to censorship when we believe it will protect "other" people who we (or our government or religious community) don't think are able to handle certain media messages. A recent study finds that the effect is particularly strong for social networking—we think others are more influenced by Facebook than we ourselves are (Zhang & Daugherty, 2009). With all media, you need to be aware that you may be overestimating the effect on others or underestimating the effect on yourself (or both).

Influences on Attitudes and Behaviors

Although selectivity may give audiences some power and make them resistant to being influenced by media, there are several areas where media *do* have more substantial influences on audiences. These include encouraging people to imitate behavior, cultivating cultural attitudes, and setting the political issue agenda.

Social Cognitive Theory

According to **social cognitive theory**, we learn behavior by watching the behaviors of those whom we have identified as models (Bandura, 2001). We must first attend to the modeled behavior, then remember it, and then have the ability and motivation to imitate it. We are particularly likely to imitate modeled behaviors when we see that the models are rewarded for what they do—when your big brother gets lots of praise for playing the guitar, you then try to play the guitar! How does this apply to media effects? Media provide many modeled behaviors for children and adults to learn from and imitate, both positive (sharing, giving to charity) and negative (violence). Decades of experimental studies looking at the effects of television violence on children's behavior have found that children are more likely to be aggressive after viewing rewarded rather than punished TV violence (see Bushman & Huesmann, 2001, for a review). Most studies are limited to examining short-term effects (behavior right after viewing), so it is unclear whether children would make long-term behavior changes after a one-time viewing experience, especially if they later get in trouble at home or school for being aggressive.

There are several factors besides rewards and punishments that can increase the likelihood of imitating behaviors we witness on television (violent or otherwise). Children are more likely to imitate behavior that is realistic (as opposed to fantasy), justified (the character has a good reason for doing it), and committed by characters the children identify with (the hero or villain) (Wilson et al., 2002). The good news is that providing strong, likeable, and realistic *positive* role models for your children can promote good behavior. But remember that children are not "sponges" of media behavior—their own unique interests and motivations also affect their interpretations of media models and their likelihood of imitation (Ferguson & Dyck, 2012).

AND YOU?

Do you think that your communication behavior is influenced by media messages? What about the clothes you wear? Your use of slang? Might you be modeling behaviors based on media messages without even realizing it?

Cultivation Theory

If you watch a lot of reality TV about cosmetic surgery, are you more likely to believe that plastic surgery is normal and acceptable? George Gerbner's **cultivation theory** indeed argues that a steady, long-term diet of heavy television viewing results in perceptions of reality that match the (distorted) view of reality presented on television (Gerbner, Gross, Morgan, & Signorielli, 1994). Originally developed in the 1970s, the theory did not distinguish between different kinds of programs; it treated the entire TV world as basically the same—dominated by messages about crime and violence. The theory proposed that the more TV you watch, the more you will develop a perception of the world as a scary, violent place. Studies showed that individuals who watch a lot of television were indeed more likely to be afraid of crime or of walking alone at night, to estimate greater police activity, and to mistrust other people (Gerbner, Gross, Morgan, & Signorielli, 1994).

However, the explosion of television channels, genres, and new media has led to criticism of the idea that all television messages are the same, and research during the past two decades has largely shifted toward looking at correlations between attitudes and heavy viewing of certain *types* of media messages—young girls who consume a lot of "thin media" messages having poorer body image, for example (Harrison & Cantor, 1997; Tiggemann, 2005). But critics of cultivation theory argue not only that the effects are pretty small but also that it is impossible to determine whether *any* of the correlations that cultivation studies find are actually media effects (Nabi, 2009). This is because the causal direction could arguably be going the other way: girls who have poor body image or low self-esteem are likely to seek out messages that confirm their views (that is, by finding thin models to compare themselves to). Similarly, people who are already accepting of plastic surgery are the very people most likely to want to watch shows about it. Still, it is important to be aware of our media "diet," as this may well be connected to the kinds of stereotypes, attitudes, and perceptions we are developing or reinforcing.

Agenda Setting

Whether or not media have the ability to cultivate our attitudes about issues, there is evidence that media *do* have an impact on what issues we think about in the first place. **Agenda setting** is the idea that extensive media coverage of a particular issue or event, such as health care reform in Washington or a major storm on the Eastern seaboard, will "set the agenda" for what issues people are thinking and talking about (see McCombs, 2005). Issues that do not get much coverage will not seem very important.

Agenda setting is important because we use the issues we are thinking about to evaluate political leaders and potential policy decisions (Scheufele & Iyengar, 2012). For example, when the troubled launch of the "healthcare.gov" Web site was getting nonstop news coverage in the fall of 2013, people tended to evaluate President Obama based on how they thought he was handling health care reform (as opposed to how he might have been dealing with other issues). Indeed, when his ratings dropped on his handling of "Obamacare" (as the Affordable Care Act is known) and the Web site rollout, his overall approval ratings also dropped (Blumenthal & Edwards-Levy, 2014). Obama's decisions to delay enrollment and employer deadlines and Democrats' efforts to distance themselves

AND YOU?

In what ways have mediated messages shaped your perceptions of the world? Do you think your views of different people (and places) may have been shaped by what you have seen in entertainment or news media?

CONNECT

If you consider your mass media experience as part of your overall culture and relational history—as explained in Chapter 1—it's easy to see how your perceptions of co-cultures that are different from your own might be shaped by media messages. But the mass media can challenge stereotypes as easily as they can reinforce them. Modern television shows in particular feature diverse casts and story lines and may help to broaden some individuals' cultural horizons.

● **DUE IN GREAT** part to vanity-focused TV programs and reality stars, plastic surgery—even in extreme forms—is perceived as almost routine, particularly among females. JB Lacroix/WireImage/Getty Images

from the law were likely a reaction to the heavy press scrutiny at the time, along with continuing coverage of other problems with the health care law (Parker, 2014). As news coverage of "Obamacare" rises or falls in the future, the issue of health care policy may resurface or fade as an important political battle.

With a diverse range of media news outlets available online, we might predict that media would no longer provide *an* agenda but would instead result in people selecting their own news agendas. But there is evidence that traditional media do still have an agenda-setting effect, although it is weakened for people who use multiple online news sources (Shehata & Strömbäck, 2013). In addition, agenda-setting effects may be a two-way process online, in which news stories encourage people to search for those issues online, while people's own online searches or Facebook or Twitter posts also influence the coverage in the news media (Ragas, Tran, & Martin, 2014).

Converging Media Technologies

Earlier in this chapter, we argued that today's media are converging—the lines between traditional mass communication and digital computing and telecommunication technologies are increasingly blurry (Pavlik & McIntosh, 2013). In this section, we explore the benefits and challenges for society of the increased interactivity and selectivity that media convergence allows.

Democratic and Social Participation

One benefit of converging media is the great potential for individuals and groups to participate more actively in the political process and contribute more directly to the culture. With traditional media, only the professionals (news organizations, television networks, studios, and so on), acting as **gatekeepers**, control the creation and distribution of information and entertainment. Those outlets require enormous capital investment as well as highly technical production skills and capability. Internet use, on the other hand, doesn't require the same degree of skill, money, or access. This means that individuals online have the opportunity to discover and provide competing voices to those of traditional media; they also have a means to connect with others locally and globally.

Connecting Marginalized Voices

How did friends, relatives, rescue workers, and relief organizations make connections in the wake of Hurricane Sandy? How did revolts in Tunisia and Egypt so quickly escalate to thousands of citizens in the streets, eventually resulting in their governments toppling despite efforts to squelch Internet access and limit news media coverage? And how do fans of quirky shows, people dealing with rare illnesses, and individuals seeking specific goals even find each other? The use of the Web, e-mail, texting, and social networking (in combination with traditional modes of communication) allow groups that would not get much media coverage or whose members are not centralized geographically to better connect, provide alternative sources of information, and spread the word about their causes. They may also build **social capital**, which refers to the valuable resources (such as information and support) that come from having connections and relationships among people (Williams, 2006). Social networking via Facebook in particular has been shown to increase the strength of what would otherwise be weak ties among acquaintances or friends who have moved to different geographic locations (Ellison, Steinfeld, & Lampe, 2007). Although there are

WIREDFORCOMMUNICATION

New Life on the Internet?

Imagine you are surfing the Internet and happen to link to a fan site devoted to a television program. There are forums where fans review episodes, discuss the actors, or explain the themes. The site also notes upcoming events or conferences in cities across the United States, and it even has a section where fans submit their own creative works related to the show (fiction, poetry, artwork). This is not surprising, of course, as the Internet is littered with such venues. But what might surprise you is that all of this fan activity is for a show that ended almost a decade ago. *Buffy the Vampire Slayer* ran on American television from 1997 to 2003, and despite achieving only modest ratings across its broadcast career, it has remained a pop culture juggernaut through its Internet fandom afterlife. There is even a devotion to the show among some media scholars, who publish academic analyses of *Buffy* in books and journals (Levine & Parks, 2007).

The Internet certainly did not invent the fandom experience—*Star Trek* and *Star Wars* fans have been stapling together "fanzines" and attending science fiction conventions for decades—but the Internet has facilitated the formation and maintenance of such fan groups. Online fandom allows fans to more easily connect with one another for companionship or to develop personal relationships. The Web also allows dedicated fans repeated viewing of TV shows, along with forums for them to dissect and scrutinize every scene and every line (Johnson, 2005). This may help shows to build and maintain their audiences while they are on the air and after they have ended. *Lost* ended in 2010, but the rewatching and reanalyzing remain in full force on the Lostpedia wiki and several other fan sites. More recently, the Internet has emerged as not just an organizational tool for disgruntled fans of canceled shows but also as a new channel for resurrecting these shows. In 2013, the streaming service Netflix fulfilled the wishes of millions of *Arrested Development* fans by producing a long-awaited fifth season and making it available all at once for immediate binge-watching. Producers of one long-missed series did them one better, inviting fans to put their money where their mouths are: the long-awaited *Veronica Mars* film (2014) was almost entirely fan-funded in one of the fastest Kickstarter campaigns ever (Cohen, 2013).

THINK ABOUT THIS

❶ Have you ever contributed fan fiction or comments to a fan blog or forum for one of your favorite shows? Why or why not? Why do some fans get involved online and others do not?

❷ Not all popular or critically acclaimed shows end up with a strong Internet afterlife. What do you think it is about a TV show or movie that might cause it to be singled out for the kind of devotional attention lavished on *Buffy*, *Lost*, or *Veronica Mars*?

❸ Is it ethical for filmmakers to accept financial backing from fans rather than backing from traditional sources? What is the difference between an investment in a film and a Kickstarter campaign?

❹ To what extent do you think that creators of TV shows or movies are aware of the commentary in online fandom groups? If you were a writer for a TV show, would you be inclined to adapt your production to meet the expectations and preferences of pertinent fandom groups?

● **WHETHER IT'S A** funny photo of your cat or a "Harlem Shake" flash mob video, all it takes is enough social media attention for something to go viral. Mike Brown/ZUMA Press/Newscom

CONNECT

In an age when anyone has access to mass media, public speaking becomes an even more important skill. Social media give voice to those whom traditional, more linear forms of mass media tended to ignore. And the opportunity for instant audience feedback—in the form of responses, re-tweets, and replies—makes social media an especially interactive forum for those who seek public access.

some groups or individuals with whom we would probably rather *not* have such connectedness—such as hate groups, terrorists, and sexual predators—remember that open access means facilitating the participation of many different voices, not just the ones we like.

Empowering Individuals

Even artist Andy Warhol, who once predicted that eventually, everyone would have the opportunity to be famous for fifteen minutes, might have been surprised by the ease with which anyone can put themselves into media today. Blogs, YouTube, Twitter, and even professional news organizations offer opportunities for **citizen journalists** to report and comment on events in their communities. Even viewer comments on a news show's Facebook page can influence the stories that later get covered (Jacobson, 2013).

Individuals can also contribute their own entertainment messages online. Many forms of **user-generated content** have emerged, ranging from simple home videos uploaded to YouTube to elaborate mash-ups of popular songs or artworks (Pavlik & McIntosh, 2013). Content that manages to break into mass media culture is said to have "gone viral"—that is, spread from user to user (like an infection) via Web links or social media. Teen idol Justin Bieber first rose to fame in this manner, while others have more short-lived viral lives (such as Norwegian comedy duo Ylvis wondering "What does the fox say?" or office workers doing the "Harlem Shake"). Social networking on Facebook or Twitter has also allowed individuals to elevate their everyday personal lives to become more public ones. Our status updates and photos can alert everyone we know (and friends of friends of people we know) to what we are doing, feeling, and thinking. We even use social networking to feel more connected to the personal thoughts and feelings of celebrities, limited of course to the thoughts they purposely release to us via Twitter.

In short, media convergence enables individual voices to contribute to news, politics, and culture. Although the quality of their messages varies greatly, there is some sense that allowing more voices to contribute to what has become known as the **marketplace of ideas**—the open forum in which ideas compete—is beneficial for society as a whole (*Abrams* v. *United States*, 1919).

Barriers to Participation

Media convergence may open up access to social, political, and cultural participation, but only for those people who are willing and able to take advantage of these technologies. Although Internet use is widespread, much exposure to media is still dominated by traditional mass media, especially television (Stelter, 2011). There are also several groups whose access to computers or high-speed Internet is limited or who are reluctant to use technology. And even among those who actively use converging media, effective participation may be limited by the ways in which they use media.

Digital Disparities

Back in 1995, a mere 3 percent of Americans had used the Internet; by 2012, almost 80 percent had. Compared to any other technology of the last century, that is quite a rapid penetration into the population, and the numbers of Internet users continue to grow across all demographic groups (Zickuhr & Smith, 2012). Even Americans of lower socioeconomic status now typically have access to at least some digital technology, including Internet and mobile phones. However, there are still some important **digital disparities** in terms of regular access to broadband connections or usage of multiple digital devices. For example, although low-income Americans may have a smartphone, that phone is often their sole digital device, which means that they are limited in their ability to do extensive Web searching or computer-based activities (such as writing papers for school) (Schradie, 2013). Even among those with similar levels of access, there are differences in how much use and participation they do online—younger adults and those with higher incomes and education are the ones who take the most advantage of online technology (Zickuhr & Smith, 2012).

Ineffective Participation

When Amy's twin girls were born almost three months prematurely, her husband Vern got online right away to find out everything he could about "preemies." But his search quickly became overwhelming: for every opinion in one direction, there seemed to be someone else giving the opposite advice. The sheer volume of messages made available by converging media can lead to **information overload**, the difficulty in sorting through and making sense of vast amounts of information. Pavlik and McIntosh (2013) argue that, apart from the difficulty for individuals, information overload can also hinder the ability of government agencies to act on shared information and make it difficult for employees to share information effectively within their companies. Media multitasking can exacerbate the problem, as studies show that multitasking hinders our ability to attend to and focus on the information we most need (Ralph, Thomson, Cheyne, & Smilek, 2013).

It can also be difficult to evaluate the quality of information in converging media. Some information online is edited by professional journalists, some is user contributed and edited (such as Wikipedia), and some is unedited information posted on forums, blogs, or personal Web sites. Rumors, hoaxes, and conspiracy theories abound (catalogued and investigated at Snopes.com). The potential for effective citizen participation is limited when users create or distribute false or other dangerous kinds of information online.

Participation is also ineffective when users fail to think critically about the information they find on the Internet. Much like with the traditional media, a site that *looks* credible, with professional design and impressive depth of content, may be given higher credence even if it might otherwise be suspect given its origins or sponsorship (Flanagin & Metzger, 2007). To make good on the promises of digital media for social and political participation, we need to devote our attention to the *quality* of our own and others' mediated communication.

● **THIS ERA MAY** well be considered the "Too Much Information Age," as converging media deliver more content than we can process. Getty Images/Flickr

AND YOU?

Are you media literate? Do you critique what you read, hear, and watch—or is most of it just background noise to you? Do you think that the media you choose *not* to attend to might have some effect on you?

Becoming a More Mindful Media Consumer

Media scholars argue that the way to avoid or counteract negative media effects is by becoming **media literate** (Potter, 2008; Potter & Byrne, 2009). This means developing an understanding of your own media habits and critically evaluating and analyzing media sources and messages. To become media literate, you should practice the following skills.

Monitor Your Media Use and Exposure

Like counting calories or carbohydrates, being aware of what you consume can end up making you consume less or at least make wiser choices about your media diet. Parents often find that if they limit the hours per day or week of their children's "screen time" (TV, video games, Internet use), children tend to be much more selective in their media choices. Monitoring your own media use—including what you read or watch intentionally as well as the peripheral messages you are exposed to along the way—encourages you to take more responsibility for your exposure to media messages.

Consider the Source of Media Messages

Remember that every message you receive has a source, and it's your job to question its credibility. If you understand the biases and goals of media sources—from advertisers and journalists to filmmakers and bloggers—you will be in a better position to know whether to resist or accept their messages. Bear in mind the economics of media, and think about how the business of mass communication might affect the messages you receive. And remember to be just as critical with material that supports your views as you are with material that does not.

Be Aware of Media Effects

Bear in mind how the media effects we discussed earlier in the chapter influence the way you receive, interpret, and react to media messages. Which media messages do you choose to attend to, and which do you tend to ignore? Do the messages you choose tend to change or reinforce your opinions on specific issues? Do you think that you are more immune to media effects than others?

Understand the Grammar of Media

Media each have a **grammar**—a set of rules and conventions that dictates how they operate. When you grow up with a medium, you often take for granted some of this grammar: you learned pretty early that the television screen going wavy is a sign of a flashback or dream sequence. But it is also useful to pay attention to other forms of television and Internet grammar, such as how news media arrange their visual clips to maximize emotional impact. Understanding media conventions helps you recognize the limitations of media, so that you can better separate, for example, TV sitcom logic from real-life situations. You can also better appreciate the genres you love, distinguish the good from poor versions of these forms, and recognize the value of parodies of these conventions (such as the *Daily Show* on Comedy Central). With digital media technology, there are many more grammars that you have to learn: Twitter and Facebook, for example, each has its own vernacular, privacy settings, and ways of sharing information. With emerging media, you need to understand where your messages are going and to whom, as well as what it may mean in different online contexts to, for example, *subscribe*, *like*, or *re-tweet*.

real communicator

NAME: Carly Gilleland
OCCUPATION: Videographer/photographer/studio manager

My life is about messages and perspectives. I run a video production and photography company and chronicle messages for clients in one of two ways. First, I do lifestyle video and photography work that includes covering private events like weddings, engagements, and parties. Second, I work with businesses in order to provide marketing and product materials, such as promotional videos, internal training videos, and even yoga fitness DVDs.

It is vital that I understand the perspectives of my clients to fashion the words and visuals that tell their stories. Lifestyle work often means that I have to tailor my approach to each client I work with, since I'm capturing an event that is often very personal. When doing business and marketing work, I take a more professional tone, since the focus should be mainly on the organization and its needs.

While getting my degree in film and media studies, I took full advantage of courses and opportunities. I never met a communication course I didn't like, and I got early experience in leadership, marketing, fundraising, and videography by getting involved in campus and community activities related to those courses. In the lead-up to President Barack Obama's inauguration, a group of communication students and I made a three-week road trip documentary to document the occasion. In college, I also started shooting marketing videos for the Special Olympics, which I continue to do up to this day.

Although I enjoyed my interpersonal course in college, I didn't expect just how important it would turn out to be. In order to craft messages and understand others' perspectives, I have to constantly adjust my communication style, and that takes skills of perception, language, nonverbal communication, and listening. Just one example is my current role in freelancing at Civitan, a volunteer organization with a special emphasis on helping people with developmental disabilities. My sister is autistic and has Turner's syndrome, and I feel so honored to be able to use my media and interpersonal skills to help not only her but also the many children and adults who have disabilities in our community (along with their families). Here again, messages and perspectives are so important when I'm shooting short videos (for both internal and marketing purposes). Some of the people are more receptive to nonverbal messages, whereas others respond better to clear, precise language.

Messages and perspectives are important in my personal life, too. My young daughter is a little sponge, taking in everything I do and say, and I want to send the right messages to her. To do this, I must take her perspective into account—not expecting too much or too little of her for her age. My career allows me a lot of flexibility, so I'm able to get the balance of family and career that makes me a happy person.

To see how the Internet helps you meet your goals, rate each statement using this scale: 1 = not at all helpful; 2 = mildly unhelpful; 3 = neither helpful nor unhelpful; 4 = mildly helpful; and 5 = very helpful.

_____ 1. The Internet helps me gain insight into why I do some of the things I do.

_____ 2. The Internet helps me imagine what I'll be like when I grow older.

_____ 3. The Internet helps me observe how others cope with problems like mine.

_____ 4. The Internet helps me stay on top of what is happening in my community.

_____ 5. The Internet helps me find out how my country is doing.

_____ 6. The Internet helps me keep up with world events.

_____ 7. I decide where to go for services by searching the Internet.

_____ 8. I figure out what to buy after consulting the Internet.

_____ 9. The Internet helps me plan where to go for evening and weekend activities.

_____ 10. I discover better ways to communicate with others by using the Internet.

_____ 11. The Internet helps me think about how to act with friends, relatives, or coworkers.

_____ 12. The Internet gives me ideas about how to approach others in important or difficult situations.

_____ 13. The Internet helps me unwind after a hard day or week.

_____ 14. I use the Internet to relax (reading blogs, watching TV shows) when I am by myself.

_____ 15. The Internet gives me something to do when nobody else is around.

_____ 16. The Internet gives me something to do with my friends.

_____ 17. Using the Internet is a great way to have fun with family or friends.

_____ 18. The Internet allows me to be a part of events I enjoy without having to be there.

Add your item scores to measure dependency: low (3–6); medium (7–11); high (12–15)

#1–3 _____ Your **self-understanding** score: If high, you find the Internet very useful for personal insight and for planning your behavior.

#4–6 _____ Your **social understanding** score: High scores indicate a reliance on the Internet to keep abreast of local, national, and international events.

#7–9 _____ Your **action orientation** score: High scores indicate dependency on the Internet for purchases and activities.

#10–12 _____ Your **interaction orientation** score: If high, you rely on the Internet to help you figure out how to communicate better with others.

#13–15 _____ Your **solitary play** score: If high, you use the Internet regularly to meet personal, solitary needs.

#16–18 _____ Your **social play** score: If high, the Internet plays a big role in your social interactions with others.

Source: Adapted from Patwardhan and Yang (2003).

Actively Evaluate Media Messages

Putting together all of the previously mentioned skills, you can then critically evaluate media messages and become a more competent participant in mass communication. Ask yourself what was great about a television episode (was it insightful, clever, funny, or moving?) and what was poor (unbelievable, unrealistic, or clichéd?). Consider carefully what underlying themes or values are being presented in your entertainment and news content. Are these consistent with your own values? *Should* they be? Might these images be suggesting that you compromise your morals or engage in unhealthy behavior?

Take time to think critically about the messages you send as well as those you receive. Be mindful when posting on Facebook or Twitter: Are you respecting the privacy of others when you tag them in photos? Are the messages in your status updates appropriate? Is it fair to re-tweet an embarrassing post that the author might regret having written? Remember, as both a consumer and a producer of media messages, it's up to you to communicate competently and ethically.

BACK TO ▶ Abigail's Multimedia Family

At the beginning of this chapter, we talked about teenager Abigail and the many types of mass and mediated communication that she and her family use in a single day, much of it at the same time. Consider Abigail's media experiences in light of what you've learned in this chapter.

▶ Abigail is experiencing media convergence. She combines traditional forms of mass media—television and books—with more interactive computer technology as she streams her favorite shows on the Internet and comments on fan blogs. Traditional media are still prominent, but these media interact with her use of texting and social networking. Even her "family time" with her brother is connected to media (video games and television), as is her schoolwork.

▶ Because of all of the different forms of media that Abigail has access to, she can be very selective about what she uses and why. She is not likely to bother with content that she doesn't like or want. Thus, media content creators (filmmakers, television producers, and so on) must be sure to include messages that appeal to her and others in her demographic group.

▶ Abigail uses Facebook not only to make connections with her peers but also to contribute her own comments and feelings about cultural phenomena, such as the *Hunger Games* trilogy and the actor Joseph Gordon-Levitt. This cultural bonding may build social capital among her network of friends.

THINGS TO TRY ▶ Activities

1. LaunchPad for *Real Communication* offers key term videos and encourages self-assessment through adaptive quizzing. Go to **bedfordstmartins.com/realcomm** to get access to:

✓ **LearningCurve** Adaptive Quizzes.

▶ Video clips that illustrate key concepts, highlighted in teal in the Real Reference section that follows.

2. Take notes as you watch one of your usual TV programs. What are some underlying messages of the story or the events? What are the values and traits of the characters you like the most and least? Are they stereotypical? If so, what would a nonstereotypical character actually look like?

3. Compare the news coverage for a political controversy on the Web sites of Fox News, CNN, MSNBC, NPR, and the wire services (AP and Reuters). What are the similarities? What are the differences? Then check the Web sites for both Media Matters for America and Media Research Center (or its offshoot, NewsBusters), and see how each of these media watchdogs criticizes the coverage. What biases do the watchdogs themselves seem to spout?

4. Think of a controversial issue about which you have very strong opinions. Write one paragraph describing the key problem and its main causes, taking care to present your information as objectively as possible, and then send it to a few friends. Can they detect where you stand on the issue based on the way you have presented your message? Have you really remained objective? Is it possible to inform without some bias when it comes to divisive issues?

5. List your five favorite TV shows. What do they have in common? Are these the same top five that your friends would list? Why or why not? What is it specifically that you like about these shows? What needs are being met by watching them? How do you think they affect you?

A Study Tool

Now that you have finished reading this Appendix, you can

Define mass and mediated communication:

▶ **Mediated communication** occurs when there is some technology that is used to deliver messages; when it occurs on a very broad scale, we refer to it as **mass communication** (pp. 532–533).

▶ **Media convergence** means the blurred distinctions between traditional and digital media forms, and we often engage in **media multitasking**, using more than one media type at the the same time (p. 533).

Describe how the business of media and the principle of free speech shape the kinds of media content you encounter:

▶ Most media are businesses that must attract audiences and advertising dollars to remain profitable. **Exponentiality** means that relatively few items bring in most of the income (p. 535).

▶ Media often cater to **low culture** in order to attract broad audiences, but they have also found success in programs with **narrative complexity**. They target niche audiences through **narrowcasting** (pp. 535–536).

▶ Media producers minimize risk by conducting extensive audience research and engaging in **self-censorship**, as well as by relying on proven formulas for success (pp. 537–538).

▶ The courts have allowed some restrictions on First Amendment freedoms when it comes to **broadcasting** (there are limitations on broadcasting **indecency**, for example) (pp. 539–541).

▶ Like all forms of communication, mass communication can be biased. **Framing** refers to the particular ways that issues are presented in the news (p. 542).

Provide two explanations for the effects of mass media:

▶ The **uses and gratifications perspective** argues that we make media choices in order to satisfy our needs and goals. The expectation that media can satisfy all these needs can lead to **media dependence** (pp. 542–543).

▶ We often make media choices in order to reinforce our existing attitudes and tend to think that media messages have more of an effect on others than they do on us, a phenomena known as the **third person effect** (p. 544).

Articulate how media exert influence on your attitudes and behaviors:

▶ **Social cognitive theory** argues that we learn behavior by watching how media models behave (p. 544).

▶ In **cultivation theory**, a steady, long-term diet of TV viewing can distort our perceptions of the world (p. 545).

▶ News coverage can have an agenda-setting effect—we tend to judge the importance of issues by the amount of new coverage they get (pp. 545–546).

Describe how the convergence of media technologies can enhance or hinder your participation in the social and political process:

▶ A benefit of converging media is that traditional media no longer serve as the sole gatekeeper for information and creative content (p. 546).

▶ Media connections allow marginalized or geographically dispersed groups to build **social capital**—valuable resources like information and support that come from having connections and relationships among people (pp. 547–548).

▶ Modern media also empower individuals to become citizen journalists and to create other kinds of user-generated content, fostering greater competition in the **marketplace of ideas** (p. 548).

▶ **Digital disparities** persist between those who have media access (and use it) and those who do not (p. 549).

▶ Ineffective participation in the digital world can be the result of **information overload**. A failure to think critically about media also hinders participation (p. 549).

Practice five skills for becoming a more mindful and **media literate** consumer (pp. 550–552):

▶ Monitor your media use and exposure
▶ Consider the source of media messages
▶ Be aware of media effects
▶ Understand the grammar of media
▶ Actively evaluate media messages

glossary

abstraction ladder: A model that ranks communication from specific, which ensures clarity, to general and vague.

accent: A pattern of pronunciation that is specific to a certain upbringing, geographical region, or culture.

accenting: Nonverbal behavior that clarifies and emphasizes specific information in a verbal message.

accommodation: Adapting and adjusting one's language and nonverbal behaviors for other people or cultures.

achievement-oriented leader: A leader who sets challenging goals and communicates high expectations and standards to members.

action-oriented listeners: Communicators who are usually focused on tasks; they tend to keep the discourse on track and are often valuable in meetings.

active listeners: Active participants in making choices about selecting, attending, understanding, and responding.

active strategies: In relationship management, strategies that allow one to obtain information about a person more directly, by seeking information from a third party.

adaptability: An organization's ability to adjust to changing times and circumstances.

adaptors: Body movements that satisfy some physical or psychological need, such as rubbing your eyes when you're tired or twisting your hair when you're nervous or bored.

ad hominem **fallacy:** A logical fallacy that entails attacking a person instead of the person's arguments.

adjourning: The stage of group development in which members reflect on their accomplishments and failures as well as determine whether the group will disassemble or take on another project.

affect displays: Body movements that convey feelings, moods, and reactions; they are often unintentional, reflecting the sender's emotions.

affective component of listening: The component of listening that refers to your attitude toward listening to a person or message.

affiliation: The affect, or feelings, we have for others.

agenda: A plan for a meeting that details the subject and goal, logistics, and a schedule.

agenda setting: The idea that extensive media coverage of a particular issue will "set the agenda" for what issues people are thinking and talking about.

all-channel network: A network in which all members are an equal distance from one another and all members interact with each other.

anchor position: An audience's position on a topic at the outset of the speech.

anecdotes: Brief, personal stories that have a point or punch line.

antigroup roles: Roles that create problems because they serve individual members' priorities at the expense of overall group needs.

apologize: To openly take responsibility for your own misbehavior in a miscommunication.

appeal to tradition: A logical fallacy in which the speaker uses tradition as proof, suggesting that listeners should agree with his or her point because "that's the way it has always been."

appreciative listening: Listening with the simple goal of taking pleasure in the sounds that one receives.

argumentativeness: A particular form of assertiveness, in which a person tends to express positions on controversial issues and verbally attack the positions that other people take.

articulation: The clarity and forcefulness with which sounds are made, regardless of whether they are pronounced correctly.

artifacts: Accessories carried or used on the body for decoration or identification.

assertiveness: The use of communication messages that demonstrate confidence, dominance, and forcefulness to achieve personal goals.

attending: The step in the listening process of focusing attention on both the presence and communication of someone else.

attitudes: Our general evaluations of people, ideas, objects, or events.

attributions: Personal characteristics that are used to explain other people's behavior.

audience analysis: A highly systematic process of getting to know one's listeners relative to the topic and speech occasion.

avoiding: An escapist tactic used to stay away from direct conflict, for example, walking away, changing the subject, or postponing conflict.

back-channel cues: Vocalizations that signal when we want to talk versus when we are just encouraging others to continue their talking.

bandwagon fallacy: Accepting a statement as true because it is popular.

bar graph: A presentation aid that shows the relationship of two or more sets of figures.

begging the question: A logical fallacy in which the speaker presents arguments that no one can verify because they are not accompanied by valid evidence.

behavior: Observable communication, including both verbal and nonverbal messages; the manner in which we act or function in response to our attitudes and beliefs.

behavioral affirmation: Seeing or hearing what one wants to see or hear in the communication of assorted group members.

behavioral component of listening: The component of listening that involves giving feedback to show that you understand and remember the information given.

behavioral confirmation: Acting in a way that makes one's expectations about a group come true.

behavioral flexibility: The ability to have a number of communication behaviors at one's disposal and the willingness to use different behaviors in different situations.

beliefs: The ways in which people perceive reality; our feelings about what is true and real and how confident we are about the existence or validity of something.

biased language: Words that are infused with subtle meanings that influence our perceptions about the subject.

bipolar question: The most closed form of a question, for which there are only two possible responses, "yes" and "no."

bonding: The process of relational partners sharing formal symbolic messages with the world that their relationship is important and cherished.

boundary turbulence: Readjusting the need for privacy against the need for self-disclosure and connection when there is a threat to one's privacy boundaries.

brainstorming: A process that entails focusing on a general area of interest, amassing information, thinking creatively, and considering problems and solutions related to the topic.

broadcasting: Signals carried over the airwaves from a station transmitter to a receiver.

bullying: Behaviors such as harsh criticism, name-calling, gossip, slander, personal attacks, or threats to safety or job security, used to try to acquire and keep control over an entire group or individual members within a group.

burnout: A sense of apathy or exhaustion that results from long-term stress or frustration.

call to action: In a persuasive speech, a challenge to listeners to act in response to the speech, see the problem in a new way, or change their beliefs, actions, and behavior.

cause-effect pattern: A pattern of speech arrangement that organizes the message around cause-to-effect or effect-to-cause relationships.

central processing: Thinking critically about the speaker's message, questioning it, and seriously considering acting on it; occurs when listeners are motivated and personally involved in the content of a message.

chain network: A network in which information is passed from one member to the next rather than shared among members.

channel: The method through which communication occurs.

channel discrepancy: When one set of behaviors says one thing, and another set says something different.

charismatic leaders: Vibrant, likable communicators who generate a positive image among their followers.

chronemics: The study of how people perceive the use of time.

chronological pattern: A pattern of speech arrangement that presents the main points of a message forward (or backward) in a systematic, time-related fashion.

civility: The social norm for appropriate behavior.

classical management approach: An approach to organizational communication that likens organizations to machines, with a focus on maximizing efficiency.

clique: A small subgroup of individuals who have bonded together within a group; also called *coalitions*.

closed question: A type of interview question that gives less freedom to the interviewee by restricting answer choices.

clustering: A technique for identifying potential speech topics whereby the writer begins with a core idea and branches out into a web of related thoughts and ideas.

co-culture: A smaller group of people within a culture who are distinguished by features such as race, religion, age, generation, political affiliation, gender, sexual orientation, economic status, educational level, occupation, and a host of other factors.

code: A set of symbols that are joined to create a meaningful message.

code switching: A type of accommodation in which communicators change their regular language and slang to fit into a particular group.

coercion: The act of using manipulation, threats, intimidation, or violence to gain compliance.

coercive power: Power that stems from a person's ability to threaten or harm others.

cognitions: Thoughts that communicators have about themselves and others.

cognitive complexity: Ability to consider multiple scenarios, formulate multiple theories, and make multiple interpretations when encoding and decoding messages.

cognitive component of listening: The component of listening that involves the mental processes of selecting messages to focus on, giving them attention, and then trying to understand them.

cognitive forces: Group members' thoughts and beliefs that affect how everyone in a particular group perceives, interprets, evaluates, stores, and retrieves information, which in turn influence the group's decisions.

cognitive language: The specific system of symbols that one uses to describe people, things, and situations in one's mind.

cohesion: The degree to which group members have bonded, like each other, and consider themselves to be one entity.

collaborating: Conflict style that involves finding a win-win solution that satisfies all parties.

collectivist culture: A culture in which individuals perceive themselves first and foremost as members of a group and communicate from that perspective.

communication: The process by which individuals use symbols, signs, and behaviors to exchange information.

communication accommodation theory: Theory that explains how language and identity shape communication in various contexts.

communication acquisition: The process of learning individual words in a language and learning to use that language appropriately and effectively in the context of the situation.

communication apprehension (CA): Fear or anxiety associated with communication, which is often a common barrier to effective delivery.

communication climate: The dominant temper, attitudes, and outlook of relational partners.

communication privacy management theory (CPM): An explanation of how people perceive the information they hold about themselves and whether they will disclose or protect it.

communication processing: The means by which we gather, organize, and evaluate the information we receive.

communication skills: Behaviors based on social understandings that help communicators achieve their goals.

comparative advantage pattern: An organizing pattern for persuasive speaking in which the speaker shows that his or her viewpoint is superior to other viewpoints on the topic.

competent communication: Communication that is effective and appropriate for a given situation, in which the communicators continually evaluate and reassess their own communication process.

competent communication model: A transactional model of communication in which communicators send and receive messages simultaneously within a relational, situational, and cultural context.

competitive styles: Conflict styles that promote the interests of individuals who see conflict as "win-lose" battles.

complementing: Nonverbal behavior that matches (without actually mirroring) the verbal message it accompanies.

compromising: A way to resolve conflict in which both parties must give up something to gain something.

conflict: A negative interaction between two or more interdependent people, rooted in some actual or perceived disagreement.

conflict management: The way we engage in conflict and address disagreements with relational partners.

conflict styles: Sets of goals and strategies that people use to manage conflict.

connotative meaning: The emotional or attitudinal response people have to a word.

consensus: Group solidarity in sentiment, belief, or decision.

contact cultures: Cultures that depend on touch as an important form of communication.

content-oriented listeners: Critical listeners who carefully evaluate what they hear; they prefer to listen to information from sources they feel are credible and critically examine the information they receive from a variety of angles.

contradicting: Nonverbal behavior that conveys meaning opposite of the verbal message.

control: The ability of one person, group, or organization to influence others, and the manner in which their relationships are conducted.

convergence: When speakers shift their language or nonverbal behaviors toward each other's way of communicating.

cooperative strategies: Strategies that benefit a relationship, serve mutual rather than individual goals, and strive to produce solutions that benefit both parties.

costs: The negative elements of a relationship.

countercoalitions: Subgroups that are positioned against other subgroups.

cover letter: A one-page letter indicating interest in a specific position.

credibility: The quality, authority, and reliability of a source of information.

critical listening: Evaluating or analyzing information, evidence, ideas, or opinions; also known as *evaluative listening*.

cultivation theory: The argument that a steady, long-term diet of heavy television viewing results in perceptions of reality that match the (distorted) view of reality presented on television.

cultural myopia: A form of cultural nearsightedness grounded in the belief that one's own culture is appropriate and relevant in all situations and to all people.

culture: A learned system of thought and behavior that belongs to and typifies a relatively large group of people; the composite of their shared beliefs, values, and practices.

cyberbullying: Multiple abusive attacks on individual targets conducted through electronic channels.

deception: The attempt to convince others of something that is false.

declining stage: The stage at which a relationship begins to come apart.

decoding: The process of receiving a message by interpreting and assigning meaning to it.

deductive reasoning: The line of thought that occurs when one draws specific conclusions from a general argument.

defensive climate: A communication climate in which the people involved feel threatened.

defensive listening: Responding with aggression and arguing with the speaker without fully listening to the message.

definitional speech: A presentation whose main goal is to provide answers to "what" questions by explaining to an audience what something is.

definition by etymology: Defining something by using the origin of a word or phrase.

definition by example: Defining something by offering concrete examples of what it is.

definition by negation: Defining something by telling what it is not.

definition by synonym: Defining something by using words that mean almost the same thing.

delivery cues: In a speech outline, brief reminders about important information related to the delivery of the speech.

demographics: The systematic study of the quantifiable characteristics of a large group.

demonstration speech: A speech that answers "how" questions by showing an audience the way something works.

denotative meaning: The basic, consistently accepted definition of a word.

descriptive presentation: An approach to conveying information that involves painting a mental picture for the audience.

dialectical tensions: Tensions that arise when opposing or conflicting goals exist in a relationship; can be external or internal.

digital disparity: The gap between the haves and have-nots in terms of regular access to modern technology, especially broadband connections.

directed question: A type of interview question that suggests or implies the answer that is expected.

direct fighting: Conflict style in which people use assertiveness to argue openly to get their way, which can sometimes lead to verbal aggressiveness.

directive leader: A leader who controls the group's communication by conveying specific instructions to members.

directory: A type of secondary resource that is created and maintained by people rather than automatically by computers; guides visitors to the main page of a Web site organized within a wider subject category.

discrimination: Behavior toward a person or group based solely on their membership in a particular group, class, or category.

distorted perception: Inaccurate, unbalanced, or inappropriate schemas.

division of labor: An aspect of the classical management approach that assumes each part of an organization (and each person involved) must carry out a specialized task for the organization to run smoothly

dyad: A pair of people.

either-or fallacy: A fallacy in which the speaker presents only two alternatives on a subject and fails to acknowledge other alternatives; also known as the *false dilemma fallacy.*

Elaboration Likelihood Model (ELM): A model that highlights the importance of relevance to persuasion and holds that listeners process persuasive messages by one of two routes, depending on how important the message is to them.

elucidating explanation: An explanation that illuminates a concept's meaning and use.

emblems: Movements and gestures that have a direct verbal translation in a particular group or culture.

emotion labor: Display of the appropriate emotions to satisfy organizational role expectations.

empathic listening: Listening to people with openness, sensitivity, and caring; attempting to know how another person feels.

encoding: The process of mentally constructing a message for production.

equivocation: Use of words that have unclear or misleading definitions.

escapist strategies: Strategies that people use to try to prevent or avoid direct conflict.

ethics: The study of morals, specifically the moral choices individuals make in their relationships with others.

ethnocentrism: A belief in the superiority of one's own culture or group and a tendency to view other cultures through the lens of one's own.

ethos: A form of rhetorical proof that appeals to ethics and concerns the qualifications and personality of the speaker.

euphemism: An inoffensive word or phrase that substitutes for terms that might be perceived as upsetting.

evasion: Intentionally failing to provide specific details.

exit interview: An interview that employers hold with employees who opt to leave the company to identify organizational problems that might affect future employee retention.

expert power: Power that comes from the information or knowledge that a leader possesses.

expert testimony: The opinion or judgment of an expert, a professional in his or her field.

explanatory speech: A speech that answers the question "Why" or "What does that mean?" by offering thorough explanations of meaning.

exploratory stage: The stage of a relationship in which one seeks relatively superficial information from one's partner.

exponentiality: The economic principle that relatively few items bring most of the income to a particular industry, while the rest add only a little.

extemporaneous speaking: A style of public speaking that involves delivery with few or no notes, but for which the speaker carefully prepares in advance.

family: A small social group bound by ties of blood, civil contract (such as marriage, civil union, or adoption), and a commitment to care for and be responsible for one another, usually in a shared household.

feedback: A message from the receiver to the sender that illustrates responses that naturally occur when two or more people communicate.

feeling: The use of language to express emotion; one of the five functional communication competencies.

feminine culture: A culture that places value on relationships and quality of life; sometimes referred to as a *nurturing culture*.

flaming: The posting of online messages that are deliberately hostile or insulting toward a particular individual.

forgive: A conflict reconciliation strategy in which people emotionally move past the conflict and let go of the bitterness and resentment.

forming: The stage of group development in which group members try to negotiate who will be in charge and what the group's goals will be.

forms of rhetorical proof: Means of persuasion that include *ethos*, *logos*, and *pathos*; first named by Aristotle.

framing: The way particular issues in the news are presented in order to relate to audiences' existing schemas.

friendship: A close and caring relationship between two people that is perceived as mutually satisfying and beneficial.

functional perspective: An examination of how communication behaviors work to accomplish goals in personal, group, organizational, or public situations.

fundamental attribution error: The tendency to overemphasize the internal and underestimate the external causes of behaviors we observe in others.

funnel sequence: A pattern of questioning that progresses from broad, open-ended questions to narrower, more closed questions.

gatekeepers: Those organizations and individuals who control the creation and distribution of information and entertainment.

gender: The behavioral and cultural traits assigned to one's sex; determined by the way members of a particular culture define notions of masculinity and femininity.

generation: A group of people who were born into a specific time frame, along with its events and social changes that shape attitudes and behavior.

globalization: The growing interdependence and connectivity of societies and economies around the world.

grammar: The system of rules for creating words, phrases, and sentences in a particular language.

grammar of media: For each form of media, a set of rules and conventions that dictate how it operates.

group: A collection of more than two people who share some kind of relationship, communicate in an interdependent fashion, and collaborate toward some shared purpose.

grouphate: The extent to which a person detests (or otherwise feels negatively about) working in groups.

groupthink: A situation in which group members strive to maintain cohesiveness and minimize conflict by refusing to critically examine ideas, analyze proposals, or test solutions.

haptics: The study of touch as a form of communication.

harassment: Any communication that hurts, offends, or embarrasses another person, creating a hostile environment.

hasty generalization: A reasoning flaw in which a speaker makes a broad generalization based on isolated examples or insufficient evidence.

hatespeech: Language that employs offensive words to deride a person or group.

hearing: The physiological process of perceiving sound; the process through which sound waves are picked up by the ears and transmitted to the brain.

hierarchy: The layers of power and authority in an organization.

hierarchy of needs: A hierarchical structure that identifies needs in five categories, from low (immature) to high (mature).

high-context culture: A culture that relies on contextual cues—such as time, place, relationship, and situation—to both interpret meaning and send subtle messages.

high language: A more formal, polite, or "mainstream" language, used in business contexts, in the classroom, and at formal social gatherings.

homogeny: Sameness, as applied to a public speaker and his or her audience.

hostile audience: An audience that opposes the speaker's message and perhaps the speaker personally; the hardest type of audience to persuade.

human relations approach: Management approach that considers the human needs of organizational members.

human resources approach: An approach to management that considers organizational productivity from workers' perspectives and considers them assets who can contribute their useful ideas to improve the organization.

human trafficking: The recruitment of people for exploitative purposes.

hurtful language: Inappropriate, damaging, mean, sarcastic, or offensive statements that affect others in negative ways.

hyperbole: Vivid, colorful language with great emotional intensity and often exaggeration.

hyperpersonal communication: A phenomenon surrounding online communication in which a lack of proximity, visual contact, or nonverbal cues results in exaggerated perceptions.

illustrators: Body movements that reinforce verbal messages and visually help explain what is being said.

imagining: The ability to think, play, and be creative in communication; one of the five functional communication competencies.

immediacy: The feeling of closeness, involvement, and warmth between people as communicated by nonverbal behavior.

impromptu speaking: A style of public speaking that is spontaneous, without any warning or preparation.

inclusion: To involve others in our lives and to be involved in the lives of others.

indecency: Discussing or showing sexual or other bodily functions in a very lewd or vulgar way.

indirect fighting: Conflict style that involves using passive-aggressive tactics to express conflict without engaging in it openly.

individualist culture: A culture whose members place value on autonomy and privacy, with relatively little attention to status and hierarchy based on age or family connections.

inductive reasoning: The line of thought that occurs when one draws general conclusions based on specific evidence.

informal–formal dimension: A psychological aspect of the situational context of communication, dealing with our perceptions of personal versus impersonal situations.

informational listening: Processing and accurately understanding a message; also known as *comprehensive listening*.

information-gathering interview: An interview that serves to transfer knowledge from one party to another by collecting attitudes, opinions, facts, data, and experiences.

information overload: The difficulty in sorting through and making sense of vast amounts of information, created by the volume of messages made available by converging media.

informative speaking: A form of public speaking intended to increase the audience's understanding or knowledge.

informing: The use of language to both give and receive information; one of the five functional communication competencies.

ingroup: The group with which one identifies and to which one feels one belongs.

initiating stage: The stage of a relationship in which one makes contact with another person.

insensitive listening: Listening that occurs when we fail to pay attention to the emotional content of someone's message, instead taking it at face value.

integrating: The process of relational partners "becoming one."

intensification stage: The stage of a relationship in which relational partners become increasingly intimate and move their communication toward more personal self-disclosures.

interaction appearance theory: The argument that people change their opinion about the attributions of someone, particularly their physical attractiveness, the more they interact with that person.

interaction management: Nonverbal cues used to manage the impressions and regulate interactions of communicators in a variety of relationships and situations.

interaction model: Communication between a sender and a receiver that incorporates feedback.

interactive strategies: In relationship management, strategies that allow one to obtain information by speaking directly with a person rather than observing or asking others for information about the person.

intercultural communication: The communication between people from different cultures who have different worldviews.

intercultural sensitivity: Mindfulness of behaviors that may offend others.

interdependence: Mutual dependence where the actions of each partner affect the other(s).

intergroup communication: A branch of the communication discipline that focuses on how communication within and between groups affects relationships.

intergroup contact theory: The argument that interaction between members of different social groups generates a possibility for more positive attitudes to emerge.

internal preview: In public speaking, an extended transition that primes the audience for the content immediately ahead.

internal summary: An extended transition that allows the speaker to crystallize the points made in one section of a speech before moving to the next section.

interpersonal communication: The exchange of verbal and nonverbal messages between two people who have a relationship and are influenced by the partner's messages.

interpersonal relationships: The interconnections and interdependence between two individuals.

interview: An interaction between two parties that is deliberate and purposeful for at least one of the parties involved.

intimacy: Closeness and understanding of a relational partner.

inverted funnel sequence: A pattern of questioning that progresses from narrow, closed questions to more open-ended questions.

jargon: Technical language that is specific to members of a particular profession, interest group, or hobby.

job interview: A type of selection interview, with the end goal of filling a position of employment.

key-word outline: The briefest type of outline, consisting of specific "key words" from the sentence outline to jog the speaker's memory.

kinesics: The way gestures and body movements communicate meaning.

laissez-faire leader: The leader who trusts others to handle their own responsibilities, does not take part in the group's discussions or work efforts, and provides feedback only when asked.

language: The system of symbols (words) that we use to think about and communicate experiences and feelings.

latitude of acceptance: The range of positions on a topic that are acceptable to an audience based on their *anchor position*.

latitude of noncommitment: A range of positions on a topic the audience is not sure about.

latitude of rejection: The range of positions on a topic that are unacceptable to an audience based on their anchor position.

latitudes: Ranges of acceptable and unacceptable viewpoints about a topic.

lay testimony: The opinion of a nonexpert who has personal experience of or has witnessed an event related to the speaker's topic.

leadership: The ability to direct or influence others' behaviors and thoughts toward a productive end.

leading question: A type of directed question that subtly suggests or implies the answer that is expected.

legitimate power: Power that comes from an individual's role or title.

library gateway: A collection of databases and information sites arranged by subject, generally reviewed and recommended by experts (usually librarians).

linear model (of communication): Communication in which a sender originates a message, which is carried through a channel—perhaps interfered with by noise—to the receiver.

linguistic relativity: The belief that speakers of different languages have different views of the world.

listening: The process of recognizing, understanding, accurately interpreting, and responding effectively to the messages communicated by others.

listening apprehension: A state of uneasiness, anxiety, fear, or dread associated with a listening opportunity; also known as *receiver apprehension*.

listening barrier: A factor that interferes with the ability to accurately comprehend information and respond appropriately.

listening fidelity: The degree to which the thoughts of the listener and the thoughts and intentions of the message producer match following their communication.

loaded question: A type of directed question that boldly suggests the answer that is expected.

logical fallacy: An invalid or deceptive form of reasoning.

logos: A form of rhetorical proof that appeals to logic and is directed at the audience's reasoning on a topic.

love: A deep affection for and attachment to another person involving emotional ties, with varying degrees of passion, commitment, and intimacy.

low-context culture: A culture that uses very direct language and relies less on situational factors to communicate.

low culture: Entertainment that appeals to most people's baser instincts, typified by lurid, sensational images and stories charged with sex, violence, scandal, and abuse.

low language: A more informal, easygoing language, used in informal and comfortable environments.

Machiavellianism: Unethical leadership style named for sixteenth-century philosopher Nicollo Machiavelli, who advised rulers to use deceit, flattery, and other exploitative measures strategically to achieve their desired ends.

main points: In public speaking, the central claims that support the specific speech purpose and thesis statement.

marketplace of ideas: The open forum in which ideas compete.

masculine culture: A culture that places value on assertiveness, achievement, ambition, and competitiveness; sometimes referred to as an *achievement culture*.

masking: A facial management technique in which an expression that shows true feeling is replaced with an expression that shows appropriate feeling for a given interaction.

mass communication: The occurrence of mediated communication on a very broad scale.

media convergence: The merging of traditional mass communication with digital computing and telecommunication technologies.

media dependence: The expectation that media will serve certain needs.

media interviews: Information-gathering interviews that question and analyze people, politics, media, and events.

media literate: Having an understanding of one's own media habits and critically evaluating and analyzing media sources and messages.

media multitasking: Using more than one media type at the same time.

media richness: The degree to which a particular channel is communicative.

mediated communication: The use of technology to deliver messages between sources and receivers.

mentor: A seasoned, respected member of an organization who serves as a role model for a less experienced individual.

message: The words or actions originated by a sender.

metacommunication: Communication with each other about how we communicate to help us become more aware of our own communicative missteps in relationships.

metasearch engine: A search engine that scans multiple search engines simultaneously.

mindfulness: The process of being focused on the task at hand; necessary for competent communication.

mindlessness: A passive state in which the communicator is a less critical processor of information, characterized by reduced cognitive activity, inaccurate recall, and uncritical evaluation.

model: A presentation aid—an appropriately scaled object.

monochronic culture: A culture that treats time as a limited resource, as a commodity that can be saved or wasted.

monopolistic listening: Listening in order to control the communication interaction.

monotone: A way of speaking in which the speaker does not vary his or her vocal pitch.

motivated sequence pattern: A pattern of speech arrangement that entails five phases based on the psychological elements of advertising: attention, need, satisfaction, visualization, and action.

motivational interview: A type of persuasive interview that attempts to elicit change collaboratively through goal-oriented questioning designed to inspire and strengthen personal motivation.

multitasking: Attending to several things at once.

mumbling: Omitting certain sounds in a word, running words together, or speaking so softly that listeners can hardly hear.

narrative complexity: In mass media, complicated plots and connections between characters, a blurring of reality and fantasy, and time that is not always linear or chronological.

narrative pattern: A pattern of speech arrangement that ties points together in a way that presents a vivid story, complete with characters, settings, plot, and imagery.

narrowcasting: In mass media, the process of targeting smaller, specific audiences; also known as *niche marketing*.

naturalistic fallacy: An appeal to nature saying that what is natural is right or good and that anything unnatural is wrong or bad.

network: A pattern of interaction that governs who speaks with whom in a group and about what.

networking: The process of using interconnected groups or associations of persons one knows to develop relationships with their connections whom one does not know.

neutral audience: An audience that falls between the receptive audience and the hostile audience; neither supports nor opposes the speaker.

neutral question: A type of interview question that provides no hint to the interviewee concerning the expected response.

noise: Interference with a message that makes its final form different from the original.

nonbinding straw poll: An informal vote on a decision that can help a group move forward when time is an issue.

noncontact culture: A culture that is less touch sensitive or even tends to avoid touch.

nonverbal codes: Symbols we use to send messages without, or in addition to, words.

nonverbal communication: The process of intentionally or unintentionally signaling meaning through behavior other than words.

norming: The stage of group development in which members establish agreed-upon norms that govern expected behavior.

norms: Recurring patterns of behavior or thinking that come to be accepted in a group as the "usual" way of doing things.

objective: Expressing or presenting facts and information in a straightforward and evenhanded way, free of influence from the speaker's personal thoughts or opinions.

obliging: An escapist tactic used to stay away from direct conflict, for example, giving in to the other person's wishes.

oculesics: The study of the use of eyes to communicate.

openness: An organization's awareness of its own imbalances and problems.

open question: A type of interview question that gives the interviewee great freedom in terms of how to respond.

operational definition: Defining something by explaining what it is or what it does.

oral citation: A reference to source materials that the speaker mentions in the narrative of a speech.

oratory: A form of public speaking in which a speech is committed to memory.

organization: A group with a formal governance and structure.

organizational assimilation: The process by which newcomers learn the nuances of the organization and determine if they fit in.

organizational communication: The interaction necessary to direct a group toward multiple sets of goals.

organizational culture: An organization's unique set of beliefs, values, norms, and ways of doing things.

organizational hero: An individual who achieves great things for an organization through persistence and commitment, often in the face of great risk.

organizational storytelling: The communication of the company's values through stories and accounts, both externally (to an outside audience) and internally (within the company).

outcome: The product of an interchange.

outgroups: Those groups one defines as "others."

outline: A structured form of a speech's content.

overaccommodate: Going too far in changing one's language or nonverbal behavior, based on an incorrect or stereotypical notion of another group.

paralanguage: The vocalized sounds that accompany words.

paraphrasing: A part of listening empathetically that involves guessing at feelings and rephrasing what one thinks the speaker has said.

participative leader: A leader who views group members as equals, welcomes their opinions, summarizes points that have been raised, and identifies problems that need discussion rather than dictating solutions.

passive listeners: Those who fail to make active choices in the listening process.

passive strategies: Observing others in communication situations without actually interacting with them.

pathos: A form of rhetorical proof that concerns the nature of the audience's feelings and appeals to their emotions.

peer communication: Communication between individuals at the same level of authority in an organization.

peer relationships: The friendships that form between colleagues at an organization as a result of *peer communication.*

people-oriented listeners: Communicators who listen with relationships in mind; they tend be most concerned with others' feelings.

perception: A cognitive process through which one interprets one's experiences and comes to one's own unique understandings.

performance appraisal: An interview designed to review an individual or party's accomplishments and develop goals for the future; used in corporate and academic environments.

performance visualization: Spending time imagining positive scenarios and personal success in order to reduce negative thoughts and their accompanying anxiety.

performing: The stage of group development in which members combine their skills and knowledge to work toward the group's goals and overcome hurdles.

peripheral processing: Giving little thought to a message or even dismissing it as irrelevant, too complex to follow, or simply unimportant; occurs when listeners lack motivation to listen critically or are unable to do so.

persuasion: The process of influencing others' attitudes, beliefs, and behaviors on a given topic.

persuasive interview: An interview in which questions are designed to elicit some change in the interviewee's behavior or opinions.

persuasive speaking: Speech that is intended to influence the attitudes, beliefs, and behaviors of an audience.

phrase outline: A type of outline that takes parts of sentences and uses those phrases as instant reminders of what the point or subpoint means.

pie chart: A presentation aid that shows percentages of a circle divided proportionately.

pitch: Variations in the voice that give prominence to certain words or syllables.

plagiarism: The crime of presenting someone else's words, ideas, or intellectual property as one's own, intentionally or unintentionally.

planting: A technique for limiting and controlling body movements during speech delivery by keeping the legs firmly set apart at a shoulder-width distance.

politically correct language: Language that replaces exclusive or negative words with more neutral terms.

polychronic culture: A culture whose members are comfortable dealing with multiple people and tasks at the same time.

posture: The position of one's arms and legs and how one carries the body.

power distance: The way in which a culture accepts and expects the division of power among individuals.

pragmatics: The ability to use the symbol systems of a culture appropriately.

prejudice: A deep-seated feeling of unkindness and ill will toward particular groups, usually based on negative stereotypes and feelings of superiority over those groups.

preparation outline: A draft outline the speaker will use, and probably revisit and revise continually, throughout the preparation for a speech; also known as a *working outline.*

primacy–recency effect: In public speaking, the tendency for audiences to remember points the speaker raises at the very beginning, or at the very end, of a message.

primary group: A long-lasting group that forms around the relationships that mean the most to its members.

primary question: A type of interview question that introduces new topics.

probing: Asking questions that encourage specific and precise answers.

problem–solution pattern: A pattern of speech arrangement that involves dramatizing an obstacle and then narrowing alternative remedies down to the one the speaker wants to recommend.

problem-solving group: A group with a specific mission.

problem-solving interview: An interview that is used to deal with problems, tensions, or conflicts.

process: The methods by which an outcome is accomplished.

productive conflict: Conflict that is managed effectively.

profanity: Words or expressions considered insulting, rude, vulgar, or disrespectful.

pronunciation: The correct formation of word sounds.

prop: A presentation aid—an object that removes the burden from the audience of having to imagine what something looks like as the speaker is presenting.

proposition of fact: A claim of what is or what is not.

proposition of policy: A claim about what goal, policy, or course of action should be pursued.

proposition of value: A claim about something's worth.

protégé: A new or inexperienced member of an organization who is trained or mentored by a more seasoned member.

provocation: The intentional instigation of conflict.

proxemics: The study of the way we use and communicate with space.

proximity: A state of physical nearness.

pseudolistening: Pretending to listen when one is actually not paying attention at all.

psychographics: Psychological qualities of an audience, such as attitudes, values, lifestyles, behaviors, and interests.

psychological forces: Group members' personal motives, emotions, attitudes, and values.

public–private dimension: An aspect of the situational context of communication dealing with the physical space that affects our nonverbal communication.

public speaking: A powerful form of communication that includes a speaker who has a reason for speaking, an audience that gives the speaker attention, and a message that is meant to accomplish a specific purpose.

public speaking anxiety (PSA): The nervousness one experiences when one knows one has to communicate publicly to an audience.

punctuated equilibrium: A stage of group development in which groups experience a period of inertia or inactivity until they become aware of time, pressure, and looming deadlines, which then compel group members to take action.

quasi-scientific explanation: An explanation that models or pictures the key dimensions of some phenomenon for a typical audience.

reasoning: The line of thought we use to make judgments based on facts and inferences from the world around us.

receiver: The target of a message.

receptive audience: An audience that already agrees with the speaker's viewpoints and message and is likely to respond favorably to the speech.

reconciliation: A repair strategy for rekindling an extinguished relationship.

red herring fallacy: A fallacy in which the speaker relies on irrelevant information for his or her argument, thereby diverting the direction of the argument.

reduction to the absurd: A logical fallacy that entails extending an argument beyond its logical limits to the level of absurdity; also known as *reductio ad absurdum.*

referent power: Power that stems from the admiration, respect, or affection that followers have for a leader.

refutational organizational pattern: An organizing pattern for persuasive speaking in which the speaker begins by presenting main points that are opposed to his or her own position and then follows them with main points that support his or her own position.

regulating: Using nonverbal cues to aid in the coordination of verbal interaction.

regulators: Body movements that help us manage our interactions.

relational dialectics theory: The theory that *dialectical tensions* are contradictory feelings that tug at us in every relationship.

relational history: The sum of shared experiences of the individuals involved in a relationship.

relational network: A web of relationships that connects individuals to one another.

relationships: The interconnection or interdependence between two or more people required to achieve goals.

remembering: The step in the listening process of recalling information.

repair tactics: Ways to save or repair a relationship.

repeating: Nonverbal behavior that offers a clear nonverbal cue that repeats and mirrors the verbal message.

research search engine: A search engine that searches only for research published in academic books, journals, and other periodicals.

responding: The step in the listening process of generating some kind of feedback or reaction that confirms to others that one has received and understood their messages.

résumé: A printed summary of one's education, work experiences, and accomplishments.

reward power: Power that derives from an individual's capacity to provide rewards.

rewards: The beneficial elements of a relationship.

ritualizing: Learning the rules for managing conversations and relationships; one of the five functional communication competencies.

role conflict: A situation that arises in a group whenever expectations for members' behavior are incompatible.

running bibliography: A list of resources the speaker has consulted, to which he or she can refer on note cards.

salient: Brought to mind in the moment; one's social identity and communication shift depending on which of one's multiple group memberships is salient in a given moment.

Sapir-Whorf hypothesis: The claim that the words a culture uses or doesn't use influence its members' thinking.

scanning: A technique for making brief eye contact with almost everyone in an audience by moving one's eyes from one person or section of people to another.

schema: A mental structure that puts together individual but related bits of information.

scientific research findings: Hard numbers and facts that are particularly useful for public speeches on medicine, health, media, or the environment.

search engine: A program that indexes Web content and searches all over the Web for documents containing specific keywords that the researcher has chosen.

secondary questions: A type of interview question that seeks clarification or an elaboration of responses to primary questions.

selecting: The step in the listening process of choosing one sound over another when faced with competing stimuli.

selection interview: An interview whose primary goal is to secure or fill a position within an organization.

selective listening: Listening that involves zeroing in only on bits of information that interest the listener, disregarding other messages or parts of messages.

selective perception: Active, critical thought resulting in a communicator succumbing to the biased nature of perception.

self-actualization: The feelings and thoughts one experiences when one knows that one has negotiated a communication situation as well as possible.

self-adequacy: The feelings one experiences when one assesses one's own communication competence as sufficient or acceptable; less positive than *self-actualization.*

self-censorship: In mass media, carefully monitoring content and eliminating messages that might offend viewers or sponsors.

self-concept: One's awareness and understanding of who one is, as interpreted and influenced by one's thoughts, actions, abilities, values, goals, and ideals.

self-denigration: A negative assessment about a communication experience that involves criticizing or attacking oneself.

self-directed work team: A group of skilled workers who take responsibility for producing high-quality finished work.

self-disclosure: Revealing oneself to others by sharing information about oneself.

self-efficacy: The ability to predict, based on self-concept and self-esteem, one's effectiveness in a communication situation.

self-esteem: How one feels about oneself, usually in a particular situation.

self-fulfilling prophecy: A prediction that causes an individual to alter his or her behavior in a way that makes the prediction more likely to occur.

self-monitoring: The ability to watch one's environment and others in it for cues as to how to present oneself in particular situations.

self-presentation: Intentional communication designed to show elements of self for strategic purposes; how one lets others know about oneself.

self-serving bias: The idea that we usually attribute our own successes to internal factors while explaining our failures by attributing them to situational or external effects.

semantics: The study of the relationship among symbols, objects, people, and concepts; refers to the meaning that words have for people, either because of their definitions or because of their placement in a sentence's structure (syntax).

sender: The individual who originates communication, with words or action.

sentence outline: A type of outline that offers the full text of a speech, often the exact words that the speaker wants to say to the audience.

service-oriented interview: An interview that is designed to cull information and provide advice, service, or support based on that information; used, for example, by customer service representatives.

sexual harassment: "Unwelcome sexual advances, requests for sexual favors, and other verbal or physical harassment of a sexual nature . . . when it is so frequent or severe that it creates a hostile or offensive work environment or when it results in an adverse employment decision (such as the victim being fired or demoted)" (from the U.S. Equal Employment Opportunity Commission, 2011).

signposts: Key words or phrases within sentences that signify transitions between main points.

situational context: The social environment, physical place, and specific events that affect a situation.

slang: Language that is informal, nonstandard, and usually particular to a specific group.

slippery slope fallacy: A logical fallacy that is employed when a speaker attests that some event must clearly occur as a result of another event without showing any proof that the second event is caused by the first.

social capital: The valuable resources, such as information and support, that come from having connections and relationships among people.

social cognitive theory: The theory that we learn behavior by watching the behaviors of those whom we have identified as models.

social comparison theory: A theory that explains our tendency to compare ourselves to others, such as friends and acquaintances or popular figures in the media, as we develop our ideas about ourselves.

social exchange theory: A theory that explains the process of balancing the advantages and disadvantages of a relationship.

social forces: Group standards for behavior that influence decision making.

social group: A group in which membership offers opportunities to form relationships with others.

social identity theory: The theory that we each have a *personal identity*, which is our sense of our unique individual personality, and a *social identity*, the part of our self-concept that comes from group memberships.

social information processing theory: The theory that communicators use unique language and stylistic cues in their online messages to develop relationships that are just as close as those that grow

from face-to-face contact because using text takes time, it takes longer to become intimate.

social judgment theory: The theory that a speaker's ability to successfully persuade an audience depends on the audience's current attitudes or disposition toward the topic.

social loafing: Failure to invest the same level of effort in the group that people would put in if they were working alone or with one other person.

social ostracism: The exclusion of a particular group member (or members).

social penetration theory (SPT): The theory that partners move from superficial levels to greater intimacy.

social relationships: Relationships that are functional within a specific context but are less intimate than friendships.

social roles: Group roles that evolve to reflect individual members' personality traits and interests.

spatial pattern: A pattern of speech arrangement that arranges main points in terms of their physical proximity or position in relation to each other (north to south, east to west, bottom to top, left to right, outside to inside, and so on).

speaking outline: The final speech plan, complete with details, delivery tips, and important notes about presentation aids; also known as the *delivery outline*.

speaking rate: How fast or slow one speaks.

specific purpose statement: A statement that expresses both the topic and the general speech purpose in action form and in terms of the specific objectives the speaker hopes to achieve with his or her presentation.

speech repertoire: A set of complex language behaviors or language possibilities that one calls on to most effectively and appropriately meet the demands of a given relationship, situation, or cultural environment.

stable stage: The stage of a relationship in which it is no longer volatile or temporary; both partners have a great deal of knowledge about one another, their expectations are accurate and realistic, and they feel comfortable with their motives for being in the relationship.

stages of change model: Approach to understanding your audience's disposition that helps predict audience members' motivational readiness toward modifying behavior and includes five stages: precontemplation, contemplation, preparation, action, and maintenance.

statistics: Information provided in numerical form.

stereotyping: The act of organizing information about groups of people into categories so that we can generalize about their attitudes, behaviors, skills, morals, and habits.

storming: The stage of group development in which members inevitably begin experiencing conflicts over issues such as who will lead the group and what roles members will play.

strategic topic avoidance: When one or both relational partners maneuver the conversation away from undesirable topics because of the potential for embarrassment, vulnerability, or relational decline.

study groups: Groups that are formed for the specific purpose of helping students prepare for exams.

subjective: Presenting facts and information from a particular point of view.

subpoints: In public speaking, points that provide support for the main points.

substituting: Replacing words with nonverbal cues.

support group: A set of individuals who come together to address personal problems while benefiting from the support of others with similar issues.

supportive climate: A communication climate that offers communicators a chance to honestly and considerately explore the issues involved in the conflict situation.

supportive leader: A leader who attends to group members' emotional needs.

surveillance: Monitoring of employees to see how they're using technology.

survey: To solicit answers to a question or series of questions related to one's speech topic from a broad range of individuals.

syllogism: A three-line deductive argument that draws a specific conclusion from two general premises (a major and a minor premise).

symbols: Arbitrary constructions (usually in the form of language or behaviors) that refer to people, things, and concepts.

systems approach: An approach to management that views an organization as a unique whole consisting of important members who have interdependent relationships in their particular environment.

taking conflict personally (TCP): Feeling so threatened by conflict that most disagreements are taken as personal insults or assaults.

task roles: Roles that are concerned with the accomplishment of the group's goals.

team: A group that works together to carry out a project or specific endeavor or to compete against other teams.

termination ritual: A final get-together to celebrate a group's achievements.

termination stage: The end of a relationship; may come about by a gradual decline in the relationship or by sudden-death.

territoriality: The claiming of an area, with or without legal basis, through continuous occupation of that area.

thesis statement: A statement that conveys the central idea or core assumption about the speaker's topic.

third person effect: The tendency to assume that negative media messages and bias have a much greater influence on other people than on oneself or people one thinks are like oneself.

time orientation: The way cultures communicate about and with time.

time-oriented listeners: Communicators who are most concerned with efficiency; they prefer information that is clear and to the point.

tone: A modulation of the voice, usually expressing a particular feeling or mood.

topical pattern: A pattern of speech arrangement that is based on organization into categories, such as persons, places, things, or processes.

trading: A way to reach compromise whereby one partner offers something of equal value in return for something he or she wants.

transactional: Involving two or more people acting in both sender and receiver roles whose messages are dependent on and influenced by those of their communication partner.

transformative explanation: An explanation that helps people understand ideas that are counterintuitive and is designed to help speakers transform "theories" about phenomena into more accepted notions.

transformative leaders: Leaders who spark change not only by having a new vision but also by conveying that vision clearly to others and energizing the group toward meeting the goals set forth in the vision.

transitions: Sentences that connect different points, thoughts, and details in a way that allows them to flow naturally from one to the next.

trolling: The posting of provocative or offensive messages to whole forums or discussion boards to elicit some type of general reaction.

tunnel sequence: A pattern of questioning in which all questions are at the same level, either broad and open-ended or narrow and closed; commonly used in polls and surveys.

turning points: Positive or negative events or changes that stand out in people's minds as important to defining their relationships.

uncertain climate: A communication climate in which at least one of the people involved is unclear, vague, tentative, and awkward about the goals, expectations, and potential outcomes of the conflict situation.

uncertainty avoidance: The process of adapting behaviors to reduce uncertainty and risk.

uncertainty event: An event or behavioral pattern that causes uncertainty in a relationship.

uncertainty reduction theory: The theory that when two people meet, their main focus is on decreasing the uncertainty about each other.

understanding: The step in the listening process of interpreting and making sense of messages.

understatement: Language that downplays the emotional intensity or importance of events, often with euphemisms.

undue influence: Giving greater credibility or importance to something shown or said than should be the case.

unproductive conflict: Conflict that is managed poorly and has a negative impact on the individuals and relationships involved.

user-generated content: Songs, videos, and other content that individuals create and share publicly through mass media.

uses and gratifications perspective: A perspective that focuses not on what media does to us, but on what we do with media—that is, the way we make media choices (uses) to satisfy our needs and goals (gratifications).

verbal aggressiveness: Attacks on individuals, rather than on issues.

visionary leaders: Leaders who are able to picture a new or different reality from what currently exists and consider the bigger, long-range picture of the group's or organization's future.

vocalizations: Paralinguistic cues that give information about the speaker's emotional or physical state, for example, laughing, crying, or sighing.

volume: How loud or soft the voice is.

wheel network: A network in which all group members share their information with one central individual, who then shares the information with the rest of the group.

work–life balance: Achieving success in one's personal and professional life.

worldview: The framework through which one interprets the world and the people in it.

references

Aakhus, M., & Rumsey, E. (2010). Crafting supportive communication online: A communication design analysis of conflict in an online support group. *Journal of Applied Communication Research, 38*(1), 65–84.

ABC News. (2013, April). Anchor A.J. Clemente fired after profanity-laced debut. Retrieved from http://abcnews.go.com/blogs/entertainment/2013/04/anchor-a-j-clemente-fired-after-profanity-laced-debut

ABC News. (2013, April 23). Worst first day ever. Retrieved from http://newsfeed.time.com/2013/04/23/worst-first-day-ever-rookie-tv-anchor-fired-for-profanity-in-first-newscast

Abrams v. *United States*, 250 U.S. 616 (1919).

Acitelli, L. K. (2008). Knowing when to shut up: Do relationship reflections help or hurt relationship satisfaction. *Social Relationships: Cognitive, Affective, and Motivational Processes*, 115–129.

Action for Children's Television v. *Federal Communications Commission*, 932 F.2d 1504 (ACT II) (D.C. Cir. 1991).

Action for Children's Television v. *Federal Communications Commission*, 58 F.3d 654 (ACT III) (D.C. Cir. 1995).

Adalian, J. (2013, June). *Under the Dome* and TV's new ad-less ways to make cash. Vulture.com. Retrieved from http://www.vulture.com/2013/06/under-the-dome-tv-revenue-when-ads-fail.html

Adkins, M., & Brashers, D. E. (1995). The power of language in computer-mediated groups. *Management Communication Quarterly, 8*, 289–322.

Adkins, R. PhD. (2006). Elemental truths. Retrieved from http://elementaltruths.blogspot.com/2006/11/conflict-management-quiz.html

Afifi, T., Afifi, W., Merrill, A. F., Denes, A. & Davis, S. (2013). "You Need to Stop Talking About This!": Verbal rumination and the costs of social support. *Human Communication Research, 39*(4), 395–421.

Afifi, T. D., McManus, T., Hutchinson, S., & Baker, B. (2007). Parental divorce disclosures, the factors that prompt them, and their impact on parents' and adolescents' well-being. *Communication Monographs, 74*, 78–103.

Afifi, T. D., McManus, T., Steuber, K., & Coho, A. (2009). Verbal avoidance and dissatisfaction in intimate conflict situations. *Human Communication Research, 35*(3), 357–383.

Ahlfeldt, S. L. (2009). Serving our communities with public speaking skills. *Communication Teacher, 23*(4), 158–161.

Albada, K. F., Knapp, M. L., & Theune, K. E. (2002). Interaction appearance theory: Changing perceptions of physical attractiveness through social interaction. *Communication Theory, 12*, 8–40.

Albert, N. M. Ph.D., R.N., Wocial, L. Ph.D, R.N., Meyer, K. H. M.S., Na, J. M.S., & Trochelman, K. M.S.N. (2008, November). Impact of nurses' uniforms on patient and family perceptions of nurse professionalism. *Applied Nursing Research, 21*(4), 181–190. Retrieved from http://dx.doi.org/10.1016/j.apnr.2007.04.008

Alexander, A. L. (2008). Relationship resources for coping with unfulfilled standards in dating relationships: Commitment, satisfaction, and closeness. *Journal of Social and Personal Relationships, 25*(5), 725–747.

Alge, B. J., Wiethoff, C., & Klein, H. J. (2003). When does the medium matter? Knowledge-building experiences and opportunities in decision-making teams. *Organizational Behavior and Human Decision Processes, 91*, 26–37.

Allan, T. (2004). *The troubles in Northern Ireland*. Chicago: Heinemann Library/Reed Elsevier Inc.

Allen, L. F., Babin, E. A., & McEwan, B. (2012). Emotional investment: An exploration of young adult friends' emotional experience and expression using an investment model framework. *Journal of Social and Personal Relationships, 29*(2), 206–227.

Allen, M. (1991). Comparing the persuasiveness of one-sided and two-sided messages using meta-analysis. *Western Journal of Speech Communication, 55*, 390–404.

Allen, R. R., & McKerrow, R. E. (1985). *The pragmatics of public communication* (3rd ed.). Dubuque, IA: Kendall/Hunt.

Allport, G. W. (1954). *The nature of prejudice*. Cambridge, MA: Addison-Wesley.

Alter, C. (2013, October 10). Miley Cyrus reels in best *Saturday Night Live* ratings since March. *Time*. Retrieved from http://entertainment.time.com/2013/10/10/miley-cyrus-reels-in-best-saturday-night-live-ratings-since-march

Altman, I., & Taylor, D. A. (1973). *Social penetration: The development of interpersonal relationships*. New York: Holt, Rinehart and Winston.

Alvarez, C., Salavati, S., Nussbaum, M., & Milrad, M. (2013). Collboard: Fostering new media literacies in the classroom through collaborative problem solving supported by digital pens and interactive whiteboards. *Computers and Education, 63*, 368–379.

Amadeo, K. (2013). Obama State of the Union 2013 Address: Summary and economic impact. Retrieved on May 9, 2014, from http://useconomy.about.com/od/Politics/p/2013-State-of-the-Union-Address.htm

American Psychological Association Zero Tolerance Task Force (2008). Are zero tolerance policies effective in the schools? *American Psychologist, 63*(9), 852–862.

Andersen, J. F. (1979). Teacher immediacy as a predictor of teaching effectiveness. In B. Ruben (Ed.), *Communication yearbook 3* (pp. 543–559). New Brunswick, NJ: Transaction Books.

Andersen, P. A. (1998). The cognitive valence theory of intimate communication. In M. Palmer & G. A. Barnett (Eds.), *Progress in communication sciences*: Vol. 14. Mutual influence in interpersonal communication theory and research in cognition, affect, and behavior (pp. 39–72). Norwood, NJ: Ablex.

Andersen, P. A., Guerrero, L. K., Buller, D. B., & Jorgensen, P. F. (1998). An empirical comparison of three theories of nonverbal immediacy exchange. *Human Communication Research, 24*, 501–535.

Andersen, P. A., Guerrero, L. K., & Jones, S. M. (2006). Nonverbal behavior in intimate interactions and intimate relationships. In V. Manusov & M. L. Patterson (Eds.), *The SAGE handbook of nonverbal communication* (pp. 259–278). Thousand Oaks, CA: Sage Publications.

Anderson, A. A., Brossard, D., Scheufele, D. A., Xenos, M. A., & Ladwig, P. (2013). The "nasty effect:" Online incivility and risk perceptions of emerging technologies. *Journal of Computer-Mediated Communication, 19*, 373–387.

Anderson, C. M., & Martin, M. M. (1999). The relationship of argumentativeness and verbal aggressiveness to cohesion, consensus, and satisfaction in small groups. *Communication Reports, 12,* 21–31.

Anderson, C. M., Riddle, B. L., & Martin, M. M. (1999). Socialization in groups. In L. Frey, D. Gouran, & M. Poole (Eds.), *Handbook of group communication theory and research* (pp. 139–163). Thousand Oaks, CA: Sage Publications.

Andreisen, D. (2007, March 29). "Baseball English" helps Mariners overcome various language barriers. *Seattle Post-Intelligencer*. Retrieved from http://www.seattlepi.com/sports/baseball/article/Baseball-English-helps-Mariners-overcome-1232513.php

Annino, J. (Executive producer). (2007, July 5). Cooking in cramped quarters [Television series episode]. In *The Rachael Ray Show*. Video retrieved from http://www.rachaelrayshow.com/show/segments/view/cooking-in-cramped-quarters

Antaki, C., Barnes, R., & Leudar, I. (2005). Self-disclosure as a situated interactional practice. *British Journal of Social Psychology, 44*(2), 181–199.

Antheunis, M. L., Valkenburg, P. M., & Peter, J. (2010). Getting acquainted through social network sites: Testing a model of online uncertainty reduction and social attraction. *Computers in Human Behavior, 26*(1), 100–109.

Antonijevic, S. (2008). From text to gesture online: A microethnographic analysis of nonverbal communication in the *Second Life* virtual environment. *Information, Communication & Society, 11*(2), 221–238.

Arasaratnam, L. (2007). Research in intercultural communication competence. *Journal of International Communication, 13,* 66–73.

Araton, H. (2010, April 26). The understated elegance of the Yankees' Rivera. *The New York Times*, p. D1.

Armstrong, B., & Kaplowitz, S. A. (2001). Sociolinguistic interference and intercultural coordination: A Bayesian model of communication competence in intercultural communication. *Human Communication Research, 27,* 350–381.

Asmuß, B. (2008). Performance appraisal interviews. *Journal of Business Communication, 45*(4), 408–429.

Asmuß, B. (2013). The emergence of symmetries and asymmetries in performance appraisal interviews: An interactional perspective. *Economic & Industrial Democracy, 34*(3), 553–570.

Assilaméhou, Y., & Testé, B. (2013). How you describe a group shows how biased you are: Language abstraction and inferences about a speaker's communicative intentions and attitudes toward a group. *Journal of Language & Social Psychology, 32*(2), 202–211.

Associated Press. (2011). In a first, women surpass men in college degrees. Reported in CBSNews.com. Retrieved from http://www.cbsnews.com/news/in-a-first-women-surpass-men-in-college-degrees

Associated Press. (2012, March 15). In *The Chicago Tribune Online*. Retrieved from http://triblive.com/sports/mlb/3670340-74/players-rule-baseball#axzz2qg4exWAI

Associated Press. (2013, November 6). Swedish cinemas test films' gender bias. *The Guardian*. Retrieved from http://www.theguardian.com/world/2013/nov/06/swedish-cinemas-bechdel-test-films-gender-bias

Associated Press. (2014, January 16). MLB tries to ease language barrier with new rule. In *Tribune Live*. Retrieved from http://triblive.com/sports/mlb/3670340-74/players-rule-baseball#axzz2qg4exWAI

Atkinson, J., & Dougherty, D. S. (2006). Alternative media and social justice movements: The development of a resistance performance paradigm of audience analysis. *Journal of Western Communication, 70,* 64–89.

Atlas, J. (2011, July 10). The art of the interview. *The New York Times*, p. SR7.

Atwood, J. D. (2012). Couples and money: The last taboo. *American Journal of Family Therapy, 40*(1), 1–19. doi: 10.1080/01926187.2011.600674

Aust, P. J. (2004). Communicated values as indicators of organizational identity: A method for organizational assessment and its application in a case study. *Communication Studies, 55,* 515–535.

Avtgis, T. A., & Rancer, A. S. (2003). Comparing touch apprehension and affective orientation between Asian-American and European-American siblings. *Journal of Intercultural Communication Research, 32*(2), 67–74.

Axtell, R. E. (1991). *Gestures: The do's and taboos of body language around the world*. Hoboken, NJ: Wiley.

Ayres, J. (2005). Performance visualization and behavioral disruption: A clarification. *Communication Reports, 18,* 55–63.

Ayres, J., & Hopf, T. (1993). *Coping with speech anxiety*. Norwood, NJ: Ablex.

Ayres, J., Keereetaweep, T., Chen, P., & Edwards, P. (1998). Communication apprehension and employment interviews. *Communication Education, 47,* 1–17.

Ayres, J., Wilcox, A. K., & Ayres, D. M. (1995). Receiver apprehension: An explanatory model and accompanying research. *Communication Education, 44,* 223–235.

Bachman, G. F., & Guerrero, L. K. (2006). Forgiveness, apology, and communicative responses to hurtful events. *Communication Reports, 19,* 45–56.

Back to twerk. (2013, September 10). *Sydney Morning Herald.* Retrieved from http://www.smh.com.au/entertainment/music/back-to-twerk-miley-cyrus-wrecking-ball-video-goes-ballistic-on-youtube-20130910-2tht6.html

Baez, J. (2013, August 28). Kate Middleton: No baby bump just 37 days after giving birth. Hollywoodlife.com. Retrieved from http://hollywoodlife.com/2013/08/28/kate-middleton-weight-loss-waitrose-pic-post-pregnancy

Baile, J., Steeves, V., Brukell, J., & Regan, P. (2013, April). Negotiating with gender stereotypes on social networking sites: From "Bicycle Face" to Facebook. *Journal of Communication Inquiry, 37*(2), 91–112.

Baker, H. G., & Spier, M. S. (1990). The employment interview: Guaranteed improvement in reliability. *Public Personnel Management, 19,* 85–90.

Baker, M. J., & Churchill, G. A. (1977). The impact of physically attractive models on advertising evaluations. *Journal of Marketing Research, 14,* 538–555.

Bakke, E. (2010). A model and measure of mobile communication competence. *Human Communication Research, 36*(3), 348–371.

Balaji, M., & Worawongs, T. (2010). The new Suzie Wong: Normative assumptions of white male and Asian female relationships. *Communication, Culture & Critique, 3*(2), 224–241.

Baldwin, M. W., & Keelan, J. P. R. (1999). Interpersonal expectations as a function of self-esteem and sex. *Journal of Social and Personal Relationships, 16,* 822–833.

Ball, K. (2010). Workplace surveillance: An overview. *Labor History, 51*(1), 87–106.

Ball-Rokeach, S. J. (1998). A theory of media power and a theory of media use: Different stories, questions, and ways of thinking. *Mass Communication and Society, 1,* 5–40.

Bandura, A. (1982). Self-efficacy mechanism in human agency. *American Psychologist, 37,* 122.

Bandura, A. (2001). Social cognitive theory of mass communication. *Media Psychology, 3,* 265–299.

Barker, L. L., & Watson, K. W. (2000). *Listen up: How to improve relationships, reduce stress, and be more productive by using the power of listening.* New York: St. Martin's Press.

Bartels, S., Kelly, J., Scott, J., Leaning, J., Mukwege, D., Joyce, N., & Vanrooyen, M. (2013). Militarized sexual violence in South Kivu, Democratic Republic of Congo. *Journal of Interpersonal Violence, 28*(2), 340–358.

Bartsch, R. A., & Coburn, K. M. (2003). Effectiveness of PowerPoint presentations in lectures. *Computers and Education, 41,* 77–86.

Bates, B. (1988). *Communication and the sexes.* New York: Harper & Row.

Bates, C. (2010). The nurse's cap and its rituals. *Dress, 36,* 21–40. Retrieved from http://www.ingentaconnect.com/content/maney/dre/2010/00000036/00000001/art00003

Bates, C. (2013). A cultural history of the nurse's uniform. Canadian Museum of Civilization. Gatineau, Quebec, Canada.

Bavelas, J. B., & Chovil, N. (2006). Nonverbal and verbal communication: Hand gestures and facial displays as part of language use in face-to-face dialogue. In V. Manusov & M. L. Patterson (Eds.), *The SAGE handbook of nonverbal communication* (pp. 97–117). Thousand Oaks, CA: Sage Publications.

Bavelous, A. (1950). Communication patterns in task-oriented groups. *Journal of the Acoustical Society of America, 22,* 725–730.

Baxter, L. A. (1990). Dialectical contradictions in relationship development. *Journal of Social and Personal Relationships, 7,* 69–88.

Baxter, L. A., Braithwaite, D. O., Bryant, L., & Wagner, A. (2004). Stepchildren's perceptions of the contradictions in communication with stepparents. *Journal of Social and Personal Relationships, 21,* 447–467.

Baxter, L. A,. & Bullis, C. (1986). Turning points in developing romantic relationships. *Human Communication Research, 12,* 469–493.

Baxter, L. A., & Montgomery, B. M. (1996). *Relating: Dialogues and dialectics.* New York: Guilford.

Baxter, L. A., & Simon, E. P. (1993). Relationship maintenance strategies and dialectical contradictions in personal relationships. *Journal of Social and Personal Relationships, 10,* 225–242.

Baxter, L. A., & Wilmot, W. W. (1985). Taboo topics in close relationships. *Journal of Social and Personal Relationships, 2,* 253–269.

Bayly, S. (1999). *Caste, society and politics in India from the eighteenth century to the modern age.* Cambridge: Cambridge University Press.

Bazelon, E. (2013). *Sticks and stones: Defeating the culture of bullying and rediscovering the power of character and empathy.* New York: Random House. Kindle Location 215.

Bazelon, E. (2013, March 11). Defining bullying down. *The New York Times.* Retrieved from http://www.nytimes.com/2013/03/12/opinion/defining-bullying-down.html

Bearak, B. (2010, September 6). Dead join the living in a family celebration. *The New York Times,* p. A7.

Beard, D. (2009). A broader understanding of the ethics of listening: Philosophy, cultural studies, media studies and the ethical listening subject. *International Journal of Listening, 23*(1), 7–20.

Becker, J. A., & O'Hair, D. (2007). Machiavellians' motives in organizational citizenship behavior. *Journal of Applied Communication Research, 35*(3), 246–267.

Beebe, S. A., Mottet, T. P., & Roach, K. D. (2012). *Training and development: Communicating for success* (2nd ed.). Boston: Pearson.

Behnke, R. R., & Sawyer, C. R. (1999). Milestones of anticipatory public speaking anxiety. *Communication Education, 48*, 164–172.

Behrendt, H., & Ben-Ari, R. (2012). The positive side of negative emotion: The role of guilt and shame in coping with interpersonal conflict. *Journal of Conflict Resolution, 56*(6), 1116–1138.

Beiser, V. (2013, May 21). Alone with everyone else. *Pacific Standard*. Retrieved from http://www.psmag.com/culture/pluralistic-ignorance-55562

Bélisle, J-F., & Onur Bodur, H. (August 2010). Avatars as information: Perception of consumers based on their avatars in virtual worlds. *Psychology & Marketing, 27*(8): 741–765. Published online in Wiley InterScience (www.interscience.wiley.com). Retrieved from http://jfbelisle.com/wp-content/uploads/2009/06/Belisle-and-Bodur-2010.pdf

Bellis, T. J., & Wilber, L. A. (2001). Effects of aging and gender on interhemispheric function. *Journal of Speech, Language, and Hearing Research, 44*, 246–264.

Benne, K. D., & Sheats, P. (1948). Functional roles in group members. *Journal of Social Issues, 4*, 41–49.

Bennett, J. M., & Bennett, M. J. (2004). Developing intercultural sensitivity: An integrative approach to global and domestic diversity. In D. Landis, J. M. Bennett, & M. J. Bennett (Eds.), *Handbook of intercultural training,* 3rd ed. (pp. 147–165). Thousand Oaks, CA: Sage Publications.

Bennis, W., & Nanus, B. (1985). *Leaders.* New York: Harper & Row.

Ben-Porath, E. (2010). Interview effects: Theory and evidence for the impact of televised political interviews on viewer attitudes. *Communication Theory, 20*(3), 323–347.

Bentley, S. C. (2000). Listening in the twenty-first century. *International Journal of Listening, 14*, 129–142.

Bercovici, J. (2013, October 30). Facebook admits it's seen a drop in usage among teens. Forbes.com. Retrieved from http://www.forbes.com/sites/jeffbercovici/2013/10/30/facebook-admits-its-seen-a-drop-in-usage-among-teens

Bergen, K. M. (2010). Accounting for difference: Commuter wives and the master narrative of marriage. *Journal of Applied Communication Research, 38*(1), 47–64.

Berger, A. (2007). *Media and society: A critical perspective.* Lanham, MD: Rowman & Littlefield.

Berger, C. R., & Bradac, J. J. (1982). *Language and social knowledge: Uncertainty in interpersonal relations.* London: Edward Arnold.

Berger, C. R., Roloff, M. E., & Roskos-Ewoldsen, D. R. (Eds.). (2010). *The handbook of communication science* (2nd ed.). Thousand Oaks, CA: Sage Publications.

Berger, J., Wagner, D. G., & Zelditch, M. Jr. (1985). Introduction: Expectation states theory: Review and assessment. In J. Berger & M. Zelditch Jr. (Eds.), *Theoretical research programs: Studies in the growth of theory* (pp. 1–72). Stanford, CA: Stanford University Press.

Berliet, M. (2013, July 3). The importance of kissing beyond the beginning. *Pacific Standard*. Retrieved from http://www.psmag.com/culture/the-importance-of-kissing-beyond-the-beginning-61780

Berrisford, S. (2006). How will you respond to the information crisis? *Strategic Communication Management, 10*, 26–29.

Berryman-Fink, C. (1993). Preventing sexual harassment through male–female communication training. In G. Kreps (Ed.), *Sexual harassment: Communication implications* (pp. 267–280). Cresskill, NJ: Hampton Press.

Berscheid, E., Dion, K., Walster, E., & Walster, G. M. (1971). Physical attractiveness and dating choice: A test of the matching hypothesis. *Journal of Experimental Social Psychology, 7,*173–189.

Bianca, A. (2013). The importance of public speaking skills within organizations. Retrieved on April 29, 2014, from http://smallbusiness.chron.com/importance-public-speaking-skills-within-organizations-12075.html

Biever, C. (2004, August). Language may shape human thought. *New Scientist.* Retrieved from http://www.newscientist.com

Bippus, A. M., & Daly, J. A. (1999). What do people think causes stage fright? Native attributions about the reasons for public speaking anxiety. *Communication Education, 48*, 63–72.

Birditt, K. S. (2013). Age differences in emotional reactions to daily negative social encounters. *The Journals of Gerontology Series B: Psychological Sciences and Social Sciences.* doi:10.1093/geronb/gbt045

Bishop, G. (2010, February 20). On and off the ice, Ohno is positioned for success. *The New York Times*, p. D3.

Bishop, R. (2000). More than meets the eye: An explanation of literature related to the mass media's role in encouraging changes in body image. In M. E. Roloff (Ed.), *Communication yearbook* (Vol. 23, pp. 271–304). Thousand Oaks, CA: Sage Publications.

Blanchard-Fields, F., Mienaltowski, A., & Seay, R. B. (2007). Age differences in everyday problem-solving effectiveness: Older adults select more effective strategies for interpersonal problems. *Journals of Gerontology, Series B: Psychological Sciences and Social Sciences, 62*, 61–64.

Bloch, J. (2011). Teaching job interviewing skills with the help of television shows. *Business Communication Quarterly, 74*(1), 7–21.

Blumenthal, M., & Edwards-Levy, A. (2014, February 4). HUFFPOLLSTER: Obamacare approval remains low. Huffingtonpost.com. Retrieved from http://www.huffingtonpost.com/2014/02/04/obamacare-approval_n_4726118.html

Blumler, J., & Katz, E. (1974). *The uses of mass communications.* Beverly Hills, CA: Sage Publications.

Blumstein, P., & Schwartz, P. (1983). *American couples: Money, work, sex.* New York: Morrow.

Bodie, G. D. (2010). A racing heart, rattling knees, and ruminative thoughts: Defining, explaining, and treating public speaking anxiety. *Communication Education, 59*(1), 70–105.

Bodie, G. D. (2013). Issues in the measurement of listening. *Communication Research Reports*, 30(1), 76–84.

Bodie, G. D., & Fitch-Hauser, M. (2010). Quantitative research in listening: Explication and overview. In A. D. Wolvin (Ed.), *Listening and human communication in the 21st century* (pp. 46–93). Oxford, England: Blackwell.

Bodie, G. D., & Jones, S.M. (2012). The nature of supportive listening II: The role of verbal person centeredness and nonverbal immediacy. *Western Journal of Communication* 76(3), 250–269.

Bodie, G. D., St. Cyr, K., Pence, M., Rold, M., & Honeycutt, J. (2012). Listening competence in initial interactions I: Distinguishing between what listening is and what listeners do. *International Journal of Listening, 26*(1), 1–28.

Bodie, G. D., Vickery, A. J., & Gearhart, C. C. (2013). The nature of supportive listening, I: Exploring the relation between supportive listeners and supportive people. *International Journal of Listening, 27*(1), 39–49.

Bodie, G. D., & Villaume, W. A. (2003). Aspects of receiving information: The relationship between listening preferences, communicator style, communication apprehension, and receiver apprehension. *International Journal of Listening, 17*, 47–67.

Bodie, G. D., Worthing, D., Imhof, M., & Cooper, L. O. (2008). What would a unified field of listening look like? A proposal linking past perspectives and future endeavors. *International Journal of Listening, 22*: 103–122.

Bodie, G. D., Worthington, D. L., & Gearhart, C. C. (2013, January). The listening styles profile-revised (LSP-R): A scale revision and evidence for validity. *Communication Quarterly, 61*(1), 72–90.

Boje, D. M. (1991). The storytelling organization: A study of story performance in an office-supply firm. *Administrative Science Quarterly, 36*, 106–126.

Bommelje, R., Houston, J. M., & Smither, R. (2003). Personality characteristics of effective listeners: A five factor perspective. *International Journal of Listening, 17*, 32–46.

Bono, J. E. & Ilies, R. (2006). Charisma, positive emotions and mood contagion. *The Leadership Quarterly, 17*, 317–334.

Bormann, E. G. (1990). *Small group communication* (3rd ed.). New York: Harper & Row.

Bosman, J. (2006). Retrieved from http://www.nytimes.com/2006/08/15/business/media/15adco.html?_r=0

Bosman, J. (2011, January 4). Publisher tinkers with Twain. *The New York Times.* Retrieved from http://www.nytimes.com/2011/01/05/books/05huck.html

Bosman, J. (2013, July 1). Appeals court's ruling helps Google in book-scanning lawsuit. *The New York Times.* Retrieved from http://www.nytimes.com/2013/07/02/business/media/appeals-courts-ruling-helps-google-in-book-scanning-lawsuit.html?ref=googlebooksearch

Boster, F. J., & Mongeau, P. (1984). Fear-arousing persuasive messages. In R. N. Bostrom (Ed.), *Communication yearbook 8* (pp. 330–375). Beverly Hills, CA: Sage Publications.

Bourhis, R. Y. (1985). The sequential nature of language choice in cross-cultural communication. In R. L. Street Jr. & J. N. Cappella (Eds.), *Sequence and pattern in communicative behaviour* (pp. 120–141). London: Arnold.

Boyd, D. (2010). Social network sites as networked publics: Affordances, dynamics, and implications. In Z. Papacharissi (Ed.), *A networked self: Identity, community, and culture on social network sites* (pp. 39–58). New York: Routledge.

Boyle, K. (2012, December 12). The fall and rise of Rockaway: We are still recovering from Hurricane Sandy. *The New York Daily News.* Retrieved from http://www.nydailynews.com/opinion/fall-rise-rockaway-article-1.1217997

Bradac, J. J. (1983). The language of lovers, flovers, and friends: Communicating in social and personal relationships. *Journal of Language and Social Psychology, 2*, 234.

Bradac, J. J., & Giles, H. (2005). Language and social psychology: Conceptual niceties, complexities, curiosities, monstrosities, and how it all works. In K. L. Fitch & R. E. Sanders (Eds.), *The new handbook of language and social psychology* (pp. 201–230). Mahwah, NJ: Erlbaum.

Brandau-Brown, F. E., & Ragsdale, J. D.(2008). Personal, moral, and structural commitment and the repair of marital relationships. *Southern Communication Journal, 73*(1), 68–83.

Brandenburg, C. (2008). The newest way to screen job applicants: A social networker's nightmare. *Federal Communications Law Journal, 60*(3), 597–626.

Brazeel, S. (2009). Networking to top talent or networking your way to top talent. *POWERGRID International, 14*(10), 2.

Brehm, J. W. (1966). *A theory of psychological reactance.* New York: Academic Press.

Brehm, J. W., & Brehm, S. S. (1981). *Psychological reactance: A theory of freedom and control.* San Diego, CA: Academic Press.

Brenneis, D. (1990). Shared and solitary sentiments: The discourse of friendship, play, and anger in Bhatgaon. In C. A. Lutz & L. Abu-Lughod (Eds.), *Language and the politics of emotion* (pp. 113–125). Cambridge: Cambridge University Press.

Brilhart, J. K., & Galanes, G. J. (1992). *Effective group discussion* (7th ed.). Dubuque, IA: Brown.

Britney, F. (2013, July 28). Kate Middleton post-baby body media coverage: Disrespectful to women? *The hollywoodgossip.com.* Retrieved from http://www.thehollywoodgossip.com/2013/07/kate-middleton-post-baby-body-coverage-disrespectful-to-women

Brock, C. (2010, March 17). Padres breaking down language barrier. Retrieved from mlb.com

Brody, L. R. (2000). The socialization of gender differences in emotional expression: Display rules, infant temperament, and differentiation. In A. H. Fischer (Ed.), *Gender and emotion: Social psychological perspectives* (pp. 24–47). Cambridge: Cambridge University Press.

Brooklyn Nine-Nine (2013). Pilot. Retrieved from http://www.baltimoresun.com/entertainment/tv/z-on-tv-blog/bal-andre-braugher-wendell-pierce-fall-tv-20130913,0,2233205.story#ixzz2qmOapNNm

Bryant, A. (2012, April 7). The phones are out, but the robot is in. *The New York Times*. Retrieved from http://www.nytimes.com/2012/04/08/business/phil-libin-of-evernote-on-its-unusual-corporate-culture.html?pagewanted=all&_r=0

Bryant, J., & Pribanic-Smith, E. J. (2010). A historical overview of research in communication science. In C. R. Berger, M. E. Roloff, & D. R. Roskos-Ewoldsen (Eds.), *The handbook of communication science* (2nd ed.). (pp. 21–36.). Thousand Oaks, CA: Sage Publications.

Buck, R. (1988). Emotional education and mass media: A new view of the global village. In R. P. Hawkins, J. M. Wiemann, & S. Pingree (Eds.), *Advancing communication science: Merging mass and interpersonal processes* (pp. 44–76). Beverly Hills, CA: Sage Publications.

Burgoon, J. K. (1978). A communication model of personal space violations: Explication and an initial test. *Human Communication Research, 4*, 129–142.

Burgoon, J. K., & Bacue, A. E. (2003). Nonverbal communication skills. In J. O. Greene & B. R. Burleson (Eds.), *Handbook of communication and social interaction skills* (pp. 179–219). Mahwah, NJ: Erlbaum.

Burgoon, J. K., Blair, J., & Strom, R. E. (2008). Cognitive biases and nonverbal cue availability in detecting deception. *Human Communication Research, 34*(4), 572–599.

Burgoon, J. K., Buller, D. B., & Woodall, W. G. (1989). *Nonverbal communication: The unspoken dialogue.* New York: Harper & Row.

Burgoon, J. K., & Dunbar, N. E. (2006). Nonverbal expressions of dominance and power in human relationships. In V. Manusov & M. L. Patterson (Eds.), *The SAGE handbook of nonverbal communication* (pp. 279–298). Thousand Oaks, CA: Sage Publications.

Burgoon, J. K., Floyd, K., & Guerrero, L. K. (2010). Nonverbal communication theories of interaction adaptation. In C. R. Berger, M. E. Roloff, & D. R. Roskos-Ewoldsen (Eds.), *The handbook of communication science* (pp. 93–108). Thousand Oaks, CA: Sage Publications.

Burgoon, J. K., & Hoobler, G. D. (2002). Nonverbal signals. In M. L. Knapp & J. A. Daly (Eds.), *Handbook of interpersonal communication* (pp. 240–299). Thousand Oaks, CA: Sage Publications.

Burleson, B. R. (2010). The nature of interpersonal communication: A message-centered approach. In C. R. Berger, M. E. Roloff, & D. R. Roskos-Ewoldsen, *The handbook of communication science* (pp. 145–163). Thousand Oaks, CA: SAGE Publications.

Burleson, B. R., Hanasono, L. K., Bodie, G. D., Holmstrom, A. J., Rack, J. J., Gill-Rosier, J., & McCullough, J. D. (2011). Are gender differences in responses to supportive communication a matter of ability, motivation, or both? Reading patterns of situational responses through the lens of a dual-process theory. *Communication Quarterly, 59*, 37–60.

Burleson, B. R., Holmstrom, A. J., & Gilstrap, C. M. (2005). "Guys can't say that to guys": Four experiments assessing the normative motivation account for deficiencies in the emotional support provided by men. *Communication Monographs, 72*(4), 468–501.

Busch, D. (2009). What kind of intercultural competence will contribute to students' future job employability? *Intercultural Education, 20*(5), 429–438.

Bushman, B. J., & Huesmann, L. R. (2001). Effects of televised violence on aggression. In D. G. Singer & J. L. Singer (Eds.), *Handbook of children and the media* (pp. 223–254). Thousand Oaks, CA: Sage Publications.

Business Week (2005). Why most meetings stink. Retrieved from http://www.businessweek.com/stories/2005-10-30/why-most-meetings-stink

Butler, C. W., & Fitzgerald, R. (2011). "My f***ing personality": Swearing as slips and gaffes in live television broadcasts. *Text & Talk, 31*(5), 525–551.

Byrd, D. (2010, January 16). Neil deGrasse Tyson: "Learning how to think is empowerment." Retrieved from http://earthsky.org/human-world/neil-degrasse-tyson

Cacioppo, J. T., Cacioppo, S., Gonzaga, G. C., Ogburn, E. L. & VanderWeele, T. J. (2013). Marital satisfaction and break-ups differ across on-line and off-line meeting venues. *Psychological and Cognitive Sciences*, www.pnas.org/cgi/doi/10.1073/pnas.1222447110

Cacioppo, J. T., & Petty, R. E. (1984). The need for cognition: Relationships to attitudinal processes. In R. P. McGlynn, J. E. Maddux, C. Stoltenberg, & J. H. Harvey (Eds.), *Social perception in clinical and counseling psychology*. Lubbock, TX: Texas Tech University Press.

Canary, D. J. (2003). Managing interpersonal conflict: A model of events related to strategic choices. In J. O. Greene & B. R. Burleson (Eds.), *Handbook of communication and social interaction skills* (pp. 515–550). Mahwah, NJ: Erlbaum.

Canary, D. J., & Cody, M. J. (1993). *Interpersonal communication: A goals-based approach*. New York: Bedford/St. Martin's Press.

Canary, D. J., Cody, M. J., & Manusov, V. (2008). *Interpersonal communication: A goals-based approach* (4th ed.). New York: Bedford/St. Martin's.

Canary, D. J., Cody, M. J., & Smith, S. (1994). Compliance-gaining goals: An inductive analysis of actors' goal types, strategies, and successes. In J. A. Daly & J. M. Wiemann (Eds.), *Strategic interpersonal communication* (pp. 33–90). Hillsdale, NJ: Erlbaum.

Canary, D. J., Cunningham, E. M., & Cody, M. J. (1988). Goal types, gender, and locus of control in managing interpersonal conflict. *Communication Research, 15*, 426–446.

Canary, D. J., & Dainton, M. (Eds.). (2003). *Maintaining relationships through communication: Relational, contextual, and cultural variations*. Mahwah, NJ: Erlbaum Associates.

Canary, D. J., & Lakey, S. (2012). *Strategic conflict*. London: Routledge.

Canary, D. J., & Spitzberg, B. H. (1993). Loneliness and media gratifications. *Communication Research, 20*, 800–821.

Capella, J. K., & Greene, J. O. (1982). A discrepancy-arousal explanation of mutual influence in expressive behavior for adult and infant–adult interaction. *Communication Monographs, 49*, 89–114.

Caplan, S. (2001). Challenging the mass-interpersonal communication dichotomy: Are we witnessing the emergence of an entirely new communication system? *Electronic Journal of Communication, 11.* Retrieved March 24, 2003, from http://www.cios.org/getfile/CAPLAN_v11n101

Capozzoli, T. (2002). How to succeed with self-directed work teams. *SuperVision, 63,* 25–26.

Cappella, J. N., & Schreiber, D. M. (2006). The interaction management function of nonverbal cues: Theory and research about mutual behavioral influence in face-to-face settings. In V. Manusov & M. L. Patterson (Eds.), *The SAGE handbook of nonverbal communication* (pp. 361–380). Thousand Oaks, CA: Sage Publications.

Cargile, A. C., & Giles, H. (1996). Intercultural communication training: Review, critique, and a new theoretical framework. In B. R. Burleson (Ed.), *Communication yearbook 19* (pp. 3835–3423). Newbury Park, CA: Sage Publications.

Carless, S. A., & DePaola, C. (2000). The measurement of cohesion in work teams. *Small Group Research, 31,* 71–88.

Carli, L. L. (1999). Gender, interpersonal power, and social influence. *Journal of Social Issues, 55,* 81–99.

Carter, C. (2011, February 26). Sheen tantrum likely to cost in the millions. *The New York Times*, p. B1.

Casella, J., & Ridgeway, J. (2012, February 1). How many prisoners are in solitary confinement in the United States? *Solitary Watch.* Retrieved from http://solitarywatch.com/2012/02/01/how-many-prisoners-are-in-solitary-confinement-in-the-united-states

Casmir, F. L. (Ed.). (1997). *Ethics in intercultural and international communication.* Mahwah, NJ: Erlbaum.

Cassell, J., Huffaker, D., Tversky, D., & Ferriman, K. (2006). The language of online leadership: Gender and youth engagement on the Internet. *Developmental Psychology, 42*(3), 436–449.

Caughlin, J. (2003). Family communication standards: What counts as excellent family communication, and how are such standards associated with family satisfaction? *Human Communication Research, 29,* 5–40.

CBS News. (2010, November 28). Colin Firth on playing King George VI: Katie Couric talks with *The King's Speech* star about the monarch's battle against a debilitating stutter. Retrieved from http://www.cbsnews.com/stories/2010/11/28/sunday/main7096682.shtml

CBS News. (2011). Texting while driving up 50 percent last year. Retrieved on May 9, 2014, from http://www.cbsnews.com/news/texting-while-driving-up-50-percent-last-year

Cegala, D. (1981). Interaction involvement: A cognitive dimension of communicative competence. *Communication Education, 30,* 109–121.

Census seen lax on diversity. (2010, February 25). *The Washington Times.* Retrieved from http://www.washingtontimes.com/news/2010/feb/25/census-seen-lax-on-diversity

Centers for Disease Control and Prevention (2013). Distracted driving. Retrieved on May 2, 2014, from http://www.cdc.gov/motorvehiclesafety/distracted_driving

Chaiken, S. (1979). Communicator physical attractiveness and persuasion. *Journal of Personality and Social Psychology, 37,* 1387–1397.

Charles, S. T., Piazza, J. R., Luong, G., & Almeida, D. M. (2009). Now you see it, now you don't: Age differences in affective reactivity to social tensions. *Psychology and Aging, 24*(3), 645.

Chen, G., & Starosta, W. J. (1996). Intercultural communication competence: A synthesis. In B. R. Burleson (Ed.), *Communication yearbook* (Vol. 19, pp. 353–383). Thousand Oaks, CA: Sage Publications.

Chen, G-M., & Starosta, W. J. (2008). Intercultural communication competence: A synthesis. In M. K. Asante, Y. Miike, & J. Yin (Eds.), *The global intercultural communication reader* (pp. 215–238). New York: Taylor and Francis Group.

Chen, Y., & Nakazawa, M. (2009). Influences of culture on self-disclosure as relationally situated in intercultural and interracial friendships from a social penetration perspective. *Journal of Intercultural Communication Research, 38*(2), 77–98.

Cherulnik, P. D., Donley, K. A., Wiewel, T. S., & Miller, S. R. (2001). Charisma is contagious: The effect of leaders' charisma on observers' affect. *Journal of Applied Social Psychology, 31,* 2149–2159.

Chidambaram, L., & Bostrom, R. P. (1996). Group development: A review and synthesis of the development models (I). *Group Decision and Negotiation, 16*(2), 159–187.

Child, J. T., & Westermann, D. A. (2013). Let's be facebook friends: Exploring parental facebook friend requests from a communication privacy management (CPM) perspective. *Journal of Family Communication, 13*(1), 46–59.

Childs, C. (2009). Perfect quiet. *Miller-McCune, 2*(4), 58–67.

Chou, G., & Edge, N. (2012, February). They are happier and having better lives than I am: The impact of using Facebook on perceptions of others' lives. *Cyberpsychology, Behavior, and Social Networking*, pp. 117–121.

Chozick, A. (2011, December 12). Athhilezar? Watch your fantasy world language. *The New York Times*, p. A1.

Christenson, P. (1994). Childhood patterns of music uses and preferences. *Communication Reports, 7,* 136–144.

Christians, C., & Traber, C. (Eds.). (1997). *Communication ethics and universal values.* Thousand Oaks, CA: Sage Publications.

Christie, R., & Geis, F. L. (1970). *Studies in Machiavellianism.* New York: Academic Press.

Christophel, D. M. (1990). The relationships among teacher immediacy behaviors, student motivation, and learning. *Communication Education, 39,* 323–340.

Church of Latter Day Saints Gospel Library. (2001). Lessons: Sexual purity. Retrieved from http://www.lds.org/ldsorg/v/index.jsp?vgnextoid=d6371b08f338c010VgnVCM10000 04d82620aRCRD&sourceId=1907be335dc20110VgnVC M100000176f620a_____ (paragraph 7)

Cialdini, R. (2008). *Influence: Science and practice* (5th ed.). Englewood Cliffs, NJ: Prentice Hall.

Clark, A. J. (1989). Communication confidence and listening competence: An investigation of the relationships of willingness to communicate, communication apprehension, and receiver apprehension to comprehension of content and emotional meaning in spoken messages. *Communication Education, 38,* 237–248.

Clarke, I., Flaherty, T. B., Wright, N. D., & McMillen, R. M. (2009). Student intercultural proficiency from study abroad programs. *Journal of Marketing Education, 31*(2), 173–181.

Clarke, J., LCSW, ACM. (2014, February 23). Personal communication.

Clausell, E., & Roisman, G. I. (2009). Outness, Big Five personality traits, and same-sex relationship quality. *Journal of Social and Personal Relationships, 26*(2–3), 211–226.

CNN.com/living. (2008). Retrieved from www.cnn.com/2007/ LIVING/personal/07/30/wlb.quiz.balance/index.html

Cohen, J. (2013, April 27). Reviving an old series the new way: Fan-financing. *The New York Times.* Retrieved from http://www .nytimes.com/2013/04/28/us/veronica-mars-will-return-thanks-to-fan-financing.html

Cohen, M., & Avanzino, S. (2010). We are people first: Framing organizational assimilation experiences of the physically disabled using co-cultural theory. *Communication Studies, 61*(3), 272–303.

The Colbert Report. (2011, March 9). Video clip "Benchpress." Retrieved from http://www.colbertnation.com/the-colbert-report-videos/376920/march-09-2011/bench-press, 3:40

The Colbert Report. (2013, September 12). Better know a district: Washington's 7th-Jim McDermott. Retrieved from http:// www.colbertnation.com/better-know-a-district/429042/ september-12-2013/better-know-a-district-washington-s-7th-jim-mcdermott, 3:00

Colvin, G. (2012, December 3). The art of the self-managing team. *Fortune, 166*(9), 22.

Comadena, M. E. (1984). Brainstorming groups. *Small Group Research, 15,* 251–264.

Comer, D. R. (1998). A model of social loafing in real work groups. *Human Relations, 48,* 647–667.

Conley, T. D. (2011). Perceived proposer personality characteristics and gender differences in acceptance of casual sex offers. *Journal of Personality & Social Psychology, 100*(2), 309–329.

Conlin, M. (2006, December 11). Online extra: How to kill meetings. *Business Week.* Retrieved from http://www .businessweek.com

Connelly, S. (2009, December 3). Rupert Everett: Coming out of the closet ruined my career in Hollywood. *Daily News.*

Retrieved from http://articles.nydailynews.com/2009-12-03/gossip/17940844_1_gay-best-friendcloset-major-stars

Conover, M. D., Ferrara, E., Menczer, F., & Flammini, A. (2013). The digital evolution of Occupy Wall Street. *PLoS ONE 8*(5). Retrieved from e64679. doi:10.1371/journal .pone.0064679

Costa, M. (2010). Interpersonal distances in group walking. *Journal of Nonverbal Behavior, 34*(1), 15–26.

Coulehan, J. L., & Block, M. L. (2006). *The medical interview: Mastering skills for clinical practice.* Philadelphia: Davis.

Cox, P. L., & Brobrowski, P. E. (2000). The team charter assignment: Improving the effectiveness of classroom teams. *Journal of Behavioral and Applied Management, 1*(1), 92.

Cox, S. S., Bennett, R. J., Tripp, T. M., & Aquino, K. (2012). An empirical test of forgiveness motives' effects on employees' health and well-being. *Journal of Occupational Health Psychology, 17*(3), 330.

Cragan, J. F., Wright, D. W., & Kasch, C. R. (2008). *Communication in small groups: Theory, process, and skills* (7th ed.). Boston: Cengage.

Cramton, C. D. (1997). Information problems in dispersed teams. *Academy of Management Best Paper Proceedings,* 298–302.

Crane, D. (2000). *Fashion and its social agendas: Class, gender, and identity in clothing.* Chicago: University of Chicago Press.

Croucher, S. M., Bruno, A., McGrath, P., Adams, C., McGahan, C., Suits, A., & Huckins, A. (2012). Conflict styles and high–low context cultures: A cross-cultural extension. *Communication Research Reports, 29*(1), 64–73.

Culbert, S. A. (2010). *Get rid of the performance review! How companies can stop intimidating, start managing—and focus on what really matters.* New York: Business Plus/Hachette Book Group.

Culbert, S. A. (2011, March 2). Why your boss is wrong about you. *The New York Times,* p. A25.

Culver, S. H., & Seguin, J. (2013). *Media career guide: Preparing for jobs in the 21st century.* New York: Bedford/St. Martin's.

Cupach, W. R., & Spitzberg, B. H. (Eds.) (2011*). The dark side of close relationships II.* New York: Routledge.

Curtis, P. (1997). Mudding: Social phenomena in text-based virtual realities. In S. Kiesler (Ed.), *Culture of the Internet* (pp. 121–142). Mahwah, NJ: Erlbaum.

Cutica, I., & Bucciarelli, M. (2011). "The more you gesture, the less I gesture": Co-speech gestures as a measure of mental model quality. *Journal of Nonverbal Behavior, 35*(3), 173–187.

Cvitanic, O. (2013, February 26). From gangnam style to the Harlem shake, why we just can't resist a dance craze. *Pacific Standard.* Retrieved from http://www.psmag.com/blogs/ the-101/from-gangnam-style-to-the-harlem-shake-why-we-just-cant-resist-a-dance-craze-53266

Daft, R. L., & Lengel, R. H. (1984). Informational richness: A new approach to managerial behavior and organizational design. In B. M. Staw & L. L. Cummings (Eds.), *Research in organizational behavior* (Vol. 6, pp. 191–233). Greenwich, CT: JAI.

Daft, R. L., & Lengel, R. H. (1986). Organizational information requirements, media richness, and structural design. *Management Science, 32,* 554–571.

Dailey, R. M., & Palomares, N. A. (2004). Strategic topic avoidance: An investigation of topic avoidance frequency, strategies used, and relational correlates. *Communication Monographs, 71,* 471–496.

Dainton, M., & Gross, J. (2008). The use of negative behaviors to maintain relationships. *Communication Research Reports, 25,* 179–191.

Danet, B., & Herring, S. C. (Eds.). (2007). *The multilingual Internet: Language, culture, and communication online.* New York: Oxford University Press.

Darbonne, A., Uchino, B. N., & Ong, A. D. (2013). What mediates links between age and well-being? A test of social support and interpersonal conflict as potential interpersonal pathways. *Journal of Happiness Studies, 14*(3), 951–963.

Dargis, M. (2012, October 12). Outwitting the Ayatollah with Hollywood's help. *The New York Times,* p. C1.

Daswani, K. (2012, January 9). More men coloring their hair. *The Los Angeles Times.* Retrieved from http://articles.latimes.com/2012/jan/29/image/la-ig-mens-hair-color-20120129

Davies A., Goetz, A. T., & Shackelford, T. K. (2008). Exploiting the beauty in the eye of the beholder: The use of physical attractiveness as a persuasive tactic. *Personality and Individual Differences, 45,* 302–306.

Davies, P. T., Sturge-Apple, M. L., Cicchetti, D., & Cummings, E. M. (2008). Adrenocortical underpinnings of children's psychological reactivity to interparental conflict. *Child Development, 79,* 1693–1706.

Davis, C., & Myers, K. (2012). Communication and member disengagement in planned organizational exit. *Western Journal of Communication, 76*(2), 194–216.

Davis, J., Foley, A., Crigger, N., & Brannigan, M. C. (2008). Healthcare and listening: A relationship for caring. *International Journal of Listening, 22*(2), 168–175.

Davis, M. S. (1973). *Intimate relations.* New York: Free Press.

Davison, W. P. (1983). The third-person effect in communication. *Public Opinion Quarterly,* 40, 1–15.

Day, L. A. (1997). *Ethics in media communications: Cases and controversies.* Belmont, CA: Wadsworth.

DeAndrea, D. C., & Walther, J. B. (2011). Attributions for inconsistencies between online and offline self-presentations. *Communication Research, 38*(6), 805–825.

DeGroot, T., & Gooty, J. (2009). Can nonverbal cues be used to make meaningful personality attributions in employment interviews? *Journal of Business and Psychology, 24*(2), 179–192.

Dehue, F. (2013). Cyberbullying research: New perspectives and alternative methodologies. Introduction to the special issue. *Journal of Community & Applied Social Psychology, 23*(1), 1–6.

DeKay, S. H. (2009). The communication functions of business attire. *Business Communication Quarterly, 72*(3), 349–350.

DeKay, S. H. (2012). Interpersonal communication in the workplace: A largely unexplored region. *Business Communication Quarterly, 75*(4), 449–452.

Dempsey, A. G., Sulkowski, M. L., Dempsey, J., & Storch, E. A. (2011). Has cyber technology produced a new group of peer aggressors? *Cyberpsychology, Behavior and Social Networking, 1*(5), 297–302.

Denniston, L. (2012, June 29). "Wardrobe malfunction" case finally ends. SCOTUSblog. Retrieved from http://www.scotusblog.com/2012/06/wardrobe-malfunction-case-finally-ends

Derks, D., Bos, A. E. R., & von Grumbkow, J. (2008). Emoticons and online message interpretation. *Social Science Computer Review, 26*(3), 379–388.

Derlega, V. J., Winstead, B. A., Mathews, A., & Braitman, A. L. (2008). Why does someone reveal highly personal information? Attributions for and against self-disclosure in close relationships. *Communication Research Reports, 25*(2), 115–130.

Devine, D. J., Clayton, L. D., Phillips, J. L., & Melner, S. B. (1999). Teams in organizations: Prevalence, characteristics, and effectiveness. *Small Group Research, 30,* 678–711.

Dewey, C. (2012, January 17). How many of this year's Oscar nominees passed the Bechdel test? Not many. *The Washington Post.* Retrieved from http://www.washingtonpost.com/blogs/style-blog/wp/2014/01/17/how-many-of-this-years-oscar-nominees-pass-the-bechdel-test-not-many/

Dewey, J. (1933). *How we think.* Lexington, MA: Heath.

DiBiase, R., & Gunnoe, J. (2004). Gender and culture differences in touching behavior. *Journal of Social Psychology, 144*(1), 49–62.

Dillon, R. K., & McKenzie, N. J. (1998). The influence of ethnicity on listening, communication competence, approach, and avoidance. *International Journal of Listening, 12,* 106–121.

Dimmick, J., Chen, Y., & Li, Z. (2004). Competition between the Internet and traditional news media: The gratification-opportunities niche dimension. *Journal of Media Economics, 17,* 19–33.

Ding, H., & Ding, X. (2013). 360-degree rhetorical analysis of job hunting: A four-part, multimodal project. *Business Communication Quarterly, 76*(2), 239–248.

Dipper, L., Black, M., & Bryan, K. (2005). Thinking for speaking and thinking for listening: The interaction of thought and language in typical and non-fluent comprehension and production. *Language and Cognitive Processes, 20,* 417–441.

DiSanza, J. R., & Legge, N. J. (2002). *Business and professional communication: Plans, processes, and performance* (2nd ed.). Boston: Allyn & Bacon.

Dizik, A. (2011, July 11). 8 important tips for Skype interviews. Retrieved from http://www.cnn.com/2011/LIVING/07/11/skype.interview.tips.cb

Doll, B. (1996). Children without friends: Implications for practice and policy. *School Psychology Review, 25,* 165–183.

Dominguez, A. (2013, May 6). Elizabeth Smart speaks out about abstinence education. *Salt Lake City Tribune.* Retrieved from http://www.sltrib.com/sltrib/news/56248622-78/abstinence-smart-elizabeth-trafficking.html.csp

Dominus, S. (2006, September 28). *Extras,* season 2, epsiode 3, Daniel Radcliffe.

Dominus, S. (2012, January 14). *Saturday Night Live,* season 37, episode 12, Daniel Radcliffe and Lana Del Rey.

Dominus, S. (2013, October 6). Daniel Radcliffe's next trick is to make Harry Potter disappear. *The New York Times Magazine,* p 26.

Donnoli, M., & Wertheim, E. H. (2012). Do offender and victim typical conflict styles affect forgiveness? *International Journal of Conflict Management, 23*(1), 57–76.

Don't call me fat! 25 Stars who have lashed out at criticism of their weight. (2013). RadarOnline.com. Retrieved from http://radaronline.com/photos/dont-call-me-fat-celebrities-lash-out-at-criticism-of-weight

Dooling, R. (2011, March 1). Curbing that pesky rude tone. *The New York Times,* p. A27.

Döring, N., & Pöschl, P. (2009). Nonverbal cues in mobile phone text messages: The effects of chronemics and proxemics. In R. Ling & S. W. Campbell (Eds.), *The reconstruction of space and time: Mobile phone practices.* New Brunswick, NJ: Transaction Publishers.

Doris, J. (Ed.). (1991). *The suggestibility of children's recollections.* Washington, DC: American Psychological Association.

Doucé, L., & Janssens, W. (2013). The presence of a pleasant ambient scent in a fashion store: The moderating role of shopping motivation and affect intensity. *Environment & Behavior, 45*(2), 215–238.

Douglas, C. (2002). The effects of managerial influence behavior on the transition to self-directed work teams. *Journal of Managerial Psychology, 17,* 628–635.

Douglas, C., Martin, J. S., & Krapels, R. H. (2006). Communication in the transition to self-directed work teams. *Journal of Business Communication, 43*(4), 295–321.

Dowd, M. (2012, July 1). The wearing of the green. *The New York Times,* p. SR11.

Dragojevic, M., Giles, H., & Watson, B. M. (2013). Language ideologies and language attitudes: A foundational framework. In H. Giles & B. Watson (Eds.), *The social meanings of language, dialect and accent: International perspectives on speech styles* (pp. 1–25). New York: Peter Lang.

Drummond, K. (2010, February 26). New Pentagon sim teaches troops to play nice. *Wired* Danger Room blog. Retrieved from http://www.wired.com/dangerroom/2010/02/newpentagon-sim-teaches-troops-to-play-nice

Ducharme, J., Doyle, A., & Markiewicz, D. (2002). Attachment security with mother and father: Associations with adolescents' reports of interpersonal behavior with parents and peers. *Journal of Social and Personal Relationships, 19,* 203–231.

Duck, S. W. (1984). A perspective on the repair of personal relationships: Repair of what, when? In S. W. Duck (Ed.), *Personal relationships: Vol. 5. Repairing personal relationships.* New York: Macmillan.

Duell, M. (2013). BBC presenter from Middlesbrough claims she gets abuse from viewers because of her northern accent. *Mail Online,* July 16, 2003. Retrieved from http://www.dailymail.co.uk/news/article-2364998/BBC-presenter-Steph-McGovern-claims-gets-abuse-viewers-northern-accent.html#ixzz2cyTVG5I1 [paragraph 8]

Dues, M., & Brown, M. (2004). *Boxing Plato's shadow: An introduction to the study of human communication.* New York: McGraw-Hill.

Duffy, M., Thorson, E., & Vultee, F. (2009). Advocating advocacy: Acknowledging and teaching journalism as persuasion. Paper presented at the annual meeting of the Association for Education in Journalism and Mass Communication, Sheraton Boston, Boston, MA. Retrieved from http://www.allacademic.com/meta/p375952_index.html

DuFrene, D., & Lehman, C. (2004). Concept, content, construction and contingencies: Getting the horse before the PowerPoint cart. *Business Communication Quarterly, 67*(1), 84–88.

Duggan, M. (2013). Cell phone activities 2013. Pew Research Internet Project. Retrieved from http://www.pewinternet.org/2013/09/19/cell-phone-activities-2013

Duke, A. (2013, April 16). Justin Bieber hopes Anne Frank "would have been a belieber." Retrieved from http://www.cnn.com/2013/04/14/showbiz/bieber-anne-frank

Dunbar, N. E., & Abra, G. (2010). Observations of dyadic power in interpersonal interaction. *Communication Monographs, 77*(4), 657–684.

Dunbar, N. E., & Burgoon, J. K. (2005). Perceptions of power and interactional dominance in interpersonal relationships. *Journal of Social and Personal Relationships, 22*(2), 207–233.

Duncan, S., & Fiske, D. (1977). *Face-to-face interaction.* Hillsdale, NJ: Erlbaum.

Dunleavy, V., & Millette, D. (2007). Measuring mentor roles and protégé initiation strategies: Validating instruments in academic mentoring. *Conference Papers—National Communication Association,* 1. Retrieved from http://www.allacademic.com/meta/p194103_index.html

Dwamena, F., Mavis, B., Holmes-Rovner, M., Walsh, K., & Loyson, A. (2009). Teaching medical interviewing to patients: The other side of the encounter. *Patient Education and Counseling, 76*(3), 380–384.

Dwyer, K. K., & Davidson, M. M. (2012). Is public speaking really more feared than death? *Communication Research Reports, 29,* 99–107.

Dwyer, K. M., Fredstrom, B. K., Rubin, K. H., Booth-LaForce, C., Rose-Krasnor, L., & Burgess, K. B. (2010). Attachment, social information processing, and friendship quality of early adolescent girls and boys. *Journal of Social and Personal Relationships, 27*(1), 91–116.

Eagly, A., Karau, S., & Makhijani, M. (1995). Gender and the effectiveness of leaders: A meta-analysis. *Psychological Bulletin, 111,* 3–32.

Eckholm, E. (2010, May 10). What's in a name? A lot, as it turns out. *The New York Times,* p. A12.

Editorial. (2011, April 5). OMG!!! OED!!! LOL!!!. *The New York Times,* p. A22.

Edwards, B. (2013, November 2). Personal communication.

Edwards, C., & Edwards, A. (2009). Communication skills training for elementary school students. *Communication Currents, 4*(4), 1–2.

Edwards, R. (1990). Sensitivity to feedback and the development of self. *Communication Quarterly, 28,* 101–111.

Efran, M. G. (1974). The effect of physical appearance on the judgment of guilt, interpersonal attraction, and severity of recommended punishment in a simulated jury task. *Journal of Research in Personality, 8,* 45–54.

Eibl-Eibesfeldt, I. (1973). The expressive behavior of the deaf-and-blind-born. In M. von Cranach & I. Vine (Eds.), *Social communication and movement: Studies of interaction and expression in man and chimpanzee* (pp. 163–194). New York: Academic Press.

Eisenberg, E., Goodall, H. L., Jr., & Trethewey, A. (2013). *Organizational communication: Balancing creativity and constraint* (7th ed.). Boston: Bedford/St. Martin's.

Ekman, P., & Friesen, W. V. (1969). The repertoire of nonverbal behavior: Categories, origins, usage, and coding. *Semiotica, 1,* 49–98.

Ekman, P., & Friesen, W. V. (1971). Constants across cultures in the face and emotion. *Journal of Personality and Social Psychology, 17,* 124–129.

Ekman, P., Friesen, W. V., & Ellsworth, P. (1972). *Emotion in the human face: Guidelines for research and an integration of findings.* New York: Pergamon Press.

El Ahl, A., & Steinvorth, D. (2006, October 20). Sex and taboos in the Islamic world. *Spiegel Online International.* Retrieved March 12, 2008, from http://www.spiegel.de/international/spiegel/0,1518,443678,00.html

Elliott, S. (2010, June 30). Food brands get sociable on Facebook and Twitter. *The New York Times.* Retrieved from http://mediadecoder.blogs.nytimes.com/2010/06/30/food-brands-get-sociable-on-facebook-and-twitter

Ellison, N. B., Steinfeld, C., & Lampe, C. (2007). The benefits of Facebook "friends": Social capital and college students' use of online social network sites. *Journal of Computer-Mediated Communication, 12,* 1143–1168.

Ellyson, S. L., Dovidio, J. F., & Brown, C. E. (1992). The look of power: Gender differences and similarities in visual dominance behavior. In C. L. Ridgeway (Ed.), *Gender, interaction, and inequality* (pp. 50–80). New York: Springer-Verlag.

eMarketer (2013, March). Digital set to surpass TV in time spent with US media. Retrieved from http://www.emarketer.com/Article/Digital-Set-Surpass-TV-Time-Spent-with-US-Media/1010096

Endo, Y., Heine, S. J., & Lehman, D. R. (2000). Culture and positive illusions in close relationships: How my relationships are better than yours. *Personality and Social Psychology Bulletin, 26,* 1571–1586.

Entertainment Software Association. (2012). Essential facts about the computer and video game industry: 2012 sales, demographic, and usage data. Retrieved from http://www.theesa.com/facts/pdfs/ESA_EF_2012.pdf

Erdur-Baker, O. (2010). Cyberbullying and its correlation to traditional bullying, gender and frequent and risky usage of Internet-mediated communication tools. *New Media and Society, 12,* 109–125.

Ewald, J. (2010). "Do you know where X is?": Direction-giving and male/female direction-givers. *Journal of Pragmatics, 42*(9), 2549–2561.

Ewalt, D. (2005, September 17). Jane Goodall on why words hurt. *Forbes.* Retrieved from http://www.forbes.com

Eyssel, F., & Kuchenbrandt, D. (2012). Social categorization of social robots: Anthropomorphism as a function of robot group membership. *British Journal of Social Psychology, 51*(4), 724–731.

Faiola, A. (2005, September 22). Men in land of samurai find their feminine side. *Washington Post Foreign Service.* Retrieved from http://www.washingtonpost.com/wp-dyn/content/article/2005/09/21/AR2005092102434.html

Farley, S. D. (2008). Attaining status at the expense of likeability: Pilfering power through conversational interruption. *Journal of Nonverbal Behavior, 32*(4), 241–260.

Farnsworth, S. J., & Lichter, S. R. (2010). *The nightly news nightmare: Media coverage of U.S. presidential elections, 1988–2008* (3rd ed.). Lanham, MD: Rowman & Littlefield.

Farroni, T., Csibra, G., Simion, F., & Johnson, M. (2002, July 9). Eye contact detection in humans from birth. *Proceedings of the National Academy of Sciences of the United States of America, 99,* 9602–9605. Retrieved from http://www.pnas.org/cgi/doi/10.1073/pnas.152159999

Faughnder, R. (2014, January 30). TV ratings: "American Idol" dominates; "Super Fun Night" falls. Retrieved from http://www.latimes.com/entertainment/envelope/cotown/la-et-ct-tv-ratings-american-idol-super-fun-night-0140130,0,1521079.story#axzz2s7UZtE00

Fayard, A. (2013, February 13). One approach does not fit all. *The New York Times.* Retrieved from http://www.nytimes.com/roomfordebate/2013/02/27/the-costs-and-benefits-of-telecommuting/in-telecommuting-one-approach-does-not-fit-all

Federal Communications Commission. (2008, January 8). *Understanding workplace harassment.* Retrieved September 3, 2008, from http://www.fcc.gov/owd/understandingharassment.html

Federal Communications Commission v. *Pacifica Foundation,* 438 U.S. 726 (1978).

Fent, B., & MacGeorge, E. L. (2006). Predicting receptiveness to advice: Characteristics of the problem, the advice-giver, and the recipient. *Southern Communication Journal, 71,* 67–85.

Ferguson, C. J., & Dyck, D. (2012). Paradigm change in aggression research: The time has come to retire the General Aggression Model. *Aggression and Violent Behavior, 17*(3), 220–228. doi:10.1016/j.avb.2012.02.007

Festinger, L. (1954). A theory of social comparison processes. *Human Relations, 7,* 117–140.

Feuer, A. (2012, November 9). Occupy Sandy: A movement moves to relief. *The New York Times*. Retrieved from http://www.nytimes.com/2012/11/11/nyregion/where-fema-fell-short-occupy-sandy-was-there.html?pagewanted=all

Figdor, C. (2010). Objectivity in the news: Finding a way forward. *Journal of Mass Media Ethics, 25,* 19–33.

Finder, A. (2006, June 11). For some, online persona undermines a resume. *The New York Times.*

Fisk, G. M. (2010). "I want it all and I want it now!" An examination of the etiology, expression, and escalation of excessive employee entitlement. *Human Resource Management Review, 20*(2), 102–114.

Fiske, S. T., & Taylor, S. E. (1991). *Social cognition.* New York: McGraw-Hill.

Fitch-Hauser, M., Powers, W. G., O'Brien, K., & Hanson, S. (2007). Extending the conceptualization of listening fidelity. *International Journal of Listening, 21*(2), 81–91.

Flaherty, L. M., Pearce, K., & Rubin, R. B. (1998). Internet and face-to-face communication: Not functional alternatives. *Communication Quarterly, 46,* 250–268.

Flanagin, A. J., & Metzger, M. J. (2007). The role of site features, user attributes, and information verification behaviors on the perceived credibility of Web-based information. *New Media & Society, 9,* 319–342.

Flecha-García, M. (2010). Eyebrow raises in dialogue and their relation to discourse structure, utterance function and pitch accents in English. *Speech Communication, 52*(6), 542–554.

Fletcher, C. (1999). Listening to narratives: The dynamics of capturing police experience. *International Journal of Listening, 13,* 46–61.

Flynn, J., Valikoski, T., & Grau, J. (2008). Listening in the business context: Reviewing the state of research. *International Journal of Listening, 22*(2), 141–151.

Foels, R., Driskell, J. E., Mullen, B., & Salas, E. (2000). The effects of democratic leadership on group member satisfaction. *Small Group Research, 31,* 676–701.

Folger, J. P., Poole, M. S., & Stutman, R. K. (2001). *Working through conflict: Strategies for relationships, groups, and organizations* (4th ed.). New York: Longman.

Forward, G. L., Czech, K., & Lee, C. M. (2011). Assessing Gibb's supportive and defensive communication climate: An examination of measurement and construct validity. *Communication Research Reports, 28*(1), 1–15.

Fox, L. (2013). Poll: Voters ready for a woman president. Retrieved from http://www.usnews.com/news/articles/2013/05/02/poll-voters-ready-for-a-woman-president.

Fox 13 News (Salt Lake City). (2013). Elizabeth Smart speaks at Johns Hopkins University. VIDEO. Retrieved from http://fox13now.com/2013/05/06/video-elizabeth-smart-speaks-at-johns-hopkins-university [11:24]

Fraleigh, D. M., & Tuman, J. S. (2011). *Speak up! An illustrated guide to public speaking* (2nd ed.). New York: Bedford/St. Martin's.

French, J. R. P., & Raven, B. (1959). The bases for power. In D. Cartwright (Ed.), *Studies in social power* (pp. 150–167). Ann Arbor, MI: Institute for Social Research.

Fridlund, A. J., & Russell, J. A. (2006). The functions of facial expressions: What's in a face? In V. Manusov & M. L. Patterson (Eds.), *The SAGE handbook of nonverbal communication* (pp. 299–320). Thousand Oaks, CA: Sage Publications.

Friedman, T. L. (2007). *The world is flat: A brief history of the twenty-first century.* New York: Farrar, Straus & Giroux.

Frisby, B. N., & Sidelinger, R. J. (2013). Violating student expectations: Student disclosures and student reactions in the college classroom. *Communication Studies, 64*(3), 241–258.

Frosch, D. (2013, March 18). Dispute on transgender rights unfolds at a Colorado school. *The New York Times*, p. A10.

Frum, D. (2000). *How we got here: The '70s.* New York: Basic Books.

Frymier, A. B. (1994). A model of immediacy in the classroom. *Communication Quarterly, 42,* 133–144.

Frymier, A. B., & Nadler, M. K. (2013). *Persuasion: Integrating theory, research, and practice* (3rd ed.). Dubuque, IA: Kendall Hunt.

Fuller, B. (2013, July 24). Kate Middleton: Good for you for showing off your post-baby bump. Hollywoodlife.com. Retrieved from http://hollywoodlife.com/2013/07/24/kate-middleton-good-for-you-for-showing-off-your-post-baby-bump

Gabriel, T. (2010, November 4). Learning in dorm, because class is on the Web. *The New York Times*. Retrieved from http://www.nytimes.com/2010/11/05/us/05college.html

Gagnon, M., Gosselin, P., Hudon-ven der Buhs, I., Larocque, K., & Milliard, K. (2010). Children's recognition and discrimination of fear and disgust facial expressions. *Journal of Nonverbal Behavior, 34*(1), 27–42.

Gallois, C., Franklyn-Stokes, A., Giles, H., & Coupland, N. (1988). Communication accommodation in intercultural encounters. In Y. Y. Kim & W. B. Gudykunst (Eds.), *Theories in intercultural communication* (pp. 157–85). Newbury Park, CA: Sage Publications.

Gardner, L. A. (2011). Wat 2 Do Abt Txt'n & Drv'n (aka: What to do about the problem of texting while driving?). *CPCU Journal, 63,* 1–13.

Gardner, W. L., Reithel, B. J., Foley, R. T., Cogliser, C. C., & Walumbwa, F. O. (2009). Attraction to organizational culture profiles: Effects of realistic recruitment and vertical and horizontal individualism–collectivism. *Management Communication Quarterly, 22*(3), 437–472.

Garner, J. T., & Poole, M. S. (2009). Opposites attract: Leadership endorsement as a function of interaction between a leader and a foil. *Western Journal of Communication, 73*(3), 227–247.

Gates, B. (2009, February). TED Talks: Bill Gates on Mosquitoes, Malaria, and Education. Retrieved from http://www.ted.com/talks/lang/eng/bill_gates_unplugged.html

Gawande, A. (2009). *The checklist manifesto: How to get things right.* New York: Metropolitan Books.

Gay, V. (2014, January). 45 best TV shows to binge-watch. Newsday.com. Retrieved from http://www.newsday.com/entertainment/tv/45-best-tv-shows-to-binge-watch-1.5631924#46

Gayomali, C. (2013, June 14). How typeface influences the way we read and think: And why everyone hates Comic Sans MS. *The Week*. Retrieved from http://theweek.com/article/index/245632/how-typeface-influences-the-way-we-read-and-think

Gearhart, C., & Bodie, G. D. (2011). Active-empathic listening as a general social skill: Evidence from bivariate and canonical correlations. *Communication Reports, 24*, 86–98.

Gehrke, P. J. (2009). Between the Ear and the Eye: A Synaesthetic Introduction to Listening Ethics. *The International Journal of Listening 23*, 1–6.

Gerbner, G., Gross, L., Morgan, M., & Signorielli, N. (1994). Growing up with television: The cultivation perspective. In J. Bryant & D. Zillmann (Eds.), *Media effects: Advances in theory and research* (pp. 17–41). Hillsdale, NJ: Erlbaum.

Gersick, C. J. G. (1988). Time and transition in work teams: Toward a new model of group development. *The Academy of Management Journal, 31*(1), 9–41.

Gersick, C. J. G., & Hackman, J. R. (1990). Habitual routines in task-performing groups. *Organizational Behavior and Human Decision Processes, 47*, 65–97.

Gettleman, J. (2008, October 18). Rape victims' words help jolt Congo into change. *The New York Times*, p. A1.

Gibb, J. (1961). Defensive communication. *Journal of Communication, 2*, 141–148.

Giles, H., Coupland, J., & Coupland, N. (1991). *Contexts of accommodation: Developments in applied sociolinguistics*. Cambridge, England: Cambridge University Press.

Giles, H., Coupland, N., & Wiemann, J. M. (1992). "Talk is cheap..." but "My word is my bond": Beliefs about talk. In K. Bolton & H. Kwok (Eds.), *Sociolinguistics today: Eastern and Western perspectives* (pp. 218–243). London: Routledge and Kegan Paul.

Giles, H., Fortman, J., Dailey, R. M., Barker, V., Hajek, C., Anderson, M. C., & Rule, N. O. (2006). Communication accommodation: Law enforcement and the public. In R. M. Dailey & B. A. LePoire (Eds.), *Applied interpersonal communication matters: Family, health, and community relations* (pp. 241–269). New York: Peter Lang.

Giles, H., & LePoire, B. A. (2006). Introduction: The ubiquity and social meaningfulness of nonverbal communication. In V. Manusov & M. L. Patterson (Eds.), *The SAGE handbook of nonverbal communication* (pp. xv–xxvii). Thousand Oaks, CA: Sage Publications.

Giles, H., Reid, S., & Harwood, J. (Eds.) (2010). *The dynamics of intergroup communication*. New York: Peter Lang.

Giles, H., & Wiemann, J. M. (1987). Language, social comparison, and power. In C. R. Berger & S. H. Chaffee (Eds.), *Handbook of communication science* (pp. 350–384). Newbury Park, CA: Sage Publications.

Gillath, O., McCall, C., Shaver, P. R., & Blascovich, J. (2008). What can virtual reality teach us about prosocial tendencies in real and virtual environments? *Media Psychology, 11*(2), 259–282.

Gitlow v. *New York*, 268 U.S. 652 (1925).

Givhan, R. (2013, April 8). The language of Margaret Thatcher's handbags. *The Daily Beast*. Retrieved from http://www.thedailybeast.com/articles/2011/12/19/the-language-of-margaret-thatcher-s-handbags.html

Gladwell, M. (2010, October 4). Small change: Why the revolution will not be tweeted. *The New Yorker*. Retrieved from http://www.newyorker.com/reporting/2010/10/04/101004fa_fact_gladwell?printable=true&currentPage=all#ixzz2Y1RyfEDF

Goffman, E. (1967). *Interaction ritual: Essays on face-to-face behavior*. Garden City, NY: Doubleday.

Gonzaga, G. C., Campos, B., & Bradbury, T. (2007). Similarity, convergence, and relationship satisfaction in dating and married couples. *Journal of Personality & Social Psychology, 93*(1), 34–48.

Gonzales, A. L., & Hancock, J. T. (2011, January/February). Mirror, mirror on my Facebook wall: Effects of exposure to Facebook on self-esteem. *Cyberpsychology, Behavior, and Social Networking, 14*(1–2), 79–83.

Goodman, J. (2013, March 24). Obsessed? You're not alone. *The New York Times*, p. ST9.

Goodrich, A. (2007, March 28). Anxiety about study abroad. *The Georgetown Independent*. Retrieved from http://travel.georgetown.edu/51469.html

Goodwin, D. K. (2002, January 27). How I caused that story. *Time*. Retrieved from http://www.time.com/time/nation/article/0,8599,197614,00.html#ixzz1FMvG5yK9

Gordon, M. E. (2011). The dialectics of the exit interview: A fresh look at conversations about organizational disengagement. *Management Communication Quarterly, 25*(1), 59–86. doi:10.1177/0893318910376914

Gordon, P. (2004, October 15). Numerical cognition without words: Evidence from Amazonia [Supplementary online materials]. *Science Online*. Retrieved March 25, 2008, from http://www.sciencemag.org/cgi/content/full/sci;1094492/DC1

Gore, J. (2009). The interaction of sex, verbal, and nonverbal cues in same-sex first encounters. *Journal of Nonverbal Behavior, 33*(4), 279–299.

Goss, B., & O'Hair, D. (1988). *Communicating in interpersonal relationships*. New York: Macmillan.

Gottman, J. M. (1994). *What predicts divorce? The relationship between marital processes and marital outcomes*. Hillsdale, NJ: Erlbaum.

Gottman, J. M., & Levenson, R. W. (1992). Marital processes predictive of later dissolution: Behavior, physiology, and health. *Journal of Personality and Social Psychology, 63*, 221–233.

Gottman, J. M., & Silver, N. (1999). *The seven principles for making marriages work: A practical guide from the country's foremost relationship expert*. New York: Three Rivers Press.

Goudreau, J. (2013, February 7). The states people are fleeing in 2013. *Forbes*. Retrieved from http://www.forbes.com/sites/jennagoudreau/2013/02/07/the-states-people-are-fleeing-in-2013

Gouran, D. S. (2003). Communication skills for group decision making. In J. O. Greene & B. R. Burleson (Eds.), *Handbook of communication and social interaction skills* (pp. 835–870). Mahwah, NJ: Erlbaum.

Grahe, J. E., & Bernieri, F. J. (1999). The importance of nonverbal cues in judging rapport. *Journal of Nonverbal Behavior, 23,* 253–269.

Gray, F. E. (2010). Specific oral communication skills desired in new accountancy graduates. *Business Communication Quarterly, 73*(1), 40–67.

Greco, B. (1977). Recruiting and retaining high achievers. *Journal of College Placement, 37*(2), 34–40.

Greenberg, B. S., Sherry, J., Lachlan, K., Lucas, K., & Holmstrom, A. (2010). Orientations to video games among gender and age groups. *Simulation & Gaming, 41*(2), 238–259.

Greenhouse, S. (2006, September 3). Now bringing home the leaner bacon: Borrowers we be. *The New York Times*. Retrieved from http://www.nytimes.com

Greenwalk, A. G., Bellezza, F. S., & Banaji, M. R. (1988). Is self-esteem a central ingredient of self-concept? *Personality and Social Psychology Bulletin, 14,* 34–45.

Groeling, T. (2013). Media bias by the numbers: Challenges and opportunities in the empirical study of partisan news. *Political Science, 16*(1), 129.

Grossman, R. B., & Kegl, J. (2007). Moving faces: Categorization of dynamic facial expressions in American Sign Language by deaf and hearing participants. *Journal of Nonverbal Behavior, 31,* 23–28.

Grossman, S. (2013, April 23). Worst first day ever: Rookie TV anchor fired for profanity in first newscast. *Time*. Retrieved from http://newsfeed.time.com/2013/04/23/worst-first-day-ever-rookie-tv-anchor-fired-for-profanity-in-first-newscast

Gudykunst, W. B. (1993). Toward a theory of effective interpersonal and intergroup communication: An anxiety/uncertainty management (AUM) perspective. In R. L. Wiseman & J. Koester (Eds.), *Intercultural communication competence* (pp. 33–71). Newbury Park, CA: Sage Publications.

Gudykunst, W. B. (2004). *Bridging differences: Effective intergroup communication* (4th ed.). Thousand Oaks, CA: Sage Publications.

Gudykunst, W. B., & Ting-Toomey, S. (1988). *Culture and interpersonal communication*. Newbury Park, CA: Sage Publications.

Gudykunst, W. B., Ting-Toomey, S., Sudweeks, S., & Stewart, L. P. (1995). *Building bridges: Interpersonal skills for a changing world*. Boston: Houghton Mifflin Company.

Guéguen, N. (2012). Tattoos , piercings, and sexual activity. *Social Behavior & Personality: An International Journal, 40*(9), 1543–1547.

Guerrero, L. K., & Afifi, W. A. (1995). Some things are better left unsaid: Topic avoidance in family relationships. *Communication Quarterly, 43,* 276–296.

Guerrero, L. K., Andersen, P. A., & Afifi, W. A. (2013). *Close encounters: Communication in relationships*. Los Angeles, CA: Sage Publications.

Guerrero, L. K., Farinelli, L., & McEwan, B. (2009). Attachment and relational satisfaction: The mediating effect of emotional communication. *Communication Monographs, 76*(4), 487–514.

Guerrero, L. K., & Floyd, K. (2006). *Nonverbal communication in close relationships*. Mahwah, NJ: Erlbaum.

Guerrero, L. K., La Valley, A. G., & Farinelli, L. (2008). The experience and expression of anger, guilt, and sadness in marriage: An equity theory explanation. *Journal of Social and Personal Relationships, 25*(5), 699–724.

Haas, J. (2012). Hate speech and stereotypic talk. In H. Giles (Ed.), *The handbook of intergroup communication* (pp. 128–140). New York: Routledge/Taylor and Francis Group.

Hall, E. T. (1959). *The silent language*. New York: Doubleday.

Hall, E. T. (1976). *Beyond culture*. New York: Anchor/Doubleday.

Hall, E. T., & Hall, M. R. (1990). *Understanding cultural differences: Germans, French, and Americans*. Yarmouth, ME: Intercultural Press, Inc.

Hall, J. A. (1998). How big are nonverbal sex differences? The case of smiling and sensitivity to nonverbal cues. In D. J. Canary & K. Dindia (Eds.), *Sex differences and similarities in communication: Critical essays and empirical investigations of sex and gender in interaction* (pp. 155–178). Mahwah, NJ: Erlbaum.

Hall, J. A. (2013). Humor in long-term romantic relationships: The association of general humor styles and relationship-specific functions with relationship satisfaction. *Western Journal of Communication, 77*(3), 272–292.

Hall, J. A., Carter, J. D., & Hogan, T. G. (2000). Gender differences in nonverbal communication of emotion. In A. H. Fischer (Ed.), *Gender and emotion: Social psychological perspectives* (pp. 97–117). Cambridge: Cambridge University Press.

Hallsten, L., Voss, M., Stark, S., & Josephson, M. (2011). Job burnout and job wornout as risk factors for long-term sickness absence. *Work, 38*(2), 181–192.

Halone, K., Cunconan, T. M., Coakley, C. G., and Wolvin, A. D. Toward the establishment of general dimensions underlying the listening process. *International Journal of Listening, 12,* 12–28. (1998).

Hameed, M. (2012, December 20). Team Rubicon: Rebuilding the Rockaways. Thirteen.org, MetroFocus. Retrieved from http://www.thirteen.org/metrofocus/2012/12/team-rubicon-rebuilding-the-rockaways, 2:30

Hammick, J. K., & Lee, M. J. (in press). Do shy people feel less communication apprehension online? The effects of virtual reality on the relationship between personality characteristics and communication outcomes. *Computers in Human Behavior*.

Hample, D. (1987). Communication and the unconscious. In B. Dervin & M. J. Voight (Eds.), *Progress in communication sciences* (Vol. 8, pp. 83–121). Norwood, NJ: Ablex.

Hample, D., & Dallinger, J. M. (1995). A Lewinian perspective on taking conflict personally: Revision, refinement, and validation of the instrument. *Communication Quarterly, 43*(3), 297–319.

Han, B., & Cai, D. (2010). Face goals in apology: A cross-cultural comparison of Chinese and U.S. Americans. *Journal of Asian Pacific Communication, 20*(1), 101–123.

Hansen, H. V. (2002). The straw thing of fallacy theory: The standard definition of "fallacy." *Argumentation, 16,* 133–155.

Hansmann, R., & Scholz, R. W. (2003). A two-step informational strategy for reducing littering behavior in a cinema. *Environment and Behavior, 35*(6), 752–762.

Hardt, B. (2012, November 8). NY1's Bob Hardt Blogs from Rockaway Beach. Retrieved from http://origin.ny1.com/content/news/171519/ny1-blog-ny1-s-bob-hardt-reports-on-sandy-from-rockaway-beach

Harmon, A. (2011, March 19). On Twitter, "What a party!" brings an envious "Enough, already!" *The New York Times*, p. A1.

Harmon, A. H., & Metaxas, P. T. (2010). *How to create a smart mob: Understanding a social network capital.* Unpublished manuscript, Wellesley College. Retrieved from http://cs.wellesley.edu/~pmetaxas/How-to-create-Smart-Mobs%20eDem2010.pdf

Harrigan, J. A., & Taing, K. T. (1997). Fooled by a smile: Detecting anxiety in others. *Journal of Nonverbal Behavior, 21,* 203–221.

Harris, A. L., & Hahn, U. (2011). Unrealistic optimism about future life events: A cautionary note. *Psychological Review, 118*(1), 135–154.

Harris, G. (2011, July 11). New for aspiring doctors, the people skills test. *The New York Times*, p. A1.

Harris, G. (2013, February 14). In India, kisses are on rise, even in public. *The New York Times*, p. A4.

Harris, T. E. (2002). *Applied organizational communication: Principles and pragmatics for future practice* (2nd ed.). Mahwah, NJ: Erlbaum.

Harrison, K., & Cantor, J. (1997). The relationship between media consumption and eating disorders. *Journal of Communication, 47,* 40–66.

Hartmann, T., & Tanis, M. (2013). Examining the hostile media effect as an intergroup phenomenon: The role of ingroup identification and status. *Journal of Communication, 63*(3), 535–555.

Hartnett, S. J. (2010). Communication, social justice, and joyful commitment. *Western Journal of Communication, 74*(1), 68–93.

Hartup, W. W., & Stevens, N. (1997). Friendships and adaptation in the life course. *Psychological Bulletin, 121,* 355–370.

Harwood, J. (2000). Communication media use in the grandparent-grandchild relationship. *Journal of Communication, 50*(4), 56–78.

Harwood, J., & Giles, H. (Eds.) (2005). *Intergroup communication: Multiple perspectives.* New York: Peter Lang.

Haughney, C. (2012). Time and CNN reinstate journalist after review. Retrieved on May 2, 2014, from http://query.nytimes.com/gst/fullpage.html?res=9C00E7DE103BF934A2575BC0A9649D8B63&ref=fareedzakaria

Hawkins, K., & Stewart, R. A. (1991). Effects of communication apprehension on perceptions of leadership and intragroup attraction in small task-oriented groups. *Southern Communication Journal, 57,* 1–10.

Hawkley, L. C., & Cacioppo, J. T. (2010). Loneliness matters: A theoretical and empirical review of consequences and mechanisms. *Annals of Behavioral Medicine, 40*(2), 218–227.

Hayakawa, S. I. (1964). *Language in thought and action.* New York: Harcourt Brace Jovanovich.

Hazel, M., Wongprasert, T. K., & Ayres, J. (2006). Twins: How similar are fraternal and identical twins across four communication variables? *Journal of the Northwest Communication Association, 35,* 46–59.

Hecht, M. L., Jackson, R. L., II, & Ribeau, S. A. (2003). *African American communication: Exploring identity and culture.* Mahwah, NJ: Erlbaum.

Helgesen, S. (1990). *The female advantage: Women's ways of leadership.* Garden City, NY: Doubleday.

Hendrick, S. S., & Hendrick, C. (1992). *Liking, loving, and relating.* Pacific Grove, CA: Brooks/Cole.

Hendriks, A. (2002). Examining the effects of hegemonic depictions of female bodies on television: A call for theory and programmatic research. *Critical Studies in Media Communication, 19,* 106–123.

Henry, A. (2012, May 11). How to choose the best chart for your data. Lifehacker.com. Retrieved from http://lifehacker.com/5909501/how-to-choose-the-best-chart-for-your-data

Herman, M. (2013, January 30). Super Bowl: Are American sports fans the classy ones? *Pacific Standard.* Retrieved from http://www.psmag.com/uncategorized/superbowl-how-to-explain-the-classyness-of-american-sports-fans-52172

Herman, M. (2013, June 13). Crisis-wracked town bets on Smurf-based economy. *Pacific Standard.* Retrieved from http://www.psmag.com/business-economics/crisis-wracked-town-bets-on-smurf-based-economy-60158

Hershatter, A., & Epstein, M. (2010). Millennials and the world of work: An organization and management perspective. *Journal of Business and Psychology, 25*(2), 211–223.

Heslin, R. (1974). *Steps toward a taxonomy of touching.* Paper presented at the Western Psychological Association Convention, Chicago.

Hesse, C., & Rauscher, E. A. (2013). Privacy tendencies and revealing/concealing: The moderating role of emotional competence. *Communication Quarterly, 61*(1), 91–112.

Hicks, A. M., & Diamond, L. M. (2011). Don't go to bed angry: Attachment, conflict, and affective and physiological reactivity. *Personal Relationships, 18*(2), 266–284. doi:http://dx.doi.org/10.1111/j.1475-6811.2011.01355.x

Hinckley, D. (2010, March 14). The price of beauty. *NYDaily News.com*. Retrieved from http://www.nydailynews.com/entertainment/tv/2010/03/14/2010-03-14_vh1s_price_of_beauty_hosted_by_jessica_simpson_is_ditzy_look_at_international_be.html

Hinkle, L. L. (1999). Nonverbal immediacy communication behaviors and liking in marital relationships. *Communication Research Reports, 16*, 81–90.

Hirokawa, R. Y., Gouran, D. S., & Martz, A. E. (1988). Understanding the sources of faulty group decision-making: A lesson from the *Challenger* disaster. *Small Group Behavior, 19*, 411–433.

Hockenbury, D. H., & Hockenbury, S. E. (2009). *Psychology* (5th ed). New York: Worth.

Hoeken, H., Van den Brandt, C., Crijns, R., Dominguez, N., Hendriks, B., Planken, B., & Starren, M. (2003). International advertising in Western Europe: Should differences in uncertainty avoidance be considered when advertising in Belgium, France, the Netherlands and Spain? *Journal of Business Communication, 40*(3), 195–218.

Hofstede, G. (1984). *Culture's consequences: International differences in work-related values.* Beverly Hills, CA: Sage Publications.

Hofstede, G. (2001). *Culture's consequences: Comparing values, behaviors, institutions, and organizations across nations.* Thousand Oaks, CA: Sage Publications.

Hofstede, G., Hofstede, G. J., & Minkov, M. (2010). *Cultures and organizations: Software of the mind* (3rd ed.). New York: McGraw-Hill.

Holland, K. (2006, December 3). Under new management: When work time isn't face time. *The New York Times*. Retrieved from http://www.nytimes.com

Holson, L. M. (2008, March 9). Text generation gap: U r 2 old (jk). *The New York Times*. Retrieved from http://www.nytimes.com/2008/03/09/business/09cell.html

Holson, L. M. (2010, May 8). Tell-all generation learns to keep things offline. *The New York Times*, p. A1.

Homer, P. M. (2006). Relationships among ad-induced affect, beliefs, and attitudes: Another look. *Journal of Advertising, 35*, 35–51.

Honeycutt, J. M., Choi, C. W., & DeBerry, J. R. (2009). Communication apprehension and imagined interactions. *Communication Research Reports, 26*(3), 228–236.

Honeycutt, J. M., & Wiemann, J. M. (1999). Analysis of functions of talk and reports of imagined interactions (IIs) during engagement and marriage. *Human Communication, 25*, 399–419.

Hong, S. M., & Faedda, S. (1996). Refinement of the Hong psychological reactance scale. *Educational and Psychological Measurement, 56*, 173–182.

Hoover, K. (2006, February). Alumni to know: He brought Trader Joe's to Main Street. *Stanford Business Magazine*. Retrieved from http://www.gsb.stanford/edu

Horn, J. (2010, October 31). The production: How *The King's Speech* found its voice. *Los Angeles Times*. Retrieved from http://articles.latimes.com/2010/oct/31/entertainment/laca-sneaks-kings-speech-20101031

Horovitz, B. (2012, May 3). After Gen X, Millennials, what should the next generation be? *USA Today*. Retrieved from http://usatoday30.usatoday.com/money/advertising/story/2012-05-03/naming-the-next-generation/54737518/1

Howard, D. L. (2004, August 2). Silencing Huck Finn. *The Chronicle of Higher Education*. Retrieved from http://chronicle.com/jobs/2004/08/2004080201c.htm

Howe, N. & Strauss, W. (1992). *Generations: The history of America's future, 1584 to 2069*. New York: Quill.

Hseih, T. (2013, March 19). Working from home alone is the real culprit. *Fortune*. Retrieved from http://management.fortune.cnn.com/2013/03/19/working-from-home-telecommuting

Hullman, G. A., Goodnight, A., & Mougeotte, J. (2012). An examination of perceived relational messages that accompany interpersonal communication motivations. *Open Communication Journal, 6*, 1–7.

Husband, C. (2009). Between listening and understanding. *Continuum: Journal of Media & Cultural Studies, 23*(4), 441–443.

Huston, A. C., Bickham, D. S., Lee, J. H., & Wright, J. C. (2007). From attention to comprehension: How children watch and learn from television. In N. Pecora, J. P. Murray, & E. A. Wartella (Eds.), *Children and television: Fifty years of research* (pp. 41–63). Mahwah, NJ: Erlbaum.

Huston, A., & Wright, J. C. (1998). Television and the informational and educational needs of children. *The Annals of the American Academy of Political and Social Science, 557*(1), 9–23.

Huston, D. (2010). Waking up to ourselves: The use of mindfulness meditation and emotional intelligence in the teaching of communications. *New Directions for Community Colleges, 2010*(151), 39–50.

Iedema, R., Jorm, C., Wakefield, J., Ryan, C., & Sorensen, R. (2009). A new structure of attention? Open disclosure of adverse events to patients and their families. *Journal of Language & Social Psychology, 28*(2), 139–157.

Imrov Everywhere. (2014, January 12). No pants subway ride 2014 New York report. Retrieved from http://improveverywhere.com/2014/01/12/no-pants-subway-ride-2014-new-york-reports

Infante, D. A. (1988). *Arguing constructively.* Prospect Heights, IL: Waveland Press.

Infante, D. A., & Rancer, A. S. (1982). A conceptualization and measure of argumentativeness. *Journal of Personality Assessment, 45*, 72–80.

Internet Gaming Disorder. (2013). *DSM5*-org. Retrieved from http://www.dsm5.org/Documents/Internet%20Gaming%20Disorder%20Fact%20Sheet.pdf

"It Gets Better Project" (2013). Retrieved November 1, 2013 from http://www.itgetsbetter.org/pages/about-it-gets-better-project

Ivy, D., & Backlund, P. (2004). *Gender speak: Personal effectiveness in gender communication* (3rd ed.). New York: McGraw-Hill.

Iyengar, S., & Hahn, K. S. (2009). Red media, blue media: Evidence of ideological selectivity in media use. *Journal of Communication, 59,* 19–39.

Jablin, F. M. (1987). Organizational entry, assimilation, and exit. In F. M. Jablin, L. L. Putnam, K. H. Roberts, & L. W. Porter (Eds.), *Handbook of organizational communication* (pp. 679–740). Newbury Park, CA: Sage. Publications.

Jablin, F. M. (2001). Organizational entry, assimilation, and disengagement/exit. In F. M. Jablin & L. L. Putnam (Eds.), *The new handbook of organizational communication: Advances in theory, research, and methods* (pp. 732–818). Thousand Oaks, CA: Sage Publications.

Jablin, F. M., Seibold, D. R., & Sorensen, R. L. (1977). Potential inhibitory effects of group participation on brainstorming preferences. *Central States Speech Journal, 28,* 113–121.

Jablin, F. M., & Sussman, L. (1978). An exploration of communication and productivity in real brainstorming groups. *Human Communication Research, 4,* 329–337.

Jackson, D. (2006, January 29). State of the Union address: A meshing of many ideas. *USA Today.* Retrieved from http:// www.usatoday.com/news/washington/2006-01-29-sotu-speech_x.htm?POE=click-refer

Jacobs, C. D., & Heracleous, L. (2006). Constructing shared understanding: The role of embodied metaphors in organization development. *Journal of Applied Behavioral Science, 42,* 207–227.

Jacobs, T. (2012, December 3). "Slut" label refuses to die. *Pacific Standard.* Retrieved from http://www.alternet.org/gender/why-slut-label-refuses-die

Jacobs, T. (2013, January 16, 2013). Chick lit may be hazardous to your self-esteem. *Pacific Standard.* Retrieved from http://www.psmag.com/blogs/news-blog/chick-lit-may-be-hazardous-to-your-self-esteem-51671

Jacobs, T. (2013, February 11). Why you can't stop perusing your Facebook profile. Retrieved from http://www.psmag .com/blogs/news-blog/why-you-cant-stop-checking-your-facebook-profile-52531

Jacobs, T. (2013, March 27). Mindfulness training boosts test scores. *Pacific Standard.* Retrieved from http://www.psmag.com/ blogs/news-blog/mindfulness-training-boosts-test-scores-54431

Jacobson, S. (2013). Does audience participation on Facebook influence the news agenda? A case study of *The Rachel Maddow Show. Journal of Broadcasting & Electronic Media, 57*(3), 338–355.

James, C. H., & Minnis, W. C. (2004, July–August). Organizational storytelling: It makes sense. *Business Horizons,* pp. 23–32.

Janis, I. L. (1982). *Groupthink: Psychological studies of policy decisions and fiascoes* (2nd ed.). Boston: Houghton Mifflin.

Janusik, L. (2005). Conversational listening span: A proposed measure of conversational listening. *International Journal of Listening, 19,* 12–28.

Janusik, L. A., & Wolvin, A. D. (2009). 24 hours in a day: A listening update to the time studies. *International Journal of Listening, 23*(2), 104–120.

Jessica Simpson "really, really frustrated" with progress of post-pregnancy weight-loss. (2013, August 13). RadarOnline. com. Retrieved from http://radaronline.com/exclusives/2013/08/jessica-simpson-baby-weight-loss-ok

Jin, B., & On, S. (2010). Cultural differences of social network influence on romantic relationships: A comparison of the United States and South Korea. *Communication Studies, 61*(2), 156–171.

Johansson, C., & Stohl, C. (2012). Cultural competence and institutional contradictions: The hydropower referendum. *Journal of Applied Communication Research, 40*(4), 329–349.

Johnson, D. I. (2012). Swearing by peers in the work setting: Expectancy violation valence, perceptions of message, and perceptions of speaker. *Communication Studies, 63*(2), 136–151.

Johnson, D. I., & Lewis, N. (2010). Perceptions of swearing in the work setting: An expectancy violations theory perspective. *Communication Reports, 23,* 106–118.

Johnson, S. (2005, April 24). Watching TV makes you smarter. *The New York Times.* Retrieved from http://www.nytimes .com/2005/04/24/magazine/24TV.html

Johnson, S. D., Suriya, C., Yoon, S. W., Berrett, J. V., & Fleur, J. L. (2002). Team development and group processes of virtual learning teams. *Computers & Education, 39,* 379–393.

Johnson, T. (2010, April 19). Land that job: What interviewers really want you to ask them. *Good Morning America.* Retrieved from http://abcnews.go.com/GMA/JobClub/questions-job-interview/story?id=10409243

Johnston, M. K., Weaver, J. B., Watson, K. W., & Barker, L. B. (2000). Listening styles: Biological or psychological differences? *International Journal of Listening, 14,* 32–46.

Joiner, R., Gavin, J., Brosnan, M., Cromby, J., Gregory, H., Guiller, J., Maras, P., & Moon, A. (2013). Comparing first and second generation digital natives' Internet use, Internet anxiety, and Internet identification. *Cyberpsychology, Behavior, and Social Networking, 16*(7), 549–552. ISSN 2152-271

Jolie, A. (2009, June 18). Angelina Jolie speaks on World Refugee Day. Video retrieved from http://www.youtube.com/user/AngelinaJolieUNHCR#p/u/87/qtt1Vs9Lcp0. Quote begins at 0:20 and ends at 1:00.

Jones, C. (2005, May 16). Gay marriage debate still fierce one year later. *USA Today.* Retrieved from http://www.usatoday .com/news/nation/2005-05-16-gay-marriage_x.htm

Jones, D. (2004, November 30). Best friends good for business. *USA Today.* Retrieved May 10, 2008, from http://www .usatoday.com/money/workplace/2004=/=30=best=friends_x .htm

Jones, E. E. (1990). *Interpersonal perception.* New York: Freeman.

Jordet, G., Hartman, E., & Jelle Vuijk, F. (2012). Team history and choking under pressure in major soccer penalty shootouts. *British Journal of Psychology, 103*(2), 268–283.

Joyce, M. P. (2008). Interviewing techniques used in selected organizations today. *Business Communication Quarterly, 71*(3), 376–380.

Jundi, S., Vrij, A., Hope, L., Mann, S., & Hillman, J. (2013). Establishing evidence through undercover and collective intelligence interviewing. *Psychology, Public Policy, and Law, 19*(3), 297–306. doi:10.1037/a0033571

Kadushin, A., & Kadushin, G. (2013). *The social work interview* (5th ed.). New York: Columbia University Press.

Kaiser Family Foundation. (2010, January 20). Daily media use among children and teens up dramatically from five years ago. In *Generation M2: Media in the lives of 8- to 18-year-olds*. Retrieved from http://www.kff.org/entmedia/8010.cfm

Kalbfleisch, P. J. (2002). Communicating in mentoring relationships: A theory for enactment. *Communication Theory, 12,* 63–69.

Kalman, Y. M., & Rafaeli, S. (2011). Online pauses and silence: Chronemic expectancy violations in written computer-mediated communication. *Communication Research, 38*(1), 54–69.

Kalman, Y. M., Ravid, G., Raban, D. R., & Rafaeli, S. (2006). Pauses and response latencies: A chronemic analysis of asynchronous CMC. *Journal of Computer-Mediated Communication, 12*(1), 1–23.

Kameda, T., Ohtsubo, Y., & Takezawa, M. (1997). Centrality in sociocognitive networks and social influence: An illustration in a group decision-making context. *Journal of Personality and Social Psychology, 73,* 296–309.

Kanter, R. M. (2009). *Supercorp: How vanguard companies create innovation, profits, growth, and social good.* New York: Crown Business.

Karau, S. J., & Williams, K. D. (1993). Social loafing: A meta-analytic review and theoretical integration. *Journal of Personality and Social Psychology, 65*(4), 681–706.

Karau, S. J., & Williams, K. D. (2001). Understanding individual motivation in groups: The collective effort model. In M. E. Turner (Ed.), *Groups at work: Theory and research. Applied social research* (pp. 113–141). Mahwah, NJ: Erlbaum.

Kato, S., Kato, Y., & Scott, D. (2009). Relationships between emotional states and emoticons in mobile phone email communication in Japan. *International Journal on E-Learning, 8*(3), 385–401.

Katzenbach, J. R., & Smith, D. K. (1993). *The wisdom of teams.* Boston: Harvard Business School Press.

Kazemi, D. M., Levine, M. J., Dmochowski, J., Nies, M. A., & Sun, L. (2013). Effects of motivational interviewing intervention on blackouts among college freshmen. *Journal of Nursing Scholarship, 45*(3), 221–229. doi:10.1111/jnu.12022

Keaten, J. A., & Kelly, L. (2008). "Re: We really need to talk": Affect for communication channels, competence, and fear of negative evaluation. *Communication Quarterly, 56*(4), 407–426.

Keating, C. F. (2006). Why and how the silent self speaks volumes: Functional approaches to nonverbal impression management. In V. Manusov & M. L. Patterson (Eds.), *The SAGE handbook of nonverbal communication* (pp. 321–340). Thousand Oaks, CA: Sage Publications.

Keller, E. (2009, September 24). One religion, two faiths. *Slate.* Retrieved from http://www.slate.com/blogs/xx_factor/ 2009/09/24/a_commitment_to_our_judaism_threatened_ our_relationship.html, para 1.

Keller, J. (2013, June 10). "The Internet made me do it." Stop blaming social media for our behavioral problems. *Pacific Standard.* Retrieved from http://www.psmag.com/culture/ internet-blaming-social-media-behavioral-problems-59538/# .UbYRNDRH9DQ

Kennedy, R. (2003). *Nigger: The strange career of a troublesome word.* New York: Vintage Books.

Kenrick, D. T., Griskevicius, V., Neuberg, S. L., & Schaller, M. (2010). Renovating the pyramid of needs: Contemporary extensions built upon ancient foundations. *Perspectives on Psychological Science, 5*(3), 292–314.

Keyton, J. (1993). Group termination: Completing the study of group development. *Small Group Research, 24,* 84–100.

Keyton, J., Ferguson, P., & Rhodes, S. C. (2001). Cultural indicators of sexual harassment. *Southern Communication Journal, 67,* 33–50.

Keyton, J., & Frey, L. R. (2002). The state of traits: Predispositions and group communication. In L. R. Frey (Ed.), *New directions in group communication* (pp. 99–120). Thousand Oaks, CA: Sage Publications.

Kiesling, S. F. (1998). Men's identities and sociolinguistic variation: The case of fraternity men. *Journal of Sociolinguistics, 2*(1), 69–99.

Kilmann, P. R. (2012). Personality and interpersonal characteristics within distressed marriages. *The Family Journal, 20*(2), 131–139.

Kirchner, L. (2013, June 10). Brain-scan lie detectors just don't work. *Pacific Standard.* Retrieved from http://www .psmag.com/science/brain-scan-lie-detectors-just-dont-work- 59584/#.UbZXyOabDMY

Kissell, R. (2014, January 20). "Sherlock" sees rising ratings in return to PBS on Sunday. Retrieved from http://variety .com/2014/tv/news/sherlock-sees-rising-ratings-in-return-to- pbs-on-sunday-1201065620

Klein, E. (2013, April 28). If this was a pill, you'd do anything to get it. *Washington Post.* http://www.washingtonpost.com/ blogs/wonkblog/wp/2013/04/28/if-this-was-a-pill-youd-do- anything-to-get-it/

Kleinmann, M., & Klehe, U. (2011). Selling oneself: Construct and criterion-related validity of impression management in structured interviews. *Human Performance, 24*(1), 29–46. doi:10.1080/08959285.2010.530634

Kline, S., Horton, B., & Zhang, S. (2005). *How we think, feel, and express love: A cross-cultural comparison between American and East Asian cultures.* Paper presented at the annual meeting of the International Communication Association, New York.

Klocke, U. (2007). How to improve decision making in small groups: Effects of dissent and training interventions. *Small Group Research, 38,* 437–468.

Knapp, M. L. (2008). *Lying and deception in human interaction.* Boston: Pearson.

Knapp, M. L., & Hall, J. A. (2010). *Nonverbal communication in human interaction.* Boston, MA: Wadsworth, Cengage Learning.

Knapp, M. L., Hart, R. P., Friedrich, G. W., & Shulman, G. M. (1973). The rhetoric of goodbye: Verbal and nonverbal correlates of human leave-taking. *Communication Monographs, 40,* 182–198.

Knapp, M. L., & Vangelisti, A. (2000). *Interpersonal communication and human relationships* (4th ed.). Newton, MA: Allyn & Bacon.

Knapp, M. L., & Vangelisti, A. L. (2008). *Interpersonal communication and human relationships.* Boston: Allyn and Bacon.

Knobloch, L. K., & Solomon, D. H. (2002). Information seeking beyond initial interaction: Negotiating relational uncertainty within close relationships. *Human Communication Research, 28,* 243–257.

Kobayshi, J., & Viswat, L. (2010). Cultural expectations in expressing disagreement: Differences between Japan and the United States. *Asian EFL Journal, 48.*

Koerner, B. I. (2013, September 26). Forget foreign languages and music. Teach our kids to code. *Wired.* Retrieved from http://www.wired.com/opinion/2013/09/ap_code

Kois, D. (2012, April 1). The payoff. *The New York Times Sunday Magazine,* p. MM18.

Kolb, D. M., & Putnam, L. L. (1992). Introduction: The dialectics of disputing. In D. M. Kolb & J. M. Bartunek (Eds.), *Hidden conflict in organizations: Uncovering behind the scenes disputes.* Newbury Park, CA: Sage Publications.

Kotler, P., & Keller, K. (2011). *Marketing management* (14th ed.). Upper Saddle River, NJ: Prentice Hall.

Kotlyar, I., & Ariely, D. (2013). The effect of nonverbal cues on relationship formation. *Computers in Human Behavior, 29*(3), 544–551.

Kowitz, A. C., & Knutson, T. J. (1980). *Decision making in small groups: The search for alternatives.* Needham Heights, MA: Allyn & Bacon.

Kram, K. E. (1983). Phases of the mentor relationship. *Academy of Management Journal, 12,* 608–625.

Kramer, M. W., & Pier, P. M. (1999). Students' perceptions of effective and ineffective communication by college teachers. *Southern Communication Journal, 65,* 16–33.

Krayer, K. (2010). *Influencing skills for effective leadership.* Dallas: University of Dallas College of Business.

Kremar, M., & Greene, K. (1999). Predicting exposure to and uses of television violence. *Journal of Communication, 49,* 24–46.

Kreamer, A. (2006, June). Back to my roots: A diary of going gray. *More Magazine.* Retrieved from http://www.more.com/beauty/hair/back-my-roots-diary-going-gray, paragraph 1.

Kreamer, A. (2007, September). Sex and the gray haired woman. *More Magazine.* Retrieved from http://www.more.com/relationships/dating-sex-love/sex-and-gray-haired-woman

Kross, E., Verduyn, P., Demiralp, E., Park, J., Lee, D. S., Lin, N., Shablack, H., Jonides, J., & Ybarra, O. (2013). Facebook use predicts declines in subjective well-being in young adults. *PLoS ONE 8*(8): e69841. doi:10.1371/journal.pone.0069841

Kruger, J., & Dunning, D. (1999). Unskilled and unaware of it: How difficulties in recognizing one's own incompetence lead to inflated self-assessments. *Journal of Personality and Social Psychology, 77*(6), 1121–1134.

Kruglanski, A. W., Chen, X., Pierro, A., Mannetti, L., Erb, H.-P., & Spiegel, S. (2006). Persuasion according to the unimodel: Implications for cancer communication. *Journal of Communication, 56,* 105–122.

Krumhuber, E., Manstead, A., Cosker, D., Marshall, D., & Rosin, P. (2009). Effects of dynamic attributes of smiles in human and synthetic faces: A simulated job interview setting. *Journal of Nonverbal Behavior, 33*(1), 1–15.

Kuhn, T., & Poole, M. S. (2000). Do conflict management styles affect group decision making? Evidence from a longitudinal field study. *Human Communication Research, 26,* 558–590.

LaBarre, S. (2013, September 24). Why we're shutting off our comments. PopularScience.com. Retrieved from http://www.popsci.com/science/article/2013-09/why-were-shutting-our-comments, paragraph 2

Lambert, C. (2012, March–April). Twilight of the lecture: The trend toward "active learning" may overthrow the style of teaching that has ruled universities for 600 years. *Harvard Magazine.* Retrieved from http://harvardmagazine.com/2012/03/twilight-of-the-lecture

Lammers, J., Dubois, D., Rucker, D. D., & Galinsky, A. D. (2013). Power gets the job: Priming power improves interview outcomes. *Journal of Experimental Social Psychology, 49*(4), 776–779. doi:10.1016/j.jesp.2013.02.008.

Lämsä, A.-M., & Sintonen, T. (2006). A narrative approach for organizational learning in a diverse organization. *Journal of Workplace Learning, 18,* 106–120.

Landis, D., Bennett, J. M., and Bennett, M. J. (Eds.). (2004). *Handbook of intercultural training.* Thousand Oaks, CA: Sage Publications.

Landro, L. (April 8, 2013). The talking cure for health care. *The Wall Street Journal.* http://online.wsj.com/news/articles/SB10001424127887323628804578346223960774296

Landsford, J. E., Antonucci, T. C., Akiyama, H., & Takahashi, K. (2005). A quantitative and qualitative approach to social relationships and well-being in the United States and Japan. *Journal of Comparative Family Studies, 36,* 1–22.

Larkey, L., & Hecht, M. (2010). A model of effects of narrative as culture-centric health promotion. *Journal of Health Communication, 15*(2), 114–135.

Latane, B., Williams, K., & Harkins, S. (1979). Many hands make light the work: The causes and consequences of social loafing. *Journal of Personality and Social Psychology, 37*(6), 822–832.

Lawler, K. A., Younger, J. W., Piferi, R. L., Billington, E., Jobe, R., Edmondson, K., & Jones, W. H. (2003). A change of heart: Cardiovascular correlates of forgiveness in response to interpersonal conflict. *Journal of Behavioral Medicine, 26*(5), 373–393.

Le, V. (2011, March 15). Ask an academic: The secret of boys. *The New Yorker* (blog). Retrieved from http://www.newyorker

.com/online/blogs/books/2011/03/ask-an-academic-the-deep-secrets-of-boys-friendships.html?printable=true&currentPage=all

Leal, S., & Vrij, A. (2008). Blinking during and after lying. *Journal of Nonverbal Behavior, 32*(4), 187–194.

Leavitt, H. J. (1951). Some effects of certain communication patterns on group performance. *Journal of Abnormal and Social Psychology, 46,* 38–50.

Lebo, B. (2009). Employing millennials: Challenges and opportunities. *New Hampshire Business Review, 31*(26), 21.

Ledbetter, A. M. (2008). Chronemic cues and sex differences in relational e-mail: Perceiving immediacy and supportive message quality. *Social Science Computer Review, 26*(4), 486–482.

Lee, E-J. (2007). Effects of gendered language on gender stereotyping in computer-mediated communication: The moderating role of depersonalization and gender-role orientation. *Human Communication Research, 33*(4), 515–535.

Lee, J. A. (1973). *The colors of love: An exploration of the ways of loving.* Don Mills, Ontario, Canada: New Press.

Leland, J. (2008, October 7). In "sweetie" and "dear," a hurt for the elderly. *The New York Times,* p. A1.

Lemonick, M. (2007, May 3). The *Time* 100: Neil deGrasse Tyson. *Time.* Retrieved from www.time.com/time/specials/2007/time100

le Roux, M. (2006, November 27). Let's talk about sex: Cult South African director shatters taboos. *Namibian.* Retrieved from http://www.namibian.com.na/2006/November/africa/065E8B0EB5.html

Levin, D. (2012, August 4). Beach essentials in China: Flip-flops, a towel and a ski mask. *The New York Times,* p. A1.

Levine, E., & Parks, L. A. (Eds.). (2007). *Undead TV: Essays on Buffy the Vampire Slayer.* Durham, NC: Duke University Press.

Levine, T. R., Serota, K. B., Shulman, H., Clare, D. D., Park, H. S., Shaw, A. S., & Lee J. H. (2011). Sender demeanor: Individual differences in sender believability have a powerful impact on deception detection judgments. *Human Communication Research, 37,* 377–403.

Levit, A. (2010, March 14). Master online searches. The Wall Street Journal Online. Retrieved from http://online.wsj.com/news/articles/SB126852207486461893

Lewis, L. (2005). Foster a loyal workforce. In *Trader Joe's adventure: Turning a unique approach to business into a retail and cultural phenomenon* (pp. 137–152). New York: Dearborn/Kaplan.

Lewis, T., & Manusov, V. (2009). Listening to another's distress in everyday relationships. *Communication Quarterly, 57*(3), 282–301.

Li, L., & Pitts, J. (2009). Does it really matter? Using virtual office hours to enhance student–faculty interaction. *Journal of Information Systems Education, 20*(2).

Ligos, M. (2001, June 20). Getting over the fear-of-speaking hump. *The New York Times.* Retrieved from http://www.nytimes.com

Lim, G. Y., & Roloff, M. E. (1999). Attributing sexual consent. *Journal of Applied Communication Research, 27,* 1–23.

Limon, M. S., & La France, B. H. (2005). Communication traits and leadership emergence: Examining the impact of argumentativeness, communication apprehension, and verbal aggressiveness in work groups. *Southern Communication Journal, 70*(2), 123–133.

Lincoln, A. (1842, February 22). Temperance address. *Repeat After Us.* Retrieved August 14, 2007, from http://www.repeatafterus.com/title.php?i=9700

Lindsley, S. L. (1999). Communication and "the Mexican way": Stability and trust as core symbols in *maquiladoras. Western Journal of Communication, 63,* 1–31.

Lipari, L. (2009). Listening otherwise: The voice of ethics. *International Journal of Listening, 23*(1), 44–59.

Lipinski-Harten, M., & Tafarodi, R. W. (2012). A comparison of conversational quality in online and face-to-face first encounters. *Journal of Language & Social Psychology, 31*(3), 331–341.

Liston, B. (2013, November 20). Charges dropped against girls in Florida cyberbullying case. *Reuters.* Retrieved from http://www.reuters.com/article/2013/11/21/us-usa-florida-cyberbullying-idUSBRE9AK05C20131121

Loden, M., & Rosener, J. B. (1991). *Workforce America! Managing employee diversity as a vital resource.* Chicago: Business One Irwin.

Lohr, S. (2007, October 31). Hello, India? I need help with my math. *The New York Times.* Retrieved from http://www.nytimes.com

Longley, R. (2007, December 31). From time to time: The State of the Union. *About.com: U.S. government info.* Retrieved from http://usgovinfo.about.com/od/thepresidentandcabinet/a/souhistory.htm

Lubell, S. (2004, February 19). On the therapist's couch, a jolt of virtual reality. *The New York Times.* Retrieved from http://www.nytimes.com

Lucas, K., & Sherry, J. L. (2004). Sex differences in video game play: A communication-based explanation. *Communication Research, 31,* 499–523.

Lucero, M. A., Allen, R. E., & Elzweig, B. (2013). Managing employee social networking: Evolving views from the National Labor Relations Board. *Employee Responsibilities and Rights Journal, 25*(3), 143–158.

Luo, M. (2010, March 29). Overqualified? Yes, but happy to have a job. *The New York Times,* p. A1.

Lustig, M. W., & Koester, J. (1993). *Intercultural competence: Interpersonal communication across cultures.* New York: HarperCollins.

Lustig, M. W., & Koester, J. (2006). *Intercultural competence: Interpersonal communication across cultures* (5th ed.). Boston: Allyn & Bacon.

Lutz, C. A. (1996). Engendered emotion: Gender, power, and the rhetoric of emotional control in American discourse. In R. Harre & W. G. Parrott (Eds.), *The emotions: Social, cultural and biological dimensions* (pp. 132–150). Thousand Oaks, CA: Sage Publications.

Macur, J., & Eder, S. (2012, November 4). Runners embrace chance to help residents recover. *The New York Times*. Retrieved from http://www.nytimes.com/2012/11/05/sports/marathon-runners-embrace-chance-to-help-storm-stricken-new-yorkers.html

Madden, M. (2012, February 24). Privacy management on social media sites. Pew Internet & Amerian Life Project. Retrieve from http://www.pewinternet.org/Reports/2012/Privacy-management-on-social-media/Main-findings.aspx?view=all

Madden, M., & Smith, A. (2010, May 26). Reputation management and social media. *Pew Internet & American Life Project*. Retrieved from http://www.pewinternet.org/Reports/2010/Reputation-Management.aspx

Maddux, J.E., & Rogers, R. W. (1983). Protection motivation theory and self-efficacy: A revised theory of fear appeals and attitude change. *Journal of Experimental Social Psychology, 19,* 469-479.

Madlock, P. E., & Kennedy-Lightsey, C. (2010). The effects of supervisors' verbal aggressiveness and mentoring on their subordinates. *Journal of Business Communication, 47*(1), 42–62.

Maguire, K. C., & Kinney, T. A. (2010). When distance is problematic: Communication, coping, and relational satisfaction in female college students' long-distance dating relationships. *Journal of Applied Communication Research, 38*(1), 27–46.

Maiden, B., & Perry, B. (2011). Dealing with free-riders in assessed group work: Results from a study at a UK university. *Assessment & Evaluation in Higher Education, 36*(4), 451–464.

Manroop, L., Boekhorst, J. A., & Harrison, J. A. (2013). The influence of cross-cultural differences on job interview selection decisions. *International Journal of Human Resource Management, 24*(18), 3512–3533. doi:10.1080/09585192.2013.777675.

Mansson, D. H., Myers, S. A., & Turner, L. H. (2010). Relational maintenance behaviors in the grandchild-grandparent relationship. *Communication Research Reports, 27*(1), 68–79.

Marcus, L. (October 4, 2013). How *Project Runway* is getting deafness right. New York Magazine. http://www.vulture.com/2013/10/how-project-runway-is-getting-deafness-right.html

Markoff, J. & Sengupta, S. (November 22, 2011). Separating you and me? 4.74 degrees. *New York Times*, p. B1.

Martinez, E. (2010, March 26). Alexis Pilkington brutally cyber bullied, even after her suicide. *CBS News*. Retrieved from http://www.cbsnews.com/8301-504083_162-20001181-504083.html

Marwick, A., & Boyd, D. (2011, September 12). The drama! Teen conflict, gossip, and bullying in networked publics. A decade in Internet time: Symposium on the dynamics of the Internet and society. Retrieved from SSRN http://ssrn.com/abstract=1926349, p. 18.

Maslach, C. (1982). *Burnout: The cost of caring*. Englewood Cliffs, NJ: Prentice Hall.

Maslow, A. (1954). *Motivation and personality*. New York: Harper & Row.

Mast, M. S. (2002). Dominance as expressed and inferred through speaking time. *Human Communication Research, 28,* 420–450.

Matsumoto, D. (1989). Cultural influences on the perception of emotion. *Journal of Cross-Cultural Psychology, 20*(1), 92–105.

Matsumoto, D., & Hwang, H. (2013). Cultural similarities and differences in emblematic gestures. *Journal of Nonverbal Behavior, 37*(1), 1–27.

Matthes, J. (2013). The affective underpinnings of hostile media perceptions exploring the distinct effects of affective and cognitive involvement. *Communication Research, 40*(3), 360–387.

Mazur, B., Boboryko-Hocazade, J., & Dawidziuk, M. (2012, March). The intercultural competencies of the managers and organization in the global world. *Managerial Challenges of the Contemporary Society, 3,* 117–120.

McCain, J. S. (2008, January 28). John McCain, prisoner of war: A first person account. *U.S. News & World Report*. Retrieved from http://politics.usnews.com/news/articles/2008/01/28/john-mccain-prisoner-of-war-a-first-person-account.html

McClanahan, A. (2006, March 9). What does a feminist "look" like? *Pocono Record*. Retrieved April 8, 2008, from http://www.poconorecord.com

McClintock, E. A. (2010). When does race matter? Race, sex, and dating at an elite university. *Journal of Marriage & Family, 72*(1), 45–72.

McCombs, M. (2005). The agenda-setting function of the press. In G. Overholser & K. H. Jamieson (Eds.), *The press* (pp. 156–168). New York: Oxford University Press.

McConnell, M. (1987). *Challenger: A major malfunction*. Garden City, NY: Doubleday.

McCroskey, J. C. (1970). Measures of communication-bound anxiety. *Speech Monographs, 37,* 269–277.

McCroskey, J. C. (1977). Oral communication apprehension: A summary of recent theory and research. *Human Communication Research, 4,* 78–96.

McCroskey, J. C. (1997). The communication apprehension perspective. In J. A. Daly & J. C. McCroskey (Eds.), *Avoiding communication: Shyness, reticence, and communication apprehension* (pp. 13–38). Cresskill, NJ: Hampton Press.

McCroskey, J. C., & Mehrley, R. S. (1969). The effects of disorganization and nonfluency on attitude change and source credibility. *Speech Monographs, 36,* 13–21.

McCroskey, J. C., & Teven, J. J. (1999). Goodwill: A reexamination of the construct and its measurement. *Communication Monographs, 66,* 90–103.

McDaniel, E., & Andersen, P. A. (1998). International patterns of interpersonal tactile communication: A field study. *Journal of Nonverbal Behavior, 22,* 59–75.

McDonald, M. (2012, September 10). Making Mandarin mandatory—in kindergartens. *The New York Times*. Retrieved from http://rendezvous.blogs.nytimes.com/2012/09/10/making-mandarin-mandatory-in-u-s-kindergartens

McGrane, W. L., Toth, F. J., & Alley, E. B. (1990). The use of interactive media for HIV/AIDS prevention in the military community. *Military Medicine, 155,* 235–240.

McLean, C. (2011, January 24). *Glee*: The making of a musical phenomenon. *The Telegraph.* Retrieved from http://www.telegraph.co.uk/culture/8271318/Glee-the-making-of-a-musical-phenomenon.html

McLeod, D. N., Detenber, B. H., & Eveland, W. P., Jr. (2001). Behind the third-person effect: Differentiating perceptual processes for self and other. *Journal of Communication, 51,* 678–695.

McWhorter, J. (2013, April). Txtng is killing language. JK!!! TED talks. Retrieved from http://www.ted.com/talks/john_mcwhorter_txtng_is_killing_language_jk.html?utm_campaign=&utm_content=ted-androidapp&awesm=on.ted.com_rBl4&utm_source=getpocket.com&utm_medium=on.ted.com-android-share

Mease, J., & Terry, D. (2012). (Organizational [performance) of race]: The co-constitutive performance of race and school board in Durham, NC. *Text & Performance Quarterly, 32,* 121–140.

Mehrabian, A. (1971). *Silent messages.* Belmont, CA: Wadsworth.

Mello, B. (2009). For k-12 educators: Speaking, listening, and media literacy standards. *Spectra, 45*(3), 11.

Merkin, R. S. (2009). Cross-cultural communication patterns—Korean and American communication. *Journal of Intercultural Communication, 20,* 5.

Merolla, A. J. (2010a). Relational maintenance and noncopresence reconsidered: Conceptualizing geographic separation in close relationships. *Communication Theory, 20*(2), 169–193.

Merrill, A. F., & Afifi, T. D. (2012). Examining the bidirectional nature of topic avoidance and relationship dissatisfaction: The moderating role of communication skills. *Communication Monographs, 79*(4), 499–521.

Microsoft, Inc. (2005, March 15). Survey finds workers average only three productive days per week [Press release]. Retrieved April 30, 2008, from http://www.microsoft.com

Miczo, N. (2008). Dependence and independence power, conflict tactics and appraisals in romantic relationships. *Journal of Communication Studies, 1*(1), 56–82.

Mignerey, J. T., Rubin, R. B., & Gorden, W. I. (1995). Organizational entry: An investigation of newcomer communication behavior and uncertainty. *Communication Research, 22,* 54–85.

Miller, C. W., & Roloff, M. E. (2007). The effect of face loss on willingness to confront hurtful messages from romantic partners. *Southern Communication Journal, 72*(3), 247–263.

Miller, D. T., & Morrison, K. R. (2009). Expressing deviant opinions: Believing you are in the majority helps. *Journal of Experimental Social Psychology, 45*(4), 740–747.

Miller, K. (2009). *Organizational communication: Approaches and processes* (5th ed.). Boston: Wadsworth.

Miller, K. I., Birkholt, M., Scott, C., & Stage, C. (1995). Empathy and burnout in human service work: An extension of a communication model. *Communication Research, 22,* 123–147.

Miller, L. C., Cooke, K. K., Tsang, J., & Morgan, F. (1992). Should I brag? Nature and impact of positive boastful disclosures for women and men. *Human Communication Research, 18,* 364–399.

Miller, R. (1991, January 31). Personnel execs reveal the truth about job applicants. *Dallas Morning News,* p. 2D.

Miller, S. K. (2013, November 6). The case for raising your child with two religions. Op Ed, *The New York Times.* Retrieved from http://ideas.time.com/2013/11/06/the-case-for-raising-your-child-with-two-religions

Miller, W. R., & Rollnick, S. (2013). *Motivational interviewing: Helping people change.* New York: Guilford Press.

Minow, N. N. (1961, May 9). Television and the public interest. Speech presented at the meeting of the National Association of Broadcasters, Washington, DC.

Minow, N. N., & Cate, F. H. (2003). Revisiting the vast wasteland. *Federal Communications Law Journal, 55,* 407–434.

Mittel, J. (2006). Narrative complexity in contemporary American television. *The Velvet Light Trap, 58,* 29–40.

Molloy, J. T. (1983). *Molloy's live for success.* New York: Bantam Books.

Money is the top subject for marital spats. (2006, March 20). *Webindia123.com.* Retrieved May 1, 2006, from http://news.webindia123.com/news/ar_showdetails.asp?id=603200038&cat=&n_date=20060320

Monge, P. (1977). The systems perspective as a theoretical basis for the study of human communication. *Communication Quarterly, 25,* 19–29.

Montana Meth Project (2013). Retrieved June 3, 2013, from http://montana.methproject.org

Montepare, J., Koff, E., Zaitchik, D., & Alberet, M. (1999). The use of body movements and gestures as cues to emotions in younger and older adults. *Journal of Nonverbal Behavior, 23,* 133–152.

Montoya, M., Massey, A., Hung, Y., & Crisp, C. (2009). Can you hear me now? Communication in virtual product development teams. *Journal of Product Innovation Management, 26*(2), 139–155.

Moore, G. E. (1903). *Principia ethica.* Cambridge, UK: Cambridge University Press.

Moreland, R. L., & Levine, J. M., (1994). *Understanding small groups.* Boston: Allyn & Bacon.

Morley, D. (2006). Unanswered questions in audience research. *The Communication Review, 9,* 101–121

Morris, D. (1977). *Manwatching.* New York: Abrams.

Morrissey, L. (2010). Trolling is *a* art: Towards a schematic classification of intention in Internet trolling. *Griffith Working Papers in Pragmatics and Intercultural Communications, 3*(2), 75–82.

Morse, C. R., & Metts, S. (2011). Situational and communicative predictors of forgiveness following a relational transgression. *Western Journal of Communication, 75*(3), 239–258.

Motley, M. T. (1990). On whether one can(not) communicate: An examination via traditional communication postulates. *Western Journal of Speech Communication, 56,* 1–20.

Motley, M. T., & Reeder, H. M. (1995). Unwanted escalation of sexual intimacy: Male and female perceptions of connotations and relational consequences of resistance messages. *Communication Monographs, 62,* 355–382.

Muir, C. (2008). Job interviewing. *Business Communication Quarterly, 71*(3), 374–376.

Mulac, A. J., Wiemann, J. M., Widenmann, S. J., & Gibson, T. W. (1988). Male-female language differences and effects in same-sex and mixed-sex dyads: The gender-linked language effect. *Communication Monographs, 55,* 315–335.

Mulgrew, K. E., & Volcevski-Kostas, D. (2012). Short term exposure to attractive and muscular singers in music video clips negatively affects men's body image and mood. *Body Image, 9*(4), 543–546.

Mumby, D. (2000). Communication, organization, and the public sphere: A feminist perspective. In P. Buzzanell (Ed.), *Rethinking organizational and managerial communication from feminist perspectives* (pp. 3–23). Thousand Oaks, CA: Sage Publications.

Muntigl, P., & Choi, K. T. (2010). Not remembering as a practical epistemic resource in couples therapy. *Discourse Studies, 12*(3), 331–356.

Murphy, D. R., Daneman, M., & Schneider, B. A. (2006). Do older adults have difficulty following conversations? *Psychology and Aging, 21,* 49–61.

Myhre, K. E., & Adelman, W. (2013). Motivational interviewing: Helping teenaged smokers to quit. *Contemporary Pediatrics, 30*(10), 18–23.

Nabi, R. L. (2009). Cosmetic surgery makeover programs and intentions to undergo cosmetic enhancements: A consideration of three models of media effects. *Human Communication Research, 35,* 1–27.

National Association of Colleges and Employers (NACE). (2013). Retrieved from http://www2.binghamton.edu/career-development-center/parents/help-your-student/skills-employers-want.html

National Highway Safety Administration. (2014). What is distracted driving? Retrieved on May 9, 2014, from http://www.distraction.gov/content/get-the-facts/facts-and-statistics.html

National Organization for Women. (2006, March 2). *Sexual harassment remains serious problem on campus.* Retrieved May 14, 2008, from http://www.now.org/issues/harass/030206aauwreport.html

Nelson, B. (2002). Making teamwork work. *ABA Bank Marketing, 34,* 10.

Nelson, J. (2011, January 5). Do word changes alter "Huckleberry Finn"? *The New York Times.* Retrieved from http://www.nytimes.com/roomfordebate/2011/01/05/does-one-word-change-huckleberry-finn

Nessen, S. (2012, December 3). In hard-hit areas, Red Cross runs into image issue. WNYC. Retrieved from http://www.wnyc.org/story/254908-red-cross-recovery-efforts

Neuliep, J. W. (2012). The relationship among intercultural communication apprehension, ethnocentrism, uncertainty reduction, and communication satisfaction during initial intercultural interaction: An extension of anxiety and uncertainty management (AUM) theory. *Journal of Intercultural Communication Research, 41*(1), 1–16, DOI: 10.1080/17475759.2011.62323.

Newcomb, A. F., & Bagwell, C. L. (1995). Children's friendship relations: A metaanalytic review. *Psychological Bulletin, 117,* 306–347.

Newman, M. L., Groom, C. J., Handelman, L. D., & Pennebaker, J. W. (2008). Gender differences in language use: An analysis of 14,000 text samples. *Discourse Processes, 45*(3), 211–236.

Ng, S. H., & Ng, T. K. (2012). Power of messages through speech and silence. In H. Giles (Ed.), *The handbook of intergroup communication* (pp. 116–127). New York: Routledge/Taylor and Francis.

Nicholas, S. (2009). "I live Hopi, I just don't speak it"—The critical intersection of language, culture, and identity in the lives of contemporary Hopi youth. *Journal of Language, Identity & Education, 8*(5), 321–334.

Nichols, R. G. (2006). The struggle to be human: Keynote address to first International Listening Association convention, February 17, 1980. *International Journal of Listening, 20,* 4–12.

Nichols, R. G., Brown, J. I., & Keller, R. J. (2006). Measurement of communication skills. *International Journal of Listening, 20,* 13–17.

Nicotera, A. M. (1997). Managing conflict communication groups. In L. R. Frey & J. K. Barge (Eds.), *Managing group life: Communicating in decision-making groups* (pp. 104–130). Boston: Houghton Mifflin.

Nielsen (2013, March—updated October). Free to move across screens: The cross-platform report (Q4). The Nielsen Company. Retrieved from http://www.nielsen.com/content/dam/corporate/us/en/reports-downloads/2013%20Reports/Nielsen-March-2013-Cross-Platform-Report.pdf

Niemann, C. (2014, January). If someone comments on your Facebook post and they're abjectly wrong, are you morally obligated to correct their misinformation? *Wired, 22*(01), 72.

Nierenberg, R. (2009). *Maestro: A surprising story about leadership by listening.* New York: Portfolio.

Nisen, M. (2013, March 14). Zappos' Tony Hseih says creating a great culture is a "five-to-lifetime commitment." *Business Insider.* Retrieved from http://www.businessinsider.com/tony-hsieh-creating-an-amazing-company-culture-2013-3

Nomani, A. Q. (2005, December 14). Tapping Islam's feminist roots. *The Washington Post.* Retrieved March 7, 2008, from http://www.seattletimes.nwsource.com

Northhouse, P. G. (2012). *Leadership: Theory and practice* (6th ed.). Thousand Oaks, CA: Sage Publications.

O'Connor, J., Mumford, M., Clifton, T., Gessner, T., & Connelly, M. (1995). Charismatic leaders and destructiveness: An histo-riometric study. *Leadership Quarterly, 6,* 529–555.

Office friends: Who needs them? (2005). *Management Today.* Retrieved May 14, 2008, via LexisNexis.

O'Hair, D., & Cody, M. (1994). Deception. In W. R. Cupach & B. H. Spitzberg (Eds.), *The dark side of interpersonal communication* (pp. 181–213). Hillsdale, NJ: Erlbaum.

O'Hair, D., Friedrich, G. W., & Dixon, L. D. (2007). *Strategic communication in business and the professions* (6th ed.). Boston: Houghton Mifflin.

O'Hair, D., Friedrich, G. W., & Dixon, L. D. (2010). *Strategic communication in business and the professions.* (7th ed.) New York: Pearson.

O'Hair, D., & Krayer, K. (1987). *A conversational analysis of reconciliation strategies.* Paper presented at the Western Speech Communication Association, Salt Lake City.

O'Hair, D., O'Rourke, J., & O'Hair, M. J. (2000). *Business communication: A framework for success.* Cincinnati, OH: South-Western.

O'Hair, D., & Stewart, R. (1998). *Public speaking: Challenges and choices.* New York: Bedford/St. Martin's.

O'Hair, D., Stewart, R., & Rubenstein, H. (2007). *A speaker's guidebook* (3rd ed.). New York: Bedford/St. Martin's.

O'Hair, D., Stewart, R., & Rubenstein, H. (2012). *A speaker's guidebook: Text and reference* (5th ed.). New York: Bedford/St. Martin's.

O'Keefe, D. J. (1999). How to handle opposing arguments in persuasive messages: A meta-analytic review of the effects of one-sided and two-sided messages. In M. E. Roloff (Ed.), *Communication yearbook 22* (pp. 209–249). Thousand Oaks, CA: Sage Publications.

O'Keefe, D. J. (2002). *Persuasion: Theory and research* (2nd ed.). Thousand Oaks, CA: Sage Publications.

Okhuysen, G., & Eisenhardt, K. M. (2002). Integrating knowledge in groups: How simple formal interventions enable flexibility. *Organization Science, 13,* 370–386.

Okhuysen, G., & Waller, M. J. (2002). Focusing on midpoint transitions: An analysis of boundary conditions. *Academy of Management Journal, 45,* 1056–1065.

Okoro, E., & Washington, M. C. (2012). Workforce diversity and organizational communication: Analysis of human capital performance and productivity. *Journal of Diversity Management, 7*(1).

Oliver, J. (2010, February). Jamie Oliver's TED Prize wish: Teach every child about food. Video retrieved from http://www.ted.com/talks/jamie_oliver.html

O'Loughlin, J. P. (2010, July 23). Senior HR executive, HR Capital Partners. Personal interview.

O'Neill, B. (2011). A critique of politically correct language. *Independent Review, 16*(2), 279–291.

Ophir, E, Nass, C., & Wagner, A. D. (2009). Cognitive control in media multitaskers. *Proceedings of the National Academy of Sciences, 106* (37), 15583—15587. http://www.pnas.org/content/106/37/15583.short

Oprah.com. (2008). *Oprah's debt diet.* Retrieved from http://www.oprah.com/packages/oprahs-debt-diet.html

O'Sullivan, P. B. (2000). What you don't know won't hurt me: Impression management functions of communication channels in relationships. *Human Communication Research, 26,* 403–431.

Our mission. (2013, December 18). Facebook newsroom. Retrieved from http://newsroom.fb.com/Key-Facts

Pagotto, L., Voci, A., & Maculan, V. (2010). The effectiveness of intergroup contact at work: Mediators and moderators of hospital workers' prejudice towards immigrants. *Journal of Community & Applied Social Psychology, 20*(4), 317–330.

Palacios Martínez, I. M., & Núñez Pertejo, P. (2012). He's absolutely massive. It's a super day. Madonna, she is a wicked singer. Youth language and intensification: A corpus-based study. *Text & Talk, 32*(6), 773–796.

Palomares, N. A. (2009). Women are sort of more tentative than men, aren't they? How men and women use tentative language differently, similarly, and counterstereotypically as a function of gender salience. *Communication Research, 36*(4), 538–560.

Palomares, N. A., & Lee, E-J. (2010). Virtual gender identity: The linguistic assimilation to gendered avatars in computer-mediated communication. *Journal of Language & Social Psychology, 29*(1), 5–23.

Paolini, S., Harwood, J., & Rubin, M. (2010). Negative intergroup contact makes group members salient: Explaining why intergroup conflict endures. *Personality and Social Psychology Bulletin, 36,* 1723–1738.

Parente, D. (2013). *Visual presence.* Retrieved on May 12, 2014, from http://theleadershipstylecenter.com/visual-presence

Park, C. (2003). In other (people's) words: Plagiarism by university students—literature and lessons. *Assessment and Evaluation in Higher Education, 28,* 471–488.

Park, W. (2000). A comprehensive empirical investigation of the relationships among variables of the groupthink model. *Journal of Organizational Behavior, 21,* 874–887.

Parker, A. (2014, February 16). On health act, Democrats run in fix-it mode. *The New York Times.* Retrieved from http://www.nytimes.com/2014/02/17/us/politics/on-health-act-democrats-run-to-mend-what-gop-aims-to-end.html?hp&_r=1

Parker, K., Lenhart, A., & Moore, K. (2012). The digital revolution and higher education. Retrieved on April 29, 2014, from http://www.pewinternet.org/2011/08/28/the-digital-revolution-and-higher-education/4

Parker-Pope, T. (2010a, April 18). Is marriage good for your health? *The New York Times,* p. MM46.

Parker-Pope, T. (2010b, May 11). The science of a happy marriage. *The New York Times,* p. D1.

Partnoy, F. (2012, July 6). Beyond the blink. *The New York Times,* p. SR5.

Patchin, J., & Hinduja, S. (2011). Traditional and nontraditional bullying among youth: A test of general strain theory. *Youth & Society, 43*(2), 727–75.

Patry, M. W. (2008). Attractive but guilty: Deliberation and the physical attractiveness bias. *Psychological Reports, 102*(3), 727–733.

Patterson, B. R., & Gojdycz, T. K. (2000). The relationship between computer-mediated communication and communication-related anxieties. *Communication Research Reports, 17*, 278–287.

Patterson, B. R., & O'Hair, D. (1992). Relational reconciliation: Toward a more comprehensive model of relational development. *Communication Research Reports, 9*, 119–127.

Patterson, T. (2006, November). The Colbert Report: How to beat the host at his own game. *Slate.* Retrieved from http://www.slate.com/articles/arts/television/2006/11/the_colbert_retort.html

Patwardhan, P, & Yang, J. (2003). Internet dependency relations and online consumer behavior: A media system dependency theory perspective on why people shop, chat, and read news online. *Journal of Interactive Advertising, 3*(2), http://jiad.org/article36.html

Paul, P. (2001). Getting inside Gen Y. *American Demographics, 23*(9), 42.

Pauley, P. M., & Emmers-Sommer, T. M. (2007). The impact of Internet technologies on primary and secondary romantic relationship development. *Communication Studies, 58*(4), 411–427.

Pavitt, C. (1999). Theorizing about the group communication-leadership relationship. In L. R. Frey, D. S. Gouran, & M. Poole (Eds.), *Handbook of group communication theory and research* (pp. 313–334). Thousand Oaks, CA: Sage Publications.

Pavley, J. (2013, May 26). Technological literacy: Can everyone learn to code? *Huffington Post.* Retrieved from http://www.huffingtonpost.com/john-pavley/learning-to-code_b_3337098.html

Pavlik, J. V., & McIntosh, S. (2013). *Converging media: A new introduction to mass communication* (3rd ed.). New York: Oxford University Press.

Payne, S. L. (1951). *The art of asking questions.* Princeton, NJ: Princeton University Press.

Pearce, C., & Tuten, T. (2001). Internet recruiting in the banking industry. *Business Communication Quarterly, 64*(1), 9–18.

Pearson, J. C., & Spitzberg, B. H. (1990). *Interpersonal communication: Concepts, components, and contexts* (2nd ed.). Dubuque, IA: Brown.

Pearson, J. C., Turner, L. H., & Todd-Mancillas, W. R. (1991). *Gender and communication* (2nd ed.). Dubuque, IA: Brown.

Peck, J. (2007, December 29). *Top 7 tips for conquering public speaking fear.* Retrieved January 9, 2008, from http://ezinearticles.com/?expert=Jason_Peck

Peluchette, J., Karl, K., & Fertig, J. (2013). A Facebook "friend" request from the boss: Too close for comfort? *Business Horizons, 56*, 291–300.

Pennington, B. (2012, March 29). Arguing over heckling. *The New York Times*, p. B12.

Perry, M. J. (2013, May 13). Stunning college degree gap: Women have earned almost ten million more college degrees than men since 1982. American Enterprise Institute AEIdeas blog. Retrieved from http://www.aei-ideas.org/2013/05/stunning-college-degree-gap-women-have-earned-almost-10-million-more-college-degrees-than-men-since-1982

Petronio, S. (2000). The boundaries of privacy: Praxis of everyday life. In S. Petronio (Ed.), *Balancing the secrets of private disclosures* (pp. 37–50). Mahwah, NJ: Erlbaum.

Petronio, S. (2002). *The boundaries of privacy: Dialectics of disclosure.* Albany: State University of New York Press.

Petronio, S. (2004). Road to developing communication privacy management theory: Narrative in progress, please stand by. *Journal of Family Communication, 4*, 193–207.

Pettigrew, T. F., & Tropp, L. R. (2006). A meta-analytical test of the intergroup contact theory. *Journal of Personality and Social Psychology, 90*, 751–783.

Petty, R. E., & Cacioppo, J. T. (1986). The Elaboration Likelihood Model of persuasion. In L. Berkowitz (Ed.), *Advances in experimental social psychology* (Vol. 19, pp. 123–205). San Diego, CA: Academic Press.

Petty, R. E., & Wegner, D. T. (1998). Matching versus mismatching attitude functions: Implications for scrutiny of persuasive messages. *Personality and Social Psychology Bulletin, 24*(3), 227–240.

Pew Internet (2013). http://www.pewinternet.org/Media-Mentions/2013/Helping-Seniors-Learn-New-Technology.aspx

Pew Research, Religion & Public Life Project. (2008, February 1). U.S. Religious Landscape Project. Retrieved from http://www.pewforum.org/2008/02/01/u-s-religious-landscape-survey-religious-affiliation

Phanor-Faury, A. (2010, June 24). "Nude" doesn't translate in fashion. *Essence.* Retrieved from http://www.essence.com/fashion_beauty/fashion/nude_dresses_racial_bias_fashion_world.php

Piezon, S., & Ferree, W. (2008). Perceptions of social loafing in online learning groups: A study of public university and U.S. Naval War College students. *International Review of Research in Open and Distance Learning, 9*(2), 1–17.

Pines, M. (1997). The civilizing of Genie. In L. F. Kasper (Ed.), *Teaching English through the disciplines: Psychology* (2nd ed.). New York: Whittier.

Planalp, S., & Honeycutt, J. (1985). Events that increase uncertainty in personal relationships. *Human Communication Research, 11*, 593–604.

Pomeroy, R. (2013, April 26). Driving is much deadlier than terrorism—Why isn't it scarier? Retrieved from http://www.realclearscience.com/blog/2013/03/why-we-fear-terrorism-more-than-driving.html

Poole, M. S., & Hollingshead, A. B. (Eds.). (2005). *Theories of small groups: Interdisciplinary perspectives.* Thousand Oaks, CA: Sage Publications.

Potter, W. J. (2008). *Media literacy* (4th ed.). Thousand Oaks, CA: Sage Publications.

Potter, W. J., & Byrne, S. (2009). Media literacy. In R. L. Nabi & M. B. Oliver (Eds.), *The SAGE Handbook of Media Processes and Effects* (pp. 345–360). Thousand Oaks, CA: Sage Publications.

Powers, W. G., & Bodie, G.D. (2003). Listening fidelity: Seeking congruence between cognitions of the receiver and the sender. *International Journal of Listening, 17*, 19–31.

Prager, K. J. (2000). Intimacy in personal relationships. In C. Hendrick & S. S. Hendrick (Eds.), *Close relationships: A sourcebook* (pp. 229–242). Thousand Oaks, CA: Sage Publications.

Pratkanis, A. R., & Aronson, E. (2001). *Age of propaganda: The everyday use and abuse of persuasion.* New York: W. H. Freeman.

Prensky, M. (2012). *From digital natives to digital wisdom: Hopeful essays for 21st century learning.* Thousand Oaks, CA: Corwin.

Preston, D. R. (1998). Language myth #17: They speak really bad English Down South and in New York City. In L. Bauer & P. Trudgill (Eds.), *Language myths* (pp. 139–149). New York: Penguin Putnam.

Priester, J. R., & Petty, R. E. (1995). Source attributions and persuasion: Perceived honesty as a determinant of message scrutiny. *Personality and Social Psychology Bulletin, 21,* 637–654.

Prochaska, J. (1994). Strong and weak principles for progressing from precontemplation to action on the basis of twelve problem behaviors. *Health Psychology, 13*, 47–51.

Prochaska, J. O., & Norcross, J. C. (2001). Stages of change. *Psychotherapy: Theory, Research, Practice, Training, 38*, 443–448.

Punyanunt-Carter, N. M. (2005). Father and daughter motives and satisfaction. *Communication Research Reports, 22,* 293–301.

Quenqua, D. (2012, February 28). They're, like, way ahead of the linguistic currrrve. *The New York Times*, p. D1.

Rabinowitz, J. (1995, July 25). Huckleberry Finn without fear: Teachers gather to learn how to teach an American classic, in context. *The New York Times.* Retrieved from http://www.query.nytimes.com

Ragas, M. W., Tran, H. L., & Martin, J. A. (2014). Media-induced or search-driven? A study of online agenda-setting effects during the BP oil disaster. *Journalism Studies, 15*(1), 48–63.

Rahim, M. A. (1983). A measure of styles of handling interpersonal conflict. *Academy of Management Journal, 26*(2), 368–376.

Rainie, L., Smith, A., & Duggan, M. (2013, February 5). Coming and going on Facebook. Pew Internet & Amerian Life Project. Retrieved from http://pewinternet.org/Reports/2013/Coming-and-going-on-facebook/Key-Findings.aspx

Ralph, B. C., Thomson, D. R., Cheyne, J. A., & Smilek, D. (2013). Media multitasking and failures of attention in everyday life. *Psychological Research*, 1–9.

Ralston, S. M., Kirkwood, W. G., & Burant, P. A. (2003). Helping interviewees tell their stories. *Business Communication Quarterly, 66*, 8–22.

Raman, A. (2007, April 26). Egypt's "Dr. Ruth": Let's talk sex in the Arab world. CNN.com. Retrieved from http://www.cnn.com/2007/WORLD/meast/04/25/muslim.sextalk/index.html

Ramirez, A., Sunnafrank, M., & Goei, R. (2010). Predicted outcome value theory in ongoing relationships. *Communication Monographs, 77*(1), 27–50.

Rampell, C. (2013, May 4). College graduates fare well in jobs market, even through recession. *The New York Times*, p. B1.

Rampell, C., & Miller, C. C. (2013, February 25). Yahoo orders home workers back to the office. *The New York Times.* Retrieved from http://www.nytimes.com/2013/02/26/technology/yahoo-orders-home-workers-back-to-the-office.html?ref=business&_r=0

Rappaport, S. D. (2010). Putting listening to work: The essentials of listening. *Journal of Advertising Research, 50*(1), 30–41.

Rath, A. (2011, February 5). Is the "CSI Effect" influencing courtrooms? NPR News Investigations. Retrieved from http://www.npr.org/2011/02/06/133497696/is-the-csi-effect-influencing-courtrooms

Rawlins, W. K. (1992). *Friendship matters: Communication, dialectics, and the life course.* Piscataway, NJ: Aldine Transaction.

Rawlins, W. K. (1994). Being there and growing apart: Sustaining friendships during adulthood. In D. J. Canary & L. Stafford (Eds.), *Communication and relational maintenance* (pp. 275–294). New York: Academic Press.

Rawlins, W. K. (2008). *The compass of friendship: Narratives, identities, and dialogues.* Thousand Oaks, CA: Sage Publications.

Ray, R., Sanes, M., & Schmitt, J. (2013, May). No-vacation nation revisited. Retrieved from http://www.cepr.net/index.php/publications/reports/no-vacation-nation-2013

Ray, R., & Schmitt, J. (2007, May). No-vacation nation. Washington, DC: Center for Economic and Policy Research. Retrieved from http://www.cepr.net

Rehling, D. L. (2008). Compassionate listening: A framework for listening to the seriously ill. *International Journal of Listening, 22*(1), 83–89.

Reiber, C., & Garcia, J. R. (2010). Hooking up: Gender differences, evolution, and pluralistic ignorance. *Evolutionary Psychology, 8*(3), 390–404.

Reis, H. T. (1998). Gender differences in intimacy and related behaviors: Context and process. In D. J. Canary & K. Dindia (Eds.), *Sex differences and similarities in communication: Critical essays and empirical investigations of sex and gender in interaction* (pp. 203–231). Hillsdale, NJ: Erlbaum.

Rheingold, H. (2002). *Smart mobs: The next social revolution.* New York: Basic Books.

Richmond, V., & McCroskey, J. C. (1998). *Communication apprehension, avoidance, and effectiveness* (5th ed.). Boston: Allyn & Bacon.

Richmond, V. P., McCroskey, J. C., & Johnson, A. D. (2003). Development of the Nonverbal Immediacy Scale (NIS): Measures of self- and other-perceived nonverbal immediacy. *Communication Quarterly, 51,* 502–515.

Richmond, V. P., McCroskey, J. C., & Payne, S. K. (1991). *Nonverbal behavior in interpersonal relations.* Englewood Cliffs, NJ: Prentice Hall.

Richmond, V. P., Smith, R. S., Jr., Heisel, A. D., & McCroskey, J. C. (2001). Nonverbal immediacy in the physician-patient relationship. *Communication Research Reports, 18,* 211–216.

Richtel, M. (2010, June 6). Attached to technology and paying a price. *The New York Times,* p. A1.

Riffe, D., Lacy, S., & Varouhakis, M. (2008). Media system dependency theory and using the Internet for in-depth, specialized information. *Web Journal of Mass Communication Research, 11.* Retrieved from http://www.scripps.ohiou.edu/wjmcr/vol11/11-b.html

Rill, L., Balocchi, E., Hopper, M., Denker, K., & Olson, L. N. (2009). Exploration of the relationship between self-esteem, commitment, and verbal aggressiveness in romantic dating relationships. *Communication Reports, 22*(2), 102–113.

Riordan, M. A., & Kreuz, R. J. (2010). Cues in computer-mediated communication: A corpus analysis. *Computers in Human Behavior, 26,* 1806–1817.

Ritter, B. A. (2014). Deviant behavior in computer-mediated communication: Development and validation of a measure of cybersexual harassment. *Journal of Computer-Mediated Communication, 19*(2), 197–214.

Roberto, A., Carlyle, K. E., Goodall, C. E., & Castle, J. D. (2009). The relationship between parents' verbal aggressiveness and responsiveness and young adult children's attachment style and relational satisfaction with parents. *Journal of Family Communication, 9*(2), 90–106.

Roberts, S. (2010, November 19). Unlearning to tawk like a New Yorker. *The New York Times.* Retrieved from http://www.nytimes.com/2010/11/21/nyregion/21accent.html

Rochman, B. (2011, December 2). Baby name game: How a name can affect your child's future. *Time.* Retrieved from http://healthland.time.com/2011/12/02/how-baby-names-affect-your-childs-future

Rogers Commission. (1986, June 6). *Report of the presidential commission on the space shuttle* Challenger *accident.* Retrieved from http://science.ksc.nasa.gov/shuttle/missions/51-l/docs/rogers-commission/Chapter-5.txt

Roloff, M. E. (1980). Self-awareness and the persuasion process: Do we really know what we are doing? In M. E. Roloff & G. Miller (Eds.), *Persuasion: New directions in theory and research* (pp. 29–66). Beverly Hills, CA: Sage Publications.

Romans, B. (2011, October 14). The joy of going to the library, from the *Wired* science blog *Clastic Detritus.* Retrieved from http://www.wired.com/wiredscience/2011/10/the-joy-of-going-to-the-library, para. 2.

Rose, G., Evaristo, R., & Staub, D. (2003). Culture and consumer responses to Web download time: A four-continent stoudy of mono and polychronism. *IEEE Transaction on Engineering Management, 50*(1), 31–44.

Rosen, M. (2004, February). Can you truly trust an office friend? When to share and when to shy away—a guide to getting along with your workplace pals (on the job). *Good Housekeeping,* p. 56.

Rosenbloom, S. (2006, August 10). Please don't make me go on vacation. *The New York Times.* Retrieved from http://www.nytimes.com

Rosener, J. (1990). Ways women lead. *Harvard Business Review, 68,* 119–125.

Rosenthal, M. J. (2001). High-performance teams. *Executive Excellence, 18,* 6.

Ross, C. (2007, March 11). Hare interviewed for "Colbert Report." *The Register-Mail.*

Ross, L., & Nisbett, R. E. (1991). *The person and the situation: Perspectives of social psychology.* Philadelphia: Temple University Press.

Roth, A. (2013, February 1). Russia revives the namesake of "Uncle Joe." *The New York Times,* p. A4.

Rothman, A. J., Salovey, P., Turvey, C., & Fishkin, S. A. (1993). Attributions or responsibility and persuasion: Increasing mammography utilization among women over 40 with an internally oriented message. *Health Psychology, 12,* 39–47.

Roup, C. M., & Chiasson, K. E. (2010). Effect of dichotic listening on self-reported state anxiety. *International Journal of Audiology, 49*(2), 88–94.

Rowbotham, S., Holler, J., Lloyd, D., & Wearden, A. (2012). How do we communicate about pain? A systematic analysis of the semantic contribution of co-speech gestures in pain-focused conversations. *Journal of Nonverbal Behavior, 36*(1), 1–21.

Ruben, B. D. (2005). Linking communication scholarship and professional practice in colleges and universities. *Journal of Applied Communication Research, 33,* 294–304.

Rubin, A. M., Perse, E. M., & Powell, R. A. (1985). Loneliness, parasocial interaction, and local television news viewing. *Human Communication Research, 12,* 155–180.

Rubin, D. L., Hafer, T., & Arata, K. (2000). Reading and listening to oral-based versus literate-based discourse. *Communication Education, 49,* 121–133.

Rubin, J. (2013, February 5). The Internet can offer additional intercultural experiences. *The Chronicle of Higher Education.* Retrieved from http://chronicle.com/blogs/letters/the-internet-can-offer-additional-intercultural-experiences

Rudoren, J. (2012, October 1). Proudly bearing elders' scars, their skin says "never forget." *The New York Times,* p. A1.

Rushton, J. P. (1980). *Altruism, socializiation, and society.* Englewood Cliffs, NJ: Prentice Hall.

Russ, T. L. (2012). The relationship between communication apprehension and learning preferences in an organizational setting. *Journal of Business Communication, 49*(4), 312–331.

Russell, J. E., & Adams, D. M. (1997). The changing nature of mentoring in organizations: An introduction to the special issue on mentoring in organizations. *Journal of Vocational Behavior, 51,* 1–14.

Rutherford, S. (2001). Any difference? An analysis of gender and divisional management styles in a large airline. *Gender, Work and Organization, 8*(3), 326–345.

Ryzik, M. (2012, January 4). When an actress prepares (no eye contact, please). *The New York Times*, p. C1.

Safir, M. P., Wallach, H.S., & Bar-Zvi, M. (2012). Virtual reality cognitive-behavior therapy for public speaking anxiety: One-year follow-up. *Behavioral Modification, 36*(2), 235–246. doi: 10.1177/0145445511429999

Sahlstein, E., Maguire, K. C., & Timmerman, L. (2009). Contradictions and praxis contextualized by wartime deployment: Wives' perspectives revealed through relational dialectics. *Communication Monographs, 76*(4), 421–442.

Salazar, A. J. (1996). An analysis of the development and evolution of roles in the small group. *Small Group Research, 27,* 475–503.

Salkever, A. (2003, April 24). Home truths about meetings. *Business Week.* Retrieved from http://www.businessweek.com

Samovar, L. A., Porter, R. E., & Stefani, L. A. (1998). *Communication between cultures.* Belmont, CA: Wadsworth.

Samter, W. (2003). Friendship interaction skills across the life span. In J. O. Greene & B. R. Burleson (Eds.), *Handbook of communication and social interaction skills* (pp. 637–684). Mahwah, NJ: Erlbaum.

Sanchez, J. (2013, December 10). MLB to tackle prospects' language barriers. MLB.com. Retrieved from http://mlb.mlb.com/news/article/mlb/major-league-baseball-works-to-eliminate-language-barriers-for-dominican-prospects?ymd=20131210&content_id=64557052&vkey=news_mlb

Sanderson, J. (2013). From loving the hero to despising the villain: Sports fans, Facebook, and social identity threats. *Mass Communication and Society, 16*(4), 487–509.

Sapir, E., & Whorf, B. L. (1956). The relation of habitual thought and behavior to language. In J. B. Carroll (Ed.), *Language, thought, and reality: Selected writings of Benjamin Lee Whorf* (pp. 134–159). Cambridge, MA: MIT Press.

Sarich, V., & Miele, F. (2004). *Race: The reality of human differences.* Boulder, CO: Westview Press.

Sashkin, M., & Burke, W. W. (1990). Understanding and assessing organizational leadership. In K. E. Clark & M. B. Clark (Eds.), *Measures of leadership* (pp. 297–326). West Orange, NJ: Leadership Library of America.

Sawyer, C., & Behnke, R. (1990). The role of self-monitoring in the communication of public speaking anxiety. *Communication Reports, 3,* 70–74.

Sawyer, C., & Behnke, R. (2002). Behavioral inhibition and communication of public speaking state anxiety. *Western Journal of Communication, 66,* 412–422.

Scheerhorn, D., & Geist, P. (1997). Social dynamics in groups. In L. R. Frey & J. K. Barge (Eds.), *Managing group life: Communicating in decision-making groups* (pp. 81–103). Boston: Houghton Mifflin.

Schelbert, L. (2009). Pathways of human understanding: An inquiry into Western and North American Indian worldview structures. In L. A. Samovar, R. E. Porter, & E. R. McDaniel (Eds.), *Intercultural communication: A reader* (pp. 48–58). Belmont, CA: Wadsworth Cengage Learning.

Schenck v. *United States*, 249 U.S. 47 (1919).

Scheufele, D., & Iyengar, S. (2012). The state of framing research: A call for new directions. *The Oxford Handbook of Political Communication Theories.* New York: Oxford University Press.

Scheufele, D. A., & Tewksbury, D. (2007). Framing, agenda setting, and priming: The evolution of three media effects models. *Journal of Communication, 57*(1), 9–20.

Schiesel, S. (October 25, 2011). Best friends, in fantasy and reality. *New York Times*, p. C1.

Schmidt, R. R., Morr, S., Fitzpatrick, P., & Richardson, M. (2012). Measuring the dynamics of interactional synchrony. *Journal of Nonverbal Behavior, 36*(4), 263–279.

Schofield, T., Parke, R., Castañeda, E., & Coltrane, S. (2008). Patterns of gaze between parents and children in European American and Mexican American families. *Journal of Nonverbal Behavior, 32*(3), 171–186.

Schradie, J. (2013, April 26). 7 myths of the digital divide. The Society Pages: Cyborgology. Retrieved from http://thesocietypages.org/cyborgology/2013/04/26/7-myths-of-the-digital-divide

Schrodt, P. (2009). Family strength and satisfaction as functions of family communication. *Communication Quarterly, 57*(2), 171–186.

Schrodt, P., & Wheeless, L. R. (2001). Aggressive communication and informational reception apprehension: The influence of listening anxiety and intellectual inflexibility on trait argumentativeness and verbal aggressiveness. *Communication Quarterly, 49,* 53–69.

Schrodt, P., Wheeless, L. R., & Ptacek, K. M. (2000). Informational reception apprehension, educational motivation, and achievement. *Communication Quarterly, 48,* 60–73.

Schroeder, L. (2002). The effects of skills training on communication satisfaction and communication anxiety in the basic speech course. *Communication Research Reports, 19,* 380–388.

Schullery, N. M., & Gibson, M. K. (2001). Working in groups: Identification and treatment of students' perceived weaknesses. *Business Communication Quarterly, 64,* 9–30.

Schulman, P. R. (1996). Heroes, organizations, and high reliability. *Journal of Contingencies and Crisis Management, 4,* 72–82.

Schultz, B. (1980). Communicative correlates of perceived leaders. *Small Group Behavior, 11,* 175–191.

Schultz, B. (1982). Argumentativeness: Its effect in group decision-making and its role in leadership perception. *Communication Quarterly, 30,* 368–375.

Schweitzer, T. (2007). *Seven out of 10 employees admit to abusing office computers, phones.* Retrieved May 13, 2008, from http://www.inc.com

Scott, A. O. (November 16, 2011). For one man, Hawaii is a land of problems. *New York Times*, p. C1.

Scott, W. R. (1981). *Organizations: Rational, natural, and open systems.* Englewood Cliffs, NJ: Prentice Hall.

Scully, M. (2005, February 2). Building a better State of the Union address. *The New York Times.* Retrieved from http://www.nytimes.com

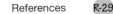

Secret of the wild child [Transcript]. (1997, March 4). *Nova*. Public Broadcasting System. Retrieved March 25, 2008, from http://www.pbs.org/wgbh/nova/transcripts/2112gchild.html

Segrin, C., Hanzal, A., & Domschke, T. J. (2009). Accuracy and bias in newlywed couples' perceptions of conflict styles and the association with marital satisfaction. *Communication Monographs, 76*, 207–233.

Segrin, C., & Passalacqua, S. A. (2010). Functions of loneliness, social support, health behaviors, and stress in association with poor health. *Health Communication, 25*(4), 312–322.

Seidler, D. (2011, February 27). Acceptance speech presented at the 83rd Annual Academy of Motion Picture Arts and Sciences Awards, Hollywood, CA.

Shachaf, P., & Hara, N. (2010). Beyond vandalism: Wikipedia trolls. *Journal of Information Science, 36*(3), 357–370.

Shannon, C. E., & Weaver, W. (1949). *The mathematical theory of communication*. Urbana: University of Illinois Press.

Shannon, M., & Stark, C. (2003). The influence of physical appearance on personnel selection. *Social Behavior & Personality: An International Journal, 31*(6), 613.

Shehata, A., & Strömbäck, J. (2013). Not (yet) a new era of minimal effects: A study of setting at the aggregate and individual levels. *The International Journal of Press/Politics, 18*(2), 234–255.

Sheldon, P. (2008). The relationship between unwillingness to communicate and students' Facebook use. *Journal of Media Psychology, 20*, 67–75.

Shepherd, C. A., Giles, H., & LePoire, B. A. (2001). Communication accommodation theory. In W. P. Robinson & H. Giles (Eds.), *The new handbook of language and social psychology* (pp. 33–56). Chichester, UK: Wiley.

Sherif, C. W., Sherif, M. S., & Nebergall, R. E. (1965). *Attitude and attitude change*. Philadelphia: W. B. Saunders.

Sherif, M., & Sherif, C. W. (1967). Attitude as the individual's own categories: The social judgment-involvement approach to attitude and attitude change. In C. W. Sherif & M. Sherif (Eds.), *Attitude, ego-involvement, and change* (pp. 105-139). New York: Wiley.

Shotter, J. (2009). Listening in a way that recognizes/realizes the world of "the other." *International Journal of Listening, 23*(1), 21–43.

Shultz, B. G. (1999). Improving group communication performance: An overview of diagnosis and intervention. In L. Frey, D. Gouran, & M. Poole (Eds.), *Handbook of group communication theory and research* (pp. 371–394). Thousand Oaks, CA: Sage Publications.

Sides, C. H. (2000). Ethics and technical communication: The past quarter century. *Journal of Technical Writing and Communication, 30*, 27–30.

Sillars, A., Canary, D. J., & Tafoya, M. (2004). Communication, conflict, and the quality of family relationships. In A. L. Vangelisti (Ed.), *Handbook of family communication* (pp. 413–446). Mahwah, NJ: Erlbaum.

Simonson, P., Peck, J., Craig, R. T., & Jackson, J. P. (Eds.) (2013). *The handbook of communication history*. New York: Routledge.

Sirolli, E. (September 2012). Want to help someone? Shut up and listen! *TED Talks*: http://www.ted.com/talks/ernesto_sirolli_want_to_help_someone_shut_up_and_listen

Sixel, L. M. (2011, July 7). Manager claims boss asked her to dye gray hair. *The Houston Chronicle*. Retrieved from http://www.chron.com/business/sixel/article/Manager-claims-boss-asked-her-to-dye-gray-hair-2080057.php#ixzz1Rp5iRmra

Smith, P. (2005, February 11). Bullies incorporated. *Sydney Morning Herald*. Retrieved from http://www.smh.com.au

Smith, R., Jr. (2004). Recruit the student: Adapting persuasion to audiences. *Communication Teacher, 18*, 53–56.

Smith, R. E. (1993). Clustering: A way to discover speech topics. *The Speech Teacher, 7*(2), 6–7.

Smith, T. E., & Frymier, A. B. (2006). Get "real": Does practicing speeches before an audience improve performance? *Communication Quarterly, 54*, 111–125.

Smith-Lovin, L., Skvortz, J. K., & Hudson, C. (1986). Status and participation in six-person groups: A test of Skvoret's comparative status model. *Social Forces, 64*, 992–1005.

Snyder, M. (1974). Self-monitoring of expressive behavior. *Journal of Personality and Social Psychology, 30*, 526–537.

Snyder, M. (1979). Self-monitoring processes. In L. Berkowitz (Ed.), *Advances in social psychology* (Vol. 12, pp. 86–128). New York: Academic Press.

Snyder, M., & Klein, O. (2005). Construing and constructing others: On the reality and the generality of the behavioral confirmation scenario. *Interaction Studies, 6*, 53–67.

Sokol, R. I., Webster, K. L., Thompson, N. S., & Stevens, D. A. (2005). Whining as mother-directed speech. *Infant and Child Development, 14*, 478–486.

Soliz, J., & Giles, H. (2010). Language and communication. In C. R. Berger, M. E. Roloff, & D. R. Roskos-Ewoldsen (Eds.), *The handbook of communication science* (pp. 75–91). Thousand Oaks, CA: Sage Publications.

Solomon, D. H., & Vangelisti, A. L. (2010). Establishing and maintaining relationships. In C. R. Berger, M. E. Roloff, & D. R. Roskos-Ewoldsen, *The handbook of communication science* (pp. 327–344). Thousand Oaks, CA: SAGE Publications.

Sonnenfeld, J. (2011, January 23). The genius dilemma. *Newsweek*. Retrieved from http://www.newsweek.com/2011/01/23/the-genius-dilemma.html

Sonnentag, S., Unger, D., & Nägel, I. J. (2013). Workplace conflict and employee well-being: The moderating role of detachment from work during off-job time. *International Journal of Conflict Management, 24*(2), 166–183.

Sorenson, G. A., & McCroskey, J. C. (1977). The prediction of interaction in small groups. *Communication Monographs, 44*, 73–80.

Sosha, T. J. (1997). Group communication across the lifespan. In L. R. Frey & J. K. Barge (Eds.), *Managing group life: Communicating in decision-making groups* (pp. 3–28). Boston: Houghton Mifflin.

Span, P. (2013). Helping seniors learn new technology. Retrieved on May 2, 2014 from http://www.pewinternet.org/Media-Mentions/2013/Helping-Seniors-Learn-New-Technology.aspx

Spillman, B. (2013, September 8). New headquarters for Zappos reflects company's growth, atmosphere. *Las Vegas Review-Journal.* Retrieved from http://www.reviewjournal.com/news/las-vegas/new-headquarters-zappos-reflects-companys-growth-atmosphere.

Spitzberg, B. H., & Cupach, W. R. (2008). Fanning the flames of fandom: Celebrity worship, parasocial interaction, and stalking (pp. 287–324). In J. R. Meloy, L. Sheridan, & J. Hoffman (Eds.), *Stalking, threatening, and attacking of public figures: A psychological and behavioral analysis.* New York: Oxford.

Sprague, J., Stuart, D., and Bodary, D. (2012). *The speaker's handbook.* Boston: Cengage Learning.

Sprain, L., & Boromisza-Habashi, D. (2013). The ethnographer of communication at the table: Building cultural competence, designing strategic action. *Journal of Applied Communication Research, 41*(2), 181–187.

Stafford, L. (2010). Geographic distance and communication during courtship. *Communication Research, 37*(2), 275–297.

Stanley, A. (2012, April 13). There's sex, there's the city, but no Manolos. *The New York Times,* p. C1.

Stapleton, A., & Yan, H. (2013, October 21). Mom of dead Florida teen sends birthday message, promises to fight bullying. CNN.com. Retrieved from http://www.cnn.com/2013/10/20/justice/rebecca-sedwick-bullying-death/index.html

Steil, L. K., Barker, L. L., & Watson, K. W. (1983). *Effective listening: Key to success.* Reading, MA: Addison-Wesley.

Steinberg, B. (2010). Swearing during family hour? Who gives a $#*! *Advertising Age, 81*(22), 2–20.

Stelter, B. (2011, January 2). TV viewing continues to edge up. *The New York Times.* Retrieved from http://www.nytimes.com/2011/01/03/business/media/03ratings.html

Stephens, K. K., & Davis, J. (2009). The social influences on electronic multitasking in organizational meetings. *Management Communication Quarterly, 23*(1), 63–83.

Stewart, C. J., & Cash, W. B., Jr. (2011). *Interviewing: Principles and practices* (12th ed.). New York: McGraw-Hill.

Stewart, C. J., & Cash, W. B., Jr. (2014). *Interviewing: Principles and practices.* New York: McGraw-Hill.

Stewart, L. P., Cooper, P. J., & Steward, A. D. (2003). *Communication and gender.* Boston: Pearson Education.

Stiff, J. B., & Mongeau, P. (2003). *Persuasive communication.* New York: Guilford Press.

Stillion Southard, B. F., & Wolvin, A. D. (2009). Jimmy Carter: A case study in listening leadership. *International Journal of Listening, 23*(2), 141–152.

Stollen, J., & White, C. (2004). The link between labels and experience in romantic relationships among young adults. Paper presented at the International Communication Association, New Orleans Sheraton, New Orleans, LA, LA Online.

Stommel, W., & Koole, T. (2010). The online support group as a community: A micro-analysis of the interaction with a new member. *Discourse Studies, 12*(3), 357–378.

StopBullying.gov. (2013, December 26). State policies and laws. Retrieved from http://www.stopbullying.gov/laws/index.html

Suler, J. (2007). The psychology of cyberspace. Retrieved December 26, 2007, from http://www-usr.rider.edu/~suler/psycyber/psycyber.html (Original work published 1996)

Sullivan, L. (2006, July 26). In U.S. prisons, thousands spend years in isolation [Audio podcast]. In *All Things Considered.* Retrieved from http://www.npr.org/templates/story/story.php?storyId=5582144

Sun, Y., Pan, Z., & Shen, L. (2008). Understanding the third-person perception: Evidence from a meta-analysis. *Journal of Communication, 58,* 280–300.

Sunstein, C. (2007). *Republic.com 2.0.* Princeton, NJ: Princeton University Press.

Sutton, S. R. (1982). Fear arousal and communication: A critical examination of theories and research. In J. Eiser (Ed.), *Social psychology and behavioral medicine* (pp. 303–337). Chichester, UK: Wiley.

Suzuki, B. H. (2002). Revisiting the model minority stereotype: Implications for student affairs practice and higher education. *New Directions for Student Services, 97,* 21.

Tajfel, H., & Turner, J. C. (1986). An integrative theory of intergroup conflict. In S. Worchel & W. Austin (Eds.), *Psychology of intergroup relations* (pp. 2–24). Chicago: Nelson-Hall.

Tamir, D. I., & Mitchell, J. P. (2012). Anchoring and adjustment during social inferences. *Journal of Experimental Psychology, 142*(1), 151–162.

Tannen, D. (1992). *You just don't understand: Women and men in conversation.* London: Virago Press.

Tannen, D. (2009). Framing and face: The relevance of the presentation of self to linguistic discourse analysis. *Social Psychology Quarterly, 72*(4), 300–305.

Tannen, D. (2010). Abduction and identity in family interaction: Ventriloquizing as indirectness. *Journal of Pragmatics, 42*(2), 307–316.

Tannen, D., Kendall, S., & Gorgon, C. (Eds.). (2007). *Family talk: Discourse and identity in four American families.* New York: Oxford University Press.

Taylor, P., & Cohn, D. (2012, November 7). A milestone en route to a majority minority nation. *Pew Research Social & Demographic Trends.* Retrieved from http://www.pewsocialtrends.org/2012/11/07/a-milestone-en-route-to-a-majority-minority-nation

Taylor, P., & Keeter, S. (Eds.) (2010). Millennials: A portrait of generation next. Confident, connected, open to change. Pew Research. Retrieved from http://pewresearch.org/millennials

Team Rubicon. (2014, January 15). Our mission. Retrieved from http://teamrubiconusa.org/about

Ted Prize. (2013). About the TED prize. Retrieved from http://www.ted.com/participate/ted-prize

Tekleab, A. G., Quigley, N. R., & Tesluk, P. E. (2009). A longitudinal study of team conflict, conflict management, cohesion, and team effectiveness. *Group and Organizational Management, 34,* 170–205.

Tell, C. (September 22, 2013). Step away from the phone! *New York Times,* p. ST1.

Teven, J. J. (2007a). Effects of supervisor social influence, nonverbal immediacy, and biological sex on subordinates' perceptions of job satisfaction, liking, and supervisor credibility. *Communication Quarterly, 55*(2), 155–177.

Teven, J. J. (2007b). Teacher temperament: Correlates with teacher caring, burnout, and organizational outcomes. *Communication Education, 56,* 382–400.

Teven, J. J. (2007c). Teacher caring and classroom behavior: Relationships with student affect, teacher evaluation, teacher competence, and trustworthiness. *Communication Quarterly, 55,* 433–450.

Teven, J. J. (2008). An examination of perceived credibility of the 2008 presidential candidates: Relationships with believability, likeability, and deceptiveness. *Human Communication, 11,* 383–400.

Teven, J. J. (2010). The effects of supervisor nonverbal immediacy and power use on employees' ratings of credibility and affect for the supervisor. *Human Communication, 13,* 69–85.

Teven, J. J., & Comadena, M. E. (1996). The effects of office aesthetic quality on students' perceptions of teacher credibility and communicator style. *Communication Research Reports, 13*(1), 101–108.

Teven, J. J., & Hanson, T. L. (2004). The impact of teacher immediacy and perceived caring on teacher competence and trustworthiness. *Communication Quarterly, 52,* 39–53.

Teven, J. J., & McCroskey, J. C. (1997). The relationship of perceived teacher caring with student learning and teacher evaluation. *Communication Education, 46,* 1–9.

Teven, J. J., McCroksey, J. C., & Richmond, V. P. (2006). Communication correlates of perceived Machiavellianism of supervisors: Communication orientations and outcomes. *Communication Quarterly, 54,* 127–142.

Teven, J. J., & Winters, J. L. (2007). Pharmaceutical sales representatives' social influence behaviors and communication orientations: Relationships with adaptive selling, sales performance, and job satisfaction. *Human Communication, 10,* 465–485.

Thacker, S., & Griffiths, M. D. (2012). An exploratory study of trolling in online video gaming. *International Journal of Cyber Behavior, Psychology and Learning (IJCBPL), 2*(4), 17–33.

Theiss, J. A., Knobloch, L. K., Checton, M. G., & Magsamen-Conrad, K. (2009). Relationship characteristics associated with the experience of hurt in romantic relationships: A test of the relational turbulence model. *Human Communication Research, 35*(4), 588–615.

Thibaut, J. W., & Kelley, H. H. (1959). *The social psychology of groups.* New York: Wiley.

Thomas, A. P. (2006, January 31). The CSI effect: Fact or fiction. *The Yale Law Journal Online.* Retrieved from http://www.yalelawjournal.org/the-yale-law-journalpocket-part/criminal-law-and-sentencing/the-csi-effect:-fact-or-fiction

Thomas, D. C., Ravlin, E. C., & Wallace, A. W. (1996). Effect of cultural diversity in work groups. In P. Bamber, M. Erez, & S. Bacharach (Eds.), *Research in the sociology of organizations* (Vol. 14, pp. 1–33). Greenwich, CT: JAI.

Thomas, L. T., & Levine, T. R. (1994). Disentangling listening and verbal recall: Related but separate constructs? *Human Communication Research, 21,* 103–127.

Thompson, A. (2008, April 17). Scientist finds truthiness in "Colbert bump." Livescience.com. Retrieved from http://www.livescience.com/2451-scientist-finds-truthiness-colbert-bump.html

Tidwell, L. C., & Walther, J. B. (2002). Computer-mediated communication effects on disclosure, impressions, and interpersonal evaluations: Getting to know one another a bit at a time. *Human Communication Research, 28*(3), 317–348.

Tierney, J. (2007, July 31). The whys of mating: 237 reasons and counting. *The New York Times,* p. F1.

Tiggemann, M. (2005). Television and adolescent body image: The role of program content and viewing motivation. *Journal of Social & Clinical Psychology, 24,* 361–381.

Ting-Toomey, S., & Oetzel, J. G. (2002). Cross-cultural face concerns and conflict styles. *Handbook of International and Intercultural Communication, 2,* 143–164.

Tjosvold, D. (1992). *The conflict-positive organization: Stimulate diversity and create unity.* Reading, MA: Addison-Wesley.

Tkaczyk, C. (2013, April 19). Marissa Mayer breaks her silence on Yahoo's telecommuting policy. Fortune/CNN.com. Retrieved from http://tech.fortune.cnn.com/2013/04/19/marissa-mayer-telecommuting

Tockett, C. (2012, November 6). How Rockaway Beach Surf Club became a Hurricane Sandy relief center. Treehugger Blog. Retrieved from http://www.treehugger.com/culture/rockaway-beach-surf-club-became-hurricane-sandy-relief-center.html

Tolman, E. G. (2012). Observing cell phone use and enhancing collaborative learning using a wiki. *Communication Teacher, 4,* 1–5.

Toma, C. L. (2013, April). Feeling better but doing worse: Effects of Facebook self-presentation on implicit self-esteem and cognitive task performance. *Media Psychology, 16*(2), 199–220.

Tong, S. T., Van Der Heide, B., Langwell, L., & Walther, J. B. (2008). Too much of a good thing? The relationship between number of friends and interpersonal impressions on Facebook. *Journal of Computer-Mediated Communication, 13*(3), 531–549.

Toobin, J. (2007, May 7). The CSI effect. *The New Yorker.* Retrieved from http://www.newyorker.com/reporting/2007/05/07/070507fa_fact_toobin

Torregrosa, L. L. (2010, August 31). Palin woos women and stirs up foes. *The New York Times.* Retrieved from http://www.nytimes.com/2010/09/01/us/01iht-letter.html

Toussaint, L., & Cheadle, A. C. D. (2009). Unforgiveness and the broken heart: Unforgiving tendencies, problems due to unforgiveness, and 12-month prevalence of cardiovascular health conditions. In M. T. Evans & E. D. Walker (Eds.), *Religion and psychology*. New York: Nova Publishers.

Toussaint, L. L., Owen, A. D., & Cheadle, A. (2012). Forgive to live: Forgiveness, health, and longevity. *Journal of Behavioral Medicine, 35*(4), 375–386.

Tracy, J. L., & Robins, R. W. (2008). The nonverbal expression of pride: Evidence for cross-cultural recognition. *Journal of Personality & Social Psychology, 94*(3), 516–530.

Triandis, H. C. (1986). Collectivism vs. individualism: A reconceptualization of a basic concept in cross-cultural psychology. In C. Bagley & G. Verma (Eds.), *Personality, cognition, and values: Cross-cultural perspectives of childhood and adolescence*. London: Macmillan.

Triandis, H. C. (1988). Collectivism vs. individualism. In G. Verma & C. Bagley (Eds.), *Cross-cultural studies of personality, attitudes, and cognition*. London: Macmillan.

Triandis, H. C. (2000). Culture and conflict. *The International Journal of Psychology, 35*(2), 1435–1452.

Triandis, H. C., Brislin, R., & Hul, C. H. (1988). Cross-cultural training across the individualism-collectivism divide. *International Journal of Intercultural Relations, 12*, 269–289.

Tripathy, J. (2010). How gendered is gender and development? Culture, masculinity, and gender difference. *Development in Practice, 20*(1), 113–121.

Troester, R. L., & Mester, C. S. (2007). *Civility in business and professional communication*. New York: Peter Lang.

Tsa, W. C., Chen, C. C., & Chiu, S. F. (2005). Exploring boundaries of the effects of applicant impression management tactics in job interviews. *Journal of Management, 31*(1), 108–125.

Tse, M., Vong, S., & Tang, S. (2013). Motivational interviewing and exercise programme for community-dwelling older persons with chronic pain: A randomized controlled study. *Journal of Clinical Nursing, 22*(13/14), 1843–1856. doi:10.1111/j.1365-2702.2012.04317.x

Tuckman, B. W., & Jensen, M. A. C. (1977). Stages in small group development revisited. *Groups and Organizational Studies, 2*, 419–427.

Tufte, E. (2003, September). PowerPoint is evil: Power corrupts; PowerPoint corrupts absolutely. *Wired*. Retrieved from http://www.wired.com/wired/archive/11.09/ppt2.html

Ubinger, M. E., Handal, P. J., & Massura, C. E. (2013). Adolescent adjustment: The hazards of conflict avoidance and the benefits of conflict resolution. *Psychology, 4*(1), 50–58.

The ubiquitous PowerPoint. (2013, April). Full text available. *Phi Delta Kappan, 94*(7), 7.

Uhl-Bien, M. (2006). Relational leadership theory: Exploring the social processes of leadership and organizing. *The Leadership Quarterly, 17*, 654–676.

Ulaby, N. (2008, September 2). The "Bechdel Rule," defining pop culture. NPR. Retrieved from http://www.npr.org/templates/story/story.php?storyId=94202522

U.S. Census Bureau. (2012). Census Bureau releases equal employment opportunity tabulation that provides a profile of America's workforce. Retrieved from http://www.census.gov/newsroom/releases/archives/employment_occupations/cb12-225.html

U.S. Department of Justice, Federal Bureau of Investigation. (2010, September). *Crime in the United States, 2009*. Retrieved from http://www2.fbi.gov/ucr/clus2009/index.html

U.S. Equal Employment Opportunity Commission. (2011). Sexual harassment charges. Retrieved from http://www.eeoc.gov/eeoc/statistics/enforcement/sexual_harassment.cfm

Valkenburg, P. M., & Vroone, M. (2004). Developmental changes in infants' and toddlers' attention to television entertainment. *Communication Research, 31*, 288–311.

Van Dick, R., Tissington, P. A., & Hertel, G. (2009). Do many hands make light work? How to overcome social loafing and gain motivation in work teams. *European Business Review, 21*(3), 233–245.

Van Swol, L. M., Braun, M. T., & Kolb, M. R. (2013). Deception detection, demeanor, and truth bias in face-to-face and computer-mediated communication. *Communication Research, 40*(5), 1–27.

Van Swol, L. M., Malhotra, D., & Braun, M. T. (2012). Deception and its detection: Effects of monetary incentives and personal relationship history. *Communication Research, 39*(2), 217–238.

Van Zandt, T. (2004). Information overload and a network of targeted communication. *RAND Journal of Economics, 35*, 542–561.

Vela, L. E., Booth-Butterfield, M., Wanzer, M. B., & Vallade, J. I. (2013). Relationships among humor, coping, relationship stress, and satisfaction in dating relationships: Replication and extension. *Communication Research Reports, 30*(1), 68–75.

Victor, D. A. (1992). *International business communication*. New York: HarperCollins.

Vijayasiri, G. (2008). Reporting sexual harassment: The importance of organizational culture and trust. *Gender Issues, 25*(1), 43–61.

Villaume, W. A., & Bodie, G. D. (2007). Discovering the listener within us: The impact of trait-like personality variables and communicator styles on preferences for listening style. *International Journal of Listening, 21*(2), 102–123.

Villaume, W. A., & Brown, M. H. (1999). The development and validation of the vocalic sensitivity test. *International Journal of Listening, 13*, 24–45.

Vogel, D. R., Dickson, G. W., & Lehman, J. A. (1986). Persuasion and the role of visual presentation support: The UM/3M study (MISRC-WP-86-11), Minneapolis, MN: University of Minnesota, Management Information Systems Research Center.

Vogel, H. L. (2011). *Entertainment industry economics: A guide for financial analysis* (8th ed.). New York: Cambridge University Press.

Von Raffler-Engel, W. (1983). *The perception of nonverbal behavior in the career interview.* Philadelphia: Benjamin.

Voorveld, H. A. M., & van der Goot, M. (2013). Age differences in media multitasking: A diary study. *Journal of Broadcasting & Electronic Media, 57*(3), 392–408. doi:http://dx.doi.org/10.1080/08838151.2013.816709

Voss, B. (2010, December 22). Sibling revelry. *TheAdvocate.com.* Retrieved from http://www.advocate.com/Arts_and_Entertainment/Television/Sibling_Revelry

Vrij, A. (2006). Nonverbal communication and deception. In V. Manusov & M. L. Patterson (Eds.), *The Sage handbook of nonverbal communication* (pp. 341–360). Thousand Oaks, CA: Sage Publications.

Wade, N. (2010, January 12). Deciphering the chatter of monkeys and chimps. *The New York Times*, p. D1.

Wailgum, T. (2008, June 8). How Steve Jobs beats presentation panic. *CIO.com.* Retrieved from http://www.cio.com/article/596271/How_Steve_Jobs_Beats_Presentation_Panic

Waldman, K. (2014, January 7). The Bechdel test sets the bar too low. Slate. Retrieved from http://www.slate.com/blogs/xx_factor/2014/01/07/the_bechdel_test_needs_an_update_we_ve_set_the_bar_for_female_representation.html

Waldron, V. R., & Applegate, J. A. (1998). Effects of tactic similarity on social attraction and persuasiveness in dyadic verbal disagreements. *Communication Reports, 11,* 155–166.

Waldron, V. R. , & Kelley, D. L. (2005). Forgiving communication as a response to relational transgressions. *Journal of Social and Personal Relationships, 22,* 723–742.

Wallenfelsz, K. P., & Hample, D. (2010). The role of taking conflict personally in imagined interactions about conflict. *Southern Communication Journal, 75*(5), 471–487.

Wallis, C. (2006, March 27). The multitasking generation. *Time*, pp. 48–55.

Walther, J. B. (1996). Computer-mediated communication: Impersonal, interpersonal, and hyperpersonal interaction. *Communication Research, 23,* 3–43.

Walther, J. B. (2006). Nonverbal dynamics in computer-mediated communication, or: :-(and the net :-('s with you, :-) and you :-) alone. In V. Manusov & M. L. Patterson (Eds.), *Handbook of nonverbal communication* (pp. 461–479). Thousand Oaks, CA: Sage Publications.

Walther, J. B., & Parks, M. R. (2002). Cues filtered out, cues filtered in: Computer-mediated communication and relationships. In M. L. Knapp & J. A. Daly (Eds.), *Handbook of interpersonal communication* (pp. 529–563). Thousand Oaks, CA: Sage Publications.

Walther, J. B., & Ramirez, A., Jr. (2009). New technologies and new directions in online relating. In S. W. Smith & S. R. Wilson (Eds.), *New directions in interpersonal communication research* (pp. 264–284). Newbury Park, CA: Sage Publications.

Walther, J. B., Van Der Heide, B., Kim, S-Y., Westerman, D., & Tong, S. T. (2008). The role of friends' appearance and behavior on evaluations of individuals on Facebook: Are we known by the company we keep? *Human Communication Research, 34*(1), 28–49.

Walther, J. B., Van Der Heide, B., Tong, S. T., Carr, C. T., & Atkin, C. K. (2010). Effects of interpersonal goals on inadvertent intrapersonal influence in computer-mediated communication. *Human Communication Research, 36*(3), 323–347.

Waltman, M., & Haas, J. (2011). *The communication of hate.* New York: Peter Lang.

Wang, G., & Liu, Z. (2010). What collective? Collectivism and relationalism from a Chinese perspective. *Chinese Journal of Communication, 3*(1), 42–63.

Wanzer, M., Booth-Butterfield, M., & Gruber, K. (2004). Perceptions of health care providers' communication: Relationships between patient-centered communication and satisfaction. *Health Communication, 16*(3), 363–383.

Ward, C. C., & Tracey, T. J. G. (2004). Relation of shyness with aspects of online relationship involvement. *Journal of Social and Personal Relationships, 21,* 611–623.

Wasserman, B., & Weseley, A. (2009). ¿Qué? Quoi? Do languages with grammatical gender promote sexist attitudes? *Sex Roles, 61*(9/10), 634–643.

Waters, S., & Ackerman, J. (2011). Exploring privacy management on facebook: Motivations and perceived consequences of voluntary disclosure. *Journal of Computer-Mediated Communication, 17*(1), 101–115.

Watson, K., Barker, L., & Weaver, J. (1995). The listening styles profile (LSP-16): Development and validation of an instrument to assess four listening styles. *International Journal of Listening, 9,* 1–13.

Watts, D. J. (2011). *Everything is obvious once you know the answer: How common sense fails us.* New York: Crown Publishing Group.

Way, N. (2011). *Deep secrets: Boys' friendships and the crisis of connection.* Cambridge, MA: Harvard University Press.

Webster, M. J., & Driskell, J. E., Jr. (1978). Status generalization: A review of some new data. *American Sociological Review, 42,* 220–236.

Webster, M. J., & Driskell, J. E., Jr. (1983). Beauty as status. *American Journal of Sociology, 89,* 140–165.

Wecker, C. (2012). Slide presentations as speech suppressors: When and why learners miss oral information. *Computers and Education, 59*(2), 260–273.

Weger, H., Jr., Castle, G. R., & Emmett, M. C. (2010). Active listening in peer interviews: The influence of message paraphrasing on perceptions of listening skill. *International Journal of Listening, 24*(1), 34–49.

Weisz, C., & Wood, L. F. (2005). Social identity support and friendship outcomes: A longitudinal study predicting who will be friends and best friends 4 years later. *Journal of Social and Personal Relationships, 22,* 416–432.

Welch, B. A., Mossholder, K. W., Stell, R. P., & Bennett, N. (1998). Does work group cohesiveness affect individuals' performance and organizational commitment? *Small Group Research, 29*, 472–494.

Welch, S. A., & Mickelson, W. T. (2013). A listening competence comparison of working professionals. *International Journal of Listening, 27*(2), 85–99.

Werner, J. (2011, February 16). Bucks County teacher suspended for "lazy whiners" comments defends herself in new blog. *The Trentonian.* Retrieved from http://www.trentonian.com

West, A. (2007, August 20). Facebook labeled a $5b waste of time. *Sydney Morning Herald.* Retrieved May 13, 2008, from http://www.smh.com.au

Wheaton, S. (2012, October 13). Missouree? Missouruh? To be politic, say both. *The New York Times*, p. A1.

Wheelan, S. A. (2012). *Creating effective teams: A guide for members and leaders* (4th ed.). Thousand Oaks: Sage Publications.

Wheelan, S. A., & Burchill, C. (1999). Take teamwork to new heights. *Nursing Management, 30*(4), 28–31.

Wherfritz, G., Kinetz, E., & Kent, J. (2008, April 21). Lured into bondage: A growing back channel of global trade tricks millions into forced labor. *Newsweek.* Retrieved from http://www.newsweek.com/id/131707

Widgery, R. A. (1974). Sex of receiver and physical attractiveness of source as determinants of initial credibility perception. *Western Speech Communication Journal, 1*, 13–17.

Wiemann, J. M. (1977). Explication and test of a model of communication competence. *Human Communication Research, 3*, 195–213.

Wiemann, J. M., & Backlund, P. M. (1980). Current theory and research in communication competence. *Review of Educational Research, 50*, 185–189.

Wiemann, J. M., Chen, V., & Giles, H. (1986, November). Beliefs about talk and silence in a cultural context. Paper presented at the annual meeting of the Speech Communication Association, Chicago.

Wiemann, J. M., & Krueger, D. L. (1980). The language of relationships. In H. Giles, W. P. Robinson, & P. M. Smith (Eds.), *Language: Social psychological perspectives* (pp. 55–62). Oxford: Pergamon Press.

Wiemann, J. M., Takai, J., Ota, H., & Wiemann, M. O. (1997). A relational model of communication competence. In B. Kovačić (Ed.), *Emerging theories of human communication* (pp. 25–44). Albany, NY: State University of New York Press.

Wiemann, M. O. (2009). *Love you/hate you: Negotiating intimate relationships.* Barcelona, Spain: Editorial Aresta.

Wierzbicka, A. (2006). *English: Meaning and culture.* New York: Oxford.

Wiesenfeld, D., Bush, K., & Sikdar, R. (2010). The value of listening: Heeding the call of the Snuggie. *Journal of Advertising Research, 50*(1), 16–20.

Willard, G., & Gramzow, R. (2008). Exaggeration in memory: Systematic distortion of self-evaluative information under reduced accessibility. *Journal of Experimental Social Psychology, 44*(2), 246–259.

Williams, D. (2006). On and off the 'net: Scales for social capital in an online era. *Journal of Computer Mediated Communication, 11*, 593–628.

Williams, D., Consalvo, M., Caplan, S., & Yee, N. (2009). Looking for gender: Gender roles and behaviors among online gamers. *Journal of Communication, 59*(4), 700–725.

Williams, D. E., & Hughes, P. C. (2005). Nonverbal communication in Italy: An analysis of interpersonal touch, body position, eye contact, and seating behaviors. *North Dakota Journal of Speech & Theatre, 18*, 17–24.

Williams, J. C. (2014). Women, work, and the art of gender judo. *Washington Post.* Retrieved from http://www.washingtonpost.com/opinions/women-work-and-the-art-of-gender-judo/2014/01/24/29e209b2-82b2-11e3-8099-9181471f7aaf_story.html

Williams, K. D. (2001). *Ostracism: The power of silence.* New York: Guilford Press.

Williams, K. D., Govan, C. L., Croker, V., Tynan, D., Cruickshank, M., & Lam, A. (2002). *Group dynamics: Theory, research, and practice, 6*(1), 65–77.

Williams, K. D., & Sommer, K. L. (1997). Social ostracism by coworkers: Does rejection lead to loafing or compensation? *Personality and Social Psychology Bulletin, 23*(7), 693–706.

Williams, K. N., Herman, R., Gajewski, B., & Wilson, K. (2009). Elderspeak communication: Impact on dementia care. *American Journal of Alzheimer's Disease & Other Dementias, 24*(1), 11–20.

Williams, P. (1993). Surveillance hurts productivity, deprives employees of rights. *Advertising Age, 64*, 14.

Willoughby, B. J., Carroll, J. S., & Busby, D. M. (2012). The different effects of "living together": Determining and comparing types of cohabiting couples. *Journal of Social and Personal Relationships, 29*(3), 397–419.

Wilmot, W. W. (1987). *Dyadic communication* (3rd ed.). New York: Random House.

Wilson, B. J., Smith, S. L., Potter, W. J., Kunkel, D., Linz, D., Colvin, C. M., & Donnerstein, E. (2002). Violence in children's programming: Assessing the risks. *Journal of Communication, 52*, 5–35.

Wilson, G. L., & Hanna, M. S. (1993). *Groups in context: Leadership and participation in small groups* (3rd ed.). New York: McGraw Hill.

Wingfield, N. (2013, October 15). Tech rivals lay down arms for youth coding. *The New York Times.* Retrieved from http://bits.blogs.nytimes.com/2013/10/15/tech-rivals-lay-down-arms-for-youth-coding

Winston, C. (2002, January 28). State of the Union stew. *The Christian Science Monitor.* Retrieved from http://www.csmonitor.com

Winter, J., & Pauwels, A. (2006). Men staying at home looking after their children: Feminist linguistic reform and social change. *International Journal of Applied Linguistics, 16*(1), 16–36.

Witteman, H. (1993). The interface between sexual harassment and organizational romance. In G. Kreps (Ed.), *Sexual harassment: Communication implications* (pp. 27–62). Cresskill, NJ: Hampton Press.

Wittenbaum, G. M., Shulman, H. C., & Braz, M. E. (2010). Social ostracism in task groups: The effects of group composition. *Small Group Research, 41*(3), 330–353.

Wolfram, W., & Schilling-Estes, N. (2006). *American English: Dialects and variation* (2nd ed.)(p. 1). Malden, MA: Blackwell Publishing.

Wolvin, A. (2010). Response: Toward a listening ethos. *International Journal of Listening, 24*(3), 179–180.

Wolvin, A. D., & Coakley, C. G. (1991). A survey of the status of listening training in some *Fortune* 500 corporations. *Communication Education, 40,* 151–164.

Wong, E., & Cheng, M. (2013). Effects of motivational interviewing to promote weight loss in obese children. *Journal of Clinical Nursing, 22*(17/18), 2519–2530. doi:10.1111/jocn.12098

Woo, E. (2011, March 13). Sam Chwat dies at 57; actors lost, and learned, accents under dialect coach's tutelage. *Los Angeles Times.* Retrieved from http://articles.latimes.com/2011/mar/13/local/la-me-sam-chwat-20110313

Wood, B. (1982). *Children and communication: Verbal and nonverbal language development* (2nd ed.). Englewood Cliffs, NJ: Prentice Hall.

Wood, J. T. (2008). Gender, communication, and culture. In L. A. Samovar, R. E. Porter, and E. R. McDaniel (Eds.), *Intercultural communication: A reader* (pp. 170–180). Belmont, CA: Wadsworth Cengage.

Wood, J. T. (2011). *Gendered lives: Communication, gender, and culture* (9th ed.). Boston, MA: Wadsworth Publishing.

Woodzicka, J. (2008). Sex differences in self-awareness of smiling during a mock job interview. *Journal of Nonverbal Behavior, 32*(2), 109–121.

Wrench, J. S., McCroskey, J. C., & Richmond, V. P. (2008). *Human communication in everyday life: Explanations and applications.* Boston: Allyn & Bacon.

Wright, C. N., Holloway, A., & Roloff, M. E. (2007). The dark side of self-monitoring: How high self-monitors view their romantic relationships. *Communication Reports, 20*(2), 101–114.

Wright, K. B., Rosenberg, J., Egbert, N., Ploeger, N. A., Bernard, D. R., & King, S. (2013). Communication competence, social support, and depression among college students: A model of Facebook and face-to-face support network influence. *Journal of Health Communication, 18*(1), 41–57.

Xerxenesky, A. (2013, January 31). When the music stopped. *The New York Times,* p. A23.

Yaguchi, M., Iyeiri, Y., & Baba, Y. (2010). Speech style and gender distinctions in the use of *very* and *real/really*: An analysis of the Corpus of Spoken Professional American English. *Journal of Pragmatics, 42*(3), 585–597.

Yasui, E. (2009, May). Collaborative idea construction: The repetition of gestures and talk during brainstorming. A paper presented at the 59th meeting of the International Communication Association, Chicago, IL.

Yee, N., & Bailenson, J. (2007). The Proteus effect: The effect of transformed self-representation on behavior. *Human Communication Research, 33*(3), 271–290.

Yoffe, E. (2013, February 25). Can we really stop bullying? Slate.com. Retrieved from http://www.slate.com/articles/double_x/doublex/2013/02/sticks_and_stones_emily_yoffe_interviews_emily_bazelon_about_her_new_book.html

Yoo, C. Y. (2007). Implicit memory measures for Web advertising effectiveness. *Journalism & Mass Communication Quarterly, 84*(1), 7–23.

Yook, E. (2004). Any questions? Knowing the audience through question types. *Communication Teacher, 18,* 91–93.

Yoon, K., Kim, C. H., & Kim, M. S. (1998). A cross-cultural comparison of the effects of source credibility on attitudes and behavioral intentions. *Mass Communication and Society, 1*(3–4), 153–173.

Young, J., & Foot, K. (2005). Corporate e-cruiting: The construction of work in *Fortune* 500 recruiting Web sites. *Journal of Computer-Mediated Communication, 11*(1), 44–71.

Yukl, G. (1999). An evaluation of conceptual weaknesses in transformational and charismatic leadership theories. *Leadership Quarterly, 10,* 285–305.

Zabava Ford, W. S., & Wolvin, A. D. (1993). The differential impact of a basic communication course on perceived communication competencies in class, work, and social contexts. *Communication Education, 42*(3), 215–223.

Zacchilli, T. L., Hendrick, C., & Hendrick, S. S. (2009). The romantic partner conflict scale: A new scale to measure relationship conflict. *Journal of Social and Personal Relationships, 26*(8), 1073–1096.

Zappos.com. (2014, February 8). Introducing: Core values frog! Retrieved from http://about.zappos.com/jobs/why-work-zappos/core-values

Zarrinabadi, N. (2012). Self-perceived communication competence in Iranian culture. *Communication Research Reports, 29*(4), 292–298.

Zeman, N. (2013, June). The boy who cried dead girlfriend. *Vanity Fair.* Retrieved from http://www.vanityfair.com/culture/2013/06/manti-teo-girlfriend-nfl-draft

Zhang, J., & Daugherty, T. (2009). Third-person effect and social networking: Implications for online marketing and word-of-mouth communication. *American Journal of Business, 24,* 54–63.

Zhang, Q., & Andreychik, M. (2013). Relational closeness in conflict: Effects on interaction goals, emotion, and conflict styles. *Journal of International Communication, 19*(1), 107–116.

Zickuhr, K., Rainie, L., & Purcell, K. (2013, January 22). Libraries in the digital age. Pew Internet and American Life Project. Retrieved from http://libraries.pewinternet.org/2013/01/22/library-services

Zickuhr, K., & Smith, A. (2012). Digital differences. Pew Research Center's Internet & American Life Project. Retrieved from http://www.pewinternet.org/files/old-media/Files/Reports/2012/PIP_Digital_differences_041312.pdf

Zickuhr, K., & Smith, A. (2013). Home broadband 2013. Pew Research Internet Project. Retrieved from http://www.pewinternet.org/2013/08/26/home-broadband-2013

Zimbushka (2008, May 27). *Mike Caro's 10 ultimate poker cues.* Retrieved from http://www.youtube.com/watch?v=QqF8m12JSDE

Zuckerberg, M. (2013, February 26). What schools don't teach. Code.org video. Retrieved from http://www.youtube.com/watch?v=nKIu9yen5nc; 3:05

acknowledgments

Box 1.2: National Communication Association, Credo for Ethical Communication. Copyright © 1999. Reprinted by permission of the National Communication Association. All rights reserved. www.natcom.org.

Figure 2.4: "Assessing Our Perceptions of Self" adapted from *Competent Communication*, Second Edition, Dan O'Hair et al. Copyright © 1997 Bedford/St. Martin's.

Figure 3.1: "The Abstraction Ladder" adapted from *Competent Communication*, Second Edition, Dan O'Hair et al. Copyright © 1997 Bedford/St. Martin's.

Table 4.1: "The Power of Eye Contact" adapted from *Successful Verbal Communication: Principles and Applications,* D. Leathers (New York: Macmillan, 1997). Reprinted with permission of Pearson Education.

Figure 4.2: "Zones of Personal Space" from *Competent Communication*, Second Edition, Dan O'Hair et al., Copyright © 1997 Bedford/St. Martin's.

Table 6.1: "Listening Goals" from *Competent Communication*, Second Edition, Dan O'Hair et al. Copyright © 1997 Bedford/St. Martin's.

Table 7.1: "Family Communication Qualities" from John Caughlin, "Family Communication Standards: What Counts as Excellent Family Communication, and How Are Such Standards Associated with Family Satisfaction?" from *Human Communication Research* 29 (2003): 5–40.

Table 7.3: "Romantic Relational Termination Strategies" adapted from D. J. Canary and M. J. Cody, *Interpersonal Communication: A Goals-Based Approach* Copyright © 1994 Bedford/St. Martin's.

Figure 9.1: "Complexity of Group Relationships" from *Competent Communication*, Second Edition, Dan O'Hair et al. Copyright © 1997 Bedford/St. Martin's.

Figure 11.1: "A College or University System" from *Competent Communication*, Second Edition, Dan O'Hair et al. Copyright © 1997 Bedford/St. Martin's.

Page 338: Sarah Jane Blakemore, *The Mysterious Workings of the Adolescent Brain*, TED Talk. http://www.ted.com/talks.

Page 339: Ricky Martin, Remarks at the Vienna Forum. Reprinted by permission of the Ricky Martin Foundation. Ricky Martin, President and Founder.

Page 340: Jim Valvano ESPY acceptance speech, March 4, 1993. Reprinted by permission.

Table 12.1: "Personal Interests Topics" adapted from *A Speaker's Guidebook*, Third Edition, Dan O'Hair et al. Copyright © 2007 Bedford/St. Martin's.

Figure 12.1: "An Example of the Web of Associations Produced by Clustering" adapted from *Competent Communication*, Second Edition, Dan O'Hair et al. Copyright © 1997 Bedford/St. Martin's.

Table 13.1: "Useful Signposts" from *A Speaker's Guidebook*, Third Edition, Dan O'Hair et al. Copyright © 2007 Bedford/St. Martin's.

Table 13.3: "Useful Delivery Cues" from *A Speaker's Guidebook*, Fifth Edition, Dan O'Hair et al. Copyright © 2012 Bedford/St. Martin's.

Page 406: Personal Report of Public Speaking Anxiety adapted from McCroskey, J. C. (1970). "Measures of communication-bound anxiety." *Speech Monographs*, 37, 269-277.

Table 15.2: "Types of Informative Speeches, Sample Topics, Informational Strategies, and Organizational Patterns" from *A Speaker's Guidebook*, Third Edition, Dan O'Hair et al. Copyright © 2007 Bedford/St. Martin's.

index

More Media in LaunchPad.

bedfordstmartins.com/realcomm
Go online to find the **Key Term Videos** and **Sample Speech Resources** that complement the book content. Here is a list of the key term videos and where their concepts appear in the text. Find even more videos and models of public speaking in LaunchPad.